FLANN CAMPBELL, son of the Ulster poet Joseph Campbell, was born in Dublin in 1919. He graduated from Trinity College Dublin with a BA in Economics and Political Science in 1943 and was awarded a Ph.D. in Sociology by the London School of Economics in 1951. He was head of the department of education at the College of All Saints, London, from 1969 until his retirement in 1980. He is the author of *Eleven Plus and All That: The London Grammar School* (1956) and has written for the *Irish Democrat*, the *Irish Times, New Statesman, New Society* and the *Times Educational Supplement*.

Flann Campbell now lives in Blackrock, County Dublin.

THE
DISSENTING
VOICE

Protestant Democracy in Ulster
from Plantation to Partition

FLANN CAMPBELL

THE
BLACKSTAFF PRESS
BELFAST

First published in 1991 by
The Blackstaff Press Limited
3 Galway Park, Dundonald, Belfast BT16 0AN, Northern Ireland

This book has received financial assistance under the Cultural Traditions
Programme which aims to encourage acceptance and understanding of
cultural diversity.

Typeset by Textflow Services Limited

Printed by The Guernsey Press Company Limited

British Library Cataloguing in Publication Data
Campbell, Flann
The dissenting voice : Protestant democracy
in Ulster from plantation to partition.
I. Title
332.4209416
ISBN 0-85640-457-8

to the memory of my father,
Joseph Campbell,
who was his own kind of Dissenter

CONTENTS

	List of Tables	ix
	Introduction	1
	Prologue: 'The North Began'	8
1	'Civil and Religious Liberty'	26
2	'The Spirit of the North'	44
3	'Reform to Separation'	61
4	'Croppies Lie Down'	81
5	'The Common Name of Irishman'	95
6	'The Grand Design'	107
7	Wooing the Presbyterians	127
8	The Battle of the Synods	137
9	The Tithe War	145
10	God and Mammon	156
11	'Ill Fares the Land'	170
12	Famine – the Political and Moral Crisis	191
13	Young Ulster	215
14	Two Sons of the Manse	232
15	'The League of North and South'	247
16	Isaac Butt – Father of Home Rule	266
17	Biggar and the Land League	282
18	The Garrison Under Siege	301
19	Imperialism and the 'Orange Card'	315
20	Against the Tide	332
21	Class Struggles	348
22	A Cultural Renaissance	361
23	Dungannon, Magheramorne, and the Belfast Strike	376
24	The Carson Crusade	400
	Epilogue: The Dilemma of Protestant Democracy in Northern Ireland	424
	Notes	435
	Select Bibliography	475
	Index	485

LIST OF TABLES

TABLE 1   147
Average tithe paid per Irish acre in Irish provinces,
   1831–2

TABLE 2   157
Number of parliamentary constituencies, MPs and
   electors in Ulster, 1815–47

TABLE 3   173
Size of farms in Ireland, 1841

TABLE 4   175
Density of population in four provinces of Ireland, 1841

TABLE 5   189
Numbers employed in outdoor-relief schemes in
   Ulster, March 1847

TABLE 6   189
Number of deaths in Ulster, 1842–50

TABLE 7   199
Number of evictions in Ulster, 1846–8

TABLE 8   275
Number of resident landlords in Ulster, 1870

TABLE 9   277
Distribution of landownership in Ulster, 1876

TABLE 10   280
Agrarian outrages in Ireland and Ulster, 1876–83

TABLE 11   291
Number of MPs elected in Ulster constituencies,
   1874–86

TABLE 12   320
Percentage of Irish population in different religious
   groups, 1881

ix

TABLE 13   333
General election results in Ulster, 1892–1900

TABLE 14   335
Number of Irish-speakers in Ulster, 1901

TABLE 15   386
General election results in Ireland and Ulster, 1906

INTRODUCTION

A curious aspect of Irish historiography has been the fact that so little has been published, at least up to recently, about the dissenting aspects of Ulster Protestantism.

The Battle of the Boyne and the Siege of Derry have been memorialised in song and story, as well as in lengthy monographs. There have been major studies of the Unionist Party and the Orange Order, and numerous biographies of such famous Tory diehards as Lords Castlereagh, Carson and Craigavon. The Act of Union has been described in minutest detail, and so has the intervention in Ireland of British cabinet ministers, such as Randolph Churchill, Arthur Balfour and Bonar Law. There has been a plethora of books about the Curragh mutiny and the Ulster Volunteer Force of 1913–14. The preaching of such clergymen as the Reverend Henry Cooke, 'Roaring' Hanna, and in our own day, Ian Paisley, has been well publicised. There is no shortage of official reports about the various sectarian riots that have afflicted Belfast. And since the civil rights struggle came to a head in the North in 1969 one can hardly open a newspaper or watch a television screen without being reminded that the unionists claim Ulster as their province.

But comparatively little has been published, apart from a few incomplete accounts of the 1798 rising and the occasional specialised thesis, about those northern Protestants who were hostile to the dominant unionists. The majority viewpoint has been given the full treatment, and the minority virtually ignored. There has been a grave neglect of those liberals, nationalists and radicals, and later of ecumenicists and socialists, who at various times and in their different ways have condemned the landlord system, called for a wider franchise, disapproved of religious bigotry, or even in some cases sought to break the connection with the British Empire. So serious has been this failure to draw attention to the democratic, as distinct from the conservative, Protestant tradition that one thesis writer has spoken of a

1

'conspiracy of silence',[1] while another has complained that the role of Protestants in nationalist politics has been 'overlooked, minimised or misrepresented'.[2] A contemporary critic goes so far as to describe this neglect as a kind of 'collective amnesia'.[3]

There was, for example, until 1987 no comprehensive and up-to-date account of how the Presbyterian Church has developed as part of the general history of the province.[4] Little new work has been done on the part that Belfast played in the rise and fall of the United Irishmen,[5] and the lives of such important personalities as Henry Joy McCracken and Thomas Russell have been the subject of ballads rather than serious investigation. The bicentenary of the Dungannon Convention of 1782 went by without much attention by serious academic historians. After two hundred years how much do we know about Samuel Neilson or James Hope? The tithe wars in the north have been almost totally ignored, and important new research on the famine of 1845–9 has not yet been published. Two memoirs of the conservative Reverend Henry Cooke have been published, but only an incomplete biography of the liberal Reverend Henry Montgomery, and a brief pamphlet on the radical Reverend William Steel Dickson. The land struggle played a crucial role in the evolution of political attitudes, but research in this vital area is still only at a preliminary stage. When the life of Isaac Butt has been recorded, the biographers have confined themselves mainly to its relevance to the south of Ireland, and Roger Casement's activities are usually related to the Congo, Berlin, London or Dublin, anywhere except Ulster. Though they were influential in their lifetime, who nowadays has heard of John Martin, John Pinkerton, or John Ferguson? And who could distinguish between Joseph Gillis Biggar and his cousin Francis Joseph Bigger? No new biography has been published of Armour of Ballymoney for over fifty years,[6] and the lives of such individuals as Bulmer Hobson, Robert Lynd and Lindsay Crawford are usually confined to the footnotes of standard history books. The Russellites have been largely forgotten and so have the Sloanites, and yet each in their day were politically important. It was only a few years ago that books began to appear on the big strike of 1907, and the unemployment struggles of 1932 – both occurring in Belfast.

As a result of this failure to give proper weight to the dissenting, as against the establishment, elements in Ulster society, the impression has been created that all episcopalians, Presbyterians, Methodists, Baptists and Quakers in the province formed, and still continue to form, a homogeneous monolithic bloc, all holding the same political, as well as social and theological, views. The implication is that almost every northern Protestant, regardless of the particular denomination to which he or she belonged, was (and is) a dyed-in-the-wool conservative, a staunch anti-Papist and a guaranteed 100-per-cent reliable supporter of the British connection. Instead of dwelling on the reforming Churches' different historical origins, contrasting social backgrounds and varying religious dogmas, so many commentators have glossed over these distinctions, repeatedly presenting Protestants as though they belonged to one class and one point of view. In this merging process, landlords and tenants, employers and workers, conformists and Nonconformists have all been lumped together. Similarly, Catholics have often been presented as one undifferentiated mass, as though, to adapt the old phrase, they all 'dug with the same foot'.

This over-simplification of what in fact has been a complex and many-sided story has been aggravated by the loose and imprecise way in which language has been used by many of the protagonists involved. Semantic confusion has often been as bad as political confusion. Words, said Edmund Burke, who was himself most scrupulous in his prose style, can distort and conceal, as well as enlighten.[7] They can become a kind of talisman or magic charm when passions run high; when debates become sharper, and especially when religious and political issues are linked together, language may become so loaded as to cease to have much real meaning. Words are debased; propaganda supersedes rational argument, and as a consequence, it is difficult to separate illusion from reality. This was particularly true of Ulster, where controversies were generally conducted in such a way as to stir the emotions rather than the

3

intellect. Phrases such as 'the constitution' and 'civil and religious liberties' were flung around in meaningless abandon, both by orators and writers who should have known better, and by opposing sides among the common people who merely wanted a verbal stick with which to beat down their enemies. The Orangemen sang lustily about 'the old cause' which 'gave us our freedom, religion and laws', but apparently seldom paused to think what was precisely meant by these brave words. What freedom existed when 95 per cent of the soil was owned by a few thousand landlords, and the overwhelming majority of the population (including most Protestants) had no right to vote? Did 'religion' imply merely a narrow kind of reformed faith, or did it embrace the whole of Christianity, including the exhortation to love one's neighbours, even if they were Papists? As for laws, could they truly be defended if they deliberately discriminated against one section of the population?

In modern times the anthropologists and other social scientists, who have plunged so eagerly into the bog of Ulster linguistics, have further helped to blur the true picture by using words like 'tribe', 'community', and 'identity', which, because of their vagueness, tend to muddle the real issues. Even the members of the New Ireland Forum, who claimed to know something about Irish history, fell back on phrases like the 'Protestant tradition', as though this was synonymous with unionism.[8] One of the most remarkable aspects of its report was that there was no mention anywhere of dissenting Protestants. The forty-one signatories who put their names to the document presumably chose not to mention the ideas of such radicals as Wolfe Tone or John Mitchel in case they themselves might be tarred with the republican brush.

Why so many omissions and distortions from a story which, at least in certain respects, has plenty of source material available and certainly does not lack for dramatic events and lively personalities? Is it merely the old convention that in any struggle the victors rather than the vanquished create what eventually becomes received opinion? Do the mass media vulgarise history by seeking easy slogans and simplistic answers to complex questions? Or, as seems more likely, has it long suited the ruling classes on both sides of the Irish Sea to present a record of Ulster Protestants in this one-sided way? Whatever the answer to these questions, there can be no doubt that it has been politically convenient for unionists to ignore or play down any defections from what they regard as their own religious ranks. At home, the more they can emphasise Protestant unity and solidarity, the better they can isolate and weaken their opponents. Abroad, and especially in Britain, where there has always been a warm response to any argument which would let that country avoid responsibility for past errors of government, there have invariably been many people only too willing to put the blame for Ireland's misfortunes on the Irish themselves. During earlier centuries, when Protestantism became identified with English nationalism, a racist interpretation was put on to the 'innate defects' of the native Catholic Celts. More recently, when the cruder forms of imperialism are no longer in favour, it is politically more advantageous to present the Irish people, both north and south, as essentially irrational, because, unlike the sensible English, they seem to be quarrelling over out-of-date religious issues.

This book sets out to challenge the myth that northern Protestants collectively have always thought the same way, either politically or theologically. It questions the claim that the various economic groups within the Protestant section of the population have necessarily had the same long-term interests at heart, and it rejects the naive approach that the struggle in the north has ever been, or indeed is now, a straightforward religious war between sects, which cannot of their nature be reconciled. It deals with neglected minorities as well as with much vaunted majorities, and more attention is paid to the rebel than to the conformist. The many bitter battles between rich and poor, privileged and non-privileged, are discussed in detail, and the tale of old schisms between conservative and liberal Churchmen and women are told once again. There is an attempt to examine the language which has been used by those involved during different historical eras; and where possible, key words and phrases that have proved so emotive and politically influential are analysed in relation to their social context.

The names of long-dead, but once potent, individuals are disinterred for modern readers. In particular, the book is concerned with the Presbyterians and the role they have played over the centuries as a middle and often vacillating section within the overall Protestant majority of the population. The period covered begins with the original plantations and comes up to partition. The central thesis is the persistent and ever recurring struggle of 'Protestant democracy', sometimes in alliance with like-minded Catholics, against the Ascendancy and Tories. The Epilogue deals briefly with the continuing dilemma that has faced all citizens, and not merely Dissenters, in Northern Ireland since 1921.

In so far as this book controverts much of the received opinion about the history of Ulster, especially the view that all Protestants think alike, it could be said to be revisionist. I have tried to go back to original sources, to be accurate in presentation of facts, and to adopt a scholarly approach to my material. There are plenty of footnotes and references, and the various personalities are allowed to speak for themselves.

But if it is revisionist in method it is certainly not revisionist in interpretation as the term has come to be popularly used during recent decades. It does not, for example, reject the thesis that it is possible to find a broad pattern in Irish history over the last 350 years. Nor does it denigrate the traditional heroes and heroines of Irish liberalism and nationalism, but hopefully adds some new names, depicted in all their strengths and weaknesses. It does not pretend to be neutral, as some revisionists do, when in fact they are conservative, and it does not, under the guise of academic objectivity, merely sit on the fence. On the contrary, I make no apology for being on the side of Irish freedom as against British imperialism; of democracy against all notions of aristocracy and ascendancy; of small tenant farmers against big landowners; of ecumenicists against sectarians, and of Dissenters of all faiths against Church establishments.

This commitment to one side of the political struggle will inevitably antagonise the not-an-inch brigade who see the Union with Britain as the best defence of their privileges; it may also disturb those would-be reformers who accept the need for change in their society, but see this as being carried out within the present constitutional structure. Why reopen old wounds, and stir up ancient fires of dissension and hatred, when what is required is reconciliation and consensus? Why retell a tale which is so marked by tragedy and so likely to revive painful memories?

It is my contention, however, that there can be no long-term solution to the 'Ulster problem' until the true picture, warts and all if necessary, is shown. There can be no healing process until the real nature of the disease is carefully examined and its underlying pathology exposed and dealt with. In other words, there can be no understanding of the present without a much fuller knowledge of the past.

In this process of filling in gaps and offering an alternative explanation of complicated events, it is hoped that the Protestants of Northern Ireland, angry and confused as many of them are because of endless violence and communal strife, have a better opportunity to appreciate that they have another heritage apart from the dying colonialism and sterile Orangeism to which so many apparently still cling. Catholics, too, will benefit from being reminded that they also can look back on fellow Christians, who, in spite of theological differences, have thought of themselves as fellow citizens, rather than members of a ruling class. Liberal-minded people of all denominations – and there are more of these trying to escape from the morass of sectarianism than is generally appreciated – should take new inspiration from the knowledge of how deeply and for how long the dissenting tradition goes back in Ulster's history.

As for the choice of material and the value judgements that are made in this book, let posterity be the judge. I can honestly claim that I accept the dictum expressed by that great democrat and Presbyterian, James Hope: 'I know of no responsibility equal to that of the historian.'[9]

FLANN CAMPBELL
JUNE 1991

7

PROLOGUE

'THE NORTH BEGAN'

The North began; the North held on
The strife for native land!
Till Ireland rose, and cow'd her foes –
God bless the Northern land!

Thomas Davis[1]

Ulster, which has remained for so long the symbol of British rule in Ireland, was paradoxically the most Gaelic of all the Irish provinces before the plantations.[2] At this time, throughout the north there was tangible evidence of the region's cultural origins – ring-forts, tumuli, ogham stones and dolmens, which went back to the dawn of Celtic history. There were many prehistoric sites, for example, at Legananny, near Ballynahinch, County Down, at Drumbo, near Belfast, and the Grianan of Aileach on the border between Derry and Donegal. Emain Macha (Navan Fort, in Armagh) had been the centre of a thriving civilisation in the third century AD, and the Cuchulain saga had been focused on this now deserted grassy mound.

The people and language were largely of Celtic origin, and the old Brehon laws generally observed. The Anglo-Normans, who had planted themselves so widely in the south since the end of the twelfth century, had hardly penetrated north of the River Boyne. There were scarcely any towns of importance, and not many castles. The few English who had settled along the eastern coastline, particularly in the Ards peninsula, had become so thoroughly absorbed that they were despised by the Tudor monarchs as having gone native.[3] In a similar way the Scots, who had been coming to Antrim as traders, farmers or soldiers for many generations, had intermarried and interbred with the local population. In any event, they were predominantly Celts

8

and spoke a Gaelic tongue – a thousand years previously their Scottii ancestors had come from Ireland.

The Reformation, which had begun to affect some areas of Leinster and Munster, hardly touched the counties of the north. Virtually everyone living there, whatever their descent or family background, was Catholic; and these 'Papists', as they were later scornfully referred to by their conquerors, could look back on a Christian heritage as rich as anywhere in Europe. Saint Patrick, after all, was reputed to have been a slave on the slopes of Slemish Mountain in Antrim, and was said to be buried in Downpatrick. Saint Colmcille had lived in Donegal as a young man, and sailed from Derry to Iona in 563. Two of the greatest missionaries in the seventh century were Saint Gall and Saint Columbanus. Both had been educated at Bangor, where the ruins of an ancient monastery still existed. And if these saintly names were not sufficient evidence, there were round towers at Devenish in Lough Erne, and high crosses at Arboe and Donaghmore in Tyrone, and Carndonagh in Donegal, to remind those who cared to look that Christianity had flourished in the north for several hundred years.

At the end of the reign of Elizabeth I the province was ruled, not by English soldiers or landlords alien in birth and religion, but by ancient hereditary families – the O'Neills, O'Dohertys, O'Reillys, O'Donnells and Maguires – all of them of unquestionable Irish origin. The old placenames – Uladh (Ulster), Béal Feirsde (Belfast), Dún (Down), Ard Macha (Armagh), Doire (Derry), Inis Ceithleann (Enniskillen), Tír Eóghain (Tyrone), Latharna (Larne) – told, and continue to tell, the story of this Gaelic past.

There is no historical evidence to tell us in any detail how free and prosperous these northern Gaels were, and it would be naive to suggest that there was then some golden age existing in which every inhabitant was materially comfortable, happy and cultivated. Nevertheless, at the beginning of the seventeenth century Ulster had within its boundaries enough natural and social potential, if left alone, to develop as a relatively peaceful and thriving part of a wider Irish state.

The plantations of 1609–13, and the subsequent Cromwellian and Williamite settlements of 1652 and 1691 respectively, changed that pattern completely. A new class, new Churches, and a new culture replaced the traditional civilisation that had endured for centuries. Ulster ceased to be a largely independent province and became, along with the rest of the country, a colony of Britain. The native Irish, defeated and outlawed, were driven from their homes and forced to scratch a livelihood as best they could in the bogs, mountains or woods, or else compelled to remain as labourers or the poorest of tenants on their ancestral lands. The clan system, which was the basis of the old social life, was destroyed within a generation, and the Brehon laws, which had brought some measure of traditional justice to the people, disappeared overnight. The Catholic religion was forced underground by penal laws, which proscribed priests, closed schools, and took away all economic and political rights from the majority of the population. English took the place of Irish as the language of the upper and middle classes, government, administration and law. A reformed Church, with its roots in England, was established, endowed with escheated lands,[4] militantly anti-Catholic, and serving as a kind of spiritual garrison for the rich and privileged.

The most fundamental economic change was in the ownership of land, and because the overwhelming majority of the people depended upon agriculture for their livelihood, this affected every sphere of social life in the province. During the first wave of plantations following the flight of the earls in 1607, a large part of the fertile soil of Armagh, Tyrone, Donegal, Fermanagh, Cavan and Monaghan was divided into blocks of 1,000, 1,500 or 2,000 acres and granted to so-called undertakers or servitors.[5] Some of these were ex-soldiers; some were adventurers seeking a fortune; others were lawyers or administrators already well established but keen to enhance further their reputations and careers in the newly conquered territories. All were greedy for cheap land, and not too scrupulous as to how they acquired it. It was a condition of the grant that they had to be 'well affected' (that is, Protestant) in religion.

10

By 1619, when Nicholas Pynnar had finished his famous survey, it was estimated that about a quarter of a million acres of profitable land had been taken over by about one hundred families, the majority of them being English, with Scots comprising about one-third of the total. It was then that such names as Abercorn, Caulfield, Cole, Archdale and Saunderson – there was even a Sir James Craig and a Sir Basil Brooke on Pynnar's list – first appeared on the Ulster scene. Hugh Montgomery and James Hamilton were two Scottish favourites who received big estates for services rendered to James I, and the city livery companies of London were granted large parts of County Derry.

The few remaining Irish landlords (called 'deserving' because they had not been involved in resisting confiscation) retained less than one-eighth of their original estates, and even this portion was mostly lost within a few score years.

The events of the mid- and late seventeenth century revived all the old Protestant anxieties about massacre, and at the same time reinforced their view that it was only through force that they could hold on to their expanding possessions. In 1641 there was a revolt by Catholics in Ulster, in which, according to the most reliable research, about four thousand Protestants were killed. This roused atavistic fears which never fully died out. In 1649 it was the turn of the Catholics to suffer – thousands were killed at Drogheda and Wexford, and 'the curse of Cromwell' became part of Irish nationalist folklore. Fifty years later, following the Glorious Revolution and the Battle of the Boyne, the gulf between Protestant and Catholic became ever wider, with the newly victorious William III as symbol of both the Protestant faith and British power. The Siege of Derry, in which the people of the town held out resolutely for months against the enveloping Jacobite armies, created another long-lasting legend, that of loyalty and courage defeating the forces of treachery and cowardice. It was a victory for the virtues of 'No surrender' over the evils of Popery and Lundyism. After each of these episodes, more forfeited estates were taken from their Catholic owners, until by the late eighteenth century about 95 per cent of all land was

11

in the hands of Protestant, overwhelmingly episcopalian, landlords.

By the end of the seventeenth century the conquest of Ulster
seemed as complete as in any other part of Ireland, and a different social pattern had been imposed, in which ethnic origin,
property, religion and political allegiance were closely connected.
This new structure was as hierarchical as any form of feudalism,
and as inflexible as any caste system.[6] In the way in which it
distributed wealth, and in the manner in which power was
concentrated in a few hands, it provided, so far as the great
majority of the province's inhabitants were concerned, the exact
opposite of those civil and religious liberties the Protestant constitution was supposed to defend.

At the top of the social pyramid was an oligarchy of landlords,
aristocrats, administrators, high-ranking army officers and
Church of Ireland bishops who formed a small (no more than a
few thousand in the whole country) but immensely powerful
ruling élite. The dominance of this Ascendancy,[7] as it came to be
called, was twofold. Economically, the landlords held the great
bulk of the population in their grip because they could evict or
raise rents, and therefore had a life-and-death hold over their
tenants.[8] To be evicted meant to lose one's home, potatoes, cereal
crops and milk upon which everything depended. To have rents
raised or to pay excessive tithes often meant sinking from poverty into destitution. Wealth itself gave the feudal lords enormous influence, both locally and nationally. An Earl of Hertford
or a Marquess of Downshire might easily draw as much income
from rents in a month as a poor tenant or labourer could earn in
a lifetime's work.

In terms of political influence the new ruling class had as much
a monopoly as they had of material possessions. In theory Dissenters, as well as members of the Church of Ireland, were free
to vote and be elected to parliament, but in practice the electoral
system was so arranged that even among the privileged
episcopalians only a small number – a minority within a minority – had any real influence. The franchise was based on a wealth
qualification that kept out all but a few scores of thousands of

owners or lessors of land. Members of parliament were traditionally selected from a tiny group of prosperous, and often titled, families.

The Presbyterians, who because of a further influx of settlers from Scotland in the 1690s and early 1700s eventually comprised about one-third of the province's population, belonged to an intermediate stratum in Ulster society, neither as wealthy and influential as the episcopalian landlords, army officers and parsons, nor as submerged and poverty-stricken as the Catholics. Half in the Ascendancy because of their Protestantism, and half out because of their inferior legal status, they formed a substantial group of the kind that was so obviously missing in the south – a middle or yeoman class. Their subordinate position made them equivocal in their attitude towards authority, and this meant their loyalty to the Government, even to the Crown, was often conditional.

In the rural areas of Antrim and north Down, where most of them were concentrated, the majority were tenant farmers who earned extra money from spinning and weaving linen. Very few actually owned any appreciable amount of land. Their farms were generally small, fifteen or twenty acres, and their living standards usually modest. Some fell into the category of cottiers, and were hardly better off than their Catholic neighbours, frequently sinking into penury in times of bad harvests or trade recession. In such towns as Belfast and Derry they were mainly artisans, clerks or shop assistants, with a smaller proportion of merchants, manufacturers and professional people.

By the mid-seventeenth century there were about sixty Presbyterian ministers serving in Ulster,[9] but though few in number, they had a powerful local influence because they were well educated and held such strong moral convictions. In a dissenting parish they were the natural leaders and spokesmen of the community. Their incomes of £50 to £80 a year meant that they were better off than Catholic priests, but their living standards were well below those of the Church of Ireland clergy.

The Dissenters obviously welcomed the 1689 revolution because they saw it as the ultimate defender of their Protestant faith, but the rule of William III, and later Anne, did not satisfy all their expectations. The Test Act of 1704, though not nearly so severe towards them as the penal laws were against Catholics, required anyone who wished to hold a post under the Crown to take an oath of allegiance and receive holy communion according to the rites of the Established Church. Non-Anglicans generally refused to accept such humiliating conditions and were accordingly debarred from posts of authority under the state. The mercantilist laws passed at Westminster were another cause of discontent because they discriminated against Irish manufacturers who might compete with British merchants. There was also a series of grievances concerning payment of tithes and the refusal of authorities to accept the validity of Presbyterian marriages.

In theology the Presbyterians claimed to be the most ardent defenders of freedom in so far as they placed great emphasis on the rights of the individual conscience and the liberty of all men and women to make up their minds on the basis of biblical teaching rather than the authority of any Church. Some went so far as to call themselves republicans, though it must be admitted they used the word in rather a special sense in line with Calvin's notion of a city-state. During the late seventeenth and early eighteenth centuries the religious scene in Ulster was deeply affected by controversies, often prolonged and bitter, spilling over from England and Scotland. These debates raised issues of the most profound significance relating to the respective rights and duties of the citizen, the Church, the Crown and parliament. Certainly the Presbyterians disapproved of any idea of a state-endowed or state-controlled Church, and the concept of a hierarchy of bishops was repugnant to them. The fact that their ministers were chosen from below (that is, elected by a congregation and elders), rather than appointed from above, gave their organisation a democratic flavour. Their synods could be centres of serious discussion and argument.

In a Church whose members, both lay and clerical, preached so much about the rights of individual dissent it was inevitable there would be many schisms and conflicts. From their arrival in Carrickfergus in 1642[10] the Presbyterians were prone to split and divide, forming sects sometimes only a few thousand strong. These secessions and regroupings weakened them organisationally, but generally led to lively debates and the publication of controversial books and sermons. In 1705, for example, the Belfast Society was founded, which had as its main purpose the vigorous discussion of political and theological matters.

In the 1720s – significantly when economic conditions were deteriorating – a violent controversy known as 'the battle of the pamphlets' broke out between two factions in the Church – the orthodox Old Lights and the unorthodox New Lights. This struggle between conservatives and liberals was destined to continue throughout the eighteenth and nineteenth centuries.

The Old Lights were strongly Calvinist in outlook, and drew their philosophical inspiration, as well as their sense of ethnic superiority, from John Knox and the Scottish Covenanters. Fundamentalist in theology and reactionary in politics, they represented a long-enduring strain in Ulster public life. Their attitude towards Catholicism and the Pope (whom they regularly denounced as 'anti-Christ', 'the man of sin', and so forth) was invariably hostile, even rancorous.

By their emphasis on predestination, with its division into the elect (or saved) and non-elect (or damned), they provided themselves with the argument that Protestants, and in particular Calvinists, were created morally and socially superior to Catholics. Their fervent evangelical principles further led them to the conclusion that it was faith in the Lord rather than good works on earth that was the surest means of getting to heaven. Why worry about social reform when what was required for salvation was God's redeeming grace? Why strive for collective political change when what was needed for a better society was the redemption of individuals?

The result of this mixing of theology and politics was that the Old Lights leaned strongly towards the conservatives, and generally took a cautious attitude towards any proposal to alter the status quo in the two key areas of the constitution and landownership. From the Bible they eagerly gathered texts stressing the rights of property, and the duty of submission to established authorities. In any crisis they could be relied upon to support the Ascendancy in Ireland and the Government in London.

The liberal New Lights, who formed a strong, and sometimes a majority, movement within Irish Presbyterianism for over a century, were accused of being Arians, taking their name from Arius, a Christian priest who lived in Alexandria during the fourth century. He preached that Christ was not consubstantial with God, and for this reason his followers were known in seventeenth-century England as Unitarians. The creed was linked with Pelagianism, which did not accept the idea of original sin, and Arminianism, which rejected Calvin's idea of predestination.[11] It was thus not in the mainstream of Scottish or English Presbyterianism.

There were five main tenets of this doctrine, which had a flavour of political, as well as religious, radicalism. First, any human test or subscription to a man-made document (as, for example, to the 1643 Westminster Confession of Faith, the official doctrine of English Presbyterianism) was contrary to the law of God. Second, the Bible spoke directly to individuals, and individuals must look to their consciences as a guide. Thus, in the last resort no Church or clergyman could override the individual's right to judge what was right or wrong; as a consequence, 'good men might think differently'. It was true that some theological beliefs were better than others, but even an erroneous creed would not necessarily shut out a sincere man from a humble mansion in God's house. Third, Calvin might have been a most eminent divine, but certain of his harsher doctrines about hell and damnation could not be accepted. The claim that unbaptised infants (or heathens, for that matter) could not enter heaven, even though they had committed no sin, was rejected as not being the wish of a merciful God. Predestination, or the belief that certain people were chosen by God's grace to enter heaven, and others were not, was contrary to the concept of free will and the moral responsibility of individuals. The Christian belief in original sin, that human beings inherited a frail and

16

corruptible nature, did not mean they were automatically involved in the guilt of Adam. Fourth, the death of Christ (or vicarious atonement) did not absolve individuals from personal responsibility for their actions, or remove the penalty that must be exacted for unGodliness. The fifth and most striking difference between Arians and other Protestants (and indeed Catholics) was on the question of the nature of God. The Arians believed there was only one God, and rejected the almost universally accepted Christian thesis that the Father, Son and Holy Ghost were three-in-one, and all equal.

Politically the New Lights tended to be democratic in outlook, even on occasions radical, resenting the ascendancy of the aristocratic and episcopalian Tories. In particular, they disliked the landlords who monopolised the most fertile soil and squeezed their tenants, regardless of their Church affiliations. Though strongly critical of Catholicism, they eventually came round, after many hesitations and reservations, to support equal rights for Catholics, including freedom of worship, education, and the right to sit and vote in parliament. Their latitudinarian sympathies led them to attack all forms of bigotry in both religion and politics.

During the first half of the eighteenth century the most eloquent advocate of New Light opinions was the Reverend John Abernethy, a prominent divine from Antrim who spent many years as a minister at Usher's Quay, Dublin. Abernethy was unorthodox enough to query certain fundamental Christian truths, including the doctrine of the Trinity. He was noticeably anti-Calvinist, and preached there was neither good nor evil without liberty. His particular bugbear was the Westminster Confession, which he saw as a shackle on freedom of expression. On one occasion he said: 'Reason is our greatest excellency.'[12]

His doubts about the divinity of Christ were rivalled only by his uncertainty as to how far he should go in tolerating Catholicism. Catholics in his view were hardly Christians at all, and might be regarded in the same way as Jews, Muslims or pagans. On the other hand, they were human beings, and with God's grace might get to heaven. In a sermon preached in

17

Dublin in 1735, and later published under the title *Persecution Contrary to Christianity*,[13] he began by declaring that one must love one's neighbour, and then went on to list all the reasons why the Pope must be condemned as anti-Christ – the Inquisition, Mariolatry, worship of idols and transubstantiation. Finally, he came to the conclusion that the penal laws, then at their most oppressive, were not too bad because they kept the peace. His cure (and he learned Irish so that he could proselytise the better) was not to tolerate Catholics, but to convert them to the one true faith.

Such contradictory views were typical of many would-be liberal Presbyterians, opinions which, so long as they continued, only served to weaken them politically. By attacking Catholics, the Dissenters strengthened the episcopalians who oppressed them both.

At the bottom of the economic and social scale, and hardly yet aware as to how these Protestant schisms might affect them, were the Catholics, who comprised about three-quarters of the population of all Ireland, and about half the population of the nine counties of Ulster.[14] Landless and voteless, they were barred from education, and persecuted for practising their religion. Serfs in their own land, the great majority were labourers or poor tenant farmers growing what potatoes or oats they could on a few acres of soil. During a bad harvest they sank from poverty into famine. At the whim of their landlords they could be evicted from their land, in most cases their only source of livelihood, or have their rents raised. The penal laws prevented them from buying land, and debarred them from appointments in public office, from voting or standing for parliament. Harsher still for a people who in spite of every adversity still clung to their pride in being Irish and Catholic, their language and religion were despised by their new masters. Their natural leaders were driven into exile, their priests harried and maltreated.

Ireland was not alone, of course, in having such a feudal social structure during the seventeenth and eighteenth centuries. Monarchies, oligarchies, despotisms, tryannies and reactionary regimes of every sort existed all over Europe. What was so remarkable about Ireland, and made the struggles for democratic rule there so difficult, was the country's colonial subordination to Britain, and the complicated interrelationships that existed between the internal elements of social class, ethnic group, language and religion. The people of Ireland, whether they wished it or not, were drawn into the wars of Reformation and Counter-Reformation, and were directly involved in the power struggles of England, France and Spain. Their country's geographical proximity to Britain gave it exceptional strategic significance. The connection between racial (or more accurately ethnic) factors and religion provided an extra dimension of bitterness to that age-old strife between rich and poor, privileged and underprivileged, which was common to all societies.

The most damaging aspect of Irish historical development – a perpetual virus, as it were, in the body politic – was the continuing intervention of British power on the side of the Ascendancy.[15] The evolution of society, for example, from feudalism to capitalism was impeded by an external force. Protestantism was introduced into Ireland not merely for missionary purposes but also as a means of imposing control over an unruly colony. As soon as some urgently needed change was mooted, such as the abolition of the penal laws, which virtually everyone nowadays would admit to have been an intolerable abuse, then the British government would come down in favour of the status quo. If some elementary and overdue reform was suggested, like extending the franchise to Catholics or democratising the system of landownership, then all the reactionary forces on both sides of the Irish Sea would be mobilised to prevent it. Finally, at the moment of crisis, when revolution threatened or a local rebellion could not be easily suppressed, sectarianism would be whipped up and the threat of civil war invoked. In the last resort, acting as a kind of ultimate veto against potential change or reform, the army could be called in. This permanent ban on progress was, and continued to be, a particular feature of political life in Ulster because the Protestants were so numerous there, and the forces of religious prejudice could be so effectively deployed.

The gap between rich and poor being so wide in rural areas,

and access to land so crucial for such a high proportion of the population, it was inevitable that the first serious threat to the Ascendancy should come from the tenant farmers, the poorest of whom were little better off than labourers. The dispossessed Catholics had the longest tradition of resistance to landlordism, and their rebellion against the loss of their homes and livelihood was often, and not surprisingly, violent. Woodkernes and rapparees[16] had been active sporadically all over Ireland in every generation. It is significant that Redmond O'Hanlon, the first Ribbonman whose name was recorded and whose fame spread far outside his own locality, was an Ulsterman. He led a guerrilla force in Tyrone and Armagh for nearly a decade, and finally betrayed by his brother-in-law, was hanged in 1681. A major outbreak of agrarian unrest occurred in Tipperary in the 1750s and 1760s, when the spread of enclosures added to the misery caused by tithes and higher rents. This Whiteboy[17] agitation quickly extended to other parts of Munster, Leinster and Connacht, and within a decade had seriously affected some areas in Ulster.

The activities of Oakboys in Armagh, Tyrone and Derry, and of Steelboys in Antrim, were triggered off by the imposition of compulsory road building rather like the unpopular corvée of prerevolutionary France. The political significance of this unrest was that for the first time since the plantations a widespread anti-government organisation in Ulster was led by Presbyterians, foreshadowing the Volunteers and United Irishmen who were to appear upon the scene within a few decades.

The aims and tactics of these underground illegal groups were similar all over the country. They wanted to keep rents down, to maintain security of tenure, and to have tithes reduced or abolished. A proclamation issued by the Hearts of Steel in March 1772 described some of their grievances in the north:

> betwixt landlords and rectors, the very marrow is screwed out of our bones, and our lives are even become so burdensome to us, by these uncharitable and unreasonable men, that we do not care whether we live or die; for they lay such burthen upon our shoulders that they cannot touch them with one of their fingers;

20

they have reduced us to such a deplorable state by such grievious oppressions that the poor is turned black in the face, and the skin parched on their back, that they are rendered incapable to support their starving families with the common necessaries of life, that nature is but scarcely supported, that they have not even food, nor yet raiment to secure them from the extremities of weather wither by day or night.[18]

As they had no legal means of redress for their grievances, the methods of intimidation used by Steelboys and Oakboys were often violent. They wrote threatening letters, maimed cattle, set fire to ricks and buildings, attacked bailiffs, even on occasion killed landlords. Exclusively Protestant in membership, they later degenerated into openly sectarian societies such as the Peep O'Day Boys, who spent more time trying to frighten their neighbouring Catholic tenants than they did in fighting their common enemy. This ideological confusion among the more backward Protestant agrarian organisations was also evident in their crudely constructed handbills or letters, in which they combined dire threats against landlords with protestations of loyalty to the Crown and constitution.

The aristocratic family who stirred up most resentment among the Steelboys, and who were mainly responsible for provoking three years' serious rioting and disturbances in County Antrim, were the Donegalls – archetypal county magnates, owning thousands of acres, episcopalian in religion, and frequently absent from their demesnes. Descended from Sir Arthur Chichester, one of James I's chief undertakers and viceroy between 1604 and 1616, the family had been raised higher and higher in the peerage for services to the Crown, and had become immensely rich, mainly because of the growth of Belfast.[19]

The fourth earl was particularly oppressive, and added insult to injury among his more respectable Protestant tenants by his extravagance and profligacy abroad.[20] His son, who inherited more than 25,000 acres of fertile soil in 1757 and was said to have an annual income of over £40,000 (the modern equivalent of around £1 million), was just as socially irresponsible. And in 1770, when he proposed a further steep increase in rents and

21

the auctioning of leases to the highest bidder, there were widespread protests. The farmers' discontent was further fuelled by the intervention of middlemen, who were, as was so often the case, harder than their masters, and by the temporary collapse of the linen trade upon which so many depended for an essential part of their income. The agitation spread in Antrim, and then into Down, Armagh and Derry.

A sensational episode that received nationwide attention and led to the intervention of the viceroy occurred in December of that year. David Douglas, a local farmer, was arrested in Templepatrick, a small town, about ten miles north-west of Belfast, which had been the centre of agrarian unrest for many years. Douglas was charged with maiming cattle belonging to one Thomas Gregg, a Belfast merchant and speculator who had become notorious as a middleman who bought up leases and livestock. Douglas was taken to Belfast jail on the orders of Waddell Cunningham, a prominent local citizen and colleague of Gregg's. Armed with pikes and guns, some thousands of tenant farmers, calling themselves Steelboys, assembled in Carnmoney, Ballyclare and other nearby Antrim villages and marched on Belfast, where they set fire to Cunningham's house and besieged the prison. Soldiers were called out by the town mayor and fired on the crowd, killing three men. This did not deter the rebels, who eventually induced the authorities to release Douglas. A proclamation was issued by the Government, and some men were put on trial, but the jury refused to convict. A song was composed about this event:

> Donegall all his tenants may plunder and fine,
> And a Greg and base Cunningham aid the design –
> Then the mischief they breed with such terrible zeal
> They falsely impute to the poor 'hearts of steel'.

In the spring of 1772 there was a new surge of activity involving at least five northern counties, particularly those areas where Presbyterian farmers were numerous. Riots broke out in several places in March of that year, and troops had to be called in. Nine protesters were killed at Claudy, County Derry,

22

seven at Grange, County Derry, and one in Ballymena, County Antrim. So high was the feeling about these deaths that some Presbyterian synods were forced to protest. The Government was embarrassed by this widespread violence in a province they regarded as traditionally peaceful and loyal, and the viceroy was compelled to make a strong attack on rack-renting landlords such as Lord Donegall.

Gradually the agitation subsided, and did not reappear until the Defenders versus Peep O'Day Boys clashes of the 1790s. The tenants were successful, however, in frightening the landlords, and protecting the Ulster custom (the right to sell the goodwill of a tenancy), which was so dear to them. They might have achieved more if they had drawn into their campaign the even more oppressed Catholics. As it was, weakened by religious divisions, their victory was only a partial one.

The suffering of these tenants resulted in a large flow of emigrants seeking better material conditions or greater freedom in North America. Historians differ as to the precise number who left Ulster during the various periods of unrest, but the most authentic estimates suggest that some 50,000 to 70,000 crossed the Atlantic between 1715 and 1775 from such ports as Belfast, Larne, Derry and Newry.[21] The severe economic distress of the 1720s had been aggravated by bad weather and a series of poor harvests, which led to widespread famine. Rents had been raised when many of the thirty-year leases granted by the Williamite settlement fell in, and simultaneously there was a collapse of the linen industry, with prices falling by half within a few years. So horrifying was the poverty all over Ireland that in 1729 Dean Swift was provoked to publish his satirical *Modest Proposal*, a suggestion that plump young babies should be cooked and eaten rather than be allowed to grow up to become a drain on the country's resources.

At the height of this migration dozens of ships were regularly employed trading into Philadelphia, Boston, New York and Montreal. During the worst phases of the Donegall evictions as many as 12,000 were leaving the north annually. Most were Presbyterians, but some Catholics are included in this figure.

23

There was also emigration from southern ports such as Cork and Dublin. The cost of the voyage, which was always uncomfortable and often hazardous, was £3 to £4 for steerage accommodation. The poorest passengers went 'free' as indentured servants or labourers pledged to work in the colonies for a specified master for a period of months or years. Farm tenants who were discontented with their lot at home, and attracted by the thought of cheap land, no rents, and freedom to think and worship as they preferred, could sometimes raise enough money to pay for themselves and their families by selling their leases under the Ulster custom.

From the early part of the century Pennsylvania had become the chief focus of attraction as fertile soil was abundant there, and the political atmosphere was tolerant towards religious dissent. The connection with Ireland was strong, its founder was William Penn from Kinsale, County Cork, and the governor at this time was George Bryan, who was born in Dublin. Benjamin Franklin reckoned that at the outbreak of the American War of Independence one-third of the total population in this state was of Irish descent. The Ulster imprint was marked by the names of local towns, for example, Armagh, Donegal, Letterkenny, Antrim, Fermanagh, Tyrone and Strabane. Philadelphia, a rapidly growing city full of Germans as well as Irish, became the centre of anti-British opinion, and it was there that a compositor from Strabane, one John Dunlap, printed the American Declaration of Independence in 1776. The strength of radical Irish influence may be seen in the fact that no fewer than eight of the fifty-six signatories of that historic document had an Irish background – Thomas McKean (Derry), Matthew Thornton (Limerick), Thomas Lynch (Galway), Edward Rutledge, George Read (Dublin), Charles Carroll (Offaly), George Taylor (Dublin), and James Smith (Dublin). James McHenry, George Washington's secretary, came from Ballymena, and Charles Thomson, secretary of Congress, from County Derry. It was to Philadelphia two decades later there also came the United Irishmen leaders, Wolfe Tone, Hamilton Rowan and Thomas Emmet.

The American volunteer army, so badly equipped but so

24

vigorous in revolutionary spirit, had as its core a group of officers and men, some fresh from Ireland, others long settled in the colony, who – like Patrick Sarsfield two generations earlier – saw themselves fighting not only for their new homeland but also settling old scores with Britain. Francis Joseph Bigger refers to these soldiers as 'the Wild Geese of the north'.[22] The highest ranks in the rebel army included men from the four provinces of Ireland. General Richard Montgomery, who was killed at the Siege of Quebec, General Andrew Lewis and Colonel Walter Stewart of the Continental Army, were all from Donegal. General William Irvine, the famous surgeon, came from Enniskillen, Major-General Edward Hand from Offaly, Major-General John O'Sullivan and Quartermaster-General Stephen Moylan from Cork, Brigadier-General Richard Butler from Dublin, and most celebrated of all, Admiral John Barry, father of the American navy, from Wexford.

Washington himself always spoke highly of his Irish troops and to show his appreciation became a member of the Friendly Sons of Saint Patrick. In March 1780 he issued a proclamation stating that the Irish national saint's day should be commemorated as a token of respect for a 'brave and generous people'.

When the war was over and postmortems were held as to why Britain had been defeated, the role of the Irish, both politically and militarily, was widely recognised. Speaking in the Irish House of Commons in April 1784, the County Dublin MP, Luke Gardiner, said:

America was lost by Irish emigrants. These emigrations are fresh in the recollection of every gentleman in this house. I am assured from the best authority, the major part of the American army was composed of Irish, and that the Irish language was as commonly spoken in the American army as English. I am also informed that it was their valour determined the contest so that England had America detached from her by force of Irish emigrants.[23]

1

'CIVIL AND RELIGIOUS LIBERTY'

We declare that after all we have heard and read about our glorious and happy constitution, we are so ignorant as not to be able to find what it is. We cannot, however, conceive that if in any nation three-fourths of the inhabitants are absolutely excluded from all share in the legislature and only a very small part of the other represented; if the great majority, of what we called the representatives, be appointed arbitrarily by a few individuals, for a long term of years, and not accountable to the people; – If places and pensions be multiplied for the purposes of corruption; if no responsibility be annexed by the great offices of state; if taxes without end be levied off the people, and the nation involved in debt, for the purposes of purchasing votes to impose more taxes – If the honours of the peerage be brought to sale . . . If the surplus of the revenue . . . be carried to another country . . . if the subject be deprived of trial by jury – We say, if any nation labours under those and innumerable other grievances . . . We are yet to learn what is the *glorious* and *happy* constitution of that nation: we do not hesitate to say – THEY ARE A NATION OF SLAVES!

Statement issued by a meeting of Belfast citizens, December 1792[1]

If land was the key issue for the majority of Ulster tenant farmers, Presbyterian and Catholic alike, the question of the franchise was the crucial political problem for the middle classes of both town and country. The much vaunted constitution, with all that was implied with regard to protection of popular rights, did not, in fact, exist. In its place was a range of oppressive and reactionary statute laws. The phrase 'civil and religious liberty' had little real meaning for the common people. It was, in truth, a cover for the rule of a few thousand members of the Ascendancy.

In Ireland during the 1780s there was no aspect of the voting system that could properly be described as free and democratic. The historian R.B. McDowell is more accurate when he calls it 'complex, defective and absurd'.[2] A recent authoritative essay on the subject says that the Irish parliament was 'landlord dominated, corrupt and unrepresentative',[3] and the author goes on to list no fewer than nine different ways in which both Commons and Lords were biased against the welfare of the overwhelming majority of the population. Thus when Orangemen sang about 'the old cause' which gave 'us our freedom, religion and laws', they referred to some notion that did not have much historical reality.

To begin with, the parliamentary franchise was restricted not only (as in Britain) to the more prosperous members of society, but, in a country in which three out of four people were Catholics, solely to Protestants. Electoral discrimination was both social and religious. The municipal franchise was even more limited and in many towns confined to a tiny handful of burgesses. The grand juries, which had both judicial and executive functions and controlled expenditure in the counties, were not reformed until the end of the nineteenth century.

In the thirty-two county constituencies, each returning two MPs, forty-shilling freeholders had the right to vote in parliamentary elections; the number in the constituencies of the three southern provinces varying between seven hundred in counties Longford and Galway to three thousand in County Cork. The ratio of electors to total population ranged from around one in thirty to one in seventy or eighty. In Ulster, mainly because the proportion of Protestants was much higher there, the number of voters was above the national average. In the mid-1780s, for example, County Down had approximately 6,000 on the electoral roll, Antrim 3,500, Tyrone 3,000, Donegal 2,500 and Armagh 2,400. The number of electors in the whole province was probably between 25,000 and 30,000 out of a total population of about 850,000.[4]

However, these figures are misleading with regard to voting rights and the modern-day notion of a popular franchise, as there was no secret ballot, and therefore no genuine freedom of choice in electing an MP. Virtually all rural electors were under heavy pressure to vote for the candidate selected by the richest local landlords. During an election campaign there was invariably a great deal of money spent on providing free food and drink, or even in outright bribery. And when election day actually came round, the practice was for the landlord, or more likely his agent, to herd the few electors to the polling booth and make sure that they put their marks in the right place. Wolfe Tone said that under the existing voting system the electors were led to the polls like 'bullocks and sheep'.[5] In such circumstances, only the bravest, or most foolhardy, voter would flout the wishes of the dominant local family or party clique.

The notorious town boroughs were even more corrupt than the county constituencies, the majority being described in one contemporary report as 'decayed, mean and dilapidated'.[6] In most cases their electorates consisted of only a dozen or so burgesses who were under the thumb of their patron, nominator or proprietor.[7] Such patrons could buy and sell their control over the franchise like so much merchandise. For example, in 1782 it was estimated that such a closed borough (as it was called) could be sold for £2,000 for a period of one parliament, or between £8,000 and £10,000 for the permanent patronage. Of the twenty-eight Ulster boroughs then existing, only Carrickfergus (900 voters), Derry (700), Newry (600–700), Lisburn (400), Antrim (250), and Downpatrick (250) had more than a handful of names on the electoral rolls. The contemptuous word 'potwalloper' was used to distinguish such voters from the much less numerous but socially superior burgesses. Belfast was a particularly 'rotten' borough: with a population of 15,000, it was the largest town in Ulster, but only thirteen people had the right to vote, several of whom normally did not live in the town.

As for the Irish House of Commons, the closer one examined it the more doubtful seemed its claim to protect the civil and religious liberties of the glorious constitution of 1689. On every count it did not speak for the majority, or even a sizeable minority, of the common people. All its members were Protestants;

the choice of parliamentary candidates was limited to a tiny number of wealthy families and was in that sense almost hereditary; the 117 boroughs were in the hands of patrons; and placemen, or those who held paid offices at the discretion of the Government, formed a considerable bloc of MPs. Henry Grattan, the leader of the Patriot Party, who saw all this corruption at close hand for more than three decades, came to the conclusion that out of three hundred MPs who sat in College Green fewer than one hundred could be described as in any way independent. The remainder were servants of the administration, or of rich and powerful, and usually aristocratic, families.

The Irish House of Lords was an even more blatant example of the way in which a tiny oligarchy ruled the country. In 1786 there were 2 royal princes, 1 duke, the lord chancellor, 4 archbishops, 65 earls, 49 viscounts, 51 barons and 18 bishops entitled to sit in the upper chamber of parliament.[8] Without exception, all were members of the Church of Ireland. The numerous Dissenters of the north were totally unrepresented, and the four existing Catholic peers were debarred because they were unwilling to take the supremacy oath requiring them to recognise the king as head of their Church. To emphasise how these lords were manipulated by the Westminster government for political purposes, W.E.H. Lecky points out that no fewer than seventy-three – almost two out of every five – of these titles had been created during the previous twenty years – all of them for services to the Government and Crown.[9] A generation before Castlereagh raised political bribery to a high art, there were plenty of Ascendancy MPs or peers willing to sell their favours for handsome rewards. Many of the temporal and spiritual lords were also borough patrons, which meant that they could directly influence the House of Commons. Lecky reckoned that 124 (out of 300) MPs were controlled by 53 peers in this way. In Ulster almost every town had its aristocratic patron nominating the MP of his choice.

A peculiar feature of the administration, which only served to illustrate how profoundly undemocratic it was, was the existence of a group (usually less than a few dozen) of legislators known as undertakers, because they undertook to see that the wishes of the Government in London were translated into laws in Dublin. These powerful men controlled not only parliamentary business but also 'pensions, peerages and promotions'.

The colonial subserviency of Ireland, and the lack of the most elementary forms of democracy, were further emphasised by the fact that all major political, financial and military decisions were made in London, and not in Dublin.[10] The Irish parliament before 1782, when some concessions were made to it, and during the next eighteen years of its existence, was drastically curtailed in its powers; and the squires, lawyers and placemen who largely comprised its membership could exchange views and argue about Irish affairs, but achieve little else. The real executive power lay in the hands of the viceroy and his chief secretary, who were appointed by, and responsible to, the government at Westminster.[11] Dublin Castle and the viceregal lodge in Phoenix Park were the real centres of power in Ireland, and not the talking shop in College Green. There was widespread resentment, especially among the expanding business classes, at the way in which taxation and the Navigation Acts were manipulated in favour of British manufacturers and merchants.

The controversy about the legacy that had been handed down from the Glorious Revolution of 1689 involved Britain as well as Ireland, and led to a famous debate about the rights of man between the conservative Edmund Burke and the radical Thomas Paine.[12] Burke argued in his influential *Reflections on the Revolution in France*, published in 1790, that the British constitution was the most perfect in the world because of the balance it achieved between kings, lords and commons, and the way in which it protected property rights, and provided for an Established Church. The rule of an educated and leisured class, with the provision that a few landed gentlemen should be allowed to vote or enter parliament, was the best method of ensuring social stability while at the same time permitting gradual legal change. In contrast, Paine, in *Rights of Man*, published immediately after Burke's book, denied that there was any such thing as a British constitution, and stated the revolution of 1689 was

30

not so much glorious as a sham and a fraud. In his view the so-called bill of rights was a bill of 'wrongs and insults', and the dominance of a hereditary monarch and aristocracy, one of the worst forms of government. Men were born with equal rights and should be able to vote or enter parliament regardless of their wealth, social origins or religious background. The king of England was descended from a long line of tyrants, and the Established Church a mockery of Christ's teachings.[13]

It was surprising that neither of these widely read books, which reflected deep ideological divisions within British society, said anything about Ireland. Paine, however, was in close touch with the United Irishmen, both in London and Paris. Burke, on a later occasion, admitted that his enthusiasm for the way in which Britain was governed did not apply to his native Ireland:

> The [Glorious] Revolution operated differently in England and Ireland. The whole spirit of the system was changed, not to say reversed. In England it was the great body of the people for the establishment of their liberties against the efforts of a very small faction which would have oppressed them. In Ireland it was the establishment of the power of the smaller number at the expense of the civil liberties and properties of the far greater part; and at the expense of the political liberties of the whole. It was, to say the truth, not a revolution, but a conquest.[14]

It was the accumulation of political and economic grievances much more than the alleged danger of a French or American invasion that led to the rise of the Volunteers and the election of Grattan's 'Patriot Parliament' in 1782. Indeed, many Irish people regarded the American colonists more as an inspiration than a threat.

The search of the Irish middle classes (mostly Protestant, but by this time including some Catholics) for some degree of national autonomy or control over their own destiny took different forms in the south and north of Ireland.

In Dublin, partly because the House of Commons was situated there, and partly because there were fewer Dissenters in the population, the struggle was mainly a parliamentary one. It was

31

in College Green in June 1778 that the first Relief Act was passed, enabling Catholics to buy land on long leases and to inherit in the same way as Protestants, and it was there eighteen months later that the legal restrictions on the export of Irish woollens was lifted. In April 1780 Grattan made his historic speech proclaiming that only the 'king, lords and commons of Ireland' were competent to enact laws binding Ireland. It was in the Dublin parliament that the most famous debates, and the highest flights of oratory, occurred. This stress on constitutional agitation, kept well within the framework of the law, suited legislators such as Grattan, Henry Flood and the other Whigs who wanted some mild reforms but feared the emergence of what they called the 'mob'. The southern Volunteers were ambivalent in their attitude towards democracy, some, such as 'the tribune of the plebs', Napper Tandy, favouring full emancipation for Catholics, but others, such as Flood, strongly opposing it.

In the north the Volunteers, though led by the typical Whig grandee Lord Charlemont, had a more popular or democratic flavour, mainly because they included large numbers of rank-and-file Presbyterians. The movement involved many 'citizen-soldiers', as well as constitutional reformers. Strengthening the parliamentary agitation, there was always in the background an implied threat of military action. Speeches, debates and pamphlets were in plenty, but there were also many conventions, marches and demonstrations. There was a wide geographical spread in those counties where Dissenters predominated – Antrim, Down and Derry. Indeed, every town of any size in the province was said to have had its Volunteer company. By the end of 1782 there were reputed to be 34,000 Volunteers enrolled in Ulster, which was a much higher figure than in any of the other three provinces.[15]

The northern movement, too, had a sharper ideological edge to it than the somewhat windy (and often woolly) rhetoric practised in the south. The threat of physical force, with all the dangers this implied for British power in Ireland, was always more evident there; and sympathy with the Catholic cause was stronger among Presbyterians than it was among members of the Church of Ireland. It was among the Dissenters, moreover, that the most important long-term political development of all began to take place, namely the growth, vague and confused at first, but gradually gaining sharply in definition, of a distinctive sense of national identity. This was the real beginning of that modern Irish nationalism which took fresh shape during the 1798 rising.

The high point of this anti-colonial and pro-ecumenical fervour was reached in Ulster on 15 February 1782 when a large gathering of Volunteers met in Dungannon, a small market town in Tyrone chosen because it was the geographical centre of the province. Unfortunately no full report of the speeches or a complete list of delegates is extant, but enough information, especially the full text of the resolutions passed, has come down to us to indicate the historic significance of this convention. A modern commentator writes: 'Far more truly than the parliament in College Green [the delegates at Dungannon] represented the spirit of the Protestant nation.' Several hundred representatives from all the northern counties were present, and many of them marched through the town in their full regimentals with banners flying and bands playing. Symbolically the meeting was held in the local Presbyterian church. The chairman, William Irvine, was an episcopalian.

Although only a provincial gathering, the motions passed presented a serious challenge to the parliaments at Dublin and Westminster. The three key resolutions, which were drawn up by Francis Dobbs of Belfast and Joseph Pollock of Newry (with the advice, it is said, of Grattan and Flood), challenged the Government at its most vulnerable points in relation to trade, the country's independence, and Catholic emancipation. The delegates declared that the Irish ports should be open to all countries not at war with Britain. They then went on to state that the claim of any body of men other than the king, lords and commons of Ireland to make laws to bind the kingdom was unconstitutional, illegal and a grievance. Finally, in language that foreshadowed the words written by the United Irishmen ten years later, they resolved in the Dungannon declaration that we hold the right of private judgement on matters of Religion to be equally sacred in others as in ourselves . . . as men and Irishmen, as Christians and as Protestants, we rejoice in the relaxation of the Penal Laws against our Roman Catholic fellow subjects, and that we conceive the measure to be fraught with the happiest consequences to the union and prosperity of the inhabitants of Ireland.

It was these ringing words, perhaps more than any other rhetoric of the period, that encouraged Grattan to claim a few months later that the Irish had become 'a free people', and that Ireland itself was 'now a nation'. In May 1782 the act known as the Sixth of George the First was repealed at Westminster, and formal recognition granted by the Whig government to the principle that the Irish Commons and Lords should become more independent.[16]

The resolutions on religious liberty were soon afterwards supported in June 1782 by the influential Ulster Presbyterian synod, and by important individual ministers such as the Reverends William Steel Dickson (Portaferry, County Down), Sinclair Kelburne (Belfast), John Rogers (County Cavan), and Samuel Barber (Rathfriland, County Down). Some of these clergymen were later to become prominent members of the United Irishmen. Even such conservatives as the Reverend William Bruce (Belfast), and the Reverend Robert Black (Dromore, County Down) joined in the general Volunteer enthusiasm, the latter being reported as an officer in the Lisburn True Blues, wearing a short blue coat with white facing, brass buttons and white breeches. One minister was recorded as arriving to preach at his church with a musket in one hand and a Bible in the other. Another clergyman held his religious service over a drum.

A second wave of democratic enthusiasm occurred in the spring of 1784 when Belfast was the centre for almost continuous Volunteer demonstrations. The *Belfast News-Letter*, which was later to become a platform for extreme conservatism, took the opportunity to rally to the liberal cause. The most dramatic evidence of this growing Protestant tolerance towards the formerly despised 'Papists' came in May of that year when the two Belfast Volunteer corps marched through the streets of the town (in which Catholics were outnumbered ten to one) to welcome the opening of St Mary's, the first Catholic chapel to be built there since the Reformation. Volunteers also subscribed funds to chapels in Dromore, Saintfield, Ballynahinch and Portaferry. On 12 July 1784 – a date normally associated with the most violent diatribes against Catholics – 2,500 Volunteers met in Belfast, and forwarded an address to their commander-in-chief, Lord Charlemont, which expressed satisfaction

> at the decay of those prejudices which have for so long involved us in feud and disunion, a disunion, which by limiting the right of suffrage, and circumscribing the number of Irish citizens, has in a high degree, tended to foster that aristocratic tyranny, which is the fountain of Irish grievances.[17]

Lord Charlemont, who never favoured the granting of full emancipation to Catholics, rejected this address in courteous but none the less firm tones.

With the exception of Lord Charlemont, all the Volunteer leaders in the north realised early during their campaign that the Dissenters on their own were not strong enough to win any important reforms, and that both social justice and political necessity required an alliance between the anti-establishment forces.

Frederick Augustus Hervey, Earl of Bristol and bishop of Derry, was the most prominent, if not the most constructive, of these advanced liberals. Fabulously rich – he owned no fewer than 70,000 acres – he is chiefly remembered for his personal extravagances, his easy-going moral views, and his grand tours of Europe in which he collected both mistresses and works of art. He was more than a pleasure-loving playboy, however, and his political opinions seem to have been firmly rooted, even if eccentrically expressed. Throughout his long and often sensational career he never faltered in his opposition to all forms of bigotry and intolerance. On several occasions he contested with his rival Charlemont for the popular leadership of the

35

Volunteers, and during the mid-1780s when the movement was threatened with decline he tried to rally its failing forces. For a brief period he was the most fêted Volunteer leader in both Dublin and Belfast. He never thought much of Catholicism, which he once described as a 'silly and harmless religion', but he was strongly against the penal laws, and always supported emancipation. Catholics, he said, were people 'deserving of every privilege in common with the rest of their fellow-subjects'.

William Todd Jones was another prominent liberal who believed passionately that reform and emancipation were indissolubly linked together. His constantly expressed view was that any Protestant who advocated an extension of the franchise without at the same time including Catholics was inconsistent and hypocritical. It was a contradiction, he said, for Protestants to be seen 'with one hand grasping at liberty for [themselves], and riveting with the other the shackles of [their] countrymen'.[18]

Todd Jones, a prosperous County Down landlord, was, like the bishop of Derry, an unexpected recruit to the radical cause. A senior officer in the Volunteers, and working closely with Napper Tandy and Hamilton Rowan, he moved freely between Ulster and the south of Ireland, and for several years was one of the movement's most active speakers and organisers. Dr William Drennan described him as 'the oldest and best friend of the Catholics'. He was elected MP for Lisburn in 1783, and helped make that town temporarily a centre of liberal opinion. His *Letters to the Electors of Lisburn*, published in February 1784, were widely read. In November 1791 he joined the newly formed Belfast branch of the United Irishmen, but he was not in sympathy with the republican sentiments of such men as Samuel Neilson and Henry Joy McCracken, and dropped out of their ranks soon afterwards.

Todd Jones's letter to his colleagues, composed at about the same time as Tone's famous *Narrative*, and signed 'native of Ulster and an Irishman', is a valuable historical document because it contains all the doubts and hesitations of a sincere but moderate reformer who feared going too far and too fast along the road of rebellion. On the one hand, he condemned the penal laws as brutal and ferocious, and was highly critical of the British government, which he described as a storehouse for 'dividing, barbarising and debilitating this island'.[19] On the other hand, he believed that many Protestants were humbugs when they disguised their political views under the pretence of defending their religion. He preferred a monarchy to a republic, and urged that Ireland and Britain should not imitate the French example. The poor of Ireland he dismissed as a 'rabble'. His most revealing comment came in a long section of his letter devoted to the tricky question of how far landlords could justifiably hold on to property which had originally been taken by force from its previous owners. There was even among the most well-intentioned and liberally inclined reformers, he warned, 'a terror of forfeiture'.

The career of William Drennan was rather like that of Todd Jones – he made an early reputation as a Volunteer, joined the United Irishmen in a flush of enthusiasm, was imprisoned for a short period, and then alarmed by the increasing dangers associated with republicanism, turned to a moderate form of nationalism in his middle age. Drennan was deeply rooted in the dissenting tradition, his father being a well-known Presbyterian minister in Belfast. Educated in Glasgow and Edinburgh, he qualified as a physician and practised for some years in Newry. His chief interests, however, were in politics and literature (he was an accomplished poet), and he devoted as much time to them as to medicine. His letters, signed 'Orellana or an Irish Helot', were published in 1785 during a critical period in the fortunes of the Volunteers. His brother-in-law was Samuel McTier, the Belfast businessman who became a founder member of the United Irishmen and a sponsor of the organisation's newspaper, the *Northern Star*. Drennan's voluminous correspondence with his sister and other northern personalities provides a useful insight into liberal opinion during that period.[20] He is the author of the celebrated test, or oath, taken by United Irishmen, and in June 1794 he was put on trial for publishing a 'wicked and seditious libel' addressed to the Volunteers. He was acquitted, but the trial turned him away from extreme politics.

Drennan was master of the vivid phrase, and wrote in Swiftian language about the Ascendancy, which he described as a 'rooted moral and national evil . . . the peculiar curse of this country'.[21] The land system was 'at best a mitigated feudality, and, at worst, the connexion of planter and slave'.[22] Every rotten borough in the kingdom was 'nothing more or less than a feudal castle'.[23] Sectarianism was 'tearing to pieces the seamless robe of our Saviour',[24] and the alliance between church and state 'preserved and fructified the abuses of both'.[25] Grattan's Patriot Parliament was the 'transference of arbitrary power from despotism abroad to aristocracy at home'.[26] The constitution was no more than a 'fig leaf . . . to hide away the indolence, timidity and corruption of the country's rulers'.[27]

Two other Volunteers, who were later to become leading United Irishmen, were the Reverend William Steel Dickson and Hamilton Rowan.

Steel Dickson, who was born in Carnmoney in the heart of dissenting Antrim, was educated locally and at Glasgow University where one of his tutors was the economist Adam Smith. He was licensed to preach as a Presbyterian minister in 1767. At an early stage during his long service at Portaferry on the Ards peninsula he made plain, in spite of those congregation members who called him a traitor and a Papist, that he supported the American colonists in their struggle against British rule. Later he courted further unpopularity by proclaiming his sympathy for Catholics suffering under the penal laws. During the 1780s he became one of the most famous preachers in the province, and was much admired for his advanced views among fashionable Belfast intellectuals. For a period he was a close friend and neighbour of the grandfather of Robert Stewart (later Lord Castlereagh), and he actually campaigned for the young Stewart in the 1790 by-election in County Down. The paths of these two men, so opposite in character and outlook, were to cross frequently in later years.[28]

The flamboyant Rowan was very different in temperament and life style to the sober-minded Dickson. Though born in London and living for long periods in England, Holland, France,

Germany and the United States of America, Rowan's heart was always in Ireland, and it was to that country that he devoted most of his considerable energies. Related to the noted Dufferin family of Clandeboye, his mother is said to have been descended from an officer who fought with William of Orange at the Boyne. He changed his surname from Hamilton to Rowan at the request of his grandfather who left him estates at Killyleagh, County Down.

Rowan was educated in the typical landed gentry way, attending Westminster School and Cambridge University. A keen traveller, he visited the American colony of Virginia as a young man, where he met Thomas Jefferson, Andrew Jackson and the Polish patriot, Tadeusz Kosciuszko, and then settled in France for eleven years between 1773 and 1784. Not much is known about these years in France except that he met some descendants of the Wild Geese, the exiled soldiers who had emigrated from Ireland after the Treaty of Limerick in 1691, and he was apparently influenced by Jean Jacques Rousseau and the French *philosophes*. He was admired by Marie Antoinette, who saw him rowing on the Seine, and was so taken with his appearance that she sent him a ring.

In 1784 at the height of the Volunteer agitation he returned to his estate at Rathcoffey, County Kildare, where his neighbours included the radical Lord Edward FitzGerald and the liberal Duke of Leinster.

Rowan first became publicly celebrated as a champion of the underdog when he took up the case of a poor Dublin girl, Mary Neal, who allegedly was abducted and put in a brothel where one of her customers was the prominent Ascendancy figure, Lord Carhampton. This became a *cause célèbre*, and made Rowan famous overnight.[29]

In 1790 he began his more serious intervention into public affairs when he joined the Whig Club in Belfast. This was a short-lived organisation, recruiting members, as its name suggests, from the more Whiggish elements in Ulster society. Robert Stewart was briefly a member, and so were the Duke of Leinster, Lord Charlemont, Lord Moira and William Drennan. It was probably Drennan who persuaded Rowan to join the United Irishmen.

Rowan was a man of great physical vitality, over six feet tall and built proportionately, who summed up his whole life by admitting that it was 'a strange medley of contrarieties'. A rich landowner, he was much loved by the Dublin poor who were always quick to greet him as he moved through the streets accompanied by his huge dog. A staunch follower of the New Light wing of Presbyterianism, he made his reputation as a defender of Catholic emancipation. At one stage, when in revolutionary France, he was imprisoned under suspicion of being a spy and nearly died among galley slaves and prostitutes.

The personalities he met were as diverse as the life style he followed. He was the intimate of Wolfe Tone and Napper Tandy, and was acquainted with the Duke of Wellington and Lord Castlereagh. While exiled in France in 1794 he became a close friend of the feminist Mary Wollstonecraft, and Robespierre, shortly before he was guillotined, gave him an interview.

Rowan was an extraordinarily energetic and restless man who, as he himself admitted, was 'perpetually under weigh when he should have been at anchor'. This was very true. Until he was middle-aged he never settled long in one place (admittedly this was not always his own fault because he was often a fugitive). Quixotic, brave and impulsive, he was not always wise politically. He is remembered, however, as one of the most romantic United Irishmen.[30]

Despite the enthusiasm and support of its members, the Volunteer movement declined in the late 1780s. Their enemies among the Ascendancy at home and the imperialists in Britain had remained immensely strong, still controlling the land, administration, armed forces and part of the mercantile economy. So long as conservatism in London backed up conservatism in Dublin the reformers could make only partial progress. This Anglo-Irish establishment, powerful as it was, might have been overcome if the reformers had developed genuinely democratic policies, and built up a campaign that would have included the broad mass of Catholic farmers, their priests, the independent-minded professions, the emerging manufacturing and merchant class, both Catholic and Protestant, and the Dissenters of the north. Together these groups would have made themselves a formidable combination.

But such a united campaign, with bold national aims, was not what Grattan, Flood, Charlemont and other moderates wanted. Their objective was partial, not full, freedom for the Irish people. Coming from the ranks of the squirearchy, legal profession and richer traders, they sought a greater say in how 'their country' (and increasingly that was how they referred to Ireland) should be run, but at the same time they feared the spread of real democracy. As Whigs influenced by such men as Edmund Burke, they wished to introduce reforms very slowly and gradually, to lead from the top, and above all, to avoid revolution.

In particular, they were afraid that once reforms got under way the mass of the oppressed tenantry and urban poor – the 'mob' or 'rabble', as they were frequently described – would get out of hand. Among property owners there was an abiding fear, often stated publicly, that the legality of the plantation settlements might be queried, and a new court of claims revived. 'Forfeiture' was one of the most frightening words to the rich and powerful. Whiteboys, Oakboys, Steelboys and Defenders were a constant reminder that 'Rory was still upon the hill', waiting to come into his own again. Grattan, an honest Whig, expressed this ancient fear when he warned of the 'armed property' (of which he approved) of the Volunteers being replaced by the 'armed beggary'.

It was this fear of social revolution that made certain leaders of the reform movement, such as Flood in Dublin, and Charlemont and Henry Joy in Belfast, repeatedly draw back when the idea of full Catholic emancipation was raised. They disapproved of the penal laws, and were unwilling to be considered bigots, but at the same time they were reluctant to abandon the privileges the Protestant constitution gave to their class and religion.

Upper-class Catholics, too, though few in number and not so

influential, were horrified at the thought of egalitarian principles spreading to Ireland. Conservative in their social attitudes as much as in their theology, they feared democracy in the same way as their successors feared socialism and communism. Though of the same religion as the Whiteboys and Defenders, they had always denounced secret agrarian organisations as being contrary to the laws of God. The Catholic Committee, which had been set up in the 1750s to try to redress some of their worst grievances, was notorious for its timidity and caution. Whenever a crisis arose and the Government put pressure on it, the committee replied, not with defiance, but with the most servile expressions of loyalty to the Crown. In 1789 the French Revolution was greeted not with acclaim as it was by so many Presbyterians and poorer Catholics but with horror and revulsion. Landlords like Lords Kenmare and Gormanstown, and bishops like Troy of Dublin and Moylan of Cork, were as hostile to the principles of liberty, equality and fraternity as any Tory aristocrat or Church of Ireland prelate. It is likely that about this time the phrase 'Castle Catholic' was coined, meaning a Catholic who was subservient to the administration in Dublin Castle.

With the advantages of hindsight, it is now possible to see that the crucial error made by Grattan, Flood and the other Patriot Party leaders arose from their confusion and uncertainty about the nation to which they belonged. Wanting to be both Irish and British,[31] they gave simultaneous allegiance to the country in which they lived (and no doubt dearly loved) and to the country that oppressed them. In this dual loyalty and double allegiance they became hopelessly muddled, often indulging in the most bombastic rhetoric, which, when analysed, meant very little. How should nationality be defined? What nation, in fact, did the Protestants claim to belong to – were they English or Scottish, as many considered themselves to be, or were they Irish, as a growing number, especially among the Dissenters, were beginning to believe?

The Irish parliament was undoubtedly more truly patriotic than its predecessors, but in spite of certain reforms, it continued to be dominated by a small group of landlords, aristocrats and government nominees who, almost without exception, gave their first fealty to the social class from which they came and to the Government at Westminster, which was the ultimate guarantee of their privileges. Grattan had boasted, in a phrase that became widely quoted, of addressing 'a free people', but he, too, got tied up in verbal confusion. By definition the 'free people' to which he referred so proudly excluded three-quarters of the population. This confusion over semantics became worse when the question of the colony was introduced.[32] In what respect could the minority colonists reasonably argue that they were a nation but deny this attribute to the majority of colonised natives? Incidentally, this anomaly was likewise unresolved by the American colonists of 1776 with respect to native Americans and Black slaves.

A further tactical error by the 'patriots' was to think that any significant social progress could be made or any major political reforms achieved without engaging in the most resolute struggle against British rule in Ireland. So long as Irish liberals and moderate nationalists convinced themselves they had something to gain from taking a few crumbs from the imperial table, or that it would be too hazardous to challenge the basic principles of Crown and constitution, they were crippled from the start. By refusing to acknowledge that in the final resort it was British power that sustained the Ascendancy, and that they must fight against both the Government in London and its supporters in Ireland, they effectively emasculated themselves. Why should the ruling élite give up one jot of their power if they could always rely upon an external force to sustain them in any crisis?

Grattan and other moderate reformers hoped that they could make Ireland more independent, peaceful and prosperous within the framework of the British Empire. The tragic events of the next two centuries proved how wrong they were.

2

'THE SPIRIT OF THE NORTH'

The spirit of the North has much influence upon the spirit of the nation.

William Drennan[1]

In the 1790s the United Irishmen replaced the Volunteers as the chief expression of democratic and nationalistic sentiment. Though the movement suffered from organisational defects, particularly in its vulnerability to spies and *agents provocateurs*, its social basis was much broader, including members of the Catholic middle classes of the south, and more particularly, the Presbyterian merchants, manufacturers, artisans and professional people of the north. Some progressive Protestant landlords, even a few aristocrats, were drawn in. In the background were thousands of poor tenant farmers, mostly Catholic, but including many Dissenters who had previously joined Whiteboy or Steelboy organisations, and were now absorbing the levelling principles of the French Revolution. Gradually the Defenders of the north, who had once been limited to terrorist activities, became more politically mature. Some Catholic priests and Presbyterian ministers preached, for the first time, the same social doctrine of hostility towards landlords and tithe proctors. Geographically, a remarkable link was beginning to be established between north and south, with the more radical leaders moving frequently between Belfast and Dublin. Indeed it was the northern capital that was foremost during this period in the struggle for social and political freedom.

The new leaders who took over the campaign for democracy and national independence – and increasingly these two causes were linked together – were much bolder and more resolute in

their views than their Volunteer predecessors. In contrast to the
confusion and vacillations which characterised the patriots of
the previous decade, the United Irishmen mostly knew where
they wanted to go politically. The majority were young men of
high moral principles. Indeed their only weakness, and it proved
to be a serious one, was that some of them were too idealistic
about human nature to make successful practical politicians. The
four leaders who played the most important role in this awak-
ening of Irish nationalism were Theobald Wolfe Tone, Thomas
Russell, Samuel Neilson and John Keogh.

Tone, who was destined to play such an important part in the
history of Irish nationalism was, until the end of the 1780s, a
relatively obscure figure. Born in 1763 in County Kildare of
lower-middle-class Church of Ireland parents, he had been a
student in Trinity College Dublin, where he was auditor of the
college historical society, and then he went to London as a trainee
barrister. It was while attending a House of Commons debate
in that city that he first met the man who became his dearest
friend and most intimate political confidante, and whose short
life ran so closely parallel to his. This was Thomas Russell – 'a
man I love as a brother', he wrote.

Tone's gifts of intellect and character made him the man most
suited to meet the challenge of the times. While still in his
twenties he had come to the conclusion that liberal-minded
Protestants must throw all their weight behind the campaign
for Catholic emancipation. Within a year or so of helping to
found the United Irishmen he had come to the historic conclusion that there could be no democracy or prosperity in Ireland
so long as British power was exercised there.

Russell, born in 1767 in Cork and son of an army officer, was
also a member of the Church of Ireland, but in contrast to the
sceptic Tone, he was for all his life a zealous Christian. Tone's
portrait of him in his diary as a jovial drinking companion
nicknamed 'P.P. – clerk of this parish' gives only one side of his
character. His other side was devoutly religious, judging political
issues on the highest moral principles. He believed that one of
the reasons for the decline of French revolutionary aims was

the slide into irreligion by the Jacobins. The historian R.R. Madden reported that if Russell heard any of his friends speak against religion he would walk out of the room. He learned Hebrew so that he could read the Bible in its original language. 'The dominant idea that had taken hold of his mind,' wrote Madden, 'was that the laws of God were outraged in Ireland, above all other countries he had seen, in the mal-treatment of the people, the rapacity of their landlords, the tyranny of their local rulers and the wickedness of the government, which not only tolerated the oppression, but ruled on the principle that disunion was essential to power.'[2]

Joining the British Army as a cadet, Russell served for some years in India, and then returned to Ireland in 1788. For a short time he thought of becoming a clergyman, but was eventually posted as an ensign to Belfast, but soon gave up his commission and left the army. For a brief period he was a magistrate in County Tyrone, but resigned that post because of the corruption he saw on the local bench. He then became secretary of the Linen Hall Library in Belfast, which was founded in May 1788 as a reading society to serve the growing public enlightenment in Ulster. Its professed aims were to 'improve the mind and excite a spirit of general enquiry'. Though not ostensibly a political institution, the society passed a resolution in 1792 in favour of Catholic emancipation.

Samuel Neilson was ideally situated, both geographically and socially, to perform the task of rallying the Dissenters. In contrast to Tone and Russell, who were southerners and episcopalians, he was a true-bred Ulsterman of Scottish descent, born in 1761 into a County Down Presbyterian manse. As a successful entrepreneur with a thriving textile business, he had accumulated £8,000 capital, a fortune in those days, which gave him the necessary independence to practise the journalism he loved. His experience of trade made him sensitive to the resentments of the local manufacturers to English-imposed taxation and Navigation Acts. In politics he was a thorough-going radical, stirred by the events in France. Under the influence of Russell, he rapidly advanced towards a full separatist position. Tone, no mean judge of the qualities required to make a rebel, called him 'an honest, a brave and a worthy fellow . . . a good Irishman, a good republican'.[3]

In certain respects John Keogh had the same aims as the other United Irishmen leaders but differed from them sharply about tactics. Less ardently revolutionary, he was none the less committed absolutely to the cause of emancipation and democracy. As a prominent member of the Dublin middle class, he knew what merchants, shopkeepers and manufacturers most wanted. As a Catholic, he had excellent credentials to speak for the majority of Irish people, but at the same time he was never afraid to challenge the bishops on matters of social policy. At heart a constitutionalist, he found it possible to work constructively both with republicans, such as Tone and Neilson, and reformers like Grattan. His greatest political contribution during those critical years was to recognise that Catholics on their own were not strong enough to win the needed reforms; they must also win the support of progressive Protestants. To achieve this religious unity he made friends with many Dissenters, paid frequent visits to the north, and most important of all, made Tone secretary of the Catholic Committee.

Keogh fell away from the republican cause after he was arrested in 1795, and the country moved towards insurrection, but he had already done enough to be remembered as one of the most far-sighted and courageous Catholic leaders.

Radicals from the older generation, like Hamilton Rowan, William Drennan and Steel Dickson, joined forces with these new bloods and provided wider provincial backing to a movement that was largely centred on Belfast. With their long experience of the Volunteers, they, too, were alert to the ever present danger that religious bigotry could be used to split the various denominations politically.

Ideologically the new movement was much more democratic in its aspirations than either the Volunteers or the Patriot Parliament. Broadly based socially, with resolute leaders, its policies could be more confidently radical. Though it was not yet committed to a republican or separatist position, it was determined

47

upon a thorough-going reform of parliament, which would end the old privileges and abuses. In particular, and in striking contrast to its predecessors which had always put Protestant interests first, it now put the Catholic case in front. This new policy to promote full Catholic emancipation was introduced partly on the grounds of justice, and partly on the grounds of expediency. Catholics should have the right to vote, it was urged, because they were entitled to be regarded as free citizens, but also because they formed a majority of the population and could therefore exert the strongest mass pressure on the Government. Though not much of a practical politician, Drennan was shrewd in his analysis of the balance of forces in the country, and well aware of how ineffectual the liberal Protestants were without the aid of the Catholic majority:

> The Protestants of Ireland resolved; they convened; they met with arms; they met without them; they petitioned; but all in vain, for they were but a portion of the people. They then looked about them and beheld their Catholic countrymen.[4]

A major step forward in this policy of trying to form an alliance between reformers and rebels came in August 1791 when Tone published *An Argument on Behalf of the Catholics of Ireland*.[5] This short pamphlet was a turning point in the history of the struggle of the Irish people for independence and democracy. A unionist historian, Frank McDermot, said it is 'as fine a piece of political propaganda as exists in the English language'[6] because it cut through so much of the prevailing rhetoric to the fundamental issues about British rule in Ireland, and how this affected the relations between different groups in the country. In spite of Tone's youth – he was then only twenty-eight – and his relative obscurity, the pamphlet had a strong impact, especially on northern Dissenters, because it set out so precisely the logical development of their own thoughts.

Tone began by pointing out that Ireland had all the necessary natural resources to make it prosperous and peaceful. Why then, he asked, was it so poor, backward and oppressed? The country's failure to progress, he suggested, was due largely to 'intestine divisions', or the divide-and-rule policy that had been deliberately encouraged for so long. The Volunteers, said Tone, had made a profound error in arguing that liberal Protestants on their own could reform parliament. 'No reform is practicable that does not include Catholics', he wrote. If the enormous power of the Government were to be redressed, then the poorest and most oppressed three-quarters of the population must be drawn in. To give Catholics the vote was both morally just and politically expedient.

Protestants must shake off their old fears and prejudices. The view, which was widely held even by those calling themselves progressive, that Catholics were poor, ignorant and superstitious did not take into account the fact that they had lived in subjection – 'absolute slavery' was the phrase he used – for more than a hundred years. As for the claim that Catholics were dominated by their clergy, the bond between people and priests was 'drawn tight by oppression; relaxation would undo it'. In a long paragraph, in which he paraphrased Shylock's speech about the persecution of the Jews, he argued that given the right political circumstances, Catholics could be as free and independent-minded as any other people.

Tone concluded his pamphlet by rejecting the old argument that Ireland was too small and backward to have its own government. The Irish people, in his view, were as justified as anyone else in having 'their own independent existence'. He called for the abolition of 'the odious distinction of Protestant and Presbyterian and Catholic', and for the binding together of the three great sects 'under the common title of Irishmen'.

Tone's pamphlet was specifically about the problems of Ireland and Irish Catholics. Thomas Paine's *Rights of Man*,[7] published at the same time but more universal in its appeal, also had great influence on the northern Presbyterians. So great was its popularity in Ulster that Tone described it as 'the Koran of Blefescu'.[8] Paine's *The Age of Reason*, published in 1794, was not so well received in Ireland because of its ridicule of the Bible and its attacks on all forms of revealed religion. The author was more a deist than an atheist; he wrote, 'I believe in one God and no more; and I hope for happiness beyond this life', but his criticism of organised religion was hardly likely to be popular among Catholics or Presbyterians, let alone members of the Church of Ireland. The *Northern Star* reviewed the book at some length, but in a cautious and explanatory rather than an approving way.[9]

Paine was not the only radical Englishman in close affinity with the United Irishmen. Dr Richard Price,[10] a Unitarian minister from London, and Dr Joseph Priestley from Birmingham, the noted libertarian and chemist, were democrats whose reputation was known throughout Europe. Mary Wollstonecraft preached feminism both in England and in Ireland, where for a short period she was a governess to a rich landlord's family in County Cork. And the London Corresponding Society,[11] the Constitutional Society of Manchester, and the Friends of the People in Scotland were promoting Jacobin ideas in Britain. In spite of their innocuous titles, these societies propagated the most advanced republican and egalitarian opinions, and were in constant communication with the French revolutionaries. Like the United Irishmen, their members were frequently prosecuted for alleged sedition, their papers suppressed, and their printers fined or imprisoned. Paine himself was charged with crimes of subversion very similar to those charges brought against William Drennan and Hamilton Rowan. When Thomas Muir, a leading Scottish republican, was put on trial in Edinburgh in the summer of 1793 (that is, during the wave of reaction that followed the execution of Louis XVI), he was visited by Rowan and Simon Butler, brother of Lord Mountgarret.

In October 1791, while interest in his pamphlet was at its height, Tone set out for Belfast with Russell, taking with him a drafted manifesto.[12] Belfast was then a thriving town of some 20,000 people of whom about one in ten were Catholics. The majority of Protestant inhabitants were engaged in manufacturing and trade, with a minority of teachers, doctors, clergymen, lawyers and other professional people. Linen spinning and weaving were already important in the nearby towns of the Lagan valley. The town was proud of its reputation for enterprise and intellectual controversy, and though its claim to be 'the Athens of the north' was exaggerated, it could justifiably argue that it had become during the previous decade one of the strongest centres of liberal opinion in the British Isles. In particular, among the Presbyterians there ran a strong current of anti-aristocratic and anti-establishment sentiment, which had been inspired by the American War of Independence, and then more recently by the French Revolution. Phrases about the rights of man, the common people, reform of parliament, freedom and democracy were on many lips.

At their first meeting with the northerners Tone's manifesto was amended in a more radical direction. Tone did not object to these proposals; he welcomed the signs that 'the thermometer of Blefescu has risen, as to politics' and was glad that 'passages in the first copy, which were three months ago esteemed too hazardous to propose, are now found too tame'. On 14 October the two young men met for dinner with Neilson and ten other sympathisers: Henry Haslett, draper; William Sinclair, linen manufacturer; William McCleery, tanner; William Tennent, merchant; Samuel McTier, clerk; John Campbell, apothecary; Thomas McCabe, watchmaker; Gilbert McIlven, linen draper; Robert Simms and his brother, William, both merchants. Most were young, all were Presbyterians, and all were members of the Belfast middle class.

Within a few months they were joined by Steel Dickson and Henry Joy McCracken,[13] a calico printer. McCracken's family, whose roots were deep in Protestant Ulster, had come from Scotland after the persecution of the Convenanters in the mid-seventeenth century, and had always been noted as fervent Presbyterians. His mother was of Huguenot descent and was related to Henry Joy, author of *Belfast Politics*, and Francis Joy, founder of the *Belfast News-Letter*. The young McCracken worshipped at the church of the progressive Reverend Sinclair Kelburne.

It was Tone who gave this new organisation the name of the Society of United Irishmen. The manifesto it produced is one of the most important documents ever recorded in the history of

Irish nationalism, calling as it did for a 'cordial union among all the people of Ireland', 'the radical reform of parliament', 'the abolition of bigotry in religion and politics', and 'the equal distribution of the rights of man through all sects and denominations of Irishmen'. Surprisingly it said nothing about land reform. On the surface its demands were moderate enough. What made it different from other anti-Ascendancy proclamations was the determination of men like Tone, Russell, McCracken, Dickson and Neilson to fight the Government to the end, and eventually to call for a complete break with British rule in Ireland. Words were to be supported with actions. The long-term significance was that for the first time an important group of Protestants began to think of themselves as belonging to the Irish nation. As historian Rosamond Jacob has said: 'It marks the day when descendants of British planters in Ireland first became Irishmen.'[14]

At the end of October, having spent what he later described as the pleasantest three weeks in his life, Tone returned to Dublin where he and Russell immediately got in touch with leaders of popular opinion, such as Napper Tandy. The Dublin Society of the United Irishmen was founded on 9 November, with Simon Butler as chairman. Two of its most prominent members were Rowan and Drennan who happened to be living at that time in the south. It was Drennan who drafted a test, or membership oath, for the society, a proposal that was unavailingly resisted by Tone, who feared, rightly as it turned out, that this would encourage the Government to suppress them, and would not necessarily prevent, as it was meant to, the leaking of secrets to the authorities.

A few weeks later, under pressure from the Government, and no doubt disturbed by the prospects of a new Catholic–Dissenter axis, Lord Kenmare and sixty-eight liberal gentry withdrew from the Catholic Committee. The result of this action was the opposite of what the conservatives had hoped; Keogh and his fellow democrats on the committee became stronger and moved closer to the United Irishmen.

The year 1792 opened auspiciously for the United Irishmen

with the publication in January of the *Northern Star*, which, as the platform for this powerful political movement, inspired so many democrats and nationalists. Though its editor and owners were continually harried by the Government, its circulation rose to over four thousand, a large figure for those days. It was said to be read in nearly one hundred towns in Ireland, as well as in Liverpool, Edinburgh and London. Founded by a group of twelve Belfast manufacturers and merchants, all of them Presbyterians, it was essentially the voice of urban, middle-class radicalism in Ulster.[15] Its editor and chief shareholder was Samuel Neilson, who put his private fortune to this cause.

The *Northern Star* began by supporting moderate demands, such as parliamentary reform and Catholic emancipation, but pressure of events, such as the war with France, the suspension of habeas corpus, and the arrest of United Irish leaders, pushed it more and more towards the direction of open rebellion.

As a fervent internationalist and admirer of the French Revolution, Neilson filled the paper with accounts of events in France and America. Speeches by members of the French National Convention were reported at great length, as were those of George Washington and Thomas Jefferson. Articles attacking Negro slavery, which was then becoming a matter of public debate, were published. There were also reports of the trials of oppressed democrats in Britain, like those of Thomas Muir in Scotland, and Joseph Priestley in Birmingham and Horne Tooke in London. The pioneer feminist tract *A Vindication of the Rights of Woman* by Mary Wollstonecraft was advertised in October 1792, and Thomas Paine's works were reviewed.

Welcome though this cosmopolitan note might have been in the context of Ireland's isolation from the rest of the world, criticism has justifiably been made that the journal paid insufficient attention to domestic Irish affairs, especially the plight of hundreds of thousands of impoverished tenant farmers whose problems required a more careful examination than did the views of Robespierre or Kosciuszko.[16] The fact that a large proportion of the population of Ulster, as well as of the other three provinces, knew no English did not seem to concern the editor.

A few exceptions to this bias towards the interest of English-speaking urban Protestants were the reports of the harpers' festival of 1792, the writings of Charlotte Brooke, an early translator from the Irish, and most popular of all, the 'Billy Bluff' letters, which were a satire on aristocracy and landlordism.

On 14 July 1792, six months after the launch of the *Northern Star*, there took place in Belfast another event to shake the establishment's confidence. A celebration was held not, as tradition demanded, to commemorate King William's victory at the Boyne, but the storming of the Bastille in Paris. So strong was democratic sentiment in the town at that time that the majority of its citizens, Dissenters and Catholics combined, seemed to be unreservedly on the side of liberty, equality and fraternity. For a brief period Belfast was the most revolutionary town in the British Isles.

During the morning three battalions of Volunteers, 790 men and officers and led by the Light Dragoons, marched through the town centre, flags flying. Thousands of United Irish sympathisers assembled, many wearing green ribbons. Samuel Neilson and William Drennan led the Dissenters, and Wolfe Tone, who had been made an honorary member of the local Volunteers, turned out in his uniform. Catholic leaders were represented by John Keogh and Richard McCormick, who had been specially invited from Dublin.

In the afternoon delegates got down to serious political business in the Linen Hall where Drennan moved a resolution greeting the people of France. William Sinclair then moved that the right to vote was a right that should be extended to all the people of Ireland, Protestants and Catholics alike. Some of the more cautious Presbyterians, such as Henry Joy, now editor of the *Belfast News-Letter*, and Waddell Cunningham, a prominent Volunteer officer, were reluctant to go so far in this direction, claiming that most Protestants would not agree to Catholic emancipation, and that the majority of Catholics was not yet ready for it. However, Sinclair, urged on by Tone and with the influential support of three Presbyterian ministers, the Reverend Steel Dickson, the Reverend Sinclair Kelburne, and the Reverend Thomas Birch of Saintfield, County Down, carried the day by an overwhelming majority.

Neilson raised the debate to a high level by pleading that delegates should get away from sectarian issues, and concern themselves with the basic rights of man. The right to vote, he said, was 'no more a Roman Catholic question than a Church question, a Presbyterian, a Quaker, an Anabaptist or a Mountain question; the true question, if any, was whether Irishmen should be free'. Tone spoke carefully and diplomatically – his aim was to prevent disruption of the new-found unity between groups who were prone to fly apart.

This historic debate marked a turning point for the progressive Dissenters in the town. Henceforth they were committed firmly and unambiguously to Catholic emancipation. At a celebratory banquet in the evening, attended by 104 guests, toasts were sung to various radical causes, including 'The 14th July, 1789', 'The French Army', 'The rights of man', 'Mr. Tom Paine', 'The Union of Irishmen', 'The society for the abolition of the slave trade', 'Mr. Grattan', 'The People of Poland', 'The freedom and prosperity of the United States' and 'The sovereignty of the people'.

While the Belfast radicals were celebrating the universal brotherhood of man, there was another event taking place in the town, which had much more specific implications for the culture of Gaelic Ireland. This was the harp festival organised by Edward Bunting, with support from Henry Joy and the antiquarian Dr James McDonnell, which was held on 11–14 July.

This historic assembly of musicians from all over Ireland was a remarkable achievement for the young Armagh-born Bunting, who, still only nineteen years old, had already won a reputation as an organist in the Belfast cathedral, and as a collector and composer. The festival brought together ten leading harpists from eight counties, five of them from Ulster – 'a race of men then nearly extinct, and now gone for ever', was a later comment. Six of these harpists were blind; one was a woman, Ann Fanning, and three were over seventy-five years of age. The most famous were Denis Hempson, a native of Derry, who was reputed to have been born in 1695 and to have once played in Scotland for Bonnie Prince Charlie, and Arthur O'Neill, who was recognised as the greatest harpist since Carolan. Bunting not only helped to raise the premiums from six to ten guineas, a large sum in those days, payable to each player, but also recorded the airs which were played. His little penny notebook is the oldest extant manuscript of Irish tunes. This collection and his later publications were of great importance for three reasons: they were virtually the only source of information about the manners and customs of the dying race of traditional Irish harpists, and they rescued many original airs and words which might have been lost for ever. Politically they were valuable because they introduced to a wider circle of liberal Protestants in the north, some of whose ancestors might once have welcomed such musicians into their homes, a deeper feeling for the old Irish culture. Wolfe Tone, for example, attended the harp festival, though he does not seem to have appreciated it. However, a deep sense of national consciousness was undoubtedly fostered there, especially in Ulster. It is significant that the United Irishmen took as their symbol a drawing of a harp with a Phrygian cap over it,[17] with the words 'It is new strung and shall be heard.'

Bunting was a dedicated musician, and certainly no active politician. He was, however, a close friend of many of the young republicans of the day, and like that other celebrant of 'the harp that once', Thomas Moore, he knew several of the leaders of the 1798 rising.

Charlotte Brooke was another Ulster Protestant who made a major contribution at that time to the scholarly study of ancient Irish civilisation. She was born in 1740, daughter of a Cavan landlord, and was related to the Brooke family of Fermanagh. Her father Henry was the son of a Church of Ireland rector and her mother was a Methodist. Henry Brooke was a minor poet and dramatist who spent much time in London as a friend of Samuel Johnson's and Oliver Goldsmith's. As a young girl living in the Irish countryside, Charlotte became interested in languages, but instead of studying the customary Latin and Greek, she turned to the Gaelic language spoken by the majority of people in west Ulster. She learned Irish from the farming people in her neighbourhood, and then began to translate from old manuscript sources.

In 1789 she published her *Reliques of Irish Poetry*, the first anthology of Irish verse ever issued.[18] 'The British muse is not yet informed that she has an elder sister in this isle', she wrote defiantly to those numerous critics who claimed that there was not much worth studying in the native literature. Like Bunting, she was not a politician but she had no doubt about the cultural importance of saving a language which was then so despised by educated Protestants.[19]

The climax of the year 1792, in which modern Irish democracy may be said to have been born, came in December when a big convention of Irish Catholics was held in Tailor's Hall, Back Lane, Dublin. The Tories sneeringly referred to this historic gathering as the 'Back Lane Parliament'. The convention was of great political importance because it was the first representative gathering of Catholics in Ireland since James II's Irish parliament of 1689. Two hundred and forty-four delegates representing all thirty-two counties and no fewer than forty towns were there, and these could justifiably claim to speak for the three million Catholics in the country. 'The delegate from Antrim sat down beside the delegate from Kerry', wrote Tone.[20] Luke Teeling, in Tone's opinion a 'spirited and intelligent' representative whose two sons took part in the 1798 rising, was the chief delegate from Ulster. Keogh was the prominent Dublin delegate. Tone, as secretary of the Catholic Committee, was one of the very few Protestants present. To illustrate the non-sectarian nature of their sympathies, the delegates decided to vote their thanks to the citizens of Belfast – 'to whom we owe that we meet here in safety'. This referred to the fact that the convention was guarded by Volunteers from Belfast.

In keeping with the spirit of the times, the mood of the conference was militant, and when some moderate spokesmen urged caution or advocated merely some minor relaxation of the penal laws, they were overruled. The majority, urged on enthusiastically by Teeling, wanted nothing less than full emancipation, including the right of Catholics to sit in parliament. Tone was so moved by this mood that he described it as 'a sublime spectacle'. 'The spirit of liberty ran like an electric fire through every link in their chains', he wrote.[21] To show how strong their feelings were, after a long debate the delegates decided to submit the petition they had drawn up, not to the viceroy, as would have been expected, but directly to London. As was intended, this move was seen as a deliberate snub to the administration in Dublin. The five representatives chosen to deliver the petition were John Keogh, and Edward Byrne of Dublin, James Devereux of Wexford, and Sir Thomas French and Christopher Bellew from Galway. Tone was invited to accompany them in view of his recognised skills as a negotiator.

The journey to London produced further evidence of the sympathy of the Presbyterians of Belfast towards Catholic claims. Owing to unfavourable weather, the delegation decided to take the short sea route from Larne to Scotland, which involved going through Belfast. The Catholic spokesmen were given a most enthusiastic welcome – and the citizens of the town, virtually all Dissenters, took the horses from their shafts and pulled the carriage with their own hands through the streets, amidst clapping and cheering.

In January 1793, while the Catholic delegation was negotiating in London, further consternation was caused in Ascendancy circles by the sensational intervention of Lord Edward Fitz-Gerald during a debate in the Irish House of Lords. A strong democrat and ardent republican, the young Protestant nobleman, from one of the richest and most famous families in Ireland, enraged his fellow peers by stating that the viceroy and members of the Irish parliament were the king's worst subjects.

Further evidence of Protestant disillusionment with traditional Ascendancy views had come in November 1792, when the Dublin Volunteers, who had previously been accustomed to celebrate the birthday of William III, refused to parade around the monarch's statue in College Green. Some of the Volunteers added insult to injury by wearing green instead of orange cockades. This anti-government demonstration caused a sensation in the city.

All these events had the desired effect. Alarmed that the Catholics were becoming better organised and more militant, and that they were moving steadily towards an alliance with the Dissenters – an alliance which, if fully cemented, could have led to an end of imperial rule in Ireland – the prime minister, William Pitt, decided on a change of policy. Though a loyal member of the Anglican Church, and disliking all aspects of Catholicism, he came to the conclusion (temporarily at least) that his best tactic was to woo the conservative Catholics in the same way as he was to woo the conservative Presbyterians ten years later. He already envisaged a full union between Britain and Ireland in which Catholics would play a minor and containable part.

The advice he was getting from Edmund Burke, and his other subordinates, including the home secretary, Henry Dundas, reinforced this view. Burke had long believed that if concessions were made to upper- and middle-class Catholics, they would form a stabilising element in Irish society. In the early 1790s his chief fear was that poorer Catholics and what he called 'Protestant Jacobins' (that is, radical Presbyterians) would join forces against the Government. In a long letter dated January 1792 to his friend Sir Hercules Langrishe MP he weighed up mathematically the balance of these various groups:

> Suppose the people of Ireland are divided into three parts. Of these (I speak within compass) two are Catholic. Of the remaining third, one half is composed of dissenters. There is not a natural union between these descriptions. It may be produced. If the two parts Catholic be driven into a close confederacy with half the third part of Protestants, with a view to a change in the constitution in church or state, or both; and you rest the whole of their security on a handful of gentlemen, clergy and their dependants; compute the strength *you have in Ireland* to oppose the grounded discontent, the capricious innovation, the blind popular fury, and to ambitious, turbulent intrigue.[22]

The viceroy, Westmorland, put the matter succinctly: If Catholics could be, as he expressed it, attached to the constitution, 'they would not be levellers'. George Knox MP put forward much the same opinion in a debate in the Irish House of Commons in April 1793: 'Depend upon it, a Catholic peer and a Catholic commoner with an interest and influence in the senate will be no republican or leveller.'[23]

The Government, therefore, decided to offer a sop to Catholic public opinion, and in April 1793 introduced a Relief Bill which gave voting rights to about 30,000 Catholic forty-shilling freeholders. Catholics would also be allowed to bear arms, and be appointed to various minor- and middle-ranking posts in the administration. To reassure conservative Protestants, it was proposed that Catholics could not be appointed viceroy, lord chancellor or commander-in-chief. The ban on their election as MPs continued. Significantly, the electoral concession was only granted in rural constituencies, where landlord influence was so strong.

Not surprisingly, in view of the menace of a resurgent France, and the unwillingness of the Irish ruling class to accept any threat to their supremacy, Pitt's enthusiasm for democracy did not last long. Within a short time he reverted to his old system of checks and balances. The pendulum swung the other way. A minor effort towards conciliation was quickly followed by a major attempt at coercion.

3

'REFORM TO SEPARATION'

Emancipation is Separation, and Reform a Republic.

William Drennan[1]

The event that led to a major change in government policy towards Ireland, and which triggered off a wave of reaction in both Britain and Ireland, was the death of Louis XVI in January 1793. A month after the French king and queen were executed, England declared war on revolutionary France. Ireland was immediately affected by the new military situation. Just as during the late seventeenth and early eighteenth centuries the country had been caught up in the wars of the Reformation and Counter-Reformation, so in the 1790s this small island on the edge of Europe was drawn into the struggles between imperial Britain and her overseas enemies.

The anxieties of the administration in London were twofold: it feared that Jacobin sentiment would spread throughout the British Isles, particularly in Ireland where social conditions were potentially so receptive to democratic and egalitarian doctrines. It was also alarmed, as it had been in the days of the Volunteers, that Ireland might become a strategic base for the invasion of Britain. The 'back door' thesis was resurrected. William Pitt had been tinkering with the idea of making some minor concessions to the middle-class Catholics[2] so that they would no longer be swayed by dangerous French influences. Now he changed his mind and decided instead to try to crush rather than negotiate with opposition parties. The policy of concessions was dropped, and in its place he substituted a policy of repression. The hope that new alliances could be formed with middle-of-the-road parties in Ireland was abandoned, and bonds were re-established with those who had been temporarily cold-shouldered.

61

He quickly made his peace with the administration in Dublin and fell back – at least temporarily until the Act of Union was safely in place – on the traditional strategy of regarding virtually all Catholics, and increasingly many Dissenters, as potential traitors to the Crown. Better a small garrison that could be relied upon, than a larger and vacillating crowd that might be undependable. For the next few years the government policy at Westminster was to trust only those who promised to be completely loyal – the landlords, the ultra-Protestants, mainly belonging to the Church of Ireland, and all their dependants. The word 'loyalist' took on a specific meaning as a person who gave his or her ultimate allegiance, not as would have been more usual in a normal society, to the country in which he or she lived or was born, but to Britain, and who could be depended upon through thick and thin to support British rather than Irish interests.

The administration in Dublin, still dominated by such acknowledged pillars of the Ascendancy as Fitzgibbon and the Beresford family, sensed that their friends in London were once again looking favourably upon them. Seizing their opportunity, they began discussing with Pitt how they might best block any further concessions to liberals or Catholics. The old alliance between the Tories in Britain and the landlord Ascendancy in Ireland, which had been under temporary strain, was renewed as the crisis deepened. A campaign of reaction, the main aim of which was to repress the common people of both countries, was inaugurated. It lasted nearly thirty years.

In Ireland a vicious circle was initiated in which the Government attempted to repress any manifestation of popular opinion by either Catholics or Dissenters. As coercion followed conciliation, there was inevitably a hardening of resistance by the United Irishmen, who in most cases had begun as constitutional reformers, but were now driven by events to become underground physical-force revolutionaries. Vague aspirations towards some form of political autonomy became sworn commitments to establish an independent republic. Sympathy for the ideas of liberty, equality and fraternity turned into a conspiracy to seek

French military aid. A decade which had commenced with some hope of peaceful evolution changed step by step into a bloody cycle of violence and counterviolence.

The first evidence that the Government had reversed its previous policy of making minor liberal concessions came in February 1793 when an Arms Bill was introduced into parliament to prevent the import of arms, gunpowder or ammunition into the country, and to permit the holding of gunpowder only by licence. This measure was designed effectively to disarm the Volunteers, who were still strong, especially in Belfast and Dublin. Simultaneously a Militia Bill was introduced by a northern peer, Lord Hillsborough, which enabled the authorities to conscript five hundred men as officers from each county under the control of the local gentry (all Protestants). The conscripts were virtually all Catholics and the act when passed proved very unpopular. There were riots in many counties, including a serious affray in Enniskillen in which several people were killed.

The Government had been seriously alarmed at the holding of the Back Lane Parliament in December 1792, and was further dismayed when a group of Protestants representing all the Ulster counties met in Dungannon. This second convention, held exactly a year after the first, included among its delegates such notables as Lord Edward FitzGerald, Henry Joy and the Reverend Steel Dickson. The authorities therefore decided to prohibit all national or province-wide gatherings which might act as a focal point for anti-government opinion or challenge the powers of Dublin Castle. In July a Convention Act was passed which forbade the holding of any widely representative assembly apart from parliament. This act, which was not repealed until 1879, was planned with the deliberate purpose of preventing the opposition parties from organising themselves in an open and constitutional way. It was the negation of democracy, and could only serve to encourage underground conspiracies. Its aim, as Rosamond Jacob says, was 'the muzzling of all popular movements'.[3]

Belfast was then – as it was for most of the decade – the main centre of disaffection, and as might be expected, its democratically inclined citizens were particularly disliked by the aristocracy. Lord Downshire in a letter to Dublin Castle in September 1792 had described the town as that 'damned sink', and Lord Londonderry writing a few months later called it a 'cursed den of thieves'.[4] Soldiers stationed there were encouraged by their officers and magistrates to take the law into their own hands and attack anyone they suspected of democratic or republican sympathies. In March 1793 a mob of dragoons ran amuck in the town's streets, abusing citizens, breaking into houses of known United Irishmen, and pulling down inn signs that sported pictures of Benjamin Franklin or the French general, Charles Dumouriez. A month later a disorderly band of cavalry broke into the offices of the *Northern Star*, wrecking printing machinery and throwing documents into the street. Henry Joy McCracken, who happened to be in the neighbourhood and tried to intervene, was abused and then challenged to a duel by a young officer. During these spring months, when liberal Presbyterians were under threat in Belfast, the Government launched a big drive against the Defenders who were active in Louth, Meath, Cavan and Monaghan. The leaders of these underground tenant organisations, who were fighting high rents, tithe payments, and arbitrary evictions, were, as historian Robert Kee puts it, 'hanged in droves'.[5]

The following year this persecution of opposition groups intensified in a series of sensational trials. In January Hamilton Rowan was charged with distributing a manifesto addressed to the Volunteers which began with the allegedly seditious words 'Citizen Soldiers'. This proclamation, originally drafted by William Drennan, had been distributed during the time of the Back Lane Parliament in December 1792, but Rowan's trial had been postponed for tactical reasons. He was found guilty and sentenced to two years' imprisonment and a fine of £500. Lodged in Dublin's Newgate jail, he soon became involved in other more overtly treasonable activities. In April he was visited in prison by the Reverend Henry Jackson, an English clergyman of advanced radical views, who carried with him a message from France asking for details about the disposition of civilian and military forces in Ireland. Jackson, who in turn was imprisoned, had brought with him a friend, Cockayne, who was in fact a government spy. Rowan, Jackson, and Wolfe Tone (who had been allowed to visit them) drew up the required document, which eventually through Rowan's own carelessness reached the authorities. In danger of being charged with a capital offence, Rowan escaped from Newgate in dramatic circumstances, and after various adventures got away to France where he remained for some years before emigrating to Philadelphia. Jackson was charged with treason, and would have been hanged but for the fact that he committed suicide. Tone avoided prosecution on condition he went to America.

In May 1794 the editor and proprietors of the *Northern Star*, which by this time had a large circulation among the Presbyterians of Antrim and Down, were charged with publishing 'a false, wicked, malicious, scandalous and seditious libel' because they had printed an address by the 'Irish Jacobins' of Belfast. This, too, had been published in December 1792, but the trial, like that of Rowan, had been postponed until the Government could find the most politically propitious time. John Philpot Curran stood for the defence, and the trial, which was held in Dublin, aroused wide public interest. All the defendants, with the exception of the printer, John Rabb, were released amid popular rejoicing.[6]

A few weeks later Drennan was also brought to trial. He, too, was acquitted. Though freed, Drennan had his democratic ardour dampened by this experience and gradually fell away from the United Irish movement. He continued, however, to be a strong liberal, and was a vigorous critic of the Union. He never ceased to strive for parliamentary reform and Catholic emancipation.

In January 1795 another event occurred which further convinced the United Irishmen, and also many moderate reformers, that the Government had definitely changed course and was now determined on a policy of coercion rather than conciliation. Several months previously Pitt had broadened his government by bringing into his cabinet certain Whigs such as the Duke of

Portland. In January he sent his liberally inclined friend, Lord Fitzwilliam, to Dublin as viceroy. Fitzwilliam's aim was the policy which Burke and Pitt had adopted a few years before – he wanted to woo the more conservative Catholics and keep them from joining the ranks of the radicals by offering them hopes of further concessions. Hints of full emancipation were made. The right-wing Ascendancy faction led by Fitzgibbon immediately responded with threats, and after some energetic lobbying in London the bewildered viceroy was hastily withdrawn. He had served in Dublin for less than three months.

The recall of Fitzwilliam in March 1795 is generally accepted as a major turning point in the evolution of both British government and Irish nationalist policies. W.E.H. Lecky, for example, argues that it completed the disillusionment of most Catholics in Ireland, and turned many constitutional reformers of all denominations into full-blooded republicans. The *Northern Star*'s editorial commented that it meant the death of any peaceful hope for Irish independence, and was the 'most ominous and fatal day of the century'.[7] The citizens of Dublin expressed their views by putting on mourning and shutting their shops as the viceroy left.

In Britain the drive against all manifestations of Jacobinism were almost as severe as in Ireland. The Tory Pitt and his Whig supporters combined to rush through parliament a bill suspending habeas corpus. Thomas Paine's *Rights of Man* was banned and Paine himself had to flee to France. The right to hold public meetings was abolished. A mob encouraged by local magistrates attacked the home of Joseph Priestley in Birmingham, and the most radical organisation in the country, the London Corresponding Society, was declared illegal. Three of its leaders, Horne Tooke, Thomas Hardy and Thomas Holcroft, were put on trial in October 1794. Their friends Mary Wollstonecraft and William Godwin were assailed as seditious.

In Scotland the attack on progressive forces was even more violent when the Society of the Friends of the People – later they called themselves the United Scotsmen after the Irish model – assembled 160 delegates in Edinburgh. Thomas Muir was put on trial in Edinburgh in August 1793. He was sentenced to fourteen years' transportation to Botany Bay; he eventually escaped and returned to France.

In some respects the deliberate policy of repression achieved the opposite of what the Government intended. Instead of dividing Catholic from Dissenter, Dublin from Belfast, and the mass of poor tenant farmers from the middle classes, there was a growing unity of anti-establishment forces. Organisationally and ideologically there was a strengthening of the most advanced democratic and separatist elements. The opposition did not moderate its views but became more militant. The United Irishmen ceased to think in terms of constitutional reform, and went underground. What had begun as an open political party was compelled by circumstances to turn into a secret army. Even the Catholic Committee led by Keogh adopted a more defiant stance. A few of the more cautious spokesmen became discouraged, and some of the less discreet, such as Napper Tandy and Hamilton Rowan, had to flee abroad, but the bulk of the rebels stood firm, with such leaders as Tone, Russell, McCracken, the Emmet and Sheares brothers, and Steel Dickson becoming more determined than ever. Russell took on responsibility for recruiting younger members, especially among the rural Defenders and the artisans of Belfast. As a result, the United Irishmen were transformed from an urban intellectual élite into a powerful mass movement, led, as Arthur Wolfe, the attorney-general, put it, by 'furious democrats'.[8] The tendency now was to look to France, not, as previously, for political ideas, but as the opportunities for legal agitation became fewer, for direct military help. Three years of conspiracy began.

Simultaneously, while ideas about the most advanced forms of democracy were steadily progressing, the principle of republicanism or complete national independence was gaining ground. Tone had used the word 'separation' as early as 1791 in a letter to Russell which was intercepted by government agents and quoted against him, but he later questioned the authorities' interpretation of the phrase, indicating that it was not until three or four years later (probably after the Coercion

Acts and prosecutions of 1793–4) that he had come to a final decision on the matter. Later, in exile in France he wrote clearly and unambiguously, in language which was to become part of the nationalist folklore, of his aim 'to break the connexion with England, the never-failing source of all our political ills'.

Certainly all the evidence suggests that by mid- or late 1795 – that is, after the Fitzwilliam débâcle – the majority of the United Irish leaders had come to the conclusion that any halfway reform, such as home rule or a dual monarchy,[9] was unacceptable, and that full legislative independence must be achieved if Ireland were ever to solve its many political and social problems. The most significant development at this time was that Dissenters from the north and Catholics from the south were beginning to think, even though at first somewhat hesitantly and tentatively, in terms of a complete break with Britain and the setting up of a republic. They had moved within a few years, as R.R. Madden states, from the idea of 'reform to separation'.

The first signs of this growing radicalisation became evident during the winter of 1793–4 when the Dublin branch of the United Irishmen put forward proposals for parliamentary reform which were revolutionary for the times, and in some cases were not adopted for over a century. In a manifesto, which preceded by a generation a similar declaration by the Chartists in England, they advocated such far-reaching changes as the granting of voting rights to all adult males,[10] annual parliaments, payment for MPs, and no property qualification for parliamentary candidates. William Drennan, who opposed what he called this 'immediate and perfect equality', reported that this declaration of political aims was printed on cheap handbills on one side of the paper only so that it could be pinned up in the poorest homes.

Irish Whigs in general were horrified at what they regarded as a dangerous tilt towards Jacobinism. Edmund Burke, for example, believed that any shift towards egalitarianism would lead to anarchy. Even Grattan attacked what he called 'the blasted Jacobins', and warned against giving the vote to 'almsmen and paupers . . . the beggar on the bridge and the scavenger in the kennel'.[11]

It is difficult to know exactly when the decision was taken to turn a legal federation of political clubs into a secret and oath-bound army, but the turning point probably came in May 1795 when delegates from seventy-two branches met in Belfast and approved a new constitution for the United Irishmen. Military decisions were almost certainly also taken at this conference, but it is not known what they were. It is possible that it was at this meeting that for the first time serious consideration was given to the need for direct military help from revolutionary France. One of the United Irish leaders, William J. Macneven, hints that it was then they realised their days of peaceful campaigning were over, and that they must fight harder, physically if necessary, for the principles they believed in.[12] By the end of the year a military organisation was probably in existence, with officers appointed in Belfast and Dublin. Lisburn, County Antrim, is said to have been the first town in which a branch of the United Irishmen sought arms. Couriers moved regularly between Ireland and France. As government spies were everywhere, and penalties for illegal activity became more severe, so they strove – not always successfully – to burrow underground. In a phrase used by Drennan, 'all became mole work'.

In their drift towards armed rebellion it was inevitable that the United Irishmen would be forced to re-examine their attitude towards the Defenders, who were recruiting among weavers and town artisans as well as poor tenant farmers.[13] Tone, Neilson and Keogh had begun to make contact with them as early as 1792, but some reformers were reluctant to become involved with those regarded by respectable people as no better than bandits and outlaws. Drennan and other members of the Belfast middle class, Protestant and English-speaking as they were, found it difficult to relate to people who were mostly illiterate, spoke Irish, and when not practising their 'Papist' superstitions were engaged in attacking landlords and maiming cattle.

But new circumstances required new tactics. The more the United Irish were driven underground the more they turned to those who were already underground. The Defenders, whatever their faults, had a bigger revolutionary potential than the bourgeois merchants and comfortable professional people of Belfast and Dublin. Their followers numbered scores of thousands of the poorest tenants, weavers and rural labourers. Their activists were hostile to tithe-paying, generally against the Government and formed a ready-made army prepared to take on local landowners. Contact with their leaders had established the fact that their narrow economic aims (such as lower rents) had begun to broaden out into wider concepts of republicanism and national freedom. Their crude leaflets and reports coming in from court trials showed that phrases such as 'all men are born equal' and 'the rights of man' were being widely used. Obviously the ideas of the French Revolution and Thomas Paine had penetrated the consciousness of many of the most downtrodden sections of society.

In their efforts to widen the anti-government alliance, one of the main tasks was to reduce the traditional hostility that had existed for many years between the Catholic Defenders and the Protestant Peep O'Day boys. James Hope, who was one of the most active United Irishmen in this work, has left a vivid picture of how he went about the country trying to reconcile the warring factions:

> The influence of the union soon began to be felt at all public places, fairs, markets and social gatherings, extending to all the counties of Ulster . . . Strife and quarrelling ceased in all public places, and even intoxication.
>
> The 'Break-of-day boys' and 'Defenders', lamented their past indiscretions on both sides, and tracing them to their legitimate source, resolved to avoid the causes which led to them. In short, for a little time, Ulster seemed one united family, the members of which lived together in harmony and peace. A secret delegation to Dublin was resolved on, and I was one of the two persons, who were appointed to proceed there, to disseminate our views among the working classes. We succeeded with our wishes, and likewise formed connections with Meath and Kildare, which soon extended to the other counties.[14]

William Macneven made the same point:

> The advantage of reconciling these two misguided parties
> [Defenders and Peep O'Day Boys], of joining them in the same
> union, and so turning them away from any ideas they might have
> exclusively religious, and of restraining them from employing a
> mutually destructive exertion of force, most powerfully struck
> the minds of several United Irishmen. For that purpose, many of
> them in the northern counties went among both, but particularly
> the Defenders, joined with them, and shewed them the superi-
> ority of the union system, and gradually while government was
> endeavouring to quell them by force melted them down into the
> United Irishmen.[15]

In Ulster this shift towards more radical policies was led by
Tone, McCracken, Neilson, Russell, and certain Presbyterian
ministers. All of them were by this time convinced separatists,
prepared to work with the Defenders, and eager to secure French
help. Tone moved regularly between Belfast and Dublin, having
by then come round to the view that the mass of small farmers,
poor and illiterate though they might be, were the best potential
allies of the liberal middle classes. Later, while in exile in Paris
he summed up his egalitarian principles in the famous phrase
about having to rely increasingly 'upon that numerous and respectable class of the community, the men of no property'.[16]
McCracken used his travels as a textile merchant as a cover
to move freely all over the north and midlands, building the
underground organisation wherever the opportunity arose.
Neilson as editor of the *Northern Star* took an ever stronger line
against the Government. The Reverend Steel Dickson was
spokesman for the most rebellious dissenting clergy.

Among the newcomers to the United Irishmen in the north
were several other young men who were to prove just as ardent
as their senior, and better known, leaders. Catholic members
included the brothers Charles and Bartholomew Teeling, whose
father had been the chief Ulster delegate at the Back Lane Parliament, and Father James Coigley, 'the priest Quigley' as he
was often named in numerous intelligence reports from Dublin

Castle. Coigley was born in Armagh, and educated in the Irish College in Paris, where as a young student he quickly showed his rebel tendencies. A close comrade-in-arms of the Presbyterian minister the Reverend Arthur MacMahon, he became one of the United Irishmen's most trusted couriers. From the Protestant section of the community came William Henry Hamilton, a law student from Enniskillen, John Tennent, son of William, the United Irishman, Joseph Orr from Derry, Samuel Turner from Newry (later to turn informer), Alexander Lowry from Down, and William Putnam McCabe, son of the United Irishman, Thomas McCabe. All of these were active organisers willing to work secretly with the Defenders or with sympathisers in Britain or France, and as a result, frequently in imminent danger of arrest. At one time or another all of them had to flee the country.[17]

A new recruit in 1795 to the ranks of the United Irishmen who most clearly symbolised this drift towards egalitarianism was James Hope, the weaver of Templepatrick. Hope resembled the other prominent northern democrats in so far as he was of Scottish Covenanting origin. He differed from them, however, because he came from a working-class background and had little formal education. R.R. Madden describes him as a 'poor mechanic, self-taught and self-ennobled'.[18] Hope had a clear conviction that the upper, middle and working classes had different economic, and therefore different political, interests.[19] Castlereagh he saw as a spokesman for the landed aristocracy, and Grattan for the mercantile interests. He was suspicious of most property owners, fearing (rightly, as it turned out) that in a crisis they could not be depended upon to stick to the cause to which they had pledged allegiance.[20] An ardent Presbyterian all his life, he never wavered in those Christian beliefs which he was convinced gave moral support to his political views. Experience had taught him, however, that many Protestants used anti-Catholicism as a means of maintaining their social privileges. As a youth in County Antrim he had heard of Peep O'Day Boys boasting that they had driven Catholic tenants from their farms, and that local magistrates had turned a blind eye to such persecution. Greed for property, he wrote, was 'the real source of persecution in the county Armagh, religious profession being only a pretext to banish a Roman Catholic from his snug little cottage or a spot of land, and get possessed of it'.[21]

Hope regarded this hypocrisy as despicable and something that must be vigorously fought, especially in Ulster where bigotry was so widespread. So when the newly formed Orangemen began to spread their doctrines in the north in 1795 he threw all his weight against them. He had no illusions about either the social composition or reactionary role of the sectarians. The Orange lodges were, in his view,

> A faction of intolerant, turbulent men . . . persecuting yeomen, renegade 'croppies', the hangers-on about landlords, and low-church clergymen with their spies and informers, all over the country . . . the bullies of certain houses in garrison towns, and those of fairs and markets in the rural districts. This association, under the nursing care of the magistrates, lent no visible protection for either life or property out of its own circle, and its members boasted that the government protected its institutions, and that a judge could not ride on circuit that was not a friend of Orangemen.[22]

The most striking evidence of how deeply engaged were many northern Dissenters in the democratic movement is indicated by the large number of Presbyterian ministers who were involved directly or indirectly in rebellion. It is not possible to prove that if a particular clergyman holds certain political opinions that his parishioners must necessarily agree with him, but taking into account the way in which the Presbyterian Church was organised, it seems likely that pastors and their congregations tended generally to think along the same lines. Otherwise, the minister would wish, or be asked, to resign. The records show that during 1797–8 between thirty and forty – or about one in six of all such ministers – were linked in one way or another with the United Irishmen. Some of the older ones were former Volunteers who progressed from being constitutional reformers to become advanced democrats or even republicans, regularly preaching rebel doctrines from their pulpits. A few actually took up arms and turned out during the 1798 rising. The authorities had no doubt about the subversive role played by many dissenting clergymen. 'The Presbyterian ministers are unquestionably the great encouragers and promoters of sedition. The *Regium Donum* [state grant to Presbyterian ministers] should be stopped', wrote Lord Downshire, one of the richest landlords in Ulster, in 1796. A list of the names and parishes of those ministers mentioned in official reports or suspected of subversive activity shows how geographically widespread was the extent of such democratic opinion among the manses of Ulster:[23]

Robert Acheson	acquitted
William Adair, Comber	emigrated
Thomas Alexander, Cairncastle	imprisoned
Samuel Barber, Rathfriland	imprisoned 1798–1800
Thomas Birch, Saintfield	emigrated
Richard Caldwell, Harmony Hill	–
Joseph Crow, Clones	–
William Steel Dickson, Portaferry	state prisoner in Fort George, Scotland, 1796–1802
John Glendy, Maghera	emigrated
Alex Gowdie, Bangor	hanged, July 1798
James Harper, Knockloughrim	emigrated
Adam Hill, Ballynure	–
Henry Henry, Connor	imprisoned
James Hull, Ballyvarnon	emigrated
Sinclair Kelburne, Belfast	imprisoned
Arthur MacMahon, Holywood	escaped to France
B. Mitchell, Maghera	imprisoned
– McMeehan, Newry	–
John McNeill, Clough	transported
James Porter, Greyabbey	hanged, July 1798
Reuben Rodgers, Derry	–
W. Sinclair, Newtownards	transported
R. Steele, the Route	emigrated
Robert Scott, Grange and Dunean	acquitted

James Simpson, Newtownards	transported
William Stevelly, Ballyconoghy	imprisoned
John Smith, Kilrea	imprisoned
Thomas Smith, Ahoghill	–
James Townsend, Greyabbey	emigrated
Bailie Warden, Killinchy	state prisoner in Fort George, Scotland
Archibald Warwick, Kircubbin	hanged, October 1798
James Worrell, Larne	imprisoned
– Worth, Larne	–

The most famous of these radical ministers were the Reverend Steel Dickson of Portaferry and the Reverend James Porter of Greyabbey, both parishes on the Ards peninsula. Dickson has already been mentioned as a prominent Volunteer and founder member of the United Irishmen in Belfast. A man of great moral courage, he never allowed any pressure from the Ascendancy to deter him from preaching what he believed to be the highest moral and philosophical truths. For him, as for so many other Presbyterian ministers before and since, religion and politics were closely related. Many of his sermons were never published, and historians must rely upon hearsay evidence as to their content, but we are fortunate in having the texts of three homilies published in 1793 under the appropriate title of *Three Sermons on the Subject of Scripture Politics*.[24] This short pamphlet contains the essence of Dickson's views, especially his conviction that a Christian clergyman must concern himself with earthly as well as heavenly matters, or as he put it, with 'the kingdom of the world and the kingdom of God'.

In a long analysis of how societies had developed in various countries over the centuries, Dickson argues that individual men and women were often prevented from living a good life because of widespread social abuses. Wealth had become accumulated in a few hands, and 'distinctions of rank' prevented the creation of a genuine democracy. Power was monopolised by depraved rulers who introduced laws to curb the people's freedom. 'All governments lead to despotism', he wrote. With the scandalous support of their own Churches, nations claiming to be Christian frequently attacked each other. The corruption of power by rich and privileged classes led to apathy and demoralisation among ordinary people. Ireland, in particular, was one of the worst governed countries in the world because of the way in which for so long the British government and its Ascendancy allies of 'placemen, pensioners and sycophants . . . gaping for spoil' had oppressed the Catholic majority of the population. 'The great body of the people, three-quarters of the country's inhabitants, had been reduced to abject and humilitating servitude', he wrote.

Enraged by the continuing open assertion of such democratic and anti-sectarian principles, the authorities determined to harass and, if possible, incriminate the defiant Dickson. Lord Londonderry described him as 'One of the most violent and seditious characters in the country'.[25] In October 1796, on the eve of the planned French invasion, several members of the Portaferry Presbyterian congregation were arrested and taken to Dublin in the hope that they would give information against their pastor. A local weaver named Carr was offered £1,000 (the equivalent of a lifetime's earnings for a man in his trade) if he would turn approver (informer), but he, like the others, refused to reveal any secrets they might have had. Ill health forced Dickson to lie low during 1797 when government agents were searching everywhere, but in 1798 he again became active at the highest levels of the United Irish movement. In the spring of that year he visited Scotland where he was suspected of being in touch with the United Scotsmen. When detained and searched he pleaded that he was visiting a sick relative. In May he was reported by the informers Maginn and Hughes as visiting Belfast frequently and touring various towns in north Down. On several occasions he was seen in the vicinity of Ballynahinch. His excuse on one such occasion was that he was buying a horse, and on another that he was taking the local medicinal waters to cure his sickness. On 5 June, the eve of the actual rising, he was arrested on a charge of planning rebellion.

The Reverend James Porter was born in 1753 in County Donegal, and educated at Glasgow University before becoming a minister at Greyabbey in 1787. As a young preacher he quickly became known for his liberal views and forthright attacks on landlordism, which he saw as a threat to both Catholics and Presbyterians. A neighbour and contemporary of Robert Stewart, he was personally well known to the Londonderry family. Later he acquired fame as a popular lecturer on science all over the province. Although an early sympathiser with the United Irishmen, he would not, according to R.R. Madden, take the society's oath, which he believed to be contrary to his religious beliefs.

His chief claim to fame came from his connection with the *Northern Star*, which he wrote for regularly until its suppression in 1797. In February 1794, under the pen name 'Sydney', he composed an open letter to the Marquess of Downshire in which he attacked what he described as 'the blood-thirsty, supercilious and unprincipled ascendancy'. Two years later he wrote a series of satirical pieces mocking three real and immediately recognisable characters: Lord Londonderry ('Lord Mountmumble'), the Reverend John Cleland ('Squire Firebrand'),[26] who was chaplain and land agent for the Londonderry family, and 'Billy Bluff', a noted spy and toady for the landlords.

These biting articles were widely popular among anti-government circles, and were reprinted several times long after their author was in his grave.[27] Here is an extract from one such letter which was published in the *Northern Star* on 21 May 1796; the text gives a good idea of lively style (and original punctuation) of Porter's:

By your leave, Mr. Editor – if you please, a corner in your paper, for this my letter, the first that I ever wrote for print, and probably will be the last. I am in danger of being hanged or put in jail, perhaps both. I want your advice like an honest man. God help us, what is the world coming to at last? I'll tell the whole affair, and the cause of it. Billy Bluff, my neighbour, was up yesterday at the 'Squire's, with his duty hens. 'Well, Billy, what news, says the 'Squire. Troth, sir, plenty of news, but none very good, says Billy. 'What's your neighbour R— (meaning me) about now? Why, please, your honour, he's at the old cut; railing against the war, against the tythes, and against game laws, and he's still reading at the newspapers. 'He is a villain, and must be laid fast; but what more do you know of him, Billy? Why, bad enough, an' please your honour. Him and the Popish priest drank together last market-day, till all was blue again with them; they shaked hands, so they did, drank toasts and sung songs. 'Pretty work! Did you overhear them?' Ah, that I did so, and listened like a pig. 'What were the toasts?' First, the Priest drank, *Prosperity to Old Ireland*, and . . . 'Stop, Billy, the toast is infamous; the word *Old* never was, and never ought to be applied to any country but England; and he who would apply it to Ireland is a rebel, and ought to be hanged'. He ought, an' please your honour, as round as a hoop. 'Well, what toast did the villain R— drink? He drank *Union and Peace to the People of Ireland*. 'Worse and worse, Billy, a d—deal worse; he who wishes union, wishes ruin to the country. Union forsooth, that is what never was, and what must never prevail in this country; and as to peace, 'tis flying in the face of government to speak of it; the devil send ruffians peace, till their betters choose to give it to them'. Then, Sir, the Priest drank, here's *Every man his own road to Heaven.* 'That, Billy, is a toast that no man would drink, but a Republican and a Sinner; for it supposes all men to be on an equality before God, and supposes that a man may go to Heaven, without being of the established church, which is impossible.' God bless your honour, I know that, and that is the reason I turned to church . . .'

By this time Porter had become a marked man and his fate was probably sealed by the sermon he preached in his own church on the day the Government had allocated for thanksgiving services in view of the fact that the French fleet had failed to land in Bantry Bay in December 1796. Entitled *Wind and Weather,*[28] the sermon ridiculed the authorities, and poked fun at those who claimed that 'a Protestant wind' had dispersed the enemy in the same way as the Spanish Armada had been blown away centuries before.

Less well known than either Dickson or Porter because his political activity was mostly underground was the Reverend Arthur MacMahon of Holywood, County Down. He formed an important link between the lay and clerical members of the United Irishmen, particularly with regard to making secret contacts with sympathisers in England and France. He worked closely with Father Coigley, trying to organise the United Englishmen in Liverpool, Manchester and London in 1797. This was a most dangerous mission and could have led, if they were caught, to trial and execution. MacMahon eventually escaped to France where, after further adventures, he joined Napoleon's army.

The other influential Presbyterian minister whose name occurs throughout the 1790s as a close friend of Neilson and McCracken was Sinclair Kelburne. Tone admired him greatly, and mentioned him several times in his diaries as a fervent democrat.

But the man who bound together these various social groups, linking Protestant with Catholic, middle with lower social classes, north with south, and who saw most clearly that democracy could not be achieved in Ireland without national independence, was Theobald Wolfe Tone.

In constant danger of arrest for his part in the Jackson–Rowan conspiracy, Tone had by this time made the momentous decision that the only way to redress the balance of power as between the republicans and the seemingly impregnable Ascendancy was to call in French help. He therefore decided to try to get to France via America. Knowing that the Ulster Dissenters were the key to revolutionary success, he decided to go by way of Belfast where he planned to hold vital discussions with his closest colleagues. In his journal he records the poignant leave-taking he had with Russell and his other northern comrades-in-arms. His account of the oath they took while walking in the hills above the town became part of the annals of Irish history:

> I remember, particularly, two days that we passed on the Cave hill. On the first, Russell, Neilson, Simms, M'Cracken and one or two more of us, on the summit of M'Art's fort, took a solemn obligation – which I think I may say I have on my part endeavoured to fulfil! – never to desist in our efforts until we had subverted the authority of England in our country, and asserted her independence. Another day we had the tent of the first regiment pitched in the Deer Park, and a company of thirty of us, including the family of the Simms's, Neilson's, M'Cracken's, and my

own, dined and spent the day together deliciously. But the most agreeable day we had passed during our stay, and one of the most agreeable of our lives, was the excursion we had made with the Simms's, Neilson and Russell, to Ram's Island, a beautiful and romantic spot in Loch Neagh. Nothing can be imagined more delightful, and we agreed, in whatever quarter we might find ourselves, respectively, to commemorate the anniversary of that day, the 11th June.[29]

It was in the summer of 1795 in Belfast that modern Irish republicanism might be said to have been born. It was conceived among Ulster Protestants.

4

'CROPPIES LIE DOWN'

I . . . will be doing everything I can to thin the country of these
rebellious scoundrels . . . Nothing but terror will keep them in
order.

General Gerard Lake[1]

The growing unity of Catholics and Dissenters, and the increasing identification of the latter with the land of their birth
were, of course, the last developments the British government
wanted, because the whole basis of its power lay in its ability to
keep the religious denominations at each other's throats. If ever
the poor and middling sections of society, regardless of their
Church affiliations, combined together, then the days of the
Ascendancy were numbered; when a substantial number of
Protestants became convinced that their best interests lay in
Ireland rather than with Britain, then the grip of the empire
would be inevitably loosened. Without a large element of bigotry, and the resultant splitting of the community into warring
sects, reaction could not rule.

The Tories, led by Pitt, and now with an ambitious Castlereagh
steadily gaining in influence, had therefore decided to return to
their old policies of divide and rule, reinforced by the most
stringent laws, and backed up when necessary by the full weight
of the armed forces. To prevent their opponents from organising
underground, and to discourage contacts with France, Pitt spent
ever larger amounts of money on his intelligence services, creating a network of spies throughout the British Isles, and even
on the Continent.

The opportunity to open up the old sectarian wounds occurred
in September 1795 when armed bands of Peep O'Day Boys and

81

Defenders clashed at the Diamond, County Armagh. Some dozens of people on both sides were killed, and local religious feelings immediately were inflamed. On the night of 21 September several Protestants, already known for their fervent Toryism and antipathy towards Catholics, formed an Orange Society at Loughgall, County Armagh.

From the beginning, the new society's policies were openly reactionary, resembling in their mixture of racism and religiosity the White Anglo-Saxon Protestant beliefs that spread in certain European countries and North America during the late nineteenth century. The Order was violently anti-Catholic, identifying the Pope as the anti-Christ who represented every kind of superstition and doctrinal error. It was strongly pro-British and pro-imperial, and its slogan was 'Protestantism and the Empire'. The native Irish were denigrated as an inferior, priest-ridden and backward people. The Orange leaders defended the wealthy establishment while at the same time trying to draw in the poor Protestants behind the ruling Ascendancy. In its early days the Order was based most strongly in the Church of Ireland, but it acquired some Presbyterian, Methodist and Baptist sympathisers. In particular, it supported the so-called constitution of 1689 as the best guarantee of Protestant privileges in Ireland. The Crown was cherished as the symbol of all these political and religious principles.

At first the authorities, particularly the grander Whigs in London and Ulster, were dubious about this plebeian organisation which threatened to disturb public order and provoke even more violent local riots. Its membership then comprised mainly innkeepers, weavers and small farmers who regarded themselves as menaced by their poor Catholic neighbours. 'The gentry stood aloof', as the Order's official historian, R.M. Sibbett, complained.[2] Respectable Presbyterians were unsympathetic, and the Quakers called the Orangemen 'wreckers'. Lord Gosford, a prominent landowner, magistrate and local grandee, was so disturbed by the turmoil in County Armagh that he called a special meeting of magistrates, describing the Orangemen as 'lawless banditti'. W.E.H. Lecky, who as a liberal unionist had little sympathy with Catholic nationalism, said that during its early phase the Orange Order was regarded as 'a form of outrage', a faction of 'tenants and labourers', comprising 'the lowest class of Protestants, essentially lawless'.[3]

Gradually during 1796 and 1797, as the United Irishmen became stronger the Orange Order was transformed from a small, scattered, and socially unacceptable fringe organisation, despised by the ruling class, into a powerful province-wide society, approved and actively sustained by some of the highest individuals in Britain and Ireland. At one stage the Duke of York, brother of George III, was a member, and peers, landlords, magistrates, parsons, army officers and MPs began to join in significant numbers. As Lecky wrote: 'Several considerable country gentlemen in Ulster changed their policy, placed themselves at the head of the Orange tenantry, and began to organise them into societies.' In Fermanagh the heads of the prominent Cole and Archdall (or Archdale) families were early members, and these were soon joined by Lord Farnham, Lord Blayney,[4] and Sir Richard Musgrave. This gentry-cum-officer class gave the Order much improved social and political prestige, with easy access to government ministers in London and officials in Dublin Castle. The lower ranks were encouraged to become more respectable, and to emphasise loyalty to the Crown and the virtues of temperance and Sabbatarianism.

The chief centres of Orange power were among the yeomanry, who recruited 30,000 men in the north, and the magistrates, who had a key role in suppression of rebels because of their legal position and the links they had with landlords and Church of Ireland clergy. Both groups benefited from the approval, at first secret, later more open, they got from senior army officers and administrators in Dublin Castle. This gave them a much-needed cloak of legality.

The yeomanry were part-time soldiers and cavalry who seldom, if ever, admitted Catholics to their ranks. The great majority were also members of the Orange Order, or to put it another way, the Orangemen were 'yeomen out of uniform'.[5] When the yeomen paraded it was customary for them to wear Orange emblems and to sing sectarian songs, such as 'The Protestant boys' or 'Croppies lie down'. Lodges were later set up in the army in both Ireland and Britain.

The magistracy all over Ireland, but especially in Ulster, was notoriously sectarian, as Catholics had long been debarred from the bench. Jurors also were recruited from the middle and upper classes, which were predominantly Protestant. Impartial justice was therefore something of a fiction, especially in political cases. Bigotry and religious bias were indeed so deeply entrenched that it was considered normal for the law, both in its drafting and imposition, to be administered in such a manner as to protect the Ascendancy.

Henry Grattan, always a stern critic of the Orange mentality, was in no doubt that the law operated unfairly in favour of one religious group. 'A Protestant mob very naturally conceives itself a part of the state,' he said.[6] Hereward Senior, a modern historian, writes: 'Orange control of local justice gave the Orangemen a sense of immunity from the law which produced much evil. Instances of Orangemen evading justice through their influence in law courts, and especially on juries, were all too numerous to recount.'[7]

The increasing willingness at highest government levels to play the sectarian card became more and more evident as the crisis deepened, especially in Ulster. Divide-and-rule tactics, which had been temporarily played down for fear of antagonising moderate Catholics, were once again boldly proclaimed. Brigadier-General C.E. Knox, a member of the prominent Dungannon family and a close friend of Thomas Verner's, Orange grand master of Tyrone, Derry and Fermanagh, was a key figure in developing this new policy. He is described by Lecky as 'a stern Cromwellian type'. Knox began by advising members of the yeomanry to join the Orange Order secretly. He then wrote two letters which made his views more explicit. In the first, dated March 1797 and addressed to General Gerard Lake, commander of the British Army in Ulster, he wrote: 'I hope to increase the animosity between Orangemen and United Irishmen. Upon that animosity depends the safety of the centre counties of the North.

Were the Orangemen disarmed or put down, were they coalesced with the other [United Irish] party, the whole of Ulster would be as bad as Antrim and Down.' In his second letter, addressed to the chief secretary, Thomas Pelham, he made the same point: 'If I am permitted, as I am inclined, to encourage the Orangemen, I think I shall be able to put down the United Irishmen in Armagh, Monaghan, Cavan and part of Tyrone.'[8] Pelham and his assistant Edward Cooke were in frequent communication with Knox all during 1797, advising him and Lake that they had almost a free hand to do as they wished to put down rebellion.[9] Pelham believed that the aim of suppressing the United Irishmen was so desirable 'that one can hardly object to any means of obtaining it'. Cooke wrote approvingly of the 'formidable' Orange yeomanry who maintained 'the quiet of the north'.

The clearest evidence that the army and the Orangemen had begun to co-operate closely together came in July 1797, when for the first time the latter felt strong enough to demonstrate locally on the streets of Ulster towns. On the anniversary of the Battle of the Boyne, Orangemen and yeomen marched together in Belfast and Lurgan, where they were addressed by Lake and Knox. This public appearance of high-ranking British officers on an Orange platform was of the utmost political significance because it showed how far the military representatives of the Government were prepared to go along the extremist path. In London even Pitt and senior politicians like Castlereagh were prepared to ignore any breaches of the law such activity involved.

The Government already had wide-ranging powers to put down sedition, but as the security situation deteriorated during 1796–7 they introduced even more draconian legislation to suppress the growing opposition to their rule. In February 1796, for example, an Insurrection Act, which Lecky describes as 'one of the most severe and comprehensive in Irish history', was rushed through the Irish parliament. The act made the administering of an illegal oath a capital offence, and the voluntary taking of such an oath could be punished by life transportation. The authorities could henceforth proclaim a particular district, impose a curfew, prohibit the holding of assemblies by day or night, and forbid the sale of seditious papers. Any individual designated 'disorderly' could be press-ganged into the navy without charge or trial. These forcible seizures of his majesty's rebellious subjects backfired on the authorities when sailors, many of them Irish, mutinied at Spithead and the Nore in 1797.

The act was used rigorously against both United Irishmen and Defenders, many of the latter being hanged for the administration of secret oaths. The plight of the Defenders during this period was worsened by the intervention of the Catholic archbishop of Dublin, Dr John Thomas Troy, who excommunicated them. In contrast, Henry Grattan, though no supporter of Whiteboyism, vigorously opposed the act as contradicting the tenets of natural justice.

Simultaneously a most extraordinary law, known as the Indemnity Act, was passed in parliament. This was a kind of all-embracing or omnibus measure providing that, in certain circumstances, any magistrate, MP, army officer, yeoman, regular soldier or government official who might in the course of imposing security have breached the law could be indemnified. In other words, it made illegality legal, and thus opened the way to even worse abuses of citizens' rights. In Britain there had been precedents for such legislation during the revolution of 1689, the Jacobite rising of 1745, and the Gordon riots of 1780. Now in Ireland, under the guise of putting down rebellion, every kind of brutality, official and unofficial, was encouraged, and a blind eye turned towards the most flagrant attacks on ordinary democratic procedures or even common humanity. Lord Carhampton, the commander-in-chief, and later General Lake were allowed to do as they wished, and the yeomen had a free hand to put down the 'Croppies' as they thought fit. Magistrates soon learned to bend the law to get convictions.

A further twist of the legal thumbscrew came in the autumn of that year when habeas corpus was suspended in Ireland. This suspension meant that suspected persons could be arrested and then held indefinitely in prison without any charge being brought against them. It was, in fact, an early form of internment without trial. Immediately the Government began to imprison not only Defenders possibly caught in some overt act of violence but also United Irish leaders believed to hold seditious views. Historian Marianne Elliott reckons that 103 such suspected rebels were apprehended in Ulster before June 1797.[10] Another historian, R.B. McDowell, while admitting that it is difficult to get precise statistics, puts the overall figure much higher, suggesting that between five hundred and six hundred persons with Ulster connections were arrested for political reasons between September 1796 and September 1797.[11] So many of these were taken south because of fears of sympathy demonstrations or attempts at release that Newgate prison in Dublin, where they were mostly lodged, became known as 'the Belfast hotel'. In the great majority of cases there was no firm evidence of illegal activities. Nevertheless, prisoners were kept in jail for months, and sometimes years, without being put on trial.

Among the most prominent of such internees were Thomas Russell and Samuel Neilson, who were arrested in September 1796 and hastily taken to Dublin under heavy guard.[12] The same month the young, and as yet unknown, William Orr was arrested. Unlike the others, he was kept in Ulster, and eventually put on trial in Carrickfergus. Three weeks later McCracken was captured and also taken to Dublin. In February 1797 Robert and William Simms, two of the founders of the *Northern Star* which was suppressed that year, were arrested in Belfast, and Arthur O'Connor was arrested in Dublin. The authorities sought without success to get evidence which would incriminate the Reverend Steel Dickson. Bartholomew Teeling, Tennent, MacMahon, Coigley, Lowry and Hamilton were among those who, to avoid arrest, had to escape hurriedly to France.

James Hope was the only northern republican leader of prominence who remained free during this period and was never at any stage, either before or after the 1798 rising, arrested.

Charles Teeling, then only a youth of eighteen, was among those kept in Dublin Castle. His memoirs published three decades later give a vivid picture of what life was like there and in Newgate and Kilmainham. McCracken's letters to his sister Mary are also lively and informative. The harshness of the regime was alleviated somewhat by the fact that the prisoners could have visitors and order their own food. Their worst experiences came when from their windows they saw preparations being made for the execution of fellow inmates, some of them known personally. There was also a constant nagging doubt about their own fate. Would they be put on trial and for how long would they be incarcerated? The most bizarre episodes occurred when these state prisoners were visited by such dignatories as Lord Carhampton, Lord O'Neill and even Lord Castlereagh. The clash of personalities and opinions which took place between the Croppy prisoners and their noble jailers in these gloomy prison cells is described in dramatic, and sometimes humorous, detail by Teeling.[13] The letters which Neilson wrote home from Fort George in Scotland between 1799 and 1802 are also remarkable examples of the prison literature of those times.[14]

The authorities, reckoning that they now had all the weapons they needed, legal and otherwise, to crush their opponents, began in 1797 systematically to sweep through or 'scour' any district they suspected of disaffection. The ostensible purpose of this scouring was to collect illegally held arms, but there can be little doubt that its main aim was to frighten into submission any potential rebels. It is also possible that certain military chiefs, knowing how close the people were to revolt and how dangerous the Government position could become if the French landed, decided to provoke a premature insurrection before foreign aid arrived.[15]

Certainly the policy adopted was one of deliberate brutality – a campaign of open and planned counter-revolutionary terror, with regular troops, militia and yeomanry all employed. There were frequent breakdowns of discipline, with marauders permitted, or even encouraged, to do as they wished. Neighbourhoods were searched for arms, people arrested, and houses set on fire. If suspects were caught in what were considered to be compromising circumstances, they were flogged or summarily hanged. It was common practice to beat people to make them inform on their friends. Hundreds of young men were forcibly seized to join the fleet, or transported overseas to Botany Bay. United Irish leaders were interned without trial. The wearing of green ribands by women was treated as an offence, and their owners assaulted or abused. In the south of Ireland a peculiarly refined form of torture was pitch-capping, in which molten tar and gunpowder were put on a man's head and then set on fire. Portable triangles on which men could be flogged were introduced. In the north another special device was picketing, in which a man was tied to the ground, face upwards, with his legs and arms pinioned to four stakes.

Ulster took the brunt of these outrages in 1797, as it was then the most rebellious province. The following year the policy of intimidation spread to such southern counties as Meath, Kildare, Wexford, Wicklow and Carlow. The determination to punish or humiliate any man or woman, Catholic or Dissenter, who dared challenge the divine right of the Ascendancy to rule perpetually is expressed in the Orange song 'Croppies lie down':

> Oh, Croppies ye'd better be quiet and still,
> Ye shan't have your liberty, do what ye will,
> As long as salt water is found in the deep,
> Our foot on the neck of the Croppy we'll keep.
> Remember the steel of Sir Phelim O'Neill
> Who slaughtered our fathers in Catholic zeal,
> And down, down, Croppies lie down . . .[16]

The appointment of General Lake to command in Ulster had been a clear sign that the Government was determined on the most brutal means of repression. In contrast to General Ralph Abercromby, (who replaced Lord Carhampton), and later Cornwallis, who prided themselves on their professional integrity as soldiers, Lake was a bigot and arch-reactionary in politics, who was prepared to use any means, no matter how cruel, to obtain his ends. No mercy was shown to actual or potential rebels. Lecky commented that he behaved with 'brutal, stupid and undiscriminating severity'.

Lake believed that harshness should not only be practised but seen to be practised. 'Nothing but terror will keep them [the rebels] in order', he wrote to Pelham in March 1797. He therefore encouraged public hangings and floggings, the display of dead bodies and the spiking of heads in public places. One such example of this type of public atrocity took place in April 1797 when four members of the Monaghan militia, charged with taking the United oath, were taken in open procession from Belfast to Blaris camp, near Lisburn, and there executed, their coffins standing open beside the gallows, in full view of several army regiments who had been marched in to look at the macabre scene. These public hangings may have frightened some soldiers, but in the end proved counterproductive, as the four Monaghan militiamen were soon commemorated in song and story. Lake's reputation for ruthlessness was increased when he permitted the atrocities of the notorious Ancient Britons in south Down during the spring and summer of 1797. This regiment of fencibles from Wales was later sent southwards to crush the insurgents in Wicklow and Wexford.

The liberal Lord Moira was so disturbed by what he saw happening in the north that he made a strong protest in the British House of Lords in November 1797. Having given a long list of atrocities committed by the regular army and yeomanry, he went on to say that Ulster was suffering under 'the most disgusting tyranny that any nation ever groaned under'.[17]

Ironically the strongest evidence that discipline had broken down in the army and that the most flagrant brutalities were being allowed to be committed unchecked came from the commander-in-chief of the army himself. General Abercromby was a conscientious and well-meaning professional soldier who had served in Ireland during the 1780s. He knew the country well, had studied its history, and was a humane man. When he succeeded Lord Carhampton as commander in November 1797, he quickly became aware of the atrocities that were being committed in the Government's name. In a general order to his troops issued a few months after his appointment he used a phrase which had wide repercussions on both sides of the Irish Sea. The army, he said, was 'in a state of licentiousness which must render it formidable to everyone but the enemy'.[18] In a private letter to a relative he went even further: 'The abuses of all kinds I found here can scarcely be believed or enumerated. Every crime, every cruelty that could be committed by Cossacks or Calmucks has been committed here.'

When news of these protests began to circulate, a cabal composed of the most ultra-conservative Ascendancy representatives – Lord Chancellor Clare, Speaker John Foster, Generals Lake and Knox and their allies in London – conspired to get rid of this allegedly over-scrupulous officer. In March 1798, after only a few months in office, Abercromby resigned because the Government in London would not listen to his pleas to tighten up discipline in the army. The men who had driven the liberal Fitzwilliam from office a few years previously, and who had constantly hampered Grattan in his attempts to introduce the mildest of reforms, were now omnipotent. It was a fatal policy for Ireland, as Lecky said, because it made rebellion inevitable.

It was at the height of this Orange-cum-military offensive that William Orr was hanged at Carrickfergus in October 1797. Orr, who was then thirty-one years of age, was a member of a farming and linen-bleaching family of Scottish origin who were then settled in Farranshare, near Shane's Castle, County Antrim. Several members of the family had been Volunteers and later joined the United Irishmen. He was well known locally, a popular sporting character, and noted as a man of strong Presbyterian convictions. He had been arrested a year previously, but as so often happened with other United leaders, his trial was postponed in order to proceed at a time when the Government hoped it could most effectively frighten the people into submission.

The charge was that of administering an illegal oath to two fencibles. The evidence against him was doubtful, and the soldiers were exposed as paid informers. One of them admitted afterwards that he was a perjurer. It was later revealed that Orr's attorney, James McGucken, was also in the pay of the Government. In spite of these circumstances, the jury, who got drunk during the proceedings, found Orr guilty, and he was sentenced to death.

Liberals in Ireland and London were shocked by the dubious trial and harsh sentence, and there were many appeals against the verdict. Charles James Fox, the radical Whig MP, created a sensation when he proposed at a public banquet in London that 'the Irish cabinet should take the place of William Orr'. The condemned man died calmly, denying he had ever administered an illegal oath, but steadfastly refusing to betray his political beliefs. His last words on the gallows were: 'I am no traitor. I die a persecuted man for a persecuted country. Great Jehovah, receive my soul. I die in the true faith of a presbyterian.'[19]

Orr was widely regarded as innocent, and quickly became a martyr. Mementoes, rings, scarves and rosettes bearing his name were sold all over the country. William Drennan wrote a lament entitled 'Wake, 1797' which went into many editions:

> Here we watch our brother's sleep.
> Watch with us, but do not weep:
> Watch with us, thro' dead of night –
> But expect the morning light . . .[20]

When the republicans marched out at Ballynahinch and Antrim six months after the execution, they carried the slogan 'Remember Orr' on their banners.

Orr was only one of the individuals who were led to the gallows or jail by the intervention of paid informers. The Government employed more than a score of agents to collect political or military information, and this 'battalion of evidence', as it became known, proved to be one of the most powerful weapons used against their opponents. Pitt had his spies well placed in Paris, Hamburg and London, as well as in Ireland, and there was scarcely an important move made by the United Irish leaders which was not reported to officials in Dublin and Belfast.[21] The most dangerous informers were not army officers, like Major Henry Charles Sirr in Dublin, Colonel Barber in Belfast or Captain McNeven in Carrickfergus, whose hostility towards rebels was only to be expected, but those members of the middle class who pretended sympathy with the republican cause and in some cases rose to positions of authority and trust within the United Irish ranks. The rebels were gravely weakened at moments of crisis by the unsuspecting, almost too idealistic, character of some of their leaders.

Payment to these agents was extremely generous, the total amount set aside by the Government for spying purposes between 1797 and 1804 amounted to over £53,000 (the modern equivalent of around £1 million). The highest paid was Thomas Reynolds, the Liberties silk merchant and neighbour of the Duke of Leinster in Kildare, who became a confidante of Lord Edward FitzGerald. For his services he was given £5,000 between September 1798 and March 1799. He was then granted £1,000 a year until he died in 1836.

In Ulster the most dangerous of these informers were James McGucken (Belfast), John Hughes (Belfast), Edward Newell (Newry),[22] Samuel Turner (Newry), James Pollock (Newry), and the Reverend John Cleland (Greyabbey). McGucken, who was a convert from Protestantism to Catholicism, served as a defence lawyer for the United Irishmen in a number of trials. Hughes owned a bookshop in Belfast, and won the confidence of such northern rebels as Samuel Neilson and Steel Dickson.[23] Newell was a portrait painter; he disappeared in June 1798, probably killed. Turner was a trusted courier for the United Irishmen. He turned traitor in 1797 and became one of Pitt's most valuable contacts in France and Germany. Pollock was paymaster of several lesser spies in the north. His name appears no less than twenty-four times between 1797 and 1804 as giving small sums to various agents. Cleland was chaplain and land agent to the Londonderry family. His local contact was Nicholas Maginn of Saintfield. A Catholic priest who was also busy in this profitable traffic was Father James McCary of Carrickfergus.[24]

It is impossible to say precisely how much the overall rebel strategy was hampered by the activities of these informers, but there can be little doubt that at moments of crisis when vital decisions had to be made, government authorities were usually one jump ahead of their opponents. Naval and military forces were deployed, and key leaders were arrested at the most critical and damaging junctures. The idealism of so many United Irish leaders was a virtue in the sense that it promoted courage and resolution at times of danger, but it was also a defect in so far as it was often associated with poor judgement of human nature and a lack of realism, almost ingenuousness, about tactics. During the harsh years 1795–8, when the utmost vigilance should have been practised by conspirators, naivety proved to be of no advantage in politics, still less in military enterprises.

5

'THE COMMON NAME OF IRISHMAN'

The idea of an 'Irish nation', indifferent to religious rivalries, rooted in history, but enlightened by the Revolution, takes its rise in the Belfast of the late eighteenth century.

J.C. Beckett[1]

Historians differ as to the consequence of the counter-revolutionary campaign which was directed as much against rebel Protestants as it was against Catholics. Undoubtedly many arms were seized, and Defenders killed or captured. Some of the most resolute United Irish leaders had to escape as best they could to France, while others were imprisoned without trial. Certain Belfast reformers – mainly, as Drennan described them, 'hesitating, half-way men' – began to draw back when they saw what sacrifices might be involved. A few Presbyterian ministers withdrew entirely from politics, and prominent Whigs like Grattan and Lord Moira were sickened by the excesses on all sides. The Catholic bishops, who by this time were mostly in the pocket of Dublin Castle, sought any excuse to denounce the twin evils of Jacobinism and Defenderism; and as the systematic rooting out of rebels continued so the landlords and Orangemen became ever more convinced that God was on the side of the big battalions. The success of informers in penetrating the underground organisations, and the subsequent arrest of many important leaders, were a serious blow to the United Irishmen.

On the other hand, the very brutality of the 'Croppies lie down' policy often proved counterproductive. Whig protests in Ireland, and the resignation of humane generals such as Abercromby, provoked British liberals like Fox to condemn government atrocities. Even when they were under the most intense pressure, very few of the rebel leaders faltered in the cause to which they had dedicated themselves. As for the common people who bore the brunt of the onslaught – the pitch-cappings, hangings, continual scourings, arrests and deportations may have frightened some but only stiffened the resolve of others.

Probably the best evidence that the spirit of resistance was not broken in the north came not from United Irish or Defender sources but from landlords, MPs, Church of Ireland clergymen, army officers and other loyalists, who during 1796 and 1797 poured messages into Dublin Castle about the dangers threatening them.[2] The letters suggest mounting panic in many of the predominantly Protestant parts of Ulster. Here is a selection giving places, dates, and where possible, authors:

1796

February	Cushendall	60 UI men sworn in (Capt. McNeven)
March	Armagh	'county in dreadful state' (Thos. Lawrence)
	Tyrone	'lower orders ready to rise if they dare' (Maj. C. Hamilton)
	Newry	'country on eve of general rising' (J. Pollock)
	Down	'lowest order busy procuring arms' (Vicar-Gen. W. Bristow)
	Armagh	'200 crimes committed' (Isaac Corry)
April	Dungannon	'a very dangerous conspiracy' (Thos. Knox)
May	Dungannon	10,000 UI men in Down, Antrim and Derry, pikes being prepared, 'rising expected in August' (Thos. Knox)
	Ballymena	'numerous UI' (Fr James McCary)
	Belfast	'associations of disaffected', 'militia corrupted' (Vicar-Gen. W. Bristow)
June	Ballycastle	'troops should be quartered there' (Lord O'Neill)
	Antrim town	'very extensive confederation'
	Antrim	5,300 UI men armed with firelocks (Sgt John Lee)

July	Dungannon	'teeming with treason' (Thos. Knox)
	Derry	'ripe for revolt' (Rev. J. Jones)
August	Derry	'every mischief to be expected' (G.F. Hill)
September	Belfast	'that damned sink' (Lord Downshire)
	Belfast	'United Irishmen beginning to cut their hair universally'(Rev. J. Jones)
	Antrim	12,516 members of UI (Capt McNeven). 27 ministers in Ulster synod sworn to UI (Thos. Whinney)
October	Derry	'hardly a man to be found in the rank of Farmer, Manufacturer or Labourer even to say he is willing to take the Oath of Allegiance' (John Richardson)
		'the country is ready to rise' (Lord Downshire)
November	Down	more than 10,000 men ('but very few Papists') registered as having arms (Lord Downshire)
	Cookstown	'the mass of the people here are conspirators' (John Walsh)
		'Presbyterian ministers are unquestionably the great encouragers and promoters of sedition' (Lord Downshire)
December	Belfast	'accursed den of traitors' (Lord Londonderry)
		'the game is nearly up in the north' (Dean Warburton)

1797

January	Antrim	County had been joyful at news of French fleet's arrival in Bantry Bay, and then full of sorrow. The population quiet but 'sullen'.
	Antrim, Down and Derry	'in a bad condition'
February	Raphoe	'widespread disaffection' (Rev. W. Hamilton)

97

Throughout 1797 and the first half of 1798, in spite of unceasing harassment of republicans, the balance of power between pro-government and anti-government forces remained fairly even in the country as a whole. In Leinster and Munster the majority of Catholics, including some from the middle classes, seemed ready to rise, and in the north those United Irishmen and Defenders who had avoided arrest appeared, in most cases, still firm and resolute. The Catholic bishops might fear Jacobinism more than they disliked the Protestant Ascendancy, but this was compensated for by the rebel sympathies of many priests.[3] In Ulster the poorer town workers and tenant farmers – both Presbyterian and Catholic – were seething with discontent, and influential sections of the dissenting middle classes persisted in their hostility towards their landlords and episcopalian rulers. In Ireland overall, probably three-quarters of the population were strongly, in some cases violently, anti-government, and but for the support the British Army gave their opponents, eventually they would have become dominant in a more normal political situation. How many of this large majority were active Defenders or sworn United Irishmen, or alternatively, how many were only 'paper members', is impossible to say.

Modern historians suggest that about 100,000 might be a reasonably accurate figure for the first category. This would have been a formidable army if well-trained and equipped, but, of course, the opposite was true. The rebels, though full of spirit and convinced of the justice of their cause, were often only 'badly-armed crowds'. Their officers in many cases proved unreliable, and in any event, were mostly only amateur soldiers. The men lacked muskets and could muster only a few pieces of artillery. Most of them had to rely on the crudest weapons, such as pikes, pitchforks and scythes.

The pro-Ascendancy forces were numerically weaker, but included virtually all the wealth and privilege of the country, controlling the law, administration, army and other levers of power. In Ireland as a whole around 1797 there were approximately 18,000 regular soldiers, highly disciplined and well-armed, 30,000 yeomanry, less disciplined but fanatical in their anti-Croppy zeal, and 16,000 militia. The militia were considered to be not always reliable as they were mostly Catholic conscripts, but when put to the test they, with a few notable exceptions, mostly obeyed the orders of their superior officers. Every town of any importance had a garrison in it. In Ulster the yeomanry, now led by the gentry and unashamedly Orange in outlook, were the major government force, buttressed, according to an official document, by nine thousand regular troops strategically stationed in the key towns of Belfast, Lurgan, Monaghan, Armagh, Belturbet, Newtownards, Carrickfergus, Derry, Omagh, Enniskillen, Dungannon, Cavan, Downpatrick, Coleraine, Ballyshannon and Newry.[4]

With the two opposing sides so equal in power, the key to victory obviously lay in the prompt arrival of a French army. If the Directory, now dominated by Napoleon, could be persuaded to send a powerful force – some 20,000 men and arms for a further 50,000 – then British superiority in trained soldiers might be successfully challenged. Britain's regular troops would be engaged with the French, and this would free the United Irishmen and Defenders to take on the yeomanry and conscript militia. But the French did not arrive until it was too late, and when they did land in August 1798, with General Jean Humbert in command, there were too few (only 1,100) of them, and they chose a place (County Mayo) where the rebels were few in number and poorly organised.

When the rising did come in May and June 1798, it proved brave but abortive. The rebels had suffered a severe setback in mid-March, when, as a result of information laid by informers, a meeting of the Leinster United Irish directory in Dublin was surprised by Major Sirr, and most of the delegates captured, including such figures as Oliver Bond, Thomas Emmet and William Macneven. Lord Edward FitzGerald escaped and hid under various disguises in the centre of Dublin for several days, but he, too, was discovered, and after a struggle in which one of his captors was killed, he was mortally wounded by Sirr. Samuel Neilson was on the run at this time, trying to organise the escape of prisoners from Dublin Castle, but he was recognised in the street and was himself put in jail. A further blow was the seizure, again as a result of betrayal of information, of the brothers Henry and John Sheares. Several other United Irish leaders, including Arthur O'Connor and Thomas Russell, were already in prison, while Wolfe Tone and other exiles were far away in France trying to hasten the coming of French military aid. As a result of all these arrests in the south, the United Irish movement there had been effectively beheaded, apart from local representatives and the largely unorganised Defenders in Kildare, Wicklow, Carlow and Wexford. In Ulster the only prominent leaders still free were McCracken, Hope, Steel Dickson and the Simms brothers.

The choice before the insurgents at this stage was desperate – either they could allow themselves to be chopped off one by one and the movement destroyed piecemeal, or else they could fight back as strongly as they were able, according to local circumstances. Their decision was to stand and fight, regardless of whether the French came to help or not.

On 23 May the rebellion broke out almost spontaneously in Kildare, Wicklow, Carlow and Wexford, led by local men whose names were hardly known outside their own townlands and whose military experience was negligible. In Wexford the command was taken by Father John Murphy, parish priest of Boolavogue, who had previously been noted more for his religious than his political zeal. The atrocities committed against his parishioners had turned him into a rebel. His own house and chapel had been burned by yeomanry. A Church of Ireland leader of the United Irishmen was Bagenal Harvey, a landlord and magistrate, who had also been sickened by the brutal hangings, burnings and free-quarterings of government troops.

On 27 May the first important action took place at Oulart Hill when Father Murphy, with a band of nearly one thousand pikemen, destroyed a mixed force of yeomanry and north Cork militia. Emboldened by this success, 'the boys of Wexford', as they became quickly known, spread out through the county, rapidly gaining recruits as they went. In all, about 30,000 rebels are reckoned to have taken to the field. By early June a large part of Wexford was under their control. There were also skirmishes in neighbouring counties. A serious setback came on 5 June when they failed to capture New Ross, suffering heavy casualties in the siege. The republican cause was marred by a horrible incident in which over one hundred Protestant prisoners, including women and children, were burned in a barn at Scullabogue.[5] This massacre, which was condemned by responsible insurgent leaders, was widely used, especially in Ulster, to persuade Protestants that Catholics only wanted to wage a war of religious extermination against them.

The rebel impetus gradually slowed down as regular army reinforcements were brought in from England, and on 21 June a decisive battle took place at Vinegar Hill near Enniscorthy when the insurgents were annihilated. Thousands were killed in the battle, and hundreds slaughtered as they tried to escape. After this defeat, the rebellion gradually petered out in the south-east of Ireland. Father Murphy and some other priests who had been directly involved in the fighting were eventually caught and hanged. Bagenal Harvey, and several other middle-class Protestants who had shown some sympathy for democratic principles, were also executed after summary trials.

In Ulster, though on a smaller scale, there was a similar confused pattern of sudden changes in strategic plans, uncertainty about leaders, leakage of secret information to the authorities, and then finally, when co-ordination of time and place was most necessary, a last-minute and hastily improvised turnout of the most determined United Irishmen and Defenders. Contrasting with the south of Ireland, where the insurgents were overwhelmingly Catholic, the majority of northern rebels were Dissenters, mainly from north Down and central Antrim.

McCracken, who had taken over as commander-in-chief from Robert Simms in Antrim, with the aid of James Hope, Samuel Orr, brother of the martyred William, and the young Catholic, Charles Teeling, turned out at Donegore Hill at the head of a mixed force of Defenders and United Irishmen numbering about three thousand men. On 6 June McCracken issued an order addressed to 'The army of Ulster – first day of Liberty'.

Gathering strength as they went, until they numbered about six thousand, they captured Randalstown and besieged the strategic port of Larne. As they marched they are said to have sung Irish patriotic songs and the 'Marseillaise'. By the next day a large part of the county, apart from the vitally important centres of Belfast and Carrickfergus, were in rebel hands. General George Nugent, the British Army commander, helped in his planning by valuable information from carefully planted informers, swiftly mobilised his army, and after a fierce battle for Antrim town, the rebels were overwhelmed. Casualties were heavy, and many insurgents killed or captured. Little mercy was shown to prisoners or those who tried to escape into the hills.

McCracken himself got away from the battlefield, but after hiding for some days, he was captured and taken to Carrickfergus and then to Belfast. Proclaiming his Presbyterian faith to the end, he was attended in jail by two of his closest friends, Sinclair Kelburne and Steel Dickson. Dickson himself was a prisoner and was soon to be dispatched to Fort George in Scotland. McCracken behaved with dignity and composure both during his trial and when he was condemned to death.[6] His sister Mary Ann walked hand in hand with him to the gallows, and later wrote a moving account of his execution. It was alleged that at the last moment he was offered a pardon if he informed on his friends but that he refused.[7]

In County Down the newly appointed Henry Munro, a linen draper from Lisburn, replaced the arrested Dickson as commander-in-chief, and succeeded in mobilising a mixed force of about seven thousand men at Ballynahinch on 12 June. After a violent battle, which went on for most of the day, the superior fire power and discipline of the regular British soldiers, supported by a strong yeomanry contingent, proved decisive. About four hundred insurgents died in the battle. Among those killed by yeomen while trying to escape was Betsy Gray who had fought alongside her brother and sweetheart.[8] Munro was executed in his home town and his head placed on a spike.

Two months later, too late to be of any real assistance to the rebels, 1,100 French troops were landed in County Mayo under the command of General Jean Humbert. Among them were Bartholomew Teeling, and Matthew Tone, brother of Wolfe Tone. This tiny army gathered some local support as it marched towards Castlebar, but was eventually surrounded in Ballinamuck, County Longford, in September. Meanwhile, another ill-fated naval incursion was taking place in Lough Swilly where several French ships were destroyed or captured in November. Wolfe Tone, on board the flagship *Hoche*, was taken prisoner, quickly recognised, and sent to Dublin for trial. On being sentenced to death on 10 November, he asked that he be shot as a soldier rather than hanged as a criminal. The request was refused. Two days later he cut his throat and died in Dublin barracks on 19 November.

There were several reasons why the rising in the north was so quickly defeated. On the eve of the insurrection several of the so-called 'colonels', including the commander-in-chief Robert Simms, refused to act. Whether this betrayal was due to cowardice or from a sincere conviction that the rebellion was doomed to failure is not clear, but it certainly had a disastrous effect on rebel organisation and morale. Rank-and-file insurgents were left confused and leaderless. Steel Dickson, who succeeded Simms, was arrested at Ballynahinch only a few days before the turnout date. In any case, he was a middle-aged clergyman in poor health, and with little military experience beyond what he had acquired in the Volunteers fifteen years before. Henry Munro, though a brave and idealistic soldier, also lacked military experience, and was too hastily propelled into senior army rank.

Spies, such as Nicholas Maginn and John Hughes, had penetrated the secrets of the provincial directorate of the United Irishmen, and were sending a flow of information to General Nugent in Belfast. Belfast itself, for long a focus of radicalism, stayed quiet during the crucial mid-June days, possibly because of the cautious, prosperous merchants and their renewed fears of a Catholic uprising.[9] Counties such as Cavan, Monaghan, Derry, Armagh and Donegal, where Catholics predominated but the yeomanry were also strong, did not stir either. More serious still was the lack of co-ordination between north and

103

south, and the non-appearance, until it was too late and too far away, of the long-promised French troops. In any event, whatever these internal weaknesses might be, the decisive factor was undoubtedly the military superiority of a well-organised, professionally led, and abundantly equipped British Army. Pikemen might be brave, but on the battlefield they were no match for bullets and cannon fire.

The 1798 rising seemed to end in total and irrevocable defeat for the forces of democracy and Irish republicanism. The insurrection was crushed without mercy, its leaders and thousands of their followers killed in battle, hanged, imprisoned, transported or driven into exile.[10] Catholic emancipation was delayed for another quarter of a century; land reform had to wait even longer; the partially independent Irish parliament was extinguished and its powers transferred to Westminster; the Ascendancy and their Tory allies in England appeared triumphant.

But though the Croppies were compelled – by the sheer weight of military force – to capitulate, they were not willing, as subsequent history showed, to lie down for ever. As had happened so often before, the spirit of resistance went underground only to re-emerge when circumstances proved more propitious. The rebellion left two legacies – one the stuff of poetry and ballads, the other more rooted in practical politics, which inspired future generations of Irish nationalists, both Protestant and Catholic.

The romantic legend, like that of the Fenians or the 1916 rising, was of the triumph of a failure – a tale of brave and idealistic men and women who fought against enormous odds for a noble cause, and whose defeat did not shame them but turned them instead into heroes and martyrs. Forty-five years after the defeats at Vinegar Hill, Antrim and Ballynahinch, for example, John Kells Ingram, a young Trinity scholar and son of a Church of Ireland clergyman from County Donegal, wrote 'The memory of the dead',[11] which was to have a powerful influence on the emerging Young Ireland movement:

Who fears to speak of Ninety-Eight?
   Who blushes at the name?
When cowards mock the patriot's fate,

> Who hangs his head for shame?
> He's all a knave and half a slave
> Who slights his country thus:
> But a true man, like you, man
> Will fill your glass with us . . .

Patrick Pearse believed that modern Irish republicanism began with the United Irishmen. In his opinion Wolfe Tone was the greatest Irish patriot who had ever lived, and his followers were the 'great, splendid, faithful common people'.[12]

In contrast to this patriotic rhetoric, there were those more down-to-earth people who believed that there might be some practical lessons which could be learned from the experiences, successful or not, of the United Irishmen. Such lessons included the belief that Catholics alone or Dissenters by themselves were not strong enough to challenge seriously the entrenched forces of the establishment; that it was only when democratic and nationally minded people of all denominations came together that they could hope to reach their goals; that the struggles for social reform and independence were not antagonistic but complementary to each other; that each involved a fight against the Ascendancy at home and the British government abroad; that in such a joint campaign the old barriers of religious prejudice would be reduced; and, finally, that the cause of Irish freedom had sympathisers in many countries, including Britain itself.

In the long run the legacy that may prove more enduring for both romantics and realists alike was the new concept of nationality which developed during the last decade of the eighteenth century. Before the emergence of the United Irish movement there was little agreement as to what constituted the Irish nation. Gael and Gall, Catholics and Protestants, descendants of natives or planters, Irish-speakers and English-speakers, were so divided by ethnic origin, class, religion, language and culture that they formed two or three fairly distinct communities. The heirs of the old Gaelic Catholics and the Anglo-Normans they had intermarried with were undoubtedly a nation, and Grattan and his followers claimed, not entirely accurately, to be one.

The joint Catholic and Dissenter struggle against the Ascendancy and their Tory protectors in Britain transformed this situation. Many Presbyterians, who had formerly regarded themselves as Scottish, began to speak of themselves as Irish, and even some members of the Church of Ireland increasingly gave their allegiance to the land where they were born and lived in, rather than the island across the sea from which their forebears came.

Wolfe Tone's aim to 'unite the whole people of Ireland, to abolish the memory of all past dissensions, and to substitute the common name of Irishman in the place of the denominations of Protestant, Catholic and Dissenter' changed from being a Utopian dream into a political prophecy which could in certain circumstances become true, at least temporarily.

The failure to achieve Tone's objectives in the nineteenth and early twentieth centuries, and the continuing communal strife in Northern Ireland to this day, have led some commentators to conclude that Tone was indeed an unrealistic and impractical visionary. Experience has taught us, say such critics, that there is no hope whatsoever of 'the common name of Irishman' becoming a reality for the thirty-two counties. Modern revisionist historians dismiss the romantic approach to the events of the 1790s as either martyrology (the cult of the blood sacrifice) or hagiography (the worship of saints).[13] In both cases the propagation of such a myth is said only to encourage violence.

Other commentators, less pessimistic and more willing to look at the underlying causes of religious dissension in Ireland, turn the argument round the other way – they suggest that there can be no hope of peace in the north until the national question is finally solved, and that it is precisely the inability to win a common political identity which has led to so much bigotry and sectarianism.

6

'THE GRAND DESIGN'

The idea [of a union with Ireland] has long been in my mind . . .
The admission of Catholics to a share of the suffrage could not
then be dangerous – the Protestant interest in point of power,
property, and Church establishment would be secure because
the decided majority of the supreme legislature would necessarily be Protestant.

William Pitt[1]

The concept of a union between Britain and Ireland, which would
abolish the five-hundred-year-old Irish parliament and absorb it
into the legislature at Westminster, had been discussed in the
highest Tory circles for several years before the 1798 rebellion
broke out. In November 1792 Prime Minister William Pitt,
alarmed at possible contacts between United Irishmen and French
Jacobins, had floated the idea in a confidential letter sent to
the viceroy, Lord Westmorland, in which he showed a keen
appreciation of the balance of political and religious forces in the
two countries. Pitt's long-term plan, or 'grand design' as the
historian R.B. McDowell describes it,[2] was simultaneously to
introduce a free trade area in the British Isles, which would also
serve as an impregnable fortress against foreign enemies. At the
same time Lord Castlereagh, then still a young man apparently
of Whiggish inclinations but rapidly gaining the confidence of
the Tory party, began to think of a United Kingdom in which
Ireland would be a minor and, it was hoped, a firmly contained
part. Lord Clare, lord chancellor of Ireland and spokesman for
the most diehard Ascendancy elements, became converted to
the view that only the amalgamation of the two parliaments
could prevent the coming of what he feared most – the rule of a
'Popish democracy'.

These important, and at that stage still secret, plans for a new constitution lay in abeyance for some years because of Ascendancy resistance to any suggestion of full Catholic emancipation, and because a strong section of Protestant opinion in Ireland still clung to the old Volunteer spirit of parliamentary independence. But the plans were quickly revived in the autumn of 1798 when it was hoped that the by-now thoroughly frightened Irish MPs and peers would be more sympathetic to them.

As soon as Pitt's revolutionary proposals became public – which happened soon after the final defeat of the French at the Battle of Ballinamuck – an acrimonious debate broke out between various sections of the upper and middle classes in Ireland. This debate was further fuelled by the publication of a pamphlet by Edward Cooke, under-secretary in Dublin Castle, entitled *Arguments for and against a Union between Great Britain and Ireland*. There was no doubt on which side Cooke was on. What was so remarkable about this controversy was that it was not a straightforward discussion between Protestant and Catholic viewpoints, or the Ascendancy versus the rest of the population. It was much more complicated than that, and as it developed it indicated a great deal of confusion, cross voting, and shifting of alliances between the different groups and individuals involved.

The Lord Clare faction, which had the support of most placemen, and the Ulster peers, Lords Abercorn, Hertford, Caledon, O'Neill and Londonderry, and other rich Protestant landowners, were quite clear as to what they wanted – they would accept a United Kingdom parliament but there must on no account be any concessions to Catholics. The leaders of Irish Catholic opinion, if they had had any integrity, might have been expected to reject such humiliating conditions. But instead, so frightened were they of any manifestation of 'Jacobin democracy', that Bishops Troy of Dublin and Moylan of Cork, with the eager support of Lords Kenmare and Fingall, began to canvass in favour of the Union. Indeed so abject was their submission at this time to Dublin Castle authorities that they secretly agreed to further proposals by Castlereagh that priests should be paid a salary by the state in order to keep them loyal, and that the Government should be allowed to veto any recommendations for the appointment of bishops.

The Protestant Patriot Party, on the other hand, led by Grattan, the Ponsonby family, John Parnell, chancellor of the exchequer, and John Foster, speaker of the Irish House of Commons, rejected the idea of giving up their own parliament, and still retaining some shreds of political personal honour, were not prepared to sell their reputations for government bribes. In this defence of Irish independence, limited as it was, they had the support of commercial and legal interests in Dublin, and of many middle-class Irish Catholics.

The Government being concerned with *realpolitik* rather than any fancy notions about democracy, could afford to disregard what the common people thought or felt. The mass of the population, whether Catholic or Protestant, had no votes, no access to parliament, and no newspapers or other forums to express their views. Their rebellious spirit had been subdued, if not entirely broken, by the failure of the 1798 rising. From the administration's viewpoint, therefore, what mattered were votes in the Irish parliament. The House of Lords could be largely relied upon, but the Commons was more doubtful. The first test of parliamentary opinion came in January 1799 when a pro-union measure in the Commons was only carried by the smallest of margins – 106 votes to 105. In this critical division approximately three out of every five Ulster MPs voted to retain their own parliament in College Green.

So narrow a victory made it impossible for the Government to proceed immediately with its proposed legislation, and during the next fifteen months it deliberately set out to win over more MPs and peers to its support. Thus began the notorious campaign of coercion and bribery, initiated by Lord Castlereagh, condoned by William Pitt, and supported with the active help of Lord Cornwallis, the viceroy. Cornwallis is sometimes portrayed as the humane liberal persuaded against his better judgement by the more ruthless Castlereagh. Cornwallis certainly had private reservations about his role as briber-in-chief.

In a letter published many years later he expressed his distaste for what the Government required him to do:

> I despise and hate myself every hour for engaging in such dirty work, and am supported only by the reflection that without the Union the British Empire must be dissolved.[3]

In spite of such qualms, Cornwallis did not, however, let his private conscience overrule what he regarded as his public duty.

Every possible method, secret or open, corrupt or seemingly honest, was used to persuade any vulnerable MP to change his mind in favour of the Union.[4] Castlereagh began by putting the maximum pressure on any placeman who opposed his wishes, and if they did not conform they were stripped of their posts in the administration. Within a period of twelve months at least one-fifth of all MPs were persuaded to give up their seats in favour of more pliable members, in return for lucrative jobs. The powerful borough-mongers, in particular, were offered an average of £15,000 for each constituency they were prepared to sell. The Marquess of Downshire, for example, was paid £52,000, and Lord Ely £45,000. In all, a total of £1,250,000 was paid to the borough owners, who were well satisfied at the price for these marketable properties. Lord Cornwallis, despite his private squeamishness, had no compunction in bribing influential peers in another way – by offering them promotion from a lower to a higher grade in the ranks of nobility. It is reckoned that between 1799 and 1801 he successfully asked George III to create twenty-eight new peerages, and got twenty more raised to the rank of viscount, earl or marquess.

This combination of political pressure and direct bribery soon began to influence the waverers in both Houses. In January 1800, although Henry Grattan made one of the most eloquent speeches in his life against Castlereagh, the pro-unionists won by 138 votes to 96, and a month later another motion was carried by 158 votes to 115. The House of Lords then voted 75 to 26 in favour of the Union.

A remarkable aspect of all this manoeuvring and cross voting was the way in which many ultra-Protestants refused to follow the majority line. In Dublin a prominent figure among the anti-Castlereagh faction was the lawyer and MP William Saurin who had long been notorious for his extreme anti-Catholic opinions. In Ulster such powerful landowners as Lords Cole, Enniskillen, Corry, and Caulfield (son of Lord Charlemont), some members of the influential Archdale family of Enniskillen, and the Marquesses of Down and Donegall were regarded as being, at best, lukewarm towards the Government's proposals. The Marquess of Downshire, who was said to control the way in which eight MPs might vote, vacillated. Commercial opinion among Belfast Protestants seems to have been split. Cornwallis hoped that, at best, Ulster would stay neutral in the contest.

As for the Orange Order, it was deeply divided – the majority of Orangemen deciding that on this occasion they were more Irish than British in their allegiance. As a result the grand lodge recommended neutrality in the struggle. However, in the final votes, according to the historian R.M. Sibbett, seventeen out of nineteen members of the Irish parliament who were also members of the Order voted against the Union. The majority of the rank and file were equally hostile, and according to W.E.H. Lecky, there is no record anywhere of a single lodge actually favouring the new legislation. Moreover, several lodges in Tyrone, Fermanagh, Armagh, Cavan and Monaghan were in outright opposition. In March 1799 a large meeting at the Maze of Orangemen from Antrim and Down resolved that the proposed Union would bring 'inevitable ruin to the Peace, Prosperity and Happiness of the Kingdom'.[5]

Undoubtedly some of the motives of these Orange opponents of the Union were backward looking. It is clear from their long-established reputation as bigots, and the way they expressed their opinions in the debate, that what they wanted was not a genuinely democratic and non-sectarian parliament in Ireland, but the continuance of the old policy of Protestant supremacy. Mistrusting what they regarded as the danger of 'English softness' (Sibbett's words), they disliked any suggestions that might interfere with their arbitrary rule. According to this narrow view, better to continue to rule locally with an iron hand than allow any London-based government, over which their influence would inevitably be weaker, to introduce vexatious laws about Catholic emancipation.

But there were other motives also. Certain leaders of ultra-Protestant opinion were so disturbed at the thought of losing their beloved forum in Dublin that they threw all their weight against Castlereagh's scheme. A striking example of such 'putting their country first' and, at least momentarily, before their religious bigotry, was that of John C. Beresford, the Dublin MP, member of one of the richest families in Ireland, and grand master of the Orange Order. The proposed Union, said this sectarian-temporarily-turned-patriot,

> must ultimately tend to see the destruction of the country, and the alienation of her affections from England. Proud of the name of Irishman, I hope never to exchange it for that of Colonist, or to see my country governed by laws exacted by a Parliament over which she can have no control, from the small share she shall have in the selection of it . . . a measure so destructive of their Commerce and Prosperity, and so humiliating to their pride as a Nation.[6]

In spite of so much open hostility, or at least reservations, by influential sections of public opinion, the Government had by the spring of 1800 clear-cut majorities in both the Irish and British parliaments, and the Act of Union received the royal assent in August of that year. It came into operation in January 1801. The new legislation abolished the Irish Houses of Commons and Lords, and made provision that to the United Kingdom parliament at Westminster each county should send two MPs, the cities of Cork and Dublin two each, and Trinity College Dublin and thirty-one boroughs one each. Twenty-eight temporal and four spiritual peers could sit in the enlarged House of Lords at Westminster. There was no provision for Catholic emancipation, or any suggestion of extending the franchise. The established Churches of England and Ireland were united, and recognised as an 'essential and fundamental part of the Union'.

Ostensibly the Union was pushed through the Irish and British parliaments for the loftiest motives. Property owners were reassured that peace and stability would be restored, and the horrid spectre of Jacobinism exorcised for ever. The northern merchants were tempted with visions of ever-expanding trade and commerce, especially in linen. Catholics were promised (or at least persuaded by hints and behind-the-scenes suggestions) that they would soon achieve their long-desired goal of full emancipation. Ireland as a whole would be treated more fairly, said these advocates of the Union, than it had been under the old Ascendancy parliament, and the Irish people could expect all kinds of commercial advantages. Had not the British prime minister made a major speech in the House of Commons in January 1799 in which he gave his pledge that if the two countries were ruled by one parliament then Ireland would benefit from 'accumulated blessings', and share fully in the 'wealth and power' of the British Empire?[7] There would be an end to the wars between 'sectaries' (that is, Orangemen and strong adherents of Catholicism), and the fading out of 'factions' (that is, firmly committed political groups). If only Ireland would come in under the benign and all-sheltering umbrella of the United Kingdom parliament, then the age-old poverty and ancient dissensions would gradually ameliorate.

The real – and at the time, largely secret[8] – objectives of the Union were, however, very different. What was said openly for public consumption did not necessarily correspond to what was discussed privately in the highest government circles. The truth, which only gradually emerged, was that instead of serving Ireland, the new legislation was planned to serve Britain; and instead of promoting democracy, the merger of the two parliaments was designed to perpetuate, in a new way, the old Ascendancy.

Briefly, the aim of the British administration was to tie Ireland irrevocably into the empire by manipulating the electoral system in such a manner as to prevent the country from ever becoming an independent nation. Under the penal laws the Catholics, and to a lesser extent the Presbyterians and other

113

Dissenters, had been kept out of power. Now that those laws were being relaxed a different tactic had to be employed to make sure that any new manifestation of Irish dissent or rebellion would be impotent. The Act of Union, in fact, was the first deliberate gerrymander in Ireland.[9]

Pitt and Castlereagh, who were the two Tory politicians mainly responsible for this strategy, were keenly aware of the balance of votes within and between the two countries. Pitt had made the necessary mathematical calculations as early as 1792. Then he and his advisers had reluctantly agreed to grant the franchise to all forty-shilling freeholders, including Catholics. It did not require much intelligence to see that as the electoral rolls were expanded so the Catholics, who outnumbered Protestants by about three or four to one, would steadily gain in influence. When Catholic emancipation actually happened, and they were allowed to enter parliament, they would eventually become dominant politically. The danger might not be imminent, but within a period of decades it was likely that Irish nationalists would control the House of Commons in Dublin, if it was allowed to continue to exist. This would present a continual challenge to Britain and its empire, especially if Catholics were supported by radical Dissenters.

To counteract this threat, Catholics would now be in a permanent minority in the new and enlarged House of Commons which was being envisaged, because the balance of the population would be decisively altered. Instead of Catholics outweighing Protestants by three or four to one as they did in Ireland, they would be outweighed by a ratio of about one to five in the United Kingdom. 'The claims of the Catholics will certainly be much weakened by their incorporation into the mass of English subjects', wrote Cornwallis in a confidential letter to Lord Portland, the home secretary.[10] In a further letter to Portland in January 1799, and this time marked 'Most secret and confidential', he wrote that under the Union 'The Catholics must ever be content with inferiority.' This same letter is also attributed to Castlereagh in his *Memoirs*. It is likely that Castlereagh as chief secretary drafted it, and Cornwallis as viceroy sent it to

London. Even if in the course of time Irish voters sent dozens of MPs to Westminster they would always remain relatively powerless. They might argue, plead, cajole or threaten to the highest flights of eloquence, but unless they could win allies among British MPs they would be unable to affect legislation in the House of Commons. When divisions took place how could a few score Irish MPs defeat fifteen times that number of British MPs? Edward Cooke put this point sharply to Lord Chancellor Clare in February 1801. 'Do I think the British Constitution would be endangered were five or six more Dissenters to sit in Parliament than sit there at present?' Cooke asked. 'My answer was an inward smile. I have asked myself if a dozen Roman Catholics were to sit in the Imperial Parliament, and a few hold good offices on account of their good conduct, do I think the Empire would be endangered? One smiled at the question.'[11]

The Government's senior advisers might laugh at the idea that Irish nationalists or radicals might ever again raise their heads now that the Union legislation was firmly in place. What had they to fear from a United Irish organisation which had been gravely weakened through losses on the battlefield, executions, imprisonment and deportation? Why should they worry about a handful of closely watched rebels at home, or a few divided, and often quarrelling, exiles abroad? The spirit of the masses had been largely broken through defeat and repression, and there seemed little hope, either constitutionally or by means of physical force, of raising the banner of rebellion again. 'Who fears to speak of Ninety-Eight?' was the query in the famous poem. The answer during the first decade of the nineteenth century was that the majority of the population, whether Catholic or Dissenter, were in no position even if they wished to, to resume a struggle so catastrophically lost a few years before. Coercion laws had not been repealed, and habeas corpus was still suspended. Moreover, those members of the upper and middle classes who had for various reasons temporarily opposed the Union gradually found good excuses to accept it. Henry Grattan was one of the very few old parliamentarians who never abandoned his particular patriotic principles.

115

But behind this façade of conformity and apparent acceptance of the new status quo there were powerful social and political forces at work, which ensured that so long as Ireland's fundamental grievances were not remedied, then the country would never be at peace. The stubborn fact remained, in spite of all the propaganda and administrative pressures, that the Union offered little to the majority of Irish people. Catholic emancipation seemed to have been postponed indefinitely, and Pitt's promises were revealed as threadbare; the corrupt Church establishment continued to exist as before; there was no movement on the tithes issue nor any extension of the franchise. The tax burden got heavier as the French war worsened, and Irish manufacturers, instead of gaining from the Union, lost further markets to British competition. The problem of land reform, which was crucial to so many other issues, was again ignored. The Presbyterians made few gains except the promise of increased *regium donum* payments to their ministers. Furthermore, so long as French armies were in the field and the French navy threatened to sail again 'into the bay', the administrations in Whitehall and Dublin Castle could not sleep easily.

It was against this background of apathy or despair on the part of the common people, withdrawal of support by the middle classes, and continued repression by the Government that the rebellions of 1803 broke out.

Thomas Russell was released from Fort George in June 1802 after serving five and a half years without trial. Accompanied by several of his fellow detainees, he travelled to Germany in July, and then on to Paris where he was reunited with his old comrade, Robert Emmet. Together they determined on a new rising, but this time without French help, as they were both disillusioned by the 'despot' Napoleon, who was in the process of having himself crowned emperor. Emmet, who had lived underground partly in France and partly in Ireland since the failure of 1798, returned to Dublin in October 1802. Russell soon joined him there, and in the spring of 1803 the two men began to make detailed plans for a military rebellion they hoped would take place simultaneously in the Dublin–Wicklow area and

116

Down and Antrim. Their closest colleagues at this time were James Hope,[12] who was living in the Liberties in Dublin but was in contact with friends in Ulster, and William Henry Hamilton from Enniskillen, who had been a trusted republican courier between Ireland and France for several years.

Hamilton was one of those influential but shadowy figures who played such an important role in the middle ranks of the United Irishmen. There are often only scattered references to such individuals in the records, but their names crop up in critical events. Son of an Enniskillen solicitor, he was educated at the Inns of Court in London, where he quickly became an ardent democrat and republican. He seems to have been both intelligent and intrepid, moving constantly with messages between Belfast, Dublin, London and Paris. If caught, he would presumably have been charged with treason, and probably executed. In October 1798 he was one of the officers serving with the ill-fated expedition led by General Jean Hardy on the north-west coast of Ireland. In contrast to Wolfe Tone, who was quickly recognised, Hamilton succeeded in bluffing his English captors that he was a French officer, and he was eventually exchanged for an English soldier imprisoned in France. Hamilton returned to Dublin in the spring of 1803, and was actively involved in plans for the Emmet and Russell rebellions.[13]

Hope and Hamilton accompanied Russell when he set out on his dangerous – and as it proved, fruitless – mission to the north in mid-July. Russell's hope was that his very presence and the memories of what they had achieved five years previously would arouse the old united spirit of 1798, and that they could quickly raise a powerful insurrection. It was from his practice of suddenly appearing in a district, and trying to stir up local people to revolt, that Russell was later given the nickname 'The man from God-knows-where':

Into our townlan', on a night of snow,
Rode a man from God-knows-where;
None of us bade him stay or go,
Nor deemed him friend, nor damned him foe.

117

But we stabled his big roan mare;
For in our townlan' we're decent folk,
And if he didn't speak, why none of us spoke,
And we sat until the fire burned low . . .[14]

Simultaneously Emmet was trying, with slightly more success, to do the same thing in Dublin.

On 24 July 1803, the day after Emmet's attempted rising in Dublin, Russell issued a proclamation grandly signed 'General in Chief of the Northern District'. But the sad truth was that he was a general without troops because any potential followers he may have had – and there seems to have been still a kernel of support among some Catholics and Dissenters – knew that any further military rising at that time was a hopeless cause, particularly as there was no mention of French help. For an unarmed and unorganised people to take to arms would have led only to their immediate slaughter.

The authorities were hot on Russell's trail, and a reward of £1,500 was offered for his arrest. However, with the aid of friends he escaped to the south. Back in Dublin he was recognised in the street by George Knox, with whom he had served in the army in India. Knox alerted Major Sirr who arrested him on 9 September 1803. Emmet had also been arrested and was awaiting trial.

Russell was then taken under heavy guard back to Downpatrick, where he was charged with high treason. The location of his trial was chosen to remind any potential northern rebels what their fate would be if they were caught. His counsel was the much-respected Henry Joy. Mary Ann McCracken, to whom Russell had once proposed marriage, gave such moral and practical help as was possible. Russell made a bold defence, expressing no regrets and offering no apologies. In his opinion he had tried to serve his country and all humanity to the best of his ability. His only plea was to the aristocracy 'to pay attention to the poor – the labouring class, the community, their tenantry and dependants'.[15] His final words before the black hood was put over his head were in keeping with his deeply held religious beliefs: 'I forgive my persecutors. I die in peace with all mankind,

118

and I hope for mercy through the merits of my Redeemer, Jesus Christ.' Russell was hanged outside the jail gates and his head cut off. Two other rebels, Michael Drake and James Corry, were executed alongside him. His body was buried in the Church of Ireland graveyard in Downpatrick, where nearly a hundred years later a simple stone was erected by the antiquarian Francis Joseph Bigger with the inscription 'the grave of Russell'.

Following the executions of Emmet and Russell, the plight of the dozen or so former United Irish leaders in Ulster got worse. They were constantly under the supervision of government agents, and there was always the possibility that they could be interned again without trial. If middle or upper class, they were ostracised by their respectable neighbours. The opportunities for a career, which had always been difficult, deteriorated further because of suspicion and fear. There was no legal political party to which they could belong, and no newspapers to express their views. Presbyterian congregations that remained sympathetic or liberal were fewer in number, and external pressure was put on these to conform. Among the radicals themselves there was the depressing admission that the cause of physical-force resistance had to be abandoned, at least temporarily, and that their French allies, upon whom they had once so ardently depended, were untrustworthy or even as imperialist as their British oppressors.

In such a situation, individuals had to work out their personal and political salvation, taking into account not only their own state of health, their age, and the strength of their consciences, but also wider circumstances of their place in society, as well as national and international politics. Interestingly enough, and as might be expected from their records, few of the 1798 men fell silent or dropped completely out of politics. There was enough of the old spirit there to keep them going until they died.

The Reverend Steel Dickson was released in January 1802 after serving three years and seven months as a prisoner in Belfast and Fort George. There was no legal proof that he had ever served, or proposed to serve, as an insurgent at the Battle of Ballynahinch, and he was not at any time brought to trial. He had been, however, a prominent United Irish leader and as such was a marked man for the rest of his life. Though faced with persecution and poverty, he refused to leave the country as he might well have done and been called to a congregation in the United States of America. Instead he decided to fight it out at home, and do the best he could to defend his record and rally Presbyterians to his cause. His Portaferry parish had paid his salary of £100 a year until the end of 1799, but this was stopped on orders of the synod. He eventually was called to a new and small liberal parish at Keady, County Armagh, where his income was £50 a year. The Reverend Robert Black, his political opponent, made sure that he was not granted any *regium donum*, so for thirteen years while he remained at Keady his income was less than £1 a week.

In spite of all the pressures put upon him, and constant government surveillance, Dickson would not admit to any guilt or retract any of his views, and carried on his pastoral work quietly among his small congregation, preaching the gospel, and continuing to express his liberal political views if the opportunity offered. In 1811, though by then elderly and infirm, he was physically assaulted by an Orange gang because he had advocated Catholic emancipation. The following year he came back again into public attention when he published *A Narrative of the Confinement and Exile of William Steel Dickson, D.D.*,[16] which offended many conservative Presbyterians because of the author's refusal to repudiate his past radical opinions. His political opponents, led by Black, then attacked him at the synod. The Reverend Henry Montgomery and some other liberal friends came to his defence, but in 1815 he had to retire from Keady because of poor health. He died in poverty in December 1824, and was buried in a pauper's grave in the old Clifton Street cemetery in Belfast. For eighty-five years the grave of this once famous preacher, Volunteer and democrat remained unmarked until Francis Joseph Bigger had a headstone put over it.

The indefatigable William Drennan, though he had long since abandoned the United Irishmen, never repudiated his conviction that Ireland had an inalienable right to its own parliament. In an open letter to Pitt in 1799 he declared that if he had to choose between separation from, and union with, Britain, he would prefer the former. In this document he made a biting criticism of the Ascendancy, which he described as:

> The rooted moral and national evil, which must ever stand in the way of social improvement, and has been the peculiar curse of this country . . . [It was] a HABITUAL CONTEMPT (worse than injury) of the common people, generated at first from the spirit of conquest, transferred into penal codes, system of monopolism, and creeds of ascendancy, until it has grown into a disease that affects all the higher order with hereditary contamination.[17]

In his opinion, Britain's long-term interests lay with an independent but friendly Ireland. In a letter to Charles James Fox published in 1806 he spoke of 'a common country and a common right to its civil and political blessings'.[18] He made a powerful attack on the continuing exclusion of Catholics from political power, and condemned the permanent veto which the Tories seemed to have over every suggestion of social improvement. 'Every question of reform was termed sedition', he wrote. 'All concerted pursuit of it, conspiracy; all recurrence to first principles in government, jacobinical philosophy, until the abuse of terms wrought the very evil it affected to deprecate.'

Hamilton Rowan had been persuaded during his exile in Germany that the Union would favour his brand of liberalism, and after making a petition to George III, he was allowed to return to his estates in Ireland in 1806. He continued, however, to support electoral reform, including Catholic emancipation, and became a member of the Catholic Association, strongly associated with Daniel O'Connell. In 1811 he wrote to Lord Fingall: 'One law ought to bind Catholic and Protestant, Jew or Mahometan, if Irishmen.'[19] The following year he was in correspondence with the poet and radical Shelley who was then making a visit to Dublin. In 1818 he was sent an address of welcome by the silk weavers of Dublin who had not forgotten the sympathy he had expressed for them during periods of trade

121

depression. His reply included the phrase, 'I learn how difficult it is for a rich man to enter the kingdom of Heaven.'

James Hope was different from the three previous leaders because of his working-class origin, and when on the run he could often find anonymity and safety among the mass of the population to which he belonged. Where possible he avoided contact with the middle or upper classes, whom he thoroughly mistrusted. Though often in the thick of the struggle, and never far from danger, he was the only important United Irish leader never to be captured or imprisoned. For over a decade, roughly between 1794 and 1806, he moved from town to town, disguising himself as best he could, and usually only one step ahead of the government agents who were constantly on his track. 'I was a marked man, and was compelled for years to wander from place to place, and avoid my enemies', he wrote long after the hue and cry had died down.[20] Working as a weaver, and helped by reliable friends, he carried a gun with him, and swore that he would never be taken alive.[21] On several occasions he was within a hair's breadth of being betrayed by informers, and had to flee hurriedly, leaving his wife and family behind him.

Hope's central conviction, from which he never wavered for more than sixty years, was that it would be the working class – the labourers, the small tenant farmers and the underprivileged – who would, in the long run, prove to be the incorruptible inheritors of the struggle for Irish freedom. Like Tone, he believed in the men of no property, and like McCracken, he claimed that the rich always betray the poor. This egalitarianism he had learned partly from his own knowledge of life as a weaver, and partly from his interpretation of the American and French revolutions. It was reinforced by his personal experience of why the United Irish movement, apparently so strong and numerous in the north, failed at the moment of crisis. Hope blamed the 'Antrim colonels' (chiefly Robert Simms), and what he called 'men of rank and fortune', for the defeats of 1798 and 1803. He never trusted the wealthy classes, in which, he said, 'there never was, and never will be, a majority of honest-principled men'.[22] Social divisions were, in his opinion, at the centre of political

122

struggles, and it was 'the condition of the labouring class' that was 'the fundamental question between the rulers and the people'. Hope died in 1847 at the age of eighty-three, and was buried at Mallusk, County Antrim.

A further survivor of the 1798 era who remained passionately committed to the cause of the underprivileged in Ulster was Mary Ann McCracken.[23] After a thriving career as a textile merchant, Mary spent the rest of her very long life devoted to the culture and welfare of the poorest people in Belfast. A close friend of Edward Bunting, she gave money and help to the fledgling Belfast Harp Society, and encouraged the training of blind harpists. Though she played little part in either Daniel O'Connell's repeal movement or the campaign for Catholic emancipation, she was always on the side of the oppressed. She was a fierce critic of what she described as the 'diabolical system' of Negro slavery in the Americas, and was among those who greeted the English prison reformer, Elizabeth Fry, in Belfast in 1827. For twenty-five years she was secretary of the Belfast Charitable Organisation, and her name became indelibly associated with the education of orphan boys and girls in the city. She kept in touch with James Hope until his death, and died herself in 1866 at the age of ninety-seven.

As so often happens in Irish history when a nationalist movment is politically or militarily defeated, those surviving rebels who are not prepared to concede complete victory to their enemies often turn to other forms of struggle. The poor may adopt sporadic guerrilla tactics of the Whiteboy type, while the educated middle classes often involve themselves in cultural activities. The political vacuum must be filled somehow. Thus when the 1798 rising had become a matter of history, and the shock of Emmet's and Russell's attempts at insurrection had died down somewhat, there remained a core of Ulster people, predominantly middle-class Dissenters, who sought some way in which they could counteract the wave of conservatism and Anglicisation that was sweeping over Ireland after the Union. Where were those who wanted to preserve some shreds of their Irish identity to turn, now that military rebellion and constitutional action had both apparently failed? The answer they found, as had taken place before and would occur again, was in the realm of education, language, literature, music and other aspects of the province's Gaelic folk heritage. If the cause of politics had temporarily failed, then culture might take its place.

The Irish language was then spoken by a large minority, probably about one-third, of the northern population, and it was to this rich source of civilisation that some scholars turned for inspiration. The fact that virtually all these Gaelic speakers were poor and Catholic did not deter these middle-class Dissenters. On the contrary, it was among the dispossessed and illiterate that they hoped to find some of Ulster's most ancient roots.

The individual most energetically involved with these early Gaelic studies was the Reverend William Nelson, a Presbyterian who was noted as much for his enthusiasm for Catholic emancipation as he was for the revival of the old language. Nelson was born in 1774, son of a Presbyterian minister in Rademan, County Down, and educated in Glasgow University, where he showed a remarkable proficiency in both dead and living languages. Though not a United Irishman, he was arrested in 1798 as a suspicious person because he sometimes insisted on preaching in Irish in his native parish. This government intimidation did not prevent him using Gaelic whenever the opportunity arose. In 1808 he published *An Introduction to the Irish Language*, in the preface of which he wrote:

> In this language are preserved the remarkable annals of our country ... It has been said, indeed, that the use of this language should be abolished and the English prevail universally ... it is surely reasonable and desirable that every person should be able to hold converse with his countrymen as well as to taste and admire the beauties of one of the most expressive, philosophically accurate and polished languages that has ever existed.[24]

A colleague of Nelson's, the Reverend Samuel Bryson, whose father had been an United Irishman, also collected and published several Gaelic manuscripts during this period. He was one of the first translators of the old saga, the *Táin*.

In the same year as Nelson published his pioneer work the Belfast Harp Society was founded by three of the city's most prominent intellectual figures, Dr James McDonnell, Henry Joy and William Drennan, all of whom were active in several aspects of the province's cultural life. Its aim was to encourage the study of traditional music, and to follow in Bunting's footsteps by training harpists. Nearly two hundred members joined, and one of their first steps was to raise an annuity for the aged blind harpist, Arthur O'Neill. The society, after various vicissitudes, survived until 1838, and had among its patrons the Marquesses of Hastings and Downshire.

This cultural variety was further stimulated by the expansion of the Linen Hall Library, and the founding in 1814, with the aid of an annual government grant of £1,500, of the Belfast Academical Institution. This school was planned to serve the needs of Belfast's expanding business and professional classes. It also had the function of educating potential Presbyterian ministers. It was predominantly Nonconformist in enrolment but also took some episcopalian and Catholic pupils. It was an unusual organisation in so far as it was both a school and a college. In contrast to the universities of England and Scotland it imposed no religious test on its entrants.

Two of its noted teachers were the Reverend Henry Montgomery, then emerging as a spokesman for liberal Presbyterianism, and the Reverend William Nelson, who was responsible for Hebrew and oriental languages. He was made head of the classics department. At the school's opening ceremony, William Drennan, who was one of the proprietors, said he wanted it to be non-sectarian and a unifying force in the community. 'Pupils of all religious denominations should communicate in the common business of education,' he said, 'by which means a new turn might be given to the national character and habits.'[25] Another founder with similar views was James McAdam, a prosperous iron-founder in the city, and father of the Gaelic scholar, Robert McAdam. Several of the men connected with the school held Arian theological views, and some, such as Robert and William Simms, the Reverend Henry Henry, William

Tennent, and W.B. Neilson, son of Samuel Neilson, had links with 1798.[26]

This liberal ethos irritated the Tories, who constantly sniped at the school's alleged political and religious heresies. Lord Castlereagh and the Duke of Wellington, together with the Reverend William Bruce, headmaster of the rival Belfast Academy, and the Reverend Henry Cooke, went so far as to express publicly their fears that this liberalism might become tainted with republicanism.[27] Sir Robert Peel, who was chief secretary between 1812 and 1819, wanted to appoint an official visitor to the school, who would have power to overrule the managers. In 1816 a row broke out when it was reported that at an unofficial dinner organised by the staff and some friends on Saint Patrick's Day two masters had proposed a toast to 'America, land of liberty and asylum of the oppressed'. Castlereagh immediately intervened to get the school's grant stopped, but this decision was soon reversed.

None of these individuals or groups was strong enough to pose a serious threat to the Government, either in Ulster or elsewhere in Ireland. They were fragmented and never formed a political movement of any significance. Nevertheless, the continuing existence of a body of Dissenters was a constant reminder that the democratic spirit was not completely dead, and that in the province many people of different religious persuasions still held a non-unionist vision of what their country should be like and how it should be governed. Lord Castlereagh and other government officials closely involved with Irish affairs recognised – secretly, if they would not admit it publicly – that the Union legislation had not tackled the most acute social and economic problems in Ireland, and that as long as these existed there would always be the danger that Catholics and Presbyterians might come together again as they had done so threateningly a few years previously. They therefore set out deliberately to isolate the Catholics, and try to win over the Presbyterians to their side.

7

WOOING THE PRESBYTERIANS

We are, I am confident, agreed in opinion that the protestant body
is the sheet anchor and bulwark of the British connection in this
country and when we consider that the [Presbyterian] synod of
Ulster materially influences one half of that body we cannot differ in the incalculable importance of granting and withholding
certificates of qualification for the ministry of that church.

Lord Castlereagh, November 1816[1]

Lord Castlereagh, with his political power bases distributed
between Ulster, Dublin and London, and his experience as chief
secretary during the crucial years 1798–1801, had become highly
skilled in manoeuvring between the conflicting claims of the
various social and religious forces on both sides of the Irish Sea.
As a Presbyterian Whig turned Church of Ireland Tory, and a
rich County Down landlord with personal knowledge of the
plight of tenant farmers and linen merchants, he recognised that
he must reconcile the needs of different classes and pressure
groups. He served in both the Irish and United Kingdom Houses
of Commons, and had been personally acquainted with several
United Irish leaders.

As that curious hybrid, an Anglo-Irish gentleman of Scottish
descent, he had wide contacts with administrators, peers and
MPs in both countries – his correspondence with them runs to

four fat volumes. Perhaps better than any other man of his time, he understood how he could cajole possible allies, or threaten and punish his enemies. Accustomed to dealing with human greed and vanity, his experience of political bribery was unequalled. It had taught him that honour and integrity meant little to most Ascendancy politicians, and that a majority of Irish MPs and peers, already half corrupt, could easily be bought with money, jobs and titles. Wealthy, talented and ambitious, he used Ireland as a springboard to move out from the narrow confines of his Ulster estate to a glittering career in Europe. His aim in life was to serve God, Mammon and the British Empire – but he could never decide which had the priority.

His first tactic, once the 1798 rebellion had been crushed, was to suborn those MPs and peers who could be most immediately useful in passing the Act of Union through the Irish parliament. His second tactic, which was developed secretly, was to look again at the role of the different Churches in Irish society, and to see how they, too, could be manipulated politically. Where corrupt parliamentarians set an example, he hoped that pliable clergy might soon follow. Realising that the situation was very different in the 1800s from what it had been ten years previously, Castlereagh's policy was now to win back the Dissenters into the broad Protestant fold.

The Church of Ireland, he knew, could be relied upon to remain loyal to Crown and empire because its privileges had not been touched. Under the Union it continued to be established with all that meant in the way of power and social status. Tithes had not been abolished. The Church was the biggest single property owner, with approximately 700,000 acres in its possession. The richest dioceses were Derry, with 95,000 acres, and Armagh, with 52,000 acres, and the other twenty averaged between 20,000 and 30,000 each. The 22 bishops, 1,400 parsons and some hundreds of curates served only about one-tenth of the country's population but shared out over £600,000 annually between them. These were 'fantastic prizes for the fortunate clergy', as historian R.B. McDowell admits.[2] The bishops of Dublin and Armagh were paid £12,000 a year each, and the lesser bishops received between

£3,500 and £8,000 a year. These were princely salaries for the time, enabling their recipients to live in great style and luxury. Even the ordinary parsons averaged about £400 to £500 a year, which was eight or ten times the income of a typical Catholic priest or Presbyterian minister. The less fortunate Church of Ireland curates were paid only about £75 a year, plus board and lodging. Many senior clergy were absentees; others were pluralists, that is, they had more than one benefice.

The Catholics were more difficult to corrupt because there were so many of them that the necessary finance could not be found. In any event, Castlereagh despised their religion and detested the politics of the majority, whom he regarded as irretrievably lost to the nationalist and democratic cause. Nevertheless, he still hoped to win some of the middle classes with hints and suggestions that emancipation might be conceded, and he knew he could rely upon the gentry and certain bishops because of their fears of Jacobin ideas. In 1799 he went so far as to propose, again secretly, that Catholic priests should be paid a salary in the same way as Presbyterian ministers were paid the *regium donum*. Conservative bishops, such as Troy of Dublin and Moylan of Cork, favoured such payments, but other bishops and most clergy rejected the idea. The young Daniel O'Connell was strongly against priests getting any stipend from the state on the grounds that it was a bribe, and would have put Catholic clergy under government control.

The Presbyterians' position in the centre of the Irish social structure had not altered much since the original plantations, and they therefore required special attention by those who formed Tory opinion in Britain. Numbering about 450,000 at the turn of the century, they were a minority of only about one in eight or ten of the total Irish population, but in Ulster, where episcopalians numbered about 350,000 and Catholics about 800,000, they held the balance of power.[3] The majority were still tenant farmers, but the urban proportion of artisans, merchants, shopkeepers, manufacturers and professional people was growing. They continued to form, as they had during the eighteenth century, a middle and lower middle class,[4] inclined to

129

waver politically, and therefore not wholly to be relied upon by the authorities. The 180 or so Church ministers were not numerous in relation to the total population, but they were influential locally, and sometimes nationally. The majority were poorly paid, and with an average income of only about £50 or £60 a year, they were almost as badly off as Catholic priests, especially if they had families. The Union had done little to remedy specific grievances, such as high rents, payment of tithes, a restricted franchise, and the continuing snubs they endured from the socially superior episcopalians.

After the French Revolution they had turned towards democracy and republicanism, and formed the solid core of the United Irishmen in Ulster. Militarily defeated in 1798, they had to some extent become weakened and demoralised, but there was still a group with strong Croppy convictions. There were also many liberals who thoroughly disliked everything the Tories stood for. Which way would they turn in the years after the Union which, after all, had done so little for them? If they swung back to the 1798 policy of alliance with the Catholics, then the repeal of the Union was always possible; if, on the other hand, they could be inveigled into forgetting those social and doctrinal differences which separated them from the Established Church and to think of themselves as part of the Ascendancy, then the imperial connection with Britain would never be broken. 'Unite the Protestants and continue to rule over the Catholics' – that was the objective of the more far-sighted and politically shrewd Tories during the first half of the nineteenth century, and indeed for the next 150 years.

In the long run the Government hoped that commercial and business interests in the north would benefit from the expanding linen market, and thus become reconciled to rule from London. This had been one of Pitt's main ambitions for the whole of Ireland since he had first sat at the feet of Adam Smith. Belfast was a special target for this kind of appeal. Lords Londonderry, Castlereagh and Cornwallis – all of whom had a keen appreciation of the biblical maxim that where a man's treasure lay there lay his heart also – had constantly harped on this theme during the negotiations leading up to the Union. The idea of a united kingdom would be recommended by the 'influx of wealth from a more extensive and flourishing commerce of which Belfast is sure to have a principal share', wrote Londonderry in December 1798.[5] A month later his son, Castlereagh, and the viceroy, Cornwallis, were echoing this sentiment.[6]

Within a short period the Government decided to reward financially more susceptible Presbyterian ministers in much the same way as they set out to bribe the more venal Irish MPs and peers in return for supporting the Union. During 1799–1802 Castlereagh was in frequent communication with Lord Cornwallis in Dublin, Pitt and Lord Portland, the home secretary, in London, and the most openly pro-union Presbyterian ministers in Ulster, as to how best they might isolate and weaken those democratic influences which were still strong among dissenting clergy. His chief advisers on Presbyterian affairs in Ulster during this critical period and for some years afterwards were his private secretary Alexander Knox, the Reverend Robert Black of Derry, and the Reverend William Bruce of Belfast. Drennan speaks of Bruce and Castlereagh 'walking hand in hand, in a new alliance of Church and State'.[7] Black was a Tory and unionist, and a theologian of impeccable Calvinist orthodoxy, who in his frequent letters to his aristocratic master showed that he had a strong gift for being at the same time deferential and yet forceful in his views. It was he more than anyone else who succeeded in getting the payment of the *regium donum* stopped to Steel Dickson when the latter was released from prison in 1802, and was invited by the liberal congregation at Keady to be their pastor.

Castlereagh's first step in February 1799 was to submit a secret scheme appropriately entitled 'Plan for strengthening the connection between the government and the Presbyterian synod of Ulster'. This carefully prepared document,[8] full of facts and figures, suggested that the total royal bounty should be increased from £5,900 to £14,400 annually. It then went on to propose that no payment should be made to any minister unless he had first been approved of by the Government, and that instead of each

131

minister being paid the same amount, as hitherto, there should henceforth be three categories of clergy, each group being paid a different sum. In other words, there would be a hierarchical structure of incomes for ministers as in the Church of Ireland and Catholic Church.

To begin with, these proposals were rejected by the then Moderator of the Ulster Synod, the Reverend John Bankhead, on the grounds they would be divisive. Many Church elders also protested that the new scheme would make their ministers more subservient to the Government, and that they would in fact turn them into what they had always claimed not to be – members of an Established Church.

Castlereagh's next move was to ask Black, the agent responsible for paying the royal bounty, to draw up a list of all the Presbyterian ministers in Ireland, with the names of their parishes and the exact amounts of their stipends. Two years later he made the same request with regard to Catholic priests. When eventually published, these returns[9] showed that the typical minister, with a total income of about £50 a year, was not much better off than the average Catholic parish priest. Certainly he was poor in relation to a Church of Ireland parson. For example, in ten parishes in County Down in 1799 the stipends ranged from £70 in Killinchy, Drumbo and Newtownards, £65 in Downpatrick, £60 in Moneyrea, £50 in Castlereagh and Kircubbin, and £40 in Millisle, down to £36 in Holywood. A similar survey made of Catholic priests in the diocese of Down and Connor in 1801 gave the following figures: £90 in Kilmore; £80 in Lower Ards, Portaferry and Lower Glens; £70 in Ahoghill and Drummaul; £50 in Saintfield and Glenarm; and £40 in Rathlin. The priests' incomes often had to be shared with a curate.

In the summer of 1803, after further internal debates, the Ulster synod agreed to a modified form of the original Castlereagh plan, which would give sixty-two ministers £100 a year, sixty-two would get £75, and the remaining sixty-two would get £50. The better paid ministers mostly had town parishes, while the poorer served in the remoter parts of Donegal and Monaghan. Black was rewarded for his services with £400 a year, which almost put him in the same income category as the average Church of Ireland parson.[10]

In these debates, which continued for many years, about the ethics of accepting a government subvention to their incomes numerous Presbyterian ministers sought to salve their consciences by claiming that they would do God's work on earth more effectively if they were free from financial worries. The Government, whatever might be its public stance, had no such doubts in private. All their representatives at Westminster or in Dublin Castle were clear that the increased *regium donum* was a straightforward political bribe. 'A principal object in the increasing and new modelling the allowance was to make them [the Presbyterian ministers] more dependent, and render them more amenable to the government', wrote Lord Portland to the viceroy in August 1799. Three years later Castlereagh was even more explicit in a six-and-a-half-page letter marked 'private', which he sent to the newly appointed prime minister, Henry Addington.

The letter began by reminding Addington that there was still a danger from what Castlereagh described as 'popular' and 'democratic' sentiments among many Presbyterians. The Government must isolate such potential rebels by making it clear that it supported only loyal clergymen. 'The distribution of the fund is the natural engine of authority', he wrote.[11] In order to make sure of this loyalty to Crown and constitution, the money should be paid, not as hitherto to the synod, but directly to individually named clergymen who would then know who was their paymaster. It should be made plain at all times that the bounty was a discretionary gift, which could be withdrawn at the monarch's will. Moreover, only when a certificate of good conduct (by which was meant supporting the Union with Britain) had been sent to the local presbytery would the viceroy graciously ask his majesty to pay up. Castlereagh further made it clear in his letter that the direct payment of ministers would relieve them of the need to rely so much upon their parishioners, especially those elders who were suspected of being democratically inclined.

133

Writing many years after Castlereagh's intervention, the historians of the Presbyterian Church were in no doubt that the offer of a rise in the *regium donum* was a payment for political services. The conservative James Seiton Reid says that the extra money enabled the state to increase its own direct influence over 'the spiritual guides of an important section of the population of Ireland', and helped discountenance any 'spirit of faction or sedition'.[12] The liberal W.T. Latimer took the same view: 'The promise of increasing the Royal Bounty was among the numerous promises to secure the Act of Union.' The offer was a political bribe designed to ensure that 'the large and wealthy congregations would receive more than those which were small and poor'.[13] Peter Brooke, a modern commentator, agrees that there could be no doubt that the Government's intention was 'to undermine the "democratic" nature of Ulster Presbyterianism'. The author's epigrammatic summing up was that Castlereagh sought to achieve the reverse of what Wolfe Tone had hoped for in the 1790s, namely to 'subsume the division of Catholic, Protestant and Dissenter into a common British citizenship'.[14]

As soon as Castlereagh turned his attention away from Ireland towards the wider affairs of Europe he dropped his clerical allies in Belfast. Black then lost much of his influence, and in 1817 after a row about the pensions of ministers' widows he had a nervous breakdown, and committed suicide by jumping off a bridge in Derry.

Castlereagh, who also had a morbid and unstable streak in his character, followed this example by killing himself a few years later. Blackmailed by an unsavoury character who alleged mutual homosexual behaviour, the famous cabinet minister committed suicide, to the horror of his friends and the astonishment of the nation. On hearing the news, the poet Byron expressed the response of much radical English opinion in the notorious lines:

> So Castlereagh has cut his throat! – The worst
> of this is, – that his own was not the first.

By this time a new star had begun to appear on the horizon of conservative Presbyterianism. An even more formidable and long-enduring clergyman than Black, the Reverend Henry Cooke was also a minister of impeccable orthodoxy and political loyalty. And like Black, he had friends at the centre of Tory power in London, particularly Sir Robert Peel. He was destined to be the centre of many religious and political controversies over a period of fifty years. His career became part of unionist folklore; his statue still stands in the centre of Belfast, and the shadow of his ideas continues to fall over Ulster today.

Cooke's father was a poor tenant farmer from County Derry, and was described as 'a plain man with little education' who claimed descent from English Puritans.[15] However, there is some doubt about his ancestry as his name was, in fact, Macook, which suggests Gaelic origins. Henry dropped the 'Mac' and added an 'e' to his name when he went to university. Henry's mother was undoubtedly of Scottish descent and a fervent evangelical who deeply affected the beliefs and style of her gifted son. Ironically in view of his subsequent conservatism, he was baptised by the Reverend John Glendy who was a noted United Irish radical and who became a leader of the New Lights in the 1820s. Curiously also, his first teacher, of whom he spoke with respect, was an Irish-speaking Catholic hedge-school master, 'a pure Milesian' as he afterwards described him affectionately. Cooke's first experience of politics seems to have been at secondary school where he is said to have spoken out against the dangers of Jacobinism. As a boy during the 1798 rising he saw distant fires among neighbouring farms, and heard talk of revolution and French invasion. His family were strong loyalists and hated the United Irishmen. In later years Cooke wrote with passion – he seems to have done everything with fierce conviction – of his fears at that time.

Cooke entered Glasgow University in 1802 to train as a Presbyterian minister, and there met for the first time his fellow Presbyterian, Henry Montgomery, who was destined to be his great rival for nearly six decades. Licensed as a minister in 1808, Cooke first went to a parish near Randalstown, County Antrim, and then to Donegore, which was only a few miles from Montgomery's parish of Dunmurry, to serve the spiritual needs

135

of fifty families, most of whom were said to be 'in affluent circumstances'. It was there he was to find his true vocation as an ultra-orthodox theologian in the strictest Calvinist tradition. So keen was he to further his theological studies – he eventually developed a phenomenal knowledge of the Bible – that he went back to Glasgow for a year, and then more surprisingly to Trinity College Dublin to study anatomy and medicine for a time.

In 1818 he moved to Killyleagh, on the shores of Strangford Lough, where he soon got drawn into that kind of violent doctrinal controversy which characterised his whole life. Killyleagh was unusual in so far as the local gentry, as well as farmers and yeomen, were almost all Presbyterians. In 1796 the local presbytery had been dissolved because of its pro-French sympathies. The lord of the manor was Hamilton Rowan of United Irish fame, now well advanced in years, but still a staunch liberal and a noted supporter of New Light views. His son, Sidney, was an elder in the church, however, and a follower of the Old Lights. Cooke soon got involved in an argument, which began locally and then spread all over Ulster, about an invitation that had been extended by Killyleagh to the Reverend J. Smithurst, a Unitarian from England who held advanced religious and political opinions. Cooke followed this unfortunate clergyman, who had not realised what a hornet's nest he was likely to stir up, preaching against him throughout the province and eventually forcing him to leave Ulster, a chastened man.

This victory over a religious opponent, whom he regarded as a dangerous subversive, gave Cooke a taste for polemics. For the first time he became fully aware of his oratorical gifts, his power as mass agitator, and most important of all, the way in which he could harness for political as well as theological ends that deep streak of Orange sentiment that existed in Ulster society. The stage was thus set for a new struggle for the political as well as the religious soul of Ulster Presbyterianism.

THE BATTLE OF THE SYNODS

> Theological controversies . . . are rarely simply about theological questions.
>
> Finlay Holmes[1]

The main obstacle to the plans of Castlereagh and his agents within the Presbyterian Church were the Arians, who in spite of the defeat in 1798 and the weakening effect of the *regium donum* still continued to be strong and active. Dissenters of various hues, both lay and clerical, still retained much of their old independent spirit, especially with regard to land reform and voting rights. In theology, too, they persisted in arguing for the rights of individual conscience against the powers of the state, the more so since that power had been transferred away from Ireland to Westminster. Their dislike of the aristocracy and the Established Church was unabated. When they joined with the growing demand for Catholic emancipation, they formed a formidable force against the Tory government.

The chief spokesman for these Dissenters was the Reverend Henry Montgomery, Presbyterian minister at Dunmurry, near Belfast, for over fifty years.[2] Montgomery was a powerful theologian and an eloquent orator, and like his archrival, Henry Cooke, he was centre of violent religious and political controversies for many years. In contrast to Cooke, he was generally on the liberal side, at least during his early and middle years.

Montgomery was descended from a middling prosperous Scottish family of farmers and linen bleachers who settled near Templepatrick in Antrim in the seventeenth century. His father was progressive in politics, a New Light adherent, and had served as a lieutenant in the Volunteers in 1782. Significantly,

Montgomery's brothers, William and John, were United Irishmen, William fighting at the Battle of Ballynahinch. Henry, then only a schoolboy, saw both brothers turn out for the rising, hide from yeomen, and then, after various adventures, escape capture. In later years he always spoke sympathetically of the rebels, though condemning the rebellion itself.

In 1802 at the age of fourteen he was sent to Crumlin Academy where he quickly showed those gifts of character and intelligence which were to characterise his long career. Matriculating in 1804, he graduated from Glasgow University three years later with a degree in divinity. There he met, but did not make friends with, Henry Cooke. In 1809 he was licensed to preach at Templepatrick, and within a few months he had moved to Dunmurry in the prosperous Lagan valley. He was associated with this parish for the rest of his life. His stipend was £72 a year (rising to £86) with the use of eight acres of glebe land. This was a reasonable amount for the small parish to raise, as the local farmers were said to be well-to-do.

In 1813 he became involved in an incident that showed both the nature of his politics and his willingness to stand up for a principle, even though it might be unpopular with the more orthodox members of his congregation. Together with the Reverend William Porter of Newtown Limavady, another New Light enthusiast, he took up the case of the persecuted Steel Dickson.

Montgomery, an early ecumenicist, disapproved of all forms of discrimination against fellow Christians. He was quite content to see the Presbyterian Church continue, as it had done for some generations, to be organised loosely in structure, with a membership containing a wide spectrum of religious and social views. He was critical of heresy hunts, and condemned any attempt to impose formal tests or oaths on either the clergy or laity, preferring to let congregations go their own way according to their conscience. Accepting that Old Lights and New Lights disagreed on several issues, he nevertheless still hoped that the different Nonconformist factions could coexist peaceably under the common name of Dissenter.

Cooke, in contrast, had no time for what he regarded as this latitudinarianism and wishy-washy liberalism. A natural authoritarian, with a strong taste for orthodoxy and discipline, he had come to the firm conviction that Presbyterianism had lost its way in Ireland, and was in danger of sinking into a bog of indifferentism and moral laxity. The 1798 rebellion had proved how vulnerable even the most pious were to the attractions of false prophets. As a convinced Calvinist, he believed that doctrinal errors should never be tolerated, and there could be no compromise with what he interpreted as non-biblical teachings. 'We must put down Arianism, or Arianism will put down us,' he said on a famous occasion at Coleraine, County Derry, in 1825.[3]

The battle between these two giants – they were both imposing men, physically as well as intellectually – began at the Newry synod in June 1822, when Cooke proposed the expulsion of those ministers who openly professed Arian views. Appropriately, in view of the loud and angry debate that followed, the discussion took place during a thunderstorm. Montgomery opposed this heresy hunt on the grounds it was divisive and intolerant, and after a bitter argument, in which several delegates spoke vehemently on each side, he temporarily carried the day. Cooke decided to lie low for a few years until new opportunities arose for him and his followers to gather strength. This occurred in 1824–5 when a controversy broke out all over Ireland about a government report on Irish national education. This report, perhaps unintentionally, raised all kinds of fears about who should control the schools, and Cooke, now moderator, emerged for the first time as the chief spokesman for anti-Catholic bigotry in Ulster.

Cooke's strategy during these critical debates was subtle. With his strong sense of contemporary politics, and his close contact with grass-roots opinion in the province, he knew that many Protestants, including orthodox members of his own Church, feared the coming of Catholic emancipation, and objected to any suggestion that 'Papists' might influence school curricula, especially teaching of the Bible. He also knew that the conservative

139

wing of Presbyterianism, now growing more vocal, was hostile to Arianism. On the other hand, in Britain and the south of Ireland, apart from the diehards, Catholic emancipation was seen as inevitable. Irish nationalists and British radicals were agreed that the entry of Catholic MPs to the House of Commons could not be long delayed. Manifestations of extreme Orange bigotry were in disfavour. Cooke thus realised that it would be inopportune to assail the Catholics directly. Tactically it would be shrewder to raise up fears about 'the Papist danger' indirectly, while concentrating his fire against the alleged traitors within the ranks of his own Church. In this way he hoped to make himself champion of the traditional Protestant cause while at the same time attacking his internal enemies at their weakest point, that of religious doctrine.

When giving evidence to the education commission he declared, therefore, that he personally was in favour of emancipation, but implied that this was not true of most Presbyterians. This statement, which was widely publicised, caused offence, as it was designed to do, among Catholics and liberal Dissenters. Daniel O'Connell, ever ready to score a point, called him 'Bully Cooke, the Cock of the North'. Cooke himself, relishing these polemics which added to his popularity in Ulster, went on to add insult to injury by suggesting that Catholics should have equal rights to personal protection, enjoyment of property, profession of religious opinion, and practice of religious worship (all good liberal aims), but that 'the essential Protestantism of the state' must be preserved by ensuring that in Ireland the monarchy and those high offices such as lord chancellor, viceroy, chief secretary and commander-in-chief of the armed forces must be firmly retained by Protestants.

In the 1827 synod at Ballymena, County Antrim, sensing that public opinion in Ulster was beginning to flow in his direction, he made a violent attack on 'the serpent of Arianism'. The following year at Strabane, County Tyrone, he returned to his theme, and got a resolution passed condemning the Unitarian views of the New Light faction. John A. Crozier, Montgomery's biographer, said of these debates:

The cause of Catholic emancipation was at that time making rapid progress; and as the Unitarians were well known to be, without exception, the steady advocates of Catholic enfranchisement, the opportunity was dexterously seized to awaken political hostility throughout all the regions of Calvinism . . . by identifying Orangeism with Orthodoxy, and political liberty with heresy . . . Dr. Cooke speedily became quite an idol with the supporters of the Protestant Ascendancy.[4]

Montgomery counterattacked, and the debate went on for five days, with many eloquent, and sometimes bitter, speeches on each side. At one stage the proceedings became so heated that ministers and elders walked out. By this time, Cooke was clearly in the ascendant, and the liberals in retreat.

Twelve months later at Cookstown, County Tyrone, Cooke decided to press home his advantage. There was no room for compromise in his character, and now that he had the power he decided to strike ruthlessly at his opponents. He was determined, as he put it, to purify the Church of doctrinal error. Indignantly denying that he was an enemy of liberty, as his critics charged, he maintained that true freedom was identified with the British constitution. Arguments about freedom of conscience and rights of individual judgement he dismissed as a further heresy because the Bible was infallible.

It was at this synod that he succeeded in getting another, and this time larger, vote carried against the central principle of Unitarianism that there was only one God. Cooke claimed there were thirty to forty Arians in the synod, and that they had no right to be there. He also persuaded the synod – and this in the long run was to prove a decisive victory for him – that in future all candidates for the ministry would have to be strictly examined by a committee as to their orthodoxy. On this committee he calculated the Old Lights would have a majority.

The battle was resumed at Lurgan, County Armagh, in 1829, with Montgomery speaking on one occasion for two and a half hours, and Cooke replying for two, the whole debate lasting several days. The excitement among both clergy and laymen was intense as everyone realised the moment of crisis had arrived, and the struggle between conservatives and liberals must be decided. So vital were the issues at stake, and so reluctant were some members to avoid a final rupture, that the synod took the unusual decision to hold another meeting.

On this occasion, according to J.L. Porter, Cooke's biographer, out of 219 ministers, 75 licentiates and about 1,200 elders, only 18 ministers, 15 licentiates and 157 elders followed Montgomery.[5] The minority then took the fateful decision to withdraw and in 1830 formed a separate group known as the remonstrant synod of Ulster. Among the eighteen ministers who took Montgomery's side was the Reverend John Mitchel, father of the Young Ireland leader.

Throughout these angry controversies Cooke also waged a relentless war against another focal point of liberal opposition that had long been a particular thorn in his orthodox flesh – the progressive Belfast Academical Institution. In 1822 Cooke had called for an inquiry into the running of the school because it was a 'seminary of Arians'. Cooke's chief ally in this campaign was Sir Robert Peel, who after serving for seven years as chief secretary, was appointed to the key post of home secretary between 1821 and 1827. Cooke and Peel had much in common politically and religiously – they were both Tories and unionists, and did everything they could to delay the inevitable coming of Catholic emancipation. In the same way as Black and Castlereagh had worked closely together, Cooke and Peel kept in close touch, constantly writing to each other and meeting personally, often in secret.

Their joint aim was to get rid of any possible liberals on the school's staff, and replace them with teachers who would be politically and theologically sympathetic to their views. Anyone suspected of Arianism was to be removed and sound Calvinists appointed in their place, especially in the faculties of moral theology, Hebrew and Greek. Cooke's persistent sniping antagonised even some of his evangelical friends, who feared that too much *odium theologicum* would be stirred up. But on this issue as on others he was determined to have his own way, and in 1825 after years of persistent lobbying he persuaded the synod to agree to a new regulation which ensured that any future candidate for a teaching post in the school would first have to be approved by a synodical committee. Henceforth they would appoint staff who, in their own words, would be of 'sound sentiments'.

Teachers and school managers fought back hard to preserve their independence from government or clerical interference, and in a widely debated struggle during 1828–9 they succeeded in defeating the attempts that were made to dismiss the Reverend John Ferrie, professor of moral philosophy, who was charged by his opponents with being an Arian. In the long run, however, the spread of Tory evangelicalism among wide sections of the Protestant population put the liberals of the school on the defensive.[6] It was perhaps a sign of the times that the school added 'Royal' to its name soon afterwards.

On the surface, these fierce polemics, which divided Ulster's Presbyterians so deeply for many years, were about matters of religious doctrine. It was such theological issues as the nature of God, predestination, original sin, and the relationship between the individual conscience and the Bible which apparently separated Old Light from New Light, orthodox from Arian, Trinitarian from Unitarian. But as so often happens in Ulster history there were all the time in the background, shaping and moulding both clerical and lay opinion, wider issues of politics and the social order, of the constitution and property ownership. During 1827–9, for example, the successful campaigns of Daniel O'Connell and the progress of Catholic emancipation were a matter of growing concern to many Protestants who feared that their traditional privileges might be undermined.

The matters which divided Cooke from Montgomery were as much about politics as they were about religion, and behind the sharp debates about the fate of unbaptised infants, or if the Holy Ghost really existed, or whether every word in the Holy Book must be interpreted literally, were more mundane, but perhaps to some, more important, considerations of the distribution of wealth, the possession of land, and the people's right to vote. The language might be divine, but the reality was often

143

very earthly indeed. During the early 1830s it was the 'reality' of tithe payments and the extension of the franchise that became the focus of public debate in Ulster.

9

THE TITHE WAR

[Tithes] . . . an odious impost which stamped them [the Catholics] with the name of slaves in the land of their birth . . . every man should pay for his own church . . . Presbyterians of the north were as determined against tithes as the Catholics of the south.

Sharman Crawford[1]

Tithes had been a painful wound in the Irish body politic for centuries. Introduced during the Reformation to help pay for the newly established Church of Ireland clergy, they bore all the defects of a thoroughly bad tax – they fell most heavily on those least able to bear them; they were paid to Churchmen who already possessed other rich sources of income, and most unfair of all, they were mainly levied on Catholic and Nonconformists to pay for episcopalians. To add insult to injury, episcopalians not only took the money, but then ungratefully heaped contempt upon those they regarded as either idolatrous and superstitious, or else troublesome Dissenters. Among the many scandals of Christendom then afflicting Ireland, this was arguably one of the worst.

It was not surprising, therefore, that the mass of Irish people regarded tithes as a hateful burden. Nationalists and radicals wanted them abolished, and moderate reformers, such as Edmund Burke and Henry Grattan, had during an earlier era criticised them as one of the most serious causes of agrarian unrest. Even the conservative Castlereagh had admitted the need to reform such a blatantly unjust system of raising Church revenue. The only defenders of the system were the bishops and clergy who benefited from them, and the Tory diehards who feared any challenge to property relations.

No doubt inspired by the earlier struggles of the Ribbonmen, violence against the episcopalian clergy and their tax collectors, or proctors, broke out in March 1831, in the parish of Graigue, County Carlow. This was a fertile agricultural district inhabited by about five thousand Catholics and seventy members of the Church of Ireland. The immediate blame for the outbreak lay with the local rector, who as well as refusing to accept that the majority of the population had no moral obligation to pay for a minority Church they detested, was notorious as a proselytiser and rancorous critic of every aspect of Catholicism.

The anti-tithe campaign spread rapidly in the counties of Kilkenny, Cork, Waterford and Tipperary, and within a few years many other parts of the country were involved. When farmers refused to pay the unpopular tax, and as a consequence had their crops and cattle forcibly seized, the violence got worse. Hundreds of police and soldiers, as well as farmers, were injured and scores killed in the struggle that went on until 1834. In many cases the parsons found that their incomes were reduced to a small fraction of their previous level. In the southern provinces this agitation was led by the Catholics, who comprised by far the largest section of the population, and in any event included the poorest tenants.

Among the Catholic hierarchy the most influential critic of tithes was James Doyle, bishop of Kildare and Leighlin. He became famous for a series of letters he published under the signature 'J.K.L.' and was blamed by the Government for stirring up agrarian unrest in 1832. His pastoral letter of that year was certainly a powerful indictment of tithes, but it also included a strong attack on Ribbonism. Indeed, it was addressed, not as might be expected to the Government, landlords or Church of Ireland bishops but to the 'deluded persons illegally combined under the unmeaning appellation of "Blackfeet" and "Whitefeet" '. The language used by the bishop now seems archaic, but the moral message conveyed about the wickedness of trying to use physical force to achieve political ends sounds rather like a contemporary Catholic ecclesiastic condemning the Provisional IRA.[2]

In Ulster the social and demographic extremes were not so clearly marked and the religious groups more evenly balanced numerically than they were in Munster, Connacht and Leinster. Moreover, the tithe burden was not quite so heavy in the northern counties, as may be seen in Table 1.[3] This was due to the fact that only the potato crop was liable to tithes in certain parts of the province (Derry, Tyrone and parts of Donegal); wool was not titheable at all, and flax, a staple crop, paid only a small amount.

TABLE 1

AVERAGE TITHE PAID PER IRISH ACRE IN IRISH PROVINCES, 1831–2

	s.	d.
Leinster		
(sample of 108 parishes)	1.	$7^{1}/_{2}$
Munster		
(sample of 72 parishes)	1.	$2^{1}/_{2}$
Connacht		
(sample of 45 parishes)		$10^{1}/_{4}$
Ulster		
(sample of 81 parishes)		$11^{1}/_{2}$*

*Calculated on a mixture of Irish, English and Scottish acres

In spite of these relative advantages there was widespread discontent among lower and middle tenant farmers in the province, and before many months had passed the north followed the south's example in agitation. Virtually all Catholics, and a large section of Dissenters were still hostile to the establishment on a broad range of issues, and tithes, because they were so obviously unfair, aroused particularly bitter feelings. Priests and Presbyterian ministers, radical MPs, many thousands of farmers, the rural middle classes, as well as potential Ribbonmen and such liberal journals as the *Northern Whig* were all drawn into the struggle. Indeed, the anti-tithe campaign, coinciding as it did with the return of a Whig government in London and subsequent parliamentary reforms, represented the biggest upsurge of democratic sentiment in the north since 1798. Tension at this time was further increased by numerous Orange counterdemonstrations, which frequently led to riots, bloodshed, and even some deaths. Generally the Orangemen supported the tithe system because they feared that any challenge, no matter how justifiable, to the episcopalian monopoly of landed property would undermine the constitution.

The interdenominational character of the anti-tithe movement in Ulster is further illustrated by the fact that two of its most famous leaders were Protestants. The chief spokesman for liberal Presbyterianism was, as might be expected, the Reverend Henry Montgomery, whose taste for political controversy had not been curbed by Cooke's synod victories.

Montgomery had always disliked the close bonds which tied the episcopalian clergy to the landlords, and when the opportunity arose in 1831 to give evidence to two parliamentary committees investigating tithes, he made a wide-ranging attack on every aspect of the Established Church's finances and role in society. The tithe system in his view was a method of taxing a large number of poor people for the benefit of a small number of rich ones, and had been a source of misery and discord for centuries. It was a potent cause of Whiteboyism and encouraged tenants to form 'agrarian combinations'. It was particularly scandalous that the largest emoluments went to bishops, deans and archdeacons who did the least work. The pluralist system, in which certain parsons drew revenues from several parishes but left the work to local curates, was a further abuse of Christian morality. If a Church provided no service there should be no fee. There was the danger that some clergy became so prosperous that they lost touch with their humbler parishioners. The bishops especially were often 'dignified clergymen . . . discharging no ostensible duties and living in splendour and affluence'. Moreover, Church of Ireland clergymen were almost invariably politically motivated, and hostile to the civil rights of both Catholics and Presbyterians. It was contrary to morality as well as to common sense to expect people to pay for the upkeep of the clergy of another denomination. Indeed, it was

148

against the spirit of the gospel to require forced payment to clergymen in any circumstances. 'The Presbyterian conceives, that by compulsory payment of tithe to support a church of whose discipline he disapproves and of whose doctrine he may disapprove, a wound is inflicted on his conscientious feelings', Montgomery concluded.[4]

In the House of Commons one of the strongest anti-tithe voices was that of William Sharman Crawford, a prosperous County Down landlord who in middle age threw off the traditions of his class and creed and joined the liberal reformers. Crawford was an independent-minded and sometimes prickly individual who did not always work well with his radical colleagues, but like Hamilton Rowan before him, he could always be relied upon to defend the underdog. The rights of Irish tenant farmers, the cause of Negro slaves in the West Indies, and the plight of Lancashire cotton operatives all got his sympathetic support. His father, Colonel William Sharman, had been a prominent Volunteer, and served for a time as MP for Lisburn.[5] He opposed the Union. His son William took on the extra name Crawford when his father-in-law died in 1827. Though an early advocate of Catholic emancipation and a well-known opponent of the Orange Order, he was appointed high sheriff of County Down. In 1831 he decided to contest the county constituency as a protest against the long-continued local domination by the Downshire and Londonderry families, and he very nearly defeated the sitting member, the 2nd Viscount Castlereagh. In 1832 he fought the Belfast seat in the general election, and again was only narrowly beaten. In 1835 he was returned unopposed for Dundalk, County Louth, and in 1841 was elected in Rochdale with the support of radicals and Chartists.

Crawford's relations with Daniel O'Connell were complicated and at times acrimonious, mainly because of the latter's refusal to tolerate anyone around him who would not unquestioningly accept his leadership of the repeal movement. O'Connell at first praised him lavishly for supporting Catholic emancipation, but then turned to jeering at him with phrases like 'Sharman, me jewel'. Finally, the two openly quarrelled when Crawford came to the conclusion that O'Connell was backing down in the struggle over tithes.

Crawford was a member of the Church of Ireland, but worked closely with Catholics and Presbyterians in parliament and at meetings all over Ireland. 'The objects for which I am contending are not those of a sect or party', he wrote. 'They are of common interest to the whole population; they are objects for which Catholics and Protestants might struggle hand in hand, in brotherly affection.'

His main interests were in patterns of landownership and how these affected the efficiency of farming methods, and in 1839 he published *A Defence of the Small Farmers of Ireland*[6] in which he attacked the current wisdom that Ireland's food problems were due to overpopulation. On the contrary, he argued that given a proper relation between owner and tenant, small farms could be extremely productive. The comparative prosperity of the Ulster farmers he attributed, not as some did to the religious virtues of Protestants, but to the economic advantages of the Ulster custom. Popular with his own tenants because he reduced rents in time of stress, he was disliked by his fellow landlords who regarded him as a traitor to the Tory cause.

In July 1836, with the help of some Irish and English radical sympathisers, he moved a proposal in the House of Commons to extinguish all tithes in Ireland.[7] Northern Presbyterians were as much against tithes as southern Catholics, he claimed, and the rights of conscience should predominate over the tyranny of establishments. Tithes had begun as a payment for the clergy of the whole people, but had been monopolised by parsons who represented only a minority of the community. Echoing Montgomery, he declared that everyone should pay for the clergy of their own Church, and clergy should not rely upon either the state or members of another Church. In this speech he did not endear himself to the Protestant bishops by arguing that their incomes, then averaging about £7,000 a year, should be reduced to £1,000.

The *Northern Whig*, whose editor was the Unitarian F.D. Finlay, threw all its considerable weight behind this liberal campaign.

In May 1834 the paper organised an anti-tithe conference in its own Belfast office, attended by delegates from twenty parishes in Down and Antrim.[8] Editorially and in its correspondence columns it provided every opportunity to criticise the privileged position of the Church of Ireland.

Typical of letters condemning clerical abuses was one published in January 1834.[9] Writing from Tandragee, County Armagh, under the pseudonym 'Observer', a correspondent made a bitter attack on Thomas Carter, the local dean, who was a pluralist and absentee, and did virtually no work except 'encouraging party spirit'. 'No more ravenous Englishman had come to Ireland "since the days of Strongbow",' said this writer. The dean, it was alleged, was fond of preaching about charity and benevolence, but had recently sent out five hundred processes for unpaid tithes. In a parish in which the majority of the population consisted of Catholics, Methodists and Presbyterians, his income was four times that of all the other clergymen combined. He was paid £500 a year from Ballymore, and a further £500 for his nominal duties in a faraway parish in Galway, for the trouble of 'travelling once a year from Tandragee to Tuam'. In addition, he had a fine rectory and 520 acres of glebe land. Dean Carter, according to this angry correspondent, left nineteen-twentieths of the parish work to his curate who was paid only £75 a year. And most serious charge of all, when cholera spread in the neighbourhood, the dean fled away to safer climes, leaving nursing and pastoral care of the sick to other clergy. Carter, in fact, was not only a pluralist but also a justice of the peace and a noted member of the Orange Order. He was dismissed from his post as magistrate for participating in an Orange demonstration on 12 July 1833 at Tandragee. This procession turned into a riot which led to a subsequent government investigation.

At the grass-roots level there were numerous tenant-farmer demonstrations during this period against tithes. In Protestant areas, like Ards, Drumbo, Comber and Carnmoney, such meetings were usually peaceful, and the issue of the *regium donum* payment was sometimes raised as well as tithes. In the predominantly Catholic counties of Cavan and Donegal the meetings were used as an excuse to make an attack on high rents and the landlord system in general.

Political tension was heightened further during this period by attempts which were made by local Orange lodges to ignore the ban which the Government had imposed on party processions. In November 1830, for example, a band of two hundred armed Orangemen assaulted the inhabitants and burned houses in the little village of Maghery near the mouth of the River Bann. At the Tandragee riot on 12 July 1833 an effigy of a local magistrate who had issued the warrant for the arrest of some local Orangemen was burned, and police officers who tried to keep the peace were abused as 'Papists'.[10]

The most violent of these episodes took place in Keady, in south Armagh, in November 1834, when several hundred tenant farmers assembled to protest against the collection of tithes by the local parson, the Reverend James Blacker, who was also a magistrate. Blacker sought to recover monies which were owing to him, and recruited twenty-nine policemen to try and enforce payment, using his position as magistrate to do so. The sums of money owed by individuals were small, usually only a few shillings, but the landlord decided to employ several bailiffs as well as the constables to drive off cattle and pigs belonging to the offending tenants. Crowds assembled from neighbouring farms, shouting, according to a lengthy report published afterwards,[11] 'No rents! No tithes!', sounding horns and brandishing pitchforks and pikes. Some had the temerity to cry out 'Huzza!' and it was said that farmers came 'from Monaghan, and speaking Irish'. The police opened fire, killing one man and wounding others. The coroner found later that the dead man had been 'murdered by policemen unknown'. A commission was set up to investigate the affray, and the authorities censured Blacker for acting as magistrate in his own case.

Blacker's own account of this episode provides a vivid picture of what happened when a party of armed police were called out to enforce payment of tithes. In his evidence to the commission he said:

152

We started about 7, and arrived about 8; we first stopped at Moore's, at Crossnenagh; he owed tithes for three years; I demanded his tithes from him; he did not offer to pay; I distrained a cow outside; he said we should not keep her long; no attempt was made at rescue; he went up the hill, and shouted out loud; the cow was afterwards released; we next went to Hanratty; he paid; we then went to Hughes, who paid. In Carrickduff, we first met opposition at another Hughes; his doors were locked; he owed a year for 1833; I demanded admission, which was refused; I went to another Hughes, whose house was also shut; on my return the first Hughes said, 'You will go home faster than you came, for by G—d, we will make you'; the police were then in sight of the hill; I arrested him in my capacity as magistrate, and called the police, to whom I gave him in charge; while I was doing so, the people ran up the hill and shouted; he went back to the crowd ... Irwines's miller, Kelly, was very abusive; he would not pay for his tithe; his cow was distrained ... I saw Long and Irwine down; the people were running away; one policeman then fired, but it was because he was falling; the ball passed close to me ... I think I heard 5 or 6 shots fired; I had seen the crowd collecting in all directions; I saw appearance of weapons, pitchforks; one had a turf spade ...[12]

Politically the most significant aspect of this anti-tithe campaign was not so much the violence, which was endemic in Ulster as elsewhere in the country, but the way in which it undermined, albeit temporarily, the strategy which the Tories had planned for Ireland after the Union. It brought Catholic and the poorer Protestant tenant farmers together in a common cause, it aroused radical sympathies in Britain, and it isolated the landlords and episcopalian clergy. Conservative Presbyterian ministers such as Cooke were embarrassed by having to defend a thoroughly unpopular vested interest.

Coincidentally, the campaign also occurred during a period when Orangeism was in disfavour at Westminster among the newly elected Whig government led by Lord Grey, who had opposed the Union, supported Catholic emancipation, and on several occasions opposed the introduction of Coercion Bills in Ireland. The Whigs, though reluctant to act decisively against those who encouraged sectarianism, regarded the Orange Order as essentially a Tory divide-and-rule movement, responsible for stirring up strife between Protestant and Catholic. Radical MPs went further in their criticism: they feared that extremist Protestant sentiment could be used to prevent the introduction of a wide range of social and political reforms in England envisaged for the 1832 Reform Act.

In 1835 a committee of the House of Commons, presided over by the radical MP Joseph Hume, produced a massive series of reports[13] charging the Orange Order with organising illegal processions, the provocation of sectarian strife, and being responsible for bringing the law into contempt by suborning juries and the magistracy. It was also said to be infiltrating the army and navy. The most serious allegation was that the Order was involved in a conspiracy to put William IV's brother, the Duke of Cumberland, on the throne. As a result of this parliamentary indictment, and the obvious disapproval of the king, the grand lodges of Britain and Ireland decided after much internal dissension to dissolve themselves.[14]

So when certain rich Orange landowners, such as Lords Roden and Enniskillen, tried through the Court of Exchequer in January 1835 to recover tithes owing to them (there were lay as well as clerical tithe owners) they got little public support. Roden had been a Tory MP for Dundalk between 1810 and 1820, a member of numerous Protestant proselytising societies, and grand master of the Orange Order. He was a keen evangelical, and a noted preacher of the gospel to the workers on his own estate in County Down.

Landlords were further handicapped at this time by the fact that Thomas Drummond, under-secretary in Dublin, 1835–9, happened to be that rare specimen among British administrators in Ireland, a man of progressive and non-bigoted views. Drummond was hostile to Orangeism, which he regarded as a source of discord and violence, and was responsible in May 1838 for removing between fifty and sixty members of the Order, including several Church of Ireland clergymen, from their posts as justices of the peace. Drummond's statue still stands in

Dublin's city hall with his famous phrase inscribed on its base: 'Property has its duties as well as its rights.'

Finally, in 1837, realising that they could no longer defend the indefensible, the Government introduced a Tithe Commutation Bill, which although it did not abolish tithes completely, reduced them slightly and transferred some payments from tenant to landlord. This ameliorated the worst burden, which was that poor members of one Church had to pay for the upkeep of richer members of another Church.

GOD AND MAMMON

Lay not up for yourselves treasures upon earth, where moth and
rust doth corrupt, and where thieves break through and steal:
But lay up for yourselves treasures in heaven, where neither moth
nor rust doth corrupt, and where thieves do not break through
nor steal: For where your treasure is, there will your heart be
also . . .

No man can serve two masters: for either he will hate the one,
and love the other: or else he will hold to the one, and despise
the other. You cannot serve God and Mammon.

Matthew 6:19–21, 24

The tithe war was only one aspect of the struggle for social justice in Ulster during the 1830s. Simultaneously while the small
farmers were trying to get rid of the onerous tax burden imposed upon them by the Church of Ireland, the middle classes
of all religious denominations strove hard to advance their
electoral rights. This campaign for parliamentary democracy in
the north was given an added impetus by the progress of
Catholic emancipation in the south. In England the liberals
fought energetically to extend the franchise in towns and cities.

The problem in Ireland was that previous electoral reforms,
with all their superficial promises of democratic progress, had
proved disappointing. Words were not matched by deeds, and
hopes too often proved illusory. The extension of the franchise
to certain Catholics in 1793, for example, seemed to break the
repressive mould of centuries, but for a generation after this
legislation had been passed with so much acclaim, the overwhelming majority of Catholics, and many Presbyterians, still
had no right to vote. In the mid-1820s out of a total population

in Ulster of about two million, of whom just under half a million were adult males, only about 76,000 were on the parliamentary register (see Table 2[1]).

TABLE 2

NUMBER OF PARLIAMENTARY CONSTITUENCIES, MPS AND
ELECTORS IN ULSTER, 1815–47

Constituencies	MPs	Population, 1831	No. of electors			
			c. 1815	1831	1832	1847
Antrim County	2	258,000	8,000	2,037	3,487	6,962
Armagh City	1	9,000	13	13	444	838
Armagh County	2	211,000	6,000	1,361	3,342	3,054
Belfast	2*	50,000	13	13	1,659	9,672
Carrickfergus	1	9,000	800	860	1,024	1,426
Cavan County	2	228,000	6,000	1,325	2,248	1,492
Coleraine	1	6,000	36	36	207	891
Donegal County	2	298,000	6,000	667	1,448	848
Down County	2	335,000	15,000	1,990	3,130	2,446
Downpatrick	1	5,000	–	2,220	517	385
Dungannon	1	4,000	13	12	154	438
Enniskillen	1	7,000	15	15	212	273
Fermanagh County	2	143,000	7,000	1,232	1,429	2,193
Lisburn	1	6,000	75	56	91	462
Derry City	1	14,000	1,000	650	611	1,904
Derry County	2	203,000	10,000	878	2,172	4,663
Monaghan County	2	196,000	6,000	1,148	2,139	2,351
Newry	1	13,000	–	2,500	1,017	1,113
Tyrone County	2	299,000	10,000	773	1,151	5,026
Total	29	2,294,000	75,965	17,786	26,482	46,437

*Belfast had one MP up to 1832, then two

The famous forty-shilling freeholders were still prisoners of the landlords because the ballot was not secret, and only the boldest spirits were likely to vote openly against their masters. This meant that in the rural areas the landlords' nominees were almost invariably elected. In towns the situation was even worse as in more than half of them only a tiny minority of burgesses had the franchise. The boroughs of Armagh, Coleraine, Dungannon, Enniskillen and Lisburn, each of which returned

157

one MP, were as 'rotten' as the notorious Old Sarum in Wiltshire. Belfast, with thirteen electors in a population approaching 50,000, was the most undemocratic of all northern towns. As for the candidates, they were virtually all wealthy men, nominees of powerful local families, and invariably (up to Catholic emancipation in 1829) Protestant. Presbyterians were hardly ever chosen as candidates, even in the Whig interest. This gerrymandering was so widespread that even those few privileged people who had the right to vote or stand for parliament often felt helpless in the face of the Ascendancy, and gave up what seemed a futile struggle. The result was that many elections went uncontested.

For example, between 1802 and 1826, when there might have been 133 possible contests in six general elections, only 23 were actually held in Ulster. The remaining 110 were not fought at all. For a quarter of a century there were no contests in County Antrim, County Donegal, County Tyrone, and the boroughs of Armagh, Belfast, Coleraine, Dungannon, Lisburn and Derry. In the 1802 election less than 1,000 people voted in all the constituencies combined, and in 1812 the number was about 1,500. The lowest point of all in this electoral farce was in 1820 when 342 people recorded their votes. The biggest total was in 1826 when just under 12,000 went to the polls.

The electoral reforms of 1829 aroused keen hopes that the long night of parliamentary discrimination against Catholics was coming to an end. Daniel O'Connell's victory in County Clare the previous year had enthused all liberals, Protestant as well as Catholic, English as well as Irish. The way seemed open for a genuine enlargement of democracy.

Unfortunately the Catholic Emancipation Act of 1829, though progressive in some parts, was regressive in others. Not only did it continue to debar Catholics from the monarchy and the highest positions in the kingdom, including the lord chancellor, viceroy, chief secretary, and commander-in-chief of the armed forces, but it also left control of Ireland in the hands of a parliament which was overwhelmingly Protestant and Anglo-Saxon in outlook. Moreover, it did not increase the number of Irish people entitled to vote, but on the contrary actually reduced it substantially. The decision to abolish the forty-shilling freeholder vote and substitute a minimum qualification of £10 decreased the number of parliamentary electors in the nine Ulster counties from about 76,000 to under 20,000. The population of the north at this time was reckoned to be just under 2,300,000.

The Presbyterians were particularly disappointed with these measures as they had gained very little directly from the 1829 act. Indeed, though the liberals among them welcomed the long overdue concessions to Catholics, they now found that they had fewer rather than more votes available. This frustration was one of the reasons why Henry Montgomery took the lead in the electoral reform agitation, as he had done over tithes. At a meeting in Belfast in December 1830 he made a powerful attack on the so-called 'constitution', which was, in his opinion, a fraud and delusion. The very word was used to confuse people; it was, he said, 'a sort of sacred relic' or 'talismatic charm'.[2] Freeholders were nominally free to vote, but in reality had to do as their landlords told them. Theoretically there was liberty, he said, but in practice there was slavery. The rotten boroughs were 'sinks of pollution and foul stains upon the morals and character of the country'. The unreformed electoral system contaminated the body politic:

> It suppresses public opinion – demoralises the peasant – makes a tyrant of the landlord – puts slaves and speculators into parliament – corrupts the army and navy – and fills the country with placemen and pensioners. Nay, the very sanctuary is not free from pollution – it is a powerful enemy of Church preferment – it places mitr ipon heads who have no other qualifications but political pliancy – it poisons the very fountains of justice.[3]

Montgomery's strong language about the abuses of democracy was no doubt partly inspired by the knowledge that similar views were being expressed in England, where a powerful anti-Tory reform movement was building up among the disenfranchised manufacturing and merchant classes of the towns and cities. In 1830 the Tories were defeated, after several decades in office, and Sir Robert Peel and the prime minister, the Duke of Wellington, were forced by popular demonstrations to resign. The new Whig administration led by Lord Grey came into office, pledged to reform the electoral system. During the critical debates leading up to the Reform Act of 1832, when the people were deeply divided and the country seemed on the verge of civil strife, Daniel O'Connell and his newly elected followers in the Irish Party helped tip the balance in favour of Grey in the House of Commons. O'Connell himself spoke eloquently in these debates. The act increased the number of voters in Britain from 438,000 (or 4.4 per cent of the adult population aged twenty or over) to 721,000 (or 7.1 per cent). It abolished rotten boroughs, and gave a fairer share of the votes to the rapidly expanding cities.

The same year, largely as a sop to Irish public opinion, the Representation of the People (Ireland) Act was passed against the wishes of the Tories but with the support of Daniel O'Connell and the Irish repealers now sitting in the House of Commons. It maintained the £10 freehold qualification in the counties, but extended the franchise to men holding leaseholds of £20 and upwards. The main improvement was in the borough qualification, which now included the £10 freeholders. The number of MPs who could represent Trinity College Dublin and the cities of Dublin, Cork, Limerick, Galway, Waterford and Belfast was increased to two each. The most striking change in the franchise was in Belfast, where the number of parliamentary electors rose from a mere thirteen to more than one hundred times that number (see Table 2). As a result of this partial democratisation of the franchise, when the next general election was held late in 1832, eight Liberal MPs, or just over one quarter of the total for Ulster, were elected, one from Antrim County, one from Armagh City, one from Armagh County, two from Belfast, one from Down County, one from Derry City and one from Monaghan County.

The very limited nature of the 1832 Reform Act, however, may be seen in the fact that even under the new electoral system only about 26,000, or between 4 and 5 per cent of adult males, had the right to vote in Ulster. Catholics, though nominally enfranchised, continued to be discriminated against because of the property qualification. The best evidence of this discrimination is that, though Catholics comprised nearly half the total population in the province, they did not return a nationalist MP until Isaac Butt, a Protestant, was elected in County Monaghan in 1871.

The successful election of the Liberal MPs – four from the Protestant heartlands of Down, Antrim and Belfast – coinciding as it did with the anti-tithe agitation, spreading agrarian crime, and the advance of O'Connell's repeal of the Union movement, alarmed those conservatives who feared that revolution was just round the corner. Dreading, above all, the revival of that alliance between Catholics and Dissenters, which had characterised 1798, they began once again to revive that 'unite-the-Protestants' policy Castlereagh had initiated thirty years before. By emphasising the importance of property rights and law-and-order themes they hoped to win over those Presbyterians who might be frightened by ultra-democratic or allegedly Jacobin sentiments. Their main instrument in trying to achieve this aim of Protestant solidarity was, as might be expected, the Reverend Henry Cooke.

Cooke had already proved himself a shrewd political manipulator. His Tory credentials were well established, and he had deep roots in the powerful evangelical movement to which many Ulster Protestants belonged. He was thus the natural choice to become chief spokesman for the anti-reform campaign which gathered pace during this period, culminating in a big demonstration at Hillsborough, County Down, in October 1834.

This huge meeting – there were said to be present 40,000 'yeomen and gentry' from Antrim and Down – marked a key stage in Cooke's career. There was a wide cross section of the Protestant community present, ranging from the aristocracy to poor tenant farmers. On the platform sat the beauty and prowess of the northern Ascendancy, including eight lords (Castlereagh, Clanwilliam, Londonderry, Roden, Donegall, Hill, Dufferin and Hillsborough), seven countesses, eight Church of

Ireland and seven Nonconformist clergymen, and several MPs and army officers.

Cooke was the star speaker, and sensing the mood of his audience, developed those themes best calculated to appeal to the traditional Orange spirit.[4] Emphasising the importance of class collaboration, he went on to stress the need for the coming together of all Protestant forces against the 'Papist' threat. In his opinion it was only through such a realignment of social and religious groups, and the dampening down of all social struggles, that the overall Ascendancy could be maintained. It was only through this combining of all Protestants, dissenting as well as established, poor as well as rich, that the nationalists could be defeated.

Cooke began by appealing for a reconciliation between landlords and tenants, and the observance of what he described as 'the relative duties of rulers and ruled'. He then went on to appeal to Presbyterians (but significantly not to the followers of Montgomery) to forget their quarrels with the Established Church, and join together in defence of their privileges and the Union. In a striking phrase, which was widely reported in Ireland and Britain, he spoke of a 'marriage' between all good-thinking Protestants:

> I trust I see more in this meeting than a mere eliciting of public opinion or a mere gathering of the clans. I trust I see in it the pledge of Protestant union and co-operation. Between the divided Churches I publish the banns of a second marriage of Christian forbearance where they differ, of Christian love where they agree, and of Christian co-operation in all matters where their common safety is concerned.[5]

Critics pointed out that Cooke's 'Christian love' did not extend to Catholics.

The 2nd Viscount Castlereagh, in an impassioned defence of the Ascendancy which was marred somewhat by shouts from the crowd of 'No tithes!' and 'Half rents!', made the same point as Cooke. 'It is quite true that there is an Established Church and a Presbyterian Church,' he said. 'But . . . if one be destroyed,

162

the sister in religion cannot long survive. These two Churches appear to me like streams springing from the one pure source.'[6]

The crowd gave Cooke a great ovation – from then on he was known as the chief anti-Catholic preacher in the British Isles – not only for the content of his speech, but for his powers of oratory. By now he had become widely experienced in the management of large gatherings of people, and on this occasion he excelled himself with a persuasive mixture of politics and religion, skilfully playing on all the prejudices of his audience. The lords and ladies liked his deference to the aristocracy; the episcopalians were delighted with his friendly remarks about their Church; the tenants responded warmly to his special brand of evangelical preaching – half political demagogy and half hell-fire threats – with its constant references to the Bible, the blood of martyrs, and the ever-present threat of the Pope and Popery. It was at Hillsborough that extreme Toryism and Protestant fundamentalism first came together successfully in a mass meeting.

Naturally these speeches were strongly criticised by liberals and nationalists. Catholics all over the country regarded them as flagrant examples of bigotry, and Daniel O'Connell was provoked to repeat his gibe about 'Bully Cooke, the Cock of the North'. The moderator of the Ulster synod, the Reverend William McClure, wrote immediately to the press saying that Cooke's views were not those of the Presbyterian Church as a whole. In England the radicals were dismayed at this demonstration of the power of Orangeism. The *Northern Whig* got up a petition which was signed by 137 Protestants dissociating themselves from the Tories. Critical editorials described the meeting as an example of 'Episcopalian Ascendancy and Conservative corruption', and the poorer people who attended were called 'enslaved tenantry' and 'rent-ground serfs'.[7] Cooke himself was criticised as 'fawning'.

What was so remarkable about these anti-repeal meetings was not so much the inevitable warnings about the alleged dangers of a Catholic ascendancy replacing a Protestant one, but the repeated references to industry and commerce, especially the

163

importance of the growing trade with Britain. At all the meetings organised in the north against repeal one of the most popular arguments used was concerned with the economic advantages Ulster's industries were getting from the Union. Cooke, for example, with his undoubted gift for sensing which way the wind was blowing, turned his eloquence from theology to economics. Speaking in Belfast in January 1841 he said:

> Look at the town of Belfast. When I was a youth it was almost a village. But what a glorious sight does it now present! The masted grove within our harbour – our mighty warehouses teeming with the wealth of every clime – our giant manufactures lifting themselves on every side – and all this we owe to the Union.[5]

The local Tory MP, J.E. Tennent, took up the same theme at a similar meeting the following day: 'No human being of ordinary intelligence can doubt the blessings that Ulster has derived from the Union, who sees the forests of masts that are moving in the harbour, or counts the multitude of her factory chimneys.'

All this rhetoric about harbours, ships' masts and warehouses was a shrewd tactical move on the part of the Ulster Tories. It shifted the emphasis away from the indefensible issues of land and the franchise to areas where an urban audience was likely to prove more responsive. In particular, it touched a deep chord in the hearts of those middle-class Presbyterians who were beginning to do well financially out of the expanding trade with Britain and the empire.

Forty years previously the first Lord Castlereagh had promised such benefits to the northern loyalists, and some of his prophecies were coming true. The linen trade, particularly, entered a period of steady expansion, especially after the changeover from domestic to factory production. Technical progress, such as the wet-spinning process introduced in 1825, and the gradual replacement of water by steam power, encouraged the growth of large-scale manufacturing enterprises, employing hundreds of men and women, and needing large amounts of capital. By the middle of the century the acreage under flax had risen to about 60,000 as compared to a total of

2,600 in the other three provinces. The number of spinners in Belfast increased to about 20,000. Engineering also expanded, both in its own right and as an adjunct of the linen industry. The foundations began to be laid for the shipbuilding industry that later proved so important in Ulster. There was a spread of railways in the Lagan valley, and the development of joint-stock banks.

Belfast took the lead in this industrial progress, and the population, which was only about 20,000 at the beginning of the century, rose to 37,000 in 1821, 50,000 in 1831, 75,000 in 1841, and 103,000 in 1851. In 1851 there was reckoned to be 28,000 men and 17,000 women employed in the city's flourishing factories. Lisburn, Portadown and Lurgan (all predominantly Protestant towns) also prospered as centres of the linen trade.

As a result of these economic changes, a strong middle class, consisting of manufacturers, merchants, bankers and richer professional people, developed in Ulster, and began to challenge the supremacy of the still feudal-minded aristocracy. The word 'Ascendancy' eventually took on a new meaning, as the names of Barbour, Mulholland, Richardson, Ewart, Harland (and later Craig) caught up in wealth and power with the Londonderrys, Hertfords, Archdales, Brookes, Abercorns and Downshires. Simultaneously, the white-collar and shopkeeping sections of the population grew in numbers. Lower down the social scale, but still better paid and more secure in their jobs than the mass of predominantly Catholic labourers, were tens of thousands of skilled artisans, the 'respectable' rather than the 'rough' members of the working class. The overwhelming majority of these relatively privileged classes were Protestants, predominantly Presbyterian,[9] but including many episcopalians, and some Quakers, Methodists and Baptists. Catholics were kept out of skilled trades by discrimination in apprenticeship and employment practices. Only a few succeeded after a hard struggle in entering business and the professions.

Ideologically the most significant aspect of this increasingly influential class was that it was firmly wedded to the principles of *laissez-faire* and the rights of private property. Like their co-religionists in other parts of the world, they tended to identify the Reformed Churches with their own advancement, and Godliness with material progress. To satisfy their consciences about the continuing poverty of the majority of the population, especially Catholics, they associated their financial success with the Puritan virtues of sobriety, thrift and hard work.[10]

Many northern businessmen gradually became convinced imperialists who identified free trade with the benefits that flowed from exporting linen, ships and engineering products to Britain and the colonies. For them the flag followed trade, and it was inevitable that Belfast would become less of an Irish and more of a British city. The *Northern Whig*, which represented such mercantile views, was in no doubt where the loyalties of Ulster's manufacturing and commercial class should lie:

> We are not devoid of national feeling, but as an industrious and enterprising people we are a thousand times more closely bound up with Liverpool and Glasgow, with Lanarkshire and Lancaster, than with all Munster taken together . . . Considerations of profit and loss press heavily upon us, and we cannot disregard them if we would.[11]

Such arguments about God and Mammon – the demands of conscience as against the pressures of materialism – inevitably revived the old controversy about the propriety of Presbyterian ministers continuing to accept the *regium donum*. Most ministers, in keeping with the utilitarian spirit of the times, wanted to keep it, but others were doubtful. The liberal Reverend Henry Montgomery had raised the issue in 1831–2 when he was giving evidence to the tithe commission. 'I freely admit,' he said, 'that the *regium donum* might be considered an improper grant . . . in abstract right and strict Christian equity I think we are not entitled to the *regium donum*.'[12] The *Northern Whig*, which was then in a more radical mood, took up Montgomery's point and published an article entitled 'More Regium, alias more Royal Bribery'. Sharman Crawford, who was at that time beginning to make himself a reputation as a radical MP, also criticised the government bounty on moral grounds. In spite of these criticisms, the minimum grant was raised to £75 a year in 1838. Significantly it was the high Tories, such as Peel, Wellington, and later Disraeli, who favoured helping the ministers financially.[13]

In the process of internalising these social-cum-moral values, the Protestant middle classes were helped by the spread of evangelical doctrines, which taught that it was personal salvation rather than political reform upon which good Christians should concentrate their energies. Faith, said these missionaries, was more important than good works, and the key question was not so much 'Do you love your neighbour?', but 'Are you saved?' Emotion (or enthusiasm) could win more converts than reason; and justification (or the pardon of sins) could be best achieved by a simple trust in God's word.

Evangelicalism, with its emphasis on the innate depravity of mankind and the need for instant conversion to the true gospel if one was to be saved from damnation, had a long tradition among the Protestants of Europe and North America, especially among the lower middle classes and struggling workers and small farmers. John Wesley had recruited millions of followers in the eighteenth century, and his emotional preaching and hymn-singing techniques were admired by many Lutherans, Baptists, Presbyterians, and even some Anglicans, as well as Methodists. Calvinist doctrines about predestination and original sin were already firmly established among many Presbyterians in Ulster. Historically it was noticeable that these revivalist movements were generally associated with periods of rapid economic and social change, when communities or individuals might feel their cherished values threatened.

Such a turbulent era occurred during the 1830s and 1840s, when on both sides of the Irish Sea, there seemed to be all kinds of dangerous enemies undermining the established order. The social climate became right for what became known as 'the new Reformation'. In Britain there was political unrest following the 1832 Reform Act, and deep divisions arising from Chartist and anti-Corn Law agitations. The working class, led by, amongst others, the Irish emigrants Feargus O'Connor and Bronterre O'Brien, strove for a wide range of democratic reforms, including a wider franchise, no property qualifications for parliamentary candidates, and payment for MPs. The urban population wanted free trade because they thought it would bring cheaper food and better opportunities to export manufactured goods. Irish immigrant labourers were flocking into the towns and cities, bringing with them poverty, the threat of disease, and an alien culture and religion. Among many educated Protestants there was anxiety about the Oxford movement, which was allegedly bringing Catholic doctrines and rituals back into the Church of England. The defection of the famous scholar and writer John Henry Newman from the Anglican to the Catholic Church caused a sensation.

In Ireland Daniel O'Connell's repeal campaign was winning enthusiastic support from millions of people, and Thomas Davis and Charles Gavan Duffy were beginning to offer a vision of Irish nationality which would, as in 1798, unite men and women of all religions.

It was in 1845, in the midst of this social and intellectual turmoil when the 'Protestant constitution' seemed under attack from so many quarters, that the Tory prime minister, Sir Robert Peel, decided to raise the annual grant of Maynooth College, the Catholic seminary, from £9,000 to £26,000.[14] This increase, which could in no circumstances seriously affect the country's finances, immediately provoked a loud public outcry in which MPs, the press, cabinet ministers and the Protestant clergy angrily joined.

In spite of his preoccupation with the Corn Law debate, Peel persevered with his bill, encouraged by his rival William Ewart Gladstone. Eventually after much violent controversy the bishops at Maynooth got their cash. However, to emphasise that ultra-Protestants were not going to tolerate any further pandering to the despised 'Papists', a world evangelical council was set up in Exeter Hall, London, in March 1845. Its main aim was to bring together the various Protestant Churches throughout the world by playing down the doctrinal and ritualistic differences that separated them, and stressing certain biblical truths to which it was hoped all Protestants could subscribe. Lord Roden, the Orange spokesman from Ulster, described this attempt at Protestant solidarity as a 'holy union'.[15]

But, as events were so dramatically to show within the next twelve months, neither the 'holy union' advocated by Lord Roden, nor the wider constitutional Union initiated by Pitt and Castlereagh, could solve the country's problems when the potato crop failed and millions of people began to starve. The famine, more than any other occurrence during the nineteenth century, proved how bankrupt in every sense – politically, economically and morally – was the rule of the Ascendancy and its British allies in Ireland.

11

'ILL FARES THE LAND'

The terrible march of famine is agitating the hearts of the people, and threatening to shake society to its roots.

Northern Whig, 7 January 1847

The Irish system of land tenure in the mid-nineteenth century was one of the worst in western Europe. The fate of several million people lay in the hands of a few thousand proprietors who possessed virtually all the country's soil. About two hundred of the richest families owned no less than five million acres, or one-quarter of the total for the four provinces. The overwhelming majority of these feudal lords were alien to the mass of the people in national loyalties, culture, language and religion. Nearly all were Anglicans in a country in which nine-tenths of the people were Catholics or Nonconformists. Many were absentees from their estates, leaving the management of their properties to bailiffs or agents whose main concern was not the welfare of the tenants but the size of the rent rolls. In all these respects there had been little change since the seventeenth- and eighteenth-century plantations.

The soil, upon which the bulk of the Irish economy depended, was divided up into a large number of small – often tiny – holdings. According to the 1841 census (the first of its kind), there were no less than 686,000 farm units with a rural population of nearly ten times that number. Almost half these farms (small holdings or potato patches would be a better description) were of less than five acres, and four-fifths were less than fifteen acres in size. This was during a period when it was officially estimated that eight acres was the absolute minimum upon

170

which a poor family could subsist. Only 7 per cent were bigger than thirty acres, which is now considered a small farm in Ireland. It was, as has been said, 'an economist's nightmare'. For most tenants there was little security of tenure. If they could not pay their rent they had no protection against eviction. Their hold on the soil upon which everything – food, clothing, shelter, life itself – depended was at the whim of the landlord.

Historians of this period sometimes suggest that while these criticisms might well apply to Leinster, Munster and Connacht, they were not necessarily true of the northern province. The impression is often conveyed, perhaps by implication rather than by direct statement, that Ulster was somehow different and that land issues there were not contentious. It is purported that the worst effects of the great famine there were avoided, and that as a result there was little agrarian unrest. Certainly there have been far fewer books written about the tenant-right agitation of the north as compared with the Land League campaign of the south.

The truth is that while Ulster tenant farmers had certain financial advantages, such as the right to sell the goodwill of their land, and sometimes had an alternative source of income from linen, this did not alter the crucial economic fact that the agricultural system was basically the same all over the country. There might be minor differences in rural social conditions between north and south, but in most respects the relationships between tenant farmers and their masters was similar throughout Ireland. In Ulster there were the same divisions between rich and poor, between those who owned the land and those who worked it, between property and labour. In Tyrone and Derry there was the same pattern as in Cork and Kerry of a few dozen families owning vast acreages while impoverished tenants scraped a living on tiny plots of soil. At one extreme were the aristocrats with incomes of £50,000 or more per year, and at the other end of the social scale were labourers earning less than a shilling a day. And contrary to current popular impression, there were many poor Presbyterians as well as Catholics suffering from high rents and threats of eviction. It was Armagh rather than

171

Mayo or Kerry that was the most thickly populated county in Ireland in 1841. The official statistics, which were published during the 1840s, show that, if anything, Ulster was worse off than the other three provinces with regard to the crucial issues of concentration of landownership, a large proportion of very small farms, and high density of population.

The precise details of landownership in the province[1] were not published until a generation later, but enough evidence is available to show that in the mid-1840s, out of a total of 5,250,000 acres, two-fifths were in the possession of about one hundred families or London livery companies, and four-fifths were owned by about 1,000 proprietors. In all, out of a total of about 1,500,000 adult population there were only about 6,000 owning any land at all.

The Devon Commission of 1845 threw a revealing light on the extraordinary wealth and influence of certain individuals in pre-famine Ulster.[2] To take some of the most striking examples: it showed that Lord Hertford then owned 66,000 acres in Antrim, on which lived no fewer than 51,000 people; the Marquess of Abercorn owned 43,000 acres in Tyrone (he also had 16,000 acres in Donegal, and 6,000 in Derry), the estate being divided up into 1,041 farms with 16,168 inhabitants; Mr. E.P. Shirley owned 32,000 acres in Cavan, with 20,500 inhabitants; Lord Antrim owned 29,000 acres in Antrim, with 7,667 inhabitants; Lord Lurgan owned 24,600 acres in Armagh, with 23,800 inhabitants; and the Marquess of Bath owned 15,000 acres around Carrickmacross, County Monaghan, with 20,000 inhabitants. Bath's income from this land was between £18,000 and £19,000 a year. About a dozen London companies also had large estates, the biggest being the Drapers, with 26,000 acres, Fishmongers, with 20,000 and Ironmongers, with 13,000 – all in County Derry.

In contrast to these few hundred barons and squires, with their huge demesnes and rich life styles, there were about a quarter of a million small tenant farmers. The surprising fact is that Ulster before the famine – and again contrary to popular impression – had a higher proportion of small, or very small, farms than either Leinster or Munster. Only in Connacht were there relatively more of these dwarf holdings. Forty-three per cent of Ulster tenants were living (or trying to live) on less than five acres. Eighty-five per cent had less than fifteen acres, and only 4 per cent more than thirty acres (see Table 3[3]).

TABLE 3

SIZE OF FARMS IN IRELAND, 1841

	Statute Acres							
	1–5		**5–15**		**15–30**		**30 or more**	
	No. of farms	%	No. of farms	%	No. of farms	%	No. of farms	%
Leinster	49,000	37	46,000	34	21,000	16	18,000	13
Munster	57,000	35	61,000	38	27,000	17	17,000	10
Ulster	101,000	43	99,000	42	25,000	11	10,000	4
Connacht	100,000	65	45,000	29	6,000	4	4,000	3
Ireland	307,000	45	251,000	37	79,000	12	49,000	7

At the bottom of the social pyramid were about 100,000 tenants, who with their families comprised between one-fifth and one-quarter of the total population of Ulster, renting a few acres of soil, often on the sides of mountains or in the less fertile valleys. The great majority of these cottiers had incomes of less than ten shillings a week, which they could sometimes supplement by labouring for local wealthy farmers or landlords, or occasionally by spinning and weaving linen. They usually lived in small cabins or two-roomed cottages. Generally they married young, and had families averaging from six to eight children. Most miserable of all were the labourers earning about 6d. to 9d. a day.

The rural poor of Ulster, like their fellows in the other three provinces, were extraordinarily reliant upon one crop, the potato, as the main – almost the sole – source of their diet. As a staple vegetable, the potato had certain advantages. The tuber was highly productive, and could be grown on poor soil and in a damp climate. The tools needed for cultivation were simple. It was estimated that on a few acres enough potatoes could be grown to feed an average family for a year. As a diet it was, if monotonous, palatable and nutritious, and a man or woman could eat several pounds per head per day. Pigs also flourished on the potato.

The danger of such a restricted diet was that farmers were dependent upon a single crop, not only for their livelihood but for their very existence. When the harvest was good they could survive just above starvation level but during bad seasons they sank into destitution. Their vulnerability to natural catastrophes was aggravated by the fact that the other products they might hope to consume or sell – wheat, oats, eggs, bacon, pork, beef, flax – were to a large extent earmarked to pay the rent. If they did not pay the landlords, they could be evicted, and this was worse than even the endemic malnutrition and poverty they regularly endured.

The province also suffered severely from that other economic difficulty of the time – a rapidly growing population and intense pressure on land resources. The seriousness of this problem for the mass of the people may be gauged from the fact that more than four-fifths lived in rural areas, and about two-thirds depended upon agriculture as their main source of livelihood. Land hunger was in certain respects even more intense in the north than in the south and west. 'In Mayo there were 2¾ acres of arable land per head of the population and in Galway 3½ acres,' says the historian E.R.R. Green. 'There were only 1¼ acres of arable land per head of the population in Co. Armagh and 1½ acres in Co. Down.'[4]

The population of Ireland as a whole had risen, it is estimated, from 2.5 million in the mid-eighteenth century to about 4.5 million in 1800, 6.8 million in 1821, and 7.8 million in 1831. By the time of the 1841 census it had reached 8.2 million. Ulster's share of the total was then about 30 per cent in a land area of about 25 per cent of all Ireland. The result was that the nine northern counties had both the highest overall density of population, and the highest concentration per arable acre (see Table 4[5]).

Politically, the important thing about this yawning gap between those who owned property and those who did not was that it was not a simple division between Protestant and Catholic. The landlords were, of course, overwhelmingly Anglican in persuasion, and the most underprivileged tenants were predominantly Catholic, but of the half or more of tenants who had what were then regarded as medium-sized farms (that is, those with ten, fifteen or twenty acres), a high proportion were Presbyterians. And these, too, were often near the poverty line and just as vulnerable to all those hazards of the time – potato blight, evictions, rising rents, or threats to the Ulster custom – as were their fellow Catholics. So when the famine came, and rural society began to disintegrate, poor Presbyterians joined with poor Catholics in a common struggle to try to protect their living standards.

TABLE 4

DENSITY OF POPULATION IN FOUR PROVINCES OF IRELAND, 1841

	No. of persons per sq. mile of arable land	No. of persons per sq. mile
Leinster	247	202
Munster	332	212
Ulster	406	253
Connacht	335	217

A system of landownership, similar in some respects to that of the *ancien régime* in France or Russia under the Tsars,[6] was not the only feudal characteristic of Ulster in the mid-nineteenth century. Politically, the franchise was still so restricted and the electoral system so gerrymandered that any notion of a genuine parliamentary democracy was, as it had always been, a farce. The phrase 'civil and religious liberties' was as much a sham as it had been a generation earlier because the vast majority of the population continued to have no say as to who should represent them in the House of Commons. The reality was that the big landlords monopolised political as well as economic and social power through their grip on the Conservative Party and the close ties they had with their fellow Tories in England. The Whigs were only marginally more democratic.

A few figures, and the mention of certain family names, illustrate how little the electoral system had changed since the 1820s and 1830s. To begin with, the property qualification still restricted the franchise to a narrow social base consisting of the upper and middle classes. By 1847, for example, the number entitled to vote in the nine northern counties had risen to 46,000 in a total population of about 2.4 million. This represented about one in ten of all adult males. In certain counties such as Donegal and Cavan, each with populations in the region of a quarter of a million, less than two thousand people in each constituency were electors. The Catholics as always suffered most deprivation because they generally belonged to the poorest sections of the population, and thus were excluded from the franchise. In total, probably not more than about five thousand Catholics had the right to vote out of a Catholic population of over one million. Moreover, even for those who were fortunate to have a vote there was usually very little choice of candidate. Generation after generation the names of certain powerful families recur as MPs in certain constituencies – the Leslies and Dawsons in Monaghan; Corrys, Knoxes, Lowrys and Hamiltons in Tyrone; Hills, Stewarts, Castlereaghs and Kers in Down; Verners in Armagh; Chichesters and Tennents in Belfast; Coles, Archdales and Brookes in Fermanagh.[7] To become an MP was often a stepping stone to further preferment as a judge, government official, colonial governor, or, for those who aspired to rise particularly high, a post at Queen Victoria's court. The officer caste in the army and navy was constantly replenished with the young sons of this junker class. For those of a more studious bent there were good careers in the Established Church as rectors, archdeacons or bishops.

At a local level, landlords made sure that they kept a firm grip on power by ensuring they served on grand juries, or were appointed as sheriffs or county lord lieutenants. They often sat as magistrates, and in this capacity they had close liaison with the police and county militias. In all these ways they formed a tightly organised ruling élite, linked by marriage and religion, and controlling the law and administration as well as the economy.

So safe was the majority of parliamentary seats in Ulster, and so tight was this family control, that in spite of the electoral reforms of 1829 and 1832 it was still a common occurrence when an election was held for there to be no contest at all in certain constituencies. During the five general elections which were held, for example, between 1832 and 1847 there were no electoral contests for the twelve seats in the large and populous counties of Antrim, Armagh, Cavan, Down, Derry and Fermanagh. The towns of Enniskillen, Dungannon, Downpatrick and Lisburn continued to be virtually rotten boroughs. Out of all the twenty-nine northern constituencies, only Belfast actually held a poll during every one of the five elections.

In the 1847 general election, held during the worst phase of the famine, when every democratic resource should have been mobilised to solve the crisis, there were only just over 3,000 votes cast – and this out of a total possible 46,000 in a population of nearly two and a half million. A Verner and a Caulfield were elected in County Armagh; a Tennent and a Chichester in Belfast; a Castlereagh and a Hill in County Down; a Ker in Downpatrick; a Knox in Dungannon; a Cole in Enniskillen; an Archdall and a Brooke in County Fermanagh; a Leslie and a Dawson in County Monaghan; a Corry and a Hamilton in County Tyrone.

The two crucial advantages Ulster had over the rest of Ireland, and which helped to alleviate some of the worst ravages of the famine, were possession of a flourishing linen industry and the way in which land tenure was affected by the Ulster custom.

Flax grew well in the cool, damp climate of the north, and linen had been produced there profitably since the Huguenots had introduced improved methods of manufacture in the early nineteenth century. Belfast, Lisburn, Lurgan and other towns in the Lagan valley were busy centres of the trade, and there were substantial exports to Scotland and England. Small farmers successfully grew the crop all over the province, and in some cases not only produced the raw material but also spun, wove or bleached the fabric.

Women, children and old people were extensively employed as well as adult males, and this family labour, combined with the production of other crops and livestock, gave these farmers what William Drennan had called 'a double anchorage on life'; that is, they had another source of income if, say, the oats or potatoes failed or the prices of pigs and cattle temporarily fell. Under the domestic system, tools were simple, and the necessary capital could be easily raised, especially as under the Ulster custom such capital was more readily available. From the 1840s onwards, with the introduction of steam power and more advanced mechanisation, the industry gradually ceased to be based on family labour, and moved into big factories in the towns. On the eve of the famine it is reckoned that just under two-thirds of Ulster's population was dependent on agriculture as compared with about three-quarters or four-fifths in other provinces. A proportion of Ulster's farming population could be also classified as semi-industrial or commercial.

The Ulster custom, or tenant right as it was usually described, was an understanding by the tenant farmer, and a recognition (even if a reluctant one) by the proprietor that the tenant could sell the goodwill of his tenancy when he wished to give up his farm. It was basically, as Gavan Duffy pointed out, a right of occupancy.[8] If the landlord wished to evict a tenant he must either allow him to sell to the highest bidder, or must buy out the right himself at the full market value. There was no legal agreement to this effect, and the arrangement could not be enforced in the courts, but in practice the tradition was so strong as almost to be as good as law.

Historians are not agreed as to how this system actually originated, but it is believed that it dated back to the plantations of the seventeenth and eighteenth centuries, and was connected with the early settlement of Protestant farmers and the security they demanded if they were to be loyal to their landlords. A vivid – if somewhat anti-Catholic – picture of how this might have happened was given by John Handcock, a witness at the Devon Commission:

178

It is a system which has more or less prevailed since the settlement of Ulster by James I when the ancestors of many of the
present landlords got grants, on condition of bringing over a
certain number of sturdy yeomen and their families as settlers. It
is not likely that the patentees were wealthy, we may, therefore,
fairly presume that the settlers built their own houses and made
improvements at their own expense, contrary to the English
practice. This, together with the fact of their being Protestants,
with arms in their hands, gave them strong claims on their
landlord and leader, and in this way it is probable, but is a matter for speculation, that tenant right may have first originated:
and probable settlers obtaining it in this way, it has gradually
extended itself to the whole rural population.[9]

Certainly during the first half of the nineteenth century the
custom had become widely recognised all over Ulster, including such counties as Donegal, Cavan, and Monaghan where
Catholics were in a majority.

The advantages of this system were so striking[10] that many
people – with the inevitable exception of conservative landlords
– approved of it, including such diverse personalities as Gavan
Duffy, John Mitchel and Sharman Crawford, most Presbyterian
ministers, practically all the Catholic clergy, and several radical
British MPs. The Devon Commission, though worried about the
implicit threat to propertied interests, gave grudging approval,
and eventually that cautious Liberal, Gladstone, came round to
the conclusion that the custom must be made into law. Even Karl
Marx, writing in London for a New York newspaper, was enthusiastic about how superior the northern tradition was over
that endured in the south.[11] What all these observers acknowledged was that whereas in the other three provinces tenants got
no benefits at all from any improvements they might make and
were therefore encouraged to be thriftless, the Ulster farmers –
small as well as big – were stimulated to invest capital, enrich the
soil with manure, erect better buildings, barns and sheds, as well
as houses, and generally to improve drainage and cultivation.

The tenants in return for their labour and expenditure could
thus build up over a period of years a tangible asset which could

generally be sold for cash when required. The landlord's role was merely to approve the purchaser. The value of the asset, as with an outright sale of a freehold or leasehold, varied according to the amount and quality of the land involved. In certain circumstances it could be quite valuable, and to most farmers it represented a very desirable asset. The going rate in Ulster during the early 1840s seems to have been about £10 or £12 per acre; in other words, a tenant with ten acres could sell his right of occupancy for about £120. In terms of modern money this would have been worth some thousands of pounds. A sum of this magnitude could enable a farmer to retire with some capital, possibly take up a new job in a local town or city such as Belfast, or – more particularly in the circumstances of those times – emigrate overseas. Fifty pounds would then have bought several adult passages to New York, Boston or Montreal. The value of this tenant right fell during the early 1850s, as we shall see later, and this was one of the major reasons for the wide-spread rural unrest during that period.

The landlords, with a few notable exceptions, such as Smith O'Brien in the south and John Martin and Sharman Crawford in the north, were mostly hostile to the tenant-right principle, and only tolerated it because of pressure of local opinion or because they were afraid to do otherwise. As proprietors they resented the fact that they seemed to have lost the right to do what they wished with their own possessions. To them, as with so many other members of the upper and middle classes, the rights of property appeared sacred, and anything that challenged those rights was regarded as dangerously seditious, even communistic. Lord Londonderry was expressing the general view of his class when he declared that the tenant right was not really a right at all but 'a voluntary act of kindness and regard'. And the rise of the Chartist movement in Britain and the out-break of revolution all over Europe in 1848 frightened them.

On the other hand, the shrewder members of the propertied classes were keenly alert to the possibility of violence and all kinds of agrarian disturbances if they abolished this old established tradition. Tenant right might be a nuisance, but it was also an insurance policy, or, as one authority said, 'an immunity from outrage'. It was tolerated, in other words, under duress. In a remark which was widely quoted, a witness to the Devon Commission warned that if tenant rights were interfered with: 'You would have a Tipperary in County Down.' The commission's secretary was equally alarmist:

> The necessity of distress for rent [that was the seizure of livestock or crops for nonpayment], a fruitful source of riots and broken heads, is also obviated by tenant-right, as there is no danger of loss of arrears. The landlords are compelled to recognise tenant-right as in several instances in this neighbourhood where they have refused to allow tenant-right, the incoming tenant's house has been burned, his cattle houghed, or his crops trodden down by night. The disallowance of tenant-right, so far as I know, is always attended by outrage. In fact, it is one of the sacred rights of the country, which cannot be touched with impunity; and, if any systematic efforts were made among the proprietors of Ulster to invade tenant-right, I do not believe there is a force of the Horse Guards to keep the peace of the Province.[12]

Tragically for the north, even the Ulster custom and the possession of a thriving linen industry could not fully protect the province from the coming of the potato blight. The worst fears of the landlords were realised – Tipperary did come to County Down, but in a way they did not foresee.

The effect of the great famine upon Ulster is an area of study gravely neglected by historians. No full-scale account of what happened in the northern counties between 1845 and 1849 has been published, and so far only one thesis on the subject has been completed.[13] The standard history books give the impression, whether deliberately or not is hard to say, that the blight hardly touched northern Ireland.[14] There are many publications, popular as well as scholarly, often graphically illustrated, of what happened in, say, Skibbereen, County Cork, or Clifden, County Galway, but virtually nothing about the calamities suffered in Lurgan, County Armagh, or Letterkenny, County Donegal. The histories of the Protestant Churches, particularly, which contain massive documentation about theological debates or controversies about ecclesiastical organisation, are curiously silent when it comes to describing the devastation that fell upon so many Christian communities during this period. A series of essays about the Church of Ireland at this time, for example, does not include the word 'famine' in its index, but appropriately enough has an entry for 'Family, royal'. The official history of the Orange Order covers an era of 150 years, and is several hundred pages and two volumes in length. The famine is not mentioned in it. The Reverend Henry Cooke, acknowledged leader of the conservative Presbyterians, and usually so vocal about social matters, kept his thoughts to himself. Finlay Holmes, his biographer, writes of 'The bitter experiences of the years of famine in the 1840s about which there is strangely little in the records of the [Presbyterian] Assembly.'[15]

Why this neglect of what, after all, was a turning point in the history of every province in Ireland? Is it suggested that because Ulster was somehow 'different' it escaped the disasters which fell on other regions? Or that landlordism was less oppressive in the north? Or that problems of overpopulation were not so acute? Or that the workhouse system was more efficient?

The factual evidence – and there is plenty of it when the investigator starts digging – suggests that, though the plight of tenant farmers and labourers in the northern counties was alleviated to some extent by the privilege of tenant right or the extra income that could be obtained from linen, the famine ravages when they did come affected Ulster very severely between 1845 and 1849. The fungus disease *phytophora infestans* blew freely over the whole of Ireland. Antrim and Down were affected in the same way as Cork and Galway. When the staple crop failed for three years in succession, a large proportion of the starving rural population, perhaps as many as one-third, began to suffer acutely. Diseases spread throughout the north, particularly affecting Belfast and the workhouses in the Lagan valley. Mortality rates more than doubled, and the total population fell by about one-fifth within a few years. Landlords were as harsh on their Protestant tenants who were unable to pay rents as they were on Catholics, and evictions more than quadrupled. In all these respects the experience of Ulster was not very different from that of Leinster, Munster or Connacht.

The potato blight was first observed in the counties of Fermanagh, Donegal, Antrim, Cavan and Tyrone in late September 1845, a week or so after it had been reported in County Kildare.[16] The wind seems to have carried the tiny spores from England, where they had been recorded in the Isle of Wight. Previously it had been reported in various parts of Europe. The blight was certainly no respecter of countries, and certainly did not distinguish – as some commentators seem to imply – between the Protestant-planted and the Catholic-planted potato.

To begin with the disease was not thought to be serious. There had been previous blights and famines which had receded after a year or so. The recent summer had been damp and changeable, and this was suggested as a cause of the trouble. Gradually during October and November, when the main crop should have been lifted, the full extent of the disaster began to be realised. Alarming newspaper reports of spotted and foul-smelling haulms and decaying, pulpy tubers came in from various parts of the province. Travellers spoke of blackened fields and a strange odour in the air. The *Banner of Ulster*, which was closely in touch with farming affairs, reported that by the end of 1845 at least a dozen agricultural districts were affected. The *Northern Whig* specifically mentioned Gweedore, County Donegal, Strabane, County Tyrone, Ballynure, County Derry, Markethill, County Armagh, Killyleagh, Holywood and Rathfriland, County Down, Ballymena and Ballycastle, County Antrim, and Cavan as contaminated areas. 'Public alarm is increasing, and great anxiety prevails', commented the *Whig*, and recommended the urgent calling of a town meeting in Belfast to consider the crisis.

In the summer of 1846 the blight again appeared, and this time the failure of the potato crop was even more widespread. Observers who had expressed high hopes for the harvest because of the abundance of the spring flowering were shocked by the sudden way in which apparently healthy plants turned into decay and corruption. The Reverend Samuel Montgomery, a Church of Ireland rector from Ballinascreen, County Derry, recorded:

> On the last three days of July and the first six days of August, 1846 the potatoes were suddenly attacked when in their full growth. The tops were observed to wither and then on looking to the roots, the tubers were found hastening to decomposition. The entire crop that in the month of July appeared so luxuriant, about the 15th August manifested only blackened and withered stems. The whole atmosphere in the month of September, was tainted with the odour of decaying potatoes.[17]

A traveller journeying across the centre of Ulster also mentions the first week of August as the time in which most damage was done. 'I remember driving through to Bundoran with my sister Bella on August 3rd and as we went seeing the fine crops of potatoes in the fields', he wrote. 'We spent three days in Bundoran and returning found these same fields blackened and useless.'[18] A month later the *Northern Whig* was describing further evidence of destruction, this time in County Antrim: 'In all the fields which we saw, in not a solitary instance did our eye fall upon as much as a single potato which presented the faintest indication of soundness – the prospect was utter ruin.'[19]

A letter written by a well-connected and influential Derry landlord in January 1847 made the important point that not only was there much local distress but that this was caused, not by scarcity of alternative food in the neighbourhood, but by lack of money to buy that food:

> I really have not had the heart to write to you before, for I have nothing to communicate except the heart rending scenes of misery which I daily witness. I wish I had never come here. If I had known what I was to encounter in this hitherto happy district, I should have spared myself the pain of witnessing a misery, which, with every feeling of compassion and every expenditure within my means, I can do no more than most inadequately and feebly relieve.
>
> I can think of nothing else than the wretched condition of this wretched people. We are comparatively well off in this neighbourhood. There is no want of food: but it is at such a price as to

make it totally impossible for a poor man to support his family with the wages he receives. I do not exaggerate when I tell you that from the moment I open my hall door in the morning until dark, I have a crowd of women and children crying out for something to save them from starving.

The men, except the old and infirm, stay away and show the greatest patience and resignation. I have been obliged to turn my kitchen into a bakery and soup shop to enable me to feed miserable children and mothers that cannot be sent away empty. So great is their distress that they actually faint on getting food into their stomachs . . . The gentry, the shopkeepers, the clergy are making every effort in their power to relieve the people by subscriptions and incessant attention, but what can be done when thousands are daily applying for one meal a day? . . . If provisions were cheaper, we might look forward with hope, but if no reduction in the price of food shall take place, hundreds will die of starvation.[20]

This letter was written by George Dawson, brother-in-law of Sir Robert Peel, to Sir Thomas Fremantle in London. Dawson had been MP for County Derry between 1815 and 1830, and was a substantial landowner. Fremantle had been chief secretary under Peel in 1845–6. The letter illustrates the point that there was other food, apart from potatoes, locally available. If a farmer produced cereals, meat, eggs or butter he might have to sell all or part of them to pay his rent. The ports of Derry, Belfast, Larne and Newry continued to export quantities of food during the famine.

By the spring of 1847 the situation had become so bad that even the conservative *Belfast News-Letter* was forced to admit: 'The destitution, in its most appalling form, has reached even to our hitherto favoured province. We have accounts from Donegal, Fermanagh, Tyrone and even Armagh, which almost rival the dreadful narratives which reach our ears from Skibbereen and Mayo.'[21]

Hunger was soon followed by sickness, and before many months had elapsed reports began to come in from various parts of the province about the spread of the most serious and highly contagious diseases. Typhus, known in Donegal as *fiabhras dubh* (black fever), and relapsing fever, known as *fiabhras buidhe* (yellow fever), because of the colour of the victims' skin, were both lice- or flea-borne diseases, which spread rapidly wherever unwashed people gathered together. Dysentery, known as *rith fola* (bloody flux), affected children especially. Asiatic cholera was carried in contaminated water or food. Smallpox and the more virulent strains of influenza also multiplied in crowded workhouses, hospitals and jails. Soup kitchens became centres for the dispersal, not only of food, but of dangerous bacteria. In the spring of 1847 various forms of these illnesses, often lumped together under the heading 'fever', were reported in the counties of Tyrone, Derry, Down and Fermanagh.

The poorest areas of the towns were often focal points of contagion because it was there that the dirtiest and most overcrowded were usually huddled together. Belfast's population, in particular, was growing quickly as the famished flocked there in search of food or work. A vivid picture of what life was like in one of the city's slums, in which not a single house was free from fever, is given in the *Northern Whig*, reporting an account from the Reverend W. Johnston, a Church of Ireland clergyman who was visiting some sick parishioners:

> In the first house he entered there were two patients lying, and the house itself was as black as smoke and dirt could make it. There was a child dead in the second house he entered – the second death during the week. He went to the third house, and found a person lying on the floor upstairs, without even a particle of straw under him, except for an old piece of sacking. He had no linen on him, nor a single rag of any description; he was lying in a fever, and near him was a child in dysentery; and, in the same place, nine persons were to sleep there – side by side, on the previous night. On the other side of the room, there was another family consisting of several persons; so that, in that small room, not more than about 16 feet square, 16 persons had slept the night before . . . In the next house he saw a man and his children lying beside one another – the former in fever, the latter in dysentery. The man's wife on the previous day, had taken out her cradle to dispose of it, for the purpose of procuring food, and had been unable to find a purchaser for it.[22]

So bad was the situation in Belfast at the time this letter was written that a special town meeting was called to discuss how workhouses and hospitals could be urgently expanded. In July 1847 there were 2,100 patients in the city's fever hospitals. Six hundred new admissions were recorded in one week.

Workhouses, which had trebled the size of their intake within a few years, were particularly dangerous places to seek refuge in because they did not separate the undernourished and hungry from those who were sick or dying. Built with the intention of helping the poor and homeless, these institutions often did more harm than good. The mortality of inmates was enormous. Indeed, it was probably safer for a destitute person to take his or her chance on the open road or build a shelter in a ditch than crowd together in such charnel houses.

A sickening account of one such bleak and barrack-like building is given by Dr Robert Smith who visited Lurgan workhouse in February 1847.[23] Lurgan was the centre of a prosperous linen industry and the workhouse there might have been expected to be better than the average. But overcrowded and badly staffed, it proved to be a place of horror for even such a hardened physician. Dr Smith reported that during the previous week before his visit ninety-five people had died, of whom fifty-five were children under ten, and nine aged over sixty. Fifty-two of the ninety-five had been healthy when admitted.

The wards and fever sheds were not only grossly overcrowded but generally filthy, lacked adequate ventilation, and in many cases had not proper floors or beds. The healthy and the sick, the living and dying, the young and old were all mixed up together, and so many people were applying for admission that they had to use what were called 'the Idiot wards', that is, rooms in which lunatics were normally confined. Practically everyone suffered from some form of dysentery, and sewage disposal was neglected. Dead bodies were allowed to lie around for days in corridors and wards before burial. 'In some of the dysenteric wards, I noticed the chamber utensils which had been used, were not taken away or emptied', wrote Dr Smith. 'In one ward, especially, a large, uncovered bucket, nearly half-filled with aloine

187

discharges, was allowed to remain for hours; and I found that this was the case upon each day that I visited the ward . . . In another part of the infirmary, I found, lying upon the lobby into which several wards opened, the bodies of two females who had been eight hours dead.'[24]

The well that was supposed to supply clean water was in the middle of the cemetery, and there had been so many funerals that the water had become discoloured from the disturbed soil. Paupers, if fit to work, were encouraged to serve as nurses. Food was scanty and unsuitable. Sometimes two people slept in the same small bed, or lay on damp straw. At the time of inspection it was reported that the old master had resigned, and no one appointed in his place. The matron was ill.

Workhouse masters were expected to keep a strict account of every penny they spent on their inmates. Official figures show that during the famine period on average the food and drink allowance was between 1s. 3d. and 1s. 9d. per week per person, or between 2d. and 3d. a day. This would not have bought much bread or meal, let alone meat, even allowing for the fact that the sick were probably eating very little, if anything at all.

In December 1848 a new dimension of horror was added when Asiatic cholera broke out in Belfast. It had been brought into the city by a Scottish sailor who died in the workhouse. Within a few months this plague had spread to nine other northern towns, and then in ever-widening circles to other parts of Ireland. In Belfast alone 2,700 people are said to have caught the disease, the mortality rate being about 35 per cent.[25]

The official figures, which were published some years later, bear out the impression given in these contemporary sources as to the extent and severity of the famine in Ulster. A mass of statistical material eventually became available to amplify in factual terms what was so vividly described in these personal letters, doctors' reports, and local newspaper accounts.

The workhouse population in the north, for example, increased from an average of just over 8,000 in the early 1840s to 11,600 in May 1846, 30,400 in 1847, and 33,000 in 1848. The numbers employed in outdoor-relief schemes nearly doubled in a year, and by March 1847, when the numbers reached their peak, totalled over 87,000. Donegal, Cavan and Monaghan, where reliance on the potato crop was probably greatest, were the worst affected counties, but no area escaped unscathed, as can be seen in Table 5.[26]

TABLE 5

NUMBERS EMPLOYED IN OUTDOOR-RELIEF SCHEMES IN
  ULSTER, MARCH 1847

Antrim	2,300
Armagh	5,500
Cavan	25,500
Derry	4,000
Donegal	21,000
Down	1,200
Fermanagh	8,500
Monaghan	11,400
Tyrone	8,000

Mortality figures more than doubled (see Table 6 for number of deaths in Ulster in 1842–50[27]), rising from a total of about 100,000 during the first half of the decade to 217,000 between 1846 and 1850. It is reckoned that no fewer than 33,000 died from typhus or relapsing fever, 12,000 from dysentery, and 2,300 from cholera. In addition, tens of thousands perished directly from starvation or from other diseases aggravated by malnutrition.

TABLE 6

NUMBER OF DEATHS IN ULSTER, 1842–50

1842	18,000
1843	18,750
1844	20,000
1845	22,000
1846	31,600
1847	64,600
1848	46,200
1849	42,700
1850	32,200

Emigration, which for a century and a half had been carrying away a variable flow of people through the ports of Belfast, Newry and Derry, turned into a flood. As soon as they could raise the fares, thousands took the boat for the United States of America, Canada, Australasia or Britain.

The most striking evidence of the disastrous impact of the famine may be seen in the overall population figures. During the ten years 1841–51, the total number of inhabitants in Ulster declined from 2.4 million to 2 million, a fall of about one-sixth or the equivalent of the population of five Belfasts at that time. The percentage loss in Monaghan (29 per cent), Cavan (28), and Fermanagh (26) was as high as in such western counties as Mayo (29), Galway (27), or Clare (26); Tyrone (18) and Armagh (16) were almost as bad as Kerry (19); only Antrim (9) and Down (11) were well below the national average.

The vast exodus of people escaping the horrors of their native land continued virtually unabated during the following decade, with a further 1.3 million emigrating from Ireland as a whole. Between 1851 and 1861, Ulster, with 372,000 emigrants (or 29 per cent of the Irish total) came second to Munster, and ahead of Leinster and Connacht in this flight overseas. By the end of the century more than one million men, women and children had emigrated from the north. The comparative figure for the whole of Ireland during this half-century was just under three million so Ulster's share of the total had risen slightly. The percentage of Catholics in the north fell from about 50 per cent in 1861 to about 44 per cent in 1901, which implies that, allowing for differential fertility and mortality rates between the various religious denominations, emigration was somewhat heavier among Catholics compared to Protestants.

Considering the large scale of this migration to North America and other countries, and that it must have included many Presbyterians and episcopalians, it is surprising that there has been so little comment on these demographic changes.

12

FAMINE — THE POLITICAL AND MORAL CRISIS

> The Irish poor must have food and employment; and it must not
> be from Imperial resources. It cannot be put on the Consolidated
> Fund. It follows that the property of Ireland must pay.
>
> *The Times*, December 1846[1]

The famine, more than any other event of the nineteenth century, undermined the conservative argument that the Act of
Union would solve Ireland's economic and social problems. To
put it briefly, when the basic food crop failed, and millions
went hungry or sick, and when above all other considerations
the country needed its own parliament and its own government
to make laws for its own people, virtually all legislative power
lay in another country, the overwhelming majority of whose
citizens had little knowledge of, and less sympathy with,
Ireland.

The advocates of the Union had always claimed that under
the United Kingdom parliament set up in 1801 the Irish people
would be treated fairly, and that the wealth of Britain and its
empire would be used, among other things, to benefit its
poorer neighbour. There was much talk of a family in which
the stronger would help its weaker members. There was also
the implied promise that freer trade would assist all parts of the
British Isles, and that sectarian passions would diminish under
the benign and neutral rule of Westminster. Indeed, the whole
idea of the Union was sold largely on the proposition that it
would provide equal treatment and just shares between all
citizens and different regions. The *Northern Whig*, which was
strongly in favour of the Union, made this point when it

became suspicious that most MPs and peers in London were deaf to Irish pleas for aid during the famine. 'If there is a real Union between England and Ireland,' said the *Whig*, 'it should have reciprocal conditions on all such covenants – mutual benefits and mutual burdens.'[2] The paper had been provoked into making this comment by a letter sent to the prime minister, Lord John Russell, by the Catholic archbishop of Tuam, Dr John MacHale, a noted nationalist, who accused the Government of hypocrisy. The *Belfast News-Letter*, speaking for the Ulster Tories, declared that the famine was not just an Irish national or provincial issue – it was an 'imperial calamity'. 'The poor of Ireland must not be allowed to die like dogs', it went on to comment. 'No such deep disgrace shall stain the future annals of this great and glorious empire.'[3]

But when the potatoes began to rot in the ground, and hunger spread throughout the country, such pledges of mutual help proved to be only of limited value. Reciprocal aid was agreeable in theory, but could be expensive in practice. Britain was content to go on ruling Ireland so long as the advantages were clearly on her side, but when profits turned into losses then other considerations had to be borne in mind. Economics had to be weighed against politics, and military strategy balanced against religious alliance. There were foreign policy problems of Britain's reputation in the world. The fact was that the interests of the ruling groups in each country, though they ran parallel, were not identical, and from time to time as historical circumstances changed so these interests could conflict with each other. Such disputes had occurred in 1798–1801, and were to occur again in the 1880s and 1913–14.

At first, when the seriousness of the crisis was not fully appreciated, there was broad agreement between the establishments on both sides of the Irish Sea as to how to react to the failure of the potato crop. To begin with, it was suggested that the blight was only a temporary phenomenon, and that the next harvest would be better. In the short run Providence was to blame, and in the long run the laws of capitalist economics must not be interfered with. Whigs and Tories, apart from a few critics, generally rallied behind those principles which they were convinced had made their empire and their class rich and powerful.

There was strong emphasis on the sacred rights of property, which, as the chief secretary, H. Labouchere, said in the House of Commons early in 1847, was 'the cornerstone of civilisation and improvement'.[4] The edicts of Adam Smith must prevail, and no laws passed that prevented the unrestricted flow of food into and out of the country. Repeal of the Union must not be contemplated under any circumstances because military strategy, the sanctity of the Protestant constitution, and the very survival of the Whig and Tory parties depended upon the continuing control of Ireland by the parliament in London. Moreover, it was very important for the ruling class in both countries to stick together, and form a united front against the twin dangers of Chartist subversion and Irish rebellion.

Later, as the crisis got worse and it became clearly more evident that the old nostrums were not working, this consensus broke down. The manufacturers, merchants and artisans of Britain were generally hostile to the landlord classes, especially if they were Irish and reputed to be wealthy and profligate. Nonconformists disliked Anglicans on principle, and Whigs and Peelite Tories, who had temporarily agreed about repealing the Corn Laws, which had taxed the import of grain into the United Kingdom, pulled in different directions. The Anglo-Irish grandees, who held so much power in both countries, vacillated. In particular, the debate about imperial responsibility became more vehement as the famine relief bill got bigger.

It was the sheer size of the disaster confronting the Irish economy that forced successive governments at Westminster to abandon – at least temporarily – their undiluted faith in free trade. The emphasis shifted from ideology to pragmatism, and emergency steps were taken to provide aid. Lord Russell had to concede that if millions were not to starve, then the Government must intervene on an unprecedented scale. By early 1847 the numbers employed on public works in Ireland rose to 2.7 million, and a few months later, as a result of a change in policy, over 3 million were being fed from soup kitchens. At least

193

one-third of the Irish population were being supported directly by the state. The cost to the exchequer in mid-1847 was running at the rate of nearly £1 million a month.

The realisation that this burden, which fell heavily on tax-payers in England, Scotland and Wales, might continue for a long time, and could even get worse, led to a loud outcry in Britain. MPs, the press and public opinion generally all deplored the never-ending appeals for financial assistance coming from Ireland, and sought for scapegoats whom they could blame for the unceasing flow of bad news. Traditionally such scapegoats had been found among the 'irresponsible' Irish poor and the 'troublesome' nationalists who spoke for them. Now in the search for more obvious whipping boys, the few thousand landed proprietors, who controlled so much wealth and power, were, more justly, held to blame. Increasingly, as disaster piled on disaster, and the Ascendancy could offer no solution, so the rulers of Britain turned away from the garrison they had pre-viously so warmly cherished. Former heroes became villains overnight, and the Irish landlords, whose writ had run un-questioned for so long, were now publicly criticised as greedy, arrogant and politically inept. One English MP described them briefly as 'horrible'. *The Times* said they were 'absentee, spend-thrift, beggarly, borrowing, jobbing, mismanaging . . . always squeezing out rent and returning nothing to the soil'.[5] Some months later in a widely quoted editorial, it denounced them as a 'thriftless and improvident race'.[6]

Irish nationalists and British radicals had, of course, been making such criticisms for years. Smith O'Brien, Sharman Crawford, John O'Connell and such pro-Chartist MPs as Feargus O'Connor (MP for Nottingham) and Poulett Scrope (MP for Stroud) never missed an opportunity in the House of Commons to attack the system of Irish landownership as unjust, inefficient, and the cause of all kinds of social abuses.

What was so remarkable about this new wave of criticism, however, was that it involved not merely the radicals in par-liament but also drew in many sections of the centre, and even some right-wing members of the political spectrum. Liberals poured scorn on the wealthy rulers in Ireland. Even such Anglo-Irish grandees as Lords Lansdowne, Devonshire, Palmerston and Fitzwilliam, who had every reason to support the status quo, were put on the defensive about their privileges. On one occasion Lord Russell got so angry about the unwillingness of the big proprietors to pay their taxes that he lumped together all those engaged in Irish agriculture – owners, tenants and labourers alike – as being responsible for overpopulation and the subdivision of land. There had been a 'connivance', he alleged, between these interested groups to promote a bad economic policy. Sir Robert Peel agreed with Russell that the Irish should not look too much to Britain for aid, but depend more upon their own exertions.[7] He did not extend this argument to the granting of political independence. Russell summed up these views about where the ultimate responsibility for relief should fall when he used the phrase: 'Irish property must pay for Irish poverty.'

The harsh attacks threw the Ascendancy into confusion. Their first response was to express astonishment that their former friends should turn against them in this uncalled-for way. Were they not the bastion upon which imperial power so much depended? Were they not loyalists who could always be relied upon to defend the Crown? Above all, were they not Protestants who were the very pillars of the 1689 constitution? Then, as it became apparent that the rift with Britain was a deep one, and that many hitherto sacrosanct beliefs might have to be abandoned, they, too, began to look for new allies and new policies. In short, if the empire was not going to pay their bills then the Union might have to be looked at in a different light.

The first sign that old allegiances were shifting – even if only temporarily – occurred in January 1847 when a group of Irish landlords met in Dublin to form what they called an 'Irish Party'. The title of the new organisation was significant because it raised the question of national allegiance. Did the Ascendancy now regard themselves as more Irish than British? And in times of acute economic crisis were they harping back to the patriot concepts of Henry Grattan? Whatever their long-term loyalties

195

might be, there seemed for a few brief months a willingness on the part of certain influential proprietors and their parliamentary representatives to encourage a spirit of good will and compromise between formerly conflicting sections of Irish society. The new party's manifesto said that its aim was to reduce factional and religious differences, and 'co-operate cordially in the interests of Ireland'. Their purpose was to save the country from the 'ruin by which all classes in the land were threatened'.[8]

Nearly fifty peers, including Lords Farnham, Erne, Conyngham, Caledon, O'Neill and Charlemont from Ulster, and thirty MPs, including J. Maxwell (County Cavan), A.B. Brooke (County Fermanagh), M. Archdall (County Fermanagh), D. Ross (Belfast), J. Boyd (Coleraine), and C.P. Leslie (County Monaghan), were present at this remarkable rally. John O'Connell, Daniel O'Connell's son, and Smith O'Brien spoke for the southern Irish nationalists. The conference was greeted by the Young Ireland journal, the *Nation*, as a sign that there was a change of heart on the part of the Irish unionists, and Smith O'Brien's letter was printed, pleading for the landlords to place themselves at the head of the Irish people in their struggle to save themselves from disaster. Even such a radical as John Mitchel was briefly persuaded that the leopard had changed its spots.

The fact that the Irish conservatives soon abandoned their brief flirtation with Irish nationalism did not mean they could revert at once to their old arrogance. Their confidence had been severely shaken both by the famine itself and by their belief that they had been betrayed by their former friends. For some years they remained at loggerheads, uncertain as to how to proceed. Their coherence as a group was momentarily gone, and individuals often took their own idiosyncratic line over such issues as free trade and the Corn Laws, the Ulster custom, and how they could reconcile the need for charity with their dislike of mendicancy.

The old controversy between the free-traders of the north and the protectionists of the south flared again, and was complicated by the argument as to how much corn should be imported into Ireland, who should pay for it, and how commerce should be regulated. The manufacturers and merchants of Belfast and the Lagan valley were urged on by the *Northern Whig*[9] to resist any limitations being placed on the full implementation of *laissez-faire*. It attacked protectionists and what it called 'a monstrous system of outdoor relief'. Several influential administrators and politicians in Dublin took an opposing view. Moreover, the anger aroused by the repeal of the Corn Laws in 1846 had not died away entirely.

Similarly there was disagreement about the future of tenant rights. Generally the landed proprietors in Leinster, Munster and Connacht rejected them as an intolerable intrusion on their own legal privileges, but in Ulster such rights were deeply entrenched and to encroach upon them at a time of agricultural crisis would only exacerbate an already fraught situation.

Tory and Whig MPs, who represented Ulster rural constituencies, were also uncomfortably aware that their selection as candidates or popularity with voters could depend on the way in which they treated their tenants. As a result, they often trimmed their policies in the predominantly farming constituencies. Lord Castlereagh, who represented County Down and who in some respects was more liberal than his famous predecessor, was an example of a wealthy peer who was also an MP who had to watch carefully which way the electoral wind was blowing. In February 1847 – in a noticeably moderate speech – he opposed Sharman Crawford's bill in the House of Commons which proposed legally to strengthen the Ulster custom. Castlereagh argued that a custom should not be made a law. Four months later, however, when a general election was pending, he had a change of heart, and was actually one of the twenty-five MPs who voted in support of a similar bill introduced by Crawford.

A further cause of disagreement among middle- and upper-class Protestants, lay as well as clerical, arose over the relative claims of charity and state finance in saving the poor. Helping the needy was supposed to be a prime moral duty, and philanthropy said to be one of the qualities distinguishing the gentry. But there was also a danger of a flood of paupers over-whelming the country. Mendicancy should on no account be encouraged.

In the spring of 1847, when the famine was entering its worst phase, this issue came to a head. The Government introduced a bill to permit the payment of outdoor relief, that is, the granting of aid outside the workhouse. This went contrary to the tradition that state-assisted paupers must give up any independence they might have, and enter an institution. The basic principle was that conditions in the workhouse should always be worse than anything outside, and that the workhouse should thus be a refuge of last resort. Immediately the Government measure was introduced there was uproar among the more conservative peers, MPs and clergy on both sides of the Irish Sea.

In the south of Ireland the campaign was led by Lord Monteagle of the well-known Spring-Rice family, Richard Whateley, Church of Ireland archbishop of Dublin, and Lords Radnor and Mountcashel. In Ulster Lord Castlereagh argued that payment should not be made to the needy unless work was contributed in exchange. Otherwise, idleness and every form of moral degeneracy would be encouraged. On no account should food be given gratuitously to the 'able-bodied poor'.[10] Sir William Verner, the Orange spokesman from County Armagh, told the House of Commons that the attempt to give outdoor relief would 'convert all Ireland into a great workhouse'.[11]

The Ulster establishment might argue about their relationship with the Whig government in London, their willingness to contribute to charity, or their liability to pay taxes, but there was a certain subject upon which they were all agreed, namely, the defence of their property rights. Whatever concessions they might make on other matters, there could be no question of a retreat on their legal possession of land. They were lords of the soil, and that was that. With a few exceptions, any failure to pay up usually led to the tenant's ejectment.

Evictions had always been the sharpest weapon in the land-lords' armoury, and it was very striking how, in spite of many pleas to the contrary, the number of forcible removals from the land rose rapidly in 1847 and 1848. Table 7[12] shows the extent of these evictions throughout Ulster in 1846–8. Protestant areas were affected almost as much as Catholic areas, religion did not seem to matter all that much when it came to penalising defaulters.

TABLE 7

NUMBER OF EVICTIONS IN ULSTER, 1846–8

	1846	1847	1848
Antrim	210	626	490
Armagh	196	568	1,269
Cavan	124	390	679
Derry	130	177	480
Donegal	138	216	720
Down	143	227	468
Fermanagh	79	211	242
Monaghan	107	382	500
Tyrone	114	351	668
Total	1,241	3,148	5,516

Any manifestation of Ribbonism, riots or rural unrest was, of course, suppressed with the full rigour of the law. Thus the Protection of Life Act of February 1846 was followed by the Crime and Outrage Act of November 1847, and a Treason-felony Act in March 1848. Habeas corpus was once again suspended in the summer of 1848, following the Smith O'Brien rising in Tipperary.[13] In spite of the fact that Ulster remained remarkably peaceful during this period, not a single northern peer or MP voted against any of these measures. Lords Londonderry and Downshire, two of the richest peers in the province, led the law-and-order campaign, often giving the impression in their speeches that they were more concerned in putting down any possible rural rebellion than they were in alleviating hunger.

If Whig and Tory MPs continued to put British interests first, and if Ascendancy peers and landlords were, as always, hostile to reform, what of the leaders of the Christian Churches who were supposed to follow Jesus' exhortation to feed the hungry and succour the sick? How did bishops, parsons, ministers and priests respond to the crisis which affected every member of the community? In particular, when it came to the question of tilting the scales of justice between the rights of property and the rights of people, where did the ecclesiastical weight fall?

At this time of moral as well as material disaster the responses of the clergy were, with a few notable exceptions, not much more constructive than those of the laity. The painful reality of the famine years in Ireland was that most Church spokesmen proved to be as much prisoners of their own history and victims of their own social and value systems as any hardened politician or selfish layman. In spite of their claim to advocate only the eternal verities and to preach only universal truths, they turned out to be as culture-bound as anyone else. Birth, solid family background, a classical education, detailed knowledge of the Bible, or even personal sanctity did not seem to make much difference when it came to choosing between God and Mammon.

The majority of Protestants would not break away from the centuries-old tradition that relegated Catholics to a subordinate position in society. They avoided the question 'Who is my neighbour?', or gave an ambiguous answer. Catholics were still regarded as beyond the pale: lazy, feckless and improvident, they were author of their own misfortunes. Many Presbyterians, now increasingly under conservative influence, went back to Calvinist doctrines about the elect and non-elect, those predestined for salvation and those doomed to everlasting fires. Catholics generally fell into the latter category. Even the Quakers, usually so humane and practical in their views, ascribed the causes of the famine, not so much to man's folly and greed, as to the inscrutable laws of Providence.

The Catholic Church, at least, spoke for the mass of the people who were suffering most cruelly, and were not so willing to put up with the excuses propagated in the writings of Thomas Robert Malthus and Adam Smith. They correctly saw repeal of the Union as the only way in which Ireland could control its own destiny. Nevertheless, urged on by Pope Pius IX and Dr

Paul Cullen, his adviser on Irish affairs in Rome, they also were not prepared to challenge the landlord system head on. Nor were they generally willing to sanction physical resistance to evictions or to allow the seizure of food that was being exported. No matter what the provocation, the laws passed at Westminster must be obeyed.

All the Churches blamed Providence for the failure of the potato crop. It was the unfathomable will of the Almighty, possibly aggravated by man's wickedness, which caused the famine. If a higher power decreed such an appalling amount of suffering, it was not for humble mortals to query the divine dispensation. Submission to God's purpose would cure, if not the body, then at least the soul.

Such fatalistic arguments were popular among the wealthier and more respectable members of society because they enabled them to retreat into a kind of quietism or withdrawal from the problems of the world. They let individuals off the moral hook and avoided the need for political action. For example, Lord George Beresford, a pious and scholarly man, who as archbishop of Armagh was supposed to speak for the Church of Ireland, apparently never uttered a word in the House of Lords about the famine between 1845 and 1849. These arguments offered, in other words, an escape route for those faced with intolerable choices. All that was needed for personal salvation, said the unco guid, was to believe in Christ, keep the Ten Commandments, take the sacraments, and say one's prayers. Piety and the dutiful observance of Church rules should take precedence; good works, apart from the necessary alms-giving, took very much a second place. It was for others, politicians and the like, to find solutions to social problems. A good Christian should concentrate on cultivating his own moral garden.

This preference for individual rather than social or collective responsibility for helping the poor was raised in an acute form during the spring of 1847 when the issue of charitable versus state aid came to the fore. Devout Christians knew the parable of the Good Samaritan, and no doubt a few pondered uneasily about the biblical warning that it was unlikely that a rich man could enter the kingdom of heaven. Philanthropy was, of course, a prime religious duty. As a result, charities were subscribed to generously throughout Ireland, Britain and the world. Many individual Churchmen and women dipped deeply into their pockets, and parsons joined with ministers and priests in raising funds. Committees were set up all over Ireland to organise soup kitchens. The Quakers, especially, were noted for their energy in collecting food, clothing and money. In Ulster it was reported that one in three relief schemes was presided over by a Protestant pastor.[14] Several clergymen, mainly Catholic but including two County Cork Church of Ireland rectors (the Reverend Robert Traill of Schull and the Reverend Richard Townsend of Skibbereen) died from fevers caught while visiting the sick.

The difficulty with all this personal altruism was that it was simply not enough to cope with the enormous demands made upon it. During 1847, when hundreds of thousands and eventually millions were clamouring for food, the clergy – like the politicians – were under intense pressure to change their tactics. What were sincere and God-fearing Christians to do when confronted with a catastophe of such dimensions? The only realistic reply was to accept the need for more state aid and heavier taxes. But this solution did not please those brought up in Puritan traditions. The Catholic bishops did not have any moral objection to government intervention as such, and urgently pressed the prime minister to send more state funds. Protestants, on the other hand, were very much tied to the contemporary attitudes about the sacredness of the free market. Many well-meaning clergymen of all denominations were torn one way and then the other.

A notable example of this facing-both-ways attitude towards famine relief was provided by Archbishop Whateley, who combined generous private benevolence with the most severe strictures on government aid for the poor. The archbishop's sister reports that he gave £8,000, a princely sum in those days, towards famine charities.[15] On the other hand, he believed it was unwise for the state to assume too much responsibility for the relief of poverty.

Whateley came from an English upper-class background, and had been educated at English public schools and at Oxford. He was by no means an evangelical, but had grown up – like most Protestants of that era – in the Puritan tradition that a distinction should be made between the deserving and the undeserving poor. The deserving poor, including the old, blind, sick, or otherwise physically handicapped, should be helped, when necessary, with alms. The undeserving poor, who since the days of the first Elizabethan poor law had been classified as 'sturdy beggars', were capable of work, and must on no account be encouraged to be lazy and dissolute. Idleness was both a sin and a crime against society. The archbishop, therefore, was prepared to dip into his long purse and find money for charitable funds, but he would not accept that government money should be spent on outdoor-relief schemes and soup kitchens.

In the 1830s he had served on a commission set up to inquire into the poor laws, and this had given him, he sincerely believed, an insight into the nature of Irish poverty. Moreover, he prided himself on his knowledge of economics, and the wisdom, as he saw it, of *laissez-faire* theories.[16] His closest friend, who often visited him in his episcopal palace near Kingstown (modern-day Dun Laoghaire), County Dublin, was the most influential economist of his day, Nassau William Senior.[17] Senior also worshipped at the shrine of Adam Smith.

Whateley's most important intervention in the recurring debate as to what should be done to relieve famine distress came during a major House of Lords discussion in March 1847, when the Government introduced proposals for outdoor relief. Together with Lords Monteagle, Radnor and Mountcashel, he strongly attacked the measure on the grounds it would encourage pauperism on huge scale. They claimed that if ever outdoor relief was granted, then the floodgates would be opened, and vast numbers of people, as many as five million were suggested, would have to be paid out of rates and taxes. Society would disintegrate, and a 'Jacquerie' (Whateley's word) would be let loose upon the land. Whateley observed:

> An Irish labourer has been accustomed, unhappily, to work for a
> very small pittance and to be content with the bare necessities of
> life, and to be, as it were, always on the brink of ruin. This is a
> deplorable condition at the best; but if you give him a legal right
> independently of industry and good behaviour . . . you ruin his
> industry and independence of character for ever, and sink him
> permanently, into the lowest degradation, physical and moral.[18]

The archbishop's only remedy, apart from charity to the hungry men, women and children pressing at his gate, was an 'inquiry'. His speech was widely reported, and he was so pleased with it he had it published as a pamphlet. A scathing reply soon came from the British radical, Poulett Scrope.[19]

Theologically, Whateley was a liberal and prepared to show some tolerance towards Catholicism. It was his economic opinions that made him so narrow-minded and reluctant to show an open attitude in seeking a solution to social problems. The evangelical Protestants, in contrast, took a much more stern and Calvinist view of human nature and society. Blaming most of Ireland's current difficulties on Sin (with a capital S), they attributed the country's ills largely to the 'false' religion to which the majority of the population belonged. The souls of too many people as well as the potatoes were rotten, they implied. In their view the Catholic Church was the chief source of iniquity in Ireland and Catholics, being ignorant, superstitious, and idolatrous, were largely to blame for their own misfortunes. It was not explained why many poor Presbyterians and even members of the Church of Ireland went hungry. If only the Catholic poor would convert to the true religion, then their sufferings would be alleviated. If only they would read their Bibles and abandon their priest-ridden ways, then everything else would eventually come right. Admittedly the famine was a horrible experience and the suffering had been appalling, but like the fabled ill wind, it brought opportunities as well as tragedies. The Catholic Church was reeling under the blows it had received, and a unique opportunity was now offered to win large-scale conversions to the true Protestant faith. A second Reformation might hopefully be at hand. The main task of missionaries, therefore, was to preach the gospel and spread the Word. Proselytism, rather than charity, would carry the day. The poor were offered, not bread, not even a stone, but a Bible text. However, if the provision of food, clothes and education could ease the missionaries' path, then this was God's way of saving the lost souls of Papists.

Inevitably, this being Ireland, there was a political dimension to this allegedly religious approach. Conservative clergymen hoped that a convert to Protestantism would necessarily become a convert to unionism. The Reverend Alexander Dallas, chief spokesman for the missionaries, was quite explicit about this political motive. 'The converts become the best friends of social order, respecting and obeying the laws of our beloved Queen because they are taught to be obedient to the laws of God', he wrote, in an article appropriately entitled 'Remedy for Ribbonism'. After a visit to Connemara he claimed that out of social evil there might possibly come much moral good:

> The state of Ireland during the whole of this year [1848] was most appalling. Disease in the shape of fever and cholera, had followed on starvation . . . Many hearts were thus being prepared to receive those consolations which the glorious Gospel of God can alone impart. The oil of his joy was to be poured by his missionary servants, and his tours there [in the west of Ireland] were full of encouragement, speaking as he did beside the dying and the dead with the full realisation of eternal truth.[20]

The zealous Lord Roden, who went on a proselytising tour of Connemara in September 1851, triumphantly records how scores of ragged, Irish-speaking children came to hear him preach, and be examined as to their knowledge of Scripture, in various remote villages on the Atlantic coast and the shores of Loughs Corrib and Mask. He praised them for their understanding of the Bible and also for their ability to sing 'God save the Queen'. As reward they got soup and bread. In one chapter of his extraordinary book he recounts how a farmer in Oughterard, County Galway, had formerly been an 'active demagogue and great leader of Repeal in the district', but had turned Protestant, and as a result changed his 'political as well as his religious views'.[21]

This 'souper' attitude was welcomed in England as well as in Ireland by the prosperous middle and upper classes because it enabled them to salve their consciences, which had been troubled by reports of widespread distress. In January 1847 the *Morning Herald* published a letter by a group of northern peers, army officers, landlords and Protestant clergy, including the Duke of Manchester (who owned 12,000 acres in County Armagh), which was phrased in such a way as to appeal to both Protestant zealots and the monied classes. To make sure this letter would attract those English people who might, from their religious prejudice, feel that nothing should be done for the benighted Irish, the duke and his colleagues referred to 'provident circumstances' and 'the present favourable crisis' which provided 'an opening . . . for conveying the light of the Gospels to the darkened minds of the Roman Catholic peasantry'.

The promising new opportunities for proselytising were the main theme of an address given by the Reverend John Edgar, home missions secretary of the Presbyterian Church, to the annual synod in July that year. Divine providence, he claimed, was making a visitation to Ireland, a country which must pay for its largely Catholic sins. 'God had been with the [Presbyterian] Church' during the crisis, he said, but the famine had 'eaten the right arm of Popish power'. (Cries of 'Hear! Hear!' from the audience.) Praising the conversions from 'priestly superstition', he concluded by saying: 'Let it be known that God has overruled the famine in Ireland to open the door to Protestant missions.'[22]

Edgar's fervent opinions cannot be dismissed as those of a crank or fanatic outside the mainstream of Protestant fundamentalism. His speech at the 1847 synod was well received, and he was welcomed as a popular lecturer among many Presbyterian congregations. W.D. Killen, his biographer, writes of him enthusiastically.[23] There were several other preachers of similar style prominent during that period. But what makes this minister's career and theological ideas historically important is that he personified in several respects the profound contradictions that existed within the missionary movement known as the new

206

Reformation. He was a student of the social sciences, and wrote a pamphlet entitled *The Perishing and Dangerous Classes*, which was a kind of sociological tract unambiguously setting out the connections between poverty, low wages, bad housing, unemployment and crime. He led vigorous campaigns against the evils of prostitution and drunkenness, and was an active member of the Belfast Anti-Slavery Society. Though committed to the evangelical doctrine that the only salvation for the individual was to be saved, or 'born again', he apparently accepted that societies as well as people could be unjust and corrupt, and there could be social as well as personal sin.

When confronted face to face with the horrors of the famine during a visit to Sligo and Mayo in the autumn of 1846, Edgar's response was humane and, in the truest sense, Christian. The pamphlet *A Cry from Connaught*,[24] which he wrote in the manse in Killala, County Mayo, and which quickly sold 26,000 copies, was well informed, vividly written and compassionate in tone. It was hostile towards the landlords, and critical about official government policy on the export of food. Was it morally right, he asked, to exact rents from those who were suffering so acutely? Was it just to send food abroad when those who produced it were starving at home? The real fact of the case, he said, was this: 'The poor Connaughtman eats none of his own corn, none of his own butter, none of his own pig: corn, butter, pig – all go to pay his rent; and whatever potatoes remain after the pig is fed, are the only food, the only support, of his family.' This plea for aid made a deep impression on public opinion in Ulster, and within a short time two important relief committees were set up in Belfast and London. Over £16,000 was collected for soup kitchens, Edgar being the driving force behind much of this charitable activity.

On the other hand, as soon as the immediate crisis was over, and the poor and the hungry not quite so visible on farms or in the streets, Edgar returned to what was an even stronger motive force in his life – his hostility towards Catholicism. In a series of extraordinary sermons, and especially in a pamphlet entitled *Ireland's Mission Field* published in 1852, he repeated the opinions which had so long occupied his mind, only this time in more passionate language. 'Priestcraft' was the cause of almost every Irish ill, social as well as moral. 'Romanism' was debasing and unhallowed, indelibly linked with filth and rags, and the exponent of all kinds of blasphemy. The Pope was 'the Man of Sin', and there was nothing that could be done for his followers throughout the world except convert them. As for Irish Papists, let them leave their homeland for ever, or alternatively – the implication was quite clear – perish from the earth. The famine, therefore, had its positive as well as its negative aspects, because it provided a unique opportunity to resettle Ireland with a morally superior kind of person – preferably staunch Calvinists like himself. The country now offered, what he described in his own peculiar way, 'a field of delightful interest' for Protestant missionaries.

An even more extreme example of this ultra-evangelical attitude – in which almost any measure was regarded as justifiable to destroy the power of the Catholic Church – was provided in a book entitled *The Mystery Solved or Ireland's Miseries, the Grand Cause and Cure*, published in 1852 by the Reverend Edward Marcus Dill, missionary agent of the Irish Presbyterian Church. Dill was a bigot of the first order, and hated everything to do with the Pope and Popery. In the summary of one of his chapters he describes Catholics as 'mental imbeciles, social cripples, moral slaves', and elsewhere decries Romanism as 'a Satanic conspiracy against the human soul'. The cause of Irish poverty and miseries over the centuries was not, as some deluded people suggested, bad government, an unjust land system, a greedy ascendancy class, or even the innate defects of the Celtic race, but could be attributed to one, and only one, fundamental cause – the fact that so many of the island's inhabitants were Papists. Logically, therefore, in this 'Christian' preacher's view, it followed that the best and only solution for Ireland's woes was either to convert all Catholics to the superior faith of Protestantism, or perhaps better still, get rid of the Papists altogether by means of death or emigration. This 'grand cure', as he expressed it, was coming about fortuitously as a result of the potato blight:

God has pleased, by means of the famine, to commence a social revolution amongst us, which promises to effect the country's renovation. Irish Popery has ever relied on its numbers and, to increase these, has encouraged early marriages and availed of itself of the potato's productiveness. But how vain its craftiest devices, when God chooses to mar them! He smites the potato, and its strength becomes its weakness – its people, who had multiplied like summer insects, vanish like them too – its supplies are cut off – its priests are starving – its chapels are being emptied, and its arm is withered!

It is a matter of easy calculation that if things go on for some years as, to all appearances, they must do, Popery in Ireland is inevitably doomed. It would seem as if God had resolved to clear out the country in order to replenish it anew. The land is rapidly passing into British hands. With the emigration of the Irish, there has commenced the immigration of the Scotch and English; and numbers are only awaiting the adjustment of the land question to settle among us. Thus God is renovating the country by the double process of driving Popery beyond the ocean, and bringing Protestantism across the Channel.[25]

How can one explain such violent outbursts of contempt, even hatred, for those who, after all, were fellow Christians? Were such prejudices held only by a minority, or were they the opinions of most Protestants? Could they be compared with, say, the cruelties of the Catholic Inquisition or the anti-Semitism that had disfigured Christian Europe for so many centuries? How could one love one's neighbour and at the same time cast so many innocent people into outer darkness? In particular, why was it the clergy, who were supposed to be educated and God-fearing men and claimed to be models for ordinary folk to follow, who set such a bad example of intolerance to the most ignorant, self-interested and biased of the laity.

To find adequate answers to such questions it is necessary to examine closely, not merely contemporary theology and Church organisation, but also Anglo-Irish relations and the state of public opinion in the two countries.

The Irish Ascendancy, in spite of temporary setbacks during the famine, still put its faith in the Union with Britain as the strongest defence against any challenge to its privileges, and continued to regard, as it had always done, the episcopalians as an essential prop of Church and state. 'Establishment' was a word which was an emblem for property rights and political power, as well as a label for religious dominance.

In Ulster a growing number of Presbyterians had come to identify their increasing material prosperity, and the *laissez-faire* economic doctrines that accompanied it, with the so-called Puritan virtues of self-help, thrift and hard work. The Calvinists, who were still intellectually fighting the old battles of Reformation and Counter-Reformation, were particularly contemptuous of the impoverished Catholics, whom they regarded as not only steeped in superstition but also, because of their backward-looking religion, incapable of improving themselves in any sense.

Among all these groups, holding them ideologically together and binding their social with their philosophical attitudes, was a passionate belief in the benefits, both material and moral, to be gained from the colonial system. The empire, the reformed faith, and the glorious constitution were linked – sometimes in a rather muddled way – with British wealth, British strength and British greatness. The Orange banner, in which a triumphant Victoria, holding a Bible and draped in the Union Jack, perhaps spoke truer than it knew.

The tragedy of Ireland in the mid-nineteenth century (and indeed for many generations before and since) was that there was a combination of historical circumstances in which almost everything came together to create a situation in which sectarianism could reach its most extreme form. Politics and religion were linked in a way in which it was often difficult to know where social policy began and theology ended, and vice versa. The interests of God and Mammon were not always kept separate. It was specifically in this cultural environment, in which material and moral issues were so closely interrelated, that bigotry and prejudice could flourish.

The British establishment, both Whig and Tory, were determined at all costs to protect their economic and other privileges, and simultaneously encouraged a chauvinist, even positively racist, attitude towards the native Irish. Within the United Kingdom, the 'Protestant constitution' was the keystone of parliamentary democracy as they saw it. It was doubly unlucky for the majority of the Irish people that the politicians and administrators who controlled government policy during the late 1840s were noted as much for their dislike of Catholics as they were for their conservatism. Robert Peel, for example, had been nicknamed 'Orange Peel' because of his opposition to Catholic emancipation. Lord Russell was famous for his anti-Catholic prejudices, and in 1851 took the lead as prime minister in attacking what he called 'Papal aggression'.

The most noted of the moralising civil servants was Sir Charles Trevelyan, a typical agent of the empire, high-minded and self-righteous, but an obscurant and prone to let his conservative political opinions affect his religious values. He was appointed assistant secretary to the treasury, and in this capacity had oversight of the Whig government's welfare policies towards Ireland during the worst stages of the famine. In economics he was a keen disciple of Adam Smith, and in spite of the growing distress, he never lost faith in the advantages of free trade. He constantly advised the Government to spend as little as possible on importing food into Ireland, and condemned any schemes which encouraged what he called 'mendicancy'. He, too, blamed the potato blight on the inscrutable ways of Providence. As to where the main responsibility lay for so much hunger and disease, he said: 'The great evil with which we have to contend is not the physical evil of the famine, but the moral evil of the selfish, perverse and turbulent character of the [Irish] people.'[26] For him, as for so many other members of his Church and class, his 'heart' and his 'treasure' seem to have beaten to the same rhythm.

In contrast, there were, of course, a few politicians and landlords who were more enlightened in their views. Not every Irish property owner was necessarily an evicter, rack-renter or bigot. A handful tried to practise the exhortation to love their neighbours as themselves, and showed themselves prepared to put their altruism before their greed for rents. Some were given

211

the name 'improvers' because through better farming techniques, shrewder buying and selling methods, or even more humane social relationships, they sought to improve the productivity of their estates. Occasionally they wrote to the press, published pamphlets or spoke at meetings or in parliament about the sore plight of their tenants.

One such humanitarian was Lord Frederick Dufferin, the young heir of the Clandeboye estate in north Down who later became a famous imperial administrator. While a student at Oxford in the winter of 1846–7 Dufferin had read about the famine, and along with a companion, he decided to go to Ireland to see what was happening. The two undergraduates chose Skibbereen for their investigation because this was an area which had received so much publicity. Their report, which was published in March 1847, is a sensitively observed and vividly written account of what they saw and the people they met.[27] The visit confirmed all their worst fears. The authors were deeply shocked by their experience, and gave what money they had with them to relief funds. On their return to university they raised a further £1,000 from friends. But charity was all they could offer. Neither could then suggest any political remedy for the country's ills. It was Dufferin's mother, Helen, who wrote that most famous of all famine laments, 'The Irish emigrant'.

John Hamilton of Rossnowlagh, County Donegal, Lord George Hill of Gweedore, County Donegal,[28] Shafto Adair of Ballymena,[29] and the Reverend James Martin, a Church of Ireland parson from Killeshandra, County Cavan,[30] were other Protestants noted as improvers or philanthropists.

The most consistently democratic of these reformers was Sharman Crawford, who, in spite of the fact that he represented Rochdale in Lancashire, never lost interest in his native Ulster. In the Commons he worked closely with fellow radicals, especially with Poulett Scrope and Smith O'Brien.

After several decades of public life, Crawford had few illusions about the role of the Ascendancy in Ireland. In contrast to other critics who blamed tenant farmers and labourers for having too many children and splitting up the land, he argued that the majority of landlords actually encouraged subdivisions so as to get more rents (and incidentally more votes). Moreover, because of laziness or absenteeism they failed to persuade tenants to diversify their crops. From his long experience as a landowner, and his personal knowledge of the Irish economy, Crawford was convinced that the central problem of Irish agriculture was not so much overpopulation or too much reliance on potatoes, but a bad tenure system (this 'monster grievance' as he called it), which made proprietors greedy and arrogant, and tenants thriftless and improvident. The latter were prone to be either too submissive or, alternatively, blindly violent against injustice. The British ruling class could be blamed for always supporting the Irish landlords, and not promoting true democracy in Ireland.

Crawford plunged into the heart of the contemporary political debate when he took up the question of the Government allowing food to be exported from Ireland when hundreds of thousands of Irish people were starving, a controversy of exceptional importance because it raised the most profound issues of how far the welfare of the common people should be balanced against minority rights in property and the related dogmas of *laissez-faire*. He was not content to talk in generalities, but quoted facts and figures to support his case. Irish landlords were drawing rents, he claimed, of about £13 million annually. If three-quarters of that total was divided among labourers and poorer tenant farmers, then this would have been enough (possibly with some financial assistance from the British exchequer) to buy the large quantities of beef, pork, lamb, oats and barley, butter and eggs which were being sold abroad. 'The farmers were obliged to send off their corn to Liverpool and Scotland in order to pay their rents,' said Crawford to an unsympathetic House of Commons. 'The rents are not returned to the people in the shape of profitable investment – the rents are collected and the people left starving.'[31]

In an attempt to back up his oratory with some tangible legislation, Crawford moved at least five bills relating to landownership in Ireland during the famine – in May 1846, January, February and June 1847, and March 1848 – but they were all defeated. When a grass-roots tenant-right movement began to revive in Ulster in the late 1840s and early 1850s, he was one of the keenest propagandists for the farmers, speaking at meetings all over the province.

But for all his radicalism, at heart Crawford remained a federalist, or moderate unionist. There were other northern Protestants, however, who were prepared to go further, and boldly declared themselves, against all odds, the inheritors of the democratic and non-sectarian United Irish tradition. These were the Young Irelanders.

13

YOUNG ULSTER

The English Parliament and Government cannot do good to Ireland, even if they were supposed to be willing to try. No matter what laws they make or change or amend, by way of relief or boon to Ireland, while their rule remains, it acts like a poison or cancer on the body of the Irish community, deranging its vital functions, crushing its vital forces, destroying its health or soundness . . . It is not revolution or changes in constitutional forms that Ireland needs, or that the Irish people desire. It is simply Ireland for the Irish; for the Irish of every creed or class – for tenants and landlords – for Catholics and Protestants – for poor and rich.

John Martin[1]

The individual best placed strategically to campaign against the damage which the Union with Britain had done to Ireland was Daniel O'Connell. For over thirty years he had built up an unrivalled reputation as the most famous of Irish nationalists, the great Counsellor and Liberator, the architect of Catholic emancipation. His fame as a popular leader had spread to Europe. His personality and energy were enormous, and his oratory could attract hundreds of thousands of people to monster meetings. His political enemies feared and disliked him, while at the same time he had unique power over the poorest and most dispossessed. If he beckoned they would follow him anywhere.

Tragically for his own reputation, and for the independence and prosperity of his native land, when the famine came he proved inadequate in both words and deeds. His policies turned out to be calamitous. During a period when the Irish people

215

were crying out for resolute leadership, he bluffed and temporised. At a time when almost any sacrifice would have been better than allowing the population to sink into avoidable hunger, death or emigration, he persisted in his long-established refusal to countenance any physical resistance to landlord neglect or government misrule. The winning of Irish national independence was not worth the shedding of a single drop of Irish blood, he said, and yet during the years 1845–9 perhaps a million Irish people died, many of them unnecessarily. In company with conservative Catholic bishops and clergy, he helped disarm the Irish people during a time of social catastrophe – when genocide was occurring on a vast scale – leaving the poorest, demoralised and defenceless, when they should have striven to hold on to every acre and ounce of food.

O'Connell's most serious political mistake, apart from his unwillingness to envisage any other form of struggle except for moral force, was to allow his long campaign for repeal of the Union to be too closely identified with his own religious group, the Catholics. Though personally tolerant, and in no sense a bigot, and often proclaiming himself a friend of Protestants, in practice his life and career were inextricably linked with the Church in which he was born, brought up and educated. He regularly admitted that he could not achieve his aims without the support of members of all religious denominations,[2] but in fact he relied upon the Catholic section of the population. He was founder of the Catholic Association, he depended financially upon 'Catholic rent', a regular collection of small amounts of money from the poorer section of the Catholic community, and his chief agents in the constituencies were generally the local Catholic priests. His greatest political achievement, that of Catholic emancipation, in some respects turned the clock back, because it actually reduced the number of parliamentary voters. In any event, it was a reform specifically favouring one religious denomination; it did nothing to improve the lot of disenfranchised Presbyterians or episcopalians. More than any other Irish leader of the nineteenth century, he was responsible for laying the nationalists open to the charge which was later so

216

effectively used against them by the unionists, that 'Home Rule would mean Rome rule'.

He was also, in spite of his many virtues, a man of certain personal weaknesses – he was arrogant and unwilling to listen to advice or to have lieutenants around him who were not sycophants. His favourite son, John, whom he wished to become his political heir, was weak and vacillating. The saddest part of his career came in his old age, when tired and feeble, he sank into senility. His death, while on a pilgrimage to Rome in May 1847, occurred during the darkest days of the famine.

As a result of this possibly unwitting sectarian approach to politics, he failed to understand the social problems of Ulster, and allowed himself to be outmanoeuvred by such unionists as the Reverend Henry Cooke, who succeeded in foiling his attempts to promote the repeal movement in the north in 1841. He antagonised the liberal Presbyterians by the scurrility of his tongue, and quarrelled over tithes with Sharman Crawford, the man who might have been one of his best allies in the province. He showed little awareness of the importance in Ulster of the issue of tenant rights.

The Young Ireland movement, which gradually took over the struggle for national independence during the mid-1840s, differed from O'Connell's movement not only in style of leadership but also in its broader vision of a new and all-embracing Ireland. John Mitchel compared the Young Irelanders to the United Irishmen of the 1790s: 'It was the grand object of Young Ireland – and it was grand – to lift up the Irish cause above both Catholic claims and Protestant pretensions, and to unite all sects in the one character of Irishmen, to put an end to English domination. Their aim was precisely the idea of the United Irishmen; though their mode of action was very different.'[3]

The Young Ireland leaders were concerned with all aspects of Irish culture, as well as politics, and succeeded in winning the support of many scholars and writers. They were particularly skilful in taking up the related questions of nationality, land and religion. Bolder and more courageous than O'Connell in the face of difficulties, they were mostly prepared to envisage the use of physical force, if compelled by circumstances.

The famine shocked them to their innermost being, but they did not whinge or whine, or blame the disaster on God's inscrutable will – they held the British government and the landlords responsible for the existing agricultural system, and called, in the short run, for suspension of rents and the prohibition of food exports. In the long run they urged the creation of a peasant-proprietorship scheme. Their internationalism was characterised by their friendly relations with the Chartists in England, and their sympathy towards the various revolutionary movements in Europe in 1848. It was one of their leaders, Thomas Francis Meagher, who brought back from France the idea of a tricolour flag, symbolising the unity of Orange and Green.

In particular, they had a better understanding of Ulster than O'Connell. This appreciation of the north's specific problems arose partly from the fact that several of the movement's leaders were Ulstermen, and partly derived from their different religious backgrounds. Gavan Duffy, a founder of the *Nation*, was a Catholic from County Monaghan, and John Mitchel and John Martin were Presbyterians from County Down. Samuel Ferguson, also from County Down, was an episcopalian, poet, antiquarian, and contributor to the *Nation*. All these individuals, though they might disagree on certain key issues, were acutely aware of the damage done by religious dissension. It was this northern flavour, combined with a non-sectarian spirit, which led some people to speak of 'Young Ulster'.

Thomas Davis, a Protestant from the south, also enthusiastically took up the theme that a spirit of religious tolerance was the only basis on which a true and worthwhile Irish nationalism could be built. Like his hero Wolfe Tone, he claimed that everyone living in Ireland, regardless of their ethnic or denominational affiliations, should regard himself or herself as Irish, and that the only way in which the nation's freedom could be won was through the joint activity of Catholic, episcopalian and Dissenter. His philosophy was summed up in the poem 'Celts and Saxons', which he wrote for the *Nation*:

> What matter that at different shrines
>> We pray unto one God?
> What matter that at different times
>> Your fathers won this sod?
> In fortune and in name we're bound
>> By stronger links than steel:
> And neither can be safe or sound
>> But in the other's weal . . .[4]

When William Carleton, the Ulster novelist who had converted from Catholicism to Protestantism, was criticised as an apostate, Davis said that anyone was entitled to change their religion if they wanted to. In any event, he felt that Carleton was a magnificent writer and should be assessed on his literary merits.

But Davis, like other liberal Protestants, equally rejected any suggestion of triumphalism on the part of narrow-minded Catholics. So far as his own private conscience was concerned, he was not prepared to approve any Catholic practice, such as worship of holy relics or belief in miracles, which he regarded as superstitious. He argued, rightly as it turned out, that the most reactionary elements in the establishment would continue to play on the fears of Protestants in all walks of life; in particular, the fear that if Catholics achieved political power in an independent parliament they would at once impose a Catholic supremacy in place of a Protestant one. In an important letter to Smith O'Brien in October 1844, when Davis was being attacked by the O'Connellites for his alleged anti-Catholicism, he wrote: 'I will not be the conscious tool of bigots. I will not strive to beat down political, in order to set up religious, ascendancy.'[5] In another letter written a day later, this time to Duffy, he threatened that he would withdraw from politics if his own religious liberty or that of the Irish people generally was interfered with. 'I am determined not to be the tool of a Catholic ascendancy, while apparently the enemy of British domination', he wrote.[6]

The attacks on Davis and his followers for their alleged lack of sympathy with the Catholic Church, or worse still, their possible indifference towards Christian teachings as a whole, came to a head in May 1845, when an ugly incident occurred, revealing not the irreligion of the Young Irelanders but the deep-rooted intolerance of O'Connell and his sympathisers towards everything that Young Ireland stood for, particularly their religious liberalism. The issue, which was one of the main factors leading to a final breach between the right and left wings within the Repeal Association, arose over the Government's proposal for three new and non-denominational university colleges in Galway, Cork and Belfast.[7] Davis welcomed these plans as offering an opportunity to provide non-sectarian higher education for young Irishmen. In contrast, the Catholic bishops, and following them, O'Connell and his son John, were suspicious of these institutions, which they claimed would be 'Godless' and therefore un-Irish. A debate took place in the Repeal Association, in which Michael Joseph Barry, a Protestant, angered some members of the audience by stating that he was 'utterly indifferent' to the issue of whether the colleges should be non-denominational or not. This remark infuriated a young Catholic delegate, who bitterly criticised the phrase 'utterly indifferent', and argued that the Young Irelanders knew nothing about true Irish character and real Irish hearts. The temperature of the meeting was further raised when O'Connell took off his cap, waved it in the air, and loudly cheered his approval of the young speaker's remarks.

Davis then rose to reply, referring to 'my old college friend, my Catholic friend, my very Catholic friend, Mr. Conway'. O'Connell interrupted him: 'It is no crime to be a Catholic, I hope?' 'No,' said Davis. 'Surely no, for –' 'The sneer with which you used the word would lead to the inference,' O'Connell interrupted again. Davis strove as best he could to deny the accusation, declaring that some of his best friends were Catholics, and making it clear that he thought the suggestions of the Catholic bishops (including the appointment of college chaplains) would actually improve the proposed parliamentary bill. But O'Connell was determined to press home his advantage, and denounce those upstarts who called themselves Young Ireland. In a phrase, which was afterwards widely quoted, he said that he had always stood by Old Ireland, and that he had a notion that Old Ireland would stand by him. Davis was so over-come by this unprovoked public attack by an individual who was still his nominal leader, and for whom he still had some respect, that he burst into tears.

The two men later shook hands, but the damage had been done. In January 1847 the Young Irelanders broke decisively with O'Connell, and formed a new and more radical organisation, the Irish Confederation. Sectarianism and religious differences had once again been allowed to split the nationalist ranks.

The second issue on which the Young Irelanders broke with the constitutional repealers was on the question of landowner-ship, which became ever more critical as the famine spread. O'Connell himself was a minor landlord, and though strongly critical of the greed and incompetence of his fellow proprietors, never envisaged that the system as such should be abolished. He played to the mass of the population with his rhetorical appeals to vast crowds, and democratic phrasemongering, but what he feared above all else was a popular rising of labourers and tenant farmers. Since the French Revolution he had abhorred the idea of a revolutionary mob. In Ulster it was widely believed that he was not fully committed to tenant rights.

In contrast, the more radical Young Irelanders had become convinced from their experiences during the famine that minor reforms or mere tinkering with landlordism was not enough – that what was now required was the destruction of the whole rotten corrupt edifice, and its replacement by a system of peas-ant ownership. Social and economic revolution must go hand in hand with political revolution.

In the south of Ireland the main theoretician of this new doctrine was James Fintan Lalor, a member of the Church of Ireland and son of the well-known Queen's County (now County Laois) nationalist MP Patrick Lalor. The young Lalor was crip-pled and suffered from asthma, and by nature was more of a recluse and scholar than an activist. His mind and spirit were vigorous, however, and he travelled for some years in France, where he absorbed revolutionary ideas. In 1847 he came to public attention when he published a series of articles in the *Nation* in which he declared that land was the key to the political struggle in Ireland, and that it was only through agrarian agitation that the majority of labourers and poor tenant farmers could be roused. Landlords in Ireland, he said, had no moral right to the vast demesnes they possessed because their ancestors had seized the soil by force. It was wrong for eight thousand rich men to control the lives and destinies of eight million people, and the only right of property that could justifiably be accepted was that property which had been created by the individual's own labour. What the Irish people needed, therefore, was not just the repeal of the Union but a reconquest of the land. This idea of giving back the soil to the men who tilled it, which he put forward to a meeting of tenant farmers at Holycross, County Tipperary, in September 1847, alarmed the Tory press, which could at once see its revolutionary implications. On the other hand, it appealed strongly to the radical Young Ireland leaders.[8]

In Ulster the tenant farmers and rural labourers, backed by liberal supporters in the towns, were in two minds as to how to react to Lalor's appeals. The more cautious elements, predominantly Presbyterian, wanted to concentrate their forces in defence of tenant rights, and to disregard what they considered to be Utopian schemes about peasant proprietorship. Led by Sharman Crawford, they hoped that parliamentary legislation, spurred on when necessary by peaceful demonstrations, would bring some solution to their problems. Land reform, and not repeal of the Union, was what they wanted. Crawford himself was not a separatist, and advocated an Irish constitution that would consist of some form of federalism, or halfway house, between the full Union and an independent state. The *Northern Whig*, though still critical of landlords, was dismissive of any land reform that went beyond the preservation of the Ulster custom.

The radicals, on the other hand, especially among Catholics but also involving some Presbyterians, sought for more fundamental changes, including a determined resistance against the authorities.[9] They pointed out that the official Devon Commission report of 1845 had threatened the tenant right privilege, with its warning that 'Landlords do not appear aware of the perils which threaten their property . . . They do not perceive the present tenant-right of Ulster as an embryo copyhold which must decline in value as the practice becomes more confirmed.'[10] And Lord Palmerston's dictum, 'Tenant rights are landlords' wrongs' had further undermined their confidence. As for Sharman Crawford, he had laboured valiantly on behalf of tenant farmers for many years in the House of Commons, but all his measures had been humiliatingly defeated. Hopes that Irish landlords would somehow change their spots and try to look after the interests of all the Irish people, and not merely their own narrow caste, had come to nothing.

Crawford's prestige as the most radical of Ulster-born MPs and his well-earned reputation as 'the father of tenant rights' was high, and his parliamentary-oriented views carried the day. It was his personality and political style which was dominant among the reformers, and he soon had around him a powerful alliance of the middle classes, professional people, liberal MPs, politicians, journalists, and some Catholic and Presbyterian clergymen. The *Northern Whig* and the *Londonderry Standard* were on his side, and at Westminster he had the support of several radical, and some Irish nationalist, MPs.

In October 1847, that is, one month after Lalor's rally in Tipperary, a big anti-landlord and anti-government demonstration was held in Derry city, attended by tenant-right delegates from all over the north-west of Ireland. This was followed by a dinner held in honour of Crawford at which the city's mayor, ten Presbyterian ministers and eighteen Catholic priests attended.[11] Messages of support were sent by two Catholic bishops. In January 1848 another big rally was held in Ballybay, County Monaghan.[12] It was reported that two thousand people were present, again including many clergy. On the platform with the indefatigable Crawford was James McKnight, editor of the *Londonderry Standard*, a man who was destined to play an important part in Ulster land-reform agitation during the next twenty years. The choice of Ballybay for the rally was significant as this small town had once been a stronghold of Orangeism,

223

and the home of the Tory anti-repeal hero, Sam Gray. Another town of famous memory was Dungannon, which was the scene of the next big tenant demonstration in May 1848. This meeting was attended by representatives from scores of villages and towns in the north, and was said by the *Northern Whig* to be 'the most important demonstration held in Ulster for many years'.[13] The two main speakers were McKnight and the rising young barrister and liberal politician from Coleraine, Samuel Greer.

A high point of this non-sectarian campaign had occurred in November 1847, when 1,200 repealers met in Belfast.[14] In contrast to O'Connell's unsuccessful visit in 1841 when his overtures were mainly to Catholics, the appeal on this occasion was deliberately made as wide as possible. There were many references back to the ecumenical spirit of Dungannon in 1782 and the United Irishmen in 1798. On the platform, instead of one Liberator from the south, there were several prominent Confederates representing different parts of the country, and belonging to different Churches – the episcopalian Smith O'Brien, the Presbyterians John Mitchel and John Martin, and the Catholics Michael Doheny, Darcy McGee and Thomas Meagher.

Mitchel, in keeping with his non-sectarian philosophy, went out of his way to emphasise the local patriotism of the Ulster people, regardless of whether they were Orangemen, Conservatives, democrats, Chartist sympathisers, tenants or landlords. In his new Ireland he promised there would be no ascendancy by any one group, but a broad and democratic base for the Irish nation. The eloquent Meagher, who had been touring the famine districts in the south with Mitchel, devoted the most important part of his long speech to the theme that one of the reasons why the repeal movement had made little ground in the north was O'Connell's error in identifying the national cause with one religious group. Meagher suggested that they should substitute the broader call to 'The Citizens of Ireland' in place of the old slogan 'Priests and People'. 'I say to you that there is a spirit growing up among young Catholics,' he concluded, 'which will not bend to any clerical authority beyond the sanctuary.'

The Confederates further disagreed with Daniel O'Connell about his attitude towards the language and ancient culture of Ireland. O'Connell, though brought up as a native Irish-speaker at Derrynane in County Kerry, had despised the tongue of his forefathers because he associated it with poverty and backwardness. He wanted the common people to learn English so that they could advance themselves socially and economically. In his constant travels throughout the country he saw everywhere ruins and monuments, the relics of an old and once highly developed civilisation, but these seem to have meant little to him. As a follower of Jeremy Bentham, the English pragmatist, his dream was of material progress. He spoke of himself as a modernist who wished to forget the past and concentrate on the industrialisation of his country.

Paradoxically the Confederates, most of whom were of English or Scottish descent, knowing little or no Gaelic, took the opposite view. They, too, favoured the coming of factories and economic growth, but not at the expense of the traditional Irish culture which had sustained the people through the darkest centuries of poverty and oppression. For them the struggle to de-anglicise Ireland culturally and politically went hand in hand, and they were deeply involved in every aspect of the study of the old Gaelic civilisation, pre-Christian as well as Christian. With solemnity and proper awe they visited the neolithic ruins at Newgrange and the Boyne, and the rich monastic remains at Cashel, Monasterboice and Clonmacnoise. They read with admiration the newly translated Annals of the Four Masters, learned the epic tales of Cuchulain and the Knights of the Red Branch, listened with pride, and often tried to copy, old Irish songs and music. Among their friends were the most eminent linguists and antiquarians of the day.

Thomas Davis, though he died young (from scarlatina in 1845), and his most creative period only covered about five years, is generally recognised as the individual who did most in the early 1840s to promote this study of Irish history and literature. Though lacking the literary gifts of Mitchel, and the political skills of Duffy, he nevertheless reached, through the columns of the *Nation*, many thousands of ordinary people who were seeking ideas and words to express their nationality. With remarkable foresight, even before the famine got its grip and hundreds of thousands began to flee the land, he could see that the old language was in danger because of growing English cultural domination. A nation without a language of its own, he wrote in a phrase which had a profound effect on subsequent generations, is only half a nation. If the language dies, then the fetter of conquest has worn through.

Two Ulster-born writers who were friends of Davis's, and played a major part in this cultural revival, were Samuel Ferguson from Belfast, and William Carleton from County Tyrone. Both lived most of their adult lives in Dublin, but their roots were deeply planted in the north.

Samuel Ferguson was an important inspiration of cultural nationalism in Ireland during the second and third quarters of the nineteenth century. Born in Ulster in 1810, and of Scottish origin, he never thought of himself as being anything else but an Irishman. Although for most of his life he proclaimed himself a unionist, he is remembered chiefly for his studies of Gaelic literature, and his lifelong interest in Celtic and early Christian antiquities. He was the foremost literary archaeologist of his day. A humane and tolerant Christian brought up as a sincere member of the Church of Ireland, he was in no way hostile towards Catholics. He had a warm appreciation of how Irish missionaries had brought Christianity to Europe, and at one stage contemplated writing a book about such early Irish saints as Gall, Columba and Columbanus.

Ferguson's involvement with Irish history began when he went to Dublin as a young man to study law: 'The genius of a people at large is not to be learned by the notes of Sunday tourists. The history of centuries must be gathered, published, studied and digested', he wrote.[15] To achieve this aim he taught himself Irish, and quickly became friendly with Eugene O'Curry, John O'Donovan, George Petrie, William Wilde and William Stokes, who were beginning to study the old Irish tongue, manuscripts, music, and artefacts in a scholarly way. In 1840 he contributed to Edward Bunting's *The Ancient Music of Ireland*, and in 1845 favourably reviewed George Petrie's *The Round Towers of Ireland*.

During this period, inspired by the Young Irelanders, he wrote for the *Nation*, and in spite of his objections to the use of physical force to achieve political ends, he defended Richard Dalton Williams, who was on trial on a charge of treason. Williams was acquitted. The elegy he wrote on the death of Thomas Davis was the finest tribute ever paid to this Irish nationalist:

> I walked through Ballinderry in the Spring-time,
>   When the bud was on the tree;
> And I said, in every fresh-ploughed field beholding
>   The sowers striding free,
> Scattering forth the corn in golden plenty
>   On the quick seed-clasping soil,
> Even such this day among the fresh-stirred hearts of Erin,
>   Thomas Davis, is thy toil!

In 1848 Ferguson helped found the Protestant Repeal Association, and in May of that year spoke at one of the association's meetings in Dublin. Proclaiming himself no politician, he nevertheless on this occasion showed a remarkable grasp of political realities. Admitting that he had been mistaken in his earlier belief that Ireland would be better off under the Union, he said that the country had gone back rather than forward since 1801. 'The disadvantages of the Imperial connection greatly outweigh any advantages we might derive, and infinitely outweigh any advantages which we hitherto have derived, from that source,' he stated. Ireland had been treated with 'insolence' and was suffering from laws made by 'strangers to the Irish people'. If during the famine Ireland had had its own government, then the burdens of poverty and hunger would have been more equally shared, but instead the country had been turned into a 'draw-farm for England', and 'all the wealth, refinement and social attractions of the empire' had been centralised in London. What the country needed was 'the establishment of its own legislature'. He was particularly caustic about the failure of the upper classes to come to the aid of the people in a time of acute crisis – a 'great and characteristic evil', he called it. The Ascendancy looked to England for support and protection, and this had propagated an 'anti-national and servile spirit, which is wholly inconsistent with social solidarity, dignity or progress'. He concluded by declaring: 'We are not a colony of Britain – we are an ancient kingdom, an aristocratic people, entitled to our own nationality and resolved on having it.'[16]

After the collapse of Young Ireland he reverted to his unionist beliefs, and was made a Queen's Counsel, appointed to the post of deputy-keeper of Irish records, and eventually knighted by Queen Victoria. These favours from the establishment did not, however, turn him away from his Irish studies. He was interested in every aspect of the history of his native country, its barrows, dolmens and ogham stones, ancient manuscripts, prehistoric sites and holy ruins. Wherever he went on his extensive travels in Ireland or on the Continent he recorded what he saw and heard. His hope, a vain one as it turned out, was that he could persuade the gentry and aristocracy among whom he moved to become as cultivated and educated as himself. He was a savage critic of those Englishmen, or metropolitan 'scribes', as he described them, who took a superior attitude towards Irish people and culture.[17]

In 1865 he published his most important book, *Lays of the Western Gael*, and seven years later he translated the epic poem *Congal*. Ferguson can hardly be described as a great poet, and in scholarship he was surpassed by O'Donovan and O'Curry. However, during the darkest days following the famine, when such a high proportion of the people were broken and demoralised, he kept alive 'the heroic spirit' in Ireland, and thus paved the way for the literary renaissance inspired a generation later by Douglas Hyde and William Butler Yeats.

Ferguson's close friend William Carleton was born in 1794 near Clogher, County Tyrone, the fourteenth child of a poor tenant farmer. His father seems to have been a remarkable man – a pious Catholic, loving parent, good linguist, and well known in the neighbourhood as the custodian of old folk tales and

228

customs. His mother was famed locally as a singer of Gaelic songs.

As a boy he was sent to a hedge school, which was then the only opportunity for a poor but likely Catholic lad to get some education. He learned to speak and write Latin fluently, and thus became that rarity – trilingual. His natural intelligence and aptitude for learning encouraged him at the age of fifteen to set out for Munster as 'a poor scholar'. Returning home after various adventures, he was indulged by his parents as a potential recruit to the priesthood and for a short time he was a student at Maynooth. On his own later admission, at the age of nineteen he joined the Ribbonmen in County Tyrone, perhaps stemming from a bitter childhood memory of an Orange raid on his farm, but he afterwards turned strongly against them. His interests were not really in scholarly pursuits, the clerical life or even politics. Instead he closely observed everything that was going on around him, and used the experiences of this early life as subject matter for some of his finest short stories and novels.

In Dublin Carleton fell in with the noted editor and proselytiser Caesar Otway, who persuaded him to convert to Protestantism. Otway published several of Carleton's early stories in his magazine the *Christian Examiner*. In 1830 a collection of these tales was published under the title *Traits and Stories of the Irish Peasantry*. Though his widely publicised apostasy had offended some Catholics, the book, which ran to three volumes, was an immediate success, and was soon reprinted.

In spite of his association with such ultra-Protestants as Otway, Carleton was admired by the Young Irelanders Duffy and Davis as one of the finest writers of his era. He was published in the *Nation*, and issued *Rody the Rover* under the imprint of the nationalist James Duffy. One of his most ardent defenders against political criticism was the Catholic bishop, Patrick Murray. In 1845 he published his most famous novel, *Valentine McClutchy, the Irish Agent*, a powerful study of a profligate landlord. The book, which was praised by the *Nation* and attacked by the Tory press, is regarded by the critic and writer Benedict Kiely as the

229

most important Irish novel published during the nineteenth century.[18] In its preface Carleton repudiates what he terms the 'absurd prejudices' of his earlier novels. Two years later he wrote *The Black Prophet*, the story of a Tyrone family enduring the horrors of famine.

Carleton, writing about a social system in decline, was a superb storyteller, and an accurate interpreter of the lives of the humblest people – 'the lost people of Ireland',[19] as Kiely describes them – before and after the great famine.

Two other contemporaries of Ferguson's, and co-workers in the field of Gaelic studies, were Robert Shipbuoy McAdam and William Reeves, bishop of Down and Connor. McAdam was born in Belfast in 1808, and died there, almost completely forgotten, eighty-seven years later. His father James had been a friend of the Reverend Samuel Bryson and James McDonnell during the Ulster Celtic revival of the 1820s and 1830s. Robert's main interests were in the study of the Irish language and the country's antiquities and he devoted most of his spare time to this hobby. He was a personal friend of several hedge-schoolmasters, and in contradiction to the trend towards teaching English in schools, he favoured the teaching of Irish to children in those areas where that language was widely spoken. In 1853 he began publishing the *Ulster Journal of Archaeology*, a serious and weighty journal dealing with the topography, languages, ruins and monuments of the north.

Reeves, a northern antiquarian who received more honour in his own lifetime than McAdam, is now also largely forgotten. He was born in Cork in 1815 but spent much of his clerical career in Ulster. A classics student in Trinity College Dublin, he later became a curate in Lisburn and then rector in Ballymena.

Reeves became a close friend of John O'Donovan's, who in the 1840s was establishing a reputation as a linguist and translator. The two men corresponded frequently, and also developed contacts with scholars in Britain and on the Continent.

The most important contribution which Reeves made to the preservation of the relics of early Christian Ireland was his purchase of the famous Book of Armagh and his donation of it to the cathedral library in Armagh, along with various other documents relating to Saint Patrick.

In 1856 he published his translation from the Latin of Adomnan's life of Saint Columba and shortly before he died he was honoured by his fellow Gaelic scholars by being made president of the Royal Irish Academy. Reeves was never directly involved in politics but strove all his life to bring Protestants and Catholics together in the study of their Christian past. As his biographer Lady Ferguson puts it, he believed that Irishmen of all creeds could meet on 'a common platform' of historical, religious and archaeological studies.[20]

The main contribution which these scholars and writers made to the ongoing debate about the nature of Irish society and Irish nationality was in the field of language and literature. They saw culture as a possible inspirational force to bind together the different regional, ethnic and religious groups. A more directly political influence, but pointing in the same broad direction, came from two other Ulstermen, both Dissenters, whose names have become indelibly linked with the vision of Young Ireland. These were John Mitchel and John Martin.

14

TWO SONS OF THE MANSE

My friends, the people's sovereignty, the land and sea and air of
Ireland: this is the gospel that the heavens and the earth are
preaching, and that all hearts are secretly burning to embrace.
Give up for ever that old interpretation you put upon the word
'Repeal'. Ours is no priest movement; it is no sectarian movement; it is no money swindle, or 'Eighty-Two' delusion, nor
puffery, nor O'Connellism, nor Mullaghamast 'green-cap' stage-
play, nor loud-sounding inanity of any sort, got up for any man's
profit or praise. It is the mighty, passionate struggle of a nation
hastening to be born into national life . . .

John Mitchel[1]

The strength of the Young Ireland movement was that it had
the power of drawing into its ranks the finest spirits of the age –
poets, novelists, scholars, historians, linguists, doctors, politicians and landlords, as well as rank-and-file tenant farmers and
workers. It attracted people from the four provinces of Ireland,
and the different religious denominations. The personalities of
its leaders were diverse – populist and demagogic like Meagher
or aloof like O'Brien, tough like Mitchel or sensitive like Davis,
practical like Duffy or dreamy like the poet James Clarence
Mangan, but they all had the special quality of moral integrity.
At home or in exile, whatever differences they might have about
the best tactics to pursue, they held firm to their view that their
first allegiance was to their native, and not to some foreign, land.

What inspired them was their belief that there would be no
solution to Ireland's political problems until the country was
free to settle its own destiny, and that national freedom could

232

not be won unless north and south, Protestants and Catholics, worked together to achieve their common aims.

John Mitchel, who joined the *Nation* in the autumn of 1845 shortly after Davis's sudden death, held both these convictions – but more fiercely, boldly and resolutely than the others. By temperament he was a fighter, always prepared to go to extremes, hating with a burning intensity the wrongs and evils he saw around him. The circumstances of the time only added to his belief that British rule, which he saw as the root of all social ills in Ireland, should be destroyed. His comrades Davis and Duffy, who had persuaded him to join them in Dublin, had founded the *Nation* in sunnier times when there was still some hope of peaceful progress in Ireland. Mitchel came on the scene just as the potato blight appeared. The famine, in all its horror and hypocrisy, its political cruelty and moral collapse, needed the *saeva indignatio* of a Swift to excoriate it. It found such indignation, combined with superb literary gifts, in the person of this young radical.

Mitchel was born in 1815 near Dungiven, County Derry, son of a liberal Presbyterian minister reputed to have sympathised with the United Irishmen, and a mother with literary tastes. In theology his father was inclined towards Unitarianism, and during the 1820s wrote a religious treatise that showed some independence of mind. The young Mitchel was educated at Dr Henderson's school in Newry, County Down, where he met a local boy, John Martin, who became a lifelong friend. At the age of fifteen he was sent to Trinity College Dublin, where he obtained a BA degree. After graduation he entered banking but did not like it, and later became a solicitor in Banbridge, County Down. At the age of twenty-two he eloped with the sixteen-year-old Jenny Verner, daughter of a local army officer, and after some romantic adventures was later married in Drumcree, County Armagh.

Mitchel's political interests, which were already maturing because of his legal defence of local Catholics and his wide reading of Irish history, were stimulated by a visit made by Daniel O'Connell to Newry in 1839. A year later he met Gavan

Duffy in Belfast. It was this meeting that was to change his life. Duffy, together with Thomas Davis and John Blake Dillon, founded the *Nation* in 1842, and three years later Mitchel was invited to join them as a regular writer. Soon they had added Fintan Lalor and James Clarence Mangan to their list of contributors. It was a team destined to leave an imprint on Irish history. Mitchel quickly proved to have exceptional gifts as a polemicist and political writer. His cultural background and wide education had given him a deep understanding of Irish history. His passionate convictions, combined with a biting, ironical literary style, made him within a few years the most celebrated agitator in Ireland. Critics compared him to Swift for the savagery of his attacks on the Government, and to Tone for the wide sweep of his political imagination.

Setting up house in Dublin in 1845, his home became a centre of the Young Ireland movement, regularly visited by almost all the famous Irish nationalists of the time, Protestant and Catholic alike. Thomas Carlyle, the Scottish Tory philosopher, visited him there, and so did Samuel Ferguson and William Carleton. Mangan was a close friend, and long after his death Mitchel edited his poems in New York.

It was during the next three short, but momentous, years in Dublin, while still only a young man, that all those ideas which became central to his political philosophy matured – his concept of Irish nationality, which embraced both Protestant and Catholic, his hatred for foreign rule, which he saw (like Tone) as being responsible for so many ills in Ireland, and his growing conviction that it could only be through physical force that imperialism and landlordism would be driven out of the country.

Mitchel's upbringing had been a tolerant one, and though he became prejudiced on matters of race and skin colour, there is no sign that he was bigoted religiously. His ideal was the movement of 1798 when Protestant and Catholic sank their theological differences in the common cause of Irish political unity. Recognising that the reformed faith had been brought into Ireland as an alien doctrine imposed by foreigners who had seized the land, he nevertheless always adhered to the belief that members of the different Churches could live together in peace so long as they were not stirred up from outside the country. In his *History of Ireland* he devoted several passages to describing the way in which during the seventeenth and eighteenth centuries Ireland had been caught up in Reformation and Counter-Reformation struggles and in the continuing wars between England, France and Spain for European hegemony. He was not interested in theology, which he regarded as a device for diverting people's minds away from the real issues of food and land. His main purpose was to give a better life to the mass of the impoverished Catholic population, and to this end he worked as closely as possible with sympathetic Catholics. His closest friend, apart from John Martin, was the Tipperary priest, Father John Kenyon. Until the split which took place over political tactics before the 1848 rising, he worked closely with the Catholic Gavan Duffy.

Mitchel did not extend his tolerance to the Orange Order – that 'bloody association', he called it – which he saw as the religious arm of the Tory Party and deliberately created in 1795 to stir up hatred against Catholics. 'There is . . . little doubt that this shocking society was encouraged by the Government, and by most of the magistrates and country gentlemen to keep alive religious animosity, and prevent the spread of the United Irish organisation', he wrote.[2] He was also critical of the bishops and parsons of the Established Church, whom he regarded as tools of the landlords.

Mitchel always detested any manifestation of hypocrisy, whether in religion or politics, and he was particularly scornful about those unionists who pretended to be concerned about the purity of their theological doctrines when what they were really worried about was protecting their vested financial interests. In his famous 'third letter' to the Protestant farmers of Ulster he ridicules the pretensions of such aristocrats as the viceroy Lord Clarendon and the Earl of Enniskillen, and analyses what was meant by 'loyalty' to the Protestant succession to the English throne:

My Lord Enniskillen does not say a word to you about what is, after all, the main concern – the tenure of your farms – not one word. It is about your Protestant interest he is uneasy. He is apprehensive not lest you be evicted by landlords, and sent to the poorhouse, but lest purgatory and the Seven Sacraments be thrust down your throats . . . Do you think . . . that a vow to defend the Protestant Constitution in Church and State would remedy the conditions of hundreds of thousands of tenants who were sinking ever deeper into hunger and poverty? It seems to me precisely our Constitution in Church and State that has brought us up to this condition . . . it was certainly not the Pope of Rome – the Pope, we know, is 'the man of Sin', and 'the anti-Christ', and also, if you like, 'the Mystery of Iniquity' and all that, but he brings no ejectments from Ireland. The Seven Sacraments are, to be sure, very dangerous, but the quarter-acre clause touches you more nearly.[3]

His passionate conviction that religion should not be allowed to divide the Irish people was only equalled by his belief that everyone born or living in Ireland, irrespective of their origin or language, should be accepted as Irish so long as they paid allegiance to Ireland and not to another country. He occasionally used the phrase 'the two nations', but he was referring here to castes or classes rather than clearly defined national groups. His idea of nationality was essentially political, and not an ethnic, religious or linguistic concept. In all his writings, both in his books and articles, he proclaimed that the Protestants, even if their ancestors had come from Wales, England or Scotland, had become part of the Irish nation through long residence in the island, and that their help was essential if freedom was to be won. In this view he was, of course, echoing Tone and Davis, and foreshadowing the views of politicians like Parnell, and poets like Hyde and Yeats.

In the preface to his first book, *The Life and Times of Aodh O'Neill*, he claimed that the armies of Elizabeth and the planters and undertakers of James may have been marauding adventurers, and even robbers, but that in time their descendants, too, had become Irish:

Whatever god or demon may have led the first of them to these shores, the Anglo-Irish and Scottish Ulstermen have now far too old a title to be questioned: they are a hardy race, and fought stoutly for the pleasant valleys they dwell in. And are not Derry and Enniskillen Ireland's as well as Benburb and the Yellow Ford? – and have not those men and their fathers lived, and loved, and worshipped God, and died there? – are not their green graves heaped up there – more generations of them than they have genealogical skills to count? – a deep enough root these planters have struck into the soil of Ulster, and it would now be ill to unplant them.[4]

He came back again to this theme in one of his most celebrated speeches in 1846 in Conciliation Hall in Dublin:

I am one of the Saxon Irishmen of the North, and you want that race of Irishmen in your ranks more than any other. You cannot well afford to drive even one away from you, however humble and uninfluential. And let me tell you, friends, this is our country as well as yours. You need not expect to free it from the mighty power of England by yourselves – you will not be able to do it. Drive the Ulster Protestants away from your movement by needless tests and you perpetuate the degradation of both yourselves and them. Keep them at a distance from you, make yourself subservient to the old, and well-known English policy of ruling Ireland always by one party or the other and England will keep her heel upon both your necks for ever.[5]

Critics have said of Mitchel that he hated England more than he loved Ireland. Certainly he loathed English rule in Ireland. All his speeches and writings are full of the most powerful invective against imperialism, the military conquest of his native country, the seizure of land, the penal laws, the deliberate encouragement of sectarianism, and the destruction of the Irish language and culture. He despised the landlord system, and had the most withering contempt for both Whigs and Tories. Lord Clarendon and other British administrators were to him stupid, tyrannical, and – worst crime of all for one who detested humbug – hypocritical. In particular, he saw the Act of Union as the final mark of bondage upon an oppressed people. In *The*

237

Life and Times of Aodh O'Neill he described imperialism as a 'foul fiend'.[6] Later in his *Jail Journal* when he ran out of words – an unusual occurrence for so prolific a talker and writer – he could only express his feelings of horror by describing British rule in Ireland as 'the Thing'. His biographer, Seumus MacCall, says that he regarded the British Empire as a new Carthage, and himself as a new Cato.[7]

But he did not dislike the ordinary people of England. On the contrary, he spoke most warmly of them, seeing them as victims of their own ruling class, and led by an aristocracy which was greedy and oppressive. His respect for English literature was enormous, and he worshipped Shakespeare. His own literary style was deeply influenced by the authorised version of the Bible, which he had absorbed as a young man in the Newry manse. During moments of darkest despair, when he was ill with asthma aboard the prison ship in Bermuda, he spoke with affection of those jailers who showed some kindness to him. He admired the Chartists who were striving for social reform at home and protesting against the imprisonment of Young Irelanders. The Chartists reciprocated these sentiments. In June 1848 when Mitchel was arrested and put on trial they held protest demonstrations in London, Manchester, Birkenhead and Bradford.[8]

In spite of what he admitted had become a 'holy hatred' for English rule, it was only gradually, and under the pressure of dreadful events, that he came round to the view that moral force was useless, and that armed rebellion was necessary if ever Ireland was to be freed from foreign domination. Like Patrick Pearse two generations later, he witnessed a grave national crisis in which Westminster refused to make concessions, and in which the country's Catholic leaders (Daniel O'Connell in 1846–7, John Redmond in 1913–14) betrayed the people's cause by endless talk, prevarication and political manoeuvring. Like Pearse also, he became convinced that Ireland's honour would be saved if even only a few died fighting with a sword in their hand.

At first in Newry and then for a brief period in Dublin he hoped for concessions from the British government, and was prepared temporarily to give the ageing O'Connell and his constitutional repeal agitation the benefit of the doubt. At this stage he even hoped that the landlords might be persuaded to lead the movement for reform. His writing in the *Nation*, though vehement and hotly worded, did not call for an armed rebellion.

It was the famine, and the Government's response to it, which turned him into a separatist and an advocate of physical force. Young Ireland must, as he said, 'tear society up by the roots'. The coming of the blight, the spreading mass starvation, the teeming workhouses with their fever-ridden inmates, the flight of hundreds of thousands overseas – all these filled him with what he called a 'sacred wrath' against landlordism and English rule in Ireland.[9] He raged against the export of food when the people who produced it were hungry. The Coercion Act of 1846, and the notorious quarter-acre clause in the Relief Act of 1847 – which laid down that no person holding more than one-quarter of an acre could be eligible for relief – filled him with a bitter fury.

O'Connell, too, disgusted him with his political manoeuvrings and his vacillations when faced with the nationwide catastrophe. Never a warm admirer of the Liberator, Mitchel now came to see him as a ranting, senile old man:

> Poor old Dan! – wonderful, mighty, jovial, and mean old man! with a silver tongue and a smile of witchery, and a heart of melting ruth! lying tongue! smile of treachery! heart of unfathomable fraud! with a royal, yet vulgar soul! with the keen eye and potent swoop of a generous eagle, and with the base servility of a hound and the cold cruelty of a spider![10]

Blaming both O'Connell and the Catholic hierarchy for preaching moral force alone, he said they had destroyed the manhood of the Irish people, and turned them into docile serfs. He could no longer bear the thought of starving men, whose ancestors had once fought so bravely against oppression, lying down and dying like sheep in a ditch. More and more, he came under the influence of radicals like Meagher and Fintan Lalor.

The breaking point came in the spring of 1848 after he left the still-cautious *Nation*, and decided to publish his own, more radical, journal the *United Irishman*. For five short months he preached an ever more violent doctrine of resistance to British rule. In February of that year he wrote the inflammatory sentence: 'Let the man among you who has no gun, sell his garment and buy one.' In May he addressed a letter 'To the Protestant Farmers, Labourers and Artisans of the North' in which he dealt with the futility of peaceful agitation, and urged the necessity for an armed uprising. In this document he appealed more specifically to the Ulster tradition of standing up and fighting for what was believed to be the truth:

> Why do I reason thus with you – with you, the Irish of Ulster, who have never denied the noble creed and sacraments of manhood? You have not been schooled for forty years in the fatal cant of moral force – you have not been utterly debauched and emasculated by the claptrap platitudes of public meetings, and the empty glare of 'imposing demonstrations'. You have not learned the litany of slaves and the whine of beaten hounds, and the way to die a coward's death. No, let once the great idea of your country's destiny seize on *you*, my kinsmen, and the day will be plain before you as a pikestaff twelve feet long.
>
> Yet there is one lesson you must learn – fraternal respect for your countrymen of the South, and that sympathy with them, and faith in them without which there can be no vital nationality in Ireland. You little know the history and sore trials and humiliations of this ancient Irish race . . . But I tell you the light has at length come to them; and the flowery spring of this year is the dawning of their day . . . I will speak plainly. There is now growing on the soil of Ireland a wealth of grain, and roots, and cattle, far more than enough to sustain in life and comfort all the inhabitants of the island. *That wealth must not leave us another year* – not until every grain of it is fought for in every stage, from the tying of the sheaf to the landing of the ship.[11]

Within a fortnight of writing this appeal Mitchel had been charged with treason-felony, found guilty, and sentenced to fourteen years' transportation to Van Dieman's Land. He was not to return to Ireland until a few weeks before his death in 1875.

Mitchel might not appear to have achieved much during his lifetime. Judged by the materialistic standards of the Victorian era, he was not successful. The journals he contributed to were suppressed; the military rising which he urged on so vehemently was badly planned, and turned out to be a fiasco. He was transported to Tasmania as a felon, and after his escape, several years later, was jailed in Virginia, USA, for supporting the losing side in the American Civil War. Fêted by the Irish in America, he did not get on well with his natural allies, the Fenians, bickering with them about minor points of tactics. Nor did he help the constitutional Home Rule movement that emerged in the 1870s, in which his friend John Martin took a leading part. Increasingly he became a political loner, finding it difficult to work closely with friends and colleagues.

In particular, he was criticised for being such an open and unabashed advocate for the institution of slavery, and some of his writings were obviously racist, in the manner of his friend Thomas Carlyle. His notorious remark that he would like to have a plantation in Alabama 'stocked by fat slaves' shocked the abolitionists, including most Fenians, the Catholic archbishop of New York and John Martin.[12] Mitchel's political philosophy was indeed confused, veering between extreme egalitarianism and tolerance of Black serfdom. He did not understand, as did Wolfe Tone and James Connolly, the connection between Irish republicanism and world democracy.

His personal life was fraught with difficulties, as he was constantly separated from his beloved wife, Jenny,[13] and two of his sons died vainly fighting for the south in the American Civil War. He suffered from asthma all his life, and frequently was on the verge of penury. When he finally returned to Ireland in 1875 he was already weak in health, and did not live long to appreciate his parliamentary victory in Tipperary. If he had survived another five years he would have seen the rise of Michael Davitt and Charles Stewart Parnell. As it was, he knew only the bitterness of defeat and exile.

Modern critics dismiss him contemptuously as a racist and fanatic. Yet during his formative years, and especially during the darkest days of the famine, his nobility of character shone through. If he was passionate and burning in his hatreds he had good cause. His bravery in the face of adversity inspired several generations of republicans. The power of his writing stirred both Protestants and Catholics, and his *Jail Journal* became a classic of prison literature. It is still in print.

His greatest virtue was that two generations after the democratic Presbyterianism of 1798 seemed to have been crushed for ever, and when the sectarianism of the Reverend Henry Cooke and his sympathisers was spreading, he renewed the old emphasis on the unity of Protestant, Catholic and Dissenter under the common name of Irishman. Ulster to him was an intrinsic part of Ireland, and anyone who thought differently had been bought by crumbs from the imperialist table. He believed it was British rule, and not theology, which was the real cause of conflict between Catholic and non-Catholic.

As a writer he had a unique gift of cutting through all cant, of stripping away false masks and portraying the real face underneath. He loathed humbug, and was at his sharpest when flaying those who talked about 'loyalty', 'Protestantism' and 'the constitution' when what they really meant was rent, privilege and bigotry.

His third letter to the northern Protestants is worth quoting again because it contains all that was best in Mitchel's writing – his inimitable prose style, savage irony, and fierceness of invective. It is in some respects his political testament:

> If any man talks to you now of religious sects, when the matter in hand relates to civil and political rights, and administration of government, or distribution of property – he means to cheat you.
>
> In fact, religious hatred has been kept alive in Ireland longer than anywhere in Christendom, just for the simple reason that the Irish landlords and British statesmen found their own account in it; and as soon as Irish landlordism and British dominion are finally rooted out of the country, it will be heard of no longer in Ireland, any more than it is in France or Belgium now . . .
>
> As for Lord Clarendon and his friendly addresses, exhorting to 'loyalty' and attachment to the institutions of the country, I tell you

that *he* is a cheat. What institutions . . . are there to be attached to? . . . Tenant-right is not an institution . . . No; out-door relief is our main institution at present – our *Magna Charta* – our Bill of Rights. A high-paid church and a low-fed people are institutions; stipendiary clergymen, packed juries, a monstrous army and navy, which we pay, not to defend, but to coerce us – these are institutions of the country . . .

But, then 'Protestants have been loyal men'. Have they! And what do they mean by 'loyalty'? I have never found that, in the north of Ireland, this word has any meaning at all, except that we, Protestants, hated Papists and despised the French . . .

I tell you, frankly, that I, for one, am not 'loyal'. I am not wedded to the Queen of England, or unalterably attached to the House of Brunswick. In fact, I love my own barn better than I love that House. The time is long past when Jehovah *anointed* kings . . . There is no divine right now but in the sovereign people.[14]

John Martin was a much gentler person than Mitchel, but was committed as strongly as his close friend and comrade-in-arms to the cause of Irish separatism. Born in 1812 into a solidly prosperous, religious and liberally inclined family (his father was also a Presbyterian minister), he had a talent for languages and might have become an amateur antiquarian or reclusive scholar. Instead he chose the hard road of political struggle during the period of the famine and the Fenians. Nicknamed 'Honest John', he was recognised by both friends and foes as a man of incorruptible integrity.

Martin went to school in Newry with John Mitchel, and there formed a friendship that was to endure until death. For fifty years, at school and university, at meetings and among colleagues, writing seditious articles for soon-to-be-banned journals, in Down, Dublin, Tipperary, Van Dieman's Land, France and the United States of America, he was Mitchel's political intimate and dearest ally. Separated for long periods the two remained in touch with each other, writing or meeting whenever possible. In his *Jail Journal*, Martin – who eventually after a long courtship married Mitchel's sister – is described as 'simply the best, worthiest and most thoroughly high-minded man I ever knew'.

For three decades of his political life Martin went through agonies of indecision as to whether he should support the physical-force or constitutional wing of the Irish national movement. By nature a man of peace, and with a Quakerish distaste for violence, he was driven by the horrors of the famine to abandon O'Connell's reform agitation, and call for an insurrection in 1848. When Mitchel was arrested, and the *United Irishman* suppressed by the Government, he launched the *Irish Felon*, which only lasted five issues before it, in turn, was closed down. He had already described the Irish landlords as 'men of property in treasonable alliance with a foreign country', and in his journal he was proud to publish the writings of such avowed separatists as Devin Reilly, Fintan Lalor and Meagher. Arrested and charged with treason-felony, he was sentenced to ten years' transportation.[15] He spent over four of these years in Tasmania, where he shared his exile with Mitchel, Smith O'Brien and other ticket-of-leave prisoners. Conditionally pardoned in 1854, he later returned to Newry, and threw himself into various national activities, including attempts to preserve the Irish language, which had been so damaged by the famine losses.

His letters to George C. Mahon during this period provide us with an insight into the way in which he believed Protestants and Catholics could co-operate together if only they were free from outside interference. Mahon seems to have been something of a bigot, or at least held the conventional view of narrow-minded Protestants that all Catholics were superstitious, ignorant and priest-ridden. Mahon argued that if Ireland ever became independent then 'a Romish hierarchy would be substituted for an English oligarchy'.

In reply Martin claimed that Catholic priests, like any other citizens, should be free to give advice, but that this could be accepted or rejected according to individual conscience. Protestants, in his view, should be confident of their own strength and the rightness of their religious beliefs. They should not invariably look, as historically they had been prone to do, to Britain to justify and protect their cause:

244

> I hold the view that there is one right and effective way to settle the religious question, and that is simply to obey the dictates of equity and common sense. Let the state, immediately on becoming its own master, declare all religions free and all sects equal by the constitution and before the laws. If once perfect religious equality were established in Ireland, I think there would not arise any serious danger of its being overthrown.[16]

In 1864 he organised the National League, a repeal society which favoured constitutional rather than revolutionary methods of reform. By this time he had turned against the advocates of physical force, differing in this respect from Mitchel who never abandoned his contempt for reformist policies. A critic of the Fenians, Martin described the rising of 1867 as 'an insane attempt by patriotic men'. His ambivalent attitude towards the dynamitards was illustrated, however, by the views he expressed about the three Fenians Allen, Larkin and O'Brien (later known as the Manchester martyrs), who were executed for their part in an attack on a police vehicle in Manchester in 1867. Condemning their terrorist methods, he nevertheless agreed to become chairman of the committee that arranged their funeral in Dublin. For this offence he was charged with planning a seditious demonstration. Once again he was put in the dock in Green Street, Dublin, where he and Mitchel had stood twenty years before. This time he was acquitted.

In 1871 Martin was persuaded to stand for election, and was voted Irish Parliamentary Party MP for Meath. His first parliamentary speech was in opposition to a coercion bill. In November 1873 the Irish Home Rule League – a forerunner of the much larger movement led by Davitt and Parnell – was set up with Martin as secretary. In the 1874 general election sixty Home Rulers (including the still-convicted felon, John Mitchel) were elected.

In spite of his constitutionalist leanings towards the end of his life, Martin remained an incorrigible separatist, and never wavered from the view that the connection with Britain must be broken if ever there was to be political progress in Ireland:

> What I really want is that our country should belong to our own citizens, to own it, to rule it, use it or abuse it, as their own

245

wisdom or folly may think fit. I hold it for an axiom that the worst native rule is better for a country than the best foreign rule.[17]

Mitchel died suddenly in March 1875 only a few months after his return from exile in America, and a grieving Martin attended his funeral in Newry. Martin, like Mitchel, had been a long-time sufferer from asthma and caught a chill at the graveside. Within a week he, too, was dead in Dromalane where Mitchel had been nursed by him during his illness. In death as in life, the two Johns – both sons of the manse, both Young Irelanders, both transported to Tasmania, and both from County Down – were not divided.

15

'THE LEAGUE OF NORTH AND SOUTH'

> The principle of union and united action among Irishmen has
> had a glorious triumph . . . There has been nothing like it since
> 1782 . . . The tenant-right men united to rid the country of an
> internal curse . . . the tyranny of landlordism . . . has been more
> ruinous to this country than fifty French invasions . . . This is the
> first combination of the Irish people in which the animosities of
> race and creed were forgotten or trampled underfoot . . . the first
> honest blending of orange and green . . . a real reconciliation of
> conquerors and conquered. Our landlords and rulers, for their
> own purposes, have managed to keep open and bleeding, even
> to the present day, the wounds inflicted in the Battle of the Boyne;
> but the 'issue of blood' is now stopped . . . We are about to have
> a league formed, not for Old Ireland or Young Ireland, for
> Catholic Ireland or for Protestant Ireland, but for all Ireland. The
> Ulster Presbyterians have found out, at last, that patriotism is
> not Popery; and the Munster Catholic that Protestantism is not
> anti-Irish oppression.
>
> *Londonderry Standard*, 1850[1]

The defeat of Young Ireland and the transportation of Mitchel,
Martin, Smith O'Brien and other rebel leaders did not result in
the disappearance of agrarian unrest. On the contrary, so grave
were the land problems, and so deep was the gulf between rich
and poor in the rural areas, that any setback for the tenant-right
movement could only be temporary. When they began to recover from the worst aspects of the famine, the small and middling farmers once again lifted their heads. On this occasion the
struggle was mainly constitutional, and the issue of repeal of
the Union was rarely raised. Ulster was in some respects more

247

active than the other three provinces. Gavan Duffy, who was one of the movement's chief inspirations, emphasised the interprovincial and interdenominational aspects of the campaign in a book which he later published under the title *The League of North and South.*[2]

This title has been criticised by some historians on the grounds that it exaggerated the depth and width of the tenant-right campaign, but recent research has confirmed that the agitation of 1849–51 did, in fact, like the tithe war of the 1830s, draw a broad cross section of Irish society. Labourers and farmers, shopkeepers, merchants and professional people all over Ireland were involved in the struggle. MPs from both liberal and nationalist parties took part, as did several influential journalists. Sharman Crawford and Gavan Duffy worked closely together. John MacHale, the long-lived and formidable Catholic bishop of Tuam, was an ardent tenant-righter, and his example was followed by hundreds of priests. So strong was grass-roots support in rural areas that even the reactionary Archbishop Paul Cullen could not refuse his sympathy. In Ulster some dozens of Presbyterian ministers became open propagandists for the farmers' cause, in spite of the hostility of conservatives such as the Reverend Henry Cooke.

Ulster became the chief focus of this agitation because it was in that province that tenant rights were most directly under attack. The famine had devastated every region in the country, but it was the Ulster custom which was immediately threatened. Prices of agricultural products had begun to fall as the new potato crops proved more abundant, and food supplies came back to normal. The repeal of the corn laws was also beginning to have an impact on the cost of cereals. In the Belfast market between April 1848 and April 1850 prices of wheat, oats, potatoes, butter, beef and mutton fell on average by between one-third and one-quarter. This decline in prices had a twofold effect: the farmer got a smaller profit, and the value of his tenant right diminished. The consequence was that if rents were not reduced, there was a squeeze on both income and capital assets. The secretary of the newly formed Coleraine Tenants' Association,

Samuel M. Greer, made this point in a letter published in the *Impartial Reporter* in November 1848:

> For years the tenant farmer had a valuable freehold interest in his farm, for which he could at once have obtained a ready purchaser and a large price. He could not now obtain a farthing for it, or get a ready purchaser on any terms . . . the greater of the value of the tenant-right interest that existed has been swallowed up in the general depreciation of agricultural prices.[3]

Simultaneously while economic pressures were getting worse, the parliamentary scene did not seem promising for farmers. Sharman Crawford's efforts to defend them were manifestly getting nowhere in the House of Commons, and in the Lords there was a constant barrage of aristocratic criticism against any 'plebeian' presumptions which might be advanced. The concepts of free sale, fair rents, and fixity of tenure were still rejected as so much Jacobinism.

An early sign that farmers' morale was improving and that certain Catholic priests were prepared to get involved in political activities in support of their parishioners had come in October 1849 when a meeting of tenants was organised in Callan, County Kilkenny, by two local curates, Father Tom O'Shea and Father Matthew Keefe. The object of their hostility was a local landlord, the Earl of Desart, who owned about eight thousand acres, and had been responsible for the eviction of between four hundred and five hundred families during the famine. Desart had been nicknamed 'the exterminator' for his cruelty. The aim of the new organisation was to get an independent valuation of farm rents, and to persuade neighbours not to take over any farm from which tenants had been evicted even though they had been prepared to pay their agreed rent. This was an example of that solidarity among the oppressed which was to become such a powerful weapon a generation later during the Land League days. By the end of the year it was reckoned that about twenty similar organisations had been set up in Leinster, Munster and Connacht.

Ulster was not slow to respond to this lead from the Catholic south, and during the first half of 1850 a further three dozen or so meetings were held in various parts of the north, often in areas that were predominantly Protestant in population. Attendance at these assemblies, which were often held in the open air, frequently numbered hundreds, and on occasions, thousands of people. Coleraine began the campaign on New Year's Day, and within six months this had been followed by Annaghglone, Ballybay, Ballyclare, Ballydown, Ballymena, Ballymoney, Banbridge, Belfast, Boardmills, Broughshane, Carnmoney, Carrickfergus, Castlereagh, Comber, Cookstown, Derry, Donaghadee, Dundonald, Dundrod, Dungannon, Garvagh, Greyabbey, Holywood, Islandmagee, Killinchy, Lisburn, Loughbrickland, Magheragall, Moneymore, Saintfield, Scarva, Strabane and Tullylish.

The climax of the campaign came during the summer of 1850 when two big conferences were held in the main cities of the north and south. In June 1,600 delegates took part in what was described as a 'magnificent and enthusiastic demonstration'[4] in Belfast. The hall was so crowded that hundreds could not gain entry. Several Catholic priests were present, and Father John M'Loughlin (Coleraine) and Father James O'Doherty (Garvagh) spoke. The Presbyterians were represented by the Reverend David Bell (Ballybay) and the Reverend William Dobbin (Annaghglone). The editors of the *Londonderry Standard* and the *Banner of Ulster* also spoke. Dobbin's was the most radical speech; he summed up the mood of the delegates in apocalyptic language:

I rejoice that on this subject [of tenant rights] there is now but one opinion in Ireland. Six million of Irishmen shall soon, in reference to this matter, be one united band. The policy of divide-and-conquer has had its day (hear! hear!). The people fought and bled, and starved and died, and the landlords gained and revelled and rack rented and evicted (cheers), but our day of folly is drawing to its close. Affliction's sons are brothers in distress; and ere two months elapse, the North and South shall be banded together on this land question (tremendous cheering) – and from

Ireland's united people a voice will soon go forth far too loud to be unheeded – too stern to be disregarded – proclaiming in the face of the empire, that feudal tyranny – a system that flesh and blood can no longer endure – poor, suffering, patient and loyal Ulster must at length be free (tremendous cheering, protracted for several minutes).[5]

The conference in Dublin two months later was even more representative of tenant farming opinion in Ireland. The number of delegates (140) was much smaller, but they usually spoke for well-established organisations, and came from almost every county in Ireland. There was a contingent of sixteen priests and several leading Presbyterian ministers. A speaker claimed that this conference – which lasted four days – had the backing of hundreds of Protestant clergy as well as Catholic priests. This was certainly an exaggeration, but reflected the ecumenical enthusiasm of the time. It was pointed out, however, that not a single Church of Ireland parson was present. Several important present or future MPs, including Gavan Duffy and William Keogh, and the editors of four newspapers were on the platform. Sharman Crawford sent a message of greeting, and J.F. McGuire, editor of the *Cork Examiner* and later a nationalist MP, spoke of 'a glorious vision – a meeting of north and south'.[6] The well-known British radical MP for Birmingham, John Bright, who was there in spirit if not in the flesh, said 'it was the most formidable agitation in Ireland for fifty years'.[7] Duffy used the phrase 'Young Ulster',[8] and the *Londonderry Standard* hoped that the day 'would be ever memorable in our calendar'.[9] A.M. Sullivan, the historian of Young Ireland, commented: 'The sharp Scottish accents of Ulster mingled with the broad Doric of Munster. Presbyterian ministers greeted Papish priests with fraternal fervour.'[10] The *Fermanagh Mail*, which according to Duffy was a strongly Protestant newspaper circulating in one of the most Orange districts of the north, broke into even more flowery prose about this ecumenical spirit:

It was a grand and enobling sight to see the children of the Covenant from the far North, the Elizabethan settlers from the Ards

251

peninsula, the Cromwellians from the centre, the Danes of Kerry, the sons of Ith from Corca's southern valleys, the followers of Strongbow from Waterford and Wexford, and the Williamites from Fermanagh and Meath – all united in harmonious concert for the dear old land.[11]

Deliberately to emphasise the interconfessional aspect of the gathering, the three secretaries appointed were Father Tom O'Shea, the Reverend William Dobbin, and William Girdwood, an episcopalian from Lisburn.

This cross fertilisation of liberal Protestant with progressive Catholic was reflected in a number of influential newspapers and magazines of the period, and the tenant-right campaigners were fortunate in the support they got from several talented journalists. The two Presbyterian journals, the *Londonderry Standard*,[12] and the *Banner of Ulster*, published in Belfast, and the *Impartial Reporter* of Enniskillen, were all strongly in favour of land reform. Though conservative on religious issues, and inclined to hit out occasionally against 'Popery', they were consistently hostile towards the landowners and the Tory Party.

In the south of Ireland an equally lively anti-landlord agitation was conducted by such Catholic newspapers as the *Cork Examiner*, the *Freeman's Journal* of Dublin (editor John Gray, also later a nationalist MP), and the *Tablet*, which had moved its place of publication from London to Dublin. This last journal was edited by Frederick Lucas, who in spite of the fact that he was born in England and considered himself a good Catholic, proved a painful thorn in the side of Archbishop Cullen. The *Nation*, which had been suspended during the treason trials of 1848, was revived by Gavan Duffy in September 1849. It never again showed the wide-ranging polemical force and organisational influence it had displayed in the heyday of Young Ireland, but nevertheless gave strong leadership on the land issue.

Duffy did not let government persecution, or the imprisonment or exile of his closest colleagues, intimidate him (he was prosecuted for sedition no fewer than four times during 1848–9, but was acquitted in each case), and for several years continued to be the most important journalist in Ireland. At heart he had never been a physical force separatist, and in the new constitutional campaign for land reform in the early 1850s he found fresh scope for his gifts as a speaker, writer and organiser. His experience of the famine had reinforced his long-held view that the landlords and their British backers were the enemy to be overcome. Land was 'the main Irish question . . . the root of all wrongs and disasters', he wrote. Wages paid to labourers of 6d. a day were an insult to humanity, and among the lowest in the civilised world.

Duffy was brought up a strict Catholic, and in spite of many clerical provocations never gave up his faith. He opposed Cullen's conservatism, and was not afraid to say so. He never accepted that Catholicism necessarily meant political conservatism, and still less that it required anyone to knuckle under British domination. Like Davis, his colleague in Young Ireland, he was firmly against all forms of religious bigotry. In a striking phrase he once identified Orangeism, which he abhorred, with racism: 'The [unionists] encouraged the Orange Lodges for the same motive which induced the planter of the Southern States of America to encourage the Mean whites.'[13]

Duffy believed, with Lalor, that the land and nationalist struggles were indissolubly linked together, and claimed with Mitchel, that neither soil nor national freedom could be won without the help of a significant number of progressive-minded Ulster Protestants. Indeed, one of his main contributions to politics during these critical years was the intimate knowledge and understanding he had of Ulster, derived from his native County Monaghan, and his experience as a journalist in Belfast. It was essential, he said, 'to win the ear of the north'.[14] To achieve this co-operation he worked closely with Sharman Crawford, and frequently spoke in Belfast.

Two other journalists who gave a strong stimulus to the land agitation in Ulster during this period were James McKnight and James Godkin.

McKnight was born in Rathfriland, County Down, in 1800, son of a Presbyterian tenant farmer who could speak Irish and was reputed to be fond of singing Gaelic songs. Educated in that liberal nursery, the Royal Belfast Academical Institution, the young James showed an early interest in theology, but was never ordained.[15] He then turned to the study of languages, in which he became a proficient scholar. W.T. Latimer, his biographer, said of him that he was 'at home in either Greek particles, Hebrew roots, German metaphysics or modern theology, he was a splendid Keltic scholar, and has read everything dealing with the early history of his country'.[16]

The coming of the potato blight to his beloved County Down in the autumn of 1846 turned his attention to land reform, and spurred on by the example of Sharman Crawford and Samuel Greer, and the inspiration of such local Presbyterian ministers as the Reverend John Rogers of Comber, he joined the developing campaign for tenant rights. After a spell as a journalist on the Tory *Belfast News-Letter*, he was appointed editor of the liberal *Londonderry Standard* in 1848. He was briefly editor of the *Banner of Ulster* between 1849 and 1853, but then returned to the *Londonderry Standard*, where he remained until his death in 1876. So strong was his reputation as a political writer that when the famine crisis worsened he was invited to London to offer advice to the prime minister, Lord Russell. He also met Sir Robert Peel shortly before the latter died.

During the 1850s he established himself as the main voice of radical liberalism in Ulster, constantly hammering the landlords and their representatives in parliament. 'Ireland is almost the only country in the world', he wrote, 'in which the bulk of the population are treated as alien on the soil of their birth.'[17] His particular *bête noire* was the rack-renting Lord Leitrim, whom he harried mercilessly on the platform and in the columns of his journal which had a wide circulation in Derry and east Donegal.

James Godkin[18] was another theologian-turned-journalist who had a considerable influence as a land reformer in both Ireland and England. Born in Gorey, County Wexford, in 1806, he was ordained a Presbyterian minister. As a young man he was a keen evangelist for Protestantism, and served for a time as a missionary among the southern Catholics. In 1845 he turned to full-time journalism, and founded the *Christian Patriot* in Belfast. He wrote several books and pamphlets on religious topics. For a period he was editor of the *Londonderry Standard*, and was then employed by the London *Times* to write a series of articles on agrarian problems. These formed the basis of his most important book, *The Land War in Ireland*, published in 1870, a discursive and somewhat rambling account of the history of agrarian struggle in Ireland since the plantations.

Confronted with this alliance of nationalists and liberals, rural professional people and a large number of angry farmers, the landlords resorted to their customary methods of divide and rule, or alternatively, of direct intimidation of those who stood in their way.

Lord Roden, who could always be relied upon to do what was most provocative and least useful socially, used the agitation as an excuse to whip up sectarian strife. In July 1849 he lent his estate at Tullymore, near Castlewellan, County Down, for the holding of an Orange demonstration, and he personally made a speech bitterly attacking Catholics. At nearby Dolly's Brae there was a skirmish between Protestant and Catholic bands in which some thirty Catholics were killed. This incident passed into Orange folklore as one more glorious victory over the hated Papists. Roden's part in provoking the riot was condemned by an official commission of inquiry, and he was dismissed from his position as justice of the peace. He was not removed, however, from his post as grand master of the Orange Order.

Evictions of non-paying or otherwise troublesome families had always been a favourite way of getting rid of those tenants who would not obey the traditional property-oriented rules, and clearances of estates were practised on a large scale, both during and immediately after the famine. In 1849 it was reported that 1,534 Ulster families had been removed in this way, and the following year the figure rose to 1,575. As each family probably represented on average about five or six persons, these were substantial figures. Most landlords had few scruples in acting in this manner: they believed in *laissez-faire* principles and reckoned that the country as a whole would benefit from a smaller population.

255

Lord Londonderry was another Tory magnate who made strong attacks on all rebellious tenant farmers – including both Dissenters and Catholics. In an important debate in the House of Lords in January 1850 he took the lead in denouncing those who, he said, were promoting 'Socialism and Communism' – the people of Ulster had been allowed to become restless and excited, and were reviving the doctrines of the United Irishmen. The Ulster custom, which he personally had condoned for twenty years, was not a legal right. He then turned his fire against those Presbyterian ministers, or 'clerical agitators', as he called them, who were advocating land reform. Denouncing as impudent and contemptible a letter he claimed to have received from the Reverend John Rutherford of Ballydown, he called for the arrest of any Presbyterian minister who held similar anti-Ascendancy views, and he recommended the proclaiming of any disturbed county in the north. He added fuel to the flames by proposing that the payment of the *regium donum* should be stopped to all Presbyterian ministers who could not be certified as loyal to the Crown.[19] His contempt for his own tenants was shown when he dismissed a petition which was sent to him as being signed 'with ill-written names on a dirty scrap of paper'.[20] Soon after, he made a bitter attack on a minister 'who calls himself Dobbin', who, he said, was using subversive language and stirring up tenants not to pay their lawful rents. Dobbin was accused of the crime of encouraging 'incendiarism in Down and Antrim'.[21]

Londonderry's criticisms evoked a sharp response from radical Presbyterians who resented this intervention by their traditional opponents. Several ministers and liberal journals were highly indignant at what they regarded as an attempt to suppress free speech. The Reverend John Rogers replied: 'I owe no apology to landlords. The church of which I am a member has never been a sycophant or slave of power.'[22]

The fact that Lord Londonderry, a more sophisticated politician than Lord Roden, chose to direct the main thrust of his attack against the Presbyterians was significant. Dissenters comprised just over one-quarter of the Ulster population,[23] and still held the political balance in the province. The largest single occupational group among them were tenant farmers, often holding only a few acres, and not fully recovered from the famine. Like the Catholic small farmers, they were often threatened with eviction and rack-rents. In several rural constituencies their votes could sway the elections. Outside of Belfast, where the Tory–Orange doctrines of the Reverend Henry Cooke and the Reverend Thomas Drew had gained ground, they were mostly strongly anti-establishment.

Among their clergy there was deep concern at the way in which emigration was weakening their congregations, and alarm at the general decline in morality and social behaviour that had resulted from the famine. In certain parts of the province, for example, north Down, Antrim, and east Derry, the Presbyterian farmers outnumbered Catholics. This was certainly the case around Mount Stewart on the shores of Strangford Lough, where Lord Londonderry had his big estate. It was in such predominantly Protestant districts that several Presbyterian ministers, including the Reverends John Rogers, William Dobbin, John Rutherford, David Bell, J.L. Rentoul, Ballymoney, and J. Johnston, Tullylish, began to make reputations as agitators on social as well as religious issues.

In all these politico-religious struggles there was a strong element of class warfare, as there had been on so many previous occasions. Presbyterian farmers on average might not be so poor as their Catholic neighbours, but the great majority regarded themselves as being economically oppressed nevertheless. Disliking both the flamboyant wealth and what they regarded as the profligate life style of their masters, they openly treated the landlords as their political enemies. This contempt for the squirearchy was aggravated if landlords, as was so often the case, were titled and members of the Church of Ireland. The radical Presbyterian journals similarly did not disguise their disdain for what they implied was a reactionary and effete social class. In one issue of the *Banner of Ulster*, for example, the aristocracy were dismissed as 'rack-renters' and 'feudal superiors', while the gentry were derisively described as 'buckeens' and

257

'puppy squireens'.[24] Nationalists and liberals both took it for granted that landowners were the main prop of the Tory Party.

So strong was the egalitarian mood at this time that even such allegations of socialism and communism, which were widespread after the various European uprisings of 1848, did not always frighten the more middle-class and respectable Protestants. Nor did it prove possible to persuade the affected clergymen that they should avoid politics, and stick to purely religious themes. The *Impartial Reporter* strongly defended the right of Presbyterian ministers to preach on such pressing topics as farmers' poverty. What was the Bible, said this Protestant newspaper, ever ready to quote a text, 'but the poor man's Book, the freeman's standard'.[25] In a long editorial a month later it rejected attacks being made on some clergymen for their alleged levelling tendencies:

> What, after all, is this alarming Socialism – this terrific Communism that people so much hate and dread? It is, at the utmost, the principle on which the first Christian church was constituted – that having all things in common which distinguished the first Christian society from all its degenerate successors.[26]

A few weeks after this bold statement the *Banner of Ulster* joined in the debate by warning its readers not to be frightened by the 'cabbalistic word' of 'Communism'.[27]

The more conservative elements within the Presbyterian Church were alarmed at these radical tendencies, and tried to prevent ministers and their parishioners being drawn into activities they regarded as potentially subversive. As always, when their deepest social fears were aroused they fell back on the old tactic of stirring up religious prejudices.

Matters came to a head at the various synods held in 1850. Heated debates took place about the propriety of God's ministers involving themselves in such profane matters as rents, evictions, food prices and landlord–tenant relations. The conservatives claimed that the problems of the next world were more important than the problems of this world; the liberals argued that when their parishioners were dying of hunger or being driven on to emigrant ships they must do more than merely pray or read the Bible. The decentralised nature of the synods, and the lack of formal hierarchical structures in the Church, encouraged this kind of lively controversy.

The most important of these debates took place in Belfast in the spring of 1850 when Henry Cooke, then as previously the leading Tory spokesman and evangelist within the Church, tried to prevent the matter of tenant rights being discussed at all. He deplored the intrusion of what he termed 'secular matters' into the synod, and condemned personal attacks on the nobility and aristocracy, which he believed violated that word of God which said 'Thou shalt not speak evil of the rulers of the people.' In his opinion some Presbyterian ministers had been promulgating 'Communist doctrines', like those of Ledru Rollin, Louis Blanc and the Irish Chartist leader, Feargus O'Connor. 'The worst practices of the French Revolution' were being advocated in the synod. He particularly attacked William Dobbin for approving contacts with the south of Ireland, and supporting fraternity with Catholics. 'Don't think you are in Bannside,' he shouted at Dobbin when the debate got very heated, 'where Doran the priest exclaimed, "Oh, did I ever think that I should see such a happy hour? Am I in Tipperary?" '[28]

Following these allegations, John Rogers, leader of the Church's liberal wing, had a violent argument with Cooke in which there was a revealing altercation about the rights of property:

Dr Rogers: The entire outlay of the tenant farmer has gone periodically into the pockets of the landlords – a small minority have swallowed up the property of nine-tenths of the province (hear! hear!).

Dr Cooke: Now we have communism preached in the synod (hear! hear!).

Dr Rogers: If Dr Cooke charges the advocates of tenant right with preaching communism, I state the fact that Communism is on the other side. It would seem to be forgotten by some members that the poor man has property which should be as fully secured as that of the rich.[29]

After a long, and often acrimonious, debate in which the conservative elders and clergy tried every procedural device to stop the synod from committing itself to a definite policy on land reform a vote was taken in which Rogers had a majority of eighteen votes to twelve. At similar synods at Armagh and Monaghan, Derry and Omagh, Ballymena and Coleraine, the tenant-right supporters won the day, sometimes by large majorities.

However, it was not the hostility of the landlords, nor the hesitation of conservative-minded Presbyterians, that led eventually to the collapse of the league of north and south. By a historical coincidence a series of events took place, which had more to do with the internal manoeuvrings of British politicians, the prejudices of British public opinion, and Papal ambitions in Europe than they had to do with Irish land problems. It was these external circumstances as much as internal disunity that helped break up the tenant-right movement. Once again the shadow of ancient pro-Reformation and anti-Reformation struggles fell over the country, darkening and confusing the people's minds. It was a tragedy for Ireland that the peak of Victorian evangelicalism and anti-Catholicism was reached during the precise period when the country was enduring its most acute economic and political crisis.[30]

In the autumn of 1850, when sectarian passions seemed to have cooled slightly in Ireland, an anti-Catholic uproar broke out in England because of what came to be known as Papal aggression. Briefly, this alleged aggression arose from a decision of Pope Pius IX to create a Catholic hierarchy with named territorial bases in England – a system which already existed without any controversy in Ireland, Canada and Australia. This announcement about what in fact was a purely administrative arrangement was accompanied by a pastoral letter from Cardinal Nicholas P.S. Wiseman, which, in rather tactless language, talked about Catholic bishops 'governing' their dioceses. Immediately, the latent hostility of the reformed Churches in Britain, which some years previously had been aroused by the Government's decision to grant money to Maynooth, burst out in resentment against what was said to be an intolerable interference with the freedom of British Protestants. The foundations of the British constitution were believed to be under attack. Parsons vied with each other in denouncing the 'man of Satan' in Rome, and 'No Popery' meetings were held all over the country. Government ministers, instead of trying to curb this wave of bigotry, fell in behind the popular clamour. Lord Russell, the prime minister, wrote an open letter to the Anglican bishop of Durham denouncing the wicked ambitions of the Papacy. *The Times*, then as always in the van of Toryism, thundered against nunneries, foreign usurpation, superstition, and the dangers posed by the Reverend E.B. Pusey, professor of Hebrew in Oxford University, who suggested that certain Catholic doctrines and rituals should be restored to the Church of England. 'Puseyism', which became part of the wider Oxford movement, was anathema to evangelical Protestants.

After some months, in response to this tidal wave of public opinion, the Government passed a bill by 395 votes to 63, which became law in August 1851, rendering all ecclesiastical titles in Britain illegal, except for those of the Established Church. Catholics in the south of Ireland, instead of ignoring or riding out this diversionary religious storm, and sticking to the crucial land issue, set up a defence association. This organisation, which had the approval of Cullen, had as its immediate aim the repeal of the obnoxious Ecclesiastical Titles Act. Its wider purpose was to reject those insults which seemed to have been shown to the Catholic faith, and it was in that sense a return to the old narrow siege mentality. Two of its leading members were William Keogh, a prominent barrister from Athlone, and John Sadleir, a banker from Tipperary, both MPs. So zealous were these two, and the group they gathered round them, in defence of Papal power, and so enthusiastically did they admire Cullen, that they became known as 'the Pope's Brass Band'.

A loose alliance was formed between these Catholic zealots and the committed tenant-right MPs in parliament, and Keogh and Sadleir solemnly pledged themselves not to support any government which did not accept the principle of tenant rights. When the 1852 election took place, nearly fifty MPs, including

Gavan Duffy, were returned for Irish constituencies on an anti-Tory or independent platform, and these held the balance of power in the new parliament. Everything seemed ripe for the success of progressive tenant-right legislation, particularly as the new government under Lord Aberdeen seemed sympathetic.

However suddenly overnight, and to the consternation of Duffy, Gray and other committed land-reform MPs, and contrary to all promises, it was announced that Sadleir had accepted the post of junior lord of the treasury, and Keogh had been made solicitor-general. Several nationalist MPs followed these turn-coats into the government lobby. Cullen and other Catholic bishops defended them on the grounds that they had been given a secret assurance that the Ecclesiastical Titles Act would eventually be rescinded. The issues of land and religion were once more confused. It was an apt comment on these betrayals that Sadleir before long was exposed as a bank swindler, and committed suicide. Keogh went on to become lord chief justice of Ireland and, as such, was responsible for severe sentences on the Fenians.

If it was the bigotry of the Orangemen and the prejudice of many Anglicans and Nonconformists in Britain that triggered off the anti-Catholic agitation of that period, it was the ultra-montane views of Cullen that antagonised many liberal Prot-estants. Once again it was entrenched sectarianism on both sides that prevented political co-operation for social reforms.

Cullen, who originally came from Kildare, spent more than twenty years in Rome where he became rector of the Irish College. He was made archbishop of Armagh in 1850, translated to Dublin in 1852, and appointed a cardinal fourteen years later, the first Irishman to achieve this rank. By nature authoritarian and intolerant of opposition, he fell naturally into the role of strict administrator and stern repressor of any deviation from canon law. His task, as he saw it, was to win back all Ireland (and by implication Britain as well) to the one true faith. He also endeavoured to establish a system socially conformable to his conservative view of Catholic teaching. As a priest he had seen at first hand the rise of the Italian *risorgimento*, in which such leaders as Garibaldi, Cavour and Mazzini attacked the established authorities, promoted liberal ideas, and tried to unite their country. Cullen, like his mentor Pope Pius IX, was alarmed at the spread of subversive opinions all over Europe in 1848.

Young Ireland was anathema to him because of its radical political views and also because he distrusted such Protestants as Mitchel, Davis and Lalor. He disliked Gavan Duffy, whom he described as 'a wicked man . . . an Irish Mazzini'. Duffy, in turn, called Cullen 'a Castle bishop'.[31]

In summary, from the Vatican viewpoint, Cullen may have been the ideal man for reinforcing Catholic power in Ireland, but with regard to the reconciliation of Catholics and Protestants he was a calamity. He could see no good whatever in Protestantism, and the whole of his long life was dedicated to the destruction of Reformation ideas. In this respect he was the counterpart of Henry Cooke. More than any other Catholic prelate of the mid- to late nineteenth century in Ireland, he was responsible for building up Protestant fears about the dangers of Papal triumphalism.

While these religious and political rows were diverting the minds of the Irish people away from the real problems confronting them, there were other economic factors which were taking some of the urgency out of the agrarian agitation. A series of good harvests removed for the moment those fears that existed about the return of another great hunger. The price of foodstuffs began to turn upwards, and the threat to the Ulster custom grew weaker. This meant that once again those farmers who wished to sell could get a good price for disposing of their occupancy rights.

Simultaneously, there was a decrease in population pressure on the land, the total number of inhabitants of the nine northern counties, which had fallen by 374,000 in the 1840s, declined by a further 179,000 between 1851 and 1871.[32] Thousands emigrated to the United States of America, Britain, Australia, Canada and New Zealand, but there was also a substantial internal migration within the province itself. Generally the rural areas lost, and the urban areas gained, population. It is probable that those who emigrated overseas included not only the poorest, or alternatively, those who were most ambitious to improve their economic lot, but also those who might be politically discontented. As in the south of Ireland, and as had happened a hundred years previously during the great flight of Presbyterians to North America, it was often the potential rebels who got out.

The expanding towns and cities, especially Belfast, provided more work and higher wages for the landless labourers and poor cottiers. Girls and women, too, could find more jobs, even if ill-paid, in the new mills and factories. The population of Belfast, for example, multiplied nearly fivefold – from 75,000 in 1841 to 350,000 in 1901. Derry, Lisburn, Lurgan, Ballymena, Newry and Portadown also grew in size. There was a steady extension of the linen industry, shipbuilding, railways, dock, road and bridge construction and house building during the second half of the century. Edward James Harland began shipbuilding in the 1850s, and fifty years later his company employed about nine thousand men. Workman Clark developed into another major ship-building enterprise on the River Lagan. The application of steam power to the manufacture of linen revolutionised the industry, and in the 1850s the numbers employed (three-quarters of them being women) rose from 21,000 to 34,000. Wages in manufacturing, though low in absolute standards, rose more quickly in urban than in rural areas. The skilled workers, mainly Protestants, benefited especially.

It was this influx of poorly paid, and predominantly Catholic, labour from the rural areas, the consequent competition for jobs, and the determination of the skilled workers to hang on to their economic privileges that led to heightened sectarian tensions. Street preachers, such as the Reverend Thomas Drew and the Reverend Hugh ('Roaring') Hanna, with their populist anti-Popery demagoguery, found a ready acceptance for Orange doctrines among the more backward Protestant workers. In 1857, and again in 1864, there were serious sectarian riots in the city, which led to many injuries and deaths.[33]

This spread of political reaction in the urban areas, combined with the temporary decline of rural radicalism and the still very restricted franchise, helped the Conservatives to win twenty-six out of Ulster's twenty-nine parliamentary seats in the 1852 general election. Seven years later they won twenty-eight seats. The number of Liberal MPs, which had been five in 1847, fell to three in 1852, and then to one (Derry City) in 1859. Belfast did not return a non-Tory MP for another half-century. In the County Down constituency the veteran Sharman Crawford, then over seventy years of age, put up a strong fight in 1852, but could only come third with 3,113 votes against his opponents' 4,654 and 4,117. Crawford then retired from public life, dying in 1861. Gavan Duffy was still in the prime of life but disillusioned by the failure of both land reform and the Irish Parliamentary Party to make progress, and the constant personal attacks made against him by Cardinal Cullen. In 1855 he decided to emigrate to Australia, declaring that Ireland was as dead 'as a corpse on a dissecting table'.

In spite of the loss of these two prominent leaders, there were some important individuals in Ulster still prepared to carry on the land struggle. The most important of these in the 1860s and early 1870s was Isaac Butt.

ISAAC BUTT – FATHER OF HOME RULE

There is but one secret in governing Ireland, as there is in governing any country, let it be governed for the good of the whole people. Let us abandon the policy of maintaining any English interest, or any class interest, or any Protestant interest, or any interest but that of the Irish people.

Isaac Butt, 1867 [1]

Isaac Butt was born in Glenfin, County Donegal, the son of a Church of Ireland rector of plantation stock, and everything about his northern birth, his family background and early political attitudes suggested he would grow up as another loyal unionist. Educated at the Royal School, Raphoe, County Donegal, and at Trinity College Dublin (where he studied law, and like Wolfe Tone, was auditor of the college historical society), he did not disguise his Tory outlook, and joined with a group of fellow students to oppose the Reform Bill of 1832. During 1834–8 he was editor of the *Dublin University Magazine*, a journal with a strong Orange flavour. While still a young man, he was appointed professor of political economy in Trinity – a post which involved, among other things, the study of land tenure, industry and taxation. In 1843 he first came into public prominence by speaking against Daniel O'Connell in a debate on the Union. Displaying that oratorical brilliance that was to win him so many admirers, he became for a brief period the darling of Dublin's most extreme unionists. At this stage all the indications were that the young Butt, so intelligent, eloquent and forceful, was destined to follow the traditional conservative path, and become a successful lawyer with fat fees from rich

Protestants, eventually taking up a judgeship or a lucrative government post.

However, the tragic circumstances of the time and his own humanitarian instincts turned him in an entirely different direction. By nature a compassionate and warmhearted man,[2] he had always, even during his Tory days, been shocked by the poverty he saw in Dublin and his native Donegal. The famine, and its accompanying evictions and emigration, horrified him, and within a few years had completely altered his attitude towards Anglo-Irish relations. From the summer of 1848 onwards, though still describing himself as a liberal unionist, he began to move – tentatively at first, but gradually more boldly – towards the concept of some form of legislative independence for Ireland. John Mitchel approved of his plea for the protection of Irish industries against British imports, and the *Nation*, although warning that he was still only half on their side, applauded his decision to serve as defence counsel for Smith O'Brien and other rebels after the rising in the summer of 1848. This led to one observer referring to 'Orange Young Ireland',[3] and for a while he was something of a hero to nationalists.

Butt's main contribution to Irish politics during this period was on the subject of land reform, which he saw as the key to so many economic and social problems. As Whig MP for Youghal, County Cork, between 1852 and 1865, and then Irish Parliamentary Party MP for Limerick between 1871 and 1879, he kept alive in the House of Commons the issue of tenant rights, and the need to give control of the soil to those who tilled it. His attitude towards landlordism was unambiguous: he regarded it as an unmitigated evil, the source of endless misery and perpetual strife. His language on the topic was bold and uncompromising, and even if some of his writings tended to be repetitive, showing signs of hurried composition, he often coined phrases of striking power and vividness: Ireland during the famine was 'one half a barracks, and one half a workhouse';[4] the country's perpetual degradation was caused by the fact that 'the great mass of the people have been treated as belonging to a conquered race';[5] evictions were 'the sword suspended over

267

the serf, the lash hanging to terrify the slave';[6] the gentry were 'encamped and not settled on the soil . . . in the midst of the nation, and yet scarcely of the nation, they stand on their possessions, isolated and alone'.[7]

His most important book, *The Irish People and Irish Land*, sums up his view on the way in which in the last resort it was English power which prevented the redress of Irish wrongs:

> If English arms created, English arms maintained the proprietary right. All the force of the English government is exerted to maintain extreme proprietary rights of landowners, no matter what cruelty they exercised – and to crush the resistance of the peasantry, no matter by what oppression it is provoked. Can any system of government be more fatal to national improvement, more destructive of every hope of that adjustment of differences by mutual forbearance and concession which in all nations has reconciled the angry war of classes? I know of no greater curse to a country than to have its local oppressions maintained by the force of another country.[8]

In his *A Plea for the Celtic Race* he makes the same point – it was external domination that distorted the normal development of Irish society:

> The presence of the overwhelming force of England, has, in fact, destroyed the peaceful interest, the moral force, by which the will and interest of the great body of people assert themselves against the encroachments of property and power.[9]

This thesis that it was English power which prevented the introduction of necessary social changes in Ireland should have led Butt to conclude that the only solution to Irish problems was for the country to achieve its legislative independence. Logically, it followed from his argument that if ever the land problem was to be settled, some measure of genuine democracy introduced, religious bigotry diminished, or the Catholic majority be granted a fair deal, then the Union must be repealed, and the Irish people allowed to settle their own affairs. Butt, indeed, did gradually lose faith in government from Westminster, and by the end of the 1860s had begun to develop his up to then rather shadowy ideas about a federal relationship between the two countries. If anyone could claim the honour, Butt was the father of Home Rule.

However, by inclination and intellectual conviction, Butt was a reformist and not a revolutionary. He could see that domination by Britain was harmful to his nation's interests, but at the same time he was not prepared to challenge it decisively. He had begun life as a conservative, and was still overwhelmed by the enormous military strength of the neighbouring country, and the ever growing wealth that flowed from the empire. His biographer, David Thornley, describes him as a 'Palmerstonian imperialist who never lost faith in the imperial partnership of Britain and Ireland in a joint civilising destiny'.[10] While practising as a barrister in London, he had seen with his own eyes the city's immense treasures, and while serving for many years as an MP he had been constantly reminded that to question England's dominant role on the world stage was to commit a kind of political sacrilege. All these experiences, combined with his personal reluctance to rock the boat too violently, made him something of a halfway nationalist, like Daniel O'Connell before him and John Redmond after him, perpetually hoping for reforms but not willing to push too hard to achieve them.

This ambivalent approach to Anglo-Irish relations, and the extent to which he was prepared to go to break with constitutional traditions, was well illustrated by his reaction to the Fenian movement. On the one hand, he deplored their advocacy of physical force, and was shocked when violence actually broke out. On the other hand, he admired the rebels' idealism and bravery, and was prepared to admit that honest patriots could be driven by intolerable wrongs to revolt. His natural instincts were with the oppressed, and he had a deep respect for the 'felons of our land', who should not be classified as ordinary criminals.

So when in September 1865 the three republicans bringing out the Fenian weekly, the *Irish People*, Thomas Clarke Luby, John O'Leary and Charles Kickham, were arrested and charged with felony, he agreed to act as their counsel. Jeremiah O'Donovan

Rossa, the other Fenian involved, conducted his own defence. Butt's arguments were strong and vigorous, and he tried every legal tactic, including the plea that the defendants had only advocated rebellion, and had not at any time been actually involved in it. But the presiding judge, William Keogh, directed the jury to find the four men guilty of conspiracy. Kickham was sentenced to fourteen years' penal servitude, Luby and O'Leary to twenty years', and Rossa to imprisonment for life. The severity of these sentences, and the way in which the trial had been conducted, shocked Butt, and turned him more firmly towards the idea of constitutional reform.

When the attempted Fenian rising broke out in 1867 he condemned it as an act of folly and political madness, but once again as had happened in 1848 he was as much concerned with the causes as he was with the events of rebellion. By the late 1860s there was a groundswell of public opinion on both sides of the Irish Sea that some form of parliamentary independence should be granted to Ireland within the framework of the empire. In Britain Gladstone had been persuaded that his task was now 'to pacify Ireland', and to achieve this aim in 1870 he introduced measures to disestablish the Church of Ireland, and a land act designed to legalise some aspects of tenant rights. The radical MP John Bright and the philosopher John Stuart Mill announced that they favoured the idea of a system of peasant proprietorship. In Ireland there was emerging a coalition between various farmers' organisations, some Catholic priests, and the more liberally inclined Presbyterians. Even a few episcopalians joined in, after what they regarded as Gladstone's betrayal over disestablishment. The Catholic bishops supported constitutional reforms so long as they could be won peacefully. The new phrase 'Home Rule' began to be bandied about.[11]

Isaac Butt was the front man, or cover, for this movement because of his patent sincerity and reputation as a Protestant democrat. In 1869 he won over the Fenians by joining the amnesty committee which had been set up to try to alleviate the conditions suffered by Irish prisoners in British jails. The following year he joined the so-called Home Government

Association, and in 1873 when a big Home Rule conference was organised in Dublin, Butt was seen as the natural leader. It was at this conference, attended by more than twenty-five MPs and more than fifty priests, that a new name appeared from the Ulster stage. This was Joseph Gillis Biggar, a merchant from Belfast and soon to be chosen as Irish Parliamentary Party MP for County Cavan. Biggar startled the delegates by his suggestion (at first rejected, later adopted) that any Home Rule member elected must keep strict party discipline in the House of Commons.

On the surface, much of this agitation seemed to be about matters which were mainly political – the extension of the franchise, the winning of elections, party policies, and the role of the Westminster parliament with regard to Ireland. Underneath the campaign, and constantly welling up from the rural grass roots, three out of four of the population, was the perennial question of the deplorable state of Irish agriculture. Though not as serious as they had been twenty years previously, all the old social and economic evils were still there. Wealth was still concentrated in a few hands, privation was to be found in every village and townland, tenants had little security of tenure, absenteeism flourished, and evictions continued year after year. Probably about one-third of the farming population lived on the edge of subsistence.

It was this widespread poverty, combined with disappointment over the results of the 1870 Land Act and a general growth of hostility towards the Tory landlords, which led to a revival of agrarian agitation in Ulster in the 1870s. Though this rural unrest was not as vigorous as it had been two decades before, it did keep alive, especially among Presbyterian farmers, a local spirit of radicalism, and thus paved the way for the much bigger Land League and tenant movements of 1880–1. In all, about twelve or fifteen farmers' organisations were active, mainly in Antrim, Down and Derry.[12]

The lead in this agitation was taken by the farmers of the Route district of north Antrim, where there was a strong dissenting tradition going back to 1798. Ballymoney, then a market town

271

of about three thousand people, was the centre of this agricultural region, which was dominated by a small group of aristocrats – Lords O'Neill, Hertford, Donegall and Antrim – who were immensely rich and correspondingly arrogant. The population was largely Presbyterian, and there was much resentment among both town and country people at the way in which the episcopalians monopolised not only the county's wealth but also the magistracy, grand juries and political privileges. Many shopkeepers, small merchants, professional people and dissenting clergy, as well as independent-minded farmers, voted Liberal but were repeatedly beaten in elections by the all-enveloping influence of the Tory landlords.

The most prominent local Presbyterian minister was the Reverend J.L. Rentoul, who had been a zealous advocate of land reform for many years. His view, which was widely held by his fellow ministers, was that riches bred ostentation and dissolute behaviour among the aristocracy, and encouraged a sycophantic and cap-in-hand attitude among those parishioners who had to seek favours from their masters.

Rentoul was succeeded in 1869 by an even more fervent land-reformer, the Reverend James Brown Armour, who eventually became famous as Armour of Ballymoney. Armour was born in 1841 in Lisboy, County Antrim, son of a tenant farmer with about sixty acres of land. As a boy he observed the famine at first hand. He was educated at the Royal Belfast Academical Institution, and then at Queen's College Belfast, where he first read science and then classics. For a period he also studied in Cork, where he mixed freely with Catholic students. This mixing had a profound effect because it persuaded him that Catholics, whom he had previously been taught to regard with suspicion, could be reasonable and well-intentioned people. It also convinced him that the Protestant minority in Ireland, because of their convictions and moral integrity, had no need to fear Catholic domination. It was his experiences in Cork, as he later admitted, that led him in the long run to come to the conclusion that Home Rule would mean, not the rule of the Pope, as so many of his co-religionists feared, but the rule of democracy.

In any event, the 'radical Route' and Armour got on well, and in spite of many later storms and stresses, he stayed in the one parish for fifty-six years. His first stipend was £65 a year, and on this small income he married a local widow, a descendant of the Reverend William Stavely who had attended William Orr on the eve of his execution in 1797. Political as well as religious sympathisers in the neighbourhood were the Reverends S. Finlay (Kilraughts), J.S. Maire (Dunboy), and A. Robinson (Broughshane).

Strong lay support came from Samuel C. McElroy, editor of the *Ballymoney Free Press* and a local auctioneer who was for thirty years a leading advocate of tenant rights in the province. McElroy started his adult life as a house painter, but found his true vocation as a political journalist. His short book, *The Route Land Crusade*,[13] had a considerable influence on politicians, including Gladstone. He was an energetic organiser, and gathered round him a group of lively disciples, such as Thomas McIlderry, a Ballymoney town commissioner, and John Megaw, a local farmer. Thomas Shillington, a prosperous merchant from Portadown, was another contemporary sympathiser. These liberals and radicals constituted an important countervailing power against local landlords and Tories.

In 1869, when Gladstone had been considering the new legislation affecting the ownership of land in Ireland, Ballymoney Tenants' Association sent a delegation to London to explain tenant grievances. Gladstone met them courteously, and was persuaded that the Ulster custom must be regarded as a key factor in any potential legal changes. On their return, the delegates, led by McElroy, organised an open-air meeting, reputed to have been attended by one thousand people. The Route Tenants' Association was then set up, and continued in existence for many years. In 1872 the Down Farmers' Union was formed, and the following year there were said to be as many as five tenant associations operating in County Derry. In January 1874 the campaign was extended from a provincial to a national scale when twenty-eight associations, of which nineteen were reported to be Ulster-based, met in Belfast.[14]

So high was feeling running in the farming communities during this period that the landlord versus tenant issue dominated, at least in rural areas, the general election of 1874. Land had become the focus for a much wider range of social, religious and political problems, and the Tories were retreating before the combined onslaught of Liberals and constitutional nationalists. On this occasion the number of Tory seats in Ulster dropped from twenty-five to nineteen, and the Liberals rose from two to six. Liberals also polled strongly in several constituencies, where they were beaten by small margins. Home Rulers had their first successes in the north when they won two seats in County Cavan – one of the victors was Biggar, who defeated Captain Edward Saunderson, then standing as a Liberal, by 3,079 votes to 2,310. The anti-Tory successes were all the more remarkable as the election was fought on a restricted franchise.

In June 1876 the Antrim Central Tenants' Association was formed. The same year, incidentally, the veteran James McKnight died. He had championed the small farmers' cause for thirty years. His newspaper, the *Londonderry Standard*, continued to support the tenants, as did the Protestant *Impartial Reporter* of Enniskillen, the *Chronicle* of Coleraine, the Catholic *Ulster Examiner*, and the influential daily, the *Northern Whig*. The Bessborough Commission, which reported in 1881,[15] took evidence from fourteen tenant associations in the north, an indication that these groups were well organised, with properly elected committees and officers. Unfortunately the number of members in the various groups was not recorded.

The publication of a series of well-documented government reports confirmed what Butt and other critics had long been saying about the intolerable nature of the landownership system, and added to pressures for reform. In 1872, for example, a statistical return was made of resident landlords in every province in Ireland. This showed that only one county in Ulster had more than half of its big proprietors living on or near their estates, and in some counties the proportion was less than two in five (see Table 8[16]).

TABLE 8

NUMBER OF RESIDENT LANDLORDS IN ULSTER, 1870

	No. of proprietors with 1,000 or more acres	Proprietors classified as being 'resident on or near property'	
			%
Antrim	369	163	44
Armagh	276	136	49
Cavan	409	145	35
Donegal	364	146	40
Down	372	141	38
Fermanagh	246	91	37
Derry	259	113	44
Monaghan	241	100	41
Tyrone	463	224	48
Total	2,999	1,259	42

Absenteeism on such a scale was widely deplored by hardworking and God-fearing farmers, who regarded it as just one more example of feudal arrogance. The distaste of Ulster Nonconformists for the life style of one of the province's richest territorial magnates is well illustrated in this comment made c. 1869 by the editor of the *Northern Whig*:

Lord Hertford, the fourth marquis, was himself an absentee landlord. He resided in his magnificent villa, La Bagatelle, in the Bois de Boulogne of Paris almost over-looking the race-course. Strange stories, some of them doubtless much exaggerated, were told of the marquis's cynicism, dissipation, contempt of public opinion, and indifference to his duties as a large Irish landed proprietor. It was said that he had only been once on a visit to his Irish estates. This was during Sir Robert Peel's Government, when the marquis wanted the Garter, soon after he had succeeded his father. He did go over to Lisburn at that time. While looking round from a high hill on the fine land of which he was proprietor, he was reported to have said, 'Well, I like this country so well that I shall never come into it any more.' He was as good as his word. More than a quarter of a century had passed away; but the tenants during all that time had never seen the noble landlord's face.[17]

In 1876 another bluebook was published under the title *Owners of Land in Great Britain and Ireland*. This report is of exceptional importance for historians and social scientists because it is both comprehensive and minutely detailed. It covers all the landowners of Ireland, from the biggest to the smallest, and gives a mass of information about the size of estates and their annual valuation, names of proprietors, and their titles.[18] It is a kind of Domesday Book, in fact. By giving actual acreages and valuations it was possible for the first time to know who owned what in the country, and how rich they were. The social structure of Ireland was thus revealed in both statistical and personal terms. Such phrases as 'feudalism' or 'the landlord class' could now be defined with some precision. It was shown, for example, that there were at that time no fewer than three dukes, nine marquesses, eleven earls, three viscounts, and sixteen other assorted lords, baronets and knights who owned estates in Ulster.

The figures revealed what had long been suspected, namely that landownership in all four provinces was extraordinarily concentrated. In Ulster there were forty very large proprietors (or 'lords of the soil', as Devon had described them), each with more than 20,000 acres, and holding between them no less than 1,444,000 acres or over one-quarter of the land. A further 62, each with between 10,000 and 20,000 acres, held 824,000 acres, and 121, each with between 5,000 and 10,000 acres, held 840,000 acres. Fifty-nine per cent of all land was owned by 223 persons or companies. This compared with 151 owners holding a total of 1,761,000 acres in Leinster, or 29 per cent of the land; 204 owning 2,601,000 acres in Munster, or 45 per cent; and 164 owning 2,339,000 acres in Connacht, or 56 per cent. In total, there were just under 6,000 landlords possessing over 5,250,000 acres in Ulster as compared to about 190,000 tenant farmers. An analysis of the figures, showing the contrast between the few large, and the many small, units is given in Table 9.

TABLE 9

DISTRIBUTION OF LANDOWNERSHIP IN ULSTER, 1876

Area in statute acres	No. of proprietors	Total area in statute acres	Average size of estate in statute acres
More than 20,000	40	1,444,000	36,100
10,000–20,000	62	824,000	13,300
5,000–10,000	121	840,000	7,000
2,000–5,000	270	853,000	3,100
1,000–2,000	332	465,000	1,400
500–1,000	517	361,000	690
300–500	439	169,000	390
200–300	421	104,000	220
100–200	772	110,000	140
50–100	734	52,000	71
25–50	693	25,000	36
Less than 25	1,366	16,000	12
	5,767	5,263,000	

The individual names recorded enable us to put flesh and (blue) blood on what otherwise would be a rather bare statistical skeleton. The Marquess of Conyngham, for instance, had 129,000 acres in Donegal; the Marquess of Downshire, 75,000 in Down; Lord O'Neill, 66,000 in Antrim; the Marquess of Hertford, 60,000 in Antrim; Lord Leitrim, 56,000 in Donegal; the Duke of Abercorn, 52,000 in Tyrone; Mr H. Stewart, 51,000 in Donegal; the Earl of Antrim, 24,500 in Antrim; Lord Farnham, 30,000 in Cavan; the Earl of Caledon, 27,000 in Tyrone; the Earl of Castlestuart, 27,000 in Tyrone; Mr E. P. Shirley, 27,000 in Monaghan; and the Marquess of Londonderry, 23,500 in Down. The London livery companies also had huge estates, particularly in County Derry: the Drapers' Company owned 27,000; the Mercers' Company, 23,000; the Fishmongers' Company, 20,500; the Salters' Company, 19,000; the Ironmongers' Company, 13,000; the Grocers' Company, 12,000; and the Clothworkers' Company, 10,000.

The value of these estates depended partly upon their size, and partly upon the quality of soil. Poor mountainsides and boglands, which were extensive in west Donegal, south Down and central Tyrone, were worth less than the fertile valleys of north Down, Antrim and Armagh. Proximity to a city such as Belfast was a valuable asset. The biggest incomes, as calculated on the basis of annual valuations,[19] went to such magnates as the Marquess of Downshire (about £73,000 a year), the Marquess of Hertford (£69,000), Lord O'Neill (£45,000), Mr D. S. Ker (£31,000), the Duke of Abercorn (£27,000), Lord Lurgan (£20,000), and Mr E. P. Shirley (£20,000). In addition, some of these very rich men owned property in other parts of Ireland and Britain, and probably investments in industry. Lord Londonderry was reported to hold 13,000 acres in Durham (some of these with coalfields on them), 7,000 in Montgomery and 3,000 in Merioneth, both in Wales, together with his 23,500 in Down, 2,000 in Derry and 1,700 in Donegal. Altogether the total annual valuation was £100,000, which made him one of the richest men in the British Isles. The Marquess of Downshire was almost as wealthy, with estates in Berkshire, Suffolk, King's County (modern-day County Offaly), Kilkenny and Kildare, as well as Down.

The immense value of these properties may be judged from the fact that the average income of a small tenant farmer at that time was about fifteen or twenty shillings a week, that clerks, shopkeepers and minor professional people thought themselves well off on £200 a year, and that labourers were earning ten shillings a week or less.[20] The weekly wage of a female indoor servant was about half a crown a week.

A feudal property system and absentee landlords were not, however, the only problems affecting tenant farmers. In addition to continuing economic insecurity and perpetual lack of political power, the agricultural population now had to face the threat of falling prices and bad harvests. The world market and the weather both turned against them.

The small farmers of Ulster, who had made some economic progress in the ten or fifteen years following the famine, entered a new phase of depression in the late 1870s and 1880s. Competition from New Zealand, Australia, Argentina, Canada and the United States of America became keener as technological advances, such as the steamship, railways and refrigeration, made food cheaper to carry. The price of wheat fell sharply, and there was a shift from arable crops to pasture, from 'the plough to the cow', as F. S. L. Lyons neatly expressed it. The Government refused to protect agriculture from this overseas competition because by then it had become dominated by industrial and commercial interests, and in any event it still supported a *laissez-faire* economic policy. In their search for profit, the landlords turned more and more to the encouragement of livestock farming, and the consolidation where possible of small farming units into bigger ones. This often involved evictions when the necessary excuses could be found. The linen industry continued to be transformed from a manual process – which, whatever its defects, at least provided work and income on local farms – to a steam-driven, highly mechanised manufacturing system in cities such as Belfast. 'If you take away the hand-loom weaving, that is rapidly leaving the country, the farmer cannot live on ten acres, and when the farms are smaller it is miserable in the extreme', wrote one contemporary critic.[21]

Then in 1877–80 came an even harsher (if temporary) blow from a succession of wet, cold summers, and poor harvests. There was flooding in Armagh, the Erne basin, Cavan and Tyrone, and reports of farms completely under water in Fermanagh. Bad crops were recorded throughout the province. In Tyrone fuel was said to be scarce, and there was a lack of employment. The potato crop in Ulster, which had averaged about 1.5 million tons during the previous two years, fell to 0.6 million tons in 1877. It then rose to 1.11 million tons in 1878, but collapsed to only 0.4 million tons in 1879.[22] This failure of the staple source of food for many poor people aroused all the old memories of the famine of a generation earlier.

As a consequence of these agricultural disasters a large number of small farmers in mid-Ulster could not pay their rent. The plight of such farmers was illustrated by a petition which was sent during the winter of 1880 to the Duke of Marlborough, viceroy of Ireland, by the tenants of Ballygawley, County Tyrone:

> Our district in conjunction with the rest of Ireland has suffered severely by reason of the wet summer last year, the bad harvests of the last three years, and the low price of stock. Our turf is still in the bog – our potatoes are at best a missed crop, and the few we kept for seed the exigencies of our families compelled us to eat. Our corn too was far below the average, the consequence being that there is a great deal of suffering amongst us. We are unable without borrowing to meet our rent, and the credit with our shops is collapsed.[23]

A prominent Tory and 'improving' landlord agreed that the tenants had a grievance. 'The farmers . . . have for the last few years found it difficult to make their rent', he wrote. 'Last winter they were in danger of starvation; this year many were in danger of eviction; and many more thought themselves so.'[24]

Inevitably, as living standards dropped and evictions increased a growing number of tenant farmers turned to the traditional method of violence as a means of resistance. This violence was not so serious in the north as it was in the south and west of Ireland, but nevertheless, Ulster had its share of these outrages (that is, murder, attacks on bailiffs and landlords, arson, maiming of cattle, and the writing of intimidatory letters), as may be seen in Table 10.[25]

TABLE 10

AGRARIAN OUTRAGES IN IRELAND AND ULSTER, 1876–83

	Ireland	Ulster
1876	212	64
1877	236	52
1878	301	57
1879	863	109
1880	2,585	259
1881	4,439	414
1882	3,433	320
1883	870	89

Isaac Butt was not the man to cope with these disasters. By nature too easy-going, and by experience too wedded to parliamentary ways, he was unable to give strong leadership to the Irish people. Tougher new leaders and tougher policies were required when once again economic and political crisis threatened.

By the mid-1870s he was physically ailing, and harassed by financial troubles. The majority of the Home Rule MPs, who had been elected in 1874, were increasingly critical of his moderate approach, and wanted to go ahead with all-out parliamentary obstruction. Butt, with his respect for House of Commons traditions, would have none of this. In April 1877, during a long and acrimonious debate on the Mutiny Bill in which every filibustering tactic was used, Tory MPs appealed to Butt to restrain his factious friends. The House was in an uproar and Butt made the cardinal mistake of attacking his own side – 'I am not responsible for the member for Meath [Parnell]' – and made a rather fulsome apology to the Tories. The Home Rulers did not forgive Butt for this treachery, as they saw it, and he lost much of his party's support. At a special conference held in Dublin in February 1879 he was challenged by Parnell, and though he won a vote of confidence by thirty-two votes to twenty-four, he was in effect a beaten man, and soon withdrew from leadership. Within a few months he was dead, and his funeral passed almost unnoticed. He did not live to see the significant event which took place in Westport, County Mayo, in June 1879, and which was to carry a stage further the campaign for land reform and Home Rule to which he had devoted so much of his energy and talents.

17

BIGGAR AND THE LAND LEAGUE

> In Antrim and Londonderry, in Tyrone and Armagh, the Orange
> Lodges have been converted into tenant-right clubs.
>
> *Impartial Reporter*, 1880 [1]

The launching of the Land League by Michael Davitt in the
summer of 1879 is generally recognised as a turning point in
the history of nineteenth-century Ireland. Throughout the thirty-
two counties powerful democratic forces were stirring which
within a few short years would begin to transform Irish society
and change the whole nature of Anglo-Irish relations. In the
south the great majority of impoverished tenant farmers, fearing the return of a new famine, and seeing the price of their
crops fall and evictions increase, were showing a new militancy.
For the first time the social issue of landownership was being
linked realistically with the political issue of national independence. Two engines rather than one were driving the people forward. In Ulster the Presbyterian farmers, newly conscious
of the threat to the value of their tenant rights, were prepared,
at least temporarily, to co-operate with Catholics against the
unpopular Ascendancy landlords. In both parts of the country
the new franchise laws and the introduction of the secret ballot
made it possible to hold elections that were free from intimidation and more genuinely democratic. The British political
scene was marked by a strong revival of liberalism, and the
growing confidence of the charismatic Gladstone. On both sides
of the Irish Sea the old-style Tory aristocracy were on the defensive. Even the hard-line Fenians could see the possibilities
which might open up if they could begin a 'new departure' in

which physical-force separatists could collaborate with constitutional reformers.

The political leaders who emerged from these dramatic new circumstances were as full of potentialities as the times they lived in. Charles Stewart Parnell, the Protestant landlord with a strong sense of his own destiny, was willing to join forces with the Catholic factory worker and ex-convict, Michael Davitt, to serve the cause of Irish freedom as they saw it. Both proved to be men of striking personality and powerful intelligence. Parnell showed that he had qualities of inspiration and authority which amounted to genius. John Dillon and William O'Brien in the south, and Jeremiah Jordan, John Pinkerton and John Ferguson in the north, though coming from widely divergent religious backgrounds, were willing to work together for a common cause. Joseph Gillis Biggar, though physically handicapped and rough in his manners, proved himself the parliamentary equal of the most sophisticated MPs. The House of Commons, with all its glamour and prestige, did not intimidate him.

For the first time since the 1790s large sections of the Irish people were drawn into a campaign which had revolutionary aims, was well organised and vigorously led, and which involved every county in the land. Within eighteen months of its foundation the Land League had enrolled more than 200,000 members and by the mid-1880s the Irish Parliamentary Party had won more than four-fifths of all Irish seats, including half of those in the north. In a way which had not appeared realistic for centuries, it became possible to envisage the landlord system, which had always seemed so impregnable a fortress, being eventually replaced by a system of peasant proprietorship. The idea of Home Rule, which had for generations been merely a pious hope, became a well-founded expectation.

The first report of a Land League meeting held in the north is of that organised at Belcoo, County Fermanagh, in December 1879, but this seems to have been a small and local rally. Significant progress began to occur in the summer of 1880, and there was a big league demonstration at Sessiagh, County Tyrone, in August of that year at which over two thousand farmers attended. Gradually the league extended its activities into the predominantly Catholic southwestern part of the province, and before many months had elapsed the Protestant areas of Antrim, north Down, east Donegal, Derry and east Tyrone were affected. In November Parnell made an important speech at Belleek, County Fermanagh, launching, as he said, 'the land campaign in the north of Ireland'. The fact that Jeremiah Jordan, a Methodist from Enniskillen, presided at this meeting provoked the pro-Liberal *Impartial Reporter* into making the approving comment that for the first time there was a 'Protestant Chairman in a Protestant county, presiding over a meeting held under the auspices of the Land League'.[2]

Soon after the Belleek demonstration, Parnell, Biggar and twelve others were arrested and charged with conspiracy for encouraging tenants not to pay their rents. The same month, using Mitchel's tactics, Davitt issued an appeal to Protestant farmers to join the Land League.

The climax of the year's campaign came in December 1880 when, despite the short days and bad winter weather, more than three dozen tenants' meetings were held in the province, including six on Christmas Day. So strong was anti-landlord feeling that the Land League was able to demonstrate in areas previously noted for their Orangeism. In south Fermanagh, for example, where Lords Erne and Enniskillen, and the Brooke, Archdale and Cole families had monopolised political power for generations, Jeremiah Jordan was able successfully to confront the Tories. In Saintfield in north Down Davitt appeared on the same platform with the two nationalist MPs, Dillon and Biggar, the local parish priest Father James O'Boyle, and the Unitarian minister from Moneyrea, the Reverend Harold Rylett. A resolution was passed attacking the rapacity of the landlords, and declaring that 'the land question can only be definitely settled by making the cultivators of the soil proprietors'.[3]

The year 1881 was even more crucial in the land struggle because it was then that the Bessborough Commission produced its report so critical of the prevailing system of landownership, and Gladstone introduced his bill granting the three Fs – fixity of tenure, free sale, and fair rents. There were also two important by-elections in Ulster, in which Liberals defeated the Tories, mainly on the land issue.

The year began with a surge of activity in January, with Davitt again taking the lead in such widely separated districts as Letterkenny in Donegal, Downpatrick in Down, Strabane in Tyrone, and Ballymacnab in north Armagh. At Kinnegoe, County Armagh, on the shores of Lough Neagh, at a meeting organised by the Land League branch from Loughgall (the cradle of the Orange Order), he succeeded in getting James Weir, master of the local Orange lodge, to take the chair. Speaking to two thousand Protestant farmers who in spite of the arctic weather assembled in a field, Davitt took up the challenge of sectarian disunity:

> You are no longer the tame and superstitious fools who fought for their amusement and profit with your equally foolish and superstitious catholic fellow workers, and allowed the landlords to pick both your pockets during the encounter. Did you ever hear tell of a catholic landlord who gave a reduction of rent to a tenant who had his head broken in a fight for the honour of the pope? Or a protestant gentleman . . . who would refuse to evict an orangeman who drank to the memory of the vanquisher of that miserable coward, King James, at the Boyne? No, my friends, the landlords of Ireland are all of one religion – their God is mammon, and rack-rents, and evictions their only morality, while the toilers of the fields, whether orangemen, catholics, presbyterians, or methodists, are the victims whom they desire to see fling themselves beneath the juggernaut of landlordism.[4]

In February there were eleven more meetings, in March six, and in April a further eleven. Two of the April meetings were major conferences in Belfast and Ballymoney, the latter fast becoming one of the most important centres of radical agitation in Antrim.[5] During May and June the agitation declined slightly because of urgent crop-planting and hay-making operations.

In July, however, partly because by this time the various clubs and associations were better co-ordinated and the Land League had several full-time organisers in the field, the leaders decided

285

to switch from mass demonstrations to smaller but more representative conferences or conventions. That month the Derry convention was attended by delegates from twelve branches, the Moneymore convention by eleven branches, and the Newry convention by eighteen branches. In September there was a major tenants' conference in Dublin, and in October a similar one in Belfast.

The Tyrone by-election in September led to a temporary falling-off in agitation because of disunity in the anti-Tory camp. However, a new momentum began to build up the following month, and within a fortnight of Parnell's arrest and imprisonment in Kilmainham there were no fewer than nineteen protest demonstrations in Ulster. There are no official statistics relating to meetings in 1881, but on the basis of local newspaper reports it is possible to estimate that at least several score further demonstrations were held in that year.[6]

It is likely that a grand total of well over two hundred league or tenant-right meetings were held in more than eighty towns and villages in Ulster over a period of two and a half years. This was a remarkable achievement, considering how strong was the landlord–Tory–Orange opposition, and how unaccustomed the poorer farmers and labourers, many of them illiterate, were to political organisation. Agitation on such a scale showed how deep were the farmers' grievances, and how willing they were, under certain circumstances, to co-operate with each other across the religious divide.

Attendance at these meetings ranged, according to local newspaper reports,[7] from several hundreds to many thousands, with farmers often travelling on foot or horseback from distant townlands as well as neighbouring villages. The meetings were often held in fields or on hillsides, sometimes in wet or bitterly cold weather, and generally with a cart or hastily improvised wooden construction as a platform. When an important speaker, such as Parnell, Dillon or Davitt, was due to appear, the organisers would make a point of getting a local shopkeeper and a priest and, if possible, a Protestant clergyman on the platform. There was almost always a government shorthand writer there to report on any possible seditious remarks, and it was customary to make jokes at the expense of these unwelcome guests. Occasionally when feelings were running high and there was a danger of a clash with Orange opponents, the police would be reinforced. Fortunately, in spite of local excitement and strong emotions, most of these meetings passed off peacefully.

The gala atmosphere, together with the blending of green and orange, at one such assembly was recorded by a journalist from the *Impartial Reporter* at a meeting held in Garrison, County Fermanagh, in November 1880:

> The day was very frosty and cold, and made worse by a piercing wind which blew hard from the mountains. The contingents present represented all the surrounding districts of Fermanagh, Leitrim and Donegal counties, many of whom travelled eighteen or twenty miles to be present. Derrygonnelly sent its fife and drum band and splendid flag, Ballyshannon its excellent brass band . . . The flags were of the usual costly kind. Most of the parties present wore green sashes and caps trimmed with orange, and many of the fair sex . . . relieved the dark blue of their dresses with ribbons of a brighter orange. Arches of ever-greens bearing words of welcome, at intervals, spanned the three miles between Ballaghameehan and Garrison.[8]

John Dillon, a liberal Catholic who resented clerical interference in politics, spoke prophetically at a big meeting in Armagh in April 1881:

> I tell you that the dispute between Orangemen and Catholics has been maintained by the landlords and magistrates of Ulster lest people might agree, for they know that those who see the Orange farmer and Catholic farmer unite in one organisation will see the downfall of landlordism.[9]

Parnell, who was warmly received on the several occasions he spoke in Ulster, made a strong point of his own Protestant background, and the need to end religious feuds in the province. At the beginning of his campaign in Belleek in November 1880 he said:

This meeting has been convened to declare that the land movement is not a sectarian movement, and that upon this platform of 'land for the people' all creeds and classes of Irishmen may unite. I as a Protestant . . . a member of the Church of Ireland . . . I feel proud that the Protestant north has opened her arms to the land movement. I am convinced that the day is not far distant when the orange and green unite together we shall see the dreams of Irish patriotism realised.[10]

Five months later at Hilltown, County Down, Parnell came back to the same theme, boasting that he was a descendant of an officer who had crossed the Boyne with William's army, but that they would now gain their rights by a 'junction of the Orange north and the Catholic south' to shouts of 'Orange and green will carry the day!'[11]

In their appeals to farmers to unite on social and economic principles such speakers were not indulging in empty rhetoric or engaged in wishful thinking. What was so remarkable about the land campaign of the early 1880s was the fact that, not only was it on a much bigger scale than the similar agitation of thirty years before, but that it now covered a much wider spectrum of public opinion. Catholics were almost without exception hostile to the landlord system, and judging by election results, newspaper reports and the number and scale of meetings, so were a high proportion of Dissenters. Class feelings, in other words, were stronger during this period than religious sentiments, and as a consequence, the unionists found themselves temporarily on the defensive.

A striking aspect of this Protestant radicalism was that a number of individual clergymen were on the tenants' side. As sympathetic witnesses, the Bessborough Commission[12] mentions the names of the Reverends Nathaniel McBrown of Limavady, G.W. Hamill of the Kennaught Farmers' Association, and Edward Laughrey of Claudy. In Belfast the Reverend R. J. Lynd, father of the essayist Robert, preached frequently in his Berry Street church against the wickedness of landlords, who, he said, had 'sown the wind and reaped the whirlwind'.[13] A Methodist minister, the Reverend Forde, spoke at a Land League meeting in Derrygonnelly in December 1880.[14] A Unitarian, the Reverend J. C. Street of the Second Congregational Church in Belfast, was a strong advocate of tenants' rights, and often preached on their behalf.[15] The Reverend Harold Rylett was an active supporter of the farmers' cause for many years. In December 1880, speaking alongside Davitt, Dillon, Biggar and the local parish priest in Saintfield, County Down, he made a biting attack on the way in which the Orange Order was coming to the aid of the landlords. Davitt was so impressed that he persuaded him to join the central committee of the Land League. In November 1881 Rylett was chosen as envoy to visit Davitt who was back in prison again in England after his ticket-of-leave had been temporarily revoked.

Two Church of Ireland parsons who rejected the political orthodoxies of their Church by coming out unequivocally against landlord abuses were the Reverend T. S. Graham[16] and the Reverend Furlonge of Aghadea. A more widely known clergyman was the Reverend Isaac Nelson, a Presbyterian and author of *Year of Delusion* (1861) and *Present Importance of Irish History* (1874). Nelson was minister in Comber, County Down, for some years, and then moved to Donegall Street, Belfast, in 1842. After thirty-eight years in this post, he resigned to enter parliament for County Mayo in 1880 as a follower of Parnell. He did not contest the 1885 election because of his age. For a short period he was president of the Protestant Home Rule Association in Belfast. The Presbyterian historian W.T. Latimer describes him as 'A man of great mental power and an eloquent though hesitating speaker. In almost every case he cast in his lot with the minority.'

While tenant farmers were waging a hard battle throughout Ireland for possession of the land on which they worked, the Irish Parliamentary Party was making substantial gains at the polls. Economic and political struggles went hand in hand. The key to this democratic advance was the transformation of the electoral system, which for the first time gave improved opportunities to the poorer sections of the population, especially Catholics. In the 1860s only about one adult male in five had the vote in parliamentary elections, and these were mostly the more prosperous Protestants. Tories could boast of their continued monopoly of power. Liberals might be elected occasionally, but no nationalist MP was chosen in Ulster until 1871 when Isaac Butt won the County Monaghan seat. In spite of the fact that they comprised nearly half the population, not a single Catholic was either nominated or elected until C.J. Fay was successful, along with the Protestant Home Ruler Biggar, in County Cavan in 1874.

In September 1881 a sensation was caused when the Liberal and pro-tenant candidate T.A. Dickson defeated the Tory in a close fight in the County Tyrone by-election. The result was Dickson 3,168, Knox 3,084, and Rylett 907. Colonel W.S. Knox was a well-known Orangeman and had been MP in the Ranfurly interest for many years. The vote was a complicated one as Rylett had been persuaded by Parnell to run as a Home Ruler, but this had been opposed by local nationalists as they thought Dickson had a better chance of beating the Tory. When contests were evenly balanced, tactical voting was the name of the game.

The electoral corruption began to change in 1872 when the Liberal government introduced legislation requiring ballots to be secret. This effectively undermined the power of the land-lords to influence their tenants' votes. In 1883 the Corrupt Practices Act was passed (again by Gladstone), prohibiting the use of bribes or threats to influence elections. Finally, and most decisively, in 1884 a new Franchise Act greatly increased the number of people entitled to vote in the United Kingdom. Between 1881 and 1891 in Ulster the number of parliamentary electors rose nearly threefold from 96,000 to 275,000 (or about two-thirds of the adult males).

These revolutionary changes meant that for the first time in the province's history Catholics were given a large, if not completely full, measure of equality of electoral rights with Protestants. The majority of male farmers, skilled workers, minor professional people, clerks, shopkeepers, and even some labourers, could now vote and in secret. Naturally it was those constituencies that had a high proportion of Catholics which were affected most, and within a few years the counties of Derry, Tyrone, Fermanagh, Armagh, Donegal and Monaghan were following the example of Cavan in returning nationalists. At the same time as the electorate was increased, the boundaries of the constituencies were altered. The nine counties, which had previously each returned two MPs regardless of population, were split up into two, three or four constituencies, each returning one MP. The rotten boroughs of Coleraine, Downpatrick, Dungannon, Lisburn, Enniskillen and Carrickfergus were abolished. Belfast, with its rapidly growing population, was awarded four rather than two seats.

In Ulster the results of the 1885 general election – the first held under the new franchise – were sensational, the Tories being reduced to sixteen MPs, and the Irish Parliamentary Party making remarkable advances. The Liberals, though polling well in several constituencies, did not succeed in winning a single seat. The following year the Unionists (as the Tories were now known) lost Belfast West to the nationalists, who in their turn lost Tyrone South and Derry South to the breakaway Liberal Unionists. In Tyrone the successful candidate was Thomas W. Russell who, though he favoured the Union, was a strong supporter of tenant rights. (For a comparison of election results between 1874 and 1886 see Table 11.)

TABLE 11

NUMBER OF MPs ELECTED IN ULSTER CONSTITUENCIES, 1874–86

	Conservative/ Unionist	Liberal	Liberal Unionist	Irish Parliamentary Party
1874	21	6	–	2
1880	18	9	–	2
1885	16	–	–	17
1886	15	–	2	16

Apart from the extension of the franchise, the main reason for the decline in the Liberal and rise of the nationalist vote was the intervention once more of the Home Rule issue. Repeal of the Union had, of course, been a major concern in northern politics for many years, but had never seemed a practical possibility. Now as a result of Gladstone's willingness to try once and for all to 'settle the Irish question', it became an immediate and potentially explosive matter. The Tories opposed Home Rule; the Irish Parliamentary Party enthusiastically supported it, gaining wind in their sails from Gladstone. The Liberals were divided, with a majority wanting to retain the Union, but a vocal minority, also gaining strength from Gladstone, were willing to accept that Ireland as a whole might have some form of legislative independence.

In this rapidly evolving situation, with all its hopes and fears, Parnell was fortunate in having, not only Davitt, but three young activists, Tim Healy, William O'Brien and John Dillon, who served as confidantes and advisers. They all had fought election campaigns in the north, and, as well as having a good understanding of land problems, they had a shrewd appreciation of the nuances of the relations between conflicting religious groups. However, though intelligent and energetic, they suffered from the 'disadvantage' of being Catholics, and could be criticised as blow-ins from the south.

Much more significant among those who tried to lead Parnell through the labyrinth of Ulster politics were a group of Protestants, mainly from the north but including some from the south, who were not only vocal and vigorous in attacking the Ascendancy over a wide range of issues but also had the extra advantage of belonging to the reformed faith. These Dissenters from establishment values had considerable influence on British public opinion, especially among the numerous Nonconformists, because they controverted the idea that only Catholics were advocates of Home Rule in Ireland. For a few years some of the reformers organised themselves in the Irish Protestant Home Rule Association, which was founded in Belfast in May 1886, and in Dublin a month later. The association's membership was never large – one estimate suggests 1,200 in Dublin, 1,000 in Ulster, and 1,000 in the rest of the country[17] – but their propaganda effect was appreciable. At one stage they could count six MPs among their members. As well as having a political impact, they also inspired the rising generation of Protestant writers, such as Yeats, Hyde, T.W. Rolleston and Stephen Gwynn.

In the south the association's spokesmen were mainly progressive intellectuals, such as Professor C.H. Oldham and the Reverend J.A. Galbraith, both teaching in Trinity College Dublin, and Alfred Webb, the Quaker printer and publisher. Like their radical predecessors in the 1790s and 1840s, these Protestant Home Rulers regarded themselves as Irish rather than British. A conviction they, too, held passionately was that the Protestant faith was strong enough, morally and theologically, to stand on its own feet, and not depend upon political support from Britain. 'We belong to Ireland; and our fortunes and our lives are bound up with the Irish people; we remain here,' said their manifesto published in Dublin. 'The future of Irish Protestantism depends solely on the positive influence it can secure in Ireland.'[18]

In Ulster the association drew its main strength from an alliance of land reformers, liberal politicians, and certain Presbyterian ministers who favoured a more tolerant and ecumenical spirit towards Catholics. All had to face intense opposition, nationally from the Unionists and locally from their coreligionists. In spite of this hostility, their electoral influence in some marginal constituencies could be crucial, and they are said to have been partly responsible for the victory of the nationalist Thomas Sexton in Belfast West in 1886. Indirectly they played an important role in shaping overall nationalist strategy through their contact with important individuals of various religious denominations throughout the British Isles. Geographically they moved freely within and between the two islands, mixing widely with different groups and personalities. Their broad experience gave them a healthy respect for realism in politics.

A key figure in this mobile and politically astute group was John Ferguson, who was born in Belfast in 1835 but spent most of his adult life in Scotland. Ferguson came from a Presbyterian family, and was apprenticed to the stationery trade, where he soon showed business acumen. As a young man he moved to Glasgow, and quickly built up a flourishing printing and publishing enterprise. In the mid-1870s he made contact with Isaac Butt and also with some emigrant members of the Irish Republican Brotherhood (IRB). From then on, until his death in 1906, he was continuously active in several aspects of nationalist and land politics, and a leading spokesman for Ireland's cause in west Scotland. In January 1878 he was among those who, with Parnell, met the released Davitt at Kingstown, and he was again at Davitt's side in April 1879 at the launch of the land agitation in Irishtown, County Mayo. Between 1879 and 1881 he spoke at land reform meetings all over Ireland and Britain, and was one of the two Protestants elected to the central committee of the Land League. T.W. Moody describes him as a 'strong and striking personality, widely and deeply read in the social sciences, an intellectual radical steeped in John Stuart Mill and Herbert Spencer. He was an advanced land reformer, and a fervent admirer of Gladstone and Bright. He was one of the earliest champions in Scotland of Butt's new [Home Rule] movement.'[19]

Jeremiah Jordan, a Methodist shopkeeper from Enniskillen, was a well-known tenant-right agitator for many years, drawing support from both liberal Protestants and nationalist Catholics. He was Home Rule MP for Clare West between 1885 and 1892, Meath South between 1893 and 1895, and then represented Fermanagh South from 1895 until his death in 1911.

John Pinkerton was another important Protestant reformer of this period whose name has been largely forgotten. Son of a tenant farmer near Seacon, Ballymoney, he became a prominent member of the Land League and a colleague of Davitt's. An ardent nationalist, he was much admired by Parnell, and chosen, after an abortive attempt to be elected in Antrim North the year before, as a candidate for Galway City, where he came top of the poll in 1885. He held this seat until his retirement in 1900. Pinkerton was noted for the frequent attacks both inside and outside of parliament he made on various Coercion Bills, and for his long-running campaign against the London livery companies which held land in County Derry.

A new and very young recruit to this movement was Henry Harrison, who, while still a student at Oxford, hero-worshipped Parnell. Harrison was born into a wealthy County Down family in 1867, and was educated at Westminster School. By temperament he was something of a romantic and idealist. When he was only twenty-one years of age he persuaded the Irish Parliamentary Party to nominate him for the constituency of Mid Tipperary, where he was elected in 1888. For a brief period he served as Parnell's secretary, and he always stood by his chief even during the darkest hours of scandal and division. After the split of 1890 he stood again as a Parnellite in Sligo North but was heavily defeated. In spite of his disillusionment, he continued to be deeply concerned with Anglo-Irish relations, and later published several books on the subject.

The most famous of these northern Dissenters during the 1880s, and a man who had great influence on Parnellite politics, was Joseph Gillis Biggar.[20] His ancestors came from Dumfries in Scotland in the early seventeenth century, and settled in Belfast where the family became well-known merchants. His father was a dealer in pork and bacon, and chairman of the Ulster Bank. A Presbyterian by religion, Joseph was educated in the old- established Belfast Royal Academy, which had produced so many of Ulster's leaders and prominent businessmen. As a young man he entered the family firm, and became sole heir on his father's death in 1861.

As a boy he had been injured when thrown from a pony, and this accident left him with a marked curvature of the spine. In appearance he was small and crooked, and on a famous occasion in the House of Commons, Disraeli – who often felt the lash of his tongue – gibingly asked: 'Is he a leprechaun?' Historians constantly refer to his physical disabilities, as well as to his personal charm. Joan Haslip speaks of 'the strange, uncouth little man who refused to be intimidated either by the sneers of the English or the pained disapproval of Isaac Butt'.[21] She also writes of 'kindly, lecherous Biggar, with his engaging elf-like grin'. F. S. L. Lyons comments: 'Unprepossessing in appearance, in fact almost a hunchback, delivering his opinions in a harsh Belfast accent, Biggar was undoubtedly a man with valuable qualities. Tough-minded, shrewd, loyal once his loyalties were engaged (which to Butt they never fully were), he represented a very different tradition from that to which so many of his colleagues belonged.'[22] T. A. Jackson said he had a voice like 'a rusty saw'.[23] In spite of his bodily deformities, he seems to have been quite a ladies' man, fathering according to one witness two children by different mothers and being 'a great favourite with barmaids'. In 1883 he was sued for breach of promise by one Fanny Hyland who was awarded £400 damages. He died a bachelor. St John Ervine describes him in his prim way as 'an avowed and unashamed sinner'.[24] Like his fellow northerner Butt, he does not seem to have been politically harmed by these sexual escapades.

Biggar's place in history is assured from the crucial role he played in devising the obstructionist technique in the House of Commons, his part in developing the 'New Departure' policy, and his close association with Parnell. A curious alliance was formed between the two nationalist MPs. Jackson emphasises the personal differences between them:

> No contrast could possibly be greater in extremes of speech, physique and manner than that between Biggar and Parnell. The one squat, deformed and homely, with a voice and accent as harsh as a corncrake; the other tall, slender, aristocratic, and speaking with an accent, that except for a slight trace of America, marked him as a Cambridge man.[25]

Yet within a short time of meeting, the two men were working intimately together. By chance Biggar was speaking – on this occasion he actually spoke for four hours on the subject of swine fever – on the very first day that Parnell took his seat in the House of Commons in April 1875. Parnell, who was impressionable and then inexperienced in Westminster ways, was stirred by Biggar's persistence in wearing down his opponents, and from then on determined to use every legal stratagem to foil Liberal or Tory measures that seemed hostile to Ireland.

Tory and Liberal members were often reduced to a state of impotent rage by such tactics. They disliked the Irish nationalists for their politics and religion, and they despised them for being peasants and tradesmen. Above all, they resented the mother of parliaments being held up to ridicule. A particular cause of anger was that Parnell and his lieutenants often spoke – contrary to Westminster custom – on topics such as navy discipline and problems in South Africa, which had nothing to do with Ireland. It was bad enough having Irishmen talking about their own country, but to have upstarts like Biggar querying whether the cat-o'-nine-tails was a suitable form of military punishment, or criticising British rule in parts of the empire, was intolerable.

It was one such dramatic intervention that led to the fall of Isaac Butt and the emergence of Parnell as leader of the Irish Parliamentary Party. Henceforward there were no holds barred in the parliamentary struggle, culminating in the bitter and prolonged debates on the Land and Coercion Bills of 1881.

It was during this period that Biggar became one of the best known, and in England one of the most disliked, Irish MPs. Abuse was poured on him, and both his crippled body and biting tongue were sneered at. The press painted him as boorish, uncouth, definitely not a gentleman. 'Mr. Biggar brings the manner of his store into this illustrious assembly, and his manner, even for a Belfast store, is very bad', commented the *World*. 'When he rises to address the House – a whiff of salt-pork seems to float upon the gale – the air is heavy with the odour of kippered herring.'[26]

The British establishment might have turned up their sensitive noses even higher if they had realised how dangerous an opponent the despised pork butcher from Belfast really was. Biggar not only periodically brought parliamentary business to a full stop but he also played a crucial role in making the Land League non-sectarian, thus enabling it to penetrate Ulster. Even more important was his key role in developing the 'New Departure' policy, which proved so influential in the 1880s. This programme brought together issues of land reform and national

297

independence, and involved Fenians, rural agitators and members of the Irish Parliamentary Party. Like the Young Ireland movement, it embraced both physical-force separatists and those wedded to constitutional action.

Biggar had briefly been a member of the IRB, or Fenians, in the early 1870s, but had been expelled from that organisation for taking up the parliamentary seat he won in 1874. His expulsion, however, did not lead to his losing contact with his former comrades, and he was thus able to help forward the 'New Departure' negotiations in 1878–9, the year after Davitt was released from prison. By coincidence a further key personality in these discussions was another Ulster-born Presbyterian, Dr William Carroll. His family had emigrated from Rathmullan, County Donegal, to the United States of America, and after a distinguished career serving as a surgeon with the northern forces in the American Civil War, he had become one of the leading Irish republican spokesmen in Philadelphia. For some years he was medical adviser to John Mitchel and when the ailing Mitchel returned to Ireland in July 1874, Carroll accompanied him. Between 1875 and 1880 he was chairman of Clan na Gael, the Fenian organisation in America and second only in influence in that organisation to John Devoy.

In March 1878 Carroll was chosen as a delegate to represent the Clann at a meeting with Parnell, John O'Leary and J. J. Kelly in secret negotiations which took place in a London hotel. Carroll's report back to Devoy that he was impressed with Parnell's commitment to the concept of Irish national independence was one of the chief factors persuading Devoy to agree to the 'New Departure' policy. Carroll is also reported as having met Davitt 'near Manchester' in the spring of that year. Carroll had previously met, or at least seen, Davitt in Morrison's hotel when the latter was brought to Dublin after his release from prison in January 1878.

Biggar comes back on stage in a further secret conference held at the unlikely venue of a public park in Boulogne, France, in January 1879. Davitt was responsible for arranging this meeting to which Parnell took Biggar as his chief adviser, and John

Devoy, now much encouraged by what he had heard from Carroll, was assisted by John O'Leary, who represented the Irish branch of the Fenians. According to Devoy,[27] these delegates, when not discussing the more important topics that had brought them together, talked about Biggar's conversion to Catholicism,[28] and the fact that he might have served the nationalist cause better by remaining a Presbyterian. 'But what of my eternal soul?' replied Biggar, and then went on to debate the Calvinist doctrine of predestination with John O'Leary. In such curious circumstances, and so far from home, did Irish politics take on a new shape.

For the next ten years, Biggar, though not so much in the public eye, remained at the centre of nationalist politics, frequently speaking at land meetings, and constantly at the right hand of Parnell, both inside and outside of parliament. For a period he was treasurer of the Land League, and thus responsible for the considerable amounts of money collected in Ireland and the United States of America. In 1880 he won his seat again in County Cavan, and when the new constituency of Cavan West was formed in 1885 he won by more than a four to one majority over his Tory opponent. So popular was he locally that he was returned unopposed in the 1886 general election. He was prosecuted on a number of occasions for various offences, but unlike some of his prominent colleagues, he never served any period in jail.

Biggar died suddenly of a heart attack in his London home in February 1890 – an ominous year in Parnellite history. His death came as a shock to political friend and foe alike. His opponents had by this time come to value his courage and independence, even when enraged by his spiky personality. Parnell's comment was: 'It will be impossible to replace him. He was my first and for a long time my only friend and counsellor.'[29] Irish sympathisers formed a cortège of coaches and marching men to take the body from Clapham to Euston station, an arrangement which was repeated at Liverpool.

The cortège was delayed by fog on the Irish Sea, and when it arrived in Belfast many thousands were waiting at the docks to mourn. The funeral, which took place on 24 February, was one of the biggest ever seen in the city, and attended by people from all classes and religious denominations. Many nationalist MPs marched in the procession, which took at least an hour to pass. Cardinal Manning sent a wreath, the *Northern Whig* spoke of immense multitudes attending and commented specifically on the closing of factories and the presence of several hundred mill girls. It was significant of Biggar's wide popularity that Protestants turned out in large numbers, including Thomas Shillington and three other representatives from the Protestant Home Rule Association. There were also representatives from the Belfast Radical Association. The burial took place at the old family grave at Carnmoney, near Mallusk.

It was a melancholy comment on the times that his death coincided with the spread of news about the impending O'Shea divorce action. Biggar did not live to see his beloved chief brought low, but already, before he died, storm clouds were gathering. Parnellism, and with it obstructionism, died in the same year.

18

THE GARRISON UNDER SIEGE

> An owner of property of sufficient size would be opposed to
> revolution ... The creation of such a class would add to the ranks
> of those interested in support of law and order ... diminishing
> the number of those ... at beck and call of every agitator – no
> matter how wild his theory or communistic his principles.
>
> Bessborough Commission, 1881[1]

The ruling classes on both sides of the Irish Sea became deeply
divided as a result of these Land League and nationalist advances. Their power and privileges were under threat in a way
that had not been seen for three generations. The sacred rights
of property were being challenged, and the unity of the empire
threatened. There were profound economic changes taking place
in which the old territorial aristocracy were losing ground to
expanding forces of industry and commerce. Under free trade,
certain forms of wealth were gaining at the expense of others.
Population was moving from country into towns and cities. All
these changes set up serious stresses and strains between the
different social and economic groups.

In Ireland, as the crisis deepened it became obvious that there
was a conflict of interest between the small, but historically
important, landlord class and the emerging manufacturers and
merchants of the Belfast region. The dominant groups in Ulster
looked at things differently from the Ascendancy in the south.
There was also a clash of views between the Ascendancy as a
whole and their opposite numbers in Britain as to how in the
new circumstances the Union, and with it, the solidarity of the
empire, could be best preserved.

The Protestant Churches, too, were in disarray as the enthusiasts condemned the quietists, and the fundamentalists strove to drive out the latitudinarians. In spite of conservative efforts to resolve it, the old quarrel between the socially superior Anglicans and the lower-middle-class Nonconformists still rankled. In Ireland the episcopalians had suffered a severe setback from their disestablishment in 1869; they continued to be disliked because of their association with the landlord system. How were they – with only one-eighth of the total Irish population and linked with a deeply unpopular and decaying social caste – to respond to the new situation? In Ulster the majority of Presbyterians were simultaneously for land reform but against Home Rule.

The consequence was that the overall political situation in Ireland, and the relations between Ireland and Britain, became extremely fluid, and even more than usually complicated, with pressure groups pulling in opposite directions, and much cross voting in parliament. Coercion was followed by conciliation, and a policy of repression was replaced by a policy of trying 'to kill Home Rule with kindness'. Tories and Liberals found themselves further divided, both internally and in relation to each other. Parnell and the nationalists used these divisions skilfully for their own purposes, playing off one party against the other.

In Ulster, the landlords, though slow to grasp the full implications of what was happening in the two countries, and confused by the rapidly changing political situation, were quick to appreciate that two of their most cherished privileges – rents and the monopoly of votes – were under attack. Writing in December 1880 to Lord Salisbury, who had just relinquished the post of foreign secretary, Sir Thomas Bateson, a prominent northern landlord, said:

> A few weeks since the Land League invaded Ulster. Up to that time rents were well and cheerfully paid without even a murmur. Now all that is changed. The League operates in concert with the Central Radical Tenant-Rights Association, and the result is a general strike on the part of the tenants; men who voted

for the Conservatives last April are now openly fraternising with the democrats whom six weeks ago they would not have touched with a long pole, and the wave of communism has spread like wildfire. The demand is for 25, 30, and in some cases, 50 per cent permanent reduction in rents.[2]

In September 1881, shortly after the Liberal T.A. Dickson unexpectedly defeated his Tory opponent in the Tyrone by-election, a local land agent and Orangeman complained:

It is too bad that what was once called Protestant Tyrone could not return a Protestant member. That low fellow Dickson was returned by Protestant members, and I believe a number of Orangemen voted against their grand-master [Knox, the Conservative candidate]. The fact is that the Protestants as well as the Roman Catholics do not want an Orangeman or even a Fenian if he is a gentleman or a landlord. I look upon this election as a death blow to Protestantism.[3]

Such warnings might alert their friends across the sea to the dangers threatening 'the garrison', but they did not make the difficulties go away. How were they to respond to the ever more pressing demand for land reform – by conciliation, by coercion, or by playing the sectarian card? In the event they tried all three solutions.

A few of the more enlightened gentry were willing to reduce rents temporarily during the crisis. For example, Hugh Montgomery, a well-known improver who owned 8,000 acres in County Fermanagh and 4,500 acres in County Tyrone, issued a letter to his tenants in February 1881 saying that he proposed cutting payments for those who paid under £10 a year by 20 per cent, and for those who paid £10 or more by 10 per cent.[4] On certain other estates the reductions averaged about 15 per cent.

The majority of landlords, however, followed the reactionary traditions of their class, refusing to make concessions, blaming the disturbances on outside agitators, and calling for ever more repressive laws. The Liberal John Morley, who served twice as chief secretary under Gladstone, described such diehards as 'unteachable'. One of the most notorious was the Earl of Leitrim, whose name is often linked with that of Lord Clanricarde as the epitome of arrogance and cruelty. Leitrim, who owned 56,000 acres in County Donegal, had an unsavoury reputation both as a ruthless evicter of tenants and a seducer of local girls. He was assassinated on the shores of Mulroy Bay in April 1878, at a time when he is said to have had eighty eviction notices pending.[5]

Fortunately for the people of Ulster not all landlords were of the calibre of 'the wicked earl', but the records indicate that when it came to the ruthless clearing of estates they did not lag behind their fellow landlords in Leinster, Munster and Connacht. Over a period of three or four years a total of several thousand tenants and their families were driven off their farms. This suggests that some hundred landlords were involved. The official figures show that the number of evictions in the nine northern counties, which had been averaging between 100 and 200 annually in the two previous decades, rose to 497 in 1880. During the bad harvest of 1881 they more than doubled to 1,219. The total fell slightly to 1,176 the following year, to 689 in 1883, rising again sharply to 1,044 in 1884.[6] The average size of the families involved was five, so in the worst years about one hundred persons – men, women and children, Protestants and Catholics – were being put on to the road each week. With human misery on such a scale, it was not surprising that there was so much agrarian unrest.

In spite of the existence of the Ulster custom, and the fact that so many of the farmers were Presbyterians, the percentage of evictions in the north seems to have been about the same as in the other three provinces. During the twenty-five years after the famine, Ulster, which had about one-quarter of all the farmers in the country, provided at various times between one-fifth and one-third of all evictions. In 1881 the proportion was 36 per cent – and this in a region which some people claimed was quiet and prosperous.

The harshness of these clearances, and the famine memories stirred up by them, made the landlords even more unpopular, and some of this unpopularity rubbed off on to those politicians associated with them. It was noted that in the 1880 general election, though the franchise at that stage had not been much extended, the Liberals won nine of the Ulster seats, largely on issues arising from the land struggle. MPs of all parties, therefore, had to be careful about what they said on land reform in all rural constituencies, including those in Down, Antrim and Derry, where there were many Presbyterians. By and large, the Liberals accepted the need for some change in the system of landownership, but even the Conservative MPs (many of whom were landlords themselves) were forced to make concessions to voters. In 1881 when Gladstone introduced his second Land Bill, for example, with its proposals for fixity of tenure, fair rents and free sale, it was significant that six Ulster Liberals and thirteen out of eighteen Ulster Tories voted for the second reading. Four Tories, including Lord Castlereagh, MP for County Down, abstained, and only the diehard Viscount Cole of Enniskillen voted against. Why this reversal of policy on an issue which northern Conservatives traditionally regarded as so crucial? 'The answer is simple', wrote J.L. Hammond, Gladstone's biographer. 'The demand for the Bill in Ulster made it dangerous for any Ulster member to vote against it.'[7] At this time the Tories in Britain were still strongly against land reform in Ireland. Disraeli's chancellor of the exchequer, Sir Stafford Northcote, then denounced the three Fs as 'fraud, force and folly'.

The Orange Order was placed in a difficult position as a result of these conflicting pressures. Its minority populist wing, which had roots among the poorer Protestants, did not like the upper classes, especially the snobbish and wealthy landlords.[8] Some lodges openly proclaimed their support for the farmers' struggle. For example, in County Tyrone a local lodge passed a resolution in November 1880 stating that it would not participate in any landlords' meetings which had 'no other aim than to continue the present over-high rents – and calculated to produce and embitter sectarian feelings'.[9] In Monaghan a month later it was resolved that Orangemen should assist tenants' associations, but not the Land League. In Fermanagh and Armagh some lodge officers helped tenant-right candidates during the 1880 general election. This led to a warning that recalcitrant lodges might be expelled.

It was noticeable during the 12 July celebrations of 1881 that although there were the usual ritual attacks on Catholicism and Fenianism, there were also frequent calls for a 'just settlement' of the land question. On this occasion there seem to have been few speakers prepared to make an out-and-out defence of landlords and their unpopular system. It was these signs of liberalism that led the *Ulster Weekly News* to speak of 'a tide of enlightened opinion in our once benighted province'.[10]

The majority of Orangemen, however, put their dislike of Catholicism before any class loyalty they might have had; and their most ancient and atavistic fears were roused by the incursion of the Land League into what they regarded as their inviolable territories. Basically, their most profound instincts were hostile towards any movement that disturbed the social order or seemed to threaten the Protestant constitution, even though such a movement might bring practical benefits to some of their members. The Orange leaders, therefore, responded immediately to the challenge, and began to put out feelers to those gentry, MPs, clergymen, magistrates and army officers who had fallen away from them in the 1850s and 1860s because of their connection with street disorders and public riots. The cry of 'property in danger' was raised once again to rally the middle and upper classes to the sectarian flag. Thus the Pope, Fenianism, Ribbonism, and the comparatively new menace of socialism, were linked in a most unlikely alliance to try to frighten any possible defectors from the loyalist cause. If a revolutionary rising, such as the Paris Commune of 1871, or recent terrorist acts, such as the assassinations of Lord Leitrim in 1878 or the tsar of Russia in 1881, could be cited, then this was all grist to the propaganda mill. The language used by the Grand Lodge meeting in Dublin in November 1880 is significant: the Land League was condemned as 'a conspiracy against property, Protestantism and the Union ... pernicious and communistic'.[11]

Evangelical clergymen, whose stock in trade for years had been the abuse of 'the anti-Christ' in the Vatican, now tried to make their congregations' flesh creep with attacks on the new bogeymen from Europe, Karl Marx and Mikhail Bakunin. 'Roaring' Hanna, who had become notorious for his fiery anti-Papist sermons and street preaching, and who was officially held responsible for the Belfast pogroms of 1857 and 1872, turned the full blast of his oratory against the Land League, which, he said in November 1880, was associated with all things foreign, including 'Russian nihilism, German social democracy and French communism'.[12] The Reverend Abraham Jagoe, another fanatical opponent of Catholicism, speaking at an Orange soiree in Newtownbutler, County Fermanagh, the same month, condemned the league as a 'conspiracy', 'Anarchy' and 'Communism', inspired by the 'Pope and Popery', and 'responsible for the death of Lord Mountmorres'.[13]

The recruitment of two well-known and energetic Tory MPs gave an extra political dimension to the Order. Colonel Edward J. Saunderson, who served as an MP for three decades, first in County Cavan, and then between 1885 and 1906 in Armagh North, was a typical Church of Ireland landlord, wealthy, reactionary, and an officer in the militia. An enthusiastic evangelical, and a strong admirer of the American preachers Moody and Sankey, he was notorious for his bigotry. In 1882 he joined the Orange Order, with the object, as he said, of 'fighting anarchy and rebellion'.[14] He was soon made deputy grand master. Representing a rural constituency, Saunderson had to be circumspect about what he said concerning land reform. His solution for the agrarian problem was to try to divert the discontent of poorer Protestants away from the social issues, and towards the alleged dangers of Catholicism and Irish nationalism.

A close colleague in parliament, and another advocate of armed force against the Land Leaguers, was William Johnston of Ballykilbeg, County Down, who represented a Belfast constituency between 1868 and 1878, and 1885 and 1902. He was also a Church zealot, and married to the daughter of the noted Orange clergyman, the Reverend Thomas Drew. In 1867 Johnston had been put in prison briefly for his part in organising a prohibited Orange procession, but this episode was overlooked in the more respectable unionist circles he later represented. In Belfast, Johnston did not have to worry about the farmers' vote.

Paradoxically, it was during this period of social unrest, when Conservatives were promoting the law-and-order issue most vigorously, that the Orange leaders began to urge the use of force – illegally, if necessary – as a way of stopping their opponents. The Reverend Richard Kane, for example, rector of Tullylish, County Down, and later of Christ Church in Belfast, where he also became grand master, advocated the killing of the Land Leaguers. This led to him being nicknamed 'the shooting rector'.[15] A few years after this episode, Kane got in touch with Field Marshal Lord Wolseley in London, with a view to setting up a militia force. When Colonel Saunderson joined the Orange Order one of the first things he did was to advocate armed resistance against the land agitators.

A physical-force tactic, which proved very effective because it encouraged the mobilisation of large numbers of strong-arm loyalists, and to which the authorities could turn a blind eye if necessary, was for the Orange lodges to organise a counter-rally whenever the tenants planned a meeting. The trick was to threaten to stir up enough trouble so that the Government would ban both demonstrations. According to Thomas MacKnight, a contemporary critic:

> The expedient adopted was of a questionable, defiant, and even dangerous character. Whenever a Nationalist meeting from the South was announced in the North, a counter Orange demonstration, as it is called, was summoned to be held on the same day, at the same hour, and in the same neighbourhood. Nothing could be more provocative; nothing more likely to produce a breach of the peace. Such counter-irritating displays in such circumstances were justly regarded as illegal. Many meetings on both sides were proclaimed.[16]

The most dramatic evidence – the actual events had elements of farce as well as tragedy – of the hostility of extreme unionists

308

towards the Land League and the way in which the Ascendancy could mobilise the more backward Orange labourers and farmers came from Fermanagh and neighbouring counties in the autumn of 1880. In August of that year the labourers on the Lough Mask, County Mayo, estate of Captain Charles Boycott had sought a wage increase from between seven and eleven shillings weekly to between nine and fifteen shillings. Boycott was already unpopular as a rack-renter and agent for Lord Erne (who owned 31,000 acres in Fermanagh), and when he refused to pay the wage increase on his own estate, and began serving eviction notices from Lord Erne, the Mayo people began to ostracise him as they had been advised by Parnell. Immediately there was a great uproar among the unionists and their friends in parliament. A relief fund was planned to help the besieged captain, and when this faltered, a scheme was organised by a group of landlords, magistrates, army officers and unionist MPs to send a team of scab labourers to work on his Lough Mask demesne. A force of fifty-seven Orange farm workers was mobilised in Cavan and Monaghan, and under a heavy guard of about one thousand troops and armed police, travelled partly by train and partly by foot to the shores of Lough Mask. The large scale of this venture, and the resulting worldwide publicity, gave a new word to the English language, but otherwise achieved very little. The armed forces made sure that the crops were brought in, but Boycott eventually had to flee to England, where he lapsed into obscurity.[17]

A similar strike-breaking exercise was tried in August 1881 when some scores of Protestant farm labourers were entrained from Kingsbridge in Dublin, and then marched to the farm of a unionist landlord in Tipperary, a Mr Twiss, where local labourers had refused to cut his seven hundred acres of hay.[18]

In Britain the ruling classes were divided as to how to react to the deepening Irish crisis. Embarrassed by the continual round of riots, murders, arson and evictions, and yet reluctant to make fundamental changes in the country's constitution and social structure, they were not sure which way to turn. A new famine might be on the way to tarnish further Britain's good name at home and abroad. The brutalities of certain landlords were beyond toleration. The American-Irish were up in arms, and the British Nonconformist conscience troubled. Above all, agrarian discontent was feeding the movement for national independence. Then in the 1885 general election the Irish nationalists, led by Parnell, swept to victory at the polls, winning 85 seats out of 103. There seemed to be no end to the troubles of the British in Ireland.

The first instinct of the upper classes was to side with their fellow landlords in Ireland, who, after all, had been for centuries their closest allies and most trustworthy garrison. A thousand bonds of wealth, family, religion and politics bound them to the Irish Ascendancy. Did they not sit in the same parliament and vote for the same Conservative laws? Was not Davitt a dangerous Fenian and convicted terrorist, and Parnell a traitor to his class and Church? As much as their friends across the Irish Sea, they feared and disliked the Land Leaguers and the Parnellites.

But the shrewder and more far-sighted leaders of the Liberal and Tory parties were forced by events to look beyond the narrow and selfish interests of a tiny caste – comprising perhaps ten thousand families in a total population of over five million – to the wider interests of the United Kingdom and the empire it ruled. In the past the British ruling élite had always been prepared, if circumstances required, to sacrifice the part in order to protect the whole – to make a tactical retreat in order to maintain the strategical advantage. This *realpolitik* approach had been the essence of the Pitt–Castlereagh proposals for the Act of Union in 1800. Now eighty years later the long-established garrison had become so shaky in its foundations that it could no longer be relied upon. It was necessary, therefore, to seek new and hopefully more enduring power bases in Ireland. If this involved a reversal of policy then so be it.

The Liberals, led by Gladstone, who combined a hard-headed realism with an unusual dose of idealism, were first to come to the conclusion that the landlords had become, not so much a bulwark or bastion, but an Achilles' heel, in Ireland. Based as it was mainly in towns and cities, and supported chiefly by

Nonconformists, the Liberal Party had few sympathies with rich rural magnates, especially episcopalians. Gladstone's disestablishment of the Church of Ireland had been quickly followed by a Land Act, and returning to office again in 1881, and pushed forward by the Land League, he had moved a second Land Bill, which accepted the principle of the three Fs. There had been an attempt, albeit an unsuccessful one, to link rents to the price of agricultural produce, and thus make them more equitable.

Five years later, again stirred into action by the progress of Irish nationalists, Gladstone introduced proposals for Home Rule. This led to the more imperialist and Whiggish elements among the Liberals, led by the radical-turned-imperialist Joseph Chamberlain, MP for Birmingham, to split away to form the Liberal Unionist Party. Gladstone's government collapsed, and Home Rule was effectively blocked.

To begin with, the British Tories would have nothing to do with any of these reforms, denouncing the Land Leaguers as so many Fenians and Jacobins, and condemning suggestions for Home Rule as the preliminary to the break-up of the empire. Lord Salisbury and the great majority of his party (but not, as we have seen, some Ulster Tory MPs) bitterly opposed the 1881 Land Act as a confiscatory attack on the rights of property, and an unwarranted interference with the free play of the market. Then in the mid- and late 1880s – that is, when Parnell was winning new heights of popularity and the tenants' strike, known as the Plan of Campaign, was beginning to cut into rents – they, too, reversed their policy towards Irish landlordism.[19] Instead of defending the system to the last ditch, as they had done for centuries, they proceeded to abandon it; instead of sticking by their oldest friends, they sold (or rather bought) them out. Within a remarkably short space of time, really only a few years, the most conservative and property-conscious party in Britain came round to the view that it would be safer to rely upon half a million peasant proprietors than a few thousand gentry and aristocrats. It was a risky gamble to take but one they could not avoid because of the irresistible progress of democracy at the ballot box.

The fact that something drastic had to be done about land reform if the Home Rule momentum was to be slowed down was admitted by the most prominent Unionist politicians in a series of remarkably frank speeches. Tories in Ireland might still quibble and hesitate, but their counterparts in Britain no longer had any doubts as to what should be done. In 1887, for example, Lord Lansdowne, who owned vast estates in Queen's County and had held the most senior posts in both Liberal and Tory administrations, wrote to Lord Salisbury complaining that he had suffered serious losses of rent during the Plan of Campaign. The Government had to choose, he argued, between 'the collapse of the Union and a great agrarian revolution'.[20] Lansdowne's views carried great weight as he was not only married to a daughter of the Duke of Abercorn and was a prominent member of the Anglo-Irish aristocracy but he also played a leading part in creating the new and wider Unionist Party. He was later foreign secretary in the Tory government of 1900–1905, and was active in the formation of the Carson–Bonar Law alliance in Ulster.

In 1888 Joseph Chamberlain said in a speech in Birmingham:

> The root of the difficulty in Ireland is to be found in economic and agrarian questions ... Hitherto we have only trifled with the [land] question; we have only scratched on the surface; we have never dealt with it thoroughly. And we shall never have done so until we have transformed the great majority of the occupiers of land into the owners of the soil they till.[21]

In his opinion the best way of holding on to Ireland was to reduce poverty there, and by so doing 'the demand for separation will die away'.

Arthur Balfour, who held many high offices under his uncle Lord Salisbury, was prime minister between 1900 and 1905, and was closely involved with the Irish question for a quarter of a century, came to the same conclusion in 1891. The Irish land system, he believed, had become so 'essentially and radically rotten' that it no longer offered any strength to Britain. By having to defend the landlords, they were only weakening the Union.

312

The decision of the most powerful political forces in Britain to encourage, rather than block, land reform in Ireland was quickly translated into action. As soon as the Tory administration took office in the summer of 1885, Lord Salisbury – who had once declared that all Ireland needed was twenty years of firm rule – introduced the Ashbourne Act. This provided £5 million to enable tenants to buy their land, the loan being repayable at 4 per cent over forty-nine years. Two years later a further £5 million was added, and leaseholders were brought into the scheme. Better protection was given against evictions and arbitrary rent rises. In 1891 Balfour, who was then chief secretary, set up the Congested Districts Board, which was an attempt to tackle the problem of land hunger in the poorest regions in the west of Ireland.

As a result of these and previous acts it was reckoned that by the mid-1890s about one-fifth of all the land in Ulster was in the process of being transferred to tenants. The average size of the new peasant farms was about twenty to twenty-five acres. This period of reform, culminating in Wyndham's Land Act of 1903 has been described by historians as the era of 'constructive unionism'. But how constructive was it, and whom did it benefit most?

The Land Acts were positive measures in so far as they transformed an undemocratic pattern of landownership into a system of small peasant proprietors. The aristocracy and gentry, who had ruled arbitrarily for so long, lost some of their privileges and political power. For the first time since the plantations, the soil of Ulster began to be tilled by those who owned it.

The creation of a small farming class, however, did not solve all the province's agricultural problems. The new peasants might have more security, but many were deeply in debt. They lacked education and capital, and continued to be at the mercy of world market forces. Moreover, the landlords gained handsomely from the sale of their estates. Generally they invested their newly acquired cash into profitable enterprises in Britain or the empire. Increasingly their social and political power was linked with manufacturing interests in Belfast. Many continued to be influential: wealthy aristocratic families, such as the Abercorns, Brookes and Londonderrys, stayed at the centre of Ulster politics. The historian Brian O'Neill saw the Land Acts as having two aims:

> The more far-seeing landlords saw that their best course was to get rid of their ownership for as large a sum as possible, thereby obtaining liquid assets for investment in more secure undertakings. Thus the British government's various Acts had a dual purpose; first, to relieve the landlords; second, by the creation of a peasant proprietorship to raise a barrier against the political revolution which the land war threatened.[22]

The economic gap that had always existed between the richer Protestant farmers inhabiting the valleys and the fertile plains and the poorer Catholics of the hillsides and boglands did not disappear. Thus in the perpetuated wealth of the old landlords now associated with the new industrialists, and the class-cum-religious distinctions still existing between Protestant and Catholic farmers, lay the seeds of future political and religious dissension.

In the wider political sphere it was noticeable, moreover, that the names most closely connected with the policy of land reform in Ireland – Churchill, Salisbury, Balfour, Chamberlain, Lansdowne, Devonshire – were of individuals who above all other considerations were determined to preserve the empire, and to this end were prepared to play the sectarian card. Their 'constructive' impulses, therefore, were of only limited application so far as ordinary Irish people were concerned. To understand why the most conservative elements in Britain were prepared to forsake their oldest allies in Ireland, while at the same time resisting any proposals for Ireland's legislative freedom, we must appreciate the importance of imperialist ideology in their general way of thinking, and how they perceived the part that Protestantism and Ulster might play in that empire.

IMPERIALISM AND THE 'ORANGE CARD'

If we cannot hold Ireland, obviously we cannot hold India. We cannot hold our supremacy over our colonies if we cannot govern this country [the United Kingdom]. Commerce is founded on dominion, and British dominion must stand or fall together.

Lord Randolph Churchill, 1886[1]

The British empire had reached the zenith of its power and influence during the second half of the nineteenth century. Canada, Australia, New Zealand and South Africa had been acquired as strategic bases and lands for trade and White settlement. India had become one of the most profitable colonies in the world, and Egypt was seized so that an important canal could be cut through it. Between the Crimean and the Boer wars the area under British control multiplied more than four times, and the number of inhabitants rose nearly two and a half times, from 145 million to 345 million.[2] At the end of the century just under one in four of all persons on this planet lived under the Union Jack.

A string of maritime stations round the world – Gibraltar, Malta, Alexandria, Bombay, Singapore, Hong Kong (and not forgetting Cobh and Berehaven) – signified to Britain's naval superiority. Wheat and timber from Canada, meat and wool from Australia and New Zealand, gold and diamonds from South Africa, cotton, jute and tea from India, tin from Malaya, sugar and coffee from the West Indies, cocoa and palm oil from west Africa, and tea from east Africa – all these poured cheaply into Britain in exchange for the manufactures of Birmingham and Manchester, Leeds and Sheffield, Glasgow and Belfast. For a period of two or three decades in the middle of the century Britain, in spite of its small size, was the greatest manufacturing and shipbuilding country in the world.

A much larger upper and middle class of industrialists and merchants, professional people, army and navy officers, and administrators was developed to serve, and grow rich, from this imperial trade. And as wealth poured into the country from overseas so some sections of the white-collar and skilled working class became more prosperous also. British adults were told that they belonged to a mighty empire on which the sun never set, and that by the mere fact of their birth, they were heirs to a unique colonising and civilising role in the world. Children were taught to sing 'Rule Britannia', and shown a map on which nearly one-quarter of the globe was coloured red.

The dominant political ideology that accompanied this acquisition of wealth and power was as crude and as anti-democratic as the methods used to acquire it. Might was equated with right, conquest regarded as a civilising, almost divine, mission; and military successes equated with virtue.

> We don't want to fight, yet by jingo! if we do,
> We've got the ships, we've got the men,
> And we've got the money, too!

A racist philosophy, partly inherited from the old British traditions of social and cultural superiority, and partly copied from the wilder Saxon–Teutonic ideas of men like Joseph Arthur Gobineau in France and Houston Stewart Chamberlain in Germany spread ever more widely. The new doctrine of social Darwinism was grafted on, and gave a spurious scientific validity to traditional notions about the survival of the fittest and the innate superiority of certain chosen peoples. And such theories about biologically determined races were superimposed upon more genuine scientific ideas about the origin of the Aryan languages. Famous philosophers like Thomas Carlyle, and eminent historians, such as Thomas B. Macaulay and James A. Froude, gave an academic respectability to such doctrines, which were in turn popularised by writers like the Reverend Charles

316

Kingsley and Rudyard Kipling.[3] The old anti-Semitism and the traditional contempt for 'Wogs' and 'Yids' became a generalised contempt for all people with black, brown or yellow skins. Kipling wrote of 'the White man's burden' and of 'the lesser breeds without the law', and *Punch* stereotyped in text and cartoon the images of comic Sambo and stupid, sometimes dangerous, Paddy. The argument was advanced that such natives were being ruled for their own good.

The Celts were, of course, allotted their appropriate category in this European caste system. By reason of their ethnic origins, and their history as a wandering and dwindling people, they were regarded as being not fit for self-rule. They might be romantic, and have some gifts in poetry and eloquence, but they were doomed to be defeated by their stronger rivals, the virile, dominant, conquering Saxons.

As for the native Gaelic Irish, they were, in the old phrase, beyond the pale. They might have white skins and speak an Aryan language, but this did not save them from suffering from a double dose of original sin. As Celts they were by definition a subordinate people, suitable only to serve as hewers of wood and drawers of water. Worse still, as Catholics they were believed to be superstitious and prone to worship idols. They were dictated to politically by their priests, and therefore could not be trusted to exercise a democratic franchise. Unlike the loyal Protestants, their invariable tendency was to be troublesome and rebellious. The most eminent English persons, from Victoria downwards, distrusted, disliked and feared them. Lord Salisbury was saying the right thing when he declared that the Irish were no more suited to self-government than the Hottentots, and that other Tory grandee, Arthur Balfour, was perfectly correct when he argued that everything good in Ireland came from England.

The Protestant religion, which was the faith of more than nine-tenths of the British people and had taken on some extreme evangelical forms during the mid-nineteenth century, played a crucial part in the development of this imperialist philosophy. Since the days of Elizabeth I, Protestantism had been identified with two key aspects of English, and later, British life – nationalism and the rule of parliament. Elizabeth herself had been excommunicated as a heretic by the Pope, and threatened by the foreign and Catholic power of Spain. Cromwell, the arch-Protestant, was the founder of the modern House of Commons, and the Glorious Revolution of 1689 had inaugurated a new and Protestant constitution. William of Orange's victory at the Battle of the Boyne was a triumph not only for Irish but also for English Protestantism. Centuries before Sir James Craig, prime minister in Stormont after partition, resurrected the phrase, the British ruling class had chosen a Protestant king to rule over a Protestant parliament and a Protestant people. For the overwhelming majority of British people politics and religion were closely intertwined, and when they talked of 'civil and religious liberty' or 'the constitution' they excluded Catholics from their share in the national polity. As the social reformer William Cobbett said: anti-Catholicism was taken in with their mothers' milk. In certain respects, indeed, it was more deeply rooted and widespread than the anti-Semitism it resembled in its prejudice and racist overtones.[4]

Ireland, because of the fact that it was England's oldest colony, and by reason of its geographical proximity, had a very special place in this imperial structure. The majority of its Protestant population of about 800,000 people were a reliable garrison. If India was regarded as the jewel in the imperial crown, then Ireland was the archstone of the 1689 constitution. It was feared that if the arch collapsed then the whole glittering edifice would collapse with it. According to Joseph Chamberlain, if ever Ireland should achieve legislative independence then Britain 'would sink to the level of a third-rate power'.[5] The danger existed that other disaffected colonies might imitate the Irish, and throw off the British yoke. Who knows what might happen to the recently subjected nations of Africa and Asia if the discontented Celts had the presumption to challenge their masters? And what dangers might undermine the Protestant constitution if Catholics asserted their rights too vigorously? Any such disturbance affecting the citizens of Britain, as well as Ireland, could affect the delicate balance that had been achieved between Crown, Lords and Commons.

Strategically Ireland was perceived in much the same way as it had been during the dangerous eras of the Spanish Armada and Napoleon's threatened invasion – as a vital base guarding the western approaches to the British Isles, which it was necessary at all costs to defend. In spite of the fact that Britain was not then involved in any major European war, there were still fears of foreign conspiracies and threats.

A further deep-seated anxiety among members of the establishment in Britain was that any attack on property rights in Ireland might spread across the Irish Sea. To criticise the ownership of wealth, especially land, was to open the door to the dangers of socialism and communism.

But whether the imperialists liked it or not, and no matter how often they raised the Jacobin, Fenian, or socialist scare, the fact was that the landlord-garrison base was cracking open, and the Irish nationalists were coming to electoral power in the majority of Irish constituencies. Where could the imperialists find a new, and it was this time hoped indestructible, base in Ireland? The obvious answer was Ulster, where demographic, religious and economic circumstances all favoured them.[6]

First, there was the undoubted fact that in Ulster there were far more Protestants than there were in any of the other three provinces. The 1881 census, for example, showed that in the north just over half the population were Protestants, whereas in the south the proportion was less than one in ten (see Table 12[7]). This demographic balance was of crucial electoral importance.

Within this Protestant bloc there were still many differences of religious and political opinion, but in overall terms there was always a strong reservoir of anti-Catholic feeling to draw upon. There was an underlying prejudice that could, in certain circumstances, be quickly brought to the surface. It only required a few zealots to get on to the streets, and all the old, and worst, passions would be roused once again.

Second, the northern economy was much more closely integrated with the expanding markets of the British Empire.

TABLE 12

PERCENTAGE OF IRISH POPULATION IN DIFFERENT RELIGIOUS
GROUPS, 1881

	Catholic %	Church of Ireland %	Presbyterian %	Others %
Leinster	85.6	12.3	0.9	1.2
Munster	93.8	5.3	0.3	0.6
Ulster	47.8	21.8	25.9	4.5
Connacht	95.3	3.9	0.4	0.4

A policy of protective tariffs might suit the manufacturers of
the south, but it would not benefit those of the north. Since the
mid-1850s the Lagan valley had become the most industrialised part of Ireland, with linen, shipbuilding and engineering
making big strides. The proportion of people living in towns of
over two thousand population rose from 13 per cent in 1851 to
38 per cent in 1901. During the same period the population of
Belfast multiplied three and a half times to 349,000. Belfast was
catching up with Dublin, and could compete industrially with
Sheffield, Leeds and Glasgow.

This rapid growth of industry and trade helped to expand
further that middle class which had begun to increase half a
century earlier. Gradually, as the landlord class weakened, a
wealthy new group of shipyard owners, linen magnates and
engineering employers came to share power. The old aristocracy of the Londonderrys, Abercorns and Brookes still had great
social and political influence, but their direct economic authority was waning. Sir Edward Harland (shipbuilding), Sir William
Ewart (linen industry), Sir James Corry (merchant), George Clark
(shipbuilding), William Pirrie (shipbuilding), John Barbour
(linen industry) – these were the new names to be reckoned with
in Belfast.[8] All of them were Unionists, with the exception of
the Liberal Pirrie. Many were Presbyterians, in contrast to
the aristocracy and gentry who were almost invariably
episcopalians. Among these businessmen in the 1890s, though
still a young man and not yet well known, was James Craig, son

of a rich whiskey distiller, and himself a stockbroker in Belfast. Inevitably these ever-closer trading links with the empire encouraged stronger political bonds with Britain.

A further aspect of these far-reaching economic changes, which had great political as well as religious significance, was the fact that the Protestants employed in manufacturing and trade continued to be generally better paid than the Catholics. Moreover, they also had greater opportunities of getting and holding on to jobs. In the same way as the notion of White supremacy embraced both poor Whites and more prosperous Whites, so the concept of Ascendancy included, as it had always done, working-class as well as middle- and upper-class Protestants. In a pioneering study,[9] the historian Geoffrey Bell devotes several pages of text and statistics to show how the Protestants, not only monopolised the most profitable white-collar occupations in industry, commerce and the professions, but also how they had the pick of the best paid and most secure manual jobs in manufacturing and shipbuilding. In Belfast particularly, where skilled jobs were most numerous, the overwhelming majority of posts in such trades as bricklaying, carpentry, plastering, painting, plate- and boiler-making, riveting, turning, brewing and printing were held by Protestant artisans. Foremen were almost invariably Protestant and had the power of hiring and firing. Catholics, in contrast, were mainly confined to semi-skilled or labouring jobs. Moreover, the gap between the wages of skilled and unskilled workers was appreciably higher in Belfast than it was in Dublin or in British cities. In other words, to belong to the 'aristocracy of labour' in northern Ireland gave a person a very special social cachet, and if this was identified with a specific religion then the superiority was doubly reinforced.

It was in these circumstances, while a triumphant imperialism was being challenged by the Irish agrarian and nationalist movement, and while the Ulster Protestants saw increasing threats to their social and economic privileges, that Lord Randolph Churchill went to Belfast to play his 'Orange card'.

Churchill was just the right man, and in the right place at the right time, to give Orangeism the political fillip it needed.

Aristocratic and politically well-connected, his father was the Duke of Marlborough and his mother was the daughter of the 3rd Marquess of Londonderry, half-brother of Lord Castlereagh, he had become one of the leading figures in the Conservative Party, a cabinet minister under Lord Salisbury, and eventually chairman and party leader in the House of Commons. Under the guise of being a Tory democrat, he was an imperialist to the core. He was also a populist and demagogue, adept at playing on the most atavistic fears and emotions of his audiences. In 1876–80 when his father was viceroy he had served as his secretary in Dublin, and there acquired some knowledge of Irish affairs. A close friend of that period, whom he frequently visited in his house in Howth, was Gerald Fitzgibbon, who later became lord chief justice in Ireland. Fitzgibbon was an ultra-Protestant and a Freemason. His mother came from a strongly anti-Catholic family in Ulster. It was from Fitzgibbon that Churchill took much of his Irish policy, including the two key points of abandoning the landlords but at the same time going back to the old tactics of playing off Protestants against Catholics. Educated in the classics at Eton and Oxford, he knew full well the meaning of *divide et impera*. He had also learned much about the peculiarities of Ulster politics from his contact with Colonel Saunderson. It was shortly after the 1885 general election that Churchill, while visiting Fitzgibbon in Dublin, read Saunderson's speech, which argued that the Ulster Protestant tail might wag the British dog. Churchill was so interested that he invited Saunderson to stay with Fitzgibbon and himself.[10]

Speaking in London on 13 February 1886, Churchill bluntly put forward the thesis that, regardless of any principles of democracy that might be involved, the only people who mattered in Ireland were the Protestants:

> England cannot leave the Protestants of Ireland in the lurch. England is bound to the Protestants of Ireland; you, as Englishmen are bound to the Protestants of Ireland by every conceivable tie. The Protestants of Ireland on an occasion such as this, and in a national crisis such as this, are the only nation which is known to the English people in Ireland. On four successive

322

occasions they have conquered Ireland practically at the request of England. During 680 years [sic] the Protestants of Ireland have held Ireland mainly for the benefit of England. They have developed the resources of Ireland by their capital and their industry under the protection and guarantee of England. They are one with England, one with the English people, one with you in race and religion. They are essentially like the English people, a dominant and imperial caste.[11]

Three days later he wrote his celebrated letter to Fitzgibbon: 'I decided some time ago, that if the G.O.M. [Gladstone] went for Home Rule, the Orange card would be the one to play. Please God it may turn out the ace of trumps and not the two.'[12] In another letter written about the same time he used the phrase: Ulster will fight, and Ulster will be right. Then on 23 February, addressing a big Protestant rally in Belfast, he made a clever but dangerous speech in which he did not attack the Catholics directly, but went out of his way to frighten his audience with all the old anti-Papist bogeys. Beginning with the massacres of 1641, he went on to hint at a new Catholic ascendancy which would put Protestants at the bottom of the social pile. The Fenians, Parnell and the Catholic archbishop of Dublin were all part of the same conspiracy, he said, and had formed a deadly combination to destroy civil and religious liberties. In the great crisis through which the empire was going, the firmest bastion was Ulster, and Ulster loyalists were 'the first line of defence, the second line of defence, and the last line of defence'. He then went on to develop the physical-resistance theme that had been introduced by the Orange MPs William Johnston and Colonel Edward Saunderson a few years earlier. Repeal of the Union, he claimed, could not be carried through the House of Commons by 'the mere passing of a law', and the Unionists could not keep their life-and-death struggle within the confines of 'constitutional action'.[13]

The big loyalist audience cheered their famous visitor to the echo, and went on their way well satisfied that they were the chosen people of Ulster, and that they had powerful friends in Britain. Moreover, they believed they now had approval for taking any action, illegal or legal, violent or constitutional, to stop the introduction of Home Rule into Ireland.

The results of Churchill's incitement to sectarian violence came within a few months of his visit to the north. Early in June 1886, during the very week in which Gladstone's Home Rule Bill was being debated in the House of Commons, the worst riots ever seen in Belfast broke out in the city.[14] The disturbances began in the Queen's Island shipyards, where there had been an argument between a Catholic and a Protestant workman which ended in blows. Unrest then spread through various parts of the city, with Protestant mobs attacking Catholics, and the Catholics retaliating. In the shipyards, where Orange sentiment was strong, several Catholic navvies were thrown into the docks. One of them tried to swim to safety, but was pelted with rivets and steel tubes and drowned. The dead man's funeral was the occasion of further violence. The fighting got worse in July when the traditional Orange ceremonies were held.

Two thousand four hundred extra police, mainly from the south of Ireland, accompanied by dozens of inspectors and several resident magistrates, were drafted in to try to restore law and order. They were soon followed by 1,200 troops. The Protestants resented the police, whom they believed were being brought in on the orders of the Liberal government, and they nicknamed them 'Morley's Murderers' after the hapless John Morley, Gladstone's chief secretary. Zealously fanned by the Reverend Hugh Hanna, the rumour spread that 'Papish policemen were coming to kill the Northern Protestants'. In one serious incident in the Shankill area a police station was attacked by a two-thousand-strong mob, and when the police opened fire seven people were killed.

The rioting continued sporadically during August and September, and by the time it had died down the total number of casualties was over thirty dead, with hundreds of police and civilians injured, many seriously. The damage to property was enormous, with hundreds of houses, shops, and pubs burned out and looted. The always fragile communal relations in the city reached their lowest level for decades. The 'Orange card', as Andrew Boyd points out, had truly turned out to be the ace and not the two of trumps.[15]

Riots so savage and on such a scale embarrassed the Liberal government, and were severely condemned by the official commission which reported in 1887. Pogroms and street disturbances were still regarded by some sections of the establishment as the unacceptable face of Ascendancy rule.

In the long run, however, the support provided by Churchill and other prominent Conservatives to the most extreme Protestants gave the Orange Order just the accolade it needed. Within a few years it was changed from being a small and relatively insignificant group, largely outside respectable Protestant society, into a powerful and all-embracing organisation with friends in the highest places. It continued to recruit culturally deprived tenant farmers, 'poor White' city workers and street-corner demagogues, but it now began to draw increasingly upon the wealthier and more influential Protestants. One indication of this change among Protestant Churchmen and women was the way in which certain clergymen, who previously had been regarded disdainfully as rabble-rousers, became mainstays of the ecclesiastical establishment, often with fashionable congregations and large stipends. 'The shooting rector', the Reverend Richard Kane, for example, was invited to speak from the same platform as Arthur Balfour in Belfast in 1893; and 'Roaring' Hanna, officially indicted for his part in stirring up pogroms in 1857, 1872 and 1886, had a statue erected in his honour in Belfast.

The Unionist MP Ronald McNeill (later Lord Cushendun) describes the transformation which occurred in the Order during the twenty-five years before the First World War:

> The Loyal Orange Institution, founded at the end of the eighteenth century to commemorate and keep alive the principles of the Whig Revolution of 1688, had fallen into not unmerited disrepute prior to 1886. Few men of education or standing belonged to it, and the lodge meetings and anniversary celebrations had become little better than occasions for conviviality wholly inconsistent with the irreproachable formularies of the Order. But its

325

system of local lodges, affiliated to a Grand Lodge in each county, supplied the ready-made framework of an effective organisation. Immediately after the introduction of Gladstone's first bill in 1886 it received an immense accession of strength. Large numbers of country gentlemen, clergymen of all Protestant denominations, business and professional men, farmers and the better class of artisans in Belfast and other towns joined the lodges, the management of which passed into capable hands; the Society was thereby completely and rapidly transformed and, instead of being a somewhat disreputable and obsolete survival, it became a highly respectable and exceedingly powerful political organisation.[16]

A simultaneous development, which arose directly from the politicisation of a body that was supposed, at least nominally, to be devoted to religious objectives, was the increasing 'Orangeisation' of the Unionist Party. The most extreme Protestants and the most right-wing politicians moved ever closer towards each other until they became virtually indistinguishable.[17] In the 1885 general election Colonel Saunderson claimed that out of sixteen Unionist MPs elected in Ulster no fewer than twelve were Orangemen. Certainly by the end of the century it had become impossible for any Unionist to be nominated for a parliamentary constituency in the north unless he had the tacit support of the Order.[18] Symbol of this merger of religious and political factions, Deputy Grand Master Saunderson was the mainstay of the local episcopalian church, which stood in the grounds of Castle Saunderson near Belturbet, County Cavan. He was a lay preacher, a Sunday school teacher, and so proud of his sermons he had them published. His dislike of Catholicism was, as his biographer, Reginald Lucas, admits, 'a fixed principle of his philosophy'.[19] In January 1886 he became the acknowledged leader of the Ulster Unionists in the House of Commons. By this time he had become recognised, in his own words, as a 'political personage hob-nobbing with Cabinet Ministers'.[20] In this new and more ambitious capacity he was constantly in touch with such personalities as Salisbury, Balfour, Chamberlain and Churchill. His relationship with Churchill became particularly intimate, a 'mutual sympathy and attraction' developing between the two men.[21] A few weeks before Churchill's crucial visit to Belfast in February 1886, the two men consulted together in the Carlton Club, headquarters of the Tory Party.

Saunderson remained leader of the Ulster Unionists and MP for Armagh North until his death in 1906. In the 1890s he became a friend of the rising new Unionist star, Edward Carson. A member of several prestigious clubs, Saunderson moved in the best social circles in London, dining with, amongst other influential people, the Prince of Wales. Towards the end of his life he was elected grand master of the Orange Order, and was invested as a member of the privy council by Queen Victoria.

William Johnston's anti-Catholic prejudices were also a passport to electoral success. His youthful peccadilloes as a religious firebrand were now seen as an advantage rather than an impediment in his career. Johnston was something of a rough diamond, and not the sort of person invited to dine at the Carlton Club, but he had qualities which in some respects were even more valuable to his party – he could rouse up the most religiously prejudiced Belfast shipyard workers with his oratory, and held his seat in Belfast South for twenty-seven years.

At the other end of the social scale – but similar in their Orange views – were such aristocrats as Lords Erne, Rossmore and Farnham. Erne had preceded Saunderson as grand master of the Order.

An even more significant alliance during this period was the amalgamation that took place between the Ulster Tories and their opposite numbers in Britain. Irish and British Conservatives had, of course, always been intimately linked through family connections, religious sympathies and political beliefs, but in the years following the introduction of Gladstone's first Home Rule Bill this connection became ideologically and organisationally much closer. Their common rejection of Home Rule, distaste for Catholicism and Irish nationalism, and sympathy for imperialism forced an ever tighter bond until, like the Orangemen and Ulster Tories, they virtually fused together.

Churchill, a skilful political opportunist, proposed as early as March 1886 that all the anti-Irish-nationalist groups should form one united 'Conservative and Unionist Party'. This suggestion was soon adopted, and within a few years became the official title of the wider party. A hundred years later, though Ulster Unionists and British Tories have gone their separate ways, it is still the official name of the British party. Henceforth, the twenty or so Irish Conservative MPs could be expected to vote the party line without reservation in the House of Commons, to attend party conferences, and generally behave as members of one organisation. Speakers moved regularly to and fro between Ireland and Britain, and there was much mutual entertaining in clubs and private houses.

A newly elected Irish Unionist MP who fitted easily into this professional-cum-social milieu and who was destined to have great influence on the future of Ulster was the young Dublin barrister, Edward Carson. Gradually he took over from Saunderson as the chief contact between the various Conservative interests. Carson had made an early reputation as a sound Tory and formidable legal advocate during the crucial years when Balfour was chief secretary. Balfour made him Crown prosecutor in 1887, and in September of that year, when he was in County Cork prosecuting the two nationalist MPs William O'Brien and John Mandeville for their part in the Plan of Campaign, he was an observer of the 'Mitchelstown massacre', in which a crowd of tenant farmers was fired upon by the police and several people were killed. From then on, 'Bloody' Balfour and 'Coercion' Carson, as they were nicknamed, worked sympathetically together both legally and politically. Carson was elected Unionist MP for Trinity College Dublin in 1892, and then set up a highly profitable legal practice in London. His fees at one time are said to have reached as high as £100,000 a year. One of the most famous cases in which he was involved during this period was the prosecution of his former Dublin acquaintance, Oscar Wilde.

The 'gentrification' of the Orange Order, and the merger of the various Unionist interests, did not, as might have been expected, lead to the expression of more moderate views by the parties concerned. On the contrary, the more the reactionary politicians and Protestant zealots got together, the more violent became their opinions. Extremism fed on extremism on both sides of the Irish Sea.

The Orangemen had always been prepared to go outside the law if they felt their interests were threatened. Their 'loyalty' was always conditional. What was so remarkable about the wider political developments after 1886, however, was how far the wealthiest, most respectable and allegedly law-abiding members of the establishment were prepared to go down the unconstitutional road. It was not only the erratic Churchill who believed that Ulster will fight, and Ulster will be right, but the most eminent Tories and Whigs in Britain. Cabinet ministers, peers of the realm, MPs, bishops, judges and senior administrators – all those, indeed, who were first to condemn subversion by Irish nationalists – joined in the treasonable chorus. Constitutionalists of the most impeccable pedigree stood democracy on its head with the plea that minorities should rule majorities; generals and field marshals forgot their oaths of loyalty; lawyers advanced curious arguments that ultimate authority lay, not with parliament, but with the Crown or some mystical higher will. Finally, the novel doctrine was put forward that the Protestants of Ulster (comprising perhaps one-fifth of the total population of Ireland, and one-thirtieth of the population of the whole of the United Kingdom) should be allowed to have a permanent interdiction on how the province should be ruled. Joseph Chamberlain, when visiting Belfast in October 1887, was quite explicit about how this restraint should work: 'I claim . . . for a minority in Ireland,' he said, 'that at least it shall have a veto upon any settlement which may be proposed in this matter [of Home Rule].'[22] And Arthur Balfour, who through his family and political links was connected with the most eminent circles in British society, put his stamp of approval on this physical-force policy in a speech he made to 80,000 cheering loyalists in Belfast in April 1893:

> I do not come here to preach any doctrines of obedience or non-violence. You have had to fight for your liberties before. I pray God you may never have to fight for them again. I do not believe

329

you will ever have to fight for them, but I admit that the tyranny of majorities may be as bad as the tyranny of Kings and that the stupidity of majorities may be even greater than the stupidity of Kings . . . and I do think that any rational or sober man will say that what is justifiable against a tyrannical King may not under certain circumstances be justifiable against a tyrannical majority.[23]

Two small but influential groups which enthusiastically supported Balfour's view that in certain circumstances the will of the majority in the House of Commons could be flouted were the House of Lords and certain of the more politically motivated army officers. The House of Lords had always been an undemocratic body in the sense that it was selected and not elected. It had opposed Catholic emancipation, the extension of the franchise, and land reform. More than one hundred peers had big estates in Ireland, including such grandees as the Duke of Devonshire and the Earl of Lansdowne and such Ulster notabilities as the Marquess of Londonderry, the Duke of Abercorn and the Marquess of Dufferin and Ava. Many of these aristocratic families were linked by marriage as well as property, and they usually had a similar public school, Oxbridge or Sandhurst background. Almost without exception they were episcopalians and whether they began as liberals or conservatives they generally ended up as Unionists. They used the House of Lords both as a social club and as a means of blocking any progressive legislation affecting Ireland. When Gladstone got a majority of 34 votes in the Commons on the third reading of his second Home Rule Bill in 1893, the Lords immediately threw out the measure by 491 votes to 41.

Army officers generally had even less respect for parliamentary democracy than the aristocracy. Militarists by vocation, trained in an élitist system, and almost invariably anti-Catholic by upbringing and tradition, they had little time for the House of Commons or the views of the majority of voters. Almost without exception they were Conservatives, and had contempt for Liberal views. Many had served in Africa, Asia or the Middle East and despised the natives of those lands. The British

Empire was their inspiration and dream because it represented for them the highest political ideals, as well as providing opportunities for rapid promotion. The jingoistic flag-waving of the Boer War was not far removed in either theory or practice from what the more imperially minded Ulstermen were accustomed to in an Orange demonstration.

Two such junker-type officers of the highest rank were of Irish birth – Field Marshal Lord Wolseley, who had reorganised the army in the 1870s and 1880s, and Field Marshal Lord Kitchener, who was commander-in-chief in South Africa in 1900–1901. Both these men took a close interest in Ulster affairs, and were strong opponents of Irish nationalism. R.M. Sibbett records that in 1886 Wolseley had offered to organise and lead an unofficial militia force designed to foil Gladstone's plans for Home Rule.[24] Field Marshal Lord Roberts was another senior staff officer closely involved with the Unionist Party.

During the Boer War, two younger officers who served under Kitchener and later took a prominent part in the Carson crusade, were Captain James Craig and Colonel R. H. Wallace. Both were noted Orangemen. Another officer with political ambitions was Colonel Frederick H. Crawford, who in 1892 devised a bizarre scheme to kidnap Gladstone. Crawford tried to organise a Young Ulster movement which required each member to carry a pistol. In 1913–14 he was chief gunrunner for the Ulster Volunteer Force.

It was this unique combination of evangelical enthusiasm, militarist zeal, and ethnic pride that gave imperialism its special edge in Ulster at the beginning of the twentieth century.

20

AGAINST THE TIDE

I am sure that a race of Presbyterians and Protestants worthy of
the best traditions of our faith, will arise in the near future, with
their minds cleared of Unionist cant, and blood purified from
the rust of serfdom . . . and they will claim to dwell in the land,
not under the protection of the Saxon, nor by permission of the
Celt, but by virtue of the services they will render to a country
we love.

The Reverend James Brown Armour, 1894[1]

The wave of reaction that broke over Ulster in the 1890s and
early 1900s did not succeed in its aim of washing away all islands of resistance in the province. As had happened before,
during previous surges of reaction, there were several obstacles
that stood out against the Unionist and sectarian tide. The spirit
of Irish nationalism was far from dead in the north, and the old
Gaelic culture still existed in many areas; a minority of Dissenters
refused to sink beneath the incoming conservative flood; and
there were several less-privileged groups in society who resented
their poverty and low social status. In the rural areas tenant
farmers, both Protestant and Catholic, still suffered under the
landlord system, and in the towns, especially Belfast, there was
a growing working class, often narrow-minded in religion and
confused politically, but nevertheless disliking their bosses. The
barriers of nationality, religion and social class thus continued
to divert and split up the all-engulfing movement the Unionists
were striving so hard to create.

The core of resistance to unionism remained, as it had always
done, among the Catholics who comprised about 45 per cent of

the nine-county population and were in a substantial majority in counties Donegal, Cavan and Monaghan. Catholics were also numerous in Fermanagh, and parts of Derry, Tyrone, south Armagh and south Down, and numbered about one-quarter of the population of Belfast. Even in heavily settled Antrim one-fifth of the people were Catholics. Their predominantly Gaelic origins, their religion and their distinct culture continued to give them a strong sense of ethnic identity, which was still generally hostile towards the dominant British imperialist or Ulster-Scot identity claimed by the majority of Protestants. It was these Catholic Irish, with their strong feeling of social and national oppression, who were the backbone of the Irish Parliamentary Party which, in spite of setbacks caused by Parnell's involvement in the divorce scandal, held on to virtually all the seats it had won in the 1885 and 1886 elections, including Armagh South, Cavan East and West, Donegal North, South, East and West, Down South, Fermanagh South, Monaghan North and South, Newry, Tyrone Mid and East. Fermanagh North, where both Home Rule and land issues were acute, was a good example of such a marginal constituency. A swing of only a few hundred votes could decide a parliamentary election there. Nationalists won the seat by small margins in 1885 and 1886, but then lost it to Unionists in 1892, 1895, 1898 (by-election) and 1900. It was won by a Russellite candidate in the 1903 by-election by 152 votes, and then regained by the Unionists in 1906 by 88 votes.

TABLE 13

GENERAL ELECTION RESULTS IN ULSTER, 1892–1900

	Unionists	Liberal Unionists, including Russellites	Liberals	Irish Parliamentary Party
1892	16	3	–	14
1895	14	3	1	15
1900	15	3	1	14

The most striking evidence of the failure of the Conservatives to carry all before them is indicated in the election results for this period (see Table 13). The figures show that in spite of all the help they got from their British friends, and all the intense pressures imposed by the Orange lodges, the official Unionists did not succeed in winning even half of the thirty-three parliamentary seats in Ulster. Nearly 50 per cent of the constituencies consistently returned Irish Parliamentary Party MPs, and another half-dozen or so remained marginal, with Liberals and Russellites polling strongly.[2]

These electoral successes, important though they were in keeping up nationalist morale, were not, of course, the only evidence of the continuing 'Irishness' of much of Ulster's heritage. Three hundred years after the original plantations, there still existed – perhaps more ruined and decayed than they had been a few centuries before, but none the less visible – those dolmens, tumuli, ring-forts, round towers, and the ruins of ancient churches and abbeys,[3] a constant reminder that the cultural origins of the province lay indisputably in Ireland rather than in Scotland or England, as the Unionists so often proclaimed.

As for the Irish language, it was a remarkable fact, not always fully appreciated, that there were at the turn of the century more native Gaelic speakers in Ulster than there were in Leinster, even with the exclusion of the Donegal figures.[4] Though devastated by the famine, and continually under pressure from the dominant English-speaking culture, Irish was spoken by nearly 100,000 people, or almost 6 per cent of the population (see Table 14[5]). Donegal, with several Gaeltachts on the west coast, had the majority of such speakers, but there were appreciable numbers still to be found in various other districts, including Belfast with about 3,500 speakers, and the Glens of Antrim with about 1,000.

In the mountainy districts of Donegal, Tyrone, the Sperrins, the Mournes and the Glens of Antrim some of the old patterns of Gaelic life survived, with many relics of what has been called 'the hidden Ulster' in song, story and folk customs.[6] Together with the language, these formed a link with a way of life going back many centuries. The beauty of the Ulster landscape inspired another kind of affection based on a profound feeling for the region's lakes and mountains, rivers and valleys, the grand seascapes, and the splendid variety of flora and fauna. The Belfast Naturalists' Field Club, which flourished at the turn of the century, was particularly attracted to such phenomena, and promoted a spirit that can only be described as a kind of local nationalism. The club's most famous member, Robert Lloyd Praeger, who was of Dutch descent, summed up this kind of love for the place you know best, and therefore can relate to most closely, in his autobiography *The Way That I Went*. After travelling throughout the thirty-two counties for the best part of six decades, he wrote: 'To the patriot, the loveliest country is – or should be – that in which he was born, and in which he has lived, for it has given him the very foundation of his being.'

TABLE 14

NUMBER OF IRISH-SPEAKERS IN ULSTER, 1901

	Irish only	Irish and English	Total	Percentage of population
Antrim	–	1,012	1,012	0.5
Armagh	2	4,485	4,487	3.6
Belfast	–	3,587	3,587	1.0
Cavan	–	5,425	5,425	5.6
Donegal	4,448	56,229	60,677	34.9
Down	–	1,411	1,411	0.7
Fermanagh	–	1,005	1,005	1.5
Derry County including Derry City	4	3,472	3,476	2.4
Monaghan	–	5,324	5,324	7.1
Tyrone	2	6,452	6,454	4.3
Total	4,456	88,402	92,858	5.9

It was this regard for a heritage which was both man-made and natural, and a nostalgia for a declining past, which stirred a group of educated and middle-class people in Belfast to seek a less foreign and more indigenous culture. Inspired by the example of Yeats and Hyde, they were keen to prove they could find in the north relics of the ancient Gaelic civilisation as fine as anything discovered by their compatriots in the south. As romantics looking back to what they saw as a more spiritual and artistic past, they rejected the money-making and Philistine ethos with which they and their families were surrounded in late-nineteenth-century bourgeois Belfast. Many of them were young and with the natural iconoclasm of their age group sought to throw off that parental Puritanism they believed to be suffocating their intellectual and artistic freedom.

In later years many of these young enthusiasts were to make a wider reputation for themselves as writers, linguists, historians, musicians, painters, or political activists. In some cases, like their fellows in the south, Thomas MacDonagh and Patrick Pearse, they were to die for their principles; in other cases they were forced through lack of career prospects or social pressures to emigrate, their subsequent reputations being associated, not with the place in which they were born or grew up, but with Dublin, London or the United States of America. A few eventually forgot their rebel youth, and settled down as conventional civil servants, academics or judges.

Among the first of these enthusiasts for the Gaelic cause in Ulster after the death of Parnell in 1891 were two women of middle-class background – Alice Milligan and Anna Johnston.

Alice Milligan was born in 1866 in Omagh, daughter of a prosperous Protestant businessman and amateur antiquarian, and from her youth she showed a keen interest in Irish history. In an autobiographical poem entitled 'When I was a little girl' she describes how she and her brothers and sisters were being scolded by their governess who tried to frighten them with tales about the wicked republicans who would come and carry them off to some dreadful fate. Many years later, remembering these bogeymen stories, she wrote:

> But one little rebel there,
> Watching all with laughter,
> Thought 'When the Fenians come
> I'll rise and go after.'

Educated at Methodist College, Belfast, she was sent to London to learn German, but instead privately took up the study of Irish, which she had first heard spoken by labourers working for her father in County Tyrone. Apart from her substantial output as a journalist, she wrote poetry, plays and a novel, and in 1898 published a short life of Wolfe Tone. In that year she was one of the organisers of the centenary celebrations for the United Irishmen.

Anna Johnston, a Catholic who wrote under the pen name of Ethna Carbery, was born in 1864 in Ballymena. Daughter of the veteran Fenian, Robert Johnston, she moved to Belfast where as a young woman she became involved in nationalist politics. In 1901, shortly before she died, she married the Donegal writer, Seumas MacManus. He arranged for the posthumous publication of her verses, *The Four Winds of Eirinn*, which was illustrated by John Campbell. Her most famous poem, which became a favourite recitation piece among republicans, is 'Rody McCorley':

> Up the narrow street he stepped,
> Smiling and proud and young;
> About the hemp-rope on his neck
> The golden ringlets clung.
> There's never a tear in the blue, blue eyes
> Both good and bright are they –
> As Rody McCorley goes to die
> At the Bridge of Toome to-day.

In October 1895 the two women, both unmarried but with some capital in hand, decided to launch the weekly, the *Northern Patriot*, which would be unequivocally separatist in policy. On its bannerhead were the words 'A Volunteer journal' and a picture of Henry Joy McCracken. The paper's aim was to revive the spirit of Irish nationality among its readers by the publication of historical articles and the sort of patriotic verse that had once appeared in the *Nation*. In 1897 it was taken over by the *Shan Van Vocht*, which had the same editors and much the same policy, publishing memoirs of famous nationalist heroes and essays encouraging the revival of the Irish language. These pieces tended to be somewhat naive politically and sentimentally written, and there was not much comment on contemporary social issues in Ireland. However, on occasion current topics did creep in, including, among other things, a campaign for an amnesty for those Fenian prisoners still held in British jails. Maud Gonne took a leading part in this agitation. There was a direct Ulster involvement in the case of Thomas J. Clarke who had gone to school in Dungannon, and when a young man in that town is said to have joined the IRB.[7] Clarke's father, a Protestant from County Sligo, served in the British Army for many years; his mother was a Catholic from Clonmel, County Tipperary. He emigrated from Dungannon in June 1880 to the United States of America and soon became active in Fenian circles there, returning to England in the spring of 1883 to take part in the dynamitard campaign. He was caught and sentenced to penal servitude for life, serving fifteen years under conditions of great hardship. In 1892 a group of Dungannon citizens, including several local Protestant clergy and professional people, tried unsuccessfully to get him released. He was eventually freed in September 1898 and returned to Dungannon where he was given a reception.

The *Shan Van Vocht* opened its columns to the ideas of another openly committed separatist when in January 1897 it published an article by James Connolly who was then organising the Irish Socialist Republican Party in Dublin. In this early statement of his philosophy, Connolly put forward the view that the winning of national independence would be useless unless there was a social revolution as well. 'If you could remove the English army to-morrow and hoist the green flag over Dublin Castle', he wrote, 'unless you set about the organisation of the Socialist Republic, your efforts would be in vain. England would still rule you; she would rule you through her capitalists, through her landlords, through her financiers, through the whole army of commercial and industrialist institutions she has planted in this country.'[8]

In his biography, Desmond Greaves describes how Connolly was visited by Alice Milligan's brother, Ernest, an eighteen-year-old law student at Queen's College Belfast, and a member of the Gaelic League. The young Milligan found Connolly living with his growing family in one room in Dublin. Connolly lent him books, and encouraged him to form a branch of the Irish Socialist Republican Party in Belfast. This branch was called the Belfast Socialist Society, and was joined by three fellow students, James Winder Good, Robert Lynd, and Samuel Porter.

Less overtly political but none the less strongly nationalist in tone, the Gaelic League had been founded in Dublin in 1893 by a northern Catholic, Eoin MacNeill, and the southern Protestant, Douglas Hyde. By the turn of the century the league had become well established in Belfast, with several branches and some hundreds of members, organising classes, encouraging the translation of old texts,[9] and promoting Irish songs, music and dancing. In 1898 a *feis ceoil*, or musical festival, was held in the northern capital, the first such event for many years.

In a city where clubs and societies were usually organised on a religious basis, with Protestants and Catholics going their separate ways, it was noticeable that the league succeeded, as it also did in the south, in being completely non-sectarian – it recruited from all religious denominations.[10] Indeed, in the encouragement of all things Gaelic, the lead, if anything, was taken by Protestants: the journalists James Winder Good and Robert Lynd, the medical student William MacArthur,[11] the artist Paul Henry, the Reverend Richard Lyttle were Presbyterians; the musician Herbert Hughes was a Methodist; and the clerk from Lisburn, Bulmer Hobson, was a Quaker. It was Hobson, who had just left school declaring himself a disciple of Wolfe Tone's, who was the keenest activist, inviting Michael Cusack to set up branches of the Gaelic Athletic Association in Ulster, and inviting John O'Leary and Maud Gonne to Belfast.[12]

Catholic members of the league included the poet Joseph Campbell, and his artist brother, John, and the 'three Macs': Sean MacDermott, Patrick MacCartan and Denis McCullough, who became key figures in the formation of the Irish Volunteers. Joining the IRB as young men, they were responsible for maintaining links with the physical-force separatist movement in the south. The scholar among this group was Eoin MacNeill, who had been born in 1867, son of a tenant farmer in the still largely

Irish-speaking Glens of Antrim. MacNeill was educated in St Malachy's College, Belfast, and as a boy showed an aptitude for history and languages. Like so many other young Irishmen of that period, especially Catholics, he could find no outlet for his talents at home, and by the age of twenty he had secured a minor clerical post in the Four Courts, Dublin. In 1896 he had an article published in the *Shan Van Vocht* entitled 'How to save the Irish language'. He also published articles in the same journal on the survivals of the old tongue still to be found in Antrim, Tyrone and Derry. Though now living permanently in Dublin,[13] he encouraged the setting up of Gaelic League branches in Ulster.

A colleague of MacNeill's was Eleanor Hull, a Protestant whose father came from near Hillsborough, County Down. She was born in 1860, was educated in Dublin, and spent most of her life in England. Gaining her first enthusiasm for the Irish language from her mentor Standish Hayes O'Grady, she became a Celtic scholar under the tuition of the German philologist, Kuno Meyer. Her main contribution to Celtic studies was her founding in 1899 of the Irish Texts Society – a group of scholars and writers who published no fewer than fifty-two translations from ancient and middle Irish manuscripts. The society is still in existence. Its volumes are regarded as indispensable for any serious student of the Irish language. The society also published the influential dictionary by Father P. S. Dineen, which has been widely used since it was first issued in 1904. She was involved for many years in the Irish Literary Society in London as a linguist and folklorist, and is author of several popular books, including *The Cuchulain Saga* (1904), *Poem Book of the Gael* (1912), and a *History of Ireland* in two volumes (1926 and 1931). *The Times*, in an otherwise appreciative obituary when she died in 1935, complained that the section in this history dealing with the period 1916–21 was 'marred by her enthusiastic Nationalist bias'.

From its beginning, the strength of the Gaelic League lay in the fact that its aims were both cultural and political; that is, it sought to revive the ancient, and visibly perishing, language and literature of the country, and by so doing give a new validity to the claims of Irish nationalism. An added dimension, which had great attraction to those who wished to overcome barriers between the different religious denominations, was that it seemed to enthuse both Protestants and Catholics. It was this threefold appeal that reached out to another Ulster expatriate. Roger Casement had spent most of his politically formative years far away in the jungles of west Africa, but by the turn of the century, under the influence of his friends Bulmer Hobson and Francis Joseph Bigger, was increasingly directing his attention towards the problems of Ireland.

Casement was born in Dublin in 1864, son of a captain in the British Army. Orphaned while still a young boy, he was sent to live with his uncle in the family home near Ballycastle, and attended Ballymena Academy. Not much is known about his childhood and youth, but he appears to have learned little Irish history. This was hardly surprising in a family and school which were strongly Protestant.[14] He emigrated to Liverpool at the age of seventeen to take up a post as a shipping clerk. There he met his cousin Gertrude Bannister (the beloved 'Gee' of his letters), with whom he corresponded regularly until his death. He sailed for west Africa as an assistant purser in 1884, and did not return home, except for occasional holidays and official visits, for nearly twenty years. During this phase of his life his political views appear to have been shaped, not so much from events in Ireland, which he had to follow at a great distance, but by his more immediate experience of the atrocities he saw perpetrated on the Black plantation workers of the Congo. At first hand he could see the greed and exploitation involved in the scramble for Africa by Britain, Germany, France and Belgium. He served as a British consul in South Africa during 1900, and does not appear to have shown any pro-Boer sympathies, though he must have known that a brigade of Irish republican volunteers led by John MacBride was fighting against the British.

As a boy he had always had a deep affection for the Glens of Antrim, and it was there that he returned for a holiday in 1903. On this visit he joined the Gaelic League, and met such republican enthusiasts as Bulmer Hobson and Robert Lynd. However, this was only an interlude in what was still his abiding

341

concern – the writing of his report on *The Congo State*, which was published, to universal horror at the cruelties revealed, in February 1904. Overnight, the obscure Casement became a famous figure on the world stage.

It was probably soon after this event, when he could free his mind to think of other concerns, that he began seriously to turn his attention to Irish problems. It was then also that he met Alice Stopford Green, the historian and Irish nationalist who was destined to have a profound influence on his subsequent life.[15] In August 1905 he wrote to Hobson: 'All the time I shall be away from you all I shall not lose sight of Ireland, or her needs, and it may be that some day I shall be able to serve to help the cause.'[16]

At the centre of this 'Irish-Ireland' movement in the north, and for fifteen years a close friend of Casement's, was a most unexpected figure – Francis Joseph Bigger, a Freemason and Presbyterian of Lowland Scots descent, a 'respectable' wealthy solicitor, but also an archaeologist, naturalist, and advocate of all things Irish. Bigger's grandfather was a founder of the Belfast Academical Institution, and Francis himself was educated there; his cousin was the radical Joseph Gillis Biggar.

In 1894 Bigger revived the *Ulster Journal of Archaeology*, and was its editor for seventeen years. During that period he had the opportunity to pursue all his hobbies – his passion for old churches, round towers, high crosses, ancient castles, the Gaelic language, paying tribute to dead patriots, Irish flora and fauna. To commemorate the rising of 1798 he began writing a series of pamphlets on the northern leaders of the United Irishmen. Only one of them was published – *Remember Orr*; the uncompleted manuscripts of the others are now in the Central Library, Belfast, together with a remarkable collection of letters, pamphlets, books, photographs, newspaper cuttings and prints, dealing with the history of Ireland from the seventeenth century.[17]

Bigger was not a gifted writer and had no professional training as a historian or archaeologist. Nevertheless, like other talented antiquarians of the nineteenth century, he had enormous energy and enthusiasm for the study of those subjects that interested him. He also had money, and as a bachelor without family commitments, he had the leisure to follow his fancies. As a versatile amateur, indeed, he seems to have found worthwhile subjects to research, and more interesting things to say, than some of his professional colleagues. His career spanned a crucial period in Irish history, and his capacity for friendship cut across boundaries of social class, religion and culture, which, in the Ulster context, was of exceptional importance. He was greatly admired by such writers as Joseph Campbell and Shane Leslie.

Bigger and his fellow Celtic revivalists were a small minority, and would have been weak and isolated but for the fact that they had allies in other sections of the Ulster community. What gave them extra strength, and encouraged them to swim vigorously against the tide, was the knowledge that they had numerous sympathisers in their anti-establishment struggle among the Catholics, their natural friends, and also among certain important Protestant groups. The old spirit of Nonconformity and radicalism was still very much alive in the north, in spite of all attempts to obliterate it.

Some of the more enlightened members of the professional and middle classes, especially Presbyterians, remained hostile towards the Ascendancy, and resented the way in which the Orange Order was stirring up sectarianism. They might have reservations about certain aspects of Catholicism, and were not prepared to go too far down the Gaelic road, but they were still liberals at heart. Gladstone was their hero, even though there was confusion about the implications of Home Rule. Certainly they were not prepared to accept that Protestantism and unionism were synonymous, as the Conservatives claimed. Among the economically less privileged sections of society, the majority of tenant farmers were still locked in battle with the landlords, and many industrial workers in Belfast, whatever their religious beliefs, took a jaundiced view of their employers.

This rallying of Dissenters – which was simultaneously Liberal in politics, radical socially, and tolerant in religion – gained enormous impetus from the leadership of the tenant-right veteran, Armour of Ballymoney. A thin sharp-featured cleric,

343

wearing a pince-nez, and usually dressed in black, anti-gambling, a temperance advocate, and austere on sexual matters, Armour seemed the very essence of a Puritan divine. But his social convictions were liberal and tolerant, and this, combined with his eloquence, made him a formidable controversialist. He could carry only a section of his Church with him, but his strength of character and charismatic personality helped compensate for small numbers. He was generally orthodox in theology but anti-establishment in politics, and he had come to the conclusion that a Christian must be socially as well as individually responsible if he or she was truly to serve God. 'When Jesus sent forth his disciples', he wrote, 'he told them to preach the Gospel of the Kingdom, and heal the sick and whatever disease humanity suffered from, whether it be disease of the body or the soul or the social organisation.'[18]

Armour's first political hero was Gladstone, whom he regarded with awe and affection. For a few years after 1886 he seems to have changed his allegiance to the Liberal Unionists, but then became convinced they were being manipulated by the landlords and the aristocracy, and were becoming, as he put it, 'mere circus riders in the Tory hippodrome'. By the beginning of the 1890s he seems to have developed those political principles which lasted him for the rest of his long and extraordinarily vigorous life – dislike of the landlord Ascendancy, justice for Catholics, the need to separate Protestantism from unionism, and self-government for Ireland within the empire. In all these respects he followed the Protestant Home Rule Association, but he does not appear to have been an actual member of the association.

His main contribution to the Home Rule movement was not so much his overtly political activities – he was too much of an individualist to be a great joiner of organisations and he was scrupulous in avoiding preaching politics directly from the pulpit. His real influence over his fellow Presbyterians, and widening out from them to other denominations as well, was in the moral example he set for the people of Ulster during a period of the most bitter struggles. At a time of acute controversy, when every kind of pressure was being applied against those who would not submit to the mainstream of Unionist–Orange opinion, he stood absolutely firm, relying upon his moral principles to carry him through the flood. Though verbally abused, and ostracised by the respectable and unco guid members of society for many years, he never budged or altered his convictions. Indeed, he was the living example of that which was so often talked about but not always seen – the Nonconformist conscience.

Armour's finest hour was probably in April 1893, when the Presbyterian Assembly discussed Gladstone's second Home Rule Bill. This was a period of intense political excitement, when the Ulster community was deeply and emotionally divided, and the Unionists, spurred on by British Tories, had succeeded in whipping up the most vehement opposition to Gladstone. The Orangemen warned of a new Inquisition, of a St Bartholomew's Night massacre, and the imminent replacement of the old Protestant Ascendancy by a new – and it was alleged, much worse – Catholic one. Armour took the view that such fears were irrational and deliberately fomented for reactionary political ends. So when a resolution was put to the assembly condemning Gladstone's ideas out of hand, and pledging loyalty to the Crown and constitution, he moved an amendment supporting the Liberal premier, and advocating 'adequate means of self government'. Immediately, the assembly split open, and a long and virulent debate followed. In his most eloquent form – speaking with 'tongues of fire' – he condemned what he called 'the senseless fear of Romanism' and the displays of 'mass hysteria'. When he described landlordism as 'the curse and scourge of Ireland', and boldly declared that 'the principle of Home Rule is a Presbyterian principle', there was uproar, catcalls and heckling. Worse pandemonium followed when he sarcastically enquired if 'no man can be saved or remain a Presbyterian unless he renounce Home Rule'.[19] This intervention led to cries of 'Withdraw' and 'Scandalous'. The Reverend James B. Dougherty and a few other clerics and Church elders supported Armour, but the vote in the assembly was ten to one against him.

Undaunted by his defeat, Armour rallied his forces again, and in August of the same year succeeded in getting a petition favouring both land reform and Home Rule signed by 3,500 Presbyterians, including labourers, professional men, ministers and farmers. In 1894 he was agitating again about land problems in the Ballymoney area. In 1895 he had the satisfaction of seeing a Liberal chosen for Tyrone North, and fourteen nationalists elected, often with Liberal support, in other Ulster constituencies.

Armour's critics never forgave him for what they saw as the ultimate apostasy – voting for Home Rule. Henceforth conservative clergy and laity in his own Church would not invite him to lecture or preach – boycotted him, in fact. The episcopalians had always disliked his views, and now took every opportunity to belittle him publicly. Unionist politicians, riding on the tide of jingoism that swept through Ulster during the Boer Wars, depicted him as an enemy of Protestantism and the empire. On one occasion, he was physically assaulted. Twice attempts were made – notably by the *Northern Whig* – to blacken his reputation by reprinting a forged letter which he had allegedly signed in 1887. Many years later his friend Robert Lynd wrote that Armour was for long treated by his fellow Protestants as a 'sinister legend . . . a dangerous man, contentious and perverse . . . a traitor . . . a bitter and black-bearded agent of the enemy . . . enemy Number One in his own church'.[20]

In spite of these attempts at intimidation, Armour did not waver in his convictions, and continued to speak his mind until his death in 1928. He was always ready for a fight, and seemed to relish the controversies in which he was involved. During the late 1890s, when the Tories were in power at Westminster, his closest confidantes, such as Dougherty and W.H. Dodd,[21] remained loyal to him, and he kept in touch with sympathetic fellow ministers, such as the Reverend Richard Lyttle and the Reverend W.T. Latimer, the historian, and prominent land reformers, such as T. A. Dickson, Jeremiah Jordan, John Pinkerton and Thomas Shillington. His wife and children proved staunch in face of ostracism and relative poverty, and his parishioners at Trinity Presbyterian Church, Ballymoney, though they did not accept all his opinions, never abandoned him. Indeed, the membership of his church was remarkably stable over a period of several decades.

For a few years after the turn of the century, Armour was not so active politically, partly because of ill health and partly because those issues that stirred him had fallen temporarily into the background. In its early stages he took little interest in the developing Gaelic cultural renaissance, and from his remote base among the farmers and shopkeepers of north Antrim he did not show much concern about the growing working-class unrest in Belfast.[22] No doubt this geographical and social isolation cut him off from possible allies. He did return to the political scene, however, when the Home Rule issue reached its most critical stage.

21

CLASS STRUGGLES

These landlords and this land-system were the creation of the English government. England for purposes of its own planted these men in Ireland – planted the English land-system in that country. For centuries and throughout periods of great trouble these men acted as the garrison of England in a conquered country. They served England with devotion. In doing so they became a hated class in the country of their adoption . . . They governed the Church, the Land, the Representation of the People in Parliament, the Government, the country were all in their hands. They were veritable lords. The tenants were helots and slaves.

Thomas Wallace Russell, 1902[1]

The success of the Unionist Party at the polls depended largely upon the extent to which it could persuade the Protestant electorate that they should vote on religious, rather than social and economic, issues. By directing the people's attention towards a defence of the Protestant constitution, and the alleged dangers of a new Catholic ascendancy, it was hoped that they could avoid awkward social inequalities in the community. And by claiming that the Unionists embraced landlord and tenant, employer and worker, it was implied that the party was classless as well as denominational. The Orange Order, which was now successfully recruiting from all ranks of Protestant society, was a powerful auxiliary weapon in this campaign. So long as Protestant voters could be convinced that they should keep an eye on the Pope and his minions as the main enemy, and Queen Victoria or Edward VII as their friend, then they were not likely

to worry so much about rents and wages, housing and education or other contentious social issues.

The flaw in this tactic was that, while it could influence the
bigoted and gullible – in the same way as racists may in certain
circumstances affect people's attitudes towards Jews or non-
White populations – it was not based on economic realities. It
was true that the north had become more prosperous during
recent decades, but this prosperity was unevenly distributed,
and poverty was still widespread. It was correct that Protestants
as a whole were better off than Catholics as a whole, but this
could not disguise the fact that within the ranks of the Protestants
themselves there was still much poverty and deprivation.
Whatever the propagandists might say, the truth was that over
large areas of the economy and social structure there were big
gaps between haves and have-nots, rich and poor, powerful and
powerless, and that these economic divisions were found among
all religious denominations. Protestants, in other words, did not
form a homogeneous social group or a distinct economic class.
At the end of the nineteenth century there were in Ulster plenty
of poor Prods as well as impoverished Papists.

In rural areas the land problem remained acute in spite of the
various reforming acts that had been passed since 1870. The great
majority of big estates were still in existence, their wealthy
owners often feared and disliked by their tenants, Protestant
and Catholic alike. The official statistics show that by 1896 only
about one in five of all northern tenant farmers were in the
process of buying their land, and these were mostly weighed
down by debt burdens. The average size of the new peasant
holdings was between twenty and twenty-five acres, which did
not provide much of a living, especially during a period of falling agricultural prices. Rural labourers were existing on twelve
to fifteen shillings a week at a time when it was estimated that a
minimum of £1 2s. 6d. a week was needed to maintain a family
of two adults and two children above subsistence level.

The ould Lammas Fair at Ballycastle was famed in song and
story, but the reality was that boys and girls hired themselves
there for six months' labour for a few pounds. The hardships of

the migratory workers from Donegal, who travelled each season to pick potatoes in Scotland, are vividly described by Patrick MacGill in such novels as *Moleskin Joe* and *The Rat-Pit*. Shan F. Bullock, another contemporary writer, chronicled the plight of the poorer Protestant farmers around Lough Erne. *The Awkward Squads and Other Stories* and the novel *The Loughsiders* dwelt, not on lyrical landscapes and thriving homesteads, but on agricultural distress, social tensions and sexual frustration.

With so much poverty in the rural constituencies, the Unionists, linked as they were with the landlords, were vulnerable to political attack. The individual who most successfully exploited this discontent among farmers, especially those who were Presbyterians, was Thomas Wallace Russell, whose supporters at one time became so numerous that they formed a political group known as the Russellites. Russell was an ardent Presbyterian who had been born in Cupar, Fife, and had come to County Tyrone in the humble job of draper's assistant. As a young man he made a local reputation in the conventional evangelical causes of temperance and Sabbatarianism. He then turned to politics, and in 1886, standing as a Liberal Unionist, defeated the Irish Parliamentary Party candidate, William O'Brien, after a close fight in Tyrone South. He held this seat until January 1910, largely because of his commitment to land reform.[2]

Russell was a man of strong intelligence, vigorous energy and considerable eloquence, and he might in other times and in another province have become a politician of national importance. Unfortunately he was too quirky and independent-minded to sit easily in any of the traditional political parties, and he made the old mistake – which had sunk so many radicals before him – of trying to support two causes which were fundamentally contradictory. He passionately wanted to get rid of landlordism and the Ascendancy system associated with it, while at the same time he supported the constitution, which was the essential buttress of these social and religious evils. Like so many other liberals in Ulster before and since, he sought social and economic democracy at home, but believed that this could be achieved within the Union. The title of his most important book, *Ireland and the Empire,* reflects his ambivalent interests.

Russell's dislike, even hatred, for the rich landlords who dominated rural society seems to have been quite genuine, and his denunciation of their wealth and privileges was couched in language reminiscent of a Michael Davitt or a Joseph Gillis Biggar. Irish landlordism was, he said, 'barbarous and inhuman', and was no better than 'systematised and legalised robbery'. The lords of the soil were, with few exceptions, 'callous and heartless tyrants'. They had been originally planted in Ireland as an English military bastion, and during the seventeenth and eighteenth centuries they had become despots because of their Ascendancy privileges and untrammelled use of power. However, the famine, the rise of the Land League, and the extension of the popular franchise had together broken their monopoly. By the end of the nineteenth century they had become hopelessly corrupt, outdated and irrelevant. Their day was over, and their functions at an end. The sooner they were pushed aside, the better for Ireland – and for Britain. In 1901, before the introduction of Wyndham's Land Act, he wrote:

> The real fact is that Irish landlordism is played out. Where it exists, it exists merely for the purpose of taxing the community. It renders little or no service. Forty years ago it controlled, to a great extent, the parliamentary representation of Ireland; it cannot today secure, on its own merits, a single seat. Five years ago it was supreme in local administration; outside one or two counties in the north this power has wholly passed out of its hands. It was wont to administer justice locally; even in this duty it was superseded and outvoted by a popularised magistracy. The roots of landlordism have been destroyed. A rotten trunk and decaying branches are all that is left of it.[3]

There was a danger that the collapse of this once mighty edifice might bring down the Union with it. The landlords as a class were so unpopular that any cause associated with them would also be unpopular. If the Union, and with it the constitution and the empire, were to be preserved then this small, and bitterly disliked, social class must be abandoned. This was as true

351

of the predominantly Protestant north-east as it was of the overwhelmingly Catholic south. Land reform, in other words, was as much in Britain's interest as in Ireland's. Echoing the more far-sighted Tory leaders in Britain, Russell wrote:

> To buy out the Irish landlords is to buy out the fee-simple of Irish discontent. Land-purchase is true Unionist policy. The Union is best maintained and preserved by doing away with those grievances which imperil its existence. Chief of these is the Irish Land System. And he is a true Unionist who seeks, as I do, to destroy it.[4]

Finally, according to Russell, it was a potential threat to the cause of the Protestant people as a whole to allow themselves to be tied so closely with such a tiny and decaying minority, especially if this minority had an Ascendancy or Orange tinge to it. On no account should landlordism and Protestantism be allowed to sink together. Christianity would be best served in the long run if right-thinking people of all denominations came together under the banner of social reform, regardless of their precise theological beliefs. Russell professed himself a Presbyterian, but even during his most strongly pro-imperialist phase he was always critical of Orangeism. He blamed the Belfast pogroms of June 1898 on the preaching of the Reverend Richard Kane. His theological views seem to have been rather broad, as the following quotation indicates:

> So far as I know, the devout Roman Catholic believes everything which the devout Presbyterian believes. They both hold fast to the great verities of the Christian religion. The Fatherhood of God, the Divinity of the Son, the necessity of repentance and a clean life – the fundamentals of the religion of Jesus Christ are held in common by both churches.[5]

In the south of Ireland a man of similar political views, and also deeply involved in agricultural reform, was Sir Horace Plunkett, pioneer of the co-operative creamery movement. Plunkett was the third son of Lord Dunsany, and was a Unionist MP from 1892 to 1900. Like Russell, he ardently wanted Irish farming to be both more democratic and technically more efficient, but at the same time he believed that this could be done without the country having its own parliament. He was therefore willing to work closely with the so-called 'constructive' British Tories, such as the Balfour brothers, Gerald and Arthur. In 1891 he was appointed to the newly formed Congested Districts Board, and three years later formed the Irish Agricultural Organisation Society, which had as its main aim the promotion of co-operative schemes to raise credit and improve the selling methods of small farmers. In 1899 he was given an important position in the Department of Agricultural and Technical Instruction. His *Ireland in the New Century*, which was published in 1904, and went into many editions, is a well-meaning and philanthropic work, but unfortunately marred by anti-Catholic prejudice.

Plunkett's chief assistant and adviser for many years was George Russell, better known under his literary pseudonym AE. Russell was born in Lurgan in April 1867, son of a local book-keeper of evangelical convictions. He was given a conventional anti-Catholic education, and this, combined with his father's religious prejudices, turned him away from his home background when still a boy. 'I was born in Ulster', he wrote later, 'and never have been sufficiently grateful to Providence for the mercy shown to me removing me from Ulster: though I like the people, I cannot breathe the political and religious atmosphere of the North East Corner of Ireland.'[6] He was brought to Dublin as a boy, and got his first job as a clerk in Pim's, the drapers. He then went to art school, combining his painting with the writing of poetry.

Recruited as an organiser for the Irish Agricultural Organisation Society in 1894, the young Russell began the career that was to be his main source of income for many years – touring rural Ireland, talking to local priests and schoolmasters, preaching to groups of farmers about the advantages of their forming co-operative societies, which would help them to learn better farming methods, enable them to borrow money more easily, and sell their produce without the intervention of usurious gombeen men and grasping traders. Years later, Russell was to boast that he knew every county in Ireland intimately, and that he appreciated the problems of the small farmer better than the farmers themselves. Certainly in his work he proved to be both practical and visionary. Based as he was in Dublin, he established himself as a poet, mystic and theosophist through his writing and the regular tea parties he arranged in his Rathgar home. His numerous friends included W.B. Yeats and Lady Gregory, who had established the Irish Literary Theatre in 1898. In 1905 he was appointed editor of the co-operative journal the *Irish Homestead*, a post he held for eighteen years.

Russell was a pacifist, and no revolutionary in politics, but was a strong nationalist, and always prepared to defend the underprivileged and oppressed in society. He was deeply moved by the plight of the Dublin workers during the prolonged lock-out of 1913. In an open letter to the *Irish Times* he described the masters of industry as bad citizens, bad employers and bad businessmen.[7] In their attempts to starve out one-third of the poorest people in the city, they were acting as 'blind Samsons pulling down the pillars of the social order'. In November of that year he spoke alongside Bernard Shaw, James Connolly, and James Larkin's sister, Delia, in support of the strikers.

By the turn of the century the Unionists had been forced to concede that they no longer had much hope of winning any seat in which Catholic voters were in a majority. But what they had reason to fear most electorally was that because of their close links with the unpopular landlord class they were also losing support among the tenant farmers. The crucial political fact was that in certain predominantly Protestant rural areas, where they once had held almost complete sway, there lived only a few hundred wealthy people, mostly episcopalians, but thousands of discontented and relatively poor voters. At the polls it was the opinions of the latter which now counted.

That these fears were fully justified was shown in the 1900 general election. In the three southern provinces they could hold only Trinity College Dublin and (temporarily) Galway City, and in Ulster they won less than half of the thirty-three constituencies. Not only did the nationalists win fourteen seats, but independent candidates won four seats in the religiously mixed county of Tyrone, and polled strongly in Down North and Antrim South, which had previously been regarded as loyalist strongholds. Then in 1902 and 1903 came a series of by-elections which further revealed the weakness of official Unionists in the rural constituencies. In February 1902 James Wood, an independent campaigning mainly on farming issues, defeated Colonel R.H. Wallace, a pillar of the Orange Order, by 3,576 votes to 3,429 in Down East. A year later another independent gave Charles Craig, brother of the more famous Captain James Craig, a close fight in Antrim South. The following month a Russellite, again taking up agricultural problems, beat the Unionist by 2,407 votes to 2,255 in Fermanagh North. To the Tories it was now evident that so long as landlordism was a burning issue none of their rural fortresses was safe.

It was this gradual erosion of their electoral bases in Ulster, combined with the overwhelmingly strong nationalist vote in the south, which was the background to the Wyndham Land Act of 1903. Sir George Wyndham was one of those 'conciliating' Unionists who served his apprenticeship under the guidance of the Tory leader, Arthur Balfour. His interest in Ireland was enhanced by the fact that his mother, Madeleine Campbell, was a grand-daughter of the United Irish leader Lord Edward FitzGerald. Wyndham's main aim as chief secretary during 1900–1905 was to create a peasant farming class as quickly as possible. His land act has been described as the 'coping stone of the whole edifice of constructive unionism'.[8]

In brief, unionism was under attack, and in order to save its wider and long-term interests, it had to make a tactical retreat by abandoning its former cherished allies. Under the new legislation, landlords were encouraged to sell, not just piecemeal as hitherto, but their entire estates. The money borrowed by tenant farmers was to be repaid over a period of sixty-eight years at an interest rate of 3.25 per cent. In Ulster as a result of this and subsequent acts of parliament in 1909 and 1935 over two million acres were sold to 101,000 small farmers. A new class of small-scale proprietors was thus created.

Tenant farmers were not the only occupational group discontented with their economic and social position and therefore liable to be critical of the ruling Ascendancy. Protestant industrial workers, though they were generally anti-Catholic and anti-Home Rule, might on occasions vote or even strike against their bosses. Protestant dissent, in other words, took on class aspects in towns as well as rural areas, and could in certain circumstances develop into a kind of Orange democracy or populism. If there was a downturn in the trade cycle, for example, and unemployment increased, then such class allegiances might, even if only temporarily, supersede the more traditional religious and national loyalties. This was particularly important in Belfast, where in a population of about 350,000 people, approximately 100,000 were employed in factories, mills and shipyards. For more than a generation the city's politics had been dominated by the Unionists, who held all four parliamentary seats, but by the turn of the century this monopoly was under threat, both from Catholic voters in the west, and disgruntled Protestant working-class voters in the east, north and south of the city.

Generally, social conditions had improved in the urban areas during the previous twenty or thirty years, and real living standards had risen, especially among the skilled Protestant workers, who in 1900 were earning between £2 and £2 10s. 0d. a week. However, these comprised only about one-quarter of the Belfast labour force. Unskilled workers earned only £1 a week or less, and farm labourers averaged less than 15s. 0d. There was a constant flow of rural workers seeking jobs in the prospering towns, and this helped keep wages down. Women's wages, which often kept family incomes just above the poverty margin, were notoriously low, averaging about 10s. 0d. a week.[9]

For virtually all factory workers there was anxiety about loss of jobs, and fear of accidents, sickness and the onset of old age. There were no state pensions, and no state insurance against the hazards of ill health or unemployment. Hours of work were usually long, sixty to sixty-five hours being common, and conditions often noisy, dirty or humid. Tuberculosis (or 'poucey', as it was known in the linen mills) was widespread, and in 1896

356

there was a typhoid epidemic in Belfast. Housing conditions were generally bad, with much overcrowding, and lack of proper sanitary facilities. And educational opportunity was restricted for the sons and daughters of manual workers.

In such circumstances the growth of an independent labour and trade-union movement was inevitable. The Orange Order strove hard to persuade workers that their religious allegiances were more important than their class loyalties, and employers devised all kinds of job-preference and paternalistic schemes to keep their labour force docile. But the employees were not always deceived, and when economic times turned bad, there was a good deal of labour unrest. As early as 1881 the Belfast Trades Council had been formed, and its secretary was Alexander Bowman, a liberal who supported Home Rule. In 1892 the linen-lappers went on strike in Belfast, followed in 1895 by the engineers. In 1893 the Independent Labour Party was founded in England, and this soon recruited Belfast members, including the trade-union activist, William Walker. In 1896 James Connolly founded the Irish Socialist Republican Party in Dublin, and under the name of the Belfast Socialist Society enrolled several Protestant students from Queen's College. In 1897 six Labour councillors were elected in the municipal elections in Belfast. These were the first councillors standing under the name of Labour elected anywhere in Ireland. By the end of the century about 22,000 workers, practically all skilled operatives in engineering, shipyards, printing, building and textiles had joined trade unions in Ulster, out of an all-Ireland total of 67,000.

The two most prominent representatives of the Labour unionism or radical sectarianism trend among Ulster's Protestant workers were William Walker and Thomas Sloan. Walker, a carpenter by trade, had built up a popular reputation in Belfast as an eloquent speaker and trade-union activist. In 1893 he joined the Independent Labour Party. Walker's skills as an orator were learned the hard way on the city's Custom House steps, where he frequently took on Orange street preachers. But whatever religious differences he might have with the Orangemen, or class quarrels he might have with the bosses, Walker was always at heart a unionist. In 1904 he reached the pinnacle of his trade-union influence by being elected president of the Irish Trades Union Congress.

Sloan began his public career as a revivalist preacher and temperance advocate for the Belfast Protestant Association. Like Walker, he then found a sympathetic audience among the shipyard workers of Harland and Wolff, and with a mixture of anti-Catholic prejudice and anti-employer demagoguery, soon gained a considerable following in south-east Belfast. In July 1902 he won national attention when at an Orange demonstration he publicly attacked the veteran leader of the Unionist Party, Colonel Edward Saunderson, for his alleged weakness on the subject of the inspection of Catholic convent laundries, where it was reported young girls were being exploited.[10] This criticism was typical of Sloan's two-faced attitude towards social problems. On the one hand, he posed as the staunch defender of downtrodden and ill-paid laundry workers; on the other, he used the chance to abuse Catholicism.

This opportunistic attack on the Unionist establishment – with its double appeal to both class and anti-Catholic prejudices – was welcomed by many of the city's Protestant workers; and the following month, when the ageing Orange MP, William Johnston, died, leaving vacant the apparently solid Conservative constituency of Belfast South, Sloan decided to stand as an independent Unionist candidate. His election campaign was a clever, if cynical, blend of Labour rhetoric combined with the most blatant appeals to local religious bigotry. To the consternation of the official Unionists, who had long boasted of the power of their monolithic organisation, in 1902 Sloan won by 3,795 votes to his opponent's 2,969.

Flushed with this political success, and conscious that the Labour tide was running with him, Sloan refused to apologise to either the Unionists or the Orange Order, in whose ranks he had once been a highly respected grand master. A year later, after his appeal against expulsion from the Order had been finally rejected, he withdrew and took several branches with him. A demonstration in support of the new Independent Orange

Order was held in Belfast in July 1903, and succeeded in attracting an audience of eight thousand people. There had been several previous rebellions against the leaders of official Orangeism, but this was by far the biggest breakaway.[11]

Sloan was an erratic and often contradictory individual who would have achieved little but for the favourable political circumstances in which he found himself, and the help he got from other more talented persons. Such a person was Robert Lindsay Crawford, a man of much firmer character and livelier intellect than the opportunistic Sloan.

Crawford, who was born in Lisburn in 1868 and became, like his colleague, an Orange grand master, founded and was editor of the *Irish Protestant*, a fervently evangelical paper, in Dublin in 1901. This was a curious journal that set out to appeal to the prejudices of working- or lower-middle-class Protestants. On the one hand, it was violently anti-Catholic, but on the other, it attacked Church of Ireland bishops and the Unionist Party. The majority of articles and comments were on religious themes, with constant criticism of such doctrinal heresies as sacerdotalism and ritualism. There was the usual run of horror stories about wicked nuns and scheming priests, and a regular routine of the alleged threat of Catholics taking over Protestants' jobs. The Jesuits and Dominicans were said to be plotting night and day to impose a new Inquisition on liberty-loving Protestants.

The political line tended to be equally muddled, with indictments of Arthur and Gerald Balfour, whose agent, Sir Anthony MacDonnell, was not only under-secretary for Ireland but (much worse) also a Papist. MacDonnell was said to be trying to introduce Home Rule through the back door. At the same time as the British Tories were being denounced, there was sycophantic praise for the monarchy, and vigorous support for what was called the 'golden chain of imperialism'.

Crawford's ambivalent attitude towards current political issues was well illustrated by his views about Home Rule, which he then vigorously opposed. Simultaneously, even at that stage he seems to have had some sympathy with the concept of a separate Irish nationality. He was obviously stirred by the literary revival and growth of the Gaelic League that was taking place in many parts of the country. His comments indicate that he had some knowledge of the Irish language, and that in certain respects he appreciated Douglas Hyde's opinions about the threat posed by anglicisation. In April 1903 he wrote:

> Ulster is not a Scotch province. Irish Protestants per se are not hostile to the ideal of Irish Ireland . . . We cannot too strongly impress upon Irish Protestants the necessity of keeping before them the ideal of nationality . . . Irish Protestants should not wish always to be regarded as the English garrison in Ireland.[12]

He enthusiastically reported the holding of a service on St Patrick's Day, 1904, in the episcopal church of St Kevin in Dublin, in which the proceedings were conducted entirely in Irish – the first time, according to Crawford, such a non-Catholic service had been held in the native language for more than two hundred years. The text of the readings in Gaelic script, and the names of three clergymen and scores of laymen who attended, were published.[13] The driving force in organising this service seems to have been two young Protestants of republican sympathies – Sean O'Casey, destined to become the famous playwright, and Ernest Blythe from Magheragall, near Lisburn, who joined the Gaelic League and the IRB, became a prominent member of Sinn Féin, and in the 1920s was made a cabinet minister (the only northern Protestant to hold such a post) in the first Irish Free State government. Two years after the St Kevin's service, Canon James Owen Hannay, who wrote popular novels under the name of George Birmingham, was allowed to celebrate Holy Communion in Irish in St Patrick's Cathedral. This was part of the ongoing campaign to persuade Protestants to follow the example of Douglas Hyde in promoting the Irish language.[14]

Hannay's intervention was different from that of O'Casey's and Blythe's, who were separatists. Typical of those progressive Protestants who wanted to have their cake and eat it, he sought for a distinctive Irish or Ulster culture but at the same time envisaged that this could be achieved under the broad umbrella of the Union.

22

A CULTURAL RENAISSANCE

If the Ulster Theatre never produced an epoch-making play, or
never produced a distinctive school of acting, but did even a little in breaking down the barriers that divide the North from the
South, its work will not have been in vain.

James Winder Good[1]

The conservative tide that had been washing over Ulster since
the late 1880s began to ebb soon after the new century dawned,
and during the years immediately leading up to the 1906 general election there was a notable revival of anti-Unionist forces,
which affected politics, the arts, and even religious allegiances.

In Britain the Tory Party, for so long the mainstay of the Ascendancy in Ireland, was in disarray because of accumulating
electoral difficulties. Jingoism was for the moment discredited,
and the arch-imperialist Joseph Chamberlain was in disfavour
with the free-trade elements in his own party. There was growing acrimony between Anglicans and Nonconformists about
Church schools, and the trade unions were incensed by legal
judgments which discriminated against them. To add to government problems, there was a trade depression and increase
in unemployment. The Balfour policy of trying to kill Home
Rule with kindness was faltering because of delays in implementing the Wyndham Land Act, and the row that developed
over the appointment of MacDonnell as under-secretary for
Ireland was a further setback. The Conservative-dominated
House of Lords was under fierce attack from the radical and
wasp-tongued David Lloyd George. And it was at this time of

widening disunity and loss of political support that Winston Churchill left the Tory Party and joined the Liberals. At the other end of the social scale the newly formed Labour Party, led by Keir Hardie, sympathised with the emerging working-class organisations in Belfast, and several British-based trade unions were successfully recruiting members in the city.

From the south of Ireland there also flowed several currents which particularly assisted the northern nationalists and Irish-Irelanders. The Irish Parliamentary Party had become much more united under the leadership of John Redmond, and continued to hold its power base with over eighty members in the House of Commons. Redmond's protégé in Ulster was the young journalist and fluent orator, Joseph Devlin, who, with the help of the Ancient Order of Hibernians, was consolidating his grip on west Belfast. The founding of Sinn Féin by Arthur Griffith in November 1905 brought a new all-Ireland force into Irish politics. Three important literary or scholarly events, which ultimately had repercussions throughout the country, were the appointment of Patrick Pearse as editor of *An Claidheamh Soluis*, the official organ of the Gaelic League, in March 1903, the publication by AE of his collection *New Poems* in March 1904, and a series of lectures on pre-Norman Ireland given by Eoin MacNeill in University College Dublin in 1905. The Abbey Theatre, Dublin, under the charismatic guidance of Yeats and Lady Gregory, continued to provide literary inspiration for Ireland, and indeed the whole world. From Europe there were flowing in all kinds of taboo-breaking ideas from a succession of famous writers – Ibsen in Norway, Zola in France, Tolstoy and Chekhov in Russia. Bernard Shaw and H.G. Wells were the new iconoclasts in Britain.

By the middle of the decade the number of Ulster people who were willing to entertain such liberating opinions had grown appreciably. For the first time since the land wars there was now a substantial proportion of Protestants as well as virtually all Catholics who were prepared to reject the Unionists at the polls. The widespread discontent of the tenant farmers and Belfast workers was aggravated by the slow pace at which land reform was being implemented and an economic depression in engineering and shipbuilding.

Russellites in rural areas could now count on the support of many trade-unionists in Belfast. This lower-middle- and working-class disillusionment with the Ascendancy affected the thinking of the more independent-minded Orangemen, who seemed no longer content merely to repeat the old anti-Catholic shibboleths. Their chief spokesmen, Thomas Sloan and Lindsay Crawford, entered a new era of popularity.

The general challenge to traditional structures and ideologies also had repercussions on such cultural groups as existed in the province. A new theatre group was formed in Belfast, and two radical papers founded. Folk-song societies expanded their activities, and Queen's College, for so long the home of conservative Presbyterianism, began encouraging Gaelic studies, and even appointed Robert Mitchell Henry, who was something of a rebel, professor of Latin. Poets, novelists, playwrights, linguists, musicians, actors, and other creative artists, who had previously been numbered in tens or dozens, now could be counted in scores or even hundreds.

Between 1903 and 1908 there was a cultural renaissance in Ulster, perhaps not as important as the Gaelic revival in Dublin, but nevertheless of more than local significance. In this process many of the old Philistine and Puritan restrictions were thrown off, and there was an eager seeking after new ideas, new audiences and new forms of artistic expression.

Three individuals, who subsequently became well known in their respective cultural spheres, are a useful illustration of both the suffocating conformity of behaviour prevailing in many middle-class families, and the corresponding reaction by youthful rebels who were seeking social and artistic freedom.

Paul Henry detested the ultra-strict Sabbatarian atmosphere in which he was brought up in Belfast by his evangelical mother. His autobiography, *An Irish Portrait*, tells of the gloom and darkness that filled his childhood years, and how as a teenager he had only two ambitions – to leave home and to become an artist. In the first chapter, appropriately entitled 'Give Me

Liberty', he recounts how he was threatened with hell fire because he once smiled at a girl in church. 'The urge to get away became more and more intense', he wrote:

> I had been brought up in the most narrow and arid religious atmosphere, and the longing to get away from home, and its atmosphere was stifling me. I had to smoke in secret, drink in secret, and think in secret. These were the three unpardonable sins. There was a fourth more deadly still, though it was never mentioned . . .[2]

Robert Lynd, who subsequently achieved wide recognition as an essayist and literary critic, was similarly oppressed by the Sabbatarian gloom enveloping the Presbyterian manse in which he was brought up in Belfast. He has left an even more melancholy picture of what Protestant family life was like in the rural areas of the province in the 1900s:

> Sunday in some country parts of Ulster is a still stricter affair. Some of the older people – people, too, of high culture and intelligence – would not open until Monday a letter that came to them by Sunday morning's post . . . It is regarded by the extremely orthodox as a piece of doubtful morality even to go for a walk on Sunday. Whistling on Sunday is suppressed as a sin, even if one whistles a psalm-tune . . . Boating is not permitted; going into a fruit-garden to pick gooseberries is immoral. There are even some subjects of conversation which you will do ill to broach on a Sunday in strict company.[3]

The novelist Forrest Reid had a very different personality and dissimilar career to that of the openly bohemian and gregarious Henry and Lynd, but he also was a lifelong defier of conventional values. Because of his homosexuality, Reid kept to himself, never travelled far, and retained only a few close friends. He avoided being involved in any movement or organisation, and did not commit himself to any specifically Irish movement, though he did write a study of Yeats. His literary interests were mainly English and European or classical. So far as behaviour was concerned, he followed, as the title of one of his volumes of autobiography suggests, a private road.[4]

His books, however, reveal another side to his nature – imaginative, passionate, haunted by dreams and fantasies, committed to what he perceived to be the free and artistic world of the ancient Greeks. He hated (his own word) the Presbyterianism in which he was brought up, and as an adult rejected the Church. The God he worshipped was not the biblical Christ but the God of love and art. In a revealing phrase he once wrote that the spirit lived, but 'the letter killeth'. He despised the snobbery of his well-born mother who had sunk into genteel poverty after the death of his father, and he deplored the commercial values which he saw as being dominant in the Belfast of his youth and early manhood. A large part of his writing, both fictional and autobiographical, is devoted to the intimate study of family relationships, and the endeavour of young people, especially boys, to break loose from the bourgeois trappings which bound them. Delicately, because of fear of censorship and of giving offence, but none the less clearly, there is usually a strong emotion of illicit sex running through his novels. Reid, in other words, was a genuine dissenter, but perhaps not in the way that the word is generally used.

The rebellion of individual artists and writers against conventional cultural values was no doubt encouraged by the growth of various organisations which were also strongly anti-establishment in style. Of all such groups the most influential was the Gaelic League, which by the early 1900s had some dozens of full-time organisers, hundreds of branches and over 100,000 members in the thirty-two counties. In Ulster membership was not so large – probably about five hundred enrolled – but the league's reputation was raised by the recruitment of several prominent figures from the middle and upper classes. To such prominent Protestant names as Bigger, Lynd, Casement and Hobson were now added those of Margaret Hutton, translator of the *Táin*, and Alec Wilson, a Belfast accountant who became a close friend of Patrick Pearse's and later gave substantial sums of money to his school, St Enda's. When Pearse visited Belfast on league matters he stayed with Margaret Hutton at her comfortable home on the Malone Road. Paul Henry and his brother, Robert, also brought social prestige to the league. Catholic enrolment was stimulated by the arrival of such youthful enthusiasts as Cathal O'Shannon, John F. McEntee and Ernest Blythe, all of whom eventually became well-known Sinn Féin politicians in the south.

Two unexpected recruits – surprising because they came from an English public school, landlord and episcopalian background – were Sir Shane Leslie and Canon James Owen Hannay.

Shane Leslie, born John Randolph Leslie, seemed to be an unlikely volunteer in the cause of Irish nationalism. For generations his family, who lived at Glaslough Castle, County Monaghan, had been noted for three things – their broad acres, their strong Tory views, and their extreme Protestantism. They were connected with the Churchill family through Shane's mother, who was a sister of Jenny Jerome's, the American heiress who married Randolph Churchill. Leslie was thus Winston Churchill's first cousin, and through him had entry to the highest social circles in England. His father and grandfather had both been Unionist MPs and had represented Monaghan for many years.

The young Shane on growing to manhood repudiated all this Ascendancy heritage, assumed the name of Shane, and proclaimed himself a Home Ruler. He denounced the landlord class from which he came, saying it was unique among the aristocracies of Europe because it left everything undone which should normally be expected from a ruling class.[5] In 1905 while still a student at King's College, Cambridge, he joined the Gaelic League, and soon afterwards, following his experience in a shelter for the poor in London's East End, he became a convert to Catholicism. His conversion dismayed many of his friends in Ulster, and led directly to his disinheritance.

Hannay was born in Belfast in 1865, son of a rector. He was educated at an English public school, and at Trinity College Dublin, before he himself was ordained. After serving as a curate in Wicklow, he was appointed rector of Westport, County Mayo, where he remained for over twenty years. By nature extroverted and convivial, and liking the company of people from all kinds of backgrounds and social classes, he found what was perhaps his true métier under the pseudonym of George Birmingham as a prolific writer of popular novels, including the bestseller *Spanish Gold* (1908). Hannay became an executive member of the Gaelic League in 1906.

One of his more serious novels was *Benedict Kavanagh* (1907), whose eponymous hero was born illegitimately, the son of an Irish nationalist MP and a mother who came from a rich unionist family. The boy is brought up by a Church of Ireland clergyman who is an Orangeman to boot. The young Kavanagh gets a job in the west of Ireland where he becomes involved with a newly formed branch of the Gaelic League. The league's activities and members are portrayed most sympathetically, especially the schoolmaster, who is a Sinn Féiner, and the local Catholic priest, who is an even more ardent republican. There is also a Church of Ireland curate (possibly Hannay himself?) who wants to encourage Home Rule and make Irish people of all religions more spiritual and less materialistic and bigoted.

The author suggests that the regeneration of Ireland can only be achieved by the coming together of Protestant and Catholic, and the building of a common culture, which would be based, broadly, on allegiance to Ireland rather than Britain. In an eloquent passage – which has many echoes of an otherwise very dissimilar writer, Patrick Pearse – he argues that the survival of the Gaels, and their refusal throughout the centuries to accept an alien civilisation, was due to a large extent to qualities inherent in their ancient tongue:

> The genius of the people was in the language he listened to. The great world has not heard it for centuries. Science, philosophy, history, scholarship, theology itself, have spoken in other tongues. All that the modern world counts worth saying has been said, and no word of it in this strange tongue which lingers on the lips of peasantry along the desolate seaboard of the West. Yet among these people, preserved for them in this their language, preserved by no other means except their language, dwells faith, the wonderful clear faith of the child, that belief in the reality and

immanence of the eternal for which the great world sighs and craves in vain. Apologetic theologians, wooing science to be kind to them, look for it, and do not find it. Churches grow gorgeous and magnificent, art hypnotises the worshipper with them, but this faith is far away. The world missed it, passed by it, despised it once, and then cannot find it. It abides here shrined in a language that the world has never heard, among a people whom no one has understood, and who have not cared to explain themselves. And along with faith there lingers other things – the high emotion of great romance, a splendid indifference to small material matters, a lofty vision of life, a serious courtesy.[6]

This semi-mystical attitude towards the Gaelic past, with its vision of heroic virtues held by a simple, unspoiled people, free from the contamination of an alien culture, was one of the chief reasons why it was decided to hold a Gaelic League festival in north Antrim in June 1904. Here in a remote rural area, among labourers and small farmers, the middle-class and educated members of the league hoped to teach and learn from the local people, to win spiritual sustenance for themselves, and advance the cause of Irish-Ireland. The nearest place to Belfast of such a cultural storehouse was in the 'nine glens' where about one thousand native Irish speakers still lived. The site chosen for the *feis* was near Cushendall on land owned by Ada McNeill, who was a cousin of the prominent Unionist, Ronald McNeill. Ada called herself Íde in the fashionable Gaelic way. She was a tall, dark and handsome woman who greatly admired Roger Casement.

About two thousand farmers and villagers, some of whom could not read or write, are said to have attended, along with some scores of writers, musicians, scholars, linguists and other members of the middle classes. There were recitations and songs in Irish, a display of arts and crafts, and, as was recollected nearly forty years later by the poet Joseph Campbell, who took a busy part in organising the activities, 'competitions of all kinds – for babies, bread-making, sewing, horseshoes, *súgán* harness and chair-making, story-telling, singing, lilting, essay writing, dancing, wrestling, leaping and what have you'.[7]

Sir Horace Plunkett took time off from his co-operative enterprises to come north and open the *feis*. Roger Casement, a tall and bearded figure, was the centre of attention because his book *The Congo State* had just been published. Casement had made several attempts to learn Irish but according to his own admission never succeeded. So keen was he on encouraging the *feis* that he arranged for a boat load of Rathlin Islanders to come to the glens at his expense. His friend Bulmer Hobson was there, and so were Eoin MacNeill, and Francis Joseph Bigger, who had put up most of the money to pay for the event. The music contests were arranged and judged by Herbert Hughes, who was just back from a folk-song collecting trip to Donegal. He brought along the famous Welsh harpist, Owen Lloyd. Prominent among the crowd were several Protestant middle-class women, including Alice Stopford Green, Alice Milligan, Margaret Dobbs, Margaret Hutton, and Evelyn Gleeson, who ran a weaving shop in Dublin. It was there that the two poets Padraic Colum and Joseph Campbell met for the first time, immediately becoming firm friends.

Less mystical, and perhaps more deeply rooted in the harsher realities of northern social life, was another cultural enterprise, the Ulster Literary Theatre, which was founded in 1902 by Bulmer Hobson. Hobson wanted a theatre which would be racy, of the soil, and combine some elements of peasant realism with wider visions of the ancient glories of the Irish people. He therefore set out in the autumn of that year with his friend David Parkhill to discuss with Yeats his plans for a new theatre which he hoped would do for Belfast what the Abbey Theatre was doing in Dublin. Yeats, who seems to have been prejudiced against anything which came out of Ulster, did not give him much encouragement.[8] Indeed, the name proposed seemed to infringe on the rights of his own Irish Literary Theatre. In spite of this rejection, on their way home to Belfast, Hobson is said to have turned to his companion and declared: 'Damn Yeats, we'll write our own plays.' Thus the Ulster Literary Theatre was conceived as an enterprise with a distinctively northern flavour, and not prepared merely to be an appendage of the southern organisation.

Hobson's project never became as famous as the Abbey because the atmosphere in Belfast was less hospitable to creative drama than in Dublin, and it never attracted talents of the order of Yeats, Synge or O'Casey. It did not have a permanent home, and it was always short of money. Nevertheless, it attracted many fine actors and staged a number of original plays. In its time it was one of the brightest gleams in the black north. Yeats, who at the start had been so doubtful, later had the grace to admit that 'the Ulster players are the only society, apart from our own, which is doing serious artistic work'.[9]

The theatre had some popular success with the kitchen dramas and satirical fantasies that were written by Ulster writers in close touch with local audiences. David Parkhill (Lewis Purcell),[10] a young Protestant architect-turned-playwright, had his play *The Enthusiast* well received when it was produced in Belfast in 1905. It was about a young farmer who had emigrated from Antrim to America, and then returned to his father's farm, where he tried to persuade his family and other local farmers to set up a co-operative enterprise in which resources would be pooled, and Catholics and Protestants would work harmoniously together. The theme no doubt was inspired by the activities of Sir Horace Plunkett and AE.

A Belfast Protestant family, with direct involvement in the writing and staging of plays, were the six Morrow brothers, Harry, Fred, Edwin, George, Norman and Jack, who ran a decorating business in the city. Fred was chief producer of the Ulster Literary Theatre for many years, and George was a cartoonist who contributed frequently to *Punch*. Harry, who wrote under the pen name Gerald McNamara, was author of the farce *Thompson in Tír na nÓg*, in which an Orangeman, complete with sash and bowler hat, is killed in an explosion, and when resurrected finds himself in the land of eternal youth among the heroes of Irish myth; his *Suzanne and the Sovereigns* is a burlesque about James II and William III.

The most important local playwright was Samuel Waddell (Rutherford Mayne), who had been born in Japan, son of a Presbyterian missionary, and had returned to his father's native

Ulster to study engineering at Queen's College. Waddell was a man of many gifts, a most talented amateur actor who could well have made a successful professional career on the stage. Instead, encouraged by his father to get a steady job, he joined the Irish Land Commission, and continued writing and acting in his spare time. One of his early plays, *The Turn of the Road*,[11] produced in Belfast in 1906, is about a young farmer who wants to become a violinist, but is discouraged by members of his family, who can only think of making money and getting a good price for their cows. The play champions the plight of an intelligent and creative young man wanting to break out of the Philistine atmosphere in which he is forced to live. Waddell's next play, *The Drone*, a kitchen comedy, was a success in both Belfast and London. *The Troth* is an account of an agreement between a Catholic and a Protestant farmer, fellow sufferers at the hands of a brutal landlord, who plot to murder their oppressor.

Waddell's younger sister, Helen, was even more gifted than her talented brother. A brilliant Latin scholar and translator, in later years she made a worldwide reputation as the author of *The Wandering Scholars*, published in 1927, *Peter Abelard*, 1933, and *The Desert Fathers*, 1936. Helen was much more a poet and novelist than a political theorist, but her biographer, D. Felicitas Corrigan, describes how as a girl growing up in pre-1914 Belfast she was stifled both by the strict Puritanism of her family and the triumphalist unionism of her social class. She disliked all forms of religious intolerance, and though in many respects a lover of England and English culture, she rejected English rule in Ireland. One of her heroes was an ancestor, the Reverend James Porter, who was hanged outside his presbytery in Greyabbey in 1798. While a student in the newly named Queen's University Belfast, she attended a lecture given by the liberal Professor Robert Henry on the subject of sweated labour in the city's linen mills. The conditions described, the long hours and low pay, deeply shocked her. She blamed Edward Carson – 'the most sinister figure that ever influenced Irish affairs' – for the ever-increasing bigotry she witnessed around her. 'I know the

371

old kindly tolerance', she wrote, 'and I saw it stifled – under his hand – into obstinacy and hate.'[12]

For many Irish enthusiasts, music came second only to the language as a means of maintaining links with the Gaelic past. Songs and ballads were believed to carry folk memories going back many centuries, reminding people of old ways and vanished customs. The melodies, too, often had a haunting quality capable of stirring the deepest emotions. There could be no doubt that traditional music, together with the dancing that often accompanied it, had sustained the poorest people through their darkest hours, dispelling gloom and despondency, and bringing gaiety to social and family life. Where would romantic love, the crossroads dance, courtship, marriage and the coming of children be without the ballad singer or the fiddle player to inspire them? Turlough O'Carolan and Edward Bunting, Thomas Moore and Thomas Davis, had saved the oppressed nation as much as any priest or politician. And music could not only relate to the primal innocence of simple people; it could be appreciated by the educated as well as the uneducated, upper as well as lower classes, Protestants as well as Catholics. The appeal of a lively tune or well-phrased song was universal.

The Gaelic movement was fortunate in having among its members at that time a dedicated and gifted young musician who soon showed that he could do for traditional music what Hyde and MacNeill were doing for the language. Herbert Hughes, who, like Bunting one hundred years previously, decided that his first professional task should be to seek out and record such ancient melodies and songs as were still to be found in the remoter glens and valleys of his native province.

Hughes, again like Bunting, was an unexpected recruit to the cause of preserving the old Gaelic culture. He was of Welsh descent, and born into a prosperous flour-milling family in Belfast in 1882. He was a Methodist and brought up to sing English carols and hymns. As a boy he had shown keen interest in music, and his repertoire was extended when he learned songs in Irish from his barefoot nurse, Ellen Boylan. In 1901 at the age of nineteen he was sent to study in the Royal College of Music in London. Returning to Belfast for a short time, he came under the influence of the Gaelic League, and signed himself Padraig MacAodh O'Neill, and for a brief period he was a member of the Dungannon Clubs, which had been organised as a focus for pro-republican sentiments in Ulster in 1905.

Accompanied by Bigger in August 1903, Hughes set out for a tour of north Donegal, and succeeded in collecting several beautiful melodies among the farmers and fishermen he met on the way. In some cases he was unable to record the lyrics, possibly because he did not speak Irish well, and when he got back to Belfast he asked his friend Joseph Campbell to write new words for him. The result of this collaboration was published in 1904 under the title *Songs of Uladh*.[13] The book was illustrated by John Campbell, and paid for by Bigger. Many years later Joseph Campbell wrote this account of how musician and poet worked together on this joint enterprise:

> Our technique was simple. Herbert would come to Loreto (our home). Seated at the piano, he would play over the airs, improvising an accompaniment as he proceeded – first, in their natural tempo, and then more slowly so that I could catch and absorb the peculiar quality of each. In this way such pieces as 'My Lagan Love' and the 'Gartan Mother's Lullaby' came before the world . . .[14]

Three northern contemporaries of Hughes's, who were keenly interested in classical as well as Irish music, were Carl Hardebeck, who was of German descent but English born, and came to Belfast in the 1890s; Charlotte Milligan Fox, sister of Alice Milligan; and the composer Hamilton Harty. Hardebeck collected local traditional songs and joined the Gaelic League. He later became professor of music in University College Cork. Fox published in 1911 the *Annals of the Irish Harpers*, a study of Edward Bunting and his period. Harty, who had a distinguished career as a conductor in London, is perhaps best remembered for the most enduring arrangement of 'My Lagan Love'.

Bigger's ever-open purse was the source of funds for another publication, the quarterly journal *Uladh*, which ran briefly from the autumn of 1904 to the spring of 1905. Like the Ulster Literary Theatre, the magazine was liberal and nationalist in tone, and keen to promote anything in the north which was not tainted with religious bigotry or what was regarded as the alien culture of England. It was edited by Joseph Campbell, W.B. Reynolds and David Parkhill. Though short-lived, it included among its contributors some of the most distinguished writers of the day – Robert Lynd, P. S. O'Hegarty, Padraic Colum, Bulmer Hobson, Roger Casement, Stephen Gwynn, Forrest Reid, Herbert Hughes and Alice Milligan. It was in its columns that Casement began to reveal his ever-increasing involvement in Irish affairs when he wrote an angry letter about a farmer in County Donegal who had been prosecuted for displaying his name in Irish rather than English on the side of his horse cart. This case became something of a *cause célèbre*. Casement was stirred to protest by the *Daily Mail's* description of the Irish language as a 'barbarous tongue' and the even more offensive reference in the *Morning Post* to 'kitchen kaffir'.

The second number of *Uladh* took up the important issue that was troubling so many creative artists in the north during this period – how far should the Belfast-published journal concentrate on Ulster rather than wider Irish themes? Should it follow Yeats and Hyde in the south, or should it strive to encourage something more specifically northern? In February 1905 it stated in its editorial: 'We have not striven to erect a barrier between Ulster and the rest of Ireland; but we aim at building a citadel in Ulster for Irish thought and art achievement such as exists in Dublin.'

By this time Bigger's house, Ardrigh[15] on the Antrim Road, Belfast, had become the focal point for an active cultural group, where Catholics and Protestants met together to discuss their common Irish interests. It was a place 'imbued with the Gaelic spirit'. Bigger had a genius for collecting, and the large house was full of books, prints, pictures, old manuscripts, and Ulster artefacts of every sort, and was used as a kind of university by visitors. On Sunday afternoons or evenings there would be music and singing, and literary and political talk. He called it his 'firelight' (as distinct from 'twilight') school. Friendly people from the south of Ireland or Britain, as well as Ulster, would drop in, knowing that the 'crack' would be good and the atmosphere sympathetic. Herbert Hughes might recall his adventures collecting traditional songs, the Waddells talk of the new theatre, Francis 'Da' McPeake play a tune on his *uilleann* pipes, or Joseph Campbell recite a new poem. Douglas Hyde might arrive from Dublin with news of the Gaelic League, or Roger Casement be back on leave from the Congo. Shane Leslie seems to have been more at home there than he was on his own ancestral estates or in the great houses of London, and sums up Bigger's unique blend of revivalist enthusiasm and hospitality, which provided a meeting house for this cultural renaissance:

> Francis Joseph Bigger of Ardrigh, who under the trammels of a Belfast solicitor kept the soul of one of the Irishmen of 1798. Learned and sentimental, he kept open house for all who were stirring the Irish broth . . .
>
> For me it was good fortune to steer into his orbit . . . Bigger resembled Plunkett in his lack of bitterness, then a scarce virtue in Ireland. His extreme views did not prevent him from being a favourite with every creed and class . . . He imbued the Orangemen with a respect, if not enthusiasm, for Irish antiquities . . . He kept pipers and launched poets . . . In his dream he was 'the O'Neill' returned from the past – remote from the politics which clashed around him.[16]

23

DUNGANNON, MAGHERAMORNE,
AND THE BELFAST STRIKE

The independent Orange movement was strongly Protestant, strongly democratic, strongly anti-sacerdotal, strongly Irish. It was teaching Irish Protestants that love of Ireland was not incompatible with love of empire . . . They stood broadly for toleration . . . They had as Protestants trafficked too long in the shambles of sectarianism. They had looked too long upon Ireland with eyes of step-children and had been unmindful of the duties and responsibilities of citizenship.

Lindsay Crawford, 1905[1]

Singing songs in a summer garden, speaking Gaelic to one's friends, holding festivals and reciting poetry, performing controversial plays in a Belfast theatre – these were exciting ways of proclaiming a new idealism, asserting one's Irish identity, or even shocking the bourgeoisie. But it was not enough for those committed and more hard-headed republicans who wished to go further than merely promoting cultural activities. Such Irish-Irelanders were romantic in a different way – they wanted to go back to the traditions of 1798 and the Fenians. A few sought to become directly involved in politics, and hoped to give a sharper cutting edge to the staid constitutionalism of the Irish Parliamentary Party.

The Independent Orangemen, with their roots among the poorer Protestant tenant farmers and skilled Belfast workers, had even less sympathy with any kind of Kathleen ni Houlihan type of Irish nationalism. Celtic mysticism was not a notable characteristic of the culture to be found in shipyard, linen mill or engineering factory, still less in tin chapels or Orange halls. But the underpaid and underprivileged also resented the aristocrats and business plutocrats who dominated their lives. The 'land and labour' issues, which had led to the earlier electoral successes of Russell and Sloan, still rankled deeply, and indeed became sharper as the rural poor and the Belfast workers, regardless of their religious affiliations, watched the progress of the Liberal and Labour parties in Britain. By 1905 there was a general ground swell of discontent affecting a substantial proportion of Ulster's population, Protestant as well as Catholic. It was against this background of shifting political allegiances that two very different groups – one associated with the name of Dungannon, the other with Magheramorne – emerged to challenge the unionist establishment. In 1907 a large section of the Belfast proletariat had become so aroused that they went on strike.

The Dungannon Clubs, which had been founded by the indefatigable and all-embracing Bulmer Hobson early in 1905, took their name from the town in which the Volunteers had issued their famous declaration in favour of religious liberty in 1782. Belfast was the main centre of the new organisation's activity, but branches were also formed in Coalisland, Arboe, Carrickmore, Dungannon, Ballynahinch, Newry and Derry, as well as in Dublin, London, Glasgow and Newcastle upon Tyne. Hobson claimed that at its peak the organisation recruited some hundreds of members, and that he personally spoke to groups of them as many as five times a week. The membership was mostly young, including both Protestants and Catholics, the most active apart from Hobson being Denis McCullough, and Sean MacDermott, who was appointed provincial organiser in 1907 at a wage of thirty shillings a week. They were soon joined by Patrick MacCartan who had just returned to Tyrone from the United States of America. Hobson was particularly pleased at getting the support of the Reverend Richard Lyttle of Moneyrea, who seemed to perpetuate the best traditions of Presbyterian radicalism. Many years later he paid this tribute to him:

377

Lyttle was a true spiritual descendant of those Protestant clergymen who worked and fought with the United Irishmen in 1798. In Down, as in Antrim, the memory of the United Irishmen had not died out, and many of the older generation of farmers, grandsons of men who had fought at Ballynahinch and Antrim, were deeply, if mostly secretly, in sympathy with nationalist feeling. Lyttle was the natural leader of these men. He had great charm of manner, combined with ability and energy of a high order. His courage and sincerity and his exceptional powers as a public speaker made him an outstanding figure.[2]

The policy of the Dungannon Clubs was avowedly republican, and its manifesto called for a refusal to take the oath of allegiance at Westminster, the setting up of a home-based parliament, and the encouragement of education, and of native industries and language. 'The Ireland we seek to build', wrote Hobson, 'is not an Ireland for the Catholic or the Protestant, but an Ireland for every Irishman, irrespective of his creed or class, or rank or station.'[3] At this stage the clubs did not speak openly of revolution or physical-force rebellion but only of 'passive resistance' to the British administration. A leaflet, said by Hobson to have been drafted by himself, Alice Stopford Green and Roger Casement,[4] was published, opposing enlistment in the British Army. This led to a prosecution.

The clubs' weekly journal, which was launched in December 1906 with Hobson as editor, took a bolder stance. Significantly entitled the *Republic*, it rejected the moderate Home Rule policy of John Redmond and the Irish Parliamentary Party, and came out unambiguously in support of total separation from Britain. In its first issue Hobson wrote:

> We stand for an Irish Republic because we see no compromise with England, no repeal of the Union, no concession to Home Rule or Devolution, will satisfy the national aspirations of the Irish people, nor allow the unrestricted mental, moral and material development of our country . . . The old hate and bigotry that have kept Catholic and Protestant divided – the old grovelling spirit must be killed and forgotten by the people.[5]

378

The journal also rejected the religiously divisive tactics of a section of the Irish Parliamentary Party, which was seen as playing into the hands of the Orangemen. Wolfe Tone's name was constantly invoked, and readers were reminded that on many occasions in the past the Catholic hierarchy had denounced republicanism and the spread of democratic ideas. In one article the writer warned that if the Catholic Church attacked nationalism or allowed its members to attack it, then 'Nationalists must attack the Church.'[6] Joseph Devlin was criticised for the way in which he played up to the more conservative elements in the Church, and particularly, his close association with the avowedly sectarian Ancient Order of Hibernians. His victory in Belfast West in the 1906 election was welcomed as evidence of the vitality of the anti-Unionists, but at the same time his tactics were condemned by many republicans, including Connolly and Pearse.[7] Patrick MacCartan, himself a Catholic, was so alarmed at the prospect of progressive Protestants being antagonised that he wrote to the Clan na Gael leader in New York, John Devoy: 'The A.O.H. (Board of Erin) in any shape or form is a barrier to the progress of real Nationalism as it fosters distrust and bigotry.'[8]

In this anti-sectarian editorial policy, Hobson was fortunate in getting the assistance of two extremely talented writers, Robert Lynd and James Winder Good. Both were Belfast Presbyterians. Lynd, the keen Gaelic Leaguer and admirer of James Connolly, was a man of exceptional gifts – handsome and personally charming, loyal to his friends, deeply versed in Irish and English literature, shrewdly aware of the realities of contemporary politics, and, above all, a highly professional journalist and essayist.[9] In 1901, newly graduated from Queen's College, he had been forced to emigrate, like so many of his radical generation, because of lack of career opportunities and the suffocating social pressures of Edwardian Belfast. He first got a post on the Manchester *Daily Dispatch*, and then was appointed literary editor of the London *Daily* (later *News*) *Chronicle*, a position he held until shortly before his death in 1949.

In exile he did not abandon his radical views or cease to be involved in Irish affairs. Along with his friends P. S. O'Hegarty and Paul Henry, he founded a Dungannon Club in Hampstead, and continued as an active propagandist for the Irish language. It was at a Gaelic League meeting in Oxford Street, London, that he met his future wife, the poet Sylvia Dryhurst, daughter of a prominent suffragette. Lynd met Roger Casement whenever the latter was on leave in London, and corresponded with him regularly while he was in west Africa and South America.

In 1907 he published under the name Riobard Ua Fhloin a short pamphlet entitled *Orangemen and the Nation*.[10] Based on articles he had written for the *Republic*, it developed the theme that Orangemen had not invariably been unionists, and had in fact in several cases opposed the Union. Protestants had allowed themselves to be deceived by such bigots as the Reverend Henry Cooke into identifying their faith with the British connection, and this had distorted the true principles of the Reformation. It was degrading for a people who boasted of their independent views to allow themselves to act as colonialists. The real division in Ireland was between the 'patriotic Irish' (who included people of all religious opinions) and the 'English garrison in Ireland'. Lynd concluded with a passionate plea, which echoed Parnell, that Ireland could not afford to lose one of her sons. Catholics and Protestants, descendants of Celts, Danes, Normans, Saxons and Scots were all 'lawful children' of the nation.

Good never became as well known as Lynd, but he also proved to be a talented journalist and critic, particularly with regard to politics. Much of his work has been forgotten, but it still has relevance. What he had to say about unionism and Orangeism, for example, applies as much today as it did sixty or seventy years ago. For a brief period he was a junior editorial assistant on the *Belfast Telegraph*, but this did not prevent him from being (secretly, one presumes) an active Dungannon Clubs member. In the spring of 1907 when Bulmer Hobson went on a fundraising tour in the United States of America, Good was editor of the *Republic*. In 1909, finding professional opportunities closed to him in the north, he moved to Dublin where he eventually got a job on the *Freeman's Journal*. He did not intervene directly in southern politics but remained a committed nationalist, corresponding regularly with Henry, Lynd, and Casement.

Good's two books, which were published during the period when the partition of Ireland was being actively planned in London and Belfast, are important works of political analysis. *Ulster and Ireland*[11] is a well-documented account of the way in which the northern province was deliberately used, as he said, 'to discipline Ireland in the interests of England'. The ruling class in the north had formerly consisted of landlords, but during the late nineteenth century these had been joined by big business interests, forming a new type of oligarchy. Ascendancy loyalties to Britain had always been conditional, and if their privileges were questioned, then the pretence of constitutionalism was soon dropped. For any unbiased person who studied Irish history there could be no doubt that ethnic and religious differences were exploited for Britain's benefit, or that Orange riots ('squalid jehads', as he described them) were encouraged as part of this divide-and-rule policy. Edward Carson's real offence was that instead of trying to get rid of sectarian animosities he 'increased a thousandfold their venom and virulence'.

In *Irish Unionism*[12] Good develops, among several other major themes, the argument that in the eyes of Conservatives the unpardonable sin of Irish nationalists was that the latter stood for the rights of the majority over the privileges of a narrow caste, and that the Ascendancy throughout the centuries – by means of penal laws, the Union, the landlord garrison, and the encouragement of imperialist and religiously bigoted ideas – had always blocked the progress of democracy in Ireland. It was democracy as much as republicanism and Catholicism that was the enemy.

The Dungannon Clubs were not numerous, did not contest any election, and never developed into a mass movement. They have therefore been dismissed by most commentators as a mere footnote to Irish history. However, though they were numerically small and only flowered for a few years, they were politically significant in two respects: they kept alive the Protestant republican tradition of Wolfe Tone, and some of their key members were responsible for the revival of the IRB.

The secret oath-bound society from which the Fenians had sprung in the 1860s was largely moribund by the end of the century, its leaders elderly and apathetic. In Ulster its influence had never been strong, and in Belfast those members who survived were said to be more interested in alcohol than in revolution. It was therefore all the more surprising that it was in the north the brotherhood began to revive, inspired no doubt by the Gaelic League and the 1898 centenary celebrations. In 1901 it was a young Belfast Catholic, Denis McCullough, who took a bold step when he asked his publican father, a veteran member, if he could be sworn in. Disillusionment came when what he hoped would be a serious ceremony took place in a most casual manner in the back of a Falls Road pub. McCullough quickly determined to try and replace this bar-room patriotism with something altogether more idealistic, sober, and committed. His first task was to get rid of the elderly alcoholics.

One of his most promising recruits was Bulmer Hobson, then in his early twenties, a teetotaller and an earnest Quaker. Hobson was supposedly committed to pacifism, but agreed to be sworn into the brotherhood in 1904. In his turn, Hobson swore in Sean Lester in the unlikely venue of Portadown railway station.[13] A year later Patrick MacCartan also joined McCullough's group.

MacCartan proved to be an important recruit to the movement in spite of his youth and inexperience. By coincidence he had been born in Carrickmore, County Tyrone, the same village as Joseph McGarrity, who led the IRB in Philadelphia. McGarrity took the young emigrant MacCartan under his wing when he arrived in that city, and then introduced him to John Devoy in New York. When MacCartan got back to Ulster his head was not only filled with separatist ideals but he also had established the closest personal contacts with the most senior and experienced republicans in the United States of America. The veteran Thomas Clarke further strengthened this 'Ulster connection'[14] when he returned to Ireland in 1907.

Ultimately the most influential of the younger recruits was Sean MacDermott, who was sworn in by McCullough the same year as Hobson and eventually became one of the main driving forces of the insurrectionary movement in the south, and a signatory of the 1916 proclamation. The members of the Dungannon Clubs therefore had a strong influence, both directly and indirectly, on the Easter rising.

The Ulster establishment could afford to ignore the Dungannon Clubs because they were small in number and politically isolated. They were quite prepared to turn up their Philistine noses at the pretensions of poets, playwrights, musicians, and a handful of revolutionaries. What electoral influence, after all, had the Ulster Literary Theatre or a few Gaelic-speaking enthusiasts? They had long since abandoned any hope of winning many Catholic voters to their side, and could even shrug off Armour and his followers as no longer representative of mainstream Presbyterianism.

But what they really had to fear – and it was the same danger that had threatened them in 1798 and during the land wars – was the loss of conservative influence among the poorer Protestant section of the population, particularly in those fifteen or so constituencies they had long regarded as reliable bastions. If Toryism and Orangeism began to weaken in the Protestant heartlands then the Union was truly lost. This danger had again become apparent since the Russellites challenged strongly in rural areas of Antrim, Down and Tyrone, and had become ever more obvious when Labour reformers, such as Sloan and Walker, began making headway among the industrial workers of Belfast. It was this double threat of disillusioned farmers and discontented workers that was electorally so menacing to the Unionist Party because it changed the nature of the political struggle in Ulster. Land and Labour issues were taking over, at least temporarily, from the traditional issues of imperialism and Orangeism, and this could only hurt the Unionists. Simultaneously, in Britain the Liberal and Labour parties were growing in influence, and this again could only harm the Conservatives on both sides of the Irish Sea.

The most striking example of Labour's progress in Belfast was in the south of the city, where Thomas Sloan was steadily building up a power base among the workers. His brand of Protestant populism (he once described William III as a 'great liberal'), with its mixture of anti-Catholicism and attacks on bad housing, unemployment and lack of old age pensions, went down well in such areas as the strongly Orange Sandy Row. Lindsay Crawford, though still working in Dublin, was becoming increasingly involved in northern affairs, and was a frequent speaker at Independent Orange rallies. In 1905 he was elected grand master of the new Order. Valuable recruits from the trade-union movement were Alex Boyd, organiser of the municipal employees, and Thomas Carnduff, a young apprentice from Harland and Wolff. Carnduff was particularly welcome as a recruit because he was not only a socialist but also came from Sandy Row. He remained a Labour supporter for the rest of his life, and always described himself as an Independent Orangeman.[15] Thomas W. Russell and R.G. Glendinning, who had big followings among Protestant tenant farmers, were also prominent supporters of the Independent Orange Order.

By July 1905 the Independent Orangemen were claiming as many as fifty-five lodges to be in existence, and during the July celebrations of that year, six thousand supporters were said to have attended demonstrations in Belfast. In the old radical centre of Ballymoney ten thousand were present. To mark the success of these anniversary rallies the Order issued what became known as the Magheramorne manifesto, named after a small place near Larne in which it was first proclaimed. This was a remarkable document because it challenged many of the traditional dogmas of the old Orange Order (which, it should be pointed out, still retained the loyalty of the great majority of Protestants). Broadly democratic and ecumenical in tone, the manifesto was in several respects rather confused and timid politically. Nevertheless, it was widely welcomed as an example of progressive thinking, coming from a source not usually noted for such views. The veteran Fenian Michael Davitt and the young Bulmer Hobson, for example, were equally enthusiastic in their praise.

Clericalism of all kinds, and the sectarian basis of so much Irish politics, were severely criticised. The Tory and Liberal parties were both blamed for exploiting such religious divisions for selfish ends. There was a call for the compulsory purchase of land, and the redistribution of parliamentary seats. The caution of the manifesto's author was noticeable in the fact that neither the Union nor Home Rule were mentioned. However, this was compensated for by suggestions of a common Irish nationality, embracing people from all religious groups. In a key passage, reminiscent in its phrasing of the writings of Thomas Davis, members of the new Independent Orange Order were told that they stood 'once more on the banks of the Boyne, not as victors in the fight, nor to applaud the noble deeds of our ancestors . . . but to hold out the right of fellowship to those who, while worshipping at different shrines, are yet our countrymen – bone of our bone, flesh of our flesh'.[16]

Sloan at first put his name to this radical document, but when criticised by the Unionist press he began to back away, eventually repudiating his signature. Lindsay Crawford, in contrast, was quite unrepentant in his support, and indeed became ever more radical in his public opinions. Though still reluctant to make a complete break with his pro-union past, he began, under the influence of his Dublin friend, Frank Skeffington, to express support for feminism and even certain aspects of socialism. He also continued to openly admire the Gaelic League. Certainly he was a stern critic of all aspects of wealth and privilege, and published a pamphlet in which he attacked the old Orange Order as 'an instrument of landlordism and class rule'. His opinions about the Conservative oligarchy who ran Belfast at that time were summed up in the description: 'the old nobility and squirearchy . . . wealthy parvenues . . . land speculators and whiskey magnates'.

Crawford's views by this time had become far too radical for the directors of the *Irish Protestant*, and in May 1906 he was sacked from his post as editor. Four months later, with the support of the prominent Belfast Liberal William J. Pirrie (who was controlling director of Harland and Wolff, and later under a Liberal government became Lord Pirrie), he was appointed editor of the liberal *Ulster Guardian*.

The culmination of this anti-Conservative wave came in the general election of January 1906, when the Unionists could only win less than a quarter of the seats in the House of Commons. Arthur Balfour, who had been prime minister since Lord Salisbury's resignation in 1903, was defeated. It was the party's lowest point for many years. The Liberals, with Herbert Asquith and the rising Lloyd George as dominant figures, swept back into power with 387 seats. Labour, which had been gaining ground under the leadership of Keir Hardie and Ramsay MacDonald, won twenty-nine seats.

In the provinces of Leinster, Munster and Connacht the process of Tory electoral decline, which had begun after the extension of the franchise in 1885, continued unabated, with the party winning only three seats, two of which were in Trinity College Dublin. Edward Carson was one of the victors in this constituency, which some critics regarded as a kind of rotten borough. The Irish Parliamentary Party captured the remaining sixty-seven seats in these three provinces. Many southern constituencies recorded only derisory votes for the Unionists. (See Table 15[17] for 1906 general election results in Ireland and Ulster.)

TABLE 15

GENERAL ELECTION RESULTS IN IRELAND AND ULSTER, 1906

	Ireland	Ulster
Irish Parliamentary Party	82	15
Unionists	17	14
Liberals	1	1
Independent Unionist (Labour)	1	1
Russellites	2	2
Total	103	33

In Ulster, too, there were signs of disenchantment with the Unionists, even the supposedly 'loyal' Protestant heartlands of Antrim, Down, and Belfast were weakening in their allegiance. Some constituencies that had long been regarded as safe Tory strongholds temporarily became marginal. No longer was it possible to take the voters' attitudes for granted.

The Russellites, campaigning vigorously on the issue of land purchase, contested nine rural constituencies, polling strongly in five of them, and winning two seats. In total, these candidates won 26,000 votes – a substantial number when 3,000 or 4,000 votes could get a man elected. Russell himself held on to Tyrone South, with a vote of 2,954 against his Unionist rival's 2,671. Another Russellite polled 3,757 votes against 2,969 in Antrim North. The lone Liberal, W.H. Dodd, defeated the Unionist in Tyrone North by the narrow margin of nine votes.

Labour, which had been gaining ground among the industrial workers for some years, very nearly captured Belfast North, where William Walker gained 4,616 votes against the Unionist's 4,907. In Belfast South Thomas Sloan, running as an Independent Unionist with Labour support, was re-elected with 4,450 against the Unionist's 3,634.[18]

The Irish Parliamentary Party continued to maintain its strength in the predominantly Catholic constituencies of Cavan, Donegal, Armagh South, and Tyrone Mid. In Down South Jeremiah MacVeagh polled 3,910 against the Unionist's 3,262, and in Fermanagh South the veteran tenant-right campaigner, Jeremiah Jordan, retained his seat unopposed. In a bitterly fought battle in Tyrone East the nationalist polled 3,053 and the Unionist 3,022. And under the vigorous leadership of Joseph Devlin Belfast West was gained for the nationalists by 4,138 votes to 4,122.

A year after the polls had confirmed the popularity of Thomas Sloan and Joseph Devlin, and slightly less so that of William Walker, an event occurred in Belfast which was to prove within a few months how deep and widespread was the social discontent prevailing in the city, especially among the ill-paid. In January 1907 a previously little known trade-union organiser arrived with the aim of mobilising for the first time the city's tens of thousands of unskilled and semi-skilled workers. The task confronting James Larkin, as he soon found out, was a formidable one. To begin with, he was a Catholic, and most of the workers he hoped to organise were Protestants. Second, he was a stranger to the city (a Liverpudlian, his grandfather is said to have emigrated from County Armagh during or after the famine), and he had no personal knowledge of its customs and values. Third, he hoped to influence dockers, carters, and seamen, who had little tradition of trade-union organisation, and who were normally divided on sectarian issues. And in England James Sexton, secretary of his union – the National Union of Dock Labourers – was unsympathetic both to his personal style and his militant views.

Larkin had, however, certain advantages on his side, which more than compensated for these drawbacks. Belfast was full of combustible material, and only needed a match to set it alight. 'Big Jim', as he became known, was a man of tumultuous energy and charismatic appeal, a magnificent street orator in a city that appreciated fiery language. His experiences as seaman, dock labourer and socialist agitator had taught him to understand the fears and hopes of ordinary working people wherever they lived or whatever type of job they held. As a full-time organiser with the English-based union, he was well placed to influence port workers throughout the British Isles.

The first sign that the city's poorly paid workers were beginning to stir came in April of that year when a strike broke out among the unskilled – and, incidentally, overwhelmingly Protestant – operatives in the Sirocco engineering factory in east Belfast. The strikers, who were unorganised, were soon forced to return to work, and compelled to sign a pledge that they would not join a trade union. In spite of this setback, unrest spread the following month among seamen, dockers and carters, who in many cases were only paid about £1 2s. 6d. for a seventy-hour week. The even lower paid girls and women employed in Gallaher's tobacco factory came out on strike. By May, Larkin claimed to have enrolled more than half of the 1,500 carters and 3,100 dockers into his union. It has been estimated that during the summer of 1907 at no stage were there more than 3,500 on strike, but because of their key role in the trade of the city they were able to tie up much larger numbers of workers.

In June the dockers called for a general strike in support of their claim for a wage of £1 7s. 6d. and a cut in their working week to sixty hours. They got widespread support among many sections of the city's working class, skilled as well as unskilled. The unrest spread, the employers declared a lock-out, and blackleg workers were brought in from Dublin, England and Scotland. As tension mounted, more police and troops were brought into the city, and naval ships were anchored off Bangor on the orders of the admiralty.

In July Belfast was involved, not in the usual anti-Catholic demonstrations of the Orange Order, but in large rallies demanding higher wages and trade-union recognition. The class war took over, at least temporarily, from the sectarian struggle. Probably not since the heady days of 1792 had there been such anti-Ascendancy unity displayed in the city. On the Twelfth itself the Independent Orange Order, one-thousand strong and with twelve lodges in the parade, marched to Shaw's Bridge, where Lindsay Crawford was chief speaker. His main attack was on Edward Carson and the old Orange Order, which he said had become 'the dustbin of the Carlton Club and the tool of place-hunting lawyers'. Even the vacillating Thomas Sloan, who could generally be relied upon in a crisis to try and face both ways, was temporarily swept along in the call for proletarian solidarity. Joseph Devlin rallied support in west Belfast. And during these stirring months several prominent British socialist sympathisers, including John MacLean, George Lansbury, Keir Hardie and Victor Grayson, visited Belfast.

Surprisingly, the Dungannon Clubs, who might have been expected to join in on the attack against the establishment, were not as active as they could have been in defending the workers' interests. Only Patrick MacCartan seems to have appreciated the wider significance of involving Protestant workers in the struggle against the Unionists. Bulmer Hobson's comments on Larkin's efforts seem to have been rather lukewarm, and he actually closed down the *Republic* when the strike was beginning to gather strength. Hobson was a friend of Arthur Griffith's and it may be that the latter's views influenced him. Griffith was then, and during the 1913 strike in Dublin, an outspoken critic of Larkinism.

An even more sensational event took place on 19 July. A police constable, William Barrett, was told to guard a blackleg carter who was taking goods from the docks. He refused to obey the order, and was immediately suspended from duty. Within a few days several hundred constables, who themselves were only paid between twenty-four and thirty shillings a week, held a protest meeting in Musgrave Street barracks, declaring that they would not obey their officers. After various official threats, the mutineers went back to work, but two hundred were quickly transferred to other parts of the country, and Barrett was dismissed for provoking the mutiny.

On 26 July one of the biggest Labour demonstrations ever seen in Belfast took place, when an estimated 100,000 trade-unionists and their supporters marched through the city, bands playing and banners flying.

Lindsay Crawford was so enthused by all this evidence of solidarity, and so inspired by his experience of speaking alongside Larkin and his National Union of Dock Labourers colleague Michael McKeown, and other strike leaders, that he concluded – wrongly, as it turned out – that sectarianism was in permanent decline, and the dawn of a new era was at hand:

> The labour disputes in Belfast have done one thing. They have bound men of all creeds and classes together in the holy bond of a common brotherhood. None but those who know Belfast of other days can understand the change that has come over the people. It was confidently predicted by the Tory opponents of the workers that the working alliance between Protestant and Catholic dockers and carters would not survive the sectarian and party divisions of the 'Twelfth'. But to the surprise and chagrin of the Tory prophets there was never a more peaceable 'Twelfth' in Belfast. It astonished even the men themselves. They realised for the first time what a powerful instrument of peace and order lay in organised labour, men of different creeds meeting together for the protection of common interests. It was a wonderful revelation, and the strike, whatever losses and suffering it may leave behind, will leave behind a rich legacy – a united people.[19]

In mid-August there were serious riots by strikers and their supporters in the Falls Road area, in which troops as well as police were involved. Two people were killed and scores wounded. This disturbance in a traditionally nationalist area was a turning point, as it enabled the anti-Larkin elements to bring forward once again the idea of a Fenian conspiracy. The Unionist press used every opportunity to try to revive the old schisms between Protestant and Catholic, skilled and unskilled, and to introduce a new division between British and Irish trade-union leaders. Alex Boyd, who spoke mainly for skilled workers, criticised Larkin, and James Sexton constantly sniped from the sidelines in Liverpool. The British Trades Union Congress was at best lukewarm in its support, and such 'Labour imperialists' as Philip Snowden and Arthur Henderson were hostile from the start. Robert Blatchford, editor of the Labour *Clarion*, who later became such a jingo during the First World War, described the strikers as a 'howling mob'. Sloan and Walker, who were always quick to sense which way the reformist wind was blowing, soon reneged on their earlier support.

Conservatively inclined Catholics were also eager to distance themselves from the strikers, particularly now that their cause was visibly weakening. Devlin quickly made the point that he had never on any occasion spoken on the same platform as Larkin, and in the south of Ireland Arthur Griffith began his campaign of attacking what he called 'an English organiser' of 'a foreign labour union'. After the Falls Road riots several priests denounced any assaults on the police or soldiers as immoral. Cardinal Michael Logue, speaking in Derry in September, implied that active trade-unionists were promoting 'Socialism . . . irreligion and atheism'.[20]

By the autumn of 1907 the strike had virtually collapsed, without the workers winning trade-union recognition or any significant wage increases. Employers used their renewed powers to blacklist militant workers. Four years later a literary comment on these bitter struggles came from the pen of the young Belfast writer St John Ervine in his play *Mixed Marriages*.[21] The theme of this drama, which had a popular success at Dublin's Abbey Theatre, is that religious intolerance can do grave damage not only to the trade-union cause but also to the individual families caught up in the strife.

The failure of the strike had a demoralising effect on the Belfast Labour movement generally, and led indirectly to the disruption of the Independent Orange Order. One sign of this weakening of socialist forces was the disappearance of several branches of the Independent Labour Party which had sprung up in the city a year previously. Trade-union leaders were under pressure as the unity of Protestant and Catholic workers was dissipated, and the old divisions between skilled and unskilled reasserted themselves. Finding that his support had ebbed away, Larkin went to Dublin, where in the winter of 1908–9 he began to organise the home-based Irish Transport and General Workers' Union and was denounced by James Sexton as an undisciplined troublemaker. In Belfast there was an open split between the Protestant Alex Boyd and the Catholic Michael McKeown, who stuck with Larkin.

The Independent Orange Order, which had many members among the strikers, and whose two chief spokesmen, Sloan and Crawford, had widely differing views on many topics, also began to disintegrate. Sloan continued as MP for Belfast South, but his social radicalism was fading fast, and he seemed more interested in making a show at Westminster (where he acquired a reputation as something of a dandy), than in protecting the interests of his constituents. His heavy drinking did not endear him to his teetotal supporters. In contrast, Crawford remained an unrepentant defender of the underprivileged in society. Indeed, if anything he became more rather than less outspoken in his views, continually attacking the city's employers and Unionist establishment, and openly favouring Home Rule in his editorials.[22] This annoyed the businessmen who owned the *Ulster Guardian*, and in April 1908, once again, he was dismissed from his post as editor. A month later Sloan moved at a meeting of the Belfast lodge of the Independent Orange Order that Crawford be expelled from membership. Several lodges and a few individuals, such as Thomas Carnduff, opposed this expulsion, but the Sloan faction was in the ascendant, and Crawford never won back his power base among the democratic Orangemen. Failing to get suitable work in Ulster, he was forced to emigrate to Canada, where in 1910 he eventually got a post on the liberal *Toronto Globe*. In spite of his exile he continued to take a keen interest in Irish affairs. He criticised the 1916 rising but attacked the Black and Tans and opposed partition. In New York in the 1920s and 1930s he was trade representative of the Irish Free State government.

The committed republicans, too, found it increasingly difficult to maintain any viable base in the north. Several of the more prominent Irish-Ireland figures were forced to seek more promising political or vocational opportunities in Dublin or elsewhere. At the instigation of Bulmer Hobson the Dungannon Clubs had been merged in April 1907 with Arthur Griffith's Cumann na Gaedheal (which soon afterwards merged with Sinn Féin), and ceased to have much influence in Ulster. Hobson[23] himself was unable to find work in Belfast, and moved to Dublin in 1908, where he got a temporary job on the *Irish Peasant*, edited by W.P. Ryan. Sean MacDermott also moved south to become organiser of the IRB. Patrick MacCartan, who was now qualified as a doctor, spent more time in Dublin than he did in his native Tyrone. Of the original 'three Macs', only Denis McCullough was left in Belfast, where he continued to be the city's chief IRB representative until the 1916 rising. By trade a piano tuner, he made a living from the music business. He was, however, now politically isolated in the city. Roger Casement, though by then a deeply committed separatist and keeping as closely in touch as possible with his friends by means of correspondence and visits home when on holidays, was too deeply involved in exposing the rubber scandals in the Amazon Basin to be of much political influence in Ireland. He did not leave the British consular service until 1912. For more than two decades after he left Belfast in 1901, Robert Lynd continued to comment on Irish affairs. He was never a physical-force republican, and he disapproved of the 1916 rising on the grounds that it was a futile gesture, but five months after its leaders were executed

393

he wrote a long and sympathetic introduction to James Connolly's *Labour in Irish History*.[24]

There was a similar haemorrhage of talent among the writers and artists who found it virtually impossible to make any sort of living in their native province. Emigration drained away likely rebels and Dissenters in every sphere. The poet Joseph Campbell emigrated to London in search of work before settling in County Wicklow; the musician Herbert Hughes followed Hamilton Harty on the boat to England; the playwright Samuel Waddell left the struggling Ulster Literary Theatre for a position in the Land Commission in Dublin; the painter Paul Henry settled in Achill Island, County Mayo, paying only fleeting and most reluctant visits to his native Belfast; AE occasionally travelled north on his co-operative farming ventures, but did not stay long; George Birmingham was now an active member of the Gaelic League, but his energies were devoted to writing and to his clerical duties in Westport, County Mayo; James Winder Good was blacklisted by the pro-Unionist papers of Belfast, and also left for Dublin; Shane Leslie could afford financially to live in Ulster, but his tastes were cosmopolitan, and he moved around from Ireland to England and the United States of America. Forrest Reid, apart from studying in Cambridge University, stayed in Belfast almost all his life, but his interests were personal and literary rather than political. Francis Joseph Bigger, with his substantial earnings as a solicitor, was one of the few Protestant intellectuals who had set out to reform Ulster society at the turn of the century who kept a strong cultural base in Belfast.

It would be an oversimplification to suggest that the failure of Belfast trade unionists to achieve their immediate objectives, and the subsequent decline in the anti-Tory movement, can be ascribed solely to the traditional divisions between Protestant and Catholic, skilled and unskilled, workers. Undoubtedly such differences played their part, but they are not the full explanation. Indeed, what was surprising about the strike was the way in which workers of all classes and religious denominations stood together for so long under the most difficult circumstances.

The truth was that the solidarity which temporarily existed for a few years between Labour in Belfast, the Independent Orangemen, and the various Irish-Ireland groups was at best only a fragile affair.[25] During the years 1905–8 there was a variety of powerful forces, not merely in the Unionist Party and among the city's employers and newspaper owners, pulling in several different directions. The 'progressives' lacked any kind of ideological cohesion, and held widely differing views as to the direction in which they should go. Liberals, Labour, tenant farmers, Irish nationalists and republicans, Dissenters and would-be reformers of all types might broadly agree that they disliked the ruling class that dominated them, but in other respects they had not much in common. Clearly, as events proved, they were not likely to form a party that could effectively challenge the relatively monolithic Unionist Party.

To begin with, the otherwise well-disposed lower- or middle-class or skilled working-class Protestants, who disliked the Ascendancy and did not regard themselves as in any way bigots or Orangemen, found it extraordinarily difficult to shake off completely both their class and religious prejudices. They favoured more democracy and they wanted greater equality of wealth within the community, but when issues sharpened they were afraid to go too far and too fast. Their liberal instincts pulled one way, and their pockets pulled another. Thus the tenant farmers passionately wanted to break the grip of the landlords, but at the same time they feared that their Catholic neighbours might do better from the redistribution of land. The skilled artisans believed that wages were everywhere too low, but they resented the very lowly paid coming up too far on the income scale. The more tolerant Presbyterians prided themselves on their freedom from bigotry, but many were still tied to their old views about the idolatrous practices and superstitions of Catholics. In other words, their taste for liberty and equality was restricted, and their willingness to be ecumenical was hedged around with all kinds of qualifications. In words which William Drennan had once employed about similar people in the 1790s, they were 'scrupulous, hesitating, half-way men'.[26]

The historian John Gray, who has studied the events and background of the Belfast strike most thoroughly, believes that it was this failure of the Protestant workers to shake off decisively their Unionist–Orange shackles which was the main factor in the defeat of the strike:

> If then the 1907 dispute revealed in full array the capacity of Protestant workers to provide a formidable vanguard in industrial agitation, it also illustrated the limitations of such agitation, as the powerful impact of the workers' actions raised issues which threatened other compelling supremacist imperatives. In recoiling from this discovery they hastened their own defeat. The experience of 1907 was to prove a classic illustration of a more enduring dilemma for this forgotten majority, in which opportunities for real social advance, albeit with attendant political risks, were lost, and they remained trapped instead in a barren oscillation between the twin poles of proletarianism and sectarianism.[27]

A further misunderstanding of political realities arose from the fact that many would-be social reformers were sincerely convinced that they could achieve their aims within the framework of the Union. Like Isaac Butt, and so many other liberal Unionists before and after him, they expected to win some crumbs from the imperial table, and as part of this economically beneficial process, institute the necessary internal changes within Ireland, reducing the gap between rich and poor, abolishing landlordism, and lessening sectarian tensions. The social democrats (or more accurately the Labour imperialists) within their ranks genuinely hoped that they could win higher wages, better employment conditions, and improved welfare provisions as an intrinsic part of the United Kingdom. Hopefully also, the growing Liberalism in Britain would spill over into the neighbouring country, ameliorating all kinds of ancient feuds and discontents. To achieve such admirable and long-sought reforms, it would not be necessary to break away from Britain and the empire. The nationalist agitation for Home Rule was therefore a waste of time.

In this admiration for the empire, and with it all the trappings of the Crown (a Protestant monarch, of course), the pro-union Belfast Labour leaders were greatly encouraged by the support they got from their opposite numbers in Britain. Arthur Henderson, Ramsay MacDonald, Philip Snowden, Robert Blatchford, and many other prominent leaders of the British Labour Party were in several respects open admirers of the imperial system, and the benefits it brought to their country's better-paid workers and lower middle classes. They might criticise some aspects of the colonial system, but it had the undeniable advantages of keeping down the price of food and raw materials, and of offering markets for manufactured goods. MacDonald, who was a frequent visitor to Belfast, spoke in October 1905 of a 'nobler imperialism', and Henderson, who was a delegate to the Labour Party's annual conference in January 1907 (which by coincidence was held in Belfast) took the opportunity of referring to 'one unbroken imperial family'. William Walker and other social democrats in the north were naturally delighted by these comments which echoed their most profound sentiments about the Union.

A curious aspect of this theory – which proved so tragically wrong when the First World War broke out in 1914 – was the belief that imperialism, whatever its faults, could be regarded as a useful step on the road to internationalism. Thus it was argued that a group of nations and colonies such as the British Empire would evolve into a huge commonwealth in which issues of wealth and poverty would somehow be transmuted, and class struggles come to the forefront of political activity. In this way, contentious problems of race, nationality and religion would be superseded, and capitalism, the real enemy, could be more directly confronted. The Belfast *Labour Chronicle*, which expressed the views of such anti-Irish nationalists as Sloan and Walker, put this argument forward succinctly in July 1905:

> Class ties are stronger than those of race, and the workers of all lands and climes have a common class interest. They are all units in the army of labour and they ought therefore to forget their differences of race, language and colour and stand shoulder to

shoulder in order to withstand the attack of their common foe, capitalism.[28]

When a few months later the Dungannon Clubs issued their republican manifesto, the *Labour Chronicle* replied: 'Nationalism is dead or dying, and Imperialism is the transition stage to the international union of the proletariat all the world over.'[29] To reinforce this thesis it went on to denounce what it called the 'language craze' of the Gaelic League, and advocated a universal tongue such as the newly invented Esperanto.

A variation of this 'No Home Rule for Ireland' theme was the opinion held by certain influential British trade-union leaders that as their Labour movement was older, stronger and better organised than the Irish Labour movement (all of which was true), they were also more advanced ideologically (which was not always true). According to this argument, Irish workers because of their social backwardness and the influence of their priests could not be as progressive theoretically as their British counterparts. After all, they were only one step away from being peasants. For example, James Sexton, who as a keen trade-unionist wanted to raise the living standards of workers everywhere, could not get it out of his head that his Liverpool-based National Union of Dock Labourers must, by nature of its bigger membership and larger funds, be better than anything that Larkin, or later Connolly, could devise for the proletariat of Dublin or Belfast.

Nationalists, who might have been expected to welcome any evidence of anti-Unionist activity among the Protestant workers of Belfast, in most cases failed to rally behind the strikers, their argument being that Labour agitation was a diversion from the main struggle for Home Rule. Joseph Devlin's ingrained sectarianism in west Belfast has already been described. Arthur Griffith, who had established his new Sinn Féin organisation in the south of Ireland, proved to be a conservative on matters of social policy, and denounced Jim Larkin as an Englishman who was bringing alien socialist ideas to contaminate the Irish people.

The Dungannon Clubs, which took a broader view of Irish democracy, failed to grasp the opportunities opening up for

398

them. When the strike was at a critical stage, and help of any kind was urgently needed, they closed down their journal, and eventually merged their organisation with that of Sinn Féin. The Gaelic Leaguers, too, were rather purist in their search for higher forms of culture. Patrick Pearse, for example, reports how he, Francis Joseph Bigger and some other Irish-Ireland enthusiasts went on a motor tour of Donegal and Connemara in July and August 1907. Their aim was to speak at Gaelic League meetings and summer schools. Pearse wrote to Bigger on his return, discussing the events of the tour.[30] In a postscript he refers to the police strike which had taken place in late August, and asks Bigger: 'Are you at the bottom of the police mutiny?' This facetious query tucked in at the end of a long letter suggests that he did not take either the strike or the police rebellion very seriously, and how out of touch some of these intellectuals were with the plight of the Belfast working class.

24

THE CARSON CRUSADE

There are things stronger than parliamentary majorities.

Andrew Bonar Law, 1912[1]

The Irish Unionists were quick to exploit the divisions within the ranks of their opponents by reviving the methods that had been so effectively used to thwart Gladstone's first two Home Rule Bills. The aim was to persuade British public opinion that they had the overwhelming support of loyal Ulster, and that this support was the best guarantee they had against the dissolution of the empire. Within the province itself, they set out once again to convince all Protestants that only the Unionist Party stood between them and a new Inquisition. Their tactics were to try to intimidate anyone who stood in their path, particularly the Catholics and nationalists, but also any socialist or Dissenter who might show some spark of independence. They therefore decided to take every possible step to strengthen links with their opposite numbers in Britain, while at the same time integrating more closely with the official Orange Order. In this way they planned once again to replay the Orange card – with all its overtones of imperialism and religious intolerance – during a period in which circumstances were becoming increasingly favourable to them. This suited the Ulster landlords and employers because it would muffle the class struggle at home, and it pleased the British Conservatives, who were looking round for any weapon to defeat the Liberals and the rising Labour movement. Ireland was once again becoming a pawn in the internal manoeuvrings of British politics.

400

The first important decision was to co-ordinate the various reactionary forces in Ulster so that the province could be presented to the outside world as a monolithic bloc, at least so far as certain counties were concerned, standing foursquare against the nationalist foe. Minor differences between Protestants were to be subordinated, and an immediate closing of ranks encouraged. This would enable the party to present an 'unbroken front to the common enemy'.[2]

Within a few years of this policy being adopted there began one of the most powerful, sustained and fiercest campaigns ever waged by the Tories with regard to Ireland. This crusade, as it came to be called under the leadership of Edward Carson, drew in masses of ordinary people, as well as the most influential sections of big business, landlords, the highest sections of the law, administration, armed forces, the Protestant Churches and the universities. It involved wide strata of the Protestant population in Ulster and Britain, and engaged the richest sections of London society (where Londonderry House in Park Lane was the centre) and West End clubs, together with the Houses of Commons and Lords.

A preliminary step in this process of merger, or amalgamation, had taken place in March 1905 when a new Ulster Unionist Council was set up alongside the Irish Unionist Alliance, which had been in existence since 1891. This was a clear gesture to all the world that henceforth the northern Conservatives – knowing they could rely upon a mass following in twelve to fifteen Ulster constituencies – would, if necessary, go it alone, and abandon their fellow unionists in Leinster, Connacht and Munster, where their position was irretrievably weak. The necessities of *realpolitik* had required that the landlords should be abandoned. Now in the critical decade leading up to the First World War the southern unionists, comprising perhaps one-tenth of the population and incapable of winning anything more than a handful of parliamentary seats, might have to be deserted. The new Unionist policy was an indication that under certain circumstances what was being increasingly called the 'exclusion' of the north from the rest of Ireland might have to be considered. It was a further refinement of the Ulster-is-the-key-to-empire doctrine which had been developed by Randolph Churchill and Joseph Chamberlain twenty years previously.

Simultaneously, an agreement was made between Captain James Craig, MP for Down East, representing the politicians, and Colonel R.H. Wallace, grand master of the Orange Order, that out of two hundred members of the new council fifty would be nominated by the Order. Under this plan, the Orangemen, instead of being informally recognised as they had been for so many years as part of a wider anti-Irish nationalist movement, would become an integral part of the Unionist Party. From then on, membership of the two organisations was virtually interchangeable. Unionists met in Orange halls, and Orangemen served actively at every level in the party, nominating, approving or vetoing candidates in local and parliamentary elections. Certainly no ambitious politician could hope to make progress as an official Unionist unless he had the right – that is, Protestant – credentials.

Anti-Catholicism had, of course, been one of the main strands in British public life for more than three hundred years, and during the nineteenth century, in spite of much talk of liberty and tolerance, all British cabinet ministers without exception had been Protestants. Pitt, Grey, Peel, Melbourne, Russell, Salisbury, even Gladstone, made no effort to disguise their dislike of 'Popery'. But at least none of these politicians belonged to a political party that was openly and unashamedly based on sectarian principles. Tories might belong mainly to the Church of England, and Liberals to the Nonconformist Churches, but they did not proclaim officially, at least after 1829, that they would as a matter of principle impose religious tests within their ranks. Jews and Catholics might join if they wished. In the same way the Irish Parliamentary Party, though predominantly Catholic in membership, welcomed Protestant supporters.

What was so unique among the Ulster Unionist Party was that it did exactly the opposite – it deliberately fostered sectarianism, and instead of denouncing religious discrimination, openly boasted of it. It refused to take Catholic members even though they might be conservatives, and it certainly would never have one as an election candidate. Without fail, at the annual 12 July commemorations prominent Unionists would appear on Orange platforms, and make speeches in which politics and religion were appropriately mixed. A suitable reply chosen for the occasion would come from the Protestant clergy. As a consequence, the Orange Order became an ever more influential organisation, penetrating almost every section of Protestant society.[3] It eased the promotion path in administration, business and the professions, and often led to some mark of British approval, such as a title. It was not frowned upon by the majority of Protestant bishops; and politically, was not an obstacle but a prerequisite to advancement. This marriage of ultra-Conservative politics with religious and ethnic prejudice was the very opposite of that tolerance which was supposed to be the essence of dissent. It foreshadowed the racism which was to come with such appalling consequences later in the twentieth century.

The second organisational merger was just as important politically because it involved the virtually complete fusion of the Ulster Unionists with their counterparts in Britain. Randolph Churchill had mooted such a scheme in 1886, and succeeded in forming the Conservative and Unionist Party, which eventually absorbed the Liberal Unionists. In March 1907, a significant date because it was then that Larkin was beginning to rouse the Belfast workers, this amalgamation of the most conservative forces on both sides of the Irish Sea was carried a stage further. Arthur Balfour, who was still leader of the British Tories in the House of Commons, invited two delegations, one from the Irish Unionist Alliance, representing the south of Ireland, the other from the Ulster Unionist Council, representing the north, to visit him at his home in Carlton Terrace, London. The Irish delegates (twenty-four from the south, and twenty-nine from the north) included several prominent peers, MPs, landlords and businessmen, and even a representative of the Church of Ireland. They met with Balfour and the leader of the Irish Unionist MPs, Walter Long, James Craig and other Ulster MPs, and the Marquess of Lansdowne, who led the Unionists in the House of

Lords. Surprisingly in view of their close interest, neither Andrew Bonar Law nor Edward Carson seem to have been present. The following day the Irish delegates met the Duke of Devonshire, who was spokesman of the Liberal Unionists. Both Balfour and Devonshire received them warmly. Their discussions centred on the need to fight tooth and nail in parliament against any Liberal proposals to introduce Home Rule. Plans were made to intervene, preferably with carefully prepared speakers from Ireland, in any by-elections that might arise.

The involvement of several members of the House of Lords in these negotiations was regarded by Balfour as crucially important, not only because of their Anglo-Irish connections, but also because the upper House was perceived to be the key institution in the blocking of any undesirable Liberal legislation. In fact, this Lords' veto became a critical issue during the 'peoples' budget' debates of 1909, and the Home Rule debates of 1911 and afterwards. Lord Lansdowne, for example, was married to the daughter of the Duke of Abercorn. Beginning his career as a Whig under Gladstone, he moved steadily rightwards, ending up as a diehard Unionist. Under successive Tory governments, he had served as war secretary between 1895 and 1900, and then as foreign secretary between 1900 and 1905.

In these posts he had become deeply concerned with imperial strategy, and was determined to hold on to Ireland, and if not Ireland, then to Ulster, at all costs. A rich landowner in Ireland, he could speak for more than one hundred peers who also owned Irish estates, and/or had family connections in Ireland. This bloc was big enough to decide votes in the Lords. His advisers included the Duke of Abercorn, the Marquess of Londonderry, Lord Templeton, Alfred (later Lord) Milner, and on military matters, the two field marshals, Lords Roberts and Kitchener. Another military figure who was making a name for himself in the highest political circles, and who took the keenest interest in Irish affairs, was General Henry Wilson. Born in County Longford in 1864, Wilson was proud of the fact that one of his ancestors had come over to Ireland with William of Orange. After serving overseas in various parts of the far-flung empire, he had been appointed adviser to the war office in 1903, and commandant of the staff college in 1907. The closed circle of aristocrats, landowners, cabinet ministers, MPs and army officers was getting ever tighter.

The two MPs who were emerging as potentially the most influential leaders of this Ulster–British Conservative alliance were Carson and Bonar Law. Carson had used his position as solicitor-general between 1900 and 1905, his continuing friendship with Balfour, and his membership of the Carlton Club to strengthen his influence among the London establishment. At Westminster he was known as both eloquent and politically intransigent, and included among his new friends were the Londonderry family, the rising young advocate Frederick Edwin Smith, and James Craig. By now Carson had come round to the view that it was in Belfast rather than Dublin he could gain most political leverage, and was persuaded that, if necessary, the more vulnerable southern Unionists might have to be ditched, and the tougher, more entrenched, Ulstermen take their place. Though not yet leader of the Irish Unionists, he was the right-hand man of Walter Long.

Bonar Law was also developing as the other key figure linking together the various Unionist groups. He had lost his seat in the 1906 election, but this setback did not deter him, and he was soon afterwards elected for the Blackfriars ward of Glasgow. A prosperous iron merchant in that city, he had been brought up and educated in Scotland, but – a fact of crucial political importance – he was of Ulster Presbyterian descent. His father was a minister who had emigrated to New Brunswick, and then returned to Antrim in 1877. The young Bonar Law frequently visited his father's native province for holidays. He was a dour, convenanting type of Protestant, a teetotaller with strong religious as well as political beliefs. On one occasion he admitted that of all his political views the cause of Ulster unionism was closest to his heart.

The results of the two general elections held in 1910 confirmed the anti-Liberal movement on both sides of the Irish Sea during the previous four years. The swing was strong in Britain, slightly less so in Ulster. In January the Tories and Unionists gained more than one hundred seats overall, and in December they held on to all but one of these gains; the December result was a dead heat between Liberals and Unionists with 272 seats each. Labour won forty-two seats, and the Irish Parliamentary Party, eighty-four seats, which meant that together they held the balance of power in the new parliament. This gave the Irish nationalist MPs great political leverage in the discussions which were taking place about Home Rule. However, the House of Lords, with its inbuilt Unionist majority, continued to have a veto over government legislation. Ireland's future thus continued to be at the mercy of a few hundred unelected and unrepresentative peers.

In Ulster the Unionists made some small but significant gains, increasing their total number of MPs from fourteen to eighteen in January. Eleven months later they lost Tyrone Mid to the nationalists. This was not such a serious loss, for in the earlier election there had been a split vote between two nationalist candidates. Generally, there was a consolidation of the Unionist heartlands in Antrim, north Down, north Armagh, and in all the Belfast constituencies, except for the west of the city.

The Irish Parliamentary Party also continued to hold its traditional ground in the south and west of the province, winning thirteen seats in January and fourteen in December. Joseph Devlin retained his seat in Belfast West, Jeremiah Jordan won Fermanagh South, and Jeremiah MacVeagh, Down South. Two interesting nationalist results were the victories of Tom Kettle in Tyrone East, and William Redmond, brother of John, in Tyrone West. And Shane Leslie, whose nationalist convictions had been steadily strengthening, stood for Derry City in both elections and was only beaten by some one hundred votes on each occasion.

From the long-term point of view the most important aspect of these elections was the significant political polarisation that was again taking place. Catholics held firm behind the Irish Parliamentary Party, but some of those Protestants, who had temporarily strayed from the fold during the earlier part of the decade, were swinging back behind the Unionist Party.

Carsonism and Bonar Lawism were gaining influence, and the middle ground was being squeezed.

The Liberals (who by this time included the Russellites under their banner) won Tyrone North after a tough fight, and polled well in Derry County, Down East and Antrim North, all with Catholic support. Otherwise, they seemed to be in decline. In 1906, for example, Liberals and Russellites together had contested ten seats, won Antrim North, Tyrone South and Tyrone North, and polled 29,000 votes. In January 1910 they contested seven seats, succeeded in winning only Tyrone North, and polled 21,000 votes. In December of that year they fought seven seats, again were victorious in Tyrone North, but their total share of the vote fell to 19,000. Russell, their standard-bearer for so many years, was among those defeated.

Labour similarly fell back in Belfast South and Belfast North where the two candidates, Sloan and Walker, had polled over 9,000 votes between them in 1906. In the first election of 1910 Labour's total share fell to 7,500 and in the second round it slumped to 2,700. Sloan, running as an Independent Unionist, was heavily defeated on both occasions for Belfast South. He later emigrated to Canada where he seems to have been lost from view. In Belfast North a veteran Labour representative, Robert Gageby, who had been a city councillor and was one of the most prominent moderate trade-union spokesmen in the 1907 strike, took the place of William Walker. He polled 3,951 votes against his Unionist opponent's 6,275. Walker had decided to try his luck in the Scottish constituency of Leith Burghs, but ironically the Irish Catholic voters living in that constituency knew his sectarian record and would not vote for him, so he was defeated. In 1911 he was appointed an inspector in the new national insurance scheme, and retired from politics. He died prematurely during the war.

Within a few months of returning to office the Liberals announced that they would introduce legislation which would abolish the veto the House of Lords had over any bills passed in the Commons. The implications for Ireland were clear. In April 1912 the Government put forward a third Home Rule Bill – a modest measure which promised that certain vital powers, such as defence, foreign policy, sovereignty, and even certain aspects of taxation, would be retained by the imperial parliament. However, these proposals, combined with the knowledge that the Irish Parliamentary Party and the Labour Party held the balance of power in the Commons, infuriated the Unionists, who could see that their long-established and most-cherished props in London were being undermined.

As soon as the Government's intentions were made plain a reactionary campaign of vast proportions was therefore launched, with the twofold aim of blocking Home Rule at all costs, and at the same time defeating the Liberal government. Ulster was the obvious key to this strategy because the intransigents were dominant in six of the province's nine counties. The city of Belfast was also crucially important because the Protestant voters there, controlling three seats, must at all costs be prevented from slipping back into any socially progressive or independent ways of thinking.[4] During the three years leading up to the First World War every possible resource was mobilised to defeat Home Rule. Aristocrats, landlords, big employers, the most eminent figures in the Protestant Churches, the judiciary and the army, Tory politicians in both Houses, and the Conservative press all joined forces in one of the biggest, and bitterest, campaigns ever fought in these islands. The parliament of the United Kingdom was convulsed by the struggle, and Ulster itself brought to the verge of civil war.

The propaganda barrage that opened up this counterattack used all the old familiar weapons. It was alleged that if Catholics had a parliament in Dublin, they would impose a new Ascendancy, and that Protestants would lose all their privileges; Belfast's trade in linen and ships would languish if tariff barriers were imposed; the Unionists would be in a permanent electoral minority; the civil liberties of non-Catholics would be taken away; and the unity of the empire destroyed.

To reinforce, and give some kind of alleged validity to these claims, there was also an updating of the old racist theme about the special virtues of those invaders and settlers who had come from Britain. On this occasion it was not the White Anglo-Saxon Protestants who were lauded so much, as the Ulster-Scots. These chosen people, all Protestants of course, were reputed to excel in everything and possess the best human qualities. Physically they were said to be strong and hardy, they were noted for their character and sound moral values, and they had an admirable reputation for thrift and vigorous energy. Above all, unlike the lazy, shiftless and good-for-nothing Papists, they were loyal to the Crown and constitution. Lord Rosebery, himself a Scot who had once been prime minister and then had become leader of the Liberal Unionists, got so carried away with enthusiasm for this God-anointed group, that he described them in a speech in Edinburgh in November 1911 as 'without exception, the toughest, the most dominant, the most irresistible race that ever existed in the universe'.[5] Several widely circulated books, including *The Two Nations* (1911) by W.F. Monypenny, biographer of Disraeli, *The Ulster Scot* (1911) by J.B. Woodburn, and *The Soul of Ulster* (1916) by Ernest Hamilton, set out to give scholarly backing to this thesis. In countering this dubious racist theme, few critics seem to have picked on the most obvious flaw in the argument, namely that the overwhelming majority of Scottish people were, of course, Celts.

At the same time there was a revival of the argument that the position of Ulster as the linchpin of the Union and the empire was so crucial that any measures, no matter how extreme or even illegal, would be justifiable to prevent the introduction of Home Rule. According to this view, which had been expounded so eloquently by Randolph Churchill, Colonel Saunderson and others in the 1880s, the Ulster Unionists were entitled to a permanent veto against any Home Rule legislation passed in the United Kingdom parliament. Thus, a minority could dominate a majority of MPs. The tail should wag the dog; and the concept of a union in which a central government in London – which was supposed to rule fairly over England, Scotland, Wales and Ireland alike – was given a fresh twist. Ulster, and more particularly the province's pro-unionist population, who numbered perhaps one million out of a total UK population of forty million, should have ascendancy over everyone else. Oaths of allegiance to the Crown were again hedged round with qualifications, and loyalty treated as strictly conditional. This conditionality was well expressed by Ronald McNeill, one of the pillars of the Unionist Party, who claimed that 'Constitutional orthodoxy is a quite different thing from loyalty . . . true allegiance to the sovereign is sharply differentiated from personal obedience to an Act of Parliament.'[6]

To justify such singular opinions, which were in direct conflict with most generally held views about the nature of parliamentary democracy, it was necessary to invent a new political philosophy that would supersede conventional views about the rights of the electorate and those they chose to represent them in the House of Commons. The superior entity before which all were expected to bow down was thus variously symbolised as 'the Crown', 'Ulster', 'the empire', 'the constitution', and even 'the flag'; and in the same way as such imprecise concepts as Anglo-Saxons or Ulster-Scots appealed to those who were intellectually confused, so such vague terminology pleased those who were politically prejudiced.

Tactically also there was a reversion to the methods used so successfully in the late 1880s and early 1890s when the first two Home Rule Bills had been introduced, except that this time the demonstrations were bigger, the threats more violent, and the popular emotions aroused correspondingly higher. Huge marches were organised jointly by the Orange Order and the Unionist Party, and vast rallies were addressed not only by Irish leaders such as Carson and Craig but also by a succession of the most eminent British Conservatives, especially Smith and Bonar Law. The biggest Union Jack in the world was manufactured and flown, and army-type manoeuvres held all over the north-east. The *Belfast News-Letter* and the *Northern Whig* excelled each other with scare stories and abuse against Irish nationalists.

Job discrimination, which was another favourite weapon used by the Unionists to beat down their opponents, worsened as the crisis deepened. The more the siege mentality developed, the greater the reluctance of Protestant employers to give work to Catholics. At every stage from the first appointment to a job through to promotion, and affecting occupational structure at all levels, from senior business and administrative posts down to the humblest labourer or domestic servant, the old policy of 'looking after one's own' was intensified. This partiality in one of the most sensitive areas of Ulster life only polarised the communities further.

In modern times when lip service at least is paid to the principles of equality of opportunity and fair shares for all it is important to remember that before the First World War discrimination in employment was not condemned by the authorities in Ulster. On the contrary, it was widely practised and openly approved of. To choose a person for a job on the basis of his or her religion was assumed by most people to be the correct way to proceed. The situations vacant columns in newspapers were full of advertisements like 'Housemaid wanted; good needlewoman; experienced; Protestant', or 'Pharmaceutical assistant or chemist; must be strict teetotaller; Protestant', or 'Law clerk; thoroughly capable man wanted (Presbyterian preferred)'.

Edward Carson, who as a former solicitor-general and prominent barrister might have been expected to uphold the rule of law, was foremost in advocating unconstitutional action against the Home Rule Bill. In his first major speech in the north, made appropriately at a big rally of Unionists and Orangemen held in the gardens of Balmoral, Craig's Belfast home, in September 1911, he denounced the democratically approved proposals of the Asquith government as a 'nefarious conspiracy'. 'We must be prepared,' he said, 'the moment the Home Rule Bill passes, ourselves to become responsible for the government of the Protestant province of Ulster.'7 Carson was a lawyer who always phrased his speeches carefully, and there was no doubt that on this occasion he was putting forward three policies which he had previously renounced – his use of the word 'Protestant' was deliberately sectarian, he was supporting the idea of a separate Ulster, and he was rejecting the principle of majority rule in the House of Commons.

Bonar Law, who had by this time become leader of the British Conservatives, took up the same theme at another huge rally held seven months later, also at Balmoral. On this occasion 100,000 people are said to have attended, brought to the venue by 70 special trains. Speakers included Carson and Lord Londonderry, as well as Bonar Law. Bonar Law's passionate speech evoked all the old Unionist issues – the Siege of Derry, Lundy's betrayal, and how Ulster would save itself and the empire. Help in their Protestant struggle would come from Britain, he promised. Writing to Lord Lansdowne in October 1913, Bonar Law made it plain that his views were based as much on his experiences in Britain as they were of northern Ireland: 'I told him [Asquith] that in my opinion, at bottom one of the strongest feelings in England and Scotland was Protestantism, or dislike of Roman Catholicism.'[8]

Such sectarian incitement from the most eminent establishment circles in Britain added fuel to the fires which were already burning in Ulster, and just as Randolph Churchill's playing of the Orange card in the spring of 1886 had been soon followed by pogroms in Belfast, so in July 1912 serious anti-Catholic riots broke out in the city's shipyards. There was large-scale communal fighting, and much looting of shops and public houses. Mobs shouting Unionist and Protestant slogans marched through the yards of Workman Clark and Harland and Wolff, where 20,000 were employed, calling for the dismissal of 'Fenians', 'Taigs', and 'rotten Prods', that is, those Protestant workers who were known to be supporters of Labour or active trade-unionists. In all, about two thousand were driven from their jobs. Fortunately, no one was killed, but many were injured, and religious hatreds fanned throughout the city. An account of how the 'rotten Prods' were driven out of the shipyards in 1912, especially those of Workman Clark, is given by Henry Patterson, who points out that as many as one-third of all Belfast shipyard workers were actively involved in Unionist and Orange clubs.[9]

Bonar Law, whose sympathies for the Orange extremists was by this time well known, was not deterred by the dangerous forces he and Carson had unleashed. On the contrary, the more they could mobilise the bigoted elements among the Belfast working class the better they were pleased. Publicly they might 'regret' disorderly mob riots, but privately they continued to support physical action against Home Rule so long as that action was under their control.

A fortnight after the fires in Belfast had died down, Bonar Law spoke again, this time at the historic castle of Blenheim, ancestral home of the Churchill family. In his speech, which was framed deliberately to attract the most extreme Orange and extra-constitutional elements, he denounced the Asquith government as a 'Revolutionary Committee' which had seized despotic power. To a cheering crowd of English Conservatives, he then went on to make the remark that has been so often quoted as evidence of his determination to go outside the law, if necessary, to achieve his ends:

> I can imagine no length of resistance to which Ulster can go, in which I would not be prepared to support them, and which, in my belief, they would not be supported by the overwhelming majority of the British people.[10]

To add further drama to the rapidly unfolding events, in September Carson organised the signing by nearly half a million unionists of a Solemn League and Covenant, which pledged the Ulster people to oppose by every means possible the introduction of Home Rule to Ireland. A big rally of British Conservatives, held in London's Albert Hall, sent the same message back across the Irish Sea. Rudyard Kipling, who had become imperialism's most popular prophetic voice, published a poem in the *Morning Post* which contained these lines:

> What message from the North?
> One Law, One Throne, One Land.

During the next eighteen months the defiance of the law took on ever more militaristic and potentially violent characteristics. In January 1913 the Ulster Volunteer Force was formed, headed by Sir George Clark, and within a few months is said to have recruited over 100,000 men. Though its activities were technically illegal, it had open links with the Orange Order and serving officers in the British Army. The hundreds of Orange halls that existed in Protestant districts all over the province were used as recruiting centres, and later as depots for weapons and drilling. The closeness of the Order with this private army was emphasised by the historian Sibbett who claimed that as many as seven out of eight volunteers were Orangemen.[11]

General Sir George Richardson, a retired Indian army officer, was given command, and several of the most influential top brass in the army, including Field Marshal Lord French, chief of the imperial general staff, Sir Douglas Haig, commander at Aldershot, and Field Marshal Lord Kitchener, were known to be sympathetic, even actively conspiring, with the Ulster rebels. The aged Lord Roberts of Kandahar and Field Marshal Lord Wolseley also publicly proclaimed their support for the conspirators. Roberts wrote a letter, which for obvious reasons was kept secret at the time, denying that it was in all cases the duty of a soldier to obey the orders of his senior officer.[12]

General Henry Wilson, who had steadily worked his way up the army ladder and had become the confidante of several of the most influential right-wing politicians in London, was at the heart of these military conspiracies, moving easily between the war office, Sandhurst and Aldershot, London clubs and both Houses of parliament. His contacts in Ulster were the three ex-officers Captain James Craig, Colonel Frederick H. Crawford and Colonel R. H. Wallace.[13] All of these officers had served in the Boer War, and were ardent imperialists as well as ultra-Protestants.

While all this military manoeuvring was going on in Belfast and London, the constitutional aspects of Carson's campaign were not neglected. At the top level in parliament and the rank-and-file level in the constituencies there was a determined and well-organised drive to win support for the Unionist cause. In March 1913, for example, with the encouragement of such newspapers as *The Times*, the *Morning Post* and the *Daily Mail*, approximately 100 peers and 120 MPs set up the British League for the Support of Ulster and the Union. In a letter to the press, Ronald McNeill advised the British people that 'Ulster will be the field on which the privileges of the whole nation will be lost or won.'[14] A few months later Carson set out on an extensive speaking tour of Britain with the intention of weakening Liberal and Labour MPs wherever he could. Two hundred and fifty constituencies were carefully selected for this and subsequent tours, and a special appeal made to Baptist, Methodist and Presbyterian voters. There was direct intervention in certain key by-elections to try to ensure that at all costs a Unionist was elected. Carson's assistant Dawson Bates had by this time appointed seven full-time agents in Britain at a cost of ten shillings a head per day. It is said that during the three years after the 1910 general elections as many as 8,800 pro-unionist meetings were held and six million leaflets distributed.[15]

The climax of this extraordinary campaign, in which militarists and those who claimed to be constitutionalists worked hand in glove, and in which the crudest jingoism blended with the most extreme religious bigotry, came in the spring of 1914 when the Ulster Volunteer Force and their political mentors moved towards a *coup d'état*. In March of that year General Hubert Gough and fifty-nine officers at the Curragh camp in County Kildare announced they were not prepared to obey the orders of their superiors in London who had instructed them that they might be required to march against the Unionist rebels in Ulster. A month later, masterminded by Colonel Crawford, 24,600 rifles and three million rounds of ammunition were secretly imported through the ports of Larne and Bangor for the use of the Ulster Volunteer Force. Meanwhile, contacts were being made between senior Unionists and highly placed officials in Germany to see what help the latter could provide. Carson had actually met the Kaiser in August 1913, and some diehards were openly stating that they would prefer the Protestant German emperor, Wilhelm II, to the Liberal government of Asquith.

By the summer of 1914, with war with Germany already looming on the horizon, Carson had been talking for some time of setting up a provisional government in Ulster. It was this proposal, backed as it was by the British Tory leader Bonar Law, that led Winston Churchill, then first lord of the admiralty, to speak of a 'treasonable conspiracy' by the Unionists.

The anti-Unionist forces fought in their usual divided way against this powerful onslaught. The Irish Parliamentary Party continued to hold its electoral strength among its traditional Catholic supporters in the north, but as led by Joseph Devlin became ever more closely associated with the Ancient Order of Hibernians. Devlin had the confidence of his party leader John Redmond, and was engaged during 1911–14 in the complex negotiations that were going on with the Catholic bishops, Herbert Asquith, and his Liberal cabinet ministers Winston Churchill and Lloyd George. During those critical years Devlin was a useful link between Belfast, Dublin and London. He and other socially conservative Catholics did not have any sympathy with the Larkinites in the great strike in Dublin in 1913. Still less did he admire the left-wing Irish Citizen Army which was founded that year by James Connolly and Captain Jack White to defend the strikers. Devlin at first welcomed the National Volunteers which had been organised in the south in November 1913 as a response to the formation of the Ulster Volunteer Force earlier that year. He later repudiated the breakaway Irish Volunteers who refused to follow Redmond's advice to support the Allied war effort in the autumn of 1914. It was these republican Volunteers who were to be the mainspring of the 1916 rising.

The Belfast Labour movement was even more split towards the Union, and had not recovered from their defeat in the 1907 strike. Within the trades council there was said to be a majority for Home Rule. David Campbell, its president and a prominent member of the local socialist society, wanted to form an Irish Labour Party rather than affiliate to its British equivalent. Thomas Johnson, who eventually became leader of this Irish Labour Party when it was founded in 1912, and William McMullen, who later became president of the Irish Transport and General Workers' Union, supported Campbell. Both Johnson and McMullen were Protestants. The young Thomas

Carnduff developed into a spokesman for those Labour independents in Ulster who wanted to be neither unionist nor nationalist.

The individual who conducted the most vigorous ideological struggle against both Devlinism and Walkerism was Connolly, who was for a short period an organiser for the newly formed Irish Transport and General Workers' Union in Belfast. He rejected any suggestion that only Catholics could be good republicans, and strongly condemned the reformist Labour argument that the cause of British imperialism could be regarded as progressive. During May–June 1911 he carried on a polemic in the columns of the Scottish Labour *Forward* against the claims of William Walker that the interests of Ulster's working class could best be served by staying in the Union.[16] Connolly argued that, on the contrary, it was imperialism which was the main obstacle to social progress in Ireland, and that until this was defeated, any gains which might be made would be temporary and partial, and soon lost. Connolly's fiercest invective was against what he called Walker's pseudo-internationalism, which he said was really a cover-up for colonial exploitation.

Walker riposted by contrasting unfavourably the poverty of Ireland, especially in the south, with what he called 'the larger and more advanced economy of Great Britain'. In his opinion there would never again be sectarian riots in Belfast because of the progress of the Independent Labour Party there. He then revealed his underlying anti-Catholic bias by stating that 'Protestantism means protesting against superstition, and hence true Protestantism is synonymous with Labour.'

The northern Liberals avoided getting involved in such theological niceties, but concentrated instead on the political battle they were waging against the Conservatives. The visit of such a famous personality as Winston Churchill reminded them that they had influential friends at Westminster, and Lord Pirrie of Harland and Wolff provided money and support. Two by-election results gave a boost to Liberal morale. In Tyrone North in October 1911, Thomas W. Russell, who by this time had declared himself a Home Ruler, polled 3,104 against his Unionist opponent's 3,086 votes. In Derry City in 1913 D. C. Hogg, a friend of the Reverend James Armour's, beat the Unionist by 2,699 to 2,642 votes. The Liberals held this seat in another by-election in December 1914. In all three contests the Catholic votes tipped the balance against the Unionists.

Ministers and laymen in the Presbyterian Church were under intense pressure to conform to Unionist orthodoxy, and many were persuaded to sign Carson's covenant in 1912. Armour, who was constantly under attack, complained that the 'terror is so great that some men prefer to sit silent, and say nothing. The right of free speech does not exist in Ulster at present.'[17] However, some radicals remained as staunch as ever in their resolve to stick to their principles, regardless of the barrage of intimidation and propaganda directed at them. Armour himself, though now getting old, was in the forefront of this minority of Dissenters. He protested strongly against what he called 'bastard Carsonism', and condemned intimidation as a 'kind of leprosy' in the 'atmosphere of a garrison colony'. He jeered at Carson's proposal for an 'Ulster Day' as a 'Protestant fools' day'. In particular, he poured scorn on the idea that Ireland might have to be partitioned. Exclusion of the north from an independent Ireland would, he said, be 'ruinous to Ulster and Protestants generally'. The proposal was worse than nonsense – 'it was pure insanity', he commented.[18] On another occasion he said of partition: 'Of all the madcap schemes this is the worst.' He warned that if the country was divided into two parts, and the Tories gained control of the northeastern counties, then they would give no quarter to the Home Rulers they held in their power, regardless of whether they were Catholics or Protestants. They would suppress their opponents ruthlessly.

This struggle between liberal and conservative Presbyterians came to a head in the general assembly of 1913 when there was a bitter debate in which passions ran high, and in which there was much booing, catcalling and shouting. Armour, who spoke for an hour, using all the wit and sarcasm for which he was famous, made a strong attack on the numerous attempts, both inside and outside of the assembly, which were being made to stifle free speech. He did not spare his critics, and caused particular anger when he suggested that the conservative motion before the assembly implied that 'no Home Ruler can enter the Kingdom of Heaven'. Eventually after six hours' debate, Armour's amendment was lost by 921 votes to 43, with 165 abstentions.[19]

Characteristically, he was not dismayed by this defeat but returned to the fray a few months later, this time in his home town of Ballymoney where he could still rely upon local support.[20] The aim of the meeting was to rally liberal and Irish nationalist forces in the heart of north Antrim, and to show the world that not all Ulster Protestants were on the side of Carson. It was a remarkable occasion – not only did some five hundred townspeople and farmers, all Protestants, turn out, but the platform party comprised a striking collection of personalities. Armour himself gave lunch in his manse to fifteen speakers and supporters. The chairman was John McIlderry, the veteran tenant-right campaigner, and beside him sat two clergymen, two solicitors and nine justices of the peace. The main speakers were Roger Casement, who was making his first public speech in Ulster, Alice Stopford Green, the historian John Dinsmore, William Macafee, who had polled nearly three thousand votes as a Liberal candidate in Antrim North in December 1910, and Captain Jack White.

The meeting was organised by Jack White, a man who stood out as unusual even in the long litany of Ulster Protestant rebels. White's father was a knight, and a field marshal, a hero of the Siege of Ladysmith, the possessor of the Victoria Cross and a Member of the Order of Merit. The family estate was at Whitehall, near Ballymena. White had been sent to an English public school and Sandhurst, and had served in the Boer War where he won the Distinguished Service Order. Everything about his background suggested that he would become a typical member of the Ascendancy – reactionary, religiously bigoted and pro-imperialist. But his personality, character and life style did not follow the expected conventional pattern. On the contrary, he was the archetypal rebel against authority, and when he came to write his autobiography he appropriately called it *Misfit*.[21]

Individualistic by temperament, and advanced in most of his opinions, he preferred the company of bohemians and radicals to members of the establishment. Living in London after resigning his army commission, he made new friends among the writers, poets and various left-wing and anti-imperialist groups. One of the thinkers who most influenced him during this period was Sigmund Freud. When visiting Dublin in 1913 he made friends with James Connolly, and utilised his military training in helping to drill and equip the Irish Citizen Army. It was from Connolly that he picked up his Marxist views.

White detested the Unionists and Orangemen, and stated that Carson represented 'lovelessness . . . barrenness of ideals and arguments . . . the wholesale falsification of the facts of history'. He also had little time for conservative Catholic bishops who, he said, had always opposed the struggle for national independence in Ireland. In spite of his anti-clericalism, however, he seems to have got on well with Armour.

Roger Casement,[22] who had resigned from the civil service the year before and now wanted a platform from which he could publicly proclaim his political convictions, used the occasion to outline his views on the nature of Irish nationalism:

> For the question now before us is not what political party we may belong to, but whether we are Irishmen at all, all sons of one country . . . I believe there is only one Ireland, one and indivisible, and the more we love Ulster or that particular part of Ireland to which we belong, the more surely we should love that greater Ireland that owns us all. That is the true patriotism, and patriotism, remember, is perhaps the highest form of morality.[23]

Alice Stopford Green,[24] the only woman on the platform, made a passionate appeal to the Wolfe Tone tradition of Irish nationality:

> We have met here in the name of our country and for the honour of the [Protestant] religion in which we were born. We are determined that our land in one unbroken whole shall be lifted up in good fame among the peoples, and that religion among us shall be purged from the disgrace of violence and hate.[25]

420

She then went on to remind her audience what northern reformers owed to the people of the south, particularly on the question of land:

> Let us remember that Ulster Protestants joined with Munster Roman Catholics in 1851 in the Tenants' League of North and South. Isaac Butt led Protestants and Roman Catholics together in the demand for Home Rule. Go now round Down and Antrim, look at the new cottages and farms; look at the people settled in security as owners of the soil; see the first dam raised against the ravaging torrent of emigration, and Irishmen for the first time tempted to live on their own land. To whom do you owe this? It was the Catholics of South Ireland who fought the long and sore battles of which you have gathered the benefits. It was they who made the claim for the revision of rents, for the relief of lease-holders, which you won in 1886. It was they who won the purchase Acts and the planting on the soil of free proprietors.[26]

The outbreak of war in August 1914 soon put an end to such hopes and aspirations on the part of the opposition radicals. The loyalists threw all their weight behind the military effort, and any internal strife within their own ranks quickly ceased. Such differences on foreign policy as existed between Liberals and Tories largely disappeared. The future of Ireland, which only a few months previously had caused such acute dissension, was left unresolved. Edward Carson and Bonar Law, who had quarrelled so vehemently with Prime Minister Herbert Asquith, eventually joined a Liberal-led cabinet. There was a rallying to the colours by the overwhelming majority of Protestants, and anyone who suggested that the war might be an imperialistic one was denounced as a traitor and a Fenian. The pressures to support king and country were intense. Church leaders vied with each other in preaching that God was on the side of the Allies; and former trade-union officials, such as William Walker, joined with landlords and employers as recruiting sergeants. Even John Redmond, leader of the Irish Parliamentary Party, advised his Irish Volunteers to join the British Army, and was soon echoed by Joseph Devlin in nationalist west Belfast. The

Ulster Division, which emerged from the Ulster Volunteer Force of pre-war years, was created as a focus of loyalty for Protestants joining the army. On 1 July 1916 some five thousand members of this division were killed or wounded at the Somme. This sacrifice was contrasted bitterly with what was seen as a stab-in-the-back by Dublin rebels in the Easter rising.

As soon as the war ended a general election was held in December 1918 in which Sinn Féin won three out of four of the Irish seats, and the Unionists won (virtually all in Ulster) one in four. This setback to Conservatives was soon followed by a big engineering strike in Belfast, and later by the election of twelve Labour councillors in the city. Such rebellious Protestant workers and voters were denounced by Edward Carson as the friends of Fenians, Bolsheviks, and potential traitors to the loyalist cause. Throughout Ireland there was a rapid spread of militant Sinn Féin activity, spearheaded by a revived and renamed Irish Republican Army.

In response, Edward Carson and his successor as Ulster Unionist leader, James Craig, working in close liaison with the Tories and senior army officers in England, quickly resurrected the idea of dividing Ireland into two parts. There followed many months of intensive negotiation between representatives of the British government, Sinn Féin and the Ulster Unionists, culminating in the Government of Ireland Act, which was signed in London in December 1920. This act proposed that Down, Antrim, Fermanagh, Armagh, Tyrone and Derry should form a new state under the name of Northern Ireland. The crucial point about choosing six rather than the nine traditional counties of Ulster was to ensure that the selected region should have a substantial majority of Protestant voters, and thus guarantee the permanence of Unionist power. A Boundary Commission was set up to consider border rectifications, but it collapsed within a few years without making any agreed recommendations.

The official identification of the Protestant religion with one particular political party, and the public admission that administrative control could best be achieved by the manipulation of electoral boundaries along religious lines, had far-reaching consequences for all the Christian Churches in the north. Protestants were persuaded, as they had so often been in the past but this time with the full sanction of the state and legal system behind them, that their special theological doctrines could only be safeguarded under an ultra-conservative and pro-British government. Catholics were pushed further into isolation and driven in some cases to violent resistance. Under the new Stormont regime it became virtually impossible to build a community that would achieve peace and harmony. Religious apartheid proved to be as much an enemy of democracy and progress as the racial apartheid it resembled.

EPILOGUE

THE DILEMMA OF PROTESTANT DEMOCRACY
IN NORTHERN IRELAND

> There is no mainland for Ulster Protestants to go back to. Ireland is our mainland.
>
> The Reverend Robin Boyd[1]

The partition of Ireland in 1921 was, from the Unionist viewpoint, a great success. The threatening nationalists in the south were confined to twenty-six counties, and in the north the rebels were too weak to cause much difficulty. For over fifty years the new administration in Belfast weathered all vicissitudes, and fought off every attack, secure in the knowledge that they had a built-in parliamentary majority. At no time between 1921, when it was launched, and 1972 when it was summarily dismissed, was the Unionist government in danger of defeat. In public and to a large extent in private affairs it had the necessary powers to carry everything before it, and to make sure that its loyal supporters gained materially as well as psychologically from its rule. In its curious constitutional position, half in and half out of the United Kingdom, and in the way in which this enabled it to perpetuate many aspects of the old Ascendancy, it was unique in Europe. So long as Irish nationalists and democrats could be kept down, and so long as successive British governments continued to give it financial and administrative aid, there was no reason why Stormont should not survive indefinitely.

But whatever benefits may have flowed towards the loyalist sections of the population, the Stormont regime was a disaster so far as minorities and general welfare of the north were concerned. Any hope of a peaceful and progressive society being permanently created was denied by a government whose first concern was, not social justice and fair shares for all its citizens, but the preservation of its own power and privileges. The concept of democracy was abandoned in favour of gerrymandering, a narrow franchise, and a prejudiced police force. Repressive laws were introduced, which were as totalitarian in their implications as almost anywhere in the world. Catholics were not allowed to join the dominant political party solely because of their religion. Throughout the Unionist Party there was no willingness to share power or offer equal opportunities to those who were not loyalists. James Craig's speech about 'a Protestant parliament for a Protestant people' only expressed an attitude which ran through all aspects of the unionist community.

The issue of nationality was hopelessly fudged in so far as Protestants were urged to think of themselves as British and totally loyal to the Crown, but when political crises arose, as they did from time to time, then this loyalty proved as conditional as it had been during the days of the Curragh mutiny. Most Protestants when questioned about their identity, proclaimed themselves as indubitably British, but preferred not to discuss how this tied in with the fact that they lived on the island of Ireland. Some clung to the old title of Ulster-Scot, but others when pressed described their nationality as 'Ulster'. Thus Catholics, even if they wanted to, could not hope to be accepted as properly British. They had been born an inferior people and must remain that way.

The reduction of religious tensions and the ending of ancient sectarian hatreds should have been the first priority of any government which sought to create stability within the area under its control. Instead, in order to use those splitting tactics that had proved so electorally advantageous in the past, divisions between the Christian Churches were actively encouraged by the highest authorities. The Orange card continued to be played with annual zeal, and right-wing politicians were only too willing to stir up religious quarrels if it suited them. Many Protestant clergymen, who should have known better, fell back

425

on a kind of crude fundamentalism, which had the twofold purpose of impeding the spread of modernist doctrines that might undermine their authority, and also further separating them from the Papists.

In the north the Catholics were encouraged to retreat into ghettoes which were both geographical and intellectual. In the south, because its members comprised over 90 per cent of the population and because it had the sympathy of right-wing politicians, the Catholic Church was able to command a form of triumphalism, which imposed restrictions on education, and laws relating to divorce and birth control, as well as the censorship of literature. This was the 'carnival of reaction' which had been forecast by James Connolly, and also in a different way by the Reverend James B. Armour, before the war.[2] It gave conservative-minded Protestants in Northern Ireland, who might not otherwise have been particularly liberal in their moral views, the excuse to say: 'We told you so. Home Rule does mean Rome Rule.'

The long-term consequence of this divide-and-rule policy was a state in which administrative power was shared between two centres, Belfast and London, and the creation of a society which was, from its start, bitterly divided, intrinsically unstable, and prone to periodic outbreaks of rebellion and violence.

The minority of Protestants who continued to oppose the Unionist government – comprising perhaps 10 to 20 per cent of all members of the Church of Ireland and Nonconformists after partition – were placed in an extraordinarily difficult position by these divisions within their community. The more society became polarised between Protestant and Catholic (which was what the Unionists wanted) the harder it was to strengthen the middle ground. The more the voters' eyes could be diverted towards politico-religious quarrels the less chance there was of asking more serious questions about democracy and nationality.

The Dissenters' place in society had always been ambiguous, and now more than ever they were pressurised by both unionists and nationalists. On the one hand, as Protestants they could

426

hope to keep certain residual privileges left over from Ascendancy days. They might still aspire to better jobs and higher living standards than their fellow Christians. They often had a lingering affection for the monarch, and could indulge in that intellectual escapism, so characteristic of colonialism, of thinking of themselves as being both British and Irish. Although keen to prove that they were tolerant in their religious beliefs, they could not always avoid the temptation of treating Catholicism as a religion inferior to their own staunch Protestantism. The politically experienced in their ranks were sharply conscious of the danger of straying from the orthodox line, and being denounced as Taigs and Fenians. Electorally, it was safer to let sleeping sectarian dogs lie.

On the other hand, they prided themselves on being ardent democrats, and as such deplored the Government's frequent resort to religious discrimination, abuses of the voting system, and other displays of arbitrary power. Their basic liberal instincts were hostile to almost everything about the coercive regime at Stormont. Their egalitarian principles were shocked by persistent poverty and emigration, and they regarded extreme manifestations of Orangeism as a throwback to an earlier and more atavistic era. Many aspects of Sabbatarianism and Puritanism were treated with intellectual disdain, and fundamentalism in religion was criticised as non-scientific and non-scholarly. Rationalism was preferred to emotionalism in moral doctrine.

The dilemma with which the Dissenters were confronted under partition was in fact a very old one, dating back many generations. Were those Protestants who rejected the traditional Unionist domination and control of their community to regard themselves as radicals or reformers? Were they to seek root-and-branch changes in power structures, especially the relationship between Britain and Ireland, or were they to seek instead for piecemeal improvements and the gradual amelioration of admitted abuses? Should they, as seemed most logical, throw in their lot with Irish nationalists, as had the bolder Liberals in Gladstone's day, or were they to emulate the principles

427

of, say, the Liberal Unionist Joseph Chamberlain, who advocated land reform but at the same time was a dedicated imperialist? Should they imitate such rebels as Lindsay Crawford and Bulmer Hobson or should they follow the example of such Labour Unionists as Thomas Sloan and William Walker?

In the event, the majority of progressive Protestants, who by this time included fewer rural Presbyterians and more urban episcopalian workers, chose the last option. Broadly speaking, during the decades before and after the Second World War, most potential reformers decided to concentrate on issues of democracy, equality, culture and religion rather than actively take up the contentious problems of national identity and national allegiance. They were prepared to agitate about the economy or class structure or the infringement of civil rights, but reluctant to get involved in what they dismissed as 'Border politics'.

The Northern Ireland Labour Party, for example, which emerged in the 1920s as the main vehicle to express Protestant working-class discontent in Belfast, waged for nearly half a century a vigorous fight about low wages, bad housing, unemployment and inadequate social services. However, apart from brief periods when it came under local Catholic influence, it never queried the value of the link with Britain. Instead, its spokesmen constantly reiterated their loyalty to the Crown and parliament at Westminster. One of their most famous leaders, Harold Midgley, after many years describing himself a socialist, actually joined the Unionist government and became a member of the Orange Order. David Bleakley, their best-known post-war MP, always called himself a Labour Unionist. He, also, for a brief period joined a Unionist government under Brian Faulkner.

Similarly, most Protestant trade-union officials, knowing only too well how their members could be split along religious lines, tried to avoid controversial political matters altogether. For many years the northern committee of the Irish Congress of Trade Unions has actually insisted on observing a rule that they must confine themselves to bread-and-butter economic questions. The various Liberal groups that have existed since partition, though generally critical of Unionist Party policies, have always been chary of attacking the constitution. In contrast to their predecessors of Gladstone's and Asquith's day, they do not seek any modern version of Home Rule, but in its place try to get what benefits they can from the British connection. The modern Alliance Party, for example, draws its membership from both Protestants and Catholics and is largely middle class in its composition. It has invariably made it clear that, like the Northern Ireland Labour Party, it favoured the Union.

Northern intellectuals, too, though not always politically motivated or organised in a coherent group, were placed in an ambiguous position by the worsening violence and deepening polarisation of the community in which they lived. Many writers, artists and academics supported the libertarian aims of the civil rights movement, but at the same time did not necessarily come down on the side of Catholic nationalism, still less the militant IRA. Scholars were critical of the apparent illogicality or extremes of conflicting ideologies, and academics could see that to venture into the maelstrom of sectarian politics required a strong head and a stout heart. It was easier to proclaim a plague on the houses of all sides.

Poets and novelists soon realised that it was preferable to devote one's talents to private rather than public themes. The views of the poet John Hewitt well illustrate the ambivalent attitudes of such spokesmen for northern art and culture. A leading literary figure in Belfast for more than fifty years, and an outspoken radical (a term he preferred to that of liberal) in politics, Hewitt was an agnostic and a socialist, and noted for his frequent attacks on the Unionist establishment. However, the Nonconformism into which he was born did not allow much sympathy with Catholicism, and he was never a wholehearted Irish nationalist. Instead, he advocated freedom in both politics and literature. For many years he promoted a policy of regionalism which was neither pro-British nor pro-Irish, but, as he said, 'pro-Ulster'. The last lines from his poem 'The colony'[3] make it clear that it was in his native province he felt most truly at home:

for we have rights drawn from the soil and sky;
the use, the pace, the patient years of labour,
the rain against the lips, the changing light,
the heavy clay-sucked stride, have altered us;
we would be strangers in the Capitol;
this is our country also, nowhere else;
and we shall not be outcast on the world.

The more liberal-minded Protestant clergy are another group who have sought to steer a middle course between the extremes of unionism and nationalism. Horrified by the continuing shootings and bombings, and ashamed of the manner in which Christians kill Christians in their beloved province, they deliberately set out on the ecumenical path, encouraged by similar movements abroad. Consensus, reconciliation, the building of bridges and the forgetting of old quarrels – these have become popular phrases in their vocabulary. Scores of books, reports and articles have been published, and hundreds of sermons preached, all urging an end to ancient sectarian strife, and the bringing of peace between the warring sects. An Irish Council of Churches has been set up, with David Bleakley as secretary. Such names as Corrymeela, Glencree, Benburb, Tallaght and Ballymacscanlon have emerged as symbols of hoped-for Christian unity. Important landmarks in these attempts to break down inter-Church barriers were the publication in 1975 of *Conflict and Christianity* by Brian Mawhinney and Ronald Wells; in 1976 of a joint report by the Catholic Church and the Irish Council of Churches, *Violence in Ireland*; and in 1980 of *Christians in Ulster, 1968–80* by Eric Gallagher, and A. Stanley Worrall, headmaster of Methodist College, Belfast.

Individual clergymen have worked hard to build friendlier bonds between the divided communities. Following the earlier examples of his predecessors Bishops John F. MacNeice and Richard Hanson,[4] the Reverend Arthur Butler, Bishop of Down, Connor and Dromore, dissociated himself from the extremes of Orangeism. In December 1974 he took the brave step, with the Reverend William Arlow of the Church of Ireland and the Reverend Eric Gallagher of the Methodist Church, of meeting representatives of Sinn Féin at Feakle, County Clare. The Presbyterians, though increasingly moving in a conservative direction under the influence of the Paisleyites, have been represented in the ecumenical movement by the historian the Reverend John M. Barkley, and the Reverends John Morrow, Robin Boyd and David Armstrong.[5]

Barkley is in several respects the philosophical heir of Armour of Ballymoney. Orthodox in most of his religious opinions, and an admirer of many aspects of Calvinism, he has nevertheless proved to be a thorn in the side of both Church and state establishments over a period of fifty years. Though conventional in much of his theology, he was always a keen ecumenicist, opposing those Presbyterians whom he saw as too fundamentalist or 'exclusive' – a word he applies to Protestants who are unwilling to co-operate at home or abroad with fellow Christians. For many years he has been a sharp critic of Orangeism and the Paisleyites whom he saw as using religion for political ends. In his curiously entitled autobiography *Blackmouth and Dissenter*[6] he emphasises the advantages of the 'third road' – that is, standing between Protestant unionism and Catholic nationalism. However, in pursuing this preferred alternative path he apparently does not envisage going outside the boundaries of the existing six-county state.

The weakness of these 'internal solution' approaches is that, in spite of being full of good intentions and imbued with moral fervour, they leave out the crucial factor of British power in sustaining political and religious reaction in Northern Ireland. They avoid the question of how the Northern Ireland constitution had been imposed by an alliance of Ulster and British Conservatives as part of their imperial strategy, and how under the terms of this constitution the position of the Unionist Party was virtually impregnable. In particular, there is a reluctance, surprising among those who were supposed to have studied Irish history, to recognise how closely the major issues of democracy, religion and nationality are interrelated, and how futile it is to hope for improvements in one area without seeking reforms in the others.

Only on a few occasions after partition was imposed – as during the unemployment struggles of 1932,[7] and the civil rights campaign of the 1960s[8] – has Protestant democracy extended its claims beyond matters of social structure and civil liberty to include a broad challenge to the very nature of the state and constitution. Only a few northern radicals such as William McMullen (Labour) in the 1920s, Denis Ireland (Liberal) in the 1930s, and Jack Beattie (Labour) and Betty Sinclair (Communist) during the period around the Second World War, could claim that they stood for both social reform and the ending of partition. Since then a few individuals and groups have struggled, usually against intimidating odds, to develop a policy which would be simultaneously democratic and egalitarian, both anti-sectarian and anti-militarist, and at the same time in favour of a united Ireland.

Protestant democracy in Ulster has had a long and often honourable record. During the dark days of the penal laws the New Lights shone out as beacons of intellectual and moral clarity. In the 1790s the democrats sought to bring together the different religious denominations, and stood for the right of the Irish people as a whole to be free from an oppressive Ascendancy and alien rule. After the Act of Union the Presbyterians continued in the van of progress, striving to extend the restricted electoral franchise, defending the Ulster custom, and seeking to abolish the iniquitous tithe system. When the horrors of the famine were at their worst, the leaders of Young Ireland offered a vision of a country that would no longer go hungry or be in chains. The poet Samuel Ferguson wrote of a Gaelic language and culture that had never perished. Towards the end of the nineteenth century progressive Protestants were in the forefront of the struggle for land reform. The Reverend James B. Armour preached a Presbyterianism that was tolerant and humane. In the early twentieth century it was again Protestant democracy that was at the heart of the Labour and trade-union movement, and brought new blood into the Gaelic League and the Irish Volunteers. Since partition, and making allowances for the political difficulties with which it has had to grapple, the best of Ulster Protestantism has spoken up for greater equality in social and economic life, for an end to coercive laws, and reconciliation between Protestants and Catholics.

As progressive Protestants enter the last decade of the twentieth century, they can look back with pride on what was finest in their history, especially those ideas which were first advanced two centuries ago, and still have relevance today – the rights of the people, the unity of Protestant, Catholic and Dissenter, and the common name of Irishman.

NOTES

INTRODUCTION

1 P.J.O. McCann, 'The Protestant Home Rule Movement, 1886–1895' (unpublished MA thesis, University College Dublin, 1972)

2 John Patrick McLoughlin, 'Gladstone, Irish Nationalism and the Home Rule Question, 1882–1893, with particular reference to the Ulster problem' (unpublished Ph.D. thesis, Trinity College Dublin, 1984)

3 Terence Brown, *The Whole Protestant Community: The Making of a Historical Myth* (Derry, 1985). In this Field Day pamphlet Terence Brown refers to the 'dominant Unionist historical framework, that conditions Protestant thinking. He suggests that the democratic aspects of Ulster's history are in urgent need of reappraisal, with the aim of reintroducing Protestants to their many-sided, and often surprisingly liberal, heritage. However, he thinks that this is not likely to be achieved until British power is finally removed from Ireland.

4 Peter Brooke, *Ulster Presbyterianism: The Historical Perspective, 1610–1970* (Dublin, 1987) contains some useful material about the various theological issues that divided Presbyterians during the seventeenth, eighteenth, and early nineteenth centuries, but (apart from a few pages devoted to the Reverend Ian Paisley tacked on at the end) says little about dissent in Ulster during the last one hundred years. The influence of British imperialism and the growth of the Orange movement as an integral part of unionism are scarcely mentioned, and there is a neglect of the wider economic and social forces that have shaped Protestantism in Ireland.

5 Marianne Elliott's long and thoroughly researched *Partners in Revolution: The United Irishmen and France* (London, 1982) concentrates on the relationship between the United Irishmen and France. It provides much valuable material about the role of the 1790s rebels in Ulster but this is incidental to the main theme. Elliott's *Wolfe Tone: Prophet of Irish Independence* (London, 1989) has three chapters on Belfast, but these comprise only about one-tenth of her wider study of Tone. She has this comment to make (p. 147) about the connection between religion and class: 'Sectarian identity is such a part of modern Irish history that it is all too easy to see Catholics and Protestants as mutually hostile homogeneous groupings. Religion was indeed fundamental to the eighteenth century throughout Europe, but not always in a denominationally stratified form. Class interests cut across religious divides.'

6 A compilation of letters, speeches, etc., by the Reverend J.B. Armour was published by J.R.B. McMinn under the title *Against the Tide* (Belfast, 1985). The biographical details are brief, and the author seems generally hostile to the personality and opinions of Armour.

He believes that Armour's influence on Ulster liberalism has been exaggerated.

7 'A very great part of the mischiefs that vex the world arise from words. People soon forget the meaning, but the impression and the passion remain. The word Protestant is the charm that locks up in the dungeon of servitude three millions of our people [Catholics]. It is not amiss to consider this spell of potency, this abracadabra, that is hung around the necks of the unhappy, not to heal, but to communicate disease. We sometimes hear of a Protestant *religion*, frequently of a Protestant *interest*. We hear of the latter the most frequently because it has a positive meaning. The other has none. We hear of it the most frequently because it has a word in the phrase, which, well or ill understood, has animated to persecution or oppression, at all times infinitely more than all the dogmas in dispute between religious factions. These are indeed well formed to perplex and torment the intellect; but not half so well calculated to inflame the passions and animosities of men.' Edmund Burke, writing to his son Richard, c. 1795. *The Works of Edmund Burke*, vol. VI (London, 1856), p. 69.

8 *Report of the New Ireland Forum* (Dublin, 1984)

9 Quoted in R.R. Madden, *Antrim and Down in '98* (n.d.), p. 89

PROLOGUE

1 'Song of the Volunteers of 1782' by Thomas Davis, *Essays and Poems with a Centenary Memoir, 1845–1945* (Dublin, 1945)

2 Historians generally agree that Ulster was the most Gaelic of all Irish provinces at the end of the reign of Elizabeth I. For a recent comment *see*, for example, R.F. Foster, *Modern Ireland 1600–1972* (London, 1988). A.T.Q. Stewart, *The Narrow Ground: Aspects of Ulster, 1609–1969* (London, 1977), however, suggests that this claim has been exaggerated by Irish nationalists, presumably for political reasons. Stewart devotes three chapters to describing how various invaders, Celts, Vikings, Norman-English and Scots came to the province over many centuries, with the result that the population there became very mixed. It was inaccurate, therefore, to speak of the people who lived in Ulster before 1600 as though they belonged to a pure 'race' or ethnic group. Having argued this point at some length, the author then goes on to admit that virtually all these outsiders had been assimilated into the dominant Gaelic population, culture and language.

3 The Savages of the Ards peninsula were often used as examples of an Old English family which had survived as landowners until Elizabethan times. However, they too became so assimilated into the local native community by the mid-sixteenth century that they were mocked as 'Irish chieftains'.

4 The variety of words used to describe these settlements – conquest, plantation, forfeiture, attainder, escheatment, confiscation, clearance – tells us as clearly as any description of what actually happened when the land of Ulster was forcibly transferred from one group to another during the seventeenth and early eighteenth centuries.

5 An undertaker was required to plant

his land with English or Scottish tenants; a servitor could choose either English, Scottish or native Irish tenants. In both cases these requirements were often ignored, as the new landlords found it convenient to retain more Irish either as tenants or labourers.

6 Wolfe Tone, writing in Paris in 1796–7, carefully analysed the threefold division of Irish society in the eighteenth century. Theobald Wolfe Tone, *Life of Theobald Wolfe Tone, edited by his son William Theobald Wolfe Tone*, vol. I (Washington, 1826), p. 44.

7 The origin of the word 'Ascendancy' as applied to the Protestant upper classes in Ireland is not known, but its meaning is clear enough. In 1792 Dublin Corporation, which was then an exclusively Protestant body, defined this supremacy as follows: 'A Protestant king of Ireland, a Protestant parliament, a Protestant hierarchy, Protestant electors and government, the benches of justice, the army and the revenue, through all their branches and details, Protestant, and this system supported by a connection with the Protestant realm of England', quoted by W.E.H. Lecky, *History of Ireland in the Eighteenth Century*, vol. III (London, 1892 ed.), p. 64.

8 The Ulster custom, whereby a tenant farmer who was giving up his lease could sell the capital value of that lease to an incoming tenant, gave some protection against eviction in the northern counties (*see* chapter 11).

9 Peter Brooke, *Ulster Presbyterianism: The Historical Perspective, 1610–1970* (Dublin, 1987), p. 40

10 In June 1642 the first formal presbytery was set up in Carrickfergus to serve the needs of Scottish soldiers who had been brought over to crush the rebellion of the previous year. The new ministers took charge of 'the religious life of the whole area controlled by the army', writes Peter Brooke, *Ulster Presbyterianism: The Historical Perspective, 1610–1970* (Dublin, 1987), p. 30.

11 The Arians did not fully subscribe to the Westminster Confession of Faith of 1643, which was the official doctrine of English Presbyterianism. This Confession held, among other things, that 'some men and angels were predestinated unto eternal life, and others were foreordained to everlasting death'.

12 Quoted in Peter Brooke, *Ulster Presbyterianism: The Historical Perspective, 1610–1970* (Dublin, 1987), p. 82

13 John Abernethy, *Persecution Contrary to Christianity* (Dublin, 1735). The Reverend John Toland (1670–1722) was another well-known Ulster clergyman who challenged some of the fundamental truths of Christianity at the end of the seventeenth century. Born in Derry of Catholic parents, he converted to Protestantism and was educated at universities in Scotland, England and Holland. His *Christianity Not Mysterious*, published in 1696, caused great offence to the establishment, and was condemned by the Irish parliament. In England he was threatened with prosecution, and attacked as a free thinker and deist. Author of several books on religion, philosophy and biography, he was later acclaimed in Holland and Prussia as a distinguished scholar and historian.

14 The overall balance of the three

major religious groups (Catholics – about half; Presbyterians – about one-third; episcopalians – about one-sixth) seems to have remained, apart from some minor fluctuations, fairly stable in the nine counties of Ulster from about 1750 to the 1911 census. The collection of accurate statistics about religious affiliations in Ireland did not begin, however, until the 1861 census.

15 Lecky said that English rule in Ireland was like 'a spear point embedded in a living body, it inflamed all around it and deranged every function'. W.E.H. Lecky, *History of Ireland in the Eighteenth Century*, vol. I (London, 1892 ed.), p. 3.

16 Woodkerne was the name given to those Irish who refused to submit to English rule, and took to the woods and wild country as outlaws. Shakespeare refers derogatively to 'skipping kernes'. Rapparees took their name from a Gaelic word meaning pike. After William of Orange's victory at the Battle of the Boyne it was a word used to describe a bandit or robber.

17 The Whiteboys, who took their name from the rural marauders' custom of wearing a white shirt over their clothes at night, had different names in various parts of Ireland – Ribbonmen or Ribandmen, Captain Moonlight, Terry Alts, Levellers, Right-men, Defenders, Whitefeet, Lady Clares, Blackfeet, Peep O'Day Boys, etc. The Oakboys wore sprigs of oak in their hats; the Steelboys were said to have had hearts of steel. *See* Desmond Williams (ed.), *Secret Societies in Ireland* (Dublin, 1973).

18 Quoted in R.J. Dickson, *Ulster Emigration to Colonial America, 1718–1775* (London, 1966), p. 69. The traveller Arthur Young, after his long visit to Ireland in the 1770s, had no doubt what caused the unrest in Ulster: 'The Hearts of Steel last 3 years; began in 1770 against rent and tythes and from that went to all kinds of grievances. It was in reality owing to the impudent levelling spirit of the Dissenters.' Arthur Young, *A Tour in Ireland, 1776–1779*, vol. I (Shannon, 1970 ed.).

19 The historian J.A. Froude, no friend of Irish nationalism, saw the damage which landlords like the Donegalls did to the British cause: 'Sir Arthur Chichester has been rewarded for services by vast estates in the county Antrim, and now his successor Lord Donegall already by the growth of Belfast, by the fruit of other men's labours, while he was sitting still, enormously rich, found his income unequal to his enormous expenditure.' Quoted in F.J. Bigger, *The Ulster Land War of 1770* (Belfast, 1910), p. 54.

20 Bigger's comments on Donegall were equally sharp: 'He was and always had been an absentee. He died without ever seeing his Antrim estates. He lived in luxury and riot in foreign lands.' F.J. Bigger, *The Ulster Land War of 1770* (Belfast, 1910), p. 24.

21 There is a substantial body of literature about this phase of Irish history, including several books which attempt to pick out the Scots Irish (as against the Catholic Irish) as a particularly valuable element in American society. These were invariably written from a Protestant standpoint. A recent example of this 'chosen people' theme, which is characteristic of these books, is Rory Fitzpatrick's *God's Frontiersmen: The Scots Irish Epic* (London, 1989). Two

438

useful and more balanced histories are R.J. Dickson, *Ulster Emigration to Colonial America, 1718–1775* (London, 1966), and E.R.R. Green (ed.), *Essays in Scotch-Irish History* (London, 1969).

Not all the emigrants were poor – some had money to pay for the journey and also capital to set up in America. Arthur Young, a contemporary observer, said that most emigrants were 'idle and dissolute fellows', but he was a hostile witness, very critical of radical-minded Presbyterians, whether they stayed at home or went abroad. Arthur Young, *A Tour in Ireland, 1776–1779* (Shannon, 1970 ed.).

22 Quoted in F.J. Bigger, *The Ulster Land War of 1770* (Belfast, 1910), p. 111. Bigger went on to say: 'It was the Ulster emigrants, many of them hearts of steel, who supplied Washington with his best troops . . . The whole truth is that the greater part of the revolutionary army was Irish or of Irish descent, all smarting under the bitter wrongs their people had suffered under English rule in Ireland . . . the wicked cruelty of one man, Donegall, did more than anything else to drive the English government out of America', p. 113.

23 Luke Gardiner, *The Parliamentary Register*, vol. III (Dublin, 1784)

CHAPTER 1

1 Quoted in Henry Joy, *Belfast Politics* (Belfast, 1794), pp. 104–5

2 R.B. McDowell, *Ireland in the Age of Imperialism and Revolution, 1760–1801* (London, 1979), p. 120

3 J.L. McCracken, 'The political structure, 1714–60' in T.W. Moody and W.E. Vaughan (eds), *A New History of Ireland, vol. IV, 1691–1800* (London, 1986), p. 77

4 These figures are provided in the *Memoirs of the Life and Times of the Rt. Hon. Henry Grattan, by his son Henry Grattan, M.P.*, vol. III (London, 1839–41), Appendix, but are probably only rough approximations. More accurate figures about electoral rolls did not become available until much later. Wolfe Tone estimated the number of voters *c.* 1790 at about 60,000 in the whole of Ireland. The forty-shilling freeholders were adult males with land worth more than £2 a year.

5 Quoted in Sean Cronin and Richard Roche, *Freedom the Wolfe Tone Way* (Tralee, 1973), p. 120

6 This phrase was used when a large convention of Volunteers met in Dublin in November 1783 and called for the reform of the electoral system.

7 *See Memoirs of the Life and Times of the Rt. Hon. Henry Grattan . . .*, vol. III (London, 1839–41), Appendix

8 Samuel Watson, *The Gentlemen's and Citizen's Almanack* (Dublin, 1786)

9 W.E.H. Lecky, *History of Ireland in the Eighteenth Century*, vol. II (London, 1892 ed.), p. 348

10 Lecky was in no doubt as to where the real power lay between London and Dublin. The Irish House of Commons was, in his view, 'a dependent and subordinate body holding a precarious existence'. W.E.H. Lecky, *History of Ireland in the Eighteenth Century*, vol. II (London, 1892 ed.), p. 348.

11 The authority of the viceroy varied from time to time, but in general he was expected to carry out the wishes of the Government in London. His role was both political and ceremonial. His chief secretary and under-secretary had wide executive powers in implementing legislation.

12 *See* P.R. Hennessy, *Burke, Paine and the Rights of Man* (The Hague, 1963)

13 *See* E.P. Thompson, *The Making of the English Working Class* (London, 1963) for a discussion of the semantic problems confronted by writers and politicians when trying to analyse such an intangible concept as the British constitution. Thompson suggests that Whigs and Tories were invariably vague and imprecise when referring to the settlement of 1689. Words such as 'freedom' and 'civil rights' generally covered up the gross abuse of political power. There was a huge gap between what he called 'the rhetoric of liberty', and the realities of concentrated property ownership, a narrowly limited franchise, and the privileges of the aristocracy and the monarchy. The word 'dissent' also needed careful scrutiny because there were so many conflicting ideologies among the various Nonconformist sects.

14 *The Works of Edmund Burke*, vol. III (London, 1856), p. 337

15 It has been estimated that the number of Volunteers in the four provinces in 1782 was as follows: Ulster, 34,000; Leinster, 22,000; Munster, 18,000; and Connacht, 14,000. Peter Smyth, 'Our cloud-cap't grenadiers', *Irish Sword*, vol. XIII (1978–9).

16 During the sixth year of the reign of George I legislation was passed at Westminster asserting 'the Dependency of the Kingdom of Ireland upon the Crown of Great Britain'.

17 Quoted in *Memoirs of the Life and Times of the Rt. Hon. Henry Grattan . . .*, vol. III (London, 1839–41), p. 228

18 Quoted in Patrick Rogers, *The Irish Volunteers and Catholic Emancipation, 1778–1793* (London, 1934), p. 165

19 William Todd Jones, *A Letter to the Societies of the United Irishmen of the Town of Belfast* (Dublin, 1792). Todd Jones was given no credit for his moderation, and was pilloried (unfairly, as it turned out) by the Orange historian Sir Richard Musgrave, who alleged he had been an active rebel in 1798. The two men fought a duel over this charge. Todd Jones was arrested in 1803, supposedly for sympathising with Emmet and Russell, and imprisoned in Cork jail for two years. *See* the case of William Todd Jones, *A Prisoner in the County Gaol of Cork upon a Charge of High Treason* (Dublin, 1803).

20 D.A. Chart (ed.), *The Drennan Letters, 1776–1819* (Belfast, 1931)

21 William Drennan, *A Letter to the Rt. Hon. William Pitt* (Dublin, 1799), p. 22

22 William Drennan, *A Philosophical Essay on the Moral and Political State of Ireland* (London, 1797), p. 55

23 William Drennan, *Letters by Orellana or an Irish Helot* (Dublin, 1785), p. 8

24 William Drennan, *Letter to the Rt. Hon. William Pitt* (Dublin, 1799), p. 38

25 William Drennan, *Letters by Orellana or an Irish Helot* (Dublin, 1785), p. 8

26 *Ibid.*, p. 19

27 *Ibid.*, p. 9

28 W.D. Bailie, *William Steel Dickson* (Belfast, 1976) contains a short but useful summary of Dickson's life. The autobiography *A Narrative of the Confinement and Exile of William Steel Dickson* (Dublin, 1812), though historically interesting, conceals more than it reveals about this remarkable man. The copy in the British Museum library is kept in the North Library, which is usually associated with pornographic rather than political literature. On the flyleaf, handwritten in ink, is the

statement that this is 'A prohibited book containing some Curious Particulars of Irish History'. There is certainly nothing pornographic in it. Perhaps it was put there in the special section because it contains so many personal reminiscences of the youth and middle years of Lord Castlereagh.

29 Hamilton Rowan, *A Brief Investigation of the Suffering of John, Ann and Mary Neal* (Dublin, 1788)

30 *See Autobiography of Archibald Hamilton Rowan*, ed. W.H. Drummond (Dublin, 1840), and Harold Nicolson, *The Desire to Please* (London, 1943)

31 The words 'Britain' and 'British' began to be used more widely after the Union between England and Scotland in 1707, but it was still common for Protestants in Ireland to claim that they were 'English' or 'Scottish'. The popularity of 'British' increased as the empire expanded.

32 The nature of the 1782 Patriot Parliament and the concept of colonial nationalism are more fully discussed in C. Desmond Greaves, *Wolfe Tone and the Irish Nation* (London, 1963), Sean Cronin and Richard Roche, *Freedom the Wolfe Tone Way* (Tralee, 1973), T.A. Jackson, *Ireland Her Own* (London, 1946), and Rosamond Jacob, *The Rise of the United Irishmen, 1791–1794* (London, 1937).

CHAPTER 2

1 William Drennan, *Seventh Letter of Orellana*, quoted in John Lawless (ed.), *Belfast Politics Enlarged* (Belfast, 1818)

2 R.R. Madden, *The United Irishmen: Their Lives and Times*, third series, vol. II (Dublin, 1846), p. 279

3 Theobald Wolfe Tone, *Life of Theobald Wolfe Tone . . .*, vol. II (Washington, 1826), p. 223

4 Quoted in John Lawless (ed.), *Belfast Politics Enlarged* (Belfast, 1818)

5 'A Northern Whig', *An Argument on Behalf of the Catholics of Ireland* (Dublin, 1791)

6 Frank McDermot wrote that 'the success of the pamphlet was immediate and overwhelming . . . Although addressed particularly to the Protestants, the Catholics were delighted with it, and vied with the Dissenters in reprinting and distributing it in thousands; it even made its way across the Irish Sea and Dr. Priestley of Birmingham is found asking for a half a dozen copies. It contributed appreciably towards increasing the influence of the more democratic leaders against their aristocracy.' Frank McDermot, *Tone and His Times* (Dublin, 1980 ed.), p. 67.

7 Thomas Paine, *Rights of Man* (Dublin, 1791 and 1792)

8 Wolfe Tone, who had a nickname for most of his friends, called Belfast 'Blefescu'. He took the name from Swift's *Gulliver's Travels*. *See* Theobald Wolfe Tone, *Life of Theobald Wolfe Tone . . .*, vol. I (Washington, 1826), p. 141; *see also* R.B. McDowell, *Ireland in the Age of Imperialism and Revolution, 1760–1801* (London, 1979), pp. 352–3.

Tone, who met Paine in Paris in March 1797, described his fellow rebel as 'vain beyond all belief'. He then went on to say 'but he has reason to be vain, and for my part I forgive him. He has done wonders for the cause of liberty both in America and Europe.' However, Tone, who knew how important it was in Ireland not to offend religious convictions unnecessarily, regarded the publication of Paine's *The Age of Reason* as inopportune, and described some sections of the book as 'damned trash'. *See* P.R. Hennessy, *Burke, Paine and the Rights of Man* (The Hague, 1963).

9 *Northern Star*, 8 September 1794

10 Dr Richard Price's sermon in the autumn of 1789, which praised the recent storming of the Bastille in Paris as a great event in the history of human liberty, inspired Edmund Burke's famous *Reflections on the Revolution in France*. To democratic observers in Ireland it seemed ironical that Dr Price's sermon was given to commemorate the centenary of the constitutional reforms inaugurated by William of Orange's victory.

11 A leading member of the London Corresponding Society at this time was John Binns, a young merchant from Dublin. Binns was at the centre of revolutionary events in London for some years. He was arrested with Arthur O'Connor and Father James Coigley in 1798, but acquitted at the subsequent trial. He then escaped to America.

12 *See* Rosamond Jacob, *The Rise of the United Irishmen, 1791–1794* (London, 1937), for a fuller account of this visit to Belfast by Wolfe Tone and Thomas Russell. Tone unfortunately does not reveal in his diary precisely how the original words of the United Irish manifesto were modified as a result of these discussions.

See Marianne Elliott, *Wolfe Tone: Prophet of Irish Independence* (London, 1989), p. 140. 'Tone was enraptured by Belfast and the new friends he had met there. The Belfast Dissenters came to represent his ideal of middle-class virtue, and their anti-aristocratic and anti-English views

deeply influenced his own.' Elliott says that some years later Tone wrote to Russell that he regarded Belfast as 'his adopted home'.

13 A detailed history of the McCracken family is given in Mary McNeill, *The Life and Times of Mary Ann McCracken, 1770–1866* (Belfast, 1988).

14 Rosamond Jacob, *The Rise of the United Irishmen, 1791–1794* (London, 1937), p. 66

15 All of them were described as 'men of respectability' and some of them were in affluent circumstances, according to Madden. Six shareholders were founder members of the United Irishmen. R.R. Madden, *The United Irishmen: Their Lives and Times*, vol. II (London, 1842), p. 51.

16 'From first to last, its columns were chiefly devoted to details relating to the French Revolution and the actors in it, and so intent did its managers seem in filling their columns with the proceedings of the French Assembly and Jacobin and other democratic clubs, that they seldom inserted leading articles of their own or any original matter, except occasional letters, or some very indifferent verses . . .' R.R. Madden, *The United Irishmen: Their Lives and Times*, vol. II (London, 1842), p. 54. Rosamond Jacob, otherwise a sympathetic commentator on the United Irishmen, was also critical of the failure, as she saw it, of Neilson to comprehend the native Irish, as distinct from the imported British, culture. Rosamond Jacob, *The Rise of the United Irishmen, 1791–1794* (London, 1937), pp. 186–7.

17 The Phrygian capa became symbol of liberty during the French Revolution.

18 Charlotte Brooke, *Reliques of Irish Poetry* (Dublin, 1789)

19 In 1795 the *Northern Star*, encouraged
    it is said by Thomas Russell and the
    Irish-speaking Patrick Lynch,
    published *Bolg An Tsolair*, a 120-page
    miscellany of poetry, prayers,
    vocabulary and translations. This
    was a remarkable journal for several
    reasons: it was the first magazine in
    Gaelic ever published in Ireland, and
    it was printed by owners of a journal
    normally written in English – all this
    in the heart of Presbyterian Belfast.
    The purpose of the magazine was to
    dispel the ignorance of those who
    believed that Irish was 'a harsh and
    barbarous jargon', and
    simultaneously to diffuse 'the
    beauties of this ancient and once-
    admired language'. *See* Pádraig Ó
    Snódaigh, *Hidden Ulster* (Dublin,
    1977), p. 18.

20 Theobald Wolfe Tone, *Life of Theobald
    Wolfe Tone . . .*, vol. I (Washington,
    1826), p. 78

21 *Ibid.*

22 *The Works of Edmund Burke*, vol. III
    (London, 1856), p. 337

23 Quoted in T.W. Moody and W.E.
    Vaughan (eds), *A New History of
    Ireland, vol. IV 1691–1800* (London,
    1986), p. 320

CHAPTER 3

1   D.A. Chart (ed.), *The Drennan Letters,
    1776–1819* (Belfast, 1931), p. 251

2   McDowell agrees with the argument
    that in the early 1790s the British
    government had to choose between
    trying to conciliate the Catholics
    (and so, antagonising the
    Protestants) or vice versa. He
    suggests that the short career of the
    new viceroy Fitzwilliam was due to
    the fact that he hoped he could avoid
    making this hard choice and get
    round the problem by forming an
    alliance of the upper classes from all
    religious groups. 'We must unite all
    the higher orders in a common
    cause,' said Fitzwilliam in February
    1795. R.B. McDowell, *Ireland in the
    Age of Imperialism and Revolution,
    1760–1801* (London, 1979), p. 452.
    Fitzwilliam failed to achieve his
    objectives, and that is why he
    resigned so swiftly from his position
    as viceroy.

3   Rosamond Jacob, *The Rise of the
    United Irishmen, 1791–1794* (London,
    1937)

4   For Downshire's letter *see* Irish State
    Paper Office, carton 620/625, no. 45,
    and for Londonderry *see* Irish State
    Paper Office, carton 620/628, no. 5

5   Robert Kee, *The Green Flag* (London,
    1972), p. 59

6   *See* 'A Barrister', *A Faithful Report of
    the Trial of the Proprietors of the
    Northern Star* (Belfast, 1794)

7   *Northern Star*, 26 March 1795

8   The attorney-general Arthur Wolfe
    used this phrase when prosecuting
    the *Northern Star*. In those days the
    word 'democrat' was a term of
    abuse.

9   The phrase 'home rule' was not used
    until the nineteenth century, but the
    idea of some sort of semi-
    independent parliament in Dublin,
    while also accepting the British
    monarch as king of Ireland, had been
    seriously proposed since the 1780s.

10 The United Irishmen, like the
    Jacobins in France, were then not
    advanced enough to advocate votes
    for women. Mary Wollstonecraft had
    her book *A Vindication of the Rights of
    Woman* favourably reviewed in the
    Northern Star on 27 October 1792.

11 Quoted in Rosamond Jacob, *The Rise
    of the United Irishmen, 1791–1794*
    (London, 1937)

12 William James Macneven, *Pieces of
    Irish History* (New York, 1807)

13 *See* Marianne Elliott, *Partners in Revolution: The United Irishmen and France* (London, 1982)

14 Quoted in R.R. Madden, *The United Irishmen: Their Lives and Times*, third series, vol. I (Dublin, 1846), pp. 238–9

15 William James Macneven, *Pieces of Irish History* (New York, 1807), p. 179

16 R.F. Foster in his *Modern Ireland, 1600–1972* (London, 1988) disputes the case that Tone was here referring to the impoverished masses in Ireland. He suggests that the phrase 'men of no property' applied to the city middle classes. But this seems unlikely. During 1792–5 Tone had met numerous Defenders and was in no doubt about their revolutionary fervour. As events turned out, it was the real 'men of no property' who turned out in their thousands in 1798.

17 Bartholomew Teeling returned from France with Humbert in September 1798, fought at the Battle of Ballinamuck, was captured, and in spite of Humbert's plea that he was an officer in the French army and should be treated as a prisoner of war, was sentenced to death as a traitor. He was hanged at Arbour Hill in Dublin along with Wolfe Tone's younger brother, Matthew. Charles Teeling fought at the Battle of Antrim alongside McCracken, but escaped and eventually returned to his native Antrim. In 1828 he published his *History of the Irish Rebellion of 1798*. Coigley was taken prisoner along with Arthur O'Connor in February 1798 while on his way to France, charged with treason, and hanged at Maidstone in Kent. MacMahon, after many adventures, escaped to France, and joined Napoleon's army. For Hamilton's later career *see* chapter 6. McCabe, who was also involved in the 1803 rebellion, escaped to France. The fate of Orr and Lowry is not recorded. Turner betrayed his comrades and agreed to become a government agent in 1797. The information he gave about the inner workings of the United Irish command proved invaluable to the authorities.

18 R.R. Madden, *The United Irishmen: Their Lives and Times*, third series, vol. I (Dublin, 1846), p. 218

19 Tone had described these economic and political differences between Protestants, Dissenters and Catholics in great detail in a memorandum which he had prepared for the French government in 1794 (Theobald Wolfe Tone, *Life of Theobald Wolfe Tone . . .*, vol. I [Washington, 1826], p. 277), but it is unlikely that this could have been known to Hope.

20 In his memoirs Hope wrote bitterly of the betrayal (obviously he was referring to Robert Simms, though he does not name him) by those 'Antrim colonels', who when the call came to rise in May 1798, turned, as he said, 'informer and coward'. McCracken also had little faith in the revolutionary spirit of the privileged classes. When he was on the run after defeat at the Battle of Antrim, he wrote to his sister Mary Ann: 'These are times that try men's souls. You will no doubt hear a number of stories respecting the situation of this country: its present unfortunate state is entirely due to treachery. The rich always betray the poor.' Quoted in R.R. Madden, *The United Irishmen: Their Lives and Times*, second series, vol. II (London, 1842), p. 483.

21 Quoted in R.R. Madden, *The United Irishmen: Their Lives and Times*, third series, vol. I (Dublin, 1846), p. 231

22 *Ibid.*, pp. 235–6
23 In an appendix to R.R. Madden, *The United Irishmen: Their Lives and Times,* first series, vol. II (Dublin, 1846), p. 342, there is a list of 1798 leaders divided according to religion. There were 38 members of the Church of Ireland, 34 Presbyterians (almost all from Ulster) and 32 Catholics (almost all from the south). He also records separately the names of the clergy involved, including 12 Presbyterian ministers or licentiates (of whom 3 were executed) and 13 Catholic priests (of whom 6 were executed). His list of Presbyterian ministers is incomplete and should have included another score or so of names. It is possible to compile a fuller list on the basis of adding the names provided by Madden to those suggested by Richard Musgrave, *Memoirs of the Different Rebellions in Ireland* (Dublin, 1802) and Charles Dickson, *Revolt in the North: Antrim and Down in 1798* (Dublin, 1960), and also those named in A.T.Q. Stewart, 'The transformation of Belfast radicalism in Northern Ireland' (unpublished MA thesis, Queen's University Belfast, 1956).

    The Irish State Paper Office in Dublin Castle holds in its archives relevant reports, letters, documents and courts martial accounts. In total, between 30 and 40 names of Presbyterian clergy are mentioned as being known or suspected of being involved in subversive activities in the late 1790s. The Presbyterian Historical Society of Ireland makes the point that there is no definitive list of such rebels, but that the society holds much information about particular individuals. The society also makes the point that a distinction should be made between ministers who have been ordained and licentiates who were only serving their apprenticeships. The former may be properly designated as 'reverend', while the latter should be called 'Mr'.

24 William Steel Dickson, *Three Sermons on the Subject of Scripture Politics* (Belfast, 1793). The first of these sermons had been preached to the general synod in June 1781, and Dickson said he did not wish to alter a word of it. The second was at Portaferry on Christmas 1792, and the third also at Portaferry in January 1793.
25 Letter dated 31 December 1796, quoted in Charles Dickson, *Revolt in the North: Antrim and Down in 1798* (Dublin, 1960), p. 1852
26 Steel Dickson, who knew the Londonderry family personally, and had befriended the young and then liberal Robert Stewart as a boy, coined another damning phrase when he described Cleland as 'master of the croppy hounds'.
27 [James Porter], *Billy Bluff and Squire Firebrand in Six Letters which appeared in the Northern Star,* 1796 (Belfast, 1868 ed.)
28 James Porter, *Wind and Weather: A Sermon on the Late Providential Storm which Dispersed the French Fleet in Bantry Bay Preached to the Congregation of Grey-Abbey on Thursday, 16th February* (Belfast, 1797)
29 Theobald Wolfe Tone, *Life of Theobald Wolfe Tone . . .,* vol. I (Washington, 1826), p. 128

CHAPTER 4

1 Quoted in W.E.H. Lecky, *History of Ireland in the Eighteenth Century,* vol. IV (London, 1892 ed.), p. 50
2 R.M. Sibbett, *Orangeism in Ireland and*

Throughout the Empire, vol. I (London, *c.* 1937), p. 54. This is an interesting book as it is full of information about the history of the Orange Order, and is unabashed in its defence of all these Tory policies.

3 W.E.H. Lecky, *History of Ireland in the Eighteenth Century*, vol. IV (London, 1892 ed.), pp. 47–8. Lecky then went on to point to 'the growing importance of the Orange movement, and the alliance which was gradually forming between it and the Government' during 1796–8.

4 Lord Blayney was a prominent landlord, Orangeman and yeomanry officer in County Monaghan. W.E.H. Lecky quotes him as informing the Government in July 1797: 'Be assured, the yeomanry of the North are your sheet-anchor.'

5 Hereward Senior, *Orangeism in Ireland and Britain, 1795–1834* (London, 1966), p. 229. R.B. McDowell, *Ireland in the Age of Imperialism and Revolution, 1760–1801* (London, 1979), p. 559, describes the yeomen as the 'conservative party in arms'.

6 Quoted in W.E.H. Lecky, *History of Ireland in the Eighteenth Century*, vol. III (London, 1892 ed.), p. 461

7 Hereward Senior, *Orangeism in Ireland and Britain, 1795–1836* (London, 1966), pp. 185–6

8 Quoted in W.E.H. Lecky, *History of Ireland in the Eighteenth Century*, vol. IV (London, 1892 ed.), pp. 52–3

9 W.E.H. Lecky, *A History of Ireland in the Eighteenth Century*, vol. IV (London, 1892 ed.), reprints some revealing letters which passed between Pelham, Cooke, Knox and Lake in 1797.

10 Marianne Elliott, *Partners in Revolution: The United Irishmen and France* (London, 1982), p. 126

11 R.B. McDowell, *Ireland in the Age of Imperialism and Revolution, 1760–1801* (London, 1979), pp. 572–3

12 Thomas Russell was actually arrested (along with Samuel Neilson) in the Linen Hall Library, where some years previously he had been temporarily employed as a librarian. *See* John Gray, 'Millennial vision – Thomas Russell re-assessed', *Linen Hall Review* (spring, 1989).

13 C.H. Teeling, *History of the Irish Rebellion of 1798* (Shannon, 1972 ed.)

14 *See* R.R. Madden, *The United Irishmen: Their Lives and Times*, second series, vol. I (Dublin, 1846)

15 Lecky suggests that martial law forced the rebellion into 'premature explosion, and also made it comparatively easy to deal with'. W.E.H. Lecky, *History of Ireland in the Eighteenth Century*, vol. IV (London, 1892 ed.), p. 290.

16 'Croppy' was the term of contempt levelled during this period against any rebel who opposed the Government. It arose from the custom developed by some United Irishmen and Defenders of cutting their hair short in imitation of the Jacobins. It was ironical that Cromwell's soldiers had been similarly derided as 'roundheads'. 'The Croppy boy', a ballad about a young insurgent who was hanged in 1798, later became a favourite republican song.

17 Quoted in W.E.H. Lecky, *History of Ireland in the Eighteenth Century*, vol. IV (London, 1892 ed.), p. 44

18 *Ibid.*, p. 203

19 Quoted in Francis Joseph Bigger, *William Orr* (Dublin, 1906), p. 4

20 The full text of this poem is in William Drennan, *Fugitive Pieces in Verse and Prose* (Belfast, 1815).

21 The Irish State Paper Office in

Dublin Castle contains a mass of material, memoranda, government documents, official letters, requests for payment, anonymous and sometimes misspelt writings on scraps of paper, police 'wanted' notices, copies of seditious pamphlets, etc., showing the extensive nature of this government espionage. R.R. Madden summarises much of this material in Appendix XIV, vol. II of *The United Irishmen: Their Lives and Times* (Dublin, 1846). Wider aspects are discussed in W.J. Fitzpatrick, *Secret Service Under Pitt* (London, 1892). R.B. McDowell, *Ireland in the Age of Imperialism and Revolution, 1760–1801* (London, 1979), devotes several pages (529–34) to what he describes as the 'torrent of information' from these informers.

22 Edward John Newell, *The Apostasy of Newell* (Belfast, 1798), is an extraordinarily frank narrative of this informer's life and adventures.

23 *See* interrogation of John Hughes, *Reports from the Committee of Secrecy of House of Lords in Ireland* (Dublin, 1798)

24 The records in the Irish State Paper Office, Dublin Castle, give the names of more than a dozen Church of Ireland clergymen and several Catholic priests who were involved in selling secret information for money to the Government. The names of no Presbyterian ministers are mentioned.

CHAPTER 5

1 J.C. Beckett, *The Making of Modern Ireland, 1603–1923* (London, 1966), p. 260

2 During 1796 and 1797 letters poured into Dublin Castle with news and complaints about the threatening security situation in Ulster and elsewhere in Ireland. The documents were collected by the civil servants responsible and kept on file until the new state was set up in 1922. They can now be seen in the Irish State Paper Office, Dublin Castle. It is not clear why this particular collection only covers the period up to February 1797, presumably similar letters continued to arrive during the fourteen months leading up to the insurrection.

3 McDowell says that at least sixty priests, or about double the number of Presbyterian ministers, were involved in the 1798 rising. Nine priests were killed in action or executed. R.B. McDowell, *Ireland in the Age of Imperialism and Revolution, 1760–1801* (London, 1979), p. 612.

4 A document in Dublin Castle gives the distribution of the various British Army units in Ireland in December 1796. Irish State Paper Office, carton 620/626, no. 196.

5 It is often claimed that news of this massacre quickly reached Ulster and deterred many otherwise sympathetic Protestants from joining the rebellion. However, the massacre took place on 5 June, and information about it could hardly have reached the insurgents before the Battle of Antrim on 7 June. It is possible that those Dissenters who were already wavering in Belfast subsequently used the name of Scullabogue as an excuse to opt out of previous commitments.

6 'When all our leaders deserted us, Henry Joy McCracken stood alone faithful to the last.' James Hope, quoted in R.R. Madden, *The United Irishmen: Their Lives and Times*, third series, vol. I (Dublin, 1846).

7 In October 1798 Mrs McTier wrote to her brother-in-law William Drennan:

447

'M'Cracken was offered a pardon at the gallows if he would inform on R[obert] S[imms]; his old father at the foot of it, desired him to do all he could to save his life with honour. "Farewell then," said his son, embracing him and was immediately turned off.' D.A. Chart (ed.), *The Drennan Letters, 1776–1819* (Belfast, 1931), p. 280.

8 W.G. Lyttle, *Betsy Gray or Hearts of Down* (Belfast, 1896)

9 '. . . the mercantile leaders, who were appointed to places of trust in the directory, and to posts of danger in the military organisation, were not forthcoming when their services were required. Some became doubtful of the issue, others had large debts outstanding, and were not inclined to act before their debts had been got in; many were connected by ties of property with the other part of the commercial aristocracy, whose political views were opposed to theirs, and not a few, by their position in society, and the prevailing passion for festive entertainments, were in habits of close communication with the authorities, civil and military.' R.R. Madden, *The United Irishmen: Their Lives and Times*, second series, vol. II (Dublin, 1846), p. 424.

10 McDowell reckons that between May and November 1798 about 400 United Irishmen and Defenders were put on trial in Ulster and about 600 in the rest of Ireland. During 1799 a further 660 were put on trial. A grand total of about 1,450 were convicted and sentenced during this period. Scores were executed, and the remainder were flogged, sent as pressed sailors to the British Navy or conscripted to the British or Prussian army, transported to Australia or kept interned without trial until 1802 or 1803. R.B. McDowell, *Ireland in the Age of Imperialism and Revolution, 1760–1801* (London, 1979), pp. 675–7.

11 The poem, which became a favourite recitation piece during the late nineteenth century, was first published in the *Nation* on 1 April 1843. It was unsigned. The author, in fact, was John Kells Ingram, who afterwards became a fellow, professor of Greek and vice-provost of Trinity College Dublin. Ingram wrote the poem when he was twenty years of age, and although he later became a unionist, he never repudiated its sentiments.

12 Padraic H. Pearse, *Collected Works*, vol. I (Dublin, 1922), p. 345

13 *See* particularly the Conclusion, 'The cult of Tone', Marianne Elliott, *Wolfe Tone: Prophet of Irish Independence* (London, 1989); and chapter 12, R.F. Foster, *Modern Ireland, 1600–1972* (London, 1988)

CHAPTER 6

1 William Pitt in a letter to Lord Westmorland, November 1792, quoted in G.C. Bolton, *The Passing of the Act of Union* (London, 1966), p. 12

2 McDowell says that Pitt had been converted while still a young man to the *laissez-faire* ideas of Adam Smith. He had always feared a French invasion through what he regarded as the back door of Ireland. This fear worsened after 1789. R.B. McDowell, *Ireland in the Age of Imperialism and Revolution, 1760–1801* (London, 1979).

3 *Correspondence of Charles, First Marquess of Cornwallis*, ed. Charles Ross, vol. III (London, 1849), p. 102

4 G.C. Bolton, *The Passing of the Act of Union* (London, 1966), suggests that the bribery aspects of the pro-Union

campaign have been exaggerated, and in any event were not so reprehensible because they were part of the accepted Anglo-Irish culture of the time. He records the admitted fact that both opponents and supporters of the Union were often only too willing to be rewarded with 'peerages, pensions and places'. Bolton's opinions as to what was morally permissible in political behaviour leads him to the conclusion that there were no heroes and no villains in the passing of the Act of Union. Grattan apparently rated on the same ethical scale as Castlereagh.

5 Quoted in R.M. Sibbett, *Orangeism in Ireland and Throughout the Empire*, vol. I (London, *c*. 1937), p. 452. Sibbett praises the Orangemen for their stand against the Union and gibes at the Catholic bishops for being so subservient to the Government.

6 Quoted in R.M. Sibbett, *Orangeism in Ireland and Throughout the Empire*, vol. I (London, *c*. 1937), pp. 43–4

7 W.E.H. Lecky, *History of Ireland in the Eighteenth Century*, vol. V (London, 1892 ed.), p. 235

8 The letters and memoirs of Pitt, Castlereagh, Cornwallis and other Dublin Castle functionaries were not published until those who wrote them were safely dead. By this time the details of the Act of Union were a matter of history. The papers of the Earl of Hardwick, who succeeded Lord Cornwallis as viceroy in 1801, which confirmed earlier allegations about bribery and corruption, were only placed in the British Museum library in 1903. *See* Michael MacDonagh, *The Viceroy's Postbag* (London, 1904).

9 The word 'gerrymander' came into popular usage about 1810–12 when Governor Elbridge Gerry of Massachusetts tried to alter the boundaries of his constituency so that his party would be returned to power. Some historians argue that the penal laws, rather than the Union, were the first gerrymander because they prevented Catholics from voting or entering parliament.

10 *Correspondence of Charles, First Marquess of Cornwallis*, ed. Charles Ross, vol. III (London, 1849), p. 102

11 *Memoirs and Correspondence of Viscount Castlereagh, edited by his brother Charles Vane, Marquess of Londonderry*, vol. IV (London, 1848 and 1849), pp. 44–5

12 James Hope, who was a hunted man after 1798, travelled around the country to escape capture, and then settled in the Liberties region of Dublin. In 1802 he helped his friend Samuel Neilson, who had been released from Fort George and returned to Dublin, to visit in disguise Neilson's mother and sister who were living in Belfast. Hope was again with Neilson when the latter sailed into exile from the little port of Ringsend, Dublin, in December 1802. Neilson, who was in poor health, died at Poughkeepsie, New York state, eight months later. He was then only forty-one years of age and penniless.

13 After the collapse of the Thomas Russell rebellion, William Hamilton escaped to County Monaghan where he was betrayed by an informer. Because of lack of evidence, he was not brought to trial but was interned until 1806, when a general amnesty was declared. Hamilton stayed in Dublin where he became for a period editor of the *Evening Post*. In 1820, adventurous to the end, he went on

an expedition to South America, where he later died.

14 The full text of 'The man from God-knows-where' by Florence Mary Wilson was first published on 4 May 1907 in the liberal weekly *Ulster Guardian*, edited by Lindsay Crawford. It became a favourite recitation piece.

15 R.R. Madden, *The United Irishmen: Their Lives and Times*, third series, vol. II (Dublin, 1846), p. 263

16 William Steel Dickson, *A Narrative of the Confinement and Exile of William Steel Dickson, D.D.* (Dublin, 1812). This could have been a historically important book because the author had been at the centre of nationalist and democratic Ulster politics for many years, and knew most of the leading United Irishmen intimately. Unfortunately it is rather discursive and rambling in style, and says very little about the hidden aspects of the 1798 rising. For example, on the crucial question of what happened at Ballynahinch in June 1798, Dickson tantalisingly writes: 'Yet, I may have been a General, for aught that appears to the contrary; and I may not have been a General, though people said I was.' p. 51.

17 William Drennan, *A Letter to the Rt. Hon. William Pitt* (Dublin, 1799)

18 William Drennan, *A Letter to Charles James Fox* (Dublin, 1806)

19 *Autobiography of Archibald Hamilton Rowan*, ed. W.H. Drummond (Dublin, 1840), p. 100. Rowan remained in the public eye until his death at the age of eighty-three. In 1825 Sir Robert Peel made a violent attack on him in the House of Commons as an 'attainted traitor', but several radical MPs came to his defence. In January 1829 he attended a meeting called by friends of civil liberty in Dublin's Rotunda. Hearing that their benefactor was present, a large crowd of the city's poor assembled, and when the old man emerged from the meeting, they pulled his carriage through the streets. One of his last public acts before he died in November 1834 was to defend the memory of his former comrade Samuel Neilson, whose loyalty had been impugned in the newly published biography of Lord Edward FitzGerald by Thomas Moore.

20 Quoted in R.R. Madden, *The United Irishmen: Their Lives and Times*, third series, vol. I (Dublin, 1846), p. 132

21 'I went about armed, determined never to be taken alive, avoiding all connections (with few exceptions) with men above my rank.' Quoted in R.R. Madden, *The United Irishmen: Their Lives and Times*, third series, vol. I (Dublin, 1846), p. 144.

22 Quoted in R.R. Madden, *The United Irishmen: Their Lives and Times*, third series, vol. I (Dublin, 1846), p. 235

23 Mary McNeill, *The Life and Times of Mary Ann McCracken* (Belfast, 1988)

24 Quoted in Pádraig Ó Snódaigh, *Hidden Ulster* (Dublin, 1977), p. 15. *See also* Breandán Ó Buachalla, *I mBéal Feirste Cois Cuain* (Dublin, 1968).

25 Quoted in Finlay Holmes, *Henry Cooke* (Belfast, 1981), p. 13

26 Jamieson states that the school's founders were men of 'liberal outlook', and noted for their 'strong sense of justice'. John Jamieson, *The History of the Royal Belfast Academical Institution* (Belfast, 1959).

27 The Duke of Wellington warned in a letter to the prime minister, Lord Liverpool, that there was a danger of the school becoming a 'democratical establishment' which might foster

the 'Republican spirit of the Presbyterians'. Quoted in Peter Brooke, *Ulster Presbyterianism: The Historical Perspective, 1610–1970* (Dublin, 1987), p. 143.

CHAPTER 7

1 Quoted in Finlay Holmes, *Henry Cooke* (Belfast, 1981), p. 16

2 McDowell, who is himself an Anglican and Tory, admits that during this period the Church of Ireland was 'one of the greatest ecclesiastical anomalies in Christendom'. R.B. McDowell, *Public Opinion and Government Policy in Ireland, 1801–1846* (London, 1952), p. 19.
   Arthur Young was one of the first persons systematically to record the wealth of the Churches in Ireland in the 1770s. Castlereagh made a further contribution in 1799–1800 by requiring all Catholic and Presbyterian clergy to make a return of their parishes and annual incomes. *See* Viscount Castlereagh, *Memoirs and Correspondence* . . ., vol. III (London, 1848 and 1849), pp. 165–74, and vol. IV, pp. 97–173, for a mass of statistical detail. In 1824 the Government requested the Church of Ireland to make a full return of its clergy and finances. *See* Parliamentary Papers, vol. XXI (London, 1824).

3 These figures are only approximate. The first proper census was not held in Ireland until 1821, and this did not count the number of people in the various Churches. An estimate of the population belonging to the various religious groups was made in 1834, and a more accurate count in 1861.

4 'The Presbyterians are considered only as a second class of society in Ireland.' Edward Wakefield, *An Account of Ireland, Statistical and Political*, vol. II (London, 1812), p. 594.

5 Viscount Castlereagh, *Memoirs and Correspondence* . . ., vol. II (London, 1848 and 1849), p. 40

6 For Castlereagh *see ibid.*, p. 127, and for Cornwallis *see ibid.*, p. 80

7 Drennan was always a fierce critic of the *regium donum*, which he described on one occasion as 'hush-money'. In 1792 he wrote to Mrs McTier: 'The stipend . . . is certainly very small (not more than £40 per annum), and if they get a great increase to the bounty, their dependence on the crown will increase in the very same ratio. They will be dissociated from the laity, and our religion will be contaminated by the corruption of our pastors.' D.A. Chart (ed.), *The Drennan Letters, 1776–1819* (Belfast, 1931), pp. 78–9.

8 Viscount Castlereagh, *Memoirs and Correspondence* . . ., vol. III (London, 1848 and 1849), pp. 172–4

9 *See* Viscount Castlereagh, *Memoirs and Correspondence* . . ., vol. III (London, 1848 and 1849), pp. 167–72, for full list of Presbyterian ministers. Details for Catholic clergy are given in vol. IV, pp. 97–173.

10 'A living of £500 is but a middling one [for an Anglican parson] in Ireland, and anything beneath that is considered as very low.' Edward Wakefield, *An Account of Ireland, Statistical and Political*, vol. II, (London, 1812), p. 469.

11 Viscount Castlereagh, *Memoirs and Correspondence* . . ., vol. IV (London, 1848 and 1849), pp. 223–30

12 James Seiton Reid, *History of the Presbyterian Church of Ireland*, vol. III (Belfast, 1867), p. 405

13 W.T. Latimer, *A History of the Irish Presbyterians* (Belfast, 1902), p. 407

14 Peter Brooke, *Ulster Presbyterianism: The Historical Perspective, 1610–1970* (Dublin, 1987), p. 13

15 Two important biographies of Henry Cooke have been written. The first, *The Life and Times of Henry Cooke*, by his son-in-law J.L. Porter, was published in London in 1871. It is highly adulatory and presents its subject as a hero of Irish Presbyterianism. Porter was an advocate of the view, which was later taken up so enthusiastically by the Unionist Party, that the preservation of existing property relationships, the defence of the constitutional link with Britain, the maintenance of the Protestant religion, and the defence of the empire were all bound up together. Ulster was the key to this union of interests, and it was essential, as Cooke suggested, for the episcopalians and Nonconformists to come together against their common foe, Catholicism and Irish nationalism. 'On the staunch Presbyterians of Ireland the fate of the empire depended', wrote Porter, pp. 371–2.

A recent study, *Henry Cooke* (Belfast, 1981) by Finlay Holmes, is not so appreciative of Cooke or his political views.

CHAPTER 8

1 Finlay Holmes, *Henry Cooke* (Belfast, 1981), p. 24

2 John A. Crozier, *The Life of the Rev. Henry Montgomery*, vol. I (London, 1875). This is a long and detailed study of Montgomery, but unfortunately stops at about 1830; the planned second volume was never completed.

3 Quoted in J.L. Porter, *The Life and Times of Henry Cooke* (London, 1871), p. 97

4 John A. Crozier, *The Life of the Rev. Henry Montgomery*, vol. I (London, 1875), p. 140. Crozier coined a striking phrase when he wrote of 'high Toryism in politics and hard Calvinism in religion'.

5 J.L. Porter, *The Life and Times of Henry Cooke* (London, 1871)

6 A modern historian of the school states that Cooke's concern with strict religious orthodoxy was 'chiefly a cloak beneath which he sought to conceal his real objective which was the destruction of political liberalism in his church, because it stood for the negation of his own political principles'. John Jamieson, quoted in Finlay Holmes, *Henry Cooke* (Belfast, 1981), p. 40.

CHAPTER 9

1 Sharman Crawford speaking in the House of Commons, July 1836. Parliamentary Papers, vol. XXXIV (London, 1836).

2 *See* Parliamentary Papers, vol. XXII (Lords) (London, 1831–2), pp. 235–9

3 Parliamentary Papers, vol. XXI, *Tithes in Ireland* (London, 1831–2), p. 623. *See also* Angus Macintyre, *The Liberator: Daniel O'Connell and the Irish Party, 1830–1847* (London, 1965), p. 173. 'Ulster was remarkably well treated in the matter of tithes. Potatoes were subject only in Londonderry, sheep and lambs nowhere, while tithes on flax, hemp and wool, raw materials for a growing industry, were small, and in some areas, . . . non-existent.'

4 Parliamentary Papers, vol. XXI, *Select Committee of the House of Commons to Inquire into the Collection and Payment of Tithes in Ireland* (London, 1831–2),

pp. 429–50. *See also* Parliamentary Papers, vol. XXII, *Select Committee of the House of Lords to Inquire into the Collection and Payment of Tithes in Ireland, 1832* (London, 1831–2).

5 Brian Kennedy, 'Sharman Crawford, a political biography' (unpublished Ph.D. thesis, Queen's University Belfast, 1953)

6 William Sharman Crawford, *A Defence of the Small Farmers of Ireland* (Dublin, 1839), p. 119. There is a fuller account of the Ulster custom, and Crawford's role in defending it in chapter 11 of this book.

7 Crawford appealed to Irish Catholic MPs to support the Protestant movers of this bill. In Ireland he had the sympathies of the Catholic Archbishop MacHale of Tuam and the nationalist Father Davern in Tipperary, but was opposed by O'Connell and those Whigs who wanted to remedy the worst abuses of the tithe system, but feared any general attack on property rights. O'Connell therefore opposed Crawford's motion which led the latter to describe him as 'a Castle hack'. *See* Parliamentary Papers, vol. XXXIV, cols 1135–6 (London, 1836), for the debate in the House of Commons. *See also* the *Northern Whig*, 10 June 1837, 4 August 1838 and 16 August 1838 for the Crawford–O'Connell controversy.

8 *Northern Whig*, 12 May 1834

9 *Northern Whig*, 2 January 1834 There are several pages devoted to the activities of Dean Carter in Parliamentary Papers, *Report of the Select Committee Appointed to Inquire into the Nature, Character, Extent and Tendency of Orange Lodges, Associations or Societies in Ireland* (London, 1835).

10 Both these riots were carefully investigated by government committees. *See* Select Committee report on Orange Lodges, previous note.

11 Parliamentary Papers, vol. XLVII, *Tithes (Keady)* (London, 1835), pp. 99–132

12 Parliamentary Papers, vol. XLVII, *Tithes (Keady)* (London, 1835)

13 Parliamentary Papers, *Report of the Select Committee Appointed to Inquire into the Nature, Character, Extent and Tendency of the Orange Lodges, Associations or Societies in Ireland* (London, 1835). This report of nearly 500 pages provided evidence and appendices. It came to no conclusions. A further series of reports covering Britain and the colonies was published in September 1835. These had a long introduction which was sharply critical of the Orange Order in both Ireland and Britain.

14 The Grand Lodge of Ulster was revived in February 1844.

CHAPTER 10

1 Brian M. Walker (ed.), *Parliamentary Election Results in Ireland, 1801–1922* (Dublin, 1978), pp. 195 ff

2 Quoted in John A. Crozier, *The Life of the Rev. Henry Montgomery*, vol. I (London, 1875), p. 573

3 John A. Crozier, *The Life and Times of the Rev. Henry Montgomery*, vol. I (London, 1875)

4 The Orange Order admired Cooke, though he never actually became a member. In their official history there is repeated emphasis on the need for class collaboration within Protestant ranks, and of the Hillsborough meeting, it was reported enthusiastically that the crowd was 'of one thought and feeling', with the 'owners and

occupiers of the soil standing shoulder to shoulder'. R.M. Sibbett, *Orangeism in Ireland and Throughout the Empire*, vol. II (London, *c.* 1937), p. 125.

5 Quoted in R.M. Sibbett, *Orangeism in Ireland and Throughout the Empire*, vol. II (London, *c.* 1937), p. 128

6 Finlay Holmes, *Henry Cooke* (Belfast, 1981), emphasises the historical importance of this Tory meeting in Hillsborough in October 1834.

7 The *Northern Whig*, during the 1830s, conducted a vigorous campaign against the Tories, against Henry Cooke, and against the payment of *regium donum*. It was also strongly opposed to the spread of trade unionism and the policies of Daniel O'Connell.

8 Quoted in J.L. Porter, *The Life and Times of Henry Cooke* (London, 1871), p. 412

9 Curtis exaggerated when he spoke of Presbyterians becoming 'a second ecclesiastical aristocracy . . . weaned for good from all disloyalty', but there is some truth in his statement. Edmund Curtis, *A History of Ireland* (London, 1961), p. 356.

10 The connection between the rise of capitalism and the spread of Reformation doctrines, particularly the influence of Calvin upon economic thought in the sixteenth and seventeenth centuries, is discussed in depth in Max Weber, *The Protestant Ethic and the Spirit of Capitalism* (London, 1930), and in R.H. Tawney, *Religion and the Rise of Capitalism* (London, 1926). The relation between the growth of evangelicalism and the 'souper' mentality is discussed in chapter 12 of this book.

During the second half of the nineteenth century British imperialism expanded steadily, giving birth, among other things, to that peculiar species, the White Anglo-Saxon Protestant; *see* chapter 19 of this book, and Flann Campbell, *The Orange Card: Racism, Religion and Politics in Northern Ireland* (London, 1981).

11 Quoted in R.B. McDowell, *Public Opinion and Government Policy in Ireland, 1801–1846* (London, 1952), p. 173

12 Parliamentary Papers, vol. XXI, *Tithes in Ireland* (London, 1831–2), p. 449

13 The problem of the *regium donum* was finally settled by the Church Disestablishment Act of 1869, in which the Presbyterian Church was paid a lump sum of £700,000 in place of the annual subsidies. The Church of Ireland was treated much more generously – it was granted £16 million.

14 For further details of this curious episode in Anglo-Irish relations *see* E.R. Norman, *Anti-Catholicism in Victorian England* (London, 1968), *and* Donal A. Kerr, *Peel, Priests and Politics* (London, 1982).

15 Quoted in Donal A. Kerr, *Peel, Priests and Politics* (London, 1982), p. 273

CHAPTER 11

1 The first detailed statistics about landownership in Ireland were published in 1876. *See* Parliamentary Papers, *Owners of Land in Great Britain and Ireland*, vol. LXXX, *Province of Ulster* (London, 1876). An additional complication in these calculations was that at that time farm acres were often recorded in either English (statute), Irish, or Scottish (sometimes called Cunningham) acres. Where possible the figures listed in these pages are in English acres.

2 The Devon Commission report, in spite of its statistical defects, and although it was dominated by landlord interests, provides an invaluable insight into Ireland's land tenure system before the famine. In particular, the verbatim reports of evidence it received from scores of witnesses from all over the country, and from all social classes give a vivid picture of rural life. *See* Parliamentary Papers, vol. XX, *Report of Her Majesty's Commissioners of Inquiry into the State of the Law and Practice in respect of the Occupation of Land in Ireland*, Devon report (London, 1845).

3 These figures are only approximately correct. They are taken from the 1841 census, and are quoted by J.P. Kennedy (ed.), *Digest of Evidence taken before Her Majesty's Commissioners of Inquiry into the Occupation of Land in Ireland*, Devon report (Dublin, 1847). The statistics do not agree exactly with those provided in *Reports of the House of Commons Committees, Poor Laws, Ireland, 1849*, vol. XV, part 2. Historians accept that there was considerable consolidation of farms during and after the famine. The figures for 1851 and 1861 differ significantly from those of 1841.

4 *See* essay by E.R.R. Green in R. Dudley Edwards and T. Desmond Williams (eds), *The Great Famine* (Dublin, 1962), for a valuable account of Irish agriculture before the famine.

5 Apart from Belgium, in the mid-nineteenth century the six counties of Antrim, Armagh, Derry, Down, Fermanagh and Tyrone had the highest density of population of fifteen regions or countries in Europe, according to the *Report of the Commission on Emigration and other Population Problems* (Dublin, 1954). These six counties had then, in fact, a higher density of population than England and Wales, in spite of being much less industrialised.

6 The French and Russian aristocracies were at least of the same religion, spoke the same language, and came from the same ethnic origins as their serfs. This was not true of the Anglo-Irish Ascendancy, who had virtually nothing in common with their Catholic tenants and labourers, and who shared neither ancestry, Church membership nor social class with the Presbyterians.

7 In the index of Brian M. Walker (ed.), *Parliamentary Election Results in Ireland, 1801–1922* (Dublin, 1978), the names of six Archdalls (or Archdales), six Brookes, four Corrys, ten Dawsons, fifteen Hamiltons, nine Hills, six Kers, five Leslies, three Lowrys, eleven Stewarts, five Verners, two Tennents, and ten Knoxes are listed as MPs elected in various Ulster constituencies between 1801 and 1922.

8 Tenant right consisted of a 'continued occupancy at a fair rent, and the right of selling possession to a *bona fide* purchaser at its market value'. Charles Gavan Duffy, *The League of North and South, 1850–1854* (London, 1886), p. 25.

9 Parliamentary Papers, vol. XX, *Report of Her Majesty's Commissioners of Inquiry into the State of the Law and Practice in respect of the Occupation of Land in Ireland*, Devon report (London, 1845), pp. 294–5. A generation later the Bessborough Commission said that the custom had originated 'in the later days of the English settlement, when landlords were glad to invite tenants

to settle around them on easy terms in order to secure themselves to their estates'. There was no explanation as to how Catholics came to share these Protestant privileges. Parliamentary Papers, vol. XVIII, *Report of Her Majesty's Commissioners of Inquiry into the Working of the Landlord and Tenant (Ireland) Act, 1870*, Bessborough report (London, 1881).

10 Sullivan, the historian of Young Ireland, sharply contrasted the Ulster tenure system with that of the other three provinces: '. . . negligence in place of thrift, squalor in place of comfort and neatness, hovels in the place of houses; insecurity, distrust, ill-will of the government, and a deadly hostility to the law, that drew this line of distinction, this line of oppression and wrong, between the Protestant North and the Popish South'. A.M. Sullivan, *New Ireland* (Philadelphia, 1878), p. 200.

11 Karl Marx, with his colleague Frederick Engels, took a keen interest in Irish affairs. He was highly critical of the Irish landlord system, and followed the tenant rights agitation closely. He was particularly scornful about the way in which the tenant was blamed for faults which lay in the system rather than the individual. 'If the tenant is industrious and enterprising, he became taxed in consequence of his industry and enterprise. If, on the contrary, he grew inert and negligent, he was reproached with the aboriginal faults of the Celtic race. He had, accordingly, no other alternative but to become a pauper – to pauperise himself by his industry, or to pauperise by negligence.' Karl Marx and Frederick Engels, *On Ireland and the Irish Question* (Moscow, 1971). Marx was stirred to write in this way by *The Times* description of the Irish land agitation as a call for a 'communistic distribution of ownership'.

12 J.P. Kennedy (ed.), *Digest of Evidence taken before Her Majesty's Commissioners of Inquiry into the Occupation of Land in Ireland*, Devon report (Dublin, 1847). Kennedy suggested that though the value of tenant right naturally varied from farm to farm that an average price might be around twenty-five shillings an acre per year or £12 for a ten-year purchase.

13 James Grant, 'The Great Famine in the province of Ulster, 1845–49' (unpublished Ph.D. thesis, Queen's University Belfast, 1986)

14 The word 'Ulster' is not included in the index of Cecil Woodham-Smith, *The Great Hunger* (London, 1962).

15 Finlay Holmes, *Henry Cooke* (Belfast, 1981)

16 *Northern Whig*, 23 September 1845

17 The Reverend Samuel Montgomery writing in his burial register in Ballinascreen, County Tyrone. *Education Facsimile, no. 15, Famine* (PRONI, n.d.).

18 James Brown, soap manufacturer and tallow merchant of Donaghmore, County Tyrone. *Education Facsimile, no. 1, Famine* (PRONI, n.d.).

19 *Northern Whig*, 5 September, 1846

20 *Education Facsimile, no. 6, Famine* (PRONI, n.d.)

21 *Belfast News-Letter*, 9 March 1847

22 *Northern Whig*, 1 May 1847

23 Parliamentary Papers, vol. LV, *Workhouses (Ireland)* (London, 1847)

24 Dr Robert Smith, Parliamentary Papers, vol. LV, *Workhouses (Ireland)* (London, 1847)

25 The best account of the nature and spread of these epidemics is given in

William MacArthur, 'The medical history of the famine' in R. Dudley Edwards and T. Desmond Williams (eds), *The Great Famine* (Dublin, 1962). MacArthur quotes extensively from the reports of Dr Seiton Reid, MOH of Belfast. This is the same William MacArthur who was a friend of Robert Lynd, Paul Henry, James Winder Good and other radical elements in Queen's College, Belfast, *c.* 1900.

26 Parliamentary Papers, vol. XII, *Paupers in Ulster* (London, 1849)

27 Parliamentary Papers, vol. XXIII, *Census of Ireland, Ulster, 1841–1851*

CHAPTER 12

1 *The Times* quoted in *Northern Whig*, 17 December 1846

2 *Northern Whig*, 27 August 1846

3 *Belfast News-Letter*, 12 January 1847

4 H. Labouchere, speaking in the House of Commons, Parliamentary Papers (Hansard), vol. LXXXIX, January–February 1847

5 *The Times*, 15 January 1847

6 *The Times*, 28 August 1847

7 Sir Robert Peel speaking in the House of Commons, Parliamentary Papers (Hansard), vol. XCI, March–April 1847. Prime Minister Russell, his chancellor of the exchequer, Woods, and his chief administrator in Ireland, Trevelyan, all echoed Peel's views, though circumstances forced them to change their views within a few months.

8 *The Times*, 18 January 1847

9 *Northern Whig*, 20 October 1846

10 Parliamentary Papers (Hansard), vol. XC, February–March 1847

11 Parliamentary Papers (Hansard), vol. XC, February–March 1847

12 Parliamentary Papers, vol. XLIX, *Accounts and Papers* (London, 1849)

13 No fewer than seventeen Coercion Bills affecting Ireland had been passed in the UK parliament since 1801. This was an apt comment on the claim that the Union would bring peace and stability to Ireland.

14 James Grant, 'The Great Famine in the province of Ulster, 1845–49' (unpublished Ph.D. thesis, Queen's University Belfast, 1986)

15 E. Jane Whateley, *Life and Correspondence of Richard Whateley, D.D.* (London, 1875)

16 Whateley endowed a chair in economics in Trinity College Dublin.

17 Nassau William Senior, *Journals, Conversations and Essays Relating to Ireland* (London, 1868). Senior and Whateley were typical of their period in mingling religious and economic doctrines. An extraordinary example of this kind of mixture is given in *The Times*, 19 October 1846, which referred to political economy as the 'immutable doctrine . . . of Nature and Heaven . . . The greatest economist in this world, as also the strictest storekeeper and sternest teacher of husbandry and thrift, is also the Almighty himself.'

18 Richard Whateley, *Speech in the House of Lords on the Committee on the Irish Poor Law* (London, 1847)

19 G. Poulett Scrope, *Reply to the Archbishop of Dublin* (London, 1847)

20 Quoted in Desmond Bowen, *The Protestant Crusade in Ireland, 1800–1870* (London, 1978), p. 234. This book gives an excellent account of the various missionary enterprises in nineteenth-century Ireland. Bowen sees this crusade as part of what he calls the 'long cultural struggle' between the two peoples. 'It was difficult to distinguish the English "spiritual message" from English cultural imperialism, and the social

blessings which the "mother country" wanted to export to this important part of the empire', he wrote, p. 252.

21 Earl of Roden, *Progress of the Reformation in Ireland* (London, 1851)

22 *Northern Whig*, 10 July 1847

23 W.D. Killen, *Memoir of John Edgar* (Belfast, 1867)

24 John Edgar, *A Cry from Connaught* (Belfast, 1846)

25 Edward Marcus Dill, *The Mystery Solved or Ireland's Miseries, the Grand Cause and Cure* (London, 1852), p. 302

26 Quoted in James Morris, *Heaven's Command* (London, 1973), p. 172

27 Lord Dufferin and E.P. Boyle, *Narrative of a Journey from Oxford to Skibbereen during the Year of the Irish Famine* (Oxford, 1847). Dufferin's mother, Helen, was a descendant of R.B. Sheridan, and a sister of the pioneer feminist, Caroline Norton. Dufferin, who as a young man admired Gladstone, later gave up many of his liberal principles, reverted to type, and became a strong unionist. He was variously governor general of Canada, viceroy to India, and ambassador to Paris. During the land crisis of the 1880s, he favoured emigration to other British colonies as a solution to the country's problems, and opposed any system of peasant proprietorship.

28 Lord George Hill, *Facts from Gweedore* (Dublin, 1845)

29 A. Shafto Adair, *The Winter of 1846–7 in Antrim* (London, 1847)

30 James Grant, 'The Great Famine in the province of Ulster, 1845–49' (unpublished Ph.D. thesis, Queen's University Belfast, 1986), pp. 55–64

31 Sharman Crawford speaking in the House of Commons, Parliamentary Papers (Hansard), vol. LXXXIX, January–February 1847

CHAPTER 13

1 P.A. Sillard, *The Life and Times of John Martin* (London, 1893), p. 223

2 'The Protestant alone could not expect to liberate his country – the Roman Catholic alone could not do it – neither could the Presbyterian – but amalgamate the three into Irishmen, and the Union is defeated.' Daniel O'Connell in 1810, quoted in Robert Kee, *The Green Flag* (London, 1972), p. 180. *See also* Sean Cronin, *Irish Nationalism* (Dublin, 1980), pp. 65–85.

3 John Mitchel, *The History of Ireland* (Glasgow, 1869), pp. 184–5. Mitchel, like some of his colleagues, was so keen to embrace all Irishmen and women in his vision of a new country that for a time he hoped he could win over some of the landlords and gentry to his cause.

4 Thomas Davis, *Selections from his Prose and Poetry* (Dublin, n.d.)

5 Quoted in Charles Gavan Duffy, *Young Ireland, 1840–1845*, vol. II (London, 1896 ed.), p. 127

6 Quoted in Robert Kee, *The Green Flag* (London, 1972), p. 235

7 For discussion of this episode *see* Charles Gavan Duffy, *Young Ireland, 1840–1845*, vol. I (London, 1896 ed.), pp. 165–181

8 Lalor took no part in the 1848 insurrection, and some historians suggest that he may have returned to France where he had many revolutionary contacts during that period. It was the publication of an allegedly seditious article by Lalor in the *Irish Felon* in June 1848 that led to the prosecution and conviction of the paper's publisher, John Martin. Lalor was imprisoned for some months in

the autumn of 1848 and then released on grounds of ill health. He tried unsuccessfully to raise a new rebellion in December 1849, but by this time he was a very sick man. He died a short time later at the age of forty-two.

9 Ribbonism, now hiding under the new name of 'Molly Maguires', spread into counties Cavan, Leitrim and Roscommon in 1845–6. Maguire was a common name in County Fermanagh. The name 'Molly Maguires' was taken to the coalfields of Pennsylvania in the 1860s and 1870s. The mythical Captain Rock was said to be active in Keady, County Armagh, and real food riots were reported in Dunfanaghy, Omagh, Newtownards, Newtownhamilton and Belfast at various times in 1846–8. So disturbed were the British authorities at this outbreak of disaffection in 'loyal' Ulster that *The Times* sent a special correspondent to investigate.

10 J.P. Kennedy (ed.), *Digest of Evidence taken before Her Majesty's Commission of Inquiry into the Occupation of Land in Ireland*, Devon report (Dublin, 1847)

11 *Northern Whig*, 30 October 1847

12 *Northern Whig*, 13 January 1848

13 *Northern Whig*, 27 May 1848

14 The *Northern Whig*'s report on 16 November 1847 runs to nine columns. It is critical of Young Ireland but its account of the meeting is verbatim. Both the *Whig* and its conservative rival the *Belfast News-Letter* reported at length on the attempts which were made by the followers of Daniel O'Connell to break up the meeting. There was much heckling and numerous interruptions organised by the 'Old Ireland' faction, who attacked the Confederates as 'O'Connell's murderers'.

15 Lady Ferguson, *Sir Samuel Ferguson in the Ireland of His Day*, vol. I (London, 1896), pp. 246–54

16 *Ibid.*

17 In the obituary notice he wrote on Thomas Davis in the *Dublin Magazine* of January 1847, he referred to the 'insolence and folly of writers in the metropolitan [London] press'. Lady Ferguson, *Sir Samuel Ferguson in the Ireland of His Day*, vol. I (London, 1896), p. 142. Among those scribes was the Cork-born journalist William Maginn, who wrote copiously on anti-Irish themes in the Tory press.

18 Benedict Kiely, *Poor Scholar* (London, 1947)

19 *Ibid.*

20 Lady Ferguson, *Life of the Rt. Hon. Rev. William Reeves* (London, 1883)

CHAPTER 14

1 John Mitchel, *An Ulsterman for Ireland, being Letters to the Protestant Farmers, Labourers and Artisans of the North of Ireland*, ed. Eoin MacNeill (Dublin, 1917 ed.)

2 John Mitchel, *The History of Ireland* (Glasgow, 1869), p. 222

3 John Mitchel, *An Ulsterman for Ireland* ... (Dublin, 1917 ed.), p. 22

4 John Mitchel, *The Life and Times of Aodh O'Neill* (Dublin, 1845), p. viii

5 John Mitchel, *An Ulsterman for Ireland* ... (Dublin, 1917 ed.), pp. 19–20. Seumus MacCall says that Mitchel was never sure whether he was of recent Scots ancestry or descended from some seventeenth-century English adventurer. 'Family traditions pointed vaguely towards Britain; patriotism beckoned invitingly from the land of the O'Neills, but since his mother was

unquestioningly of British origin (in fact, a Scot) he anticipated the scientists of a later generation by deciding that nationality had really very little connection with race and none at all with religion.' Seumus MacCall, *Irish Mitchel* (London, 1938), p. 42.

A point which emerges in all the writings by, and about, Mitchel was that he was intensely proud of being an Ulsterman, but an Ulsterman whose province was an integral part of the Irish nation.

6 'The bitterest, deadliest foe of Ireland (however peopled) is the foul fiend of British imperialism.' John Mitchel, *The Life and Times of Aodh O'Neill* (Dublin, 1845), p. ix.

7 Seumus MacCall, *Irish Mitchel* (London, 1938), p. 124

8 *Northern Whig*, 6 June 1848

9 'A kind of sacred wrath took possession of a few Irishmen at this period. They could endure the horrible scene no longer, and resolved to cross the British car of conquest though it might crush them to atoms.' Quoted in Seumus MacCall, *Irish Mitchel* (London, 1938), p. 169.

10 John Mitchel, *Jail Journal* (Dublin, n.d.), p. 141

11 Quoted in Seumus MacCall, *Irish Mitchel* (London, 1938), pp. 179–80

12 Charles Gavan Duffy reported in later life that he had rejected certain articles written by Mitchel for the *Nation* in 1848 on the grounds that they were racist in tone. He blames Thomas Carlyle's influence on Mitchel for these views. *See* Charles Gavan Duffy, *Conversations with Carlyle* (New York, 1892).

John Martin, who was Mitchel's closest friend and greatest admirer, wrote from Paris in 1858 about the

'rage and grief of many thousands of his political friends' caused by Mitchel's support for Negro slavery. He also complained about Mitchel's 'haughty violence' towards his Irish friends. Diary of John Martin, 1848–1858 (MS held in the National Library of Ireland).

13 *See* Rebecca O'Connor, *Jenny Mitchel: Young Irelander* (Dublin, 1988)

14 Quoted in Seumus MacCall, *Irish Mitchel* (London, 1938), pp. 194–7

15 John Martin also wrote a diary about his voyage in the summer of 1849 as a transported felon from Cobh to Van Dieman's Land. Martin was treated reasonably well on board ship because he was a 'gentleman' prisoner. Though not equal on literary merit to Mitchel's *Jail Journal*, Martin's account of the ninety-seven-day voyage contains a vivid account of the day-to-day life aboard a convict ship at that time. *See* Diary of John Martin, 1848–1858 (MS held in the National Library of Ireland).

16 John Martin in a letter to George C. Mahon, May 1855 (George C. Mahon MS held in the National Library of Ireland)

17 John Martin in a letter to George C. Mahon, 1855 (George C. Mahon MS held in the National Library of Ireland)

CHAPTER 15

1 *Londonderry Standard,* 20 June 1850

2 Charles Gavan Duffy, *The League of North and South, 1850–1854* (London, 1886)

3 *Impartial Reporter*, 29 November 1848. Samuel M. Greer was a prominent figure in the tenant-right movement for several years. In 1852 he stood unsuccessfully as the Liberal candidate in County Derry.

Five years later he won the seat in a by-election, but lost it again in 1859. He polled strongly, but did not win, in Derry City in 1860 and 1865. On his appointment as recorder for Derry, he retired from politics.

4 The *Banner of Ulster* published a special supplement on 14 June 1850 containing a verbatim report of speeches at this conference.

5 Quoted in *Banner of Ulster*, 14 June 1850

6 Quoted in *Banner of Ulster*, 13 August 1850

7 Quoted in *Banner of Ulster*, 13 August 1850

8 Charles Gavan Duffy, *The League of North and South, 1850–1854* (London, 1886), p. 99

9 *Londonderry Standard*, 15 August 1850

10 A.M. Sullivan, *New Ireland* (Philadelphia, 1878), p. 205

11 Quoted in Charles Gavan Duffy, *The League of North and South, 1850–1854* (London, 1886), p. 57

12 The *Londonderry Standard* had a picture of the city's walls, with the slogan 'Our Faith and Fireside, 1688' on its masthead. The *Northern Whig*, which claimed to be the main vehicle for liberal views in Ulster, was somewhat equivocal in its attitude towards the tenants' agitation. Belfast-oriented, and under the leadership of Thomas Finlay, it showed more interest in industrial and commercial matters than it did in agriculture.

13 Charles Gavan Duffy, *The League of North and South, 1850–1854* (London, 1886), p. 35

14 *Ibid.*, p. viii

15 As well as his copious writings on politics and land reform, McKnight published several books on theological subjects, including a study of John Knox.

16 W.T. Latimer, *Ulster Biographies Relating Chiefly to the Rebellion of 1798* (Belfast, 1897), p. 106

17 James McKnight, *The Ulster Tenant Right* (Belfast, 1848), p. 45. In this pamphlet, which took the form of an open letter to the prime minister, Lord Russell, he began by saying: 'I am simply an Irishman.' It would be wrong to suggest from this and similar remarks that McKnight was an Irish nationalist. At heart he was a liberal unionist.

18 His son Edwin Laurence Godkin was an even more influential journalist than his father. After working for the *Daily News* as a war correspondent in the Crimea between 1853 and 1855, the young Godkin went to America, where he founded the *Nation*, which became one of the most important liberal journals ever published in that country. Godkin denounced the Tammany Hall corruption in the 1880s, and was an opponent of jingoism and imperialism both in his adopted country and England. He became a supporter of Irish Home Rule. A prominent crusader for all kinds of progressive causes, he is commemorated by the Godkin lectures at Harvard University.

19 *Banner of Ulster*, 5 January 1850

20 Quoted in *Banner of Ulster*, 18 January 1850

21 Quoted in *Londonderry Standard*, 28 February 1850

22 Quoted in *Banner of Ulster*, 8 February 1850

23 The first accurate religious census in Ireland was in 1861. It gave the following figures for Ulster: Church of Ireland, 391,000 (20.4 per cent), Presbyterians, 504,000 (26.3 per cent), Catholics, 967,000 (50.5 per cent), others, 52,000 (2.8 per cent). There is a useful analysis of these figures,

broken into occupational groups, in B.M. Walker, *Ulster Politics: The Formative Years, 1868–1886* (Belfast, 1989).

24 *Banner of Ulster*, 11 January 1850
25 *Impartial Reporter*, 14 February 1850
26 *Impartial Reporter*, 21 March 1850
27 *Banner of Ulster*, 17 May 1850
28 *Ibid.*
29 *Ibid.*
30 *See* E.R. Norman, *Anti-Catholicism in Victorian England* (London, 1968), for fuller discussion of the way in which Protestant evangelicalism affected attitudes towards Ireland in the mid-nineteenth century.
31 Michael Davitt believed that 'the treachery of Archbishop Cullen ... killed the hopes of Duffy and Lucas in the fifties'. Michael Davitt, *The Fall of Feudalism in Ireland* (London, 1904), p. 122.
    Lyons writes: 'Both the Tenant League and the independent party were linked in Cullen's eyes with red revolution by reason of the fact that Charles Gavan Duffy was prominent in each of them.' F.S.L. Lyons, *Ireland Since the Famine* (London, 1971), p. 109.
    'The Hierarchy took the view that preserving the rights of the bishops to their titles was work of far greater importance than preserving the Tenants' Rights to their improvements on the soil.' T.A. Jackson, *Ireland Her Own* (London, 1946), p. 259.
32 The population of Ulster was 2,386,000 in 1841, 2,012,000 in 1851, 1,914,000 in 1861, 1,833,000 in 1871, 1,743,000 in 1881, 1,620,000 in 1891, 1,583,000 in 1901, and 1,582,000 in 1911.
33 For a vivid account of these and other sectarian riots *see* Andrew Boyd, *Holy War in Belfast* (Tralee, 1969).

CHAPTER 16

1 Isaac Butt, *The Irish People and Irish Land* (London, 1867), p. 239
2 A married man with several children, he caused some mild scandal in London by his numerous and indiscreet sexual affairs.
3 Samuel Ferguson, the Belfast poet, was included in this category. *See* David Thornley, *Isaac Butt and Home Rule* (London, 1964), p. 17.
4 Quoted in Terence de Vere White, *The Road to Excess* (London, 1946), p. 119
5 Isaac Butt, *The Irish People and Irish Land* (London, 1867), p. 69
6 *Ibid.*, p. 91
7 Isaac Butt, *A Plea for the Celtic Race* (Dublin, 1866), pp. 43–4
8 Isaac Butt, *The Irish People and Irish Land* (London, 1867), pp. 251–2
9 Isaac Butt, *A Plea for the Celtic Race* (Dublin, 1866), p. 72
10 David Thornley, *Isaac Butt and Home Rule* (London, 1964), p. 16
11 The term 'Home Rule' is said to have been coined by the Reverend Joseph Galbraith, a close friend of Isaac Butt's. Galbraith was a fellow of Trinity College Dublin, and joined the National League in the 1880s. Parnell wanted him to stand as a Home Rule candidate in Dublin in 1888, but under heavy pressure from the Church of Ireland bishops, he refused. *See* R.B. McDowell, *The Church of Ireland, 1869–1969* (London, 1975), p. 99.
12 Francis Thompson, 'Land and politics in Ulster, 1868–86' (unpublished Ph.D. thesis, Queen's University Belfast, 1982), estimates there were about fifteen such tenants' associations in Ulster active during the 1870s. In 1880 the Bessborough Commission took

evidence from the following tenant-right groups: County Antrim (Route); Antrim Central; County Armagh; Camlough; Down; Ballyclare; Castlefinn; Kennaught; Coleraine; Garvagh; Aghadowey; Eglinton; Country Tyrone; and Claudy. Parliamentary Papers, vol. XVIII, *Report of Her Majesty's Commissioners of Inquiry into the Working of the Landlord and Tenant (Ireland) Act, 1870*, Bessborough report (London, 1881).

B.M. Walker, *Ulster Politics: The Formative Years, 1868–1886* (Belfast, 1989), refers to nineteen tenant associations as existing in Ulster during the 1870s, but does not name them all. In his view most members were from the better-off and politically moderate farmers, including many Presbyterians as well as Catholics.

13 S.C. McElroy, *The Route Land Crusade* (Coleraine, n.d.)

14 *Northern Whig*, 21 and 22 January 1874

15 Parliamentary Papers, vol. XVIII, *Report of Her Majesty's Commissioners of Inquiry into the Working of the Landlord and Tenant (Ireland) Act, 1870*, Bessborough report (London, 1881)

16 Parliamentary Papers, vol. XLVII, *Return for the Year 1870 of the Number of Landed Proprietors in Ireland Classed According to Residence* (London, 1872), p. 282

17 Quoted in Thomas MacKnight, *Ulster As It Is*, vol. I (London, 1896), pp. 201–2. *See also* B.M. Walker, *Ulster Politics: The Formative Years, 1868–1886* (Belfast, 1989) for a lively account of the wealth and life style of Lord Hertford and other aristocrats during this period.

18 Parliamentary Papers, *Owners of Land in Great Britain and Ireland*, vol. LXXX, *Province of Ulster* (London, 1876).

19 Valuation figures were originally based on the famous Griffiths survey, which began in Derry and Antrim in the 1830s, and eventually extended all over the country. *See* T.W. Freeman, *Pre-Famine Ireland* (London, 1957), p. 57. It was estimated that on an annual valuation of, say, £30, a rent of about the same amount could be secured.

20 Finlay Dun in his *Landlords and Tenants in Ireland* (London, 1881) says that small farmers on poor soils, even with good management, could only make profits of £2 to £3 per cultivatable acre per year, or the equivalent of £20 to £30 on a typical holding. Many units were smaller than this. He reported male adult labourers' wages as being then eight to nine shillings a week in Donegal.

21 Thomas Shillington, chairman, Armagh Tenant Farmers' Association, giving evidence to the Bessborough Commission. Parliamentary Papers vol. XVIII, *Report of Her Majesty's Commissioners of Inquiry into the Working of the Landlord and Tenant (Ireland) Act, 1870*, Bessborough report (London, 1881), p. 198.

22 *See* T.W. Moody, *Michael Davitt and Irish Revolution, 1846–1882* (Oxford, 1982), Appendix G3

23 Quoted in R.W. Fitzpatrick, 'Origins and development of the land war in mid-Ulster, 1879–85' in F.S.L. Lyons and R.A.J. Hawkins (eds), *Ireland Under the Union* (Oxford, 1980), p. 214. This petition was drafted by the local Church of Ireland rector, the Reverend Thomas Adderley.

24 Hugh de Fellenberg Montgomery,

Irish Land and Irish Rights (London, 1881), p. 15

25 T.W. Moody, *Michael Davitt and Irish Revolution, 1846–1882* (Oxford, 1982), pp. 565–6

CHAPTER 17

1 *Impartial Reporter*, 26 August 1880
2 *Impartial Reporter*, 11 November 1880
3 Quoted in T.W. Moody, *Michael Davitt and Irish Revolution, 1846–1882* (Oxford, 1982), p. 446
4 *Ibid.*, pp. 447–8
5 Speakers at the Ballymoney conference included W.D. Henderson (Belfast), Samuel Black (Randalstown), John Megaw (Route), Jeremiah Jordan (Enniskillen), S.C. McElroy (Ballymoney), and the Reverend James B. Armour (Ballymoney).
6 The records of the Land League branches and membership are incomplete. Valuable sources of information are provided by local newspapers and police records.
7 Almost every week such newspapers as the *Ulster Weekly News*, the *Impartial Reporter*, and the *Newry Weekly Examiner* carried reports of tenant demonstrations.
8 *Impartial Reporter*, 25 November 1880
9 Quoted in *Ulster Weekly News*, 30 April 1881
10 Quoted in *Impartial Reporter*, 11 November 1880
11 *Ulster Weekly News*, 30 April 1881
12 Parliamentary Papers, vol. XVIII, *Report of Her Majesty's Commissioners of Inquiry into the Working of the Landlord and Tenant (Ireland) Act, 1870*, Bessborough report (London, 1881)
13 Quoted in *Ulster Weekly News*, 30 October 1880
14 *Impartial Reporter*, 30 December 1880
15 *Ulster Weekly News*, 19 February 1881

16 *Impartial Reporter*, 21 October 1880
17 *See* John Patrick McLoughlin, 'Gladstone, Irish Nationalism and the Home Rule Question, 1882–1893, with particular reference to the Ulster problem' (unpublished Ph.D. thesis, Trinity College Dublin, 1984), *and* P.J.O. McCann, 'The Protestant Home Rule Movement, 1886–1895' (unpublished MA thesis, University College Dublin, 1972)
18 *See* P.J.O. McCann, 'The Protestant Home Rule Movement, 1886–1895' (unpublished MA thesis, University College Dublin, 1972), p. 33
19 T.W. Moody, *Michael Davitt and Irish Revolution, 1846–1882* (Oxford, 1982), p. 125
20 The Biggar family sometimes spelt their name with an 'a' and sometimes with an 'e'. Joseph Gillis Biggar was a cousin of Francis Joseph Bigger, the antiquarian.
21 Joan Haslip, *Parnell* (London, 1936), p. 63
22 F.S.L. Lyons, *Ireland Since the Famine* (London, 1971), p. 146
23 T.A. Jackson, *Ireland Her Own* (London, 1946), p. 302
24 St John Ervine, *Parnell* (London, 1944), p. 79
25 T.A. Jackson, *Ireland Her Own* (London, 1946), p. 300
26 Quoted in T.A. Jackson, *Ireland Her Own* (London, 1946), p. 298
27 John Devoy, *Recollections of an Irish Rebel* (Shannon, 1969 ed.), p. 284
28 Biggar had been converted to Catholicism in 1875.
29 Quoted in *Northern Whig*, 20 February 1890

CHAPTER 18

1 Parliamentary Papers, vol. XVIII, *Report of Her Majesty's Commissioners of Inquiry into the Working of the Landlord and Tenant (Ireland) Act,*

1870, Bessborough report (London, 1881), p. 61

2 Quoted in Brian M. Walker, 'The land question and elections in Ulster, 1868–86' in Samuel Clark and James S. Donnelly, Jr. (eds), *Irish Peasants, Violence and Political Unrest, 1780–1914* (Manchester, 1983), p. 247

3 Quoted in B.M. Walker, *Ulster Politics: The Formative Years, 1868–1886* (Belfast, 1989), p. 162

4 Patrick Buckland (ed.), *Irish Unionism, 1885–1923: A Documentary History* (Dublin, 1973), p. 41

5 Lord Leitrim's name 'haunted Donegal like an evil spectre', Shane Leslie, *Lord Mulroy's Ghost* (Dublin, 1954), p. 2

6 *See* Parliamentary Papers, vol. LXVII, *Evictions (Ireland)* (London, 1881), and subsequent volumes for 1882, 1883 and 1884 for a mass of statistical material relating to evictions in the four provinces. About one in twenty of those evicted appear to have been re-admitted as tenants. A higher proportion of tenants is recorded as having been readmitted as 'caretakers', but it is not clear whether these were given temporary reprieves or not.

7 J.L. Hammond, *Gladstone and the Irish Nation* (London, 1964), pp. 216–17

8 'The Grand Lodge had too much of a landlord and Church of Ireland flavour for these men [Presbyterian tenant farmers] at this time.' M.W. Dewar, John Brown and S.E. Long, *Orangeism, A New Perspective* (Belfast, 1967), p. 140.

9 Quoted in *Impartial Reporter*, 25 November 1880

10 *Ulster Weekly News*, 16 July 1881

11 Quoted in Francis Thompson, 'Land and politics in Ulster, 1868–86' (unpublished Ph.D. thesis, Queen's University Belfast, 1982), p. 474

12 Quoted in *Ulster Weekly News*, 27 November 1880

13 Quoted in *Impartial Reporter*, 11 November 1880

14 Reginald Lucas, *Col. Saunderson, MP* (London, 1908)

15 *Impartial Reporter*, 2 September 1880

16 Thomas MacKnight, *Ulster As It Is*, vol. II (London, 1896), p. 38

17 A full-length account of this bizarre episode is given by Joyce Barlow, *Capt. Boycott and the Irish* (London, 1973).

18 The name Twiss was an unfortunate one, because during the eighteenth century there had been an English visitor to Ireland, a clergyman of that name, who had written a book attacking the Irish. In retaliation, a Dublin porcelain-maker manufactured a chamber pot with the image of Twiss on the bottom.

19 Lord Randolph Churchill, the maverick Tory cabinet minister, had a brief flirtation with Parnellism in the early 1880s, but historians regard this as only an electoral manoeuvre.

20 Quoted in L.P. Curtis, Jr, *Coercion and Conciliation in Ireland, 1880–1882* (New Jersey, 1963), p. 347

21 Charles W. Boyd (ed.), *Mr. Chamberlain's Speeches* (London, 1914), pp. 306–7

22 Brian O'Neill, *The War for the Land in Ireland* (London, 1933), p. 96

CHAPTER 19

1 Louis J. Jennings (ed.), *Speeches of Lord Randolph Churchill, 1880–1888*, vol. II (London, 1889), p. 5

2 A.L. Morton, *A People's History of England* (London, 1946)

3 Kipling took a prominent part in the Unionist campaign of 1912, and wrote a special poem for the occasion.

The way in which the great

majority of British writers, scholars and historians – many of them claiming to be liberals – took a strongly pro-imperialist and anti-Gladstone line in the Home Rule debates after 1886 is described in T.J. Dunne, 'La trahison des clercs: British intellectuals and the first home rule crisis', *Irish Historical Studies*, vol. XXIII (1882–3). *See also* T.J. Dunne, 'Ireland, England and the Empire, 1868–1886' (unpublished Ph.D. thesis, Cambridge University, 1975).

4 For the strength of this Protestant feeling *see* E.R. Norman, *Anti-Catholicism in Victorian England* (London, 1968). It is interesting to note that two of Scotland's most famous philosophers, David Hume and Thomas Carlyle, were not only strongly anti-Papist but also were notorious for their antipathy towards Jews and Negroes. The predominantly Protestant countries of northern Europe and the USA also developed this WASP (White Anglo-Saxon Protestant) syndrome in the late nineteenth century. It was the racist forerunner of the Fascism which was to come in the twentieth century.

5 Quoted in Denis Judd, *Radical Joe* (London, 1977), p. 121

6 Ulster was the 'bulwark of the Empire', Ronald McNeill, *Ulster's Stand for Union* (London, 1922), p. 13; Ulster's mission was to 'discipline Ireland in the interest of England', James Winder Good, *Ulster and Ireland* (Dublin, 1919), p. 217; 'The Ascendancy had undoubtedly chosen Ulster as the ditch they could make their last stand in.' A.T.Q. Stewart, *The Ulster Crisis* (London, 1967), p. 44.

7 W.E. Vaughan and A.J. Fitzpatrick (eds), *Irish Historical Statistics,*

Population, 1821–1971 (Dublin, 1978), p. 59

8 Harland, Ewart, Corry and Clark were Unionist MPs.

9 Geoffrey Bell, *The Protestants of Ulster* (London, 1976)

10 Reginald Lucas, *Col. Saunderson, MP* (London, 1908), p. 239

11 Louis J. Jennings (ed.), *Speeches of Lord Randolph Churchill, 1880–1888,* vol. I (London, 1889), p. 359. Judging by his reference to '680 years', Churchill's knowledge of Reformation history must have been sketchy.

12 Quoted in Robert Rhodes James, *Lord Randolph Churchill* (London, 1959), p. 233

13 Louis J. Jennings (ed.), *Speeches of Lord Randolph Churchill, 1880–1888,* vol. II (London, 1889), p. 13

14 *See Report of the Commission of Inquiry respecting the Origins and Circumstances of the Riots in Belfast in June, July, August and September, 1886.* It was ironical that it was Randolph's son, Winston, home secretary in 1906, who should comment that this report was 'very damaging to the Orange party'.

15 Andrew Boyd, *Holy War in Belfast* (Tralee, 1969)

16 Ronald McNeill, *Ulster's Stand for Union* (London, 1922). *See also* John F. Harbinson, *The Ulster Unionist Party, 1882–1973: Its Development and Organisation* (Belfast, 1973), for a detailed account of how the gentry, businessmen and army officers took over the leadership of the Orange Order, and how the Order interacted with the Unionist Party.

17 The full merger of the Orange and Unionist organisations took place formally in 1907.

18 Reginald Lucas, *Col. Saunderson, MP* (London, 1908), p. 90

19 *Ibid.*, p. 276
20 *Ibid.*, p. 96
21 *Ibid.*, p. 240
22 Charles W. Boyd (ed.), *Mr. Chamberlain's Speeches* (London, 1914), p. 285
23 Quoted in *The Times*, 3 April 1893
24 R.M. Sibbett, *Orangeism in Ireland and Throughout the Empire*, vol. II (London, *c*. 1937), p. 579

CHAPTER 20

1 Quoted in J.R.B. McMinn, 'The Rev. James Brown Armour and Liberal politics in North Antrim, 1869–1914' (unpublished Ph.D. thesis, Queen's University Belfast, 1979), p. 94. In this thesis, and also in the Introduction to Armour's letters, which McMinn wrote under the title *Against the Tide* (Belfast, 1985), he is critical of what he alleges is the myth which has grown up around the name of Armour. However, any new facts he produces seem to confirm rather than deny the view that Armour was the most important radical figure among Ulster Presbyterian ministers between 1890 and 1914.
2 *See* chapter 21 for Russellites
3 Estyn Evans, *Prehistoric and Early Christian Ireland* (London, 1966), records 172 such ancient sites in Ulster.
4 In 1901, 26,000 people were listed as being able to speak Irish as well as English in Leinster; 272,000 in Munster; 233,000 in Connacht; and 88,400 in Ulster.
5 Parliamentary Papers, vol. CXVIII, *Census of Ireland, 1911, General Report* (London, 1912–13)
6 Pádraig Ó Snódaigh, *Hidden Ulster* (Dublin, 1977)
7 Louis Le Roux claims that Clarke was sworn into the IRB by Davitt in

1882. Louis Le Roux, *Tom Clarke and the Irish Freedom Movement* (London, 1936).
8 Quoted in C. Desmond Greaves, *The Life and Times of James Connolly* (London, 1961), pp. 69–70
9 A literary landmark involving an Ulster Gaelic revivalist was the publication in 1897 by George Sigerson of *Bards of the Gael and the Gall*. Sigerson, who was born near Strabane in 1836, had a long and successful medical career in Dublin. His mother, Nancy Neilson, was a relative of the United Irishman Samuel Neilson. Apart from his fame as a doctor, he had by the end of the century already acquired a distinguished reputation as a scholar and translator from the Irish.
10 The Gaelic League's claim to be non-sectarian did not impress the unionists who automatically identified the word 'Gaelic' with Catholics and nationalists. 'With the advent of the Gaelic League the [Irish] language came, at least partly, into its own. But the League was never considered quite "respectable" – that awful Belfast word – by the planters. To be a Gaelic Leaguer was to be suspect always. The League might shout at its loudest and longest that it was non-political and non-sectarian. The slogan did not impress Belfast . . . "Scratch a Gaelic Leaguer and you'll find a Fenian" was the formula of the old days.' Cathal O'Byrne, *As I Roved Out* (Belfast, 1946), p. 201.
11 William MacArthur's career followed a very different pattern from that of his early colleagues in the Gaelic League. He became a doctor, joined the British Army and eventually rose to the rank of

director-general of the Royal Army Medical Corps, and was knighted.

12 Bulmer Hobson, *Ireland Yesterday and Tomorrow* (Tralee, 1968)

13 The most important part of MacNeill's career is associated with the south rather than the north of Ireland. Appointed professor in University College Dublin in 1909, he became leader of the Irish Volunteers in 1913. He opposed the Easter rising of 1916. Later he became speaker of the first Dáil and a cabinet minister in the post-treaty government. His last involvement in Ulster was as a member of the abortive Irish Boundary Commission in 1926.

14 Casement's father was a romantic figure who, after resigning his army commission, travelled widely in Europe with his wife and young family. In 1849 he was involved in a famous historical incident in which he carried an urgent diplomatic message from the beleaguered Hungarian patriot, Louis Kossuth, to Lord Palmerston in England. This episode is described in 'Kossuth's Irish courier' in the *United Irishman*, 25 February 1905. He was in Paris during the Commune of 1870. He died in the late 1870s.

Casement's mother was Anne Jephson, a Catholic from County Tipperary, who met her future husband in Paris. In August 1868 she had her son, Roger David, then only four years old, baptised secretly as a Catholic when on a visit to Rhyl in north Wales. She died in childbirth in 1873, leaving four children.

Roger's uncle and guardian, who lived in Magherintemple House, near Ballycastle, County Antrim, was a strong Protestant, and had his ward brought up as a member of the Church of Ireland.

15 Leon O'Broin, *Protestant Nationalists in Revolutionary Ireland: The Stopford Connection* (Dublin, 1985)

16 Bulmer Hobson papers in National Library of Ireland, 10 August 1905

17 *Catalogue of the Books and Bound MSS of the Irish Historical, Archaeological and Antiquarian Library of the late Francis Joseph Bigger* (Central Library, Belfast, 1930).

18 Quoted in W.S. Armour, *Armour of Ballymoney* (London, 1934), p. 29

19 Quoted in J.R.B. McMinn, 'The Rev. James Brown Armour and Liberal politics in North Antrim, 1869–1914' (unpublished Ph.D. thesis, Queen's University Belfast, 1979)

20 Foreword by Robert Lynd, W.S. Armour, *Armour of Ballymoney* (London, 1934)

21 J.B. Dougherty came from Garvagh, and served as a Presbyterian minister in England before returning to become professor of logic in Magee College 1879–95. After standing as a Liberal candidate in Tyrone North in 1892, he was later knighted and made Irish under-secretary in 1908. He was MP for Derry City between 1914 and 1918.

W.H. Dodd was a lawyer from Rathfriland. He stood unsuccessfully as a Liberal in Antrim North in 1892, but was elected for Tyrone North in 1906. He then retired to become a judge.

22 In 1893 Armour described Belfast as the 'temple of violent Toryism'. On another occasion he said that Belfast was a city ruled by 'Pharisees, Sadducees and Philistines'.

CHAPTER 21

1 T.W. Russell, *The Irish Land Question* (London, 1902), p. 26

2 T.W. Russell, who had been converted to Home Rule, stood as a Liberal in Tyrone South in January 1910, and was defeated by a narrow margin. He stood in Tyrone North in a by-election in 1911, again as a Liberal, and held his seat until his retirement in 1918.

3 T.W. Russell, *Ireland and the Empire* (London, 1901), pp. 202–3

4 T.W. Russell, *The Irish Land Question* (London, 1902), p. 31

5 T.W. Russell, *Ireland and the Empire* (London, 1901)

6 Quoted in Henry Summerfield, *That Myriad Minded Man* (Gerrards Cross, 1975), p. 4

7 *Irish Times*, 7 October 1913

8 F.S.L. Lyons, *Ireland Since the Famine* (London, 1971), p. 214

9 John Gray, *City in Revolt: James Larkin and the Belfast Dock Strike of 1907* (Belfast, 1985), writes of the 'hidden poor', and of 'fear, poverty and ill health' among women workers.

10 The Government had published a report which was highly critical of the sweated conditions endured by girls and young mothers in laundries run by Catholic nuns in Ireland. This report was seized upon by Orange critics as just one more example of Catholic abuses of human rights.

11 *See* John Boyle, 'The Belfast Protestant Association and the Independent Orange Order, 1901–1910', *Irish Historical Studies*, vol. XIII (1962–3). The setting up of the Independent Orange Order in 1903 was the 'fruition of nearly forty years of Orange working-class dissent against the ascendancy', John Gray, *City In Revolt: James Larkin and the Belfast Dock Strike of 1907* (Belfast, 1985), p. 44.

12 *Irish Protestant*, April 1903

13 *Irish Protestant*, 2 April 1904. *See also* Sean O'Casey, *Drums Under the Window* (London, 1945), pp. 166–85, for an account of this event.

14 *See* David Greene, 'The Irish language movement' in Michael Hurley (ed.), *Irish Anglicanism, 1869–1969* (Dublin, 1970)

CHAPTER 22

1 Quoted by Rutherford Mayne (Samuel Waddell) in a lecture on the Ulster Literary Theatre given in the Royal Dublin Society, *Irish Times*, 28 November 1936

2 Paul Henry, *An Irish Portrait* (London, 1951), p. 6

3 Robert Lynd, *Home Life in Ireland* (London, 1909), p. 24

4 Forrest Reid, *Private Road* (London, 1940). As well as two volumes of autobiography, Reid wrote more than a dozen novels and several books of criticism.

5 Shane Leslie, *The Landlords of Ireland at the Crossroads* (Dublin, 1908), p. 4. Shane Leslie was an astonishingly prolific writer, producing more than sixty novels, plays, memoirs and books of poetry between 1915 and his death in 1969. His autobiographical studies include *The Film of Memory* (London, 1938) and *Long Shadows* (London, 1966).

6 George Birmingham, *Benedict Kavanagh* (London, 1907)

7 *See* Joseph Campbell, 'Northern Biography' (MS held in library of Trinity College Dublin)

8 Sam Hanna Bell, *The Theatre in Ulster* (Dublin, 1972), p. 1

9 *Ibid.*

10 It was noticeable that many of the men and women who worked with the Ulster Literary Theatre used pseudonyms. This was due to the pressures put upon middle-class Ulster people to keep away from the

arts, which, like the Gaelic League, were not 'respectable'.

11 Rutherford Mayne, *The Drone and Other Plays* (Dublin, 1912)

12 D. Felicitas Corrigan, *Helen Waddell* (London, 1986). R.M. Henry was the sort of scholar that Helen Waddell might well admire. Son of a nephew of John Mitchel, and brother of the painter Paul, he was not only a distinguished authority on classical literature and history, but also was an Irish nationalist. Henry was professor of Latin in Queen's University Belfast between 1907 and 1938, and held for many years the influential post of secretary of the academic council. After the First World War he might have been vice-chancellor but for his liberal views. In 1920 he published *The Evolution of Sinn Fein* (Dublin, 1920), which is a sympathetic study of that organisation.

13 *Songs of Uladh* (Belfast, 1904), words by Seosamh MacCathmhaoil, music by Padraig Aodh O'Neill, illustrations by Seaghan MacCathmhaoil

14 Joseph Campbell, 'Northern Biography' (MS held in library of Trinity College Dublin). Herbert Hughes could find no suitable employment in Belfast, and emigrated to London. He joined the British Army during the First World War. He served as a music critic on the *Daily Telegraph* for many years, dying in 1933 at the age of fifty-one.

15 Ardrigh was demolished in April 1986 to make way for a development of flats. *See Irish Times*, 8 April 1986.

16 Shane Leslie, *The Film of Memory* (London, 1938), pp. 384–5

CHAPTER 23

1 Quoted in *Ballymoney Free Press*, 11 May 1905

2 Bulmer Hobson, *Ireland Yesterday and Tomorrow* (Tralee, 1968), p. 24

3 The text of this manifesto is given in Bulmer Hobson, *Ireland Yesterday and Tomorrow* (Tralee, 1968), p. 98.

4 Roger Casement by this time was a committed republican.

5 Quoted in Bulmer Hobson, *Ireland Yesterday and Tomorrow* (Tralee, 1968), pp. 28–9

6 It was significant that this article was anonymous, and had attached to it a footnote which said that the editor was not responsible for the opinions of all his correspondents.

7 *See* T.A. Jackson, *Ireland Her Own* (London, 1946), p. 351

8 William O'Brien and Desmond Ryan (eds), *Devoy's Post Bag, 1879–1928*, vol. II (Dublin, 1953), p. 377

9 Robert Lynd wrote more than thirty books during a period of over forty years.

10 Riobard Ua Fhloin, *The Orangeman and the Nation* (Belfast, 1907). Lynd seems to have written this pamphlet in reply to a letter from James Winder Good, urgently asking for a contribution to the *Republic* 'I wonder if you would think out some articles that might move young Presbyterian ministers. The better ones among them are opening their eyes a little but they have a lot of leeway to make up. The reactionaries are making desperate efforts to catch them.' (Letter from J.W. Good to Lynd now in the possession of the estate of the late Maire Lynd, daughter of Robert Lynd.)

11 James Winder Good, *Ulster and Ireland* (Dublin, 1919)

12 James Winder Good, *Irish Unionism* (Dublin, 1920)

13 A personal communication to the author from Douglas Gageby who was the son-in-law of Sean Lester.

Lester was a journalist, and eventually became an important official in the League of Nations organisation. He served as commissioner in Danzig just before the Second World War.

14. The 'Ulster connection' is a term which might be applied to a group of ten or a dozen people who at some stage in their lives were concerned in the affairs of the north of Ireland, and also were involved in the founding of the Irish Volunteers and the events leading up to the 1916 rising. Eoin MacNeill, Bulmer Hobson, Denis McCullough, Patrick MacCartan, and Jack White were born in the province; Sean McDermott and Tom Clarke spent several critical years there; and the ancestors of James Connolly, James Larkin and Roger Casement came from Ulster. Thomas Johnson, who later became leader of the Irish Labour Party, and William McMullen and Cathal O'Shannon, who in the 1930s and 1940s were prominent officials in the Irish Transport and General Workers' Union, spent some years in Belfast.

15. *See* Thomas Carnduff, 'I remember', *The Bell* (June 1943), and 'The Orange society', *The Bell* (July 1951). The manuscript of Carnduff's unpublished autobiography is in the Linen Hall Library in Belfast.

16. Quoted in John Boyle, 'The Belfast Protestant Association and the Independent Orange Order, 1901–1910', *Irish Historical Studies*, vol. XIII (1962–3)

17. *See* Brian M. Walker (ed.), *Parliamentary Election Results in Ireland 1801–1922*, (Dublin, 1978)

18. The two key constituencies of Belfast North and Belfast South were known to be marginal seats because, while the majority of voters were workers and might be expected to support Labour, they were also noted as centres of Orangeism. William Walker and Thomas Sloan, who were not too scrupulous when it came to elections, therefore fell back on anti-Catholic demagoguery whenever the opportunity arose. In 1905 this dismayed Ramsay MacDonald, who had come over from London to act as Walker's election agent.

The manoeuvring that went on between the various political, trade union and religious factions in Belfast at this time is described in Henry Patterson, *Class Conflict and Sectarianism: The Protestant Working Class and the Belfast Labour Movement 1868–1920* (Belfast, 1980). Patterson is particularly perceptive on the social basis of 'Labour imperialism'.

19. Editorial in *Ulster Guardian*, 3 August 1907

20. John Gray, *City in Revolt: James Larkin and the Belfast Dock Strike of 1907* (Belfast, 1985), p. 166

21. St John Ervine's parents were deaf mutes and he was brought up in a poor district of east Belfast by a grandmother. Emigrating as a youth to London, he got work as a clerk, and then turned to literary ambitions. His contacts with Bernard Shaw made him a Fabian and he began to show sympathies for the Labour movement. However, these did not last long, and he ended his long life as an extreme Unionist. He was the author of more than twenty plays and novels.

22. 'Lindsay Crawford still held his ground, convinced more than ever by the strike experience that the Protestant section of the working class could not achieve its own

industrial emancipation unless it was prepared to consider political emancipation for the Irish people as a whole.' John Gray, *City in Revolt: James Larkin and the Belfast Dock Strike of 1907* (Belfast, 1985), p. 189.

23 Bulmer Hobson returned temporarily to Belfast in 1909, but two years later was appointed to the staff of the IRB journal *Irish Freedom* in Dublin. For the next few years his main work was with the Irish Volunteers.

24 Lynd also condemned Casement's activities during the war, but when his old friend was in the dock at the Old Bailey he strove hard to win a reprieve for him. The following year he published an unsigned article in the *New Statesman*, 'If the Germans conquered England', which caused a public stir because of its ironical tone about such a serious subject, and the implication that England had done equally 'Hunnish' things to Ireland over the centuries. In 1919, when the independence struggle was taking on a more violent form, he published his most important political book *Ireland a Nation*, in which he developed the argument that the Ascendancy would long ago have been replaced by democracy if it had not been sustained by British power. In a pithy phrase he distinguished progressive from reactionary types of patriotism: 'Nationalism involves a theory of a democracy of nations', he wrote. 'Imperialism involves a theory of a hierarchy of stronger nations with the right to subject weaker nations to their will' (p. 33). In 1934 he paid tribute to Ulster's radical Presbyterian tradition in the Foreword he wrote to W.S. Armour, *Armour of Ballymoney* (London, 1934).

25 J.W. Boyle saw these moderate unionists, new liberals, Labour supporters, and left-wing nationalists forming only a 'tenuous alliance' which soon collapsed. *See* John Boyle, 'The Belfast Protestant Association and the Independent Orange Order, 1901–1910', *Irish Historical Studies*, vol. XIII (1962–3).

26 D.A. Chart (ed.), *The Drennan Letters, 1776–1819* (Belfast, 1931)

27 John Gray, *City in Revolt: James Larkin and the Belfast Dock Strike of 1907* (Belfast, 1985), p. 209

28 *Labour Chronicle*, Belfast, July 1905

29 *Labour Chronicle*, Belfast, October 1905

30 Seumus Ó Buachalla (ed.), *The Letters of Patrick Pearse* (Dublin, 1980), p. 111

CHAPTER 24

1 Andrew Bonar Law, speaking at Blenheim, July 1912. Quoted in A.T.Q. Stewart, *The Ulster Crisis* (London, 1967), p. 57.

2 This quotation is taken from the agenda of the first meeting of the Ulster Unionist Council held in March 1905. *See* Patrick Buckland (ed.), *Irish Unionism vol. II: Ulster Unionism and the Origins of Northern Ireland, 1886–1922* (Dublin, 1973), p. 205.

3 For the relationship between the Orange Order and the Unionist Party post-1922 *see* John F. Harbinson, *The Ulster Unionist Party, 1882–1973: Its Development and Organisation* (Belfast, 1973), p. 96

4 '. . . for three years after the time of his [Connolly's] arrival the entire resources of Tory reaction were concentrated on this one city [Belfast]', C. Desmond Greaves, *The Life and Times of James Connolly* (London, 1961), p. 219

5 Quoted in Ronald McNeill, *Ulster's Stand for Union* (London, 1922), p. 100

6 Ronald McNeill, *Ulster's Stand for Union* (London, 1922), pp. 3–4

7 Quoted in A.T.Q. Stewart, *The Ulster Crisis* (London, 1967), p. 48

8 Quoted in Robert Blake, *The Unknown Prime Minister: The Life and Times of Andrew Bonar Law, 1858–1923* (London, 1955), p. 162

9 Henry Patterson, *Class Conflict and Sectarianism: The Protestant Working Class and the Belfast Labour Movement 1868–1920* (Belfast, 1980)

10 Quoted in A.T.Q. Stewart, *The Ulster Crisis* (London, 1967) p. 57

11 R.M. Sibbett, *Orangeism in Ireland and Throughout the Empire*, vol. II (London, c. 1937), p. 617

12 A.T.Q. Stewart, *The Ulster Crisis* (London, 1967), p. 137

13 'Col. Wallace was amongst the first to perceive the importance of this military drilling that was taking place throughout Ulster and through his leading position in the Orange Institution, his encouragement did much to extend the practice.' Ronald McNeill, *Ulster's Stand for Union* (London, 1922), p. 57.

14 Ronald McNeill, *Ulster's Stand for Union* (London, 1922), p. 147

15 Patrick Buckland (ed.), *Irish Unionism, 1885–1923: A Documentary History* (Dublin, 1973)

16 *See* Cork Workers' Club, *The Connolly–Walker Controversy* (n.d.)

17 W.S. Armour, *Armour of Ballymoney* (London, 1934), p. 282

18 *Ibid.*, p. 268

19 *Ibid.*, chapter 13

20 Jack White, who wrote a pamphlet about the meeting, *A Protestant Protest* (Ballymoney, 1913), said that the Protestant audience consisted of 'plain country people'. *The Times*, which carried reports on 24–5 October 1913, dismissed the rally as representing only a tiny minority of Ulster Protestants, mainly 'cranks and faddists'.

21 J.R. White, *Misfit* (London, 1930)

22 Roger Casement, who always said how proud he was to be an Ulsterman, tried to distinguish between ordinary Protestants and the followers of Carson. 'I love the Antrim Presbyterians – Antrim and Down', he wrote to his cousin Gertrude Bannister in 1913. 'They are good, kind, warm-hearted souls, and to see them exploited by that damn Church of Ireland – that Orange Ascendancy gang who hate the Presbyterians only less than the Papists, and to see them delirious before a Smith, a Carson (a cross between a badly-reared bloodhound, and an underfed hyena, sniffing for Irish blood in the track), and whooping Rule Britannia thro' the streets is a wound to the soul.' Rene McColl, *Roger Casement* (London, 1956), p. 121.

23 Quoted in Jack White, *A Protestant Protest* (Ballymoney, 1913), pp. 30–1

24 Alice Stopford was the daughter of the Protestant archdeacon of Kells, County Meath, and had married the distinguished English historian J.R. Green, who died in 1883, leaving her financially well-provided for. An intelligent and energetic woman, she quickly established her London home as a salon for writers, scholars and politicians who were sympathetic to the cause of Irish independence. In the 1880s and 1890s she was a strong supporter of Home Rule, and later became a friend of Roger Casement's. Her publications include *The Making of Ireland and Its Undoing* (London, 1908), *Irish Nationality* (London, 1911) and *Ourselves Alone and Ulster* (London, 1918). She opposed the

1916 rising and became a member of the Irish Free State senate after 1922. A new study of Alice Stopford Green and her family has recently been published by Leon O'Broin, *Protestant Nationalists in Revolutionary Ireland: The Stopford Connection* (Dublin, 1985).

25 Quoted in Jack White, *A Protestant Protest* (Ballymoney, 1913)

26 *Ibid.*

EPILOGUE

1 The Reverend Robin Boyd, one time director of the Irish School of Ecumenics, in an interview with the *Irish Times*, 18 March 1986

2 Writing on almost the same day in March 1914, James Connolly and J.B. Armour attacked the current proposals to divide Ireland into two parts on the grounds that it would encourage the most reactionary political elements, north and south. *See Irish Worker*, 14 March 1914, and J.B. Armour quoted in J.R.B. McMinn, *Against the Tide* (Belfast, 1985).

3 John Hewitt and John Montague, *The Planter and the Gael* (Belfast, 1970)

4 Bishop John F. MacNeice (father of poet Louis MacNeice) in the 1930s, and Bishop Richard Hanson after the war, were well-known critics of the Orange Order.

5 The Reverend David Armstrong was a young Presbyterian minister who tried to make friends with a neighbouring Catholic priest in Limavady in 1983. Armstrong was driven to resign and go to England by the hostility shown towards him by the local Orangemen and members of Paisley's Free Presbyterian Church. *See* David Armstrong and Hilary Saunders, *A Road Too Wide* (Basingstoke, 1985).

6 The Reverend J.M. Barkley, *Blackmouth and Dissenter* (Belfast, 1991), argues that the word 'blackmouth' was not a reference to the fact that Scottish Presbyterians were forced to eat bilberries in times of persecution but instead was a slang term applied derogatively against those Dissenters in Ulster during the eighteenth century who supported the American and French revolutions.

7 *See* Paddy Devlin, *Yes, We Have No Bananas: Outdoor Relief in Belfast, 1920–39* (Belfast, 1981)

8 *See* Bob Purdie, *Politics in the Streets: The Origins of the Civil Rights Movement in Northern Ireland* (Belfast, 1990)

SELECT BIBLIOGRAPHY

NEWSPAPERS AND PERIODICALS

Ballymoney Free Press
Belfast News-Letter
Evening Post
Impartial Reporter
Irish Historical Studies
Irish Protestant
Labour Chronicle
Newry Examiner
Northern Star
Northern Whig
Shan Van Vocht
The Times
Ulster Weekly News
United Irishman

THESES

Dunne, T.J. 'Ireland, England and the Empire, 1868–1886',
    unpublished Ph.D. thesis, Cambridge University, 1975
Grant, James. 'The Great Famine in the province of Ulster, 1845–49',
    unpublished Ph.D. thesis, Queen's University Belfast, 1986
Kennedy, Brian. 'Sharman Crawford, a political biography',
    unpublished Ph.D. thesis, Queen's University Belfast, 1953
McCann, P.J.O. 'The Protestant Home Rule Movement, 1886–1895',
    unpublished MA thesis, University College Dublin, 1972
McLoughlin, John Patrick. 'Gladstone, Irish Nationalism and the
    Home Rule Question, 1882–1893, with particular reference to the
    Ulster problem', unpublished Ph.D. thesis, Trinity College Dublin,
    1984
McMinn, J.R.B. 'The Rev. James Brown Armour and Liberal politics
    in North Antrim, 1869–1914', unpublished Ph.D. thesis, Queen's
    University Belfast, 1979
Thompson, Francis. 'Land and politics in Ulster, 1868–86',
    unpublished Ph.D. thesis, Queen's University Belfast, 1982

Abernethy, John. *Persecution Contrary to Christianity*, Dublin, 1735

Adair, A. Shafto. *The Winter of 1846–7 in Antrim*, London, 1847

Armour, W.S. *Armour of Ballymoney*, London, 1934

Bailie, W.D. *William Steel Dickson*, Belfast, 1976

Barkley, J.M. *Blackmouth and Dissenter*, Belfast, 1991

Barlow, Joyce. *Capt. Boycott and the Irish*, London, 1973

'A Barrister'. *A Faithful Report of the Trial of the Proprietors of the Northern Star*, Belfast, 1794

Beckett, J.C. *The Making of Modern Ireland, 1603–1923*, London, 1966

Bell, Geoffrey. *The Protestants of Ulster*, London, 1976

Bell, Sam Hanna. *The Theatre in Ulster*, Dublin, 1972

Bigger, Francis Joseph. *William Orr*, Dublin, 1906

Bigger, F.J. *The Ulster Land War of 1770*, Belfast, 1910

Birmingham, George. *Benedict Kavanagh*, London, 1907

Blake, Robert. *The Unknown Prime Minister: The Life and Times of Andrew Bonar Law, 1858–1923*, London, 1955

Bolton, G.C. *The Passing of the Act of Union*, London, 1966

Bowen, Desmond. *The Protestant Crusade in Ireland, 1800–1870*, London, 1978

Boyd, Andrew. *Holy War in Belfast*, Tralee, 1969

Boyd, Charles W. (ed.). *Mr. Chamberlain's Speeches*, London, 1914

Boyle, John. 'The Belfast Protestant Association and the Independent Orange Order, 1901–1910', *Irish Historical Studies*, vol. XIII (1962–3)

Brett, C.E.B. *Long Shadows Cast Before*, Edinburgh, 1978

Brooke, Charlotte. *Reliques of Irish Poetry*, Dublin, 1789

Brooke, Peter. *Ulster Presbyterianism: The Historical Perspective, 1610–1970*, Dublin, 1987

Brown, Terence. *The Whole Protestant Community: The Making of a Historical Myth*, Derry, 1985

Brown, Terence, and Alec Reid. *Time Was Away: The World of Louis MacNeice*, London, 1974

Buckland, Patrick (ed.). *Irish Unionism, 1885–1923: A Documentary History*, Dublin, 1973

Buckland, Patrick (ed.). *Irish Unionism vol. II: Ulster Unionism and the Origins of Northern Ireland, 1886–1922*, Dublin, 1973

Burke, Edmund. *The Works of Edmund Burke*, 6 vols, London, 1856.

Butt, Isaac. *A Plea for the Celtic Race*, Dublin, 1866

Butt, Isaac. *The Irish People and Irish Land*, London, 1867

Carbery, Ethna, Seumus MacManus and Alice Milligan. *We Sang for Ireland*, Dublin, 1950

Castlereagh, Viscount. *Memoirs and Correspondence of Viscount Castlereagh, edited by his brother Charles Vane, Marquess of Londonderry*, 4 vols, London, 1848 and 1849

Chart, D.A. (ed.). *The Drennan Letters, 1776–1819*, Belfast, 1931

Cork Workers' Club. *The Connolly–Walker Controversy*, n.d.

Cornwallis, Charles. *Correspondence of Charles, First Marquess of Cornwallis*, ed. Charles Ross, 3 vols, London, 1849

Corrigan, D. Felicitas. *Helen Waddell*, London, 1986

Crawford, William Sharman. *A Defence of the Small Farmers of Ireland*, Dublin, 1839

Crone, John S. and F.C. Bigger (eds). *In Remembrance*, Belfast, 1927

Cronin, Sean. *Irish Nationalism*, Dublin, 1980

Crozier, John A. *The Life of the Rev. Henry Montgomery*, London, 1875

Curtis, Edmund. *A History of Ireland*, London, 1961

Curtis, L.P., Jr. *Coercion and Conciliation in Ireland, 1880–1882*, New Jersey, 1963

Curtis, Liz. *Nothing but the Same Old Story: The Roots of Anti-Irish Racism*, London, 1984

Davis, Thomas. *Selection from His Prose and Poetry*, Dublin, n.d.

Davis, Thomas. 'Song of the Volunteers of 1782' in *Essays and Poems with a Centenary Memoir*, Dublin, 1945

Davitt, Michael. *The Fall of Feudalism in Ireland*, London, 1904

de Paor, Liam. *Divided Ulster*, Middlesex, 1971

Devlin, Paddy. *Yes, We Have No Bananas: Outdoor Relief in Belfast, 1920–39*, Belfast, 1981

Devoy, John. *Recollections of an Irish Rebel*, Shannon, 1969 ed.

Dewar, M.W., John Brown and S.E. Long. *Orangeism, A New Perspective*, Belfast, 1967

Dickson, Charles. *Revolt in the North: Antrim and Down in 1798*, Dublin, 1960

Dickson, R.J. *Ulster Emigration to Colonial America, 1718–1755*, London, 1966

Dickson, William Steel. *Three Sermons on the Subject of Scripture Politics*, Belfast, 1793

Dickson, William Steel. *A Narrative of the Confinement and Exile of William Steel Dickson, D.D.*, Dublin, 1812

Dill, Edward Marcus. *The Mystery Solved or Ireland's Miseries, the Grand Cause and Cure*, London, 1852

Drennan, William. *A Letter to the Rt. Hon. William Pitt*, Dublin, 1799

Drennan, William. *A Letter to Charles James Fox*, Dublin, 1806

Drennan, William. *Fugitive Pieces in Verse and Prose*, Belfast, 1815

Drennan, William. *Seventh Letter of Orellana*, quoted in John Lawless (ed.), *Belfast Politics Enlarged*, Belfast, 1818

Dufferin, Lord, and E.P. Boyle. *Narrative of a Journey from Oxford to Skibbereen during the Year of the Irish Famine*, Oxford, 1847

Duffy, Charles Gavan. *The League of North and South, 1850–1854*, London, 1886

Duffy, Charles Gavan. *Young Ireland, 1840–1845*, 2 vols, London, 1896 ed.

Edgar, John. *A Cry from Connaught*, Belfast, 1846.

Edwards, R. Dudley and T. Desmond Williams (eds). *The Great Famine*, Dublin, 1962

Elliott, Marianne. *Partners in Revolution: The United Irishmen and France*, London, 1982

Elliott, Marianne. *Watchmen in Sion: The Protestant Idea of Liberty*, Derry, 1985

Elliott, Marianne. *Wolfe Tone: Prophet of Irish Independence*, London, 1989

Ervine, St John. *Parnell*, London, 1944

Evans, Estyn. *Prehistoric and Early Christian Ireland*, London, 1966

Farrell, Michael. *Northern Ireland: The Orange State*, London, 1976

Ferguson, Lady. *Life of the Rt. Hon. Rev. William Reeves*, London, 1883

Ferguson, Lady. *Sir Samuel Ferguson in the Ireland of His Day*, 2 vols, London, 1896

Fitzpatrick, R.W. 'Origins and development of the land war in mid-Ulster, 1879–85' in F.S.L. Lyons and R.A.J. Hawkins (eds), *Ireland Under the Union*, Oxford, 1980

Fitzpatrick, Rory. *God's Frontiersmen: The Scots Irish Epic*, London, 1989

Fitzpatrick, W.J. *Secret Services Under Pitt*, London, 1892

Foster, R.F. *Modern Ireland, 1600–1972*, London, 1988

Freeman, T.W. *Pre-Famine Ireland*, London, 1957

Gallagher, Eric, and A. Stanley Worrall. *Christians in Ulster, 1968–1980*, Oxford, 1982

Gibbon, Peter. *The Origins of Ulster Unionism*, Manchester, 1975

Godkin, James. *The Land War in Ireland*, New York, 1970 ed.

Good, James Winder. *Ulster and Ireland*, Dublin, 1919

Good, James Winder. *Irish Unionism*, Dublin, 1920

Gray, John. *City in Revolt: James Larkin and the Belfast Dock Strike of 1907*, Belfast, 1985

Greaves, C. Desmond. *The Life and Times of James Connolly*, London, 1961

Green, Alice Stopford. *The Making of Ireland and Its Undoing*, London, 1908

Green, E.R.R. (ed.). *Essays in Scotch-Irish History*, London, 1969

Greene, David. 'The Irish language movement' in Michael Hurley (ed.), *Irish Anglicanism, 1869–1969*, Dublin, 1970

Haire, J.L.M. (ed.). *Challenge and Conflict*, Antrim, 1981

Hammond, J.L. *Gladstone and the Irish Nation*, London, 1964

Harbison, John F. *The Ulster Unionist Party, 1882–1973: Its Development and Organisation*, Belfast, 1973

Haslip, Joan. *Parnell*, London, 1936

Hennessy, P.R. *Burke, Paine and the Rights of Man*, The Hague, 1963

Henry, Paul. *An Irish Portrait*, London, 1951

Henry, R.M. *The Evolution of Sinn Fein*, Dublin, 1920

Hewitt, John. *Ancestral Voices: The Selected Prose of John Hewitt*, ed. Tom Clyde, Belfast, 1987

Hewitt, John, and John Montague. *The Planter and the Gael*, Belfast, 1970

Hill, Lord George. *Facts from Gweedore*, Dublin, 1845

Hobson, Bulmer. *Ireland Yesterday and Tomorrow*, Tralee, 1968

Holmes, Finlay. *Henry Cooke*, Belfast, 1981

Hope, James. *The Memoirs of Jemmy Hope*, Belfast, 1973 ed.

Ireland, Denis. *From the Irish Shore*, London, 1936

Jackson, T.A. *Ireland Her Own*, London, 1946

Jacob, Rosamond. *The Rise of the United Irishmen, 1791–1794*, London, 1937

James, Robert Rhodes. *Lord Randolph Churchill*, London, 1959

Jamieson, John. *The History of the Royal Belfast Academical Institution*, Belfast 1959

Jennings, Louis J. (ed.). *Speeches of Lord Randolph Churchill, 1880–1888*, 2 vols, London, 1889

Judd, Denis. *Radical Joe*, London, 1977

Kee, Robert. *The Green Flag*, London, 1972

Kerr, Donal A. *Peel, Priests and Politics*, London, 1982

Kiely, Benedict. *Poor Scholar*, London, 1947

Killen, W.D. *Memoir of John Edgar*, Belfast, 1867

Latimer, W.T. *A History of the Irish Presbyterians*, Belfast, 1902

Le Roux, Louis. *Tom Clarke and the Irish Freedom Movement*, London, 1936

Lecky, W.E.H. *History of Ireland in the Eighteenth Century*, 5 vols, London, 1892 ed.

Leslie, Shane. *The Landlords of Ireland at the Crossroads*, Dublin, 1908

Leslie, Shane. *Doomsland*, London, 1923

Leslie, Shane. *The Film of Memory*, London, 1938

Leslie, Shane. *Lord Mulroy's Ghost*, Dublin, 1954

Lucas, Reginald. *Col. Saunderson, M.P.*, London, 1908

Lynd, Robert. *Home Life in Ireland*, London, 1909

Lynd, Robert. *Ireland a Nation*, London, 1919

Lyons, F.S.L. *Ireland Since the Famine*, London, 1971

Lyttle, W.G. *Betsy Gray or Hearts of Down*, Belfast, 1896

MacCall, Seumus. *Irish Mitchel*, London, 1938

McColl, Rene. *Roger Casement*, London, 1956

McDermot, Frank. *Tone and His Times*, Dublin, 1980 ed.

MacDonagh, Michael. *The Viceroy's Postbag*, London, 1904

McDowell, R.B. *Public Opinion and Government Policy in Ireland, 1801–1846*, London, 1952

McDowell, R.B. *The Church of Ireland, 1869–1969*, London, 1975

McDowell, R.B. *Ireland in the Age of Imperialism and Revolution, 1760–1801*, London, 1979

McElroy, S.C. *The Route Land Crusade*, Coleraine, n.d.

MacKnight, Thomas. *Ulster As It Is*, 2 vols, London, 1896

McMinn, J.R.B. *Against the Tide*, Belfast, 1985

McNeill, Mary. *The Life and Times of Mary Ann McCracken, 1770–1866*, Belfast, 1988

McNeill, Ronald. *Ulster's Stand for Union*, London, 1922

Macneven, William James. *Pieces of Irish History*, New York, 1807

Madden, R.R. *The United Irishmen: Their Lives and Times*, 4 vols, London, 1842–3; 3 vols, Dublin, 1846

Marx, Karl, and Frederick Engels. *On Ireland and the Irish Question*, Moscow, 1971

Mayne, Rutherford. *The Drone and Other Plays*, Dublin, 1912

Millar, David. *Queen's Rebels: Ulster Loyalism in Historical Perspective*, Dublin, 1978

Milligan, Alice. *Poems*, Dublin, 1954 ed.

Mitchel, John. *The History of Ireland*, Glasgow, 1869

Mitchel, John. *An Ulsterman for Ireland, being Letters to the Protestant*

Farmers, Labourers and Artisans of the North of Ireland, ed. Eoin MacNeill, Dublin, 1917 ed.

Montgomery, Hugh de Fellenberg. *Irish Land and Irish Rights*, London, 1881

Moody, T.W. *Michael Davitt and Irish Revolution, 1846–1882*, Oxford, 1982

Moody, T.W. and W.E. Vaughan (eds). *A New History of Ireland, vol. IV, 1691–1800*, London, 1986

Morris, James. *Heaven's Command*, London, 1973

Morton, A.L. *A People's History of England*, London, 1946

Nelson, Sarah. *Ulster's Uncertain Defenders*, Belfast, 1984

Newell, Edward John. *The Apostasy of Newell*, Belfast, 1798

Nicolson, Harold. *The Desire to Please*, London, 1943

Norman, E.R. *Anti-Catholicism in Victorian England*, London, 1968.

'A Northern Whig'. *An Argument on Behalf of the Catholics of Ireland*, Dublin, 1791

Ó Buachalla, Seumus (ed.). *The Letters of Patrick Pearse*, Dublin, 1980

Ó Snódaigh, Pádraig. *Hidden Ulster*, Dublin, 1977

O'Brien, William, and Desmond Ryan (eds). *Devoy's Post Bag, 1879–1928*, 2 vols, Dublin, 1953

O'Broin, Leon. *Protestant Nationalists in Revolutionary Ireland: The Stopford Connection*, Dublin, 1985

O'Byrne, Cathal. *As I Roved Out*, Belfast, 1946

O'Casey, Sean. *Drums Under the Window*, London, 1945

O'Donoghue, David A. (ed.). *Life of William Carleton*, London, 1896

O'Neill, Brian. *The War for the Land in Ireland*, London, 1933

O'Sullivan, Donal. *Irish Folk Music and Song*, Dublin, 1961

Paine, Thomas. *Rights of Man*, Dublin, 1791 and 1792

Patterson, Henry. *Class Conflict and Sectarianism: The Protestant Working Class and the Belfast Labour Movement 1868–1920*, Belfast, 1980

Pearse, Padraic H. *Collected Works*, 3 vols, Dublin, 1922

Porter, J.L. *The Life and Times of Henry Cooke*, London, 1871

Porter, James. *Wind and Weather: A Sermon on the Late Providential Storm which Dispersed the French Fleet in Bantry Bay Preached to the Congregation of Grey-Abbey on Thursday, 16th February*, Belfast, 1797

[Porter, James]. *Billy Bluff and Squire Firebrand in Six Letters which appeared in the Northern Star, 1796*, Belfast, 1868 ed.

Purdie, Bob. *Politics in the Streets: The Origins of the Civil Rights Movement in Northern Ireland*, Belfast, 1990

Reid, Forrest. *Private Road*, London, 1940

Reid, James Seiton. *History of the Presbyterian Church of Ireland*, 3 vols, Belfast, 1867

Roden, Earl of. *Progress of the Reformation in Ireland*, London, 1851.

Rose, Richard. *Governing Without Consensus: An Irish Perspective*, London, 1971

Rowan, Archibald Hamilton. *Autobiography of Archibald Hamilton Rowan*, ed. W.H. Drummond, Dublin, 1840

Russell, T.W. *Ireland and Empire*, London, 1901

Russell, T.W. *The Irish Land Question*, London, 1902

Sawyer, Roger. *Roger Casement: The Flawed Hero*, London, 1984

Scrope, G. Poulett. *Reply to the Archbishop of Dublin*, London, 1847

Senior, Hereward. *Orangeism in Ireland and Britain, 1795–1834*, London, 1966

Senior, Nassau William. *Journals, Conversations and Essays relating to Ireland*, London, 1868

Sibbett, R.M. *Orangeism in Ireland and Throughout the Empire*, 2 vols, London, *c.* 1937

Sillard, P.A. *The Life and Times of John Martin*, London, 1893

Songs of Uladh, Belfast, 1904

Stewart, A.T.Q. *The Ulster Crisis*, London, 1967

Stewart, A.T.Q. *The Narrow Ground: Aspects of Ulster, 1609–1969*, London 1977

Sullivan, A.M. *New Ireland*, Philadelphia, 1878

Summerfield, Henry. *That Myriad Minded Man*, Gerrards Cross, 1975

Tawney, R.H. *Religion and the Rise of Capitalism*, London, 1926

Teeling, C.H. *History of the Irish Rebellion of 1798*, Shannon, 1972 ed.

Thompson, E.P. *The Making of the English Working Class*, London, 1963

Thornley, David. *Isaac Butt and Home Rule*, London, 1964

Tone, Theobald Wolfe. *Life of Theobald Wolfe Tone, edited by his son William Theobald Wolfe Tone*, 2 vols, Washington 1826

Ua Fhloin, Riobard. *The Orangeman and the Nation*, Belfast, 1907

Vaughan, W.E. and A.J. Fitzpatrick. *Irish Historical Statistics, Population 1821–1971*, Dublin, 1978

Wakefield, Edward. *An Account of Ireland, Statistical and Political*, 2 vols, London, 1812

Walker, Brian M. (ed.). *Parliamentary Election Results in Ireland, 1801–1922*, Dublin, 1978

Walker, Brian M. 'The land question and elections in Ulster, 1868–86' in Samuel Clark and James S. Donnelly, Jr. (eds), *Irish Peasants, Violence and Political Unrest, 1780–1914*, Manchester, 1983

Walker, B.M. *Ulster Politics: The Formative Years, 1868–1886*, Belfast, 1989

Weber, Max. *The Protestant Ethic and the Spirit of Capitalism*, London, 1930

Whateley, E. Jane. *Life and Correspondence of Richard Whateley, D.D.*, London, 1875

Whateley, Richard. *Speech in the House of Lords on the Committee on the Irish Poor Law*, London, 1847

White, J.R. *Misfit*, London, 1930

White, Jack. *A Protestant Protest*, Ballymoney, 1913

White, Terence de Vere. *The Road to Excess*, London, 1946

Williams, Desmond (ed.). *Secret Societies in Ireland*, Dublin, 1973

Wollstonecraft, Mary. *A Vindication of the Rights of Woman*, London, 1792

Woodham-Smith, Cecil. *The Great Hunger*, London, 1962

Young, Arthur. *A Tour in Ireland, 1776–1779*, Shannon, 1970 ed.

Abbey Theatre, 362, 369, 392
Abercorn, 1st Duke of, 277–8
Abercorn, 2nd Duke of, 312, 330, 404
Abercorn, 1st Marquess of, 108
Abercorn, 2nd Marquess of, 172
Abercorn family, 11, 165, 314, 320
Abercromby, General Ralph, 89–91, 95
Aberdeen, Lord, 262
Abernethy, Revd John, 17–18
Acheson, Revd Robert, 74
Achill Island, Co. Mayo, 394
Act of Union (1801), 1, 62, 65, 126, 134,
    310, 323, 385, 432; see also repeal
    movement
    Ascendancy support for, 209–10
    bribery campaign, 109–11
    effects of, 116, 163–6
    effects of tithes war, 153
    failures of, 128, 130, 191–3
    and Home Rule movement, 292
    and imperialism, 409
    Mitchel on, 237–8
    objectives of, 113–15
    opposition to, 111–12
    preparations for, 59, 107–12
    reform within framework of, 396–7
    repeal sought, 268–9
    Russell support for, 350–1
Adair, Shafto, 212
Adair, Revd William, 74
Addington, Henry, 133
Adomnan, 231
Africa, 341
Age of Reason, The (Paine), 49–50
Aghadea, 289
agrarian agitation, 20–3, 42, 64, 161, 171,
    214; see also Land League and land
    question
    1870s, 271–81
    influenced by Jacobinism, 70
    Plan of Campaign, 311–12
    tenant-right movement, 247–65
    tithes war, 147–55

Agricultural and Technical Instruction,
    Department of, 353
agriculture, 20, 170–4, 177–8, 277
    co-operative movement, 352–3
    depressions, 23, 248–9, 278–81
    migratory workers, 349–50
Ahoghill, Co. Antrim, 132
Alexander, Revd Thomas, 74
Allen, William P., 245
Alliance Party, 429
America see United States
amnesty campaign, 270, 338
Ancient Britons (regiment), 90
Ancient Order of Hibernians, 362, 379,
    416
Anglo-Normans, 8
Annaghglone, 250
Annals of the Four Masters, 225
Anne, Queen, 14
anti-Semitism, 318
Antrim, Co., 13, 65, 85, 257, 383, 422
    agrarian agitation, 21–2, 284, 305
    disaffection, 96–7
    elections, 161, 177, 355, 386–7, 406–7
    farmers' organisations, 271–2
    franchise, 27–8, 158
    Gaelic culture, 334
    Gaelic League festival, 368–9
    Great Famine, 182–4, 190
    Irish language, 340
    land ownership, 172, 277–8
    Orange Order, 111
    proportion of Catholics, 333
    tenant-right agitation, 156
    tithes war, 151
    United Irishmen rising, 92, 101, 104
    Volunteers, 32
Antrim, Earl of, 172, 272, 277
Antrim Central Tenants' Association, 274
Arboe, Co. Tyrone, 9, 377
Archdale (Archdall) family, 11, 83, 111,
    165, 176–7, 284
Archdall, M., 196

Argentina, 279
Arianism, 16–17, 125, 137, 139–40, 141–3
Arlow, Revd William, 430–1
Armagh, Co., 73, 96, 103, 171–2, 206, 279, 327, 422
  agrarian agitation, 20, 22, 285
  Diamond riots, 82
  diocese, 128
  elections, 176–7, 291, 387, 406
  franchise, 27
  Great Famine, 183, 185
  landownership, 172, 174, 278
  Orange Order, 111, 306
  plantation, 10
  population loss, 190
  proportion of Catholics, 333
  revolution spreading, 96
  United Irishmen, 85
Armagh city, 99, 260
  elections, 160
  Land League, 287
  rotten borough, 157–8
Arminianism, 16
Armour, Revd James Brown (of Ballymoney), 2, 272–3, 332, 343–7, 383, 418–19, 426, 431–2
Arms Bill (1793), 63
Armstrong, Revd David, 431
Ascendancy, 6, 17, 43, 79, 95–6, 104, 228, 255–8, 321, 330, 424, 427, 432
  and Act of Union, 107–12
  British criticism of, 95–6, 194–6, 310–12, 325
  and coercion policy, 62–3
  corruption of, 128
  determined to protect status, 209–10
  disillusion with, 58–9, 363
  effects of Land Acts, 313–14
  eighteenth century, 12–13
  Fitzwilliam recalled, 66
  fragmentation of opposition to, 395–8
  improving landlords, 212–13
  Irish opposition to, 20–3, 38, 75–8, 106, 121, 137, 255–8, 282, 343, 350–2, 355–6, 385, 389
  'Irish Party', 195–6
  liberalism among, 35–40

  loyalty conditional, 381, 409–11
  opposition to Home Rule, 408
  opposition to repeal, 161–4
  and Orange Order, 303, 305–6, 309
  perpetuated by Union, 113–15
  power of, 12–13, 19–20, 26–30, 84, 98–9, 156–61, 175–7
  and Presbyterians, 75–8, 130–4
  supports intimidation, 89–91
  threatened by industrialisation, 165–6 301–2
  and tithes war, 154–5
  and Ulster custom, 180–1
Asquith, Herbert, 386, 411–13, 415–16, 421, 429
Australia, 190, 260, 263, 265, 279, 315

Back Lane Parliament, 57–8, 63–4, 71
Bakunin, Mikhail, 307
Balfour, Arthur, 1, 317, 325, 353, 355, 359, 361, 403–4
  advocates physical force, 329–30
  and Carson, 328
  defeated, 386
  and land reform, 312–14
  and Saunderson, 326
Balfour, Gerald, 353, 359
Ballinamuck, Battle of, 103, 108
Ballinascreen, Co. Derry, 184
Ballybay, Co. Monaghan, 223–4, 250
Ballycastle, Co. Antrim, 96, 183, 349
Ballyclare, Co. Antrim, 250
Ballydown, 250
Ballygawley, Co. Tyrone, 280
Ballykilbeg, Co. Down, 307
Ballymacnab, Co. Armagh, 285
Ballymena, Co. Antrim, 23, 96, 183, 212, 250, 264
  synods, 140, 260
Ballymoney, Co. Antrim, 250, 257, 271–3, 294, 346–7
  Home Rule meeting, 419–21
  Land League conference, 285
Ballymoney Free Press, 273
Ballymoney Tenants' Association, 273
Ballynahinch, Co. Down
  Battle of, 119, 138

United Irishmen rising, 92, 102, 104
Ballynahinch, Co. Galway, 35, 76, 377
Ballynure, Co. Derry, 183
Ballyshannon, Co. Donegal, 99
Banbridge, Co. Down, 250
Bangor, Co. Down, 9, 415
Bankhead, Revd John, 132
Banner of Ulster, 183, 250, 252, 254, 257–8
Bannister, Gertrude, 341
Bantry Bay, Co. Cork, 78, 97
Baptists, 3, 82, 165, 167, 415
Barber, Colonel, 92
Barber, Revd Samuel, 34, 74
Barbour, John, 320
Barbour family, 165
Barkley, Revd John M., 431
Barrett, William, 390
Barry, Admiral John, 25
Barry, Michael Joseph, 220
Bates, Dawson, 415
Bateson, Sir Thomas, 302–3
Bath, Marquess of, 172
Beattie, Jack, 432
Beckett, J.C., 95
Belcoo, Co. Fermanagh, 283
Belfast, 2, 13, 21, 120, 134, 180, 196, 278, 314
    and Act of Union, 111
    and agrarian agitation, 22, 250–1, 253, 273
    agricultural prices decline, 248–9
    anti-Home Rule campaign, 408
    anti-Home Rule crusade, 416–17
    Ascendancy appeal to, 130–1
    Churchill speech, 323–4
    cultural revivals, 335–6, 339, 363–4
    disaffection in, 63–4, 95–7, 347
    effects of general strike, 392–9
    elections, 149, 176–7, 265, 293, 379, 406–7, 422
    emigration from, 23, 190
    franchise, 158, 160–1, 291
    Gaelic League, 373
    general strike, 3, 387–92
    Great Famine, 182, 185–7, 197, 207
    and Home Rule movement, 289, 292–3, 329–30, 343
    industrial development, 164–6, 264, 279, 301, 332
    influence of Orange Order, 85, 257
    informers, 92–3
    labour movement, 3, 332, 357–9, 362–3, 376–7, 383–4, 416–17
    Land League activity, 285–6, 288–9
    linen industry, 177
    population, 165, 320
    proportion of Catholics, 333
    and repeal movement, 224
    rotten borough, 28
    sectarianism, 1, 264, 307–8, 324–5, 327, 352, 412–13
    synod (1850), 259–60
    tithes war, 151
    troops in, 99
    Unionist vote declines, 386–7
    United Irishmen, 36, 47, 50–2, 54, 67, 69, 75, 87
    United Irishmen rising, 102–3
    Volunteers, 34–5, 63
    Young Ireland, 234
Belfast Academical Institution *see* Royal Belfast Academical Institution
Belfast Academy *see* Belfast Royal Academy
Belfast Anti-Slavery Society, 207
Belfast Charitable Organisation, 123
Belfast Harp Society, 123, 125
Belfast Naturalists' Field Club, 335
Belfast News-Letter, 34, 51, 54, 185, 192, 254, 410
Belfast Protestant Association, 358
Belfast Radical Association, 300
Belfast Royal Academy, 126, 295
Belfast Socialist Society, 339
Belfast Society, 15
Belfast Telegraph, 380
Belfast Trades Council, 357
Belgium, 341
Bell, Revd David, 250, 257
Bell, Geoffrey, 321
Belleek, Co. Fermanagh, 284, 287–8
Bellew, Christopher, 58
Belturbet, Co. Cavan, 99
Bentham, Jeremy, 225

Beresford, Lord George, Archbishop of Armagh, 201
Beresford, John C., 112
Beresford family, 62
Bessborough Commission, 274, 284, 288, 301
Biggar, Joseph Gillis, 2, 284, 289, 342, 351
  career of, 295–300
  election wins, 271, 290
  in Irish Parliamentary Party, 274, 283
  'New Departure', 297–8
Bigger, Francis Joseph, 2, 25, 119–20, 341, 373–4, 394, 399
  and Gaelic revival, 342–3, 365, 369, 374–5
Birch, Revd Thomas, 55, 74
Birmingham, 66
Birmingham, George, 360, 367–8, 394
Black, Revd Robert, 34, 120, 131–2, 134–5, 142
Black and Tans, 393
Blacker, Revd James, 152–3
Blanc, Louis, 259
Blatchford, Robert, 391, 397
Blayney, Lord, 83
Bleakley, David, 428, 430
Blenheim Castle, 413
Blythe, Ernest, 360, 366
Boardmills, 250
Boer Wars, 331, 341, 346, 414, 419
Bonaparte, Napoleon, 79, 99, 116
Bond, Oliver, 99
Book of Armagh, 230
boroughs, 27–8, 110, 112
  rotten, 28, 158–60, 177, 291, 386
Botany Bay, 89
Boundary Commission, 422
Bowman, Alexander, 357
Boycott, Captain Charles, 309
Boyd, Alex, 384, 391–2
Boyd, Andrew, 325
Boyd, J., 196
Boyd, Revd Robin, 424, 431
Boylan, Ellen, 372
Boyne, Battle of the, 1, 11, 39, 54, 318
  anniversary (1797), 85
Brehon laws, 8, 10
Bright, John, 251, 270, 294

Bristow, Vicar-General W., 96
Britain, 19
  attitude to Ireland, 5, 317–19, 400
  emigration to, 190, 263
  empire, 315–19
  Irish parliament's allegiance to, 42–3
  response to Great Famine, 191–5, 206
British Army, 19, 378, 414
  anti-Home Rule extremism, 330–1
  Curragh mutiny, 415
  First World War recruitment, 421–2
  intimidation, 88–91, 98
  links with Orange Order, 83–5
British League for the Support of Ulster and the Union, 414–15
British Trades Union Congress, 391
Brooke, A.B., 196
Brooke, Charlotte, 54, 56–7
Brooke, Henry, 56
Brooke, Peter, 134
Brooke family, 11, 165, 176–7, 284, 314, 320
Broughshane, Co. Antrim, 250, 273
Bruce, Revd William, 34, 126, 131
Bryan, George, 24
Bryson, Revd Samuel, 124, 230
Bullock, Shan F., 350
Bunting, Edward, 55–7, 123, 125, 227, 372–3
Burke, Edmund, 3, 30–1, 41, 59, 66, 68, 145
Butler, Revd Arthur, Bishop of Down, Connor and Dromore, 430–1
Butler, Brigadier-General Richard, 25
Butler, Simon, 50, 52
Butt, Isaac, 2, 161, 265, 290, 294, 297, 396, 421
  and Biggar, 295–6
  career of, 266–71
  death of, 281
Byrne, Edward, 58
Byron, Lord, 134

Caldwell, Revd Richard, 74
Caledon, Earl of, 108, 196, 277
Callan, Co. Kilkenny, 249
Calvin, John, 14, 16
Calvinism, 204, 208, 210, 431
Campbell, David, 416

Coalisland, Co. Tyrone, 377
Cobbett, William, 318
Cockayne (government spy), 65
Coercion Acts, 67–8, 239, 297
coercion policy, 64, 85–94, 153
Coigley, Father James, 71–2, 79, 87
Cole, Lord, 111
Cole, Viscount, 305
Cole family, 11, 83, 176–7, 284
Coleraine, Co. Derry, 99, 139, 196, 224, 274
  rotten borough, 157–8, 291
  synod, 260
  tenant-right meeting, 250
Coleraine Chronicle, 274
Coleraine Tenants' Association, 248–9
Colmcille, Saint, 9
colonialism, 19, 210, 341, 427
Colum, Padraic, 369, 374
Columbanus, Saint, 9
Comber, Co. Down, 151, 250, 254, 289
communism, 258–9, 306–7, 319
Congested Districts Board, 313, 353
Congo (Africa), 341–2
Connacht, 147, 401
  agrarian agitation, 20, 249
  elections, 386
  emigration, 190
  landownership, 173, 276
Connemara (Co. Galway), 205
Connolly, James, 241, 354, 379, 394, 398, 426
  Citizen Army, 416, 420
  Irish Socialist Republican Party, 338–9, 357
  Irish Transport and General Workers' Union, 417
Conservative and Unionist Party, 328, 403–5
Conservative Party, 322, 421–2; *see also* Tory Party
  anti-Home Rule crusade, 400
  criticisms of, 384–5
  divisions among, 361–2
  election results, 265, 333–4, 386–7, 406
  growing extremism, 328–31
  growing opposition to Ascendancy, 310–12

  and labour movement, 383
  and land reform, 305, 308, 312, 352
  links with Unionists, 403–5
  and Orange Order, 325–7
  and Ulster Tories, 327–8
Constitutional Society of Manchester, 50
Convention Act (1793), 63
Conyngham, Lord (2nd Marquess), 196, 277
Cooke, Edward, 85, 108, 115
Cooke, Revd Henry, 1–2, 148, 153, 182, 217, 257, 263, 380
  battle of the synods, 135–43
  on industry, 164
  opposed to liberalism, 126
  opposed to repeal, 161–3
  opposed to tenant rights, 259–60
Cookstown, Co. Tyrone, 97, 141, 250
co-operative movement, 352–3, 369–70, 394
Cork, Co., 146, 171
  franchise, 27
  Great Famine, 182
  Mitchelstown massacre, 328
Cork city, 24
  franchise, 112, 160
Cork Examiner, 251–2
Corn Laws, 167–8, 196
  repeal of, 193, 197, 248
Cornwallis, Lord, 89, 109–10, 114–15, 130–1
Corrigan, D. Felicitas, 371
Corrupt Practices Act (1883), 290
Corry, Isaac, 96
Corry, Lord James, 111, 119
Corry, Sir James, 320
Corry family, 176–7
Counter-Reformation, 19, 61
Craig, Charles, 355
Craig, Sir James (later Lord Craigavon), 1, 318, 320–1, 331, 355, 402–3, 405, 410, 414, 422, 425
Craig family, 11, 165
Crawford, Colonel Frederick H., 331, 414–15
Crawford, Robert Lindsay, 2, 359, 363, 376, 384–5, 428

and Belfast strike, 389–90
expelled from Independent Orange
  Order, 392–3
Crawford, William Sharman, 145, 149,
  166–7, 179–80, 194, 217
  famine activities, 212–14
  and land reform, 222–3
  land reform bills, 249
  retirement, 265
  and tenant-right agitation, 248, 251,
  253–4
  Ulster custom bill, 197
Crime and Outrage Act (1847), 199
Cromwell, Oliver, 11, 318
'Croppies lie down', 89
Crow, Revd Joseph, 74
Crozier, John A., 140–1
Cuchulain saga, 8
Cullen, Dr Paul, later Cardinal, 201, 248,
  252–3, 261–3, 265
Cumann na nGaedheal, 393
Cumberland, Duke of, 154
Cunningham, Waddell, 22, 54
Curragh mutiny, 1, 415, 425
Curran, John Philpot, 65
Cusack, Michael, 339
Cushendall, Co. Antrim, 96
Cushendun, Lord (Ronald McNeill),
  325–6, 368, 409–10, 415

Daily Chronicle, 379
Daily Dispatch, 379
Daily Mail, 374, 414
Dallas, Revd Alexander, 205
Darwinism, 316
Davis, Thomas, 8, 229, 232, 236, 253, 263,
  385
  and literary revival, 225–6, 372
  Nation, 233–4
  and Young Ireland, 168, 218–21
Davitt, Michael, 241, 245, 292, 294, 298–9,
  310, 351, 384
  Land League, 282–3, 285–6, 289
Dawson, George, 185
Dawson family, 176–7
Defenders, 23, 41–2, 44, 64, 67, 72, 95
  imprisoned, 87

Insurrection Act, 86
  and Peep O'Day Boys, 70–1
  riots, 81–2
  rising (1798), 99–101
  strength of, 98
  and United Irishmen, 67, 69–70
democracy
  after partition, 427
  fear of, 41–3, 381
  fight for, 30–5
  under partition, 425
  and United Irishmen, 47–8
Derry, Co., 11, 99, 103, 131, 147, 254, 257,
  391, 422
  agrarian agitation, 20, 22, 284, 305
  diocese, 128
  disaffection in, 97
  elections, 177, 291, 407
  emigration, 190
  farmers' associations, 271, 273
  Great Famine, 183–6
  Irish language, 340
  landownership, 171–2, 277, 294
  Orange Order, 84
  Volunteers, 32
Derry city, 13, 185, 260, 286, 377
  elections, 160, 265, 406, 418
  emigration from, 23
  franchise, 28, 158
  growth of, 264
  Siege of, 1, 11
  tenant-right meetings, 223, 250
Derrygonnelly, Co. Fermanagh, 289
Desart, Earl of, 249
Devenish, Lough Erne, 9
Devereux, James, 58
Devlin, Joseph, 387, 389, 406, 421
  Ancient Order of Hibernians, 362, 379
  and Belfast strike, 391
  and Irish Parliamentary Party, 416
  sectarianism, 379, 398
Devon Commission, 172, 178–9, 181,
  222–3, 276
Devonshire, Duke of, 195, 314, 330, 404
Devoy, John, 298–9, 379, 382
Dickson, Revd William Steel, 2, 34, 38, 47,
  51–2, 54–5, 67, 71, 74, 87

career of, 75–6
Dungannon Convention (1793), 63
and informers, 93
Montgomery's support for, 138
released from prison, 119–20, 131
rising (1798), 100, 102–3
Dickson, T.A., 290, 303, 346
Dill, Revd Edward Marcus, 208–9
Dillon, John, 283–4, 286–7, 289, 292
Dillon, John Blake, 234
Dineen, Father P.S., 340
Dinsmore, John, 419
Disraeli, Benjamin, 167, 295, 305
Dissenters, 14–15, 18; see also
  Presbyterians
after partition, 426–8
and anti-Home Rule crusade, 418–21
democratic movement, 32–3
disenfranchised, 29
emigration, 394
and Gaelic culture, 123–6
and Home Rule movement, 292–300,
  343–7, 400
and land reform, 256–7, 288
nationalism among, 68
opposition to Ascendancy, 137
overtures made to, 126–34
relations with Catholics, 6, 44, 59, 81, 114,
  161
resistance to unionism, 332
seen as traitors, 62–3
tithes war, 147–55
and United Irishmen, 44–55, 101, 105–6
and Young Ireland, 231
Dobbin, Revd William, 250–2, 256–7,
  259
Dobbs, Francis, 33
Dobbs, Margaret, 369
Dodd, W.H., 387
Doheny, Michael, 224
Dolly's Brae, Co. Down, 255
Donaghadee, Co. Down, 250
Donaghmore, Co. Tyrone, 9
Donegal, Co., 9–10, 103, 132, 147, 254
  elections, 291, 387
  franchise, 27, 158, 176
  Gaelic culture, 334, 373

Great Famine, 183, 185, 267
Land League, 284–5
landownership, 172, 277–8, 304
migrant workers, 350
proportion of Catholics, 333
Ulster custom, 179
Donegall, Marquess of, 111, 161, 272
Donegall family, 21–3
Donegore, Co. Antrim, 135–6
Dougherty, Revd James B., 345–6
Douglas, David, 22
Down, Co., 13, 65, 85, 149, 196–7, 212, 218,
  257, 383, 422
  agrarian agitation, 22, 256, 284–5, 305
  disaffection in, 96–7
  elections, 38, 160–1, 176–7, 265, 355,
    386–7, 406–7
  farmers' organisations, 271
  franchise, 27
  Great Famine, 182–3, 186, 190, 254
  intimidation policy, 90
  landownership, 174, 277–8
  Orange Order, 111
  proportion of Catholics, 333
  tithes war, 151
  United Irishmen rising, 101
  Volunteers, 32
Down, Marquess of, 111
Down and Connor diocese, 132
Down Farmers' Union, 273
Downpatrick, Co. Down, 9, 28, 99, 132,
  285
  rotten borough, 177, 291
Downshire, Marquess of, 64, 74, 77, 97,
  125, 199
  and Act of Union, 110–11
  income of, 12, 278
  landownership, 277
Downshire family, 149, 165
Doyle, James, Bishop of Kildare and
  Leighlin, 146
Drake, Michael, 119
Drapers' Company, 172, 277
Drennan, William, 36–9, 50, 61, 131, 178,
  395
  opposed to Ascendancy, 120–1
  and traditional music, 125

trial of, 65
and United Irishmen, 47–8, 52, 54, 68–9, 95
Volunteer manifesto, 64
'Wake, 1797', 92
Drew, Revd Thomas, 257, 264, 307
Drogheda, Co. Louth, 11
Dromore, Co. Down, 35
Drumbo, Co Down, 8, 132, 151
Drummaul, Co. Antrim, 132
Drummond, Thomas, 154
Dryhurst, Sylvia, 380
Dublin, 24, 121–2, 320, 377, 393
    diocese, 128
    elections, 112, 160
    Gaelic revival, 363
    Great Famine, 207
    informers, 92–3
    Land League conference, 286
    lockout (1913), 354, 416
    Protestant Home Rule Association, 292–3
    tenant-right conference, 251–2
    United Irishmen, 52, 68–9, 87
    Volunteers, 63
Dublin Castle administration, 30, 63–4, 133
    and Act of Union, 108–9
    'Castle Catholics', 42
    and Catholic bishops, 95
    intelligence reports, 71–2
    jail, 87, 99
    messages of panic to, 96–7
    and Orange Order, 83
Dufferin, Lord (2nd Baron), 161
Dufferin, Lord Frederick (5th Baron), 212
Dufferin, Helen, 212
Dufferin and Ava, Marquess of, 330
Dufferin family, 39
Duffy, Charles Gavan, 218, 225, 229
    emigrates, 265
    League of North and South, 248
    and Mitchel, 233–5
    Nation, 219, 233–4
    and tenant-right agitation, 251–3, 262
    and Ulster custom, 178–9
    and Young Ireland, 168, 232
Duffy, James, 229

Dumouriez, Charles, 64
Dunboy, Co. Antrim, 273
Dundalk, Co. Louth, 149
Dundas, Henry, 59
Dundonald (Belfast), 250
Dundrod, Co. Antrim, 250
Dungannon, Co. Tyrone, 96–7, 99, 338, 377
    rotten borough, 157–8, 177, 291
    tenant-right meetings, 224, 250
Dungannon Clubs, 373, 377–82, 393
    and Belfast strike, 389–90, 398
Dungannon Convention (1782), 2, 33–4
Dungannon Convention (1793), 63
Dungiven, Co. Derry, 233
Dunlap, John, 24
Dunmurry, Co. Antrim, 135, 137–8
Dunsany, Lord, 352
dysentery, 186, 189

Easter rising (1916), 104, 383, 393–4, 416, 422
Ecclesiastical Titles Act (1851), 261–2
ecumenism, 138–9, 430–1
Edgar, Revd John, 206–8
Edinburgh, 53
education, 139, 361
Edward VII, King, 348
    as Prince of Wales, 327
Egypt, 315
elections see franchise and general elections
Elizabeth I, Queen, 9, 236, 317–18
Elliott, Marianne, 87
Ely, Lord, 110
Emain Macha (Navan Fort), 8
emigration, 23–5, 180, 257, 263–4, 394
    Great Famine, 190
    Irish in Britain, 168
Emmet, Robert, 116–19, 123
Emmet, Thomas, 24, 99
Emmet brothers, 67
England, 14, 194
    Catholic hierarchy created, 260–3
    Mitchel's attitude to, 237–8
English, in Ulster, 8–9, 11
Enniskillen, Co. Fermanagh, 99, 252, 274, 284, 305

Militia Bill riots, 63
rotten borough, 157–8, 177, 291
Enniskillen, 1st Earl of, 111
Enniskillen, 2nd Earl of, 154
Enniskillen, 3rd Earl of, 235–6, 284
episcopalians, 3, 12, 33, 125, 165, 210, 224,
302, 311, 354
Ascendancy, 18, 98, 130, 224, 302, 311,
354
emigration, 190
franchise, 13, 17, 216
and Home Rule, 270
numbers of, 129
and tenant-right agitation, 252
and tithes, 145–6, 153
Erne, Lord, 196, 284, 309, 327
Ervine, St John, 296, 391–2
Esperanto, 398
evangelicalism, 167–9, 260–3
attacks on Land League, 307–8
and Great Famine, 204–9
evictions, 12, 23, 174, 198–9, 201, 255, 257,
279–80
Great Famine, 182–3
and Land League agitation, 304–5
Ewart, Sir William, 320
Ewart family, 165

Fanning, Ann, 55
Farnham, Lord, 83, 196, 277, 327
Faulkner, Brian, 428
Fay, C.J., 290
Feakle, Co. Clare, 431
Fenians, 104, 243, 262, 299, 311, 376, 382
amnesty campaign, 338
and Butt, 269–70
and Mitchel, 241
'New Departure', 282–3, 298
rising (1867), 245, 269
Ferguson, Lady, 231
Ferguson, John, 2, 283, 293–4
Ferguson, Samuel, 218, 226–8, 234, 432
Fermanagh, Co., 10, 196, 279, 294, 303, 422
elections, 176–7, 291, 387, 406
Great Famine, 183, 185–6
Land League, 284
Orange Order, 83–4, 111, 306, 309

population loss, 190
proportion of Catholics, 333
Fermanagh Mail, 251–2
Ferrie, Revd John, 143
Fingall, Lord, 108–9, 121
Finlay, F.D., 150
Finlay, Revd S., 273
First World War, 391, 397, 408, 411, 416,
421–2
Fishmongers' Company, 172, 277
FitzGerald, Lord Edward, 39, 58, 93, 99,
355
Dungannon Convention (1793), 63
Fitzgibbon, John see Clare, Lord
Fitzgibbon, Gerald, 322–3
Fitzwilliam, Lord, 66, 68, 91, 195
floggings, 89–90
Flood, Henry, 32–3, 41–2
Forde, Revd, 288
Fort George, Scotland, 88, 102, 116, 119
Forward, 417
Foster, John, 91, 109
Fox, Charles James, 92, 95, 121
Fox, Charlotte Milligan, 373
France, 20, 40, 60, 79–80, 118–19, 316, 341
aid sought from, 62–3, 67, 69, 71–2, 79
invasion fears, 88
invasion planned, 76
Irish spies for, 64–5
Pitt's spies, 93
United Irishmen in, 87, 95
and United Irishmen rising, 78, 97,
99–100, 102–4, 108
war with, 53, 61, 116
franchise, 112, 116, 144, 274, 330, 432
under Act of Union, 113–14
control of, 4, 12–13, 26–30, 157, 175–7
forty-shilling freeholders, 27, 60, 114,
157, 159
liberalisation of, 302–3, 305
under partition, 425
reform struggle, 54, 156–61
secret ballot, 28, 290
system transformed, 289–91
Franchise Act (1884), 290
Franklin, Benjamin, 24, 64
Freeman's Journal, 252, 380

Fremantle, Sir Thomas, 185
French, Field Marshal Lord, 414
French, Sir Thomas, 58
French Revolution, 42, 44–6, 130, 221, 259
  commemorated, 54
  influence of, 50–1, 61–3, 70
Freud, Sigmund, 420
Friendly Sons of Saint Patrick, 25
Friends of the People (Scotland), 50
Froude, James A., 316
Fry, Elizabeth, 123
Furlonge, Revd, 289

Gaelic Athletic Association, 339
Gaelic culture, 10, 55–7, 123–6, 432
  music, 372–3
  nineteenth-century revival, 225–31
  twentieth-century revival, 332, 334–7,
    360
  in Ulster, 8–9
Gaelic League, 338, 360, 373, 375, 380, 385,
    394, 398, 432
  Antrim festival, 368–9
  An Claidheamh Soluis, 362
  influence on IRB, 382
  and labour movement, 399
  spread of, 339, 340–1
  in Ulster, 365–9
Gaelic revival, 335–7, 342–3, 363
Gageby, Robert, 407
Galbraith, Revd J.A., 293
Gall, Saint, 9
Gallagher, Revd Eric, 430
Gallaher's tobacco factory, 388
Galway, Co., 27, 182, 190
Galway city, 160, 294, 354
Gardiner, Luke, 25
Garibaldi, Giuseppe, 263
Garrison, Co. Fermanagh, 287
Garvagh, 250
general elections
  1847, 177
  1852, 265
  1874, 274
  1885, 291
  1892–1900, 333–4
  1900, 354–5

1906, 386–7
1910, 405–7
George III, King, 83, 110, 121
Germany, 93, 316, 341, 415
gerrymandering, 114, 157–8, 175, 177, 425
Girdwood, William, 252
Gladstone, W.E., 179, 273, 282, 290, 294,
    303, 344, 402, 404, 427, 429
  and Home Rule, 292, 310–11, 323–4,
    326–7, 330–1, 343, 345, 400
  land bills, 270, 284–5, 305
  Maynooth bill, 168
Glasgow, 405
Glaslough Castle, Co. Monaghan, 366
Gleeson, Evelyn, 369
Glenarm, Co. Antrim, 132
Glendinning, R.G., 384
Glendy, Revd John, 74, 135
Glenfin, Co. Donegal, 266
Glorious Revolution, 11, 13–14, 30–1, 318
Gobineau, Joseph Arthur, 316
Godkin, James, 254–5
Godwin, William, 66
Goldsmith, Oliver, 56–7
Gonne, Maud, 338–9
Good, James Winder, 339, 361, 379, 380–1,
    394
Gordon riots, 86
Gorey, Co. Wexford, 254
Gormanstown, Lord, 42
Gosford, Lord, 82
Gough, General Hubert, 415
Government of Ireland Act (1920), 422
Gowdie, Revd Alex, 74
Graham, Revd T.S., 289
Graigue, Co. Carlow, 146
grand juries, 27, 176
Grange, Co. Derry, 23
Grattan, Henry, 29, 31–4, 47, 72, 91, 115,
    195
  and Act of Union, 109–10
  attacks on, 38
  fear of revolution, 41, 68–9
  and intimidation campaign, 95
  nationalism, 42–3, 105
  opposes Insurrection Act, 86
  and Orange Order, 84

on tithes, 145
Gray, Betsy, 102
Gray, John (nationalist MP), 252, 262
Gray, John (*City in Revolt*), 396
Gray, Sam, 224
Grayson, Victor, 389
Great Famine, 2, 169–70, 177, 233, 239, 243–4, 267
  Churches' reactions to, 199–209
  course of, 181–90
  law enforcement, 198–9
  mortality, 188–90
  political crisis, 191–214
  proselytism, 204–9
Greaves, Desmond, 338
Green, Alice Stopford, 342, 369, 378, 419–21
Green, E.R.R., 174
Greer, Samuel, 224, 249, 254
Gregg, Thomas, 22
Gregory, Lady, 354, 362
Grey, Lord, 153, 160, 402
Greyabbey, Co. Down, 75, 77, 93, 250, 371
Grianan of Aileach, 8
Griffith, Arthur, 362, 389–91, 393, 398
Grocers' Company, 277
Gweedore, Co. Donegal, 183, 212
Gwynn, Stephen, 293, 374

habeas corpus
  suspended, 53, 66, 86–7, 115, 199
Haig, Sir Douglas, 414
Hamill, Revd G.W., 288
Hamilton, Major C., 96
Hamilton, Ernest, 409
Hamilton, James, 11
Hamilton, John, 212
Hamilton, William Henry, 72, 87, 117
Hamilton family, 176–7
Hammond, J.L., 305
Hand, Major-General Edward, 25
Handcock, John, 178–9
Hanna, Revd Hugh ('Roaring'), 1, 264, 307, 324
Hannay, Canon James Owen, 360, 366–8, 394
Hanson, John, Bishop of Down, Connor and Dromore, 430

Hardebeck, Carl, 373
Hardie, Keir, 362, 386, 389
Hardy, General Jean, 117
Hardy, Thomas, 66
Harland, Sir Edward, 264, 320
Harland and Wolff, 358, 384–5, 412, 417
Harland family, 165
Harper, Revd James, 74
harpists, 123, 125, 372
  festival, 55–6
Harrison, Henry, 295
Harty, Hamilton, 373, 394
Harvey, Bagenal, 100–1
Haslett, Henry, 51
Haslip, Joan, 295
Hastings, Marquess of, 125
Healy, Tim, 292
Hearts of Steel, 20–1
hedge schools, 229
Hempson, Denis, 55–6
Henderson, Arthur, 391, 397
Henry, Revd Henry, 74, 125–6
Henry, Paul, 339, 363–6, 380–1, 394
Henry, Professor Robert Mitchell, 363, 366, 371
Hertford, 2nd Marquess of, 108
Hertford, 4th Marquess of, 172
Hertford, 5th Marquess of, 272, 275–8
Hervey, Frederick Augustus, Earl of Bristol, Bishop of Derry, 35–6
Hewitt, John, 429–30
high crosses, 9
Hill, Lord, 161
Hill, Revd Adam, 74
Hill, G.F., 97
Hill, Lord George, 212
Hill family, 176
Hillsborough, Co. Down, 161–3, 340
Hillsborough, Lord, 63, 161
Hilltown, Co. Down, 288
hiring fairs, 349
Hobson, Bulmer, 2, 339, 341, 365, 369, 374, 384, 428
  and Belfast strike, 389
  Dungannon Clubs, 377–81, 393
  and IRB, 382
  Ulster Literary Theatre, 369–70

Hogg, D.C., 418
Holcroft, Thomas, 66
Holmes, Finlay, 182
Holycross, Co. Tipperary, 222
Holywood, Co. Down, 78, 132, 183, 250
Home Government Association, 270–1
Home Rule Bills
  1886, 324, 326
  1893, 330, 345
  campaign against (1912), 407–16, 422–3
Home Rule movement, 241, 245, 269–71,
    283, 292, 357, 385, 392, 396
  Armour of Ballymoney, 343–7
  election victories, 274, 310
  growing English support, 310–11
  and labour movement, 398
  land reform as distraction from, 312–14
  'New Departure', 297–8
  opposition to, 327–31
  Presbyterian attitudes to, 272, 302
  role of House of Lords, 404
  Unionist crusade against, 400–23
Hope, James, 2, 7, 70, 72–3, 87, 117, 122–3
  United Irishmen rising, 100–1
House of Commons (British), 114, 127,
    322, 386, 410–11
  bills on landownership, 213–14
  Butt in, 267–9, 271
  and Carson crusade, 401
  democracy under attack, 329–30
  famine debates, 193
  Irish members in, 114–15, 283, 295–8, 362,
    408
  land reform efforts, 223, 249
  League for Support of Union, 414–15
  obstruction tactic, 281, 296–7
  Reform Bill debates, 160
  and tenant-right movement, 261–2
  and tithes war, 149–50, 153–5
  Tories and Unionists unite, 328
  unrepresentative, 13, 175
House of Commons (Irish), 60, 127; see also
    parliament, Irish
  and Act of Union, 109–10
  unrepresentative, 28–9
House of Lords (British), 201, 361
  anti-Home Rule extremism, 330
  and Carson crusade, 401
  Great Famine discussed, 203–4
  and land reform, 249, 256
  protests at intimidation, 90
  Unionists in, 403–4
  veto, 406–7
House of Lords (Irish), 29, 58
  and Act of Union, 109–10
Hughes, Herbert, 339, 369, 372–5, 394
Hughes, John, 76, 93, 103
Huguenots, 177
Hull, Eleanor, 340
Hull, Revd James, 74
Humbert, General Jean, 99, 103
Hume, Joseph, 154
Hutton, Margaret, 365, 369
Hyde, Douglas, 228, 236, 293, 335, 339,
    360, 372, 374–5
Hyland, Fanny, 296

Ibsen, Henrik, 362
Impartial Reporter, 249, 252, 258, 274, 284,
    287
imperialism, 5, 166, 315–19, 396–8, 417,
    428
  and anti-Home Rule crusade, 409–10
  and British Army, 330–1
  and Great Famine, 192–3
improvers, 212, 303
Indemnity Act (1797), 86
Independent Labour Party, 357, 392,
    417
Independent Orange Order, 358–9, 376–7,
    384–5, 395
  and Belfast strike, 389–93
India, 315, 318
industrial development, 163–6, 321, 356–7
informers
  and United Irishmen, 91–5, 99–100, 102–3
Ingram, John Kells, 104–5
Insurrection Act (1796), 85–6
internment, 87–9, 95
Ireland, Denis, 432
Irish Agricultural Organisation Society,
    353
Irish Citizen Army, 416, 420
Irish Confederation, 221–5

Irish Congress of Trade Unions, 428
Irish Council of Churches, 430
Irish Felon, 244
Irish Free State, 360, 393
Irish Home Rule League, 245
Irish Homestead, 354
Irish Labour Party, 416
Irish Land Commission, 371, 394
Irish language, 10, 18, 53, 124, 244, 340,
  360, 369, 380, 432
  and Casement, 369, 374
  Hannay on, 367–8
  studies of, 56–7, 226
  survival of, 334–5
  and Young Ireland, 225–6
Irish Literary Society, 340
Irish Literary Theatre, 354, 369
Irish Parliamentary Party, 245, 262, 265,
  271, 281, 283–4, 295, 350, 362, 406
  and anti-Home Rule crusade, 416
  balance of power, 408
  dissatisfaction with, 376, 378–9
  election victories, 289–92, 333–4, 386–7
  and First World War, 421
  'New Departure', 297–8
  Parnell leader, 297
  Protestant members, 402
Irish Peasant, 393
Irish People, 269
Irish Protestant, 359, 385
Irish Republican Army (IRA), 422, 429
Irish Republican Brotherhood (IRB), 294,
  298, 338–9, 360, 381–3, 393
Irish Socialist Republican Party, 338–9,
  357
Irish Texts Society, 340
Irish Times, 354
Irish Trades Union Congress, 358
Irish Transport and General Workers'
  Union, 392, 416–17
Irish Unionist Alliance, 401, 403
Irish Volunteers, 339, 416, 432
Irishtown, Co. Mayo, 294
Ironmongers' Company, 172, 277
Irvine, General William, 25, 33
Islandmagee, Co. Antrim, 250
Italy, unification of, 262–3

Jackson, Andrew, 39
Jackson, Revd Henry, 64–5
Jackson, T.A., 296
Jacob, Rosamond, 52, 63
Jacobinism, 135, 161, 249, 311
  fear of, 61–2, 66, 68–9, 98, 108–9, 113
  intimidation campaign, 95–6
Jacobite rising (1745), 86
Jagoe, Revd Abraham, 307
Jail Journal (Mitchel), 238, 242–3
James I, King, 11, 21, 179, 236
James II, King, 57
Jefferson, Thomas, 39, 53
Jerome, Jenny, 366
Jews, 17, 318, 402
Johnson, Samuel, 56
Johnson, Thomas, 416
Johnston, Anna (Ethna Carbery), 336–7
Johnston, Revd J., 257
Johnston, Robert, 337
Johnston, Revd W., 186
Johnston, William, 307–8, 323, 327, 358
Jones, Revd J., 97
Jones, William Todd, 36–7
Jordan, Jeremiah, 283–4, 294, 346, 387,
  406
Joy, Francis, 51
Joy, Henry, 41, 51, 55, 118, 125
  Belfast News-Letter, 54
  Dungannon Convention (1793), 63
jurors, 84

Kane, Revd Richard, 308, 325, 352
Keady, Co. Armagh, 120, 131, 152–3
Kee, Robert, 64
Keefe, Father Matthew, 249
Kelburne, Revd Sinclair, 34, 54–5, 74, 79,
  102
Kelly, J.J., 298
Kenmare, Lord, 42, 52, 108–9
Kennaught Farmers' Association, 288
Kenyon, Father John, 235
Keogh, Henry, 67, 69
Keogh, John, 45, 47, 54, 57–8
Keogh, William, 251, 261–2, 270
Ker, D.S., 278
Ker family, 176–7

Kerry, Co., 171, 190
Kettle, Tom, 406
Kickham, Charles, 269–70
Kiely, Benedict, 229–30
Kildare, Co., 70, 89, 100, 183
Kilkenny, Co., 146
Killala, Co. Mayo, 207
Killen, W.D., 206
Killinchy, Co. Down, 132, 250
Killyleagh, Co. Down, 39, 136, 183
Kilmainham jail (Dublin), 87, 286
Kilmore, 132
Kilraughts, Co. Antrim, 273
Kingsley, Revd Charles, 316–17
Kinnegoe, Co. Armagh, 285
Kipling, Rudyard, 317, 413
Kircubbin, Co. Down, 132
Kitchener, Field Marshal Lord, 331, 404, 414
Knox, Alexander, 131
Knox, Brigadier-General C.E., 84–5, 91
Knox, George, 60, 118
Knox, John, 15
Knox, Thomas, 96–7
Knox, Colonel W.S., 290, 303
Knox family, 176–7
Kosciuszko, Tadeusz, 39, 53

Labouchere, H., 193
Labour Chronicle, 397–8
labour movement, 356–60, 362, 395, 407, 422
  Belfast agitation, 387–92
  growth in Ulster, 383–92
Labour Party (British), 362, 377, 383, 400, 415
  balance of power, 408
  Belfast strike, 391
  election results, 386, 406,
  imperialism of, 396–8
  and Irish labour movement, 398
Lake, General Gerard, 81, 84–6, 89–91
Lalor, James Fintan, 221–2, 234, 239, 244, 253, 263
Lalor, Patrick, 221
Lammas Fair (Ballycastle), 349
Land Acts
  1870, 270–1, 311
  1881, 297, 305, 311
  1885 (Ashbourne), 313
  1903 (Wyndham), 313, 351, 355, 361
Land League, 249, 271, 282–9, 294, 297, 299, 305–6, 310–11, 351
  Ascendancy response to, 302–5
  Plan of Campaign, 311–12, 328
  sectarian opposition to, 305–9
landownership, 15–16, 150; see also Ulster custom
  criticisms of, 211–14
  eighteenth century, 11–12
  pre-famine structure, 170–6
  statistics (1870s), 274–8
  and tithes war, 152
land question, 2, 4, 37, 41, 116, 164, 330, 346, 350–2; see also agrarian agitation and Land League
  agricultural depression, 278–81
  effect of 1798 rising, 104
  effects of Land Acts, 349, 355, 362–3
  enclosures, 20
  land values, 278
  less population pressure, 263–4
  linked with Home Rule movement, 297–8, 312–14
  'New Departure', 282–3, 297–8
  plantations, 10–11
  support for reform, 267–9
  survey (1619), 11
  tenant-right agitation, 248–65
  three Fs, 284–5, 305, 311,
  Unionists lose farmer support, 354–5
  Young Ireland movement, 218, 221–3
landlords see Ascendancy
Langrishe, Sir Hercules, 59
language, use of, 5–6
Lansbury, George, 389
Lansdowne, 3rd Marquess of, 195
Lansdowne, 5th Marquess of, 312, 314, 330, 403–4, 412
Larkin, Delia, 354
Larkin, James, 354, 387–8, 390–2, 398, 403
Larkin, Michael, 245
Larne, Co. Antrim, 23, 185, 415
Latimer, Revd W.T., 134, 254, 289, 346

Laughrey, Revd Edward, 288
Law, Andrew Bonar, 1, 312, 400, 404
  anti-Home Rule crusade, 405, 410,
    412–13, 416
  joins war cabinet, 421
Lawrence, Thomas, 96
Lecky, W.E.H., 29, 66, 82–5, 89, 91, 111
Lee, Sergeant John, 96
Legananny, Ballynahinch, Co. Down, 8
Leinster, 9, 401
  agrarian agitation, 20
  disaffection in, 98
  elections, 386
  emigration, 190
  Irish language in, 334
  landownership, 173, 276
  tenant-right agitation, 249
  tithes, 147
Leinster, Duke of, 39, 93
Leitrim, Earl of, 254, 277, 304, 306
Leslie, C.P., 196
Leslie, Shane, 343, 366, 375, 394, 406
Leslie family, 176–7
Lester, Sean, 382
Letterkenny, Co. Donegal, 181, 285
Lewis, General Andrew, 25
Liberal Party, 161, 265, 272, 290–1, 334,
    377, 400, 415, 427; see also Whigs
  and anti-Home Rule crusade, 417–18
  attacks Ascendancy, 194–5, 310–12
  Churchill joins, 362
  criticisms of, 384–5
  divisions among, 292, 302
  election results, 274, 285, 305, 346, 386,
    406–7
  and First World War, 421
  growing strength, 383
  non-sectarian, 402
  and obstructionism, 297
  and Orange riots, 325
Liberal Unionist Party, 311, 344, 350,
    403–4, 428
liberalism, 6, 41–2, 130, 282
  after partition, 427–9
  fear of, 126
  Rights of Man debate, 30–1
Life of Saint Columba (Adomnan), 231

Limavady, Co. Derry, 288
Limerick, Treaty of, 39
Limerick city, 160
Linen Hall Library (Belfast), 46, 125
linen industry, 13, 23, 130, 164–5, 177–8,
    279
Lisboy, Co. Antrim, 272
Lisburn, Co. Antrim, 36, 69, 250, 252, 264
  linen industry, 177
  rotten borough, 157–8, 177, 291
Liverpool, 53, 79
livery companies, 11, 172, 277, 294
Lloyd, Owen, 369
Lloyd George, David, 361, 386, 416
Logue, Cardinal Michael, 391
London, 401, 405, 416
  Gaelic League in, 380
  livery companies, 11, 172, 277, 294
  Unionist support in, 414–15
  United Englishmen, 79
London Corresponding Society, 50, 66
Londonderry, 1st Marquess of, 64, 76–7,
    97, 108, 130–1
Londonderry, 3rd Marquess of, 161, 189,
    199, 256–7, 322
Londonderry, 4th Marquess of, 277–8
Londonderry, 6th Marquess of, 330, 404,
    412
Londonderry family, 149, 165, 314, 320,
    405
Londonderry Standard, 223, 247, 250–2,
    254–5, 274
Long, Walter, 403, 405
Longford, Co., 27
Lough Mask, Co. Mayo, 309
Lough Swilly, Co. Donegal, 103
Loughbrickland, Co. Down, 250
Loughgall, Co. Armagh, 82, 285
Louis XVI, King, 50, 61
Louth, Co., 64
Lowry, Alexander, 72, 87
Lowry family, 176
Luby, Thomas Clarke, 269–70
Lucas, Frederick, 252
Lucas, Reginald, 326
Lurgan, Co. Armagh, 99, 141–2, 187–8,
    264, 353

Great Famine, 181
 linen industry, 177
 Orange Order, 85
Lurgan, Lord, 172, 278
Lutherans, 167
Lynch, Thomas, 24
Lynd, Revd R.J., 288
Lynd, Robert, 2, 288, 339, 341, 346, 364–5,
 374, 379–81, 393–4; *see also* Ua Fhloin,
 Riobard
Lyons, F.S.L., 279, 295–6
Lyttle, Revd Richard, 339, 346, 377–8

McAdam, James, 125
McAdam, Robert, 125
McAdam, Robert Shipbuoy, 230
Macafee, William, 419
MacArthur, William, 339
Macaulay, Thomas B., 316
MacBride, John, 341
McBrown, Revd Nathaniel, 288
McCabe, Thomas, 51, 72
McCabe, William Putnam, 72
MacCall, Seumus, 238
MacCartan, Patrick, 339, 377, 379, 382,
 389, 393
McCary, Father James, 93, 96
McCleery, William, 51
McClure, Revd William, 163
McCormick, Richard, 54
McCracken, Henry Joy, 2, 36, 51–2, 64, 67,
 71, 122, 337
 interned, 87–8
 rising (1798), 100–2
 and Tone, 79–80
McCracken, Mary Ann, 87–8, 102, 118, 123
McCullough, Denis, 339, 377, 382, 393
McDermot, Frank, 48
MacDermott, Sean, 339, 377, 382–3, 393
MacDonagh, Thomas, 336
MacDonald, Ramsay, 386, 397
MacDonnell, Sir Anthony, 359, 361
McDonnell, Dr James, 55, 125, 230
McDowell, R.B., 27, 87, 107, 128
McElroy, Samuel C., 273
McEntee, John F., 366
McGarrity, Joseph, 382

McGee, Darcy, 224
MacGill, Patrick, 350
McGucken, James, 91, 93
McGuire, J.F., 251
MacHale, John, Archbishop of Tuam, 192,
 248
McHenry, James, 24
McIlderry, John, 419
McIlderry, Thomas, 273
McIlven, Gilbert, 51
McKean, Thomas, 24
McKeown, Michael, 390, 392
McKnight, James, 223–4, 253–4, 274
MacKnight, Thomas, 308
MacLean, John, 389
M'Loughlin, Father John, 250
MacMahon, Revd Arthur, 72, 74, 78–9, 87
MacManus, Seamus, 337
McMeehan, Revd, 74
McMullen, William, 416, 432
McNamara, Gerald, 370
MacNeice, John, Bishop of Down, Connor
 and Dromore, 430
McNeill, Ada, 368
MacNeill, Eoin, 339–40, 362, 369, 372
McNeill, Revd John, 74
McNeill, Ronald *see* Cushendun, Lord
McNeven, Captain, 96–7
Macneven, William J., 69, 71, 99
McPeake, Francis 'Da', 375
McTier, Samuel, 37, 51
MacVeagh, Jeremiah, 406
Madden, R.R., 46, 68, 72, 77
Magheragall, Co. Antrim, 250, 360
Magheramorne manifesto, 384–5
Maghery, Co. Armagh, 152
Maginn, Nicholas, 93, 103
Maginn (informer), 76
magistrates, 83–4, 86, 176
Maguire family, 9
Mahon, George C., 244–5
Maire, Revd J.S., 273
Malthus, Thomas Robert, 200
Manchester, 79
Manchester, Duke of, 206
Manchester martyrs, 245
Mandeville, John, 328

Mangan, James Clarence, 232, 234
Manning, Cardinal, 300
Marie Antoinette, Queen, 39
Markethill, Co. Armagh, 183
Marlborough, Duke of, 280, 322
Martin, Revd James, 212
Martin, John, 2, 180, 215, 231, 233, 235, 247
　career, 243–6
　and Home Rule movement, 241
　and Young Ireland, 218, 224
Marx, Karl, 179, 307
Mawhinney, Brian, 430
Maxwell, J., 196
Mayne, Rutherford, 370–1
Maynooth College, 168, 260
Mayo, Co., 174, 185, 190, 207, 289
　boycott, 309
　United Irishmen rising, 99, 102–3
Mazzini, Giuseppe, 263
Meagher, Thomas Francis, 218, 224, 239, 244
Meath, Co., 64, 70, 89, 245, 294
Megaw, John, 273
Melbourne, Lord, 402
Mercers' Company, 277
Methodist College, Belfast, 430
Methodists, 3, 82, 165, 167, 284, 288–9, 294, 339, 415
　ecumenism, 430–1
Meyer, Kuno, 340
middle classes, 71, 92–3
　Alliance Party, 429
　Catholic, 59–60, 129
　franchise struggle, 26–30, 156–61
　industrial expansion of, 320–1
　Presbyterian, 13–14, 129–30, 164
　struggle for autonomy, 31–5
Midgley, Harold, 428
militia, 96, 99, 176, 308, 331
　conscripts, 63
　intimidation, 88–9
Militia Bill (1793), 63
Mill, John Stuart, 270, 294
Milligan, Alice, 336–8, 369, 373–4
Milligan, Ernest, 338–9
Millisle, Co. Down, 132
Milner, Alfred (later Lord), 404

Mitchel, Jenny, 233, 242
Mitchel, John, 4, 142, 179, 196, 225, 232, 245, 253, 263, 284, 298
　and Butt, 267
　career, 233–43
　death of, 246
　letters to Protestants, 240, 242–3
　religious tolerance, 224, 234–6, 242–3
　transported, 240–1, 244, 247
　and Young Ireland, 217–18, 231
Mitchel, Revd John, 142
Mitchell, Revd B., 74
Mitchelstown massacre, 328
Moira, Lord, 39, 90, 95
Monaghan, Co., 10, 85, 99, 103, 132, 218, 253, 260, 290
　Defenders, 64
　elections, 160–1, 176, 291
　landownership, 172, 277
　militia, 90
　Orange Order, 111, 305–6
　population loss, 190
　proportion of Catholics, 333
　Ulster custom, 179
Moneymore, Co. Derry, 250, 286
Moneyrea, Co. Down, 132, 377
Monteagle, Lord, 198, 203
Montgomery, Revd Henry, 2, 120, 125, 135, 150, 162
　battle of the synods, 137–43
　and electoral reform, 159
　on *regium donum*, 166
　on tithes, 148–9
Montgomery, Hugh, 303
Montgomery, John, 138
Montgomery, General Richard, 25
Montgomery, Revd Samuel, 183–4
Montgomery, William, 138
Monypenny, W.F., 409
Moody, T.W., 294
Moore, Thomas, 56, 372
Morley, John, 303–4, 324
Morning Herald, 206
Morning Post, 374, 413–14
Morrow, Revd John, 431
Morrow brothers, 370
Mountcashel, Lord, 198, 203

Mountgarret, Lord, 50
Moylan, Dr, Bishop of Cork, 42, 108–9, 129
Moylan, Quartermaster-General Stephen, 25
Muir, Thomas, 50, 53, 66–7
Mulholland family, 165
Munro, Henry, 102–3
Munster, 9, 147, 401
  agrarian agitation, 20
  elections, 386
  emigration, 190
  landownership, 173, 276
  tenant-right agitation, 249
Murphy, Father John, 100–1
Murray, Bishop Patrick, 229
Musgrave, Sir Richard, 83
Mutiny Bill (1877), 281

Nation, 196, 218–19, 221–2, 226–7, 229, 267, 337
  founded, 233–4
  revived, 252
National League, 245
National Union of Dock Labourers, 388, 390, 393
National Volunteers, 416, 421
nationalism, 1–2, 6, 195–6, 332, 429; *see also* Home Rule movement
  concept of, 105–6
  cultural renaissance, 123–6, 374
  definitions of, 42–3
  development of, 33, 67–8, 71, 319
  Gaelic revival, 340–1
  and labour movement, 359–60, 396–9
  and land reform movement, 253
  linked with Catholicism, 216–17
  response to intimidation campaign, 95–6
  romantic legends, 104–5
  in Ulster, 376–81
  Young Ireland movement, 168
Navigation Acts, 30, 46
Neal, Mary, 39
Neilson, Samuel, 2, 36, 45–7, 51–2, 54, 93, 126
  arrested, 99–100

and Defenders, 69
  interned, 87–8
  Northern Star, 53
  separatism, 71
  and Tone, 79–80
Neilson, W.B., 126
Nelson, Revd Isaac, 289
Nelson, Revd William, 124–5
New Ireland Forum, 4
New Lights, 15–18, 40, 135, 432
  battle of the synods, 137–43
New Ross, Co. Wexford, 101
New Zealand, 263, 279, 315
Newell, Edward, 93
Newgate jail (Dublin), 64–5, 87
Newman, John Henry, 168
Newry, Co. Down, 33, 37, 96, 99, 185, 233, 244, 264, 333, 377
  emigration from, 23, 190
  franchise, 28
  informers, 93
News Chronicle, 379
Newtown Limavady, Co. Derry, 138
Newtownards, Co. Down, 99, 132
Newtownbutler, Co. Fermanagh, 307
Nonconformists, 3, 125, 193, 292, 343, 345, 361, 402, 426
  anti-Ascendancy, 275, 302, 310–11
  anti-Catholic, 262, 429
  factions, 138
Nore mutiny, 86
Northcote, Sir Stafford, 305
Northern Ireland, 1–3, 422
  administration of, 424–33
Northern Ireland Labour Party, 428–9
Northern Patriot, 337
Northern Star, 37, 50, 53, 71, 87
  libel charge, 65
  office wrecked, 64
  Porter's contributions, 77–8
Northern Whig, 147, 150–1, 163, 166, 197, 300, 346, 410
  on Act of Union, 191–2
  on Great Famine, 170, 183–4, 186
  and tenant-right movement, 223–4, 274–6
Nugent, General George, 102–3

504

Oakboys, 20–1, 41
O'Boyle, Father James, 284
O'Brien, Bronterre, 168
O'Brien, Michael, 245
O'Brien, William, 283, 292, 328, 350
O'Brien, William Smith, 180, 212, 219
  defended by Butt, 267
  and land reform, 194
  nationalism, 196
  and repeal movement, 224
  transported, 244, 247
  and Young Ireland, 199, 232
O'Carolan, Turlough, 372
O'Casey, Sean, 360, 370
O'Connell, Daniel, 129, 160, 196, 224, 233,
  238, 244, 266, 269
  Catholic Association, 121
  Catholic emancipation, 143
  and Cooke, 140, 163
  and Crawford, 149–50
  Great Famine, 215–17
  and Irish language, 225
  repeal movement, 123, 161, 168
  wins seat, 158
  and Young Ireland, 220–1, 238–9
O'Connell, John, 194, 196, 217, 220
O'Connor, Arthur, 87, 100
O'Connor, Feargus, 168, 194, 259
O'Curry, Eugene, 226, 228
O'Doherty, Father James, 250
O'Doherty family, 9
O'Donovan, John, 226, 228, 230
O'Donovan Rossa, Jeremiah, 269–70
O'Grady, Standish Hayes, 340
O'Hanlon, Redmond, 20
O'Hegarty, P.S., 374, 379–80
Old Lights, 15–16, 136
  battle of the synods, 137–43
Oldham, Professor C.H., 293
O'Leary, John, 269–70, 298–9, 339
Omagh, Co. Tyrone, 99, 260, 336
O'Neill, Lord, 88, 96, 108, 196, 272
  income of, 278
  landownership, 277
O'Neill, Arthur, 56, 125
O'Neill, Brian, 314
O'Neill family, 9

Orange Order, 1, 4, 7, 95, 120, 136, 140,
  149, 223, 235, 264, 355, 379, 389, 428, 431;
  see also Independent Orange Order
  and Act of Union, 111–12
  anti-Home Rule crusade, 345, 402–3, 410
  and British Army, 83–5
  and Churchill, 321–7
  criticisms of, 352
  Dolly's Brae, 255
  growing extremism, 328–31
  intimidation, 89
  and Land League, 284–5, 287, 289,
  305–9
  opposition to Ascendancy, 303, 305–6
  and repeal movement, 162–3
  sectarianism, 253, 262, 343, 348–9
  spread of, 73, 82–4
  and tithes war, 148, 151–4
  and Tory Party, 257, 325–7
  and trade unionism, 357–9, 363
  Ulster Volunteer Force, 414
  yeomanry, 99
O'Reilly family, 9
Orr, Joseph, 72
Orr, Samuel, 101
Orr, William, 87, 91–2, 101, 273
O'Shannon, Cathal, 366
O'Shea, Father Tom, 249, 252
O'Shea, Captain William, 300
O'Sullivan, Major-General John, 25
Otway, Caesar, 229
Oughterard, Co. Galway, 205
outdoor relief, 188–9, 198, 203–4
Owners of Land in Great Britain and Ireland,
  276–8
Oxford movement, 168, 261

Paine, Thomas, 30–1, 49–50, 53, 66, 70
Paisley, Revd Ian, 1
Paisleyism, 431
Palmerston, Lord, 195, 223
Paris Commune, 306
Parkhill, David, 369–70, 374
parliament, Irish, 30, 32, 34
  and Act of Union, 108–10
  allegiance to Britain, 42–3
  dissolved, 104

Patriot Parliament, 31, 38, 47
unrepresentative, 27–9, 42–3
parliamentary reform, 32, 48–9, 53, 65,
   147
Parnell, Charles Stewart, 241, 245, 290,
   295, 302, 310, 323, 380
   arrest of, 286
   and Biggar, 296–9
   boycott policy, 309
   and Butt, 281
   divorce scandal, 333
   and Land League, 283–4, 287–8, 294
   and the north, 292
Parnell, John, 109
partition, 393, 422–3
   effects of, 424–33
Patrick, Saint, 9, 231
Patriot Parliament, 31, 38, 47
Patriot Party, 29, 42, 109
Patterson, Henry, 412
Pearse, Patrick, 105, 238, 336, 362, 365, 367,
   379, 399
Peel, Sir Robert, 126, 135, 160, 167, 185,
   195, 254, 275
   anti-Catholicism, 402
   home secretary, 142
   Maynooth grant, 168
   'Orange Peel', 211
Peep O'Day Boys, 21, 23, 70–3, 81–2
Pelagianism, 16
Pelham, Thomas, 85
penal laws, 10, 14, 18–19, 36, 38, 41,
   113–14, 432
Penn, William, 24
Pennsylvania (USA), 24
Petrie, George, 226–7
Phoenix Park (Dublin), 30
picketing, 89
Pinkerton, John, 2, 283, 294, 346
Pirrie, William (later Lord), 320, 385, 417
pitch-capping, 89, 96
Pitt, William, 116, 121, 130
   and Act of Union, 107–10, 114, 169, 310
   anti-Catholicism, 402
   Catholic relief, 59–60
   coercion policy, 61–2, 66
   and Dissenters, 131

and Orange Order, 85
   spy network, 81, 92–3
   Whigs in government, 65–6
Pius IX, Pope, 200, 260, 263
plantations, 10, 41, 236–7
Plunkett, Sir Horace, 352–3, 369–70, 375
police, 176, 324, 425
   Belfast mutiny, 390
politics see franchise
Pollock, James, 93, 96
Pollock, Joseph, 33
Ponsonby family, 109
population, 165
   decline, 190, 263–4
   statistics, 174
Portadown, Co. Armagh, 264
Portaferry, Co. Down, 34–5, 38, 75–6, 120,
   132
Porter, J.L., 142
Porter, Revd James, 74–8, 371
Porter, Samuel, 339
Porter, Revd William, 138
Portland, Lord, 65–6, 114–15, 131, 133
potato, 173–4
   failures of, 182–5, 279
Praeger, Robert Lloyd, 335
predestination, 15–16
Presbyterianism
   and nationalism, 383
Presbyterians, 2–3, 6, 40, 50, 59, 72, 119,
   167, 216–17, 242, 320, 352, 432–3
   and Act of Union, 113–14, 116
   agrarian agitation, 20, 272–3
   anti-Ascendancy, 282
   and anti-Home Rule crusade, 415, 418–21
   battle of the synods, 137–43
   belief in colonialism, 210
   Castlereagh makes approaches to,
      126–34
   and coercion policy, 64
   conflicts among, 14–18
   and cultural renaissance, 363
   disaffection among, 98
   and ecumenism, 431
   emigration, 23–4, 264
   evangelicalism, 167
   evictions, 304

franchise, 158–9
and Gaelic culture, 123–6, 339
and Great Famine, 182, 190, 200, 204
and Home Rule movement, 270, 293–300,
  302, 343–7
income of, 130–2
influence of Cooke, 135–6
and intimidation campaign, 95
and land reform, 26, 222–3, 289, 305
middle classes, 165
nationalism, 71, 106
numbers of, 129–30
in Orange Order, 82
poverty among, 171, 175
radicalism, 32–3
regium donum controversy, 166–7
relations with Catholics, 44, 58, 395
religious disabilities, 14
religious tolerance, 34
and repeal movement, 161–3
republicanism, 379–81
social status of, 13–15
synods, 120, 132–3, 137–43, 259–60
tenant-right agitation, 248, 250–3, 256–60
and United Irishmen, 51–2, 73–9, 130
press-gangs, 86
Price, Dr Richard, 50
Priestley, Dr Joseph, 50, 53, 66
prison reform, 123
propaganda, 3–6
proselytism, 204–9
Protection of Life Act (1846), 199
protectionism, 196–7
Protestant Home Rule Association, 289,
  292–4, 300, 344
Protestant Repeal Association, 227–8
Protestants, 1–4, 11, 19, 168–9
  after partition, 426
  divisions among, 302
  ecumenism, 430
  electoral representation, 29
  emigration of, 190
  and Gaelic revival, 339, 341
  and Great Famine, 199–200
  and imperialism, 317–18
  involvement in Irish nation, 52, 236–7
  and labour movement, 383–92, 394–8

and Land League, 284–5, 288–9, 294
  mounting panic, 96–7
  opposition to Unionists, 362–3
  plantations, 10–11
  poverty among, 349
  preponderance in Ulster, 319
  and republicanism, 379–81
  views on charity, 197–8
  Volunteers, 34–5
  working class, 356–7
public works, 193–4
Punch, 317, 370
Purcell, Lewis, 370
Pusey, Revd E.B., 261
Pynnar, Nicholas, 11

Quakers, 3, 82, 165, 200, 202, 293, 339, 382
Quebec, Siege of, 25
Queen's College Belfast (later Queen's
  University Belfast), 272, 338, 357, 363,
  371
Queen's County, 312
Queen's University Belfast *see* Queen's
  College Belfast

Rabb, John, 65
racism, 210–11, 241, 349, 403
  anti-Home Rule campaign, 408–9
  and imperialism, 316–18
Rademan, Co. Down, 124
radicalism, 35–40, 119–23
  coercion, 61–3
  radical sectarianism, 357–60, 383–5
Radnor, Lord, 198, 203
Randalstown, Co. Antrim, 135
Raphoe, Co. Donegal, 97
rapparees, 20
Rathcoffey, Co. Kildare, 39
Rathfriland, Co. Down, 34, 183, 253
Rathlin Island, 132, 369
Rathmullan, Co. Donegal, 298
Read, George, 24
Redmond, John, 238, 269, 362, 378, 406,
  416, 421
Redmond, William, 406
Reeves, William, Bishop of Down and
  Connor, 230–1

Reform Act (1832), 154, 160–1, 167, 266
reform movement
  after 1798 rising, 119–23
  campaign of intimidation, 88–94
  effects of intimidation, 95–6
  'new Reformation', 167–8
  and Presbyterians, 143–4
  strength of, 98, 159–61
  widening of franchise, 156–61
  year of revolutions (1848), 180
Reformation, 9, 19, 61
regium donum, 74, 116, 120, 131, 137
  increase seen as bribe, 133–4
  linked with tithes, 151
  Presbyterian controversy, 166–7
  suggested for Catholic priests, 129
  threatened, 256
Reid, Forrest, 364–5, 374, 394
Reid, James Seton, 134
Reilly, Devin, 244
Relief Acts
  1778, 32
  1847, 239
Relief Bill (1793), 60
religious tolerance, 33–4, 138–9
remonstrant synod, 142
Rentoul, Revd J.L., 257, 272
Repeal Association, 220–1
repeal movement, 123, 149, 161, 168, 224, 239
  identified with Catholicism, 216–17
  National League, 245
Representation of the People (Ireland) Act (1832), 160
Republic, The, 378–9, 389
republicanism, 4, 47, 70, 126
  development of, 80
  effects of Belfast strike, 392–9
  romantic legends, 104–5
  in Ulster, 376–83
Reynolds, Thomas, 93
Reynolds, W.B., 374
Ribbonism, 146, 199, 229
Richardson, General Sir George, 414
Richardson, John, 97
Richardson family, 165
Rights of Man (Paine), 30–1, 49, 66

riots
  agrarian agitation, 22–3
  Belfast, 352, 412–13
  Belfast strike, 391
  Militia Bill, 63
  sectarian, 1
  sectarian (Belfast), 264, 324–5
  Tandragee, 151–2
risings
  1798 see under United Irishmen
  1803, 116–19
  1916 see Easter rising
  Fenians, 245, 268
Roberts, Field Marshal Lord, 331, 404, 414
Robespierre, 40, 53
Robinson, Revd A., 273
Roden, Lord, 154, 161, 169, 205, 255–6
Rodgers, Revd Reuben, 74
Rogers, Revd John, 34, 254, 256–7, 259–60
Rolleston, T.W., 293
Rollin, Ledru, 259
Rosebery, Lord, 409
Ross, D., 196
Rossmore, Lord, 327
Rossnowlagh, Co. Donegal, 212
rotten boroughs, 28, 158–9, 177, 291, 386
  abolished, 160
Rousseau, Jean Jacques, 39
Route, the, Co. Antrim, 271–2
Route Tenants' Association, 273
Rowan, Hamilton, 50, 149
  exile, 67
  trial of, 64–5
  United Irishmen, 24, 47, 52
  and Volunteers, 36, 38–40
  returns to Ireland, 121–2, 136
Rowan, Sidney, 136
Royal Belfast Academical Institution, 125–6, 142–3, 254, 272, 342
Royal Irish Academy, 231
Royal School (Raphoe), 266
Russell, George (AE), 353–4, 362, 370, 394
Russell, Lord John, 192–3, 195, 211, 254, 261, 402
Russell, Thomas, 2, 45–6, 52, 67, 71, 123
  in Belfast, 50–1

interned, 87, 100
rising (1803), 116–19
and Tone, 79–80
Russell, Thomas W., 291, 348, 350–2, 377,
384, 387, 407
wins Home Rule seat, 417–18
Russellites, 2, 334, 350, 355, 363, 383, 387,
407
Rutherford, Revd John, 256–7
Rutledge, Edward, 24
Ryan, W.P., 393
Rylett, Revd Harold, 284, 289–90

Sabbatarianism, 427
Sadleir, John, 261–2
St Enda's school (Dublin), 365
St Malachy's College (Belfast), 340
Saintfield, Co. Down, 35, 55, 132, 250, 284,
289
Salisbury, Lord, 302, 314, 317, 322, 386
anti-Catholicism, 402
Ashbourne Act, 313
opposed to land reform, 311, 312
and Saunderson, 326
Salters' Company, 277
Sarsfield, Patrick, 25
Saunderson, Colonel Edward, 274, 323,
328, 358, 409
and Churchill, 322, 326–7
and Orange Order, 307–8
Saunderson family, 11
Saurin, William, 111
Scarva, Co. Down, 250
Schull, Co. Cork, 202
Scotland, 50, 53, 76, 194, 294, 409
coercion policy, 66–7
Covenanters, 15
migrant workers, 350
religious controversies, 14
and Ulster, 8–9, 11
Scott, Revd Robert, 74
Scrope, Poulett, 194, 204, 212
Scullabogue, Co. Wexford, 101
Second World War, 428, 432
sectarianism, 19, 72–3, 191, 207–11, 255,
343, 390
and agrarian agitation, 21, 23

and anti-Home Rule campaign, 402–3,
408–12
economic imbalance, 320
encouraged by Tories, 81–7
and labour movement, 358–9, 391–2,
395–8
and land reform, 258–65, 306–9, 314
and nationalism, 219–21
and repeal movement, 161–4
riots, 1, 264, 324–5, 352, 412–13
roused by Churchill, 321–7
tithes war, 148, 151–4
Senior, Hereward, 84
Senior, Nassau William, 203
separatism, 67–8
Sessiagh, Co. Tyrone, 283–4
Sexton, James, 388, 392, 398
Sexton, Thomas, 293
Shan Van Vocht, 337–8, 340
Sharman, Colonel William, 149
Shaw, George Bernard, 354, 362
Sheares brothers, 67, 100
Shelley, Percy B., 121
Shillington, Thomas, 273, 300, 346
shipbuilding, 165
Shirley, E.P., 172, 277–8
Sibbett, R.M., 82, 111, 331, 414
Simms, Robert, 51, 87, 100–1, 103, 122,
125–6
Simms, William, 51, 87, 100, 125–6
Simms family, 79–80
Simpson, Revd James, 75
Sinclair, Betty, 432
Sinclair, Revd W., 74
Sinclair, William, 51, 54–5
Sinn Féin, 360, 362, 366, 393, 398–9, 422,
431
Sirocco factory (Belfast), 388
Sirr, Major Henry Charles, 92, 99, 118
Sixth of George the First, 34
Skeffington, Frank Sheehy, 385
Skibbereen, Co. Cork, 181, 185, 202
slavery, 53, 123, 149, 207, 241
Slemish Mountain, Co. Antrim, 9
Sligo, Co., 207
Sloan, Thomas, 377, 392–3, 397, 407, 428
and Belfast strike, 389, 391

Independent Unionist, 387
  radical sectarianism, 357–9, 363, 383–4
Sloanites, 2
Smith, Adam, 38, 130, 193, 200, 203, 211
Smith, Frederick Edwin, 405, 410
Smith, James, 24
Smith, Revd John, 75
Smith, Dr Robert, 187–8
Smith, Revd Thomas, 75
Smithurst, Revd J., 136
Snowden, Philip, 391, 397
socialism, 306, 319, 391
Society of the Friends of the People
  (Scotland), 66
Solemn League and Covenant, 413, 418
soup kitchens, 186, 193, 203, 207
South Africa, 315, 331
Spencer, Herbert, 294
Spithead mutiny, 86
Spring-Rice family, 198
Stavely, Revd William, 273
Steelboys, 20–2, 41, 44
Steele, Revd R., 74
Stevelly, Revd William, 75
Stewart, H., 277
Stewart, Robert see Castlereagh, Lord
Stewart, Colonel Walter, 25
Stewart family, 176
Stokes, William, 226
Strabane, Co. Tyrone, 140–1, 183, 250, 285
Strangford Lough, Co. Down, 257
Street, Revd J.C., 289
strikes
  Belfast, 388–92, 422
  Dublin, 354, 415
Sullivan, A.M., 251
supremacy, oath of, 29
Swift, Dean Jonathan, 23, 234
Synge, J.M., 370

Tablet, The, 252
Tailor's Hall (Dublin), 57–8
Táin Bó Cuailgne, 124, 225, 365
Tandragee, Co. Armagh, 151–2
Tandy, Napper, 32, 36, 40, 52, 67
Tasmania, 241, 244
taxation, 30, 46, 116, 156

Taylor, George, 24
Teeling, Bartholomew, 71, 87, 103
Teeling, Charles, 71, 87–8
Teeling, Luke, 57
Templepatrick, Co. Antrim, 22, 138
Templeton, Lord, 404
tenant farmers, 13, 26, 171–4, 282, 332, 343,
    354, 362; see also agrarian agitation
  anti-establishment, 257–8
  depression, late 1870s, 279–81
  effects of Land Acts, 313–14
  evictions, 271, 304–5
  and linen industry, 178
  organisations, 271–81
  poverty among, 278, 349
  sectarianism, 395
  taxation, 156
  tithes war, 147–55
  Unionists lose support of, 354–5
  and United Irishmen, 71
tenant right see Ulster custom
tenant-right movement, 247–65
Tennent, J.E., 164
Tennent, John, 72, 87
Tennent, William, 51, 72, 125–6
Tennent family, 176–7
Test Act (1704), 14
Thomson, Charles, 24
Thornley, David, 269
Thornton, Matthew, 24
Times, The, 191, 194, 255, 261, 340, 414
Tipperary, Co., 20, 146, 199, 295, 309
Tithe Commutation Bill (1837), 155
tithes, 12, 14, 116, 128, 432
  tithes war, 2, 70, 144–55, 161, 248
Tolstoy, Leo, 362
Tone, Matthew, 103
Tone, Theobald Wolfe, 4, 24, 28, 40, 65,
    100, 117, 134, 241, 266
  arrested, 103
  Back Lane Parliament, 57–8
  in Belfast, 50–2
  Belfast celebration, 54–5
  career, 45, 48–52
  and Defenders, 69
  in France, 79–80
  harp festival, 56

influence of, 105–6, 122, 218, 234, 236, 339, 379, 381, 420–1
  nationalism of, 67–8, 71
Tooke, Horne, 53, 66
Tories, 6, 17, 121; *see also* Conservative Party *and* Tory Party
Toronto Globe, 393
Tory Party, 104, 282, 290
  and Act of Union, 107–10
  and Ascendancy, 62, 210–11, 258, 272
  control of franchise, 175–7
  on defensive, 274, 282
  divisions among, 302
  election results, 159, 285
  and Great Famine, 192–3
  isolating Catholics, 126, 128–9
  and land reform, 197, 284
  and obstructionism, 297
  opposition to, 106, 130
  and Orange Order, 257
  and Protestant fundamentalism, 162–3
  regium donum, 167
  sectarianism, 81–7
  tithes war, 153–4
Townsend, Revd James, 75
Townsend, Revd Richard, 202
trade, 30, 32–3, 191
  and Act of Union, 116, 130, 163–6
  free trade, 196–7, 211, 361
  legislation, 14
  protectionism, 267, 320
trade-union movement, 357, 361–2
  after partition, 428–9
  Belfast, 387–92
Traill, Revd Robert, 202
transportation, 85, 89, 240–1, 244
Treason-felony Act (1848), 199
Trevelyan, Sir Charles, 211
Trinity College Dublin, 45, 136, 233, 266, 293, 366
  electoral representation, 112, 160, 328, 354, 386
Trinity Presbyterian Church (Ballymoney), 347
Troy, Dr John Thomas, Archbishop of Dublin, 42, 86, 108–9, 129

tuberculosis, 356
Tullylish, Co. Down, 250, 257, 308
Turner, Samuel, 72, 93
Twiss, Mr, 309
typhoid fever, 357
typhus, 185–6, 189
Tyrone, Co., 9–10, 226, 279, 383, 422
  agrarian agitation, 20
  disaffection in, 96
  elections, 176, 290–1, 303, 346, 355, 387, 406–7, 417–18
  franchise, 27, 158
  Great Famine, 183, 185–6
  Irish language, 340
  Land League, 284–5
  landownership, 171–2, 277–8
  Orange Order, 84, 111, 305
  population loss, 190
  proportion of Catholics, 333
  tithes, 147
  United Irishmen, 85

Ua Fhloin, Riobard (Robert Lynd), 380
Uladh, 373–4
Ulster, 14; *see also* agrarian agitation *and* land question
  coup d'état threatened, 415–16
  cultural renaissance, 361–75
  delegates to Back Lane Parliament, 57–8
  early history, 8–12
  effects of Belfast strike, 392–9
  effects of Land Acts, 313–14
  elections, 157–8, 265, 285, 354–5
  emigration from, 23–5, 190
  evictions, 199, 304–5
  franchise, 27, 290
  Gaelic culture, 123–6, 340
  Great Famine, 181–90
  industrial development, 163–6, 319–20
  intimidation campaign, 88–91
  Irish language in, 334–5
  job discrimination, 411
  labour movement, 383–92
  landownership, 171–6, 274–8
  league of north and south, 247–65
  population decline, 263–4
  proportion of Protestants in, 319

republicanism in, 376–83
resistance to unionism, 332–3, 386–7
struggle for democracy, 32–5
tithes war, 147–55
United Irishmen, 96–7, 101–4
Young Ireland, 218, 222–4
Ulster Bank, 295
Ulster custom, 23–4, 150, 178–81, 196–7,
  256, 263, 273, 432
  evictions, 304
  tenant-right agitation, 248–65
  threatened, 222–3
Ulster Examiner, 274
Ulster Guardian, 385, 392
Ulster Journal of Archaeology, 230, 342
Ulster Literary Theatre, 361, 369–70, 374,
  383, 394
Ulster Unionist Council, 401–3
Ulster Volunteer Force, 1, 331, 413–16,
  422
Ulster Weekly News, 306
undertakers, 10, 30
unemployment, 3, 361, 432
unionism, 288, 291, 320
  resistance to, 332–4
  seen as synonymous with Protestantism,
    4–5
  southern, 401–2, 405
Unionist Party, 1, 291, 293, 327, 330, 346,
  358, 395
  anti-Home Rule crusade, 400–23
  coup d'état threatened, 415–16
  election results, 334, 386, 406, 422
  enlarged, 312
  growing violence, 413–16
  and labour movement, 359, 383–7, 391
  losing support, 354–6, 362–3
  loyalty conditional, 409–11, 425
  and Orange Order, 326–7
  partition, 422–33
  sectarianism, 348–9
  Solemn League and Covenant, 413,
    418
Unitarianism, 16, 50, 140–1, 143, 150, 284,
  289
United Englishmen, 79
United Irishman, 240, 244

United Irishmen, 2, 20, 31, 34, 40, 44–55,
  115, 124, 135, 217, 224
  arrested, 53, 87–9
  in Belfast, 36, 54–5
  campaign against, 95
  centenary, 337, 382
  coercion policy, 62–3
  and Defenders, 67, 69–71
  Dublin manifesto, 68–9
  Dublin Society, 52
  effects of coercion policy, 65–9
  informers, 91–5, 99–100, 102–3
  Insurrection Act, 86
  manifesto, 51–2
  new constitution and tactics, 69–71
  northern members, 71–5
  oath, 37, 52, 77, 90
  opposed by Orange Order, 84–5
  pamphlets, 342
  Presbyterians in, 73–9, 130
  rising (1798), 57, 76, 92, 99–105, 122–3,
    126, 138, 139
  rising (1803), 116–19, 122–3
  strength of, 83, 96–8
  and Volunteers, 37–8, 75
United Scotsmen, 66, 76
United States, 31, 39, 43, 53, 263, 279, 310
  Civil War, 241
  emigration to, 23–5, 190
  Hobson fund-raising tour, 380
  Land League collections, 299
  Tone to, 65
  War of Independence, 24–5, 51
university plan, 220
urban areas, 263–4, 320

Verner, Jenny, 233, 242
Verner, Thomas, 84
Verner, Sir William, 198
Verner family, 176–7
viceroy, role of, 30
Victoria, Queen, 176, 228, 317, 327, 348
Vinegar Hill, Battle of, 101, 104
Volunteers, 20, 31–2, 37, 44, 47, 49, 58–9,
  73, 75, 91, 103, 108, 137, 377
  Back Lane Parliament, 57
  decline of, 40–3

disarmed, 63
Dungannon Convention (1782), 33–4
manifesto, 64
prominent members, 35–40
and United Irishmen, 54

Waddell, Helen, 371–2, 375
Waddell, Samuel, 370–1, 375, 394
Wales, 194
Walker, William, 357–8, 383, 387, 391, 397,
   407, 417, 421, 428
Wallace, Colonel R.H., 331, 355, 402, 414
Walsh, John, 97
Warburton, Dean, 97
Warden, Revd Bailie, 75
Warwick, Revd Archibald, 75
Washington, George, 24–5, 53
Waterford, Co., 146, 160
Webb, Alfred, 293
Weir, James, 285
Wellington, Duke of, 40, 126, 160, 167
Wells, H.G., 362
Wells, Ronald, 430
Wesley, John, 167
Westminster Confession of Faith, 16–17
Westmorland, Lord, 59–60, 107
Westport, Co. Mayo, 28, 366–7, 394
Wexford, Co., 11, 89
   rising (1798), 90, 100–1
Whateley, Richard, Archbishop of Dublin,
   198, 202–4
Whig Club (Belfast), 39–40
Whigs, 32, 34, 158
   fear of revolution, 41, 68–9
   and franchise, 175
   land policies, 197
   opposed to intimidation, 95–6
   and Orange Order, 82–3
   in Pitt's government, 65–6
   in power, 147, 159–60
   protector of privilege, 210–11
   and tithes war, 153–5
Whinney, Thomas, 97
White, Captain Jack, 416, 419–20
Whiteboyism, 20, 41–2, 44, 123, 148
Wicklow, Co., 89–90
   rising (1798), 100

Wild Geese, 39
Wilde, Oscar, 328
Wilde, William, 226
Wilhelm II, Emperor, 415
William III, King, of Orange, 11, 14, 39, 54,
   318, 384, 404
   statue, 58
William IV, King, 154
Williams, Richard Dalton, 227
Wilson, Alec, 365
Wilson, General Henry, 404–5, 414
Wiseman, Cardinal Nicholas, 260
Wolfe, Arthur, 67
Wollstonecraft, Mary, 40, 50, 53, 66
Wolseley, Field Marshal Lord, 308, 331,
   414
Wood, James, 355
Woodburn, J.B., 409
woodkernes, 20
woollen trade, 32
workhouses, 182, 187–9, 198
working classes, 332, 356–7
   and reform movement, 122–3
   rise of agitation, 167–8
Workman Clark, 264, 412
World, The, 297
Worrall, A. Stanley, 430
Worrell, Revd James, 75
Worth, Revd, 75
Wyndham, Sir George
   Land Act, 313, 351, 355, 361

Yeats, William Butler, 228, 236, 293, 335,
   354, 362, 370, 374
   and Ulster Literary Theatre, 369
yeomanry, 83–4, 98–9, 103
   intimidation, 88–9
York, Duke of, 83
Youghal, Co. Cork, 267
Young Ireland, 104, 142, 196, 214, 234, 244,
   247, 252, 263, 298, 432
   campaign, 217–22
   and cultural revival, 225–7, 229
   leaders of, 232–4, 239–40
   rising (1848), 241, 267

Zola, Émile, 362

513